To my parents, Richard and Evelyn Davis,

with gratitude for all those camping trips to Gettysburg,

Hyde Park, and TR's Sagamore Hill . . . and all of

the other field trips that gave me a deep love of history

as the story of real people

Hyperion
Hachette Book Group
237 Park Avenue
New York, NY 10017

www.HachetteBookGroup.com

Printed in the United States of America

Designed by Karen Minster

RRD-C

Originally published in hardcover by Hyperion.

First trade edition: April 2014
10 9 8 7 6 5 4 3 2 1

Hyperion is a division of Hachette Book Group, Inc.

The publisher is not responsible for websites (or their content) that are not owned by the publisher.

The Library of Congress has catalogued the hardcover as follows:

Davis, Kenneth C.
    Don't know much about the American presidents / Kenneth C. Davis. — 1st ed.
    p. cm.
    Includes bibliographical references and index.
    ISBN 978-1-4013-2408-7
    1. Presidents—United States—Biography. 2. Presidents—United
States—Miscellanea. I. Title. II. Title: American presidents.
    E176.1.D379 2012
    973.009'9—dc23
    [B]
                                                        2012022496

ISBN: 9781401330439

DON'T KNOW MUCH ABOUT®

★ ★ ★ ★ THE ★ ★ ★ ★

AMERICAN PRESIDENTS

Everything You Need to Know
About the Most Powerful Office on Earth
and the Men Who Have Occupied It

Kenneth C. Davis

HYPERION

NEW YORK

CONTENTS

INTRODUCTION

A few years ago, I made a surprising personal discovery. While sorting through a box of old papers that my mother had stored in the attic for safekeeping, I came across the first draft of this book. *My Project About Presidents* was written in October 1963, when I was nine years old and a member of Grade 3C at the Holmes School in Mount Vernon, New York. Neatly bound with satin ribbons and carefully composed in tidy block letters, it was adorned with drawings of John Adams and George Washington as a surveyor—no phony cherry trees for me.

Earnestly, the opening page told readers that "I want to know about the men like John F. Kennedy, and delegates and executives; people who help make a better U.S.A. for the people."

"Did you know?" I asked—even then posing questions to my readers—"In Monroe's time, it took $100 worth of candles to light the East Room." (Unfortunately, I did not know about footnotes in third grade, so I cannot confirm the source of that information today.)

Clearly, the presidency and the presidents have fascinated me for a long time!

I grew up in a city named for George Washington's famous Virginia plantation. But I think that my love of American history, and the presidents in particular, had more to do with family trips to places like Valley Forge, Gettysburg, and Teddy Roosevelt's Sagamore Hill home in Oyster Bay, New York, where I vividly remember gazing up at a towering stuffed Kodiak bear, rearing on its hind legs. These were places where I was able to walk through history—touch it close up—and where I learned that history happens to real people in real places.

When I began this series with *Don't Know Much About*® *History* in

1990, I tried to convey that sense of "living history" to readers, often highlighting the sometimes anonymous, nameless, or forgotten people who have made a difference in our nation's life—such as the women, Native Americans, or African-Americans who had no place in my childhood history books. Inspiring that effort was my belief that history is not simply about Great Men, whether kings, generals, or presidents.

But this simple fact remains—the president matters. Since George Washington took the oath of office in 1789, the president has been the central character in the drama of the nation's history, for better or for worse. The burden of history is carried on the shoulders of presidents, who are more than chief executives. As commanders in chief, they bear the ultimate responsibility of deciding when to put in harm's way the lives of men and women in uniform. As the sign on Harry Truman's White House desk famously put it, "The buck stops here."

Beyond the fundamental powers, duties, and responsibilities invested in the office by the Constitution, the commander in chief also functions as the nation's "symbol in chief." Every man (and they've all been men—so far!) who has taken the presidential oath of office comes to represent America. His ability in "playing the role" of president is sometimes as important as any piece of legislation he may champion. Statecraft is stagecraft—and the greatest presidents, including Washington, and certainly those in the media age, understood that: Theodore Roosevelt, who called the White House the "bully pulpit," FDR, JFK, and Ronald Reagan were all master performers aside from their effectiveness in dealing with Congress and getting legislation passed.

This book sets out to look at American history through the focused lens of the most powerful office on earth and the men who have occupied it.

Examining both the presidency and the presidents, it is divided into three parts:

Part I—The Making of the President—1787—commences in a time before the presidency existed and examines a very straightforward question: *Why does America have a president?*

Going back to the debates over the "Executive Department" at the Constitutional Convention in Philadelphia in the summer of 1787, the role and powers of the chief executive and commander in chief have been hotly contested and controversial issues. They remain so today. What the founders and framers had in mind and the evolving role of the executive branch are at the center of the nation's development and progress.

Part I explores how the office of the presidency was invented—perhaps "improvised" is a better word—in the summer of 1787, when questions such as *What is a natural born citizen?* were first being discussed. It is remarkable to see how questions of fitness for office and presidential powers, intensely debated in that history-changing summer, remain hot-button issues more than two hundred years later. Birthers, beware! The answers are not always so simple.

Part I also explores the initial bedeviling question of how the president would be chosen, a knotty problem ending in a compromise that we now call the "electoral college," words not found in the Constitution. This history culminates with an account of America's first presidential "race," the only presidential election to fall in an odd calendar year—1789—a rather curious affair in which no one "campaigned" and three of the thirteen states didn't even cast a vote!

Part II offers a series of **Presidential Profiles**, each of which introduces one of the forty-three men who have held the executive office, then surveys the particular crises and issues each faced, his relationship with Congress, and his historical impact: Washington walking on "untrodden ground"; Lincoln suspending habeas corpus to jail opponents of the Civil War; FDR reshaping government during his four consecutive terms in office; Richard Nixon abusing the powers of the White House in the crisis that led to his resignation; Ronald Reagan, in the "role of a lifetime," restoring a sense of luster to an Oval Office diminished by scandal and ineffective leadership.

These presidents would be classed as some of the "Great Men" who have held the office. But Part II also examines the inept or disastrous lesser men who rank consistently among the "worst" presidents—such less-than-stellar chief executives as Millard Fillmore, Franklin Pierce, and James Buchanan—each of them an accomplished, admired man of his day who failed, sometimes tragically, to effectively lead the nation.

Whether or not the old saying about there being a "great woman" behind every great man still stands, the profiles in Part II also highlight the role of the first ladies. They include such notable women as Abigail Adams, Eleanor Roosevelt, and Jackie Kennedy, as well as the more obscure but influential wives, like Sarah Polk, perhaps the first "political wife"; Abigail Fillmore, a schoolteacher who built the first White House library; and Edith Wilson, whose "stewardship" of a bedridden, paralyzed Woodrow Wilson remains controversial. These profiles also highlight the transformation of the "President's Palace," from the days it was built with slave labor, with its original outdoor "privies," through its burning by the British in 1814 and gradual transformation into the White House we know today, with its iconic Oval Office and Rose Garden—both fairly recent additions to the two-hundred-year-old executive mansion.

The final section of the book, **Part III: What Do We Do with the President?**, briefly reviews how the powers of the presidency and the presidential election process have changed over more than two hundred years. What are the president's powers today? And have they evolved too far beyond what the framers envisioned? What can be done, besides complaining every four years, about that archaic relic called the electoral college?

Some of these are questions that may only be addressed with constitutional amendments. And resolutions to the issues they raise seem very unlikely to come about, at least anytime soon. But that does not mean they are not worth considering as we continue to work our way toward a "more perfect union."

The essential spotlight of this book, however, remains on the men who have been president. Using the question-and-answer approach of my other *Don't Know Much About*® books, I pose such basic inquiries as *Who elected George Washington?* as well as more unusual or unexpected ones: *Why was Thomas Jefferson called the "Negro President"?* or *What is Tecumseh's Curse?*

My goal, as always, is to tell real stories of real people. As in my other *Don't Know Much About*® books, the questions and answers are supplemented by Milestones—timelines of the presidents and the events during their administrations—and Presidential Voices—selected quotes by and about these men, in their own day and afterward. Each entry includes Must Reads, a selection of key biographies, other books, and online resources that give much fuller documentation of each man's life, controversies, and achievements, with an emphasis on recent scholarship and works written for the general audience.

Each profile concludes with a Final Judgment, an assessment including a simple report card letter grade—A+ down to F, with a few I's for Incomplete. These grades are meant to gauge the impact, influence, and consequences of each president, because a numerical ranking of "Best to Worst" is too simplistic. As this history shows, even the "best" presidents made bad mistakes. And the influence and achievements of a failed or disgraced president, such as Richard Nixon, must still be acknowledged.

At its core, this book is meant to address the mystique, the mystery, and the mythology of the presidency. That means, in some cases, discussing the flaws, imperfections, and scandals—both public and private—of these men. That also means trying to strike a balance between honest discussion of private behavior that may have affected public performance and simple tabloid voyeurism—not always an easy task.

What these profiles prove is that presidents, whether they are carved on mountainsides, etched on the bills in our wallets, or consigned to the dustbin of history, are all human. As presidential historian Arthur M. Schlesinger, Jr., put it, "Biographies of American presidents constitute a chronicle of wisdom and folly, nobility and pettiness, courage and cunning, forthrightness and deceit, quarrel and consensus. The turmoil swirling around the White House illuminates the heart of the American democracy."[1]

To get at that heart, I have focused on the life story of each of these men. And this is the bottom line: Who they *were* is as important as what they *did*.

Some themes that reverberate throughout this book:

- *"The good old days" were terrible.* One of the starkest American myths is the comfortable fantasy that presidential politics was once more honorable, less partisan, and less mean-spirited than what we experience today. In a word, that is nonsense. The personal assaults, manipulation, backstabbing, and putting of party over principle—or sound policy—constitute the way the presidential game has always been played.

- *There is nothing new under the sun.* Politics hasn't really changed. And neither have the issues: national banks, federal powers, the size of the government, "class warfare," religion, immigration, and of course, taxes, have stood as the hottest of hot-button issues. They have divided the country since George Washington's inauguration in April 1789.

- *Yes, children, anyone can become president.* Obviously, a number of presidents (Washington, Jefferson, both Roosevelts, John F. Kennedy, and the Bushes) were born into comfortable circumstances, if not an American "elite." But the remarkable fact remains that so many of the men who attained the highest office came from truly humble beginnings. Andrew Jackson was orphaned during the Revolution. Abraham Lincoln was born in a frontier cabin. His successor, Andrew Johnson, was left fatherless at three, raised in poverty, and apprenticed to a tailor as a child. More recently, Herbert Hoover (also orphaned), Harry Truman, Ronald Reagan, Bill Clinton, and Barack Obama all came from modest beginnings.

At the other end of the spectrum is the idealized view of presidents that typically follows their deaths. There is no better example than Lincoln, who was viciously castigated while president and then venerated as a martyr. That is not biography but hagiography, a worshipful, idealized view that does not serve history.

For much of our history, America has tried to create a flawless portrait of its presidents. But real history must acknowledge that even the best presidents made grievous mistakes. John Adams lived to regret jailing journalists and congressmen under the Sedition Act. Franklin D. Roosevelt allowed a massive violation of civil liberties when Japanese-Americans were interned during World War II. Ronald Reagan's deceptions about trading "arms for hostages" in the Iran-Contra controversy were a tremendous blow to his legacy—though one that history and the public seem to have treated generously.

In his biography of Woodrow Wilson, John Milton Cooper, Jr., raises the question of how to balance our view of these men when he asks: "A consideration of Wilson poses the same ultimate questions as does that of those other towering figures in the presidential pantheon: do his sins of omission and commission outweigh the good he did, or do his great words and deeds overshadow his transgressions?"[2]

That is a question legitimately asked of most presidents. But while I have made every effort to be accurate, balanced, and fair, I have also tried not to forget or erase the essential humanity that has made each of these extraordinary men part of a very small and remarkable fraternity.

Finally, it comes down to the bottom line: What makes a president great?

It is certainly not so simple a word as "leadership." Most of the great social changes in our history did not come from the president down. Even Lincoln couldn't lead the country to emancipation before it was ready. "Moral strength" may also be overrated. Few presidents were more "moral" than Jimmy Carter, who was turned out of office after an ineffective four years.

So there is no magic elixir, but these are some basic characteristics that emerge through these profiles:

- Consistency of principles and message
- Strength of character
- Willingness to compromise—
  when necessary and consistent with principles
- Recognizing talent and being surrounded
  by it without surrendering to it
- Willingness to listen
- Communication skills
- Humor and a human touch

And one more, the one that George Bush (41) once offhandedly called the "vision thing." As Proverbs tells us, "Where there is no vision, the people perish."

Or, as a nine-year-old boy put it back in 1963, that is one important way that presidents "help make a better U.S.A. for the people."

KENNETH C. DAVIS
New York, New York

The Making of the President
1787

The people . . . immediately should have as little to do as may be about the government. They lack information and are constantly liable to be misled.
—ROGER SHERMAN
Connecticut delegate to the Constitutional Convention
May 30, 1787[1]

The first man put at the helm will be a good one. Nobody knows what sort may come afterwards. The executive will be always increasing, as elsewhere, till it ends in monarchy.
—BENJAMIN FRANKLIN
Pennsylvania delegate to the Constitutional Convention
June 4, 1787[2]

The process of election affords a moral certainty that the office of President will never fall to the lot of any man who is not in an eminent degree endowed with the requisite qualifications. Talents for low intrigue, and the little arts of popularity, may alone suffice to elevate a man to the first honors in a single State; but it will require other talents, and a different kind of merit, to establish him in the esteem and confidence of the whole Union.
—PUBLIUS (ALEXANDER HAMILTON)
The Federalist #68
March 12, 1788

[The President] shall take care that the laws be faithfully executed.
—CONSTITUTION OF THE UNITED STATES
Article II, Section 3

When the president does it, that means it's not illegal.
—RICHARD NIXON
to interviewer David Frost, November 17, 1973

★

Forget for a moment everything you know about the presidency. Dismiss all the familiar trappings. The White House, the Oval Office. The Rose Garden, and the podium with the presidential seal. The commander in chief bounding down the steps of Air Force One to be greeted by adorable flower girls, or tossing a salute to generals, their chests dripping with medals. Forget Camp David weekends and motor-cades with Secret Service guys in Ray-Bans talking into their wrist-watches. Set aside the awesome powers of the job. Take away the "football," that legendary briefcase that holds the nuclear launch codes that can obliterate the planet. Shut the doors on the Cabinet.

Now chuck out your notions of how long the chief executive serves. Or how America's president gets elected. Dismiss more than two hundred years of images of inaugurals and ceremonial wreath-laying. Toss it all into the dustbin of history.

Okay, now sit down with your yellow pad and a pencil. And try this question, or challenge, on for size:

How would you remake the presidency?

Would you make the job more or less powerful? Would you split the job up for two or three people to manage? How long should a president serve? And most important, who should choose the president?

The men who sweated in secret meetings during a steamy Philadelphia summer to create the American Constitution and reinvent the government of the United States of America faced exactly that challenge and those questions. What they came up with, sometimes by default, was a job and an office that most of them—we can probably assume—would now agree is not exactly what they had in mind.

A platypus, it has been said, is a duck designed by a committee. Perhaps the same thing can be said about the American president, a novel idea cooked up behind locked doors and sealed windows in the summer of 1787.

Who was America's first president?

There is a trick "trivia" question: "Who was the first president of the United States?" The obvious answer: George Washington. But the correct answer is John Hanson of Maryland. Or is it really Peyton Randolph of Virginia?

Both of these men, now largely obscure in American history, were presidents of the United States.

When the delegates to the Constitutional Convention arrived in Philadelphia in May 1787, they had come ostensibly to revise the ineffective Articles of Confederation, which had governed the thirteen states since the Declaration in 1776 and been adopted officially in 1781. Under the Articles, America had a "president." But he was the "President of the United States of America in Congress Assembled." The office was essentially a ceremonial chairmanship, not to be held by one man for more than one year, although he could be reelected after sitting out two years. These were extreme term limits that show how little power the man holding office could potentially wield. Under the Articles of Confederation, there was no "chief executive," and no one functioned in an executive role. Basically, he held a gavel.

This American president then lacked any of the powers associated with the president today. But as the first president elected under the Articles of Confederation, John Hanson, a merchant and patriot leader from Maryland, has often been cited as the "first president" but essentially disappeared into obscurity.

But even Hanson wasn't actually "first." A veteran of Virginia's House of Burgesses, Peyton Randolph was elected first president of the Continental Congress in 1774. He died in 1775, before Independence was declared, so he never really even lived in the United States of America. John Hancock, who was presiding over the Continental Congress in 1776 when the Declaration of Independence was adopted, could also be called the "first" president of the United States of America.

As we know it, the office of the president of the United States was created under Article II in the Constitution, written in 1787. Before that time, Congress chose fourteen other presidents. Some of their names, like Hancock, John Jay, and Richard Henry Lee, are notable or at least mildly familiar; others are completely obscure. All were presidents, but their powers were limited to presiding over Congress when it was in session.

The Presidents of the United States in Congress Assembled

1774	Peyton Randolph, Virginia
1774–1775	Henry Middleton, South Carolina
1775–1776	John Hancock, Massachusetts
	(who presided when the Declaration was adopted)
1777–1778	Henry Laurens, South Carolina
1778–1779	John Jay, New York
1779–1781	Samuel Huntington, Connecticut
1781	Thomas McKean, Delaware
1781–1782	John Hanson, Maryland
1782–1783	Elias Boudinot, New Jersey
1783–1784	Thomas Mifflin, Pennsylvania
1784–1785	Richard Henry Lee, Virginia
1785–1786	John Hancock, Massachusetts
1786–1787	Nathaniel Gorham, Massachusetts
1787–1788	Arthur St. Clair, Pennsylvania
1788–1789	Cyrus Griffin, Virginia

PRESIDENTIAL VOICES

The evils we experience flow from the excess of democracy. The people do not [lack] virtue, but are the dupes of pretended patriots. In Massachusetts, it has been fully confirmed by experience that they are daily misled into the most

baneful measures and opinions by the false reports circulated by designing men, and which no one on the spot can refute.[3]
—ELBRIDGE GERRY
Massachusetts delegate to the Constitutional Convention
May 31, 1787[4]

What did an army of angry farmers have to do with creating the U.S. presidency?

The "designing men" referred to by delegate Elbridge Gerry,* a future vice president who would ultimately refuse to put his name on the completed Constitution, surely included a group of angry citizens from his home state of Massachusetts. These men, who took part in an uprising known as Shays' Rebellion, were not exactly wild-eyed radicals. Neither were they "pretended patriots." They were mostly farmers, along with some tradesmen and shopkeepers. Many of them were veterans of the American Revolution who had stood their ground on Bunker Hill and frozen through the winter at Valley Forge. But their "little rebellion," as Thomas Jefferson later called it, helped pave the way for delegates at the Constitutional Convention to invent the new American government and with it an executive officer who would be called "president."

The years immediately following the War for Independence brought economic chaos to America. The Revolution was followed by inflation, unemployment, and depression, as is often the case with wars. Under the Articles of Confederation, which governed America during the war years and had been officially adopted in 1781, the American Congress

---

* Elbridge Gerry (1744–1814) was the fifth U.S. Vice President, serving under James Madison. He was the second to die in the office; his immediate predecessor George Clinton had died of a heart attack in office. But Gerry is better remembered in American political history for redrawing the boundaries of legislative districts in Massachusetts as the state's governor. A cartoonist depicted the oddly shaped result as a salamander, which he called a "Gerry-mander." The word gerrymander is now part of the American political lexicon as a verb that means to create legislative districts to favor one party.

had precious little power, no system of national courts, and no executive to run the show.

Each state, not each congressman (and they were all men then), got a vote. An army existed more or less in name only. But apart from seeing America through the war years, the Confederation Congress produced two important ordinances. In 1785, the Land Ordinance established surveying and land ownership provisions for the western lands being opened to settlement. The Northwest Ordinance of 1787 established the rules for admission of new states: With language that foreshadowed the Bill of Rights, it encouraged support for public education and religious freedom and prohibited slavery in this territory, which established the Ohio River as the northern boundary of slavery in America.[5]

Little more than a mutual defense pact among the thirteen states, the Articles gave the national government no power to collect taxes. The government could only ask the states for money. (Try that today!) And in those thirteen states, separate currencies had created financial chaos.

"Money problems pervaded all others under the Articles of Confederation," historian Ron Chernow wrote in an assessment that may sound remarkably familiar to contemporary Americans. "America was virtually bankrupt as the federal government and state governments found it impossible to retire debt inherited from the Revolution. On European securities exchanges, investors expressed skepticism about America's survival by trading its securities at a small fraction of the face values."[6]

While the situation was dire in many of the states, the dislocation and discontent was most threatening in Massachusetts, birthplace of the patriot cause. Popular anger boiled over into open rebellion and bloodshed in the episode known as Shays' Rebellion.

This discord was a sign of what is now called "class warfare" by the media and politicians. That is the modern buzzword for the economic tensions that existed in early America from the colonial era onward, pitting on one side the "have-nots"—including the frontier farmers, inner-city laborers, and tradesmen ("mechanics"), local merchants, and free blacks—against the "haves"—which meant the landed, slaveholding gentry and the international traders, bankers, and lawyers of the larger, mostly coastal cities.

If either the "Tea Party" or "Occupy Wall Street" movements of contemporary America wanted a historical group to point to for some antigovernment or anticorporate inspiration, the "Shaysites" of Massachusetts in 1786 might be the ticket. They had taken to heart Thomas Jefferson's preamble to the Declaration of Independence: "That whenever any form of government becomes destructive of these ends, it is the right of the people to alter or abolish it."

While there had been minor skirmishing with debtor courts across New England and other sections of America following independence, the troubles accelerated in 1780. That year, Massachusetts passed a state constitution and a series of laws that found few admirers among the working poor and striving middle class, many of them veterans of the Continental Army still waiting for promised bonuses. As John Adams explained in a letter to Thomas Jefferson as this crisis was building, "The Massachusetts Assembly had, in its zeal to get the better of their debt, laid on a tax rather heavier than the people could bear. This commotion will terminate in additional strength to the government."[7]

In the summer of 1786, with the growing loss of farmlands and homes to foreclosure, and local militia taking sides with the farmers instead of local courts, a forty-year-old army veteran named Daniel Shays emerged to become the de facto leader of this loose collection of increasingly angry citizens. Shays had served with distinction at Bunker Hill and had even been presented with a ceremonial sword by the Marquis de Lafayette after the Battle of Saratoga. With some seven hundred farmers, merchants, and other tradespeople, Shays led a march on Springfield and paraded around the town. The marchers sported a sprig of hemlock in their hatbands, an evergreen symbol of liberty worn by many soldiers during the Revolution.

By late January 1787, "Shays' Army" had grown to more than a thousand men and was preparing to assault the federal arsenal in Springfield, confiscate the muskets and cannons stored there, and march on to Boston, the seat of wealth and power. But portly General Benjamin Lincoln, one of Washington's wartime commanders, reached the arsenal first, with a militia army paid for by Boston's governor and wealthy merchants. After a few volleys of artillery fire left four "insurgents" dead, Shays' Army, outnumbered and outgunned, quickly scattered. As a harsh, snowy winter took its toll, the Shaysites disappeared into the New England woods. Some of them were caught, tried, and punished. Others were pardoned. On the run in Vermont—not yet a state and welcoming of antigovernment "outlaws"—Daniel Shays was later pardoned and eventually received a veteran's pension. He died in relative obscurity on a farm in western New York in 1825.

From Paris, where he was serving as envoy of Congress, Thomas Jefferson famously wrote of this uprising, "A little rebellion now and then is a good thing. . . . God forbid that we should ever be twenty years without such a rebellion. . . . The tree of liberty must be refreshed from time to time with the blood of patriots and tyrants."

Some other Virginians, notably George Washington, took a dimmer view. Washington fretted about the hand of England in the uprising, and he feared that everything he'd fought for was coming undone. "There are combustibles in every state which a spark may set fire to," he wrote to his old wartime friend and artillery commander, Henry Knox—now in charge of the United States Army. His worries about "combustibles" included some uncomfortably close to home. In Virginia and South Carolina, groups similar to Shays' Army were burning courthouses and stopping tax collections.[8]

The uprising named for Daniel Shays, and the fear of more like it, moved Washington, James Madison—at thirty-seven years old the youngest member of the ineffective Congress—and others to action. A groundswell to rethink and revise the Articles of Confederation led Congress to call for a meeting. James Madison, the five-foot-tall young Virginian, took the lead in organizing the meeting. It began in May 1787 in Philadelphia, in the same place the Declaration had been adopted eleven years earlier. But he and some of the men who gathered there had bigger ideas—to throw out the Articles altogether and start from scratch.

PRESIDENTIAL VOICES

In company with Mr. Govr. Morris and in his Phaeton with my horses, went up to . . . the vicinity of Valley Forge to get Trout. . . .

Whilst Mr. Morris was fishing I rid over the old Cantonment of the American [Army] of the Winter, 1777 and 8, visited all the Works, wch. Were in Ruins, and the Incampments in woods where the grounds had not been cultivated.

—GEORGE WASHINGTON
Diary entries, July 30–31, 1787[9]

Who were the "elites" in charge of the Constitutional Convention?

One of the most prominent men serving in Congress under the Articles was Robert Morris of Philadelphia. Born in Liverpool, England, he had been brought to America by his father and became a successful merchant and one of the country's wealthiest men. Morris was largely credited with keeping America afloat financially during the Revolution. He had made personal loans to pay Washington's troops, while also being assailed by Philadelphians who charged that he was hoarding wheat and other supplies to drive up prices. In wartime Philadelphia that charge actually led to a riot in which Morris and another signer of the Declaration, James Wilson, were attacked by a mob armed with cannons.

With the Revolution over, Morris was a moneyman who recognized that the fledgling country needed stronger economic footing to survive. As superintendent of finance under the Articles of Confederation, he had become a sort of "acting president," accumulating significant power and making executive decisions. But his "energetic" moves alarmed some congressmen, since he was also the head of a merchant house in Philadelphia while serving as the Confederation's equivalent of treasury secretary. His wartime reputation for "gouging" also dogged him. Congress investigated Morris's dealings and found no wrongdoing—or "conflict of interest," in modern parlance. But Morris emerged from the episode convinced that the Articles needed to be scrapped.

And he had the ear of his old friend, George Washington, then a retired war hero and gentleman farmer in Virginia who was watching the events in western Massachusetts with considerable alarm.*

The group that slowly gathered in Philadelphia in early May and eventually reached a quorum on May 25, 1787, was authorized by the Congress only to revise or amend the Articles of Confederation. But some of the men convening in the Philadelphia State House had bigger ideas. A dozen of them had met earlier, in September 1786, in Annapolis, Maryland, for a conference to discuss economic issues confronting the weak Confederacy.

Along with Madison, another key mover was Alexander Hamilton, born illegitimate on the Caribbean island of Nevis but now a New York power broker, in part due to his role as wartime aide-de-camp of America's greatest hero, George Washington, and his marriage to Elizabeth Schuyler, a member of one of New York's most wealthy and powerful political families.

In twenty-first-century America, where radio hosts, commentators, and candidates routinely deride their opponents as "elites," it is well to remember that there were few more elitist gatherings than the two groups who met in Philadelphia in 1776 and again in 1787. The Constitutional Convention was, without a doubt, one of the most extraordinary collections of political talent in history, coming together at an extraordinary moment. "They were a product of a particular place and moment of the late eighteenth century. They were deliberating at a point in history when intellectualism and political activism could naturally, easily, coexist," as Constitutional historian Richard Beeman put it. "The most influential of these men could lay claim to being both the intellectual and political leaders of their respective states."[10] The men who gathered to debate the shape and form of the new Constitution were among the wealthiest, best-educated citizens of the new nation, as

---

* Robert Morris would be Washington's first choice to head the new treasury once it was created. But Morris was not interested. Instead he would end up in debtors' prison, in one of the most spectacular falls from grace among the Founding Fathers, when his real estate empire, built on borrowed money, crashed in 1797, during one of the first economic panics in American history.

historian James McGregor Burns once famously encapsulated them, "the well-bred, the well-fed, the well-read, and the well-wed."[11]

Perhaps the single greatest personification of that description was the one man that every American knew—and whose presence was absolutely required for any possibility of success: George Washington. All of the others, including Alexander Hamilton, James Madison, and Benjamin Franklin, recognized that the convention would only succeed with Washington's blessing—and participation.

Suffering from rheumatism, the fifty-five-year-old Washington preferred to remain in "retirement" at Mount Vernon. But the shock of Shays' Rebellion and the appeals to personal ambition and ego—yes, Washington had one—convinced him that his reputation and stature were required. When old ally Benjamin Franklin wrote, "Your presence will be of the greatest importance to the success of the measure,"[12] Washington relented.

The reluctant delegate, Washington wrote to his friend the Marquis de Lafayette, "I could not resist a call to the convention of the States which is to determine whether we have a government of respectability under which life, liberty and property will be secured to us, or are to submit to one which may be the result of chance or the moment springing from anarchy and Confusion, and dictated perhaps by some aspiring demagogue."[13]

Washington arrived in Philadelphia like the conquering hero he was. Former officers came out to salute him, providing an escort across the Schuylkill River into Philadelphia, where church bells rang in a "celebration the likes of which had not been seen since the end of the war."[14] Washington settled into the lavish home of Robert Morris, who had room for Washington's longtime manservant, the slave Billy Lee, and stables for his horses.

On the evening of May 16, Benjamin Franklin—wealthy and world famous as the author of *Poor Richard's Almanack*—hosted a dinner for the delegates who had arrived, not yet enough for a quorum to begin the convention. Over substantial quantities of port—which as Franklin later reported, "the company agreed unanimously . . . was the best porter they had ever tasted"[15]—Washington, Franklin, Madison, Robert Morris and Gouverneur Morris (not relatives, but close associates), and several other key members of the Convention dined and talked about their hopes for the coming deliberations. "Franklin, more than any other delegate at the Convention, had a superb sense of the way in which good food, liquor and conversation could lubricate the machinery of government and politics," according to constitutional historian Richard Beeman.[16]

"Poor Richard's" dinner guests included the men most committed to a dramatic overhaul of the government. Before an official proposal was moved, a motion seconded, or a vote taken, these men had determined that the government would be made stronger, all under Franklin's convivial hospitality.

Once the other delegates trickled into Philadelphia and formed the necessary quorum—Rhode Island, deeply in debt and fearing the outcome, did not send a delegation, earning it the derisive nickname of "Rogue Island"—the Convention's first order of business was to elect a presiding officer. There were only two serious candidates: Benjamin Franklin and Washington. The oldest of the delegates at eighty-one, Franklin was in poor health and had to be brought to the meetings—when his health permitted—in a French sedan chair mounted on two poles and carried aloft by four inmates from the nearby Walnut Street Jail. In Franklin's absence, but at his suggestion, Robert Morris put forward Washington's name as the convention's presiding officer. He was elected unanimously.

Washington rarely addressed the Convention. Once, when a paper containing some of the resolutions under debate was dropped and left on the floor of the state house, he warned: "Gentlemen be more careful, lest our transactions get into the News Papers, and disturb the public repose by premature speculations."[17]

But his dominating presence at the Convention, and his counsel offered in more intimate and unofficial gatherings at the home of Robert Morris, held enormous sway.

PRESIDENTIAL VOICES

I have reason to hope there will be greater unanimity and less opposition, except for the little States, than was at first apprehended. The most prevalent idea in the principal States seems to be a total alteration of the present federal system, and substituting a great national council or parliament, consisting of two branches of the legislature, founded upon the principles of equal proportionate representation, with full legislative powers upon all subjects of the Union; and an executive: and to make the latter a power of a negative upon all such laws as they shall judge contrary to the interest of the federal Union. It is easy to foresee that there will be much difficulty in organizing a government upon this great scale, and at the same time reserving to the State legislatures a sufficient portion of power for promoting and securing the prosperity and happiness of their respective citizens.

—GEORGE MASON

Virginia delegate to the Constitutional Convention

May 1787

Why does America have a president?

For more than 220 years, the presidency has been a fixture of the American political landscape. The president seems to be, well, more American than apple pie.

But the thought of a single man, wielding great power at the head of the federal republic and commanding a standing army, gave the fifty-five men who gathered (not all were present for all of the debates) in Philadelphia in 1787 the willies. The job of president was being invented by men who didn't necessarily think that having a president was such a great idea.

The Constitutional debates in the summer of 1787 over the role of the "Executive Department" were heated, divisive, and often intense. And very drawn out. The convention started talking about the executive in early June and was still trying to sort the job out in early September, as tempers flared and patience seemed at an end.

An executive, whether one man or three, was desirable to most delegates because they knew the government needed a man of "energy," as Alexander Hamilton would later describe it—a quality Hamilton thought included "decision, activity, secrecy and dispatch . . . vigor and expedition." The delegates had enough experience with the endless debates and logjams in Congress and its committees—during the Revolution and afterward. An executive, whose power was sufficiently checked but who was separate from the legislature, would provide that "vigor." But they knew that a man of "energy" also needed his powers kept on a leash.

There were also real fears of foreign manipulation, the potential for bribery, and the pull of regional politics. A president from a large, populous region, like New England, where antislavery sentiment was growing, would dominate the smaller—read slaveholding—sections of the country.

Above all, men who had lived through and led the Revolution against King George feared an American king. Most of those against vesting too much power in the executive adamantly opposed the idea of a "strong man" who might turn the presidency into a stepping-stone to an American hereditary monarchy.

The concern over a new aristocracy and hereditary succession was more than mere Enlightenment-era, democratic idealism. As Virginia's Edmund Randolph—governor of Virginia and nephew of Peyton Randolph—put it in the earliest days of the Convention, the executive was the "fetus of monarchy."[18] The Constitution would specifically ban hereditary titles in America. (Article I, Section 9 specifies: "No title of nobility shall be granted by the United States.")

One unspoken reason Washington was so appealing to many delegates was the fact that he had no heirs. The age requirement for the presidency of thirty-five years, argues Constitutional historian Akhil Reed Amar, was meant to underscore this idea by preventing the young son of a famous father from rising to the presidency without a track record of personal accomplishments.[19]

The first formal proposal that a strong "national executive" be part of the new federal government was contained in the so-called Virginia Plan, drafted by Madison and presented on May 29, 1787, by Edmund Randolph. This proposal called for an executive to serve for an undetermined number of years, receive compensation, and hold the authority to "examine every act" of the legislature. Madison was concerned with the separation of powers between the three branches of government and insisted that checks be instituted at every turn to prevent one branch from dominating the others. (When finally completed in September, the Constitution provided for a legislature in Article I, an executive in Article II, and a judicial branch in Article III but gave few specific plans for the court system. The mechanics of the federal court system, including a supreme court and lower courts, would be created by Congress with the Judiciary Act of 1789.)

On the same day, May 29, Charles Pinckney of South Carolina presented his "Plan of a Federal Constitution." A colorful, flamboyant character with a reputation as a ladies' man, Pinckney possessed an outsized ego which led him to lie about his age, presenting himself as twenty-four and the youngest delegate. (He was in fact twenty-nine;[20] Jonathan Dayton of New Jersey, at twenty-seven, deserves the title of youngest delegate.) Pinckney's plan did not enter into the recorded debates, but his version of the executive, called "the president," rings very close to the final draft of Article II, which lays out the powers of the presidency. (See Appendix I, page 635.)

When Pennsylvania's James Wilson, one of the most significant framers of the Constitution that most people have never heard of, moved on June 1 that the executive consist of a single person, James Madison noted that the idea was met with a "considerable pause." Benjamin Franklin suggested that the whole discussion over the executive was so important that the "gentlemen should deliver their sentiments on it before the question was put."

Certainly one reason that there was such a considerable pause may have been the fact that everyone knew that the man who would be the first executive was sitting in the room—George Washington, the presiding officer of the Constitutional Convention. As Franklin himself told the delegates on June 1, "The first man put on the helm will be a good one. Nobody knows what sort may come afterwards. The executive will be always increasing here, as elsewhere, till it ends in monarchy."[21]

In the secret debates and discussions that would eventually lead to the framing of the Constitution in those sultry and contentious summer months, few topics generated as much heat as the question of the role and makeup of the Executive Department. To many of these delegates the prospect of an executive in the shape of a single person set alarm bells ringing. When the discussion of the executive began, there were several key issues to be explored:

- What powers should be assigned to the executive?
- How long should the executive serve?
- How would the executive be chosen?
- And how would he be removed if necessary?

Summarizing all of these issues, Yale historian Robert A. Dahl notes, "What is revealed in the most complete record of the Convention is a body floundering in its attempts to answer an impossibly difficult question: How should the chief executive of a republic be selected, and what constitutional powers should be assigned to the executive branch. The question was impossibly difficult because . . . the Framers had no relevant model of republican government to give them guidance. Most of all, they lacked any suitable model for the executive branch."[22]

As the debate in Philadelphia continued over the extent of an executive's powers, as well as his selection, the question often returned to the nearly obsessive fear of monarchy.

It was a fear voiced most clearly by influential delegate George Mason. On June 4, Mason rose and said, "We are, Mr. Chairman, going very far in this business. We are not constituting a British government, but a more dangerous monarchy, an elective one. . . . Do gentlemen mean to pave the way for a hereditary monarchy? Do they flatter themselves that the people will ever consent to such an innovation? If they do, I venture to tell them they are mistaken. The people will never consent. . . . Notwithstanding the oppressions and injustice experienced among us from democracy, the genius of the people is in favor of it, and the genius of the people must be consulted."

Mason added that he "hoped that nothing like a monarchy would ever be attempted in this country. A hatred to its oppressions had carried the people through the late Revolution."[23]

Virginia statesman George Mason (1725–1792) is not often mentioned in the same breath with the "all star" founders and framers. But Mason was one of the most significant and influential men of the day.

Before the Revolution, his greatest contribution was authorship of the Virginia Declaration of Rights, recognized as the first American Bill of Rights, written in 1776 and later added to Virginia's constitution. Jefferson borrowed from Mason to craft the Declaration of Independence.

Mason also played an active role in the debates creating the Constitution, but he disagreed intensely with parts of it. Chief among his complaints was the lack of a bill of rights to protect personal liberties. Another of those slaveholding delegates who denounced slavery, Mason also found fault with some of the compromises that would be made over slavery. But he was among the most vocal critics of the potentially monarchical powers of the new Executive Department. Dissatisfied when these concerns were not addressed, Mason was one of three delegates who refused to sign the Constitution.

PRESIDENTIAL VOICES

We are acting a very strange part. We first form a strong man to protect us, and at the same time wish to tie his hands behind him.
—GOUVERNEUR MORRIS
Pennsylvania delegate to the Constitutional Convention
August 1787[24]

What compromises did the delegates make over representation?
From the vantage point of history, and going on the record compiled by James Madison, the debates over the executive hopscotched around for most of the summer. Delegates kept shifting their attention among the various issues confronting them—the legislature composed of one chamber or two; how the states would be represented in Congress; and the slavery issue. On each one of these issues, famous compromises would be struck that paved the way for the Constitution.

The central issue was how representation of each state in Congress was to be apportioned. Smaller states feared the power of larger states if population was the only factor. On that question, the fate of the convention often hung. And the stakes were extraordinarily high. Delaware's forty-year-old Gunning Bedford, Jr., struck the most dangerous note when he threatened that if large states made population the only organizing principle of the new Congress, "the small ones will find some foreign ally of more honor and good faith." To which Gouverneur Morris replied on July 5, "The country must be united. If persuasion does not unite it, the sword will."[25]

Ultimately a compromise created a two-chamber Congress: a House of Representatives based on population, and a Senate—the word drawn from the Roman model so influential to many of the framers—based on equal representation, with two senators for each state.

The third issue was, if anything, more contentious. What was America going to do about counting its slaves?

Several delegates from the north, where emancipation was beginning to take root, began by asking why slaves should be counted at all. Gouverneur Morris, in one of the most famous of his many speeches to the convention (the record shows Morris spoke most often, 173 times), demanded to know:

Upon what principle is it that the slaves shall be computed in the representation? Are they men? Then make them citizens and let them vote. Are they property? Why then is no other property included? The houses in [Philadelphia] are worth more than all the wretched slaves which cover the rice swamps of South Carolina. . . . The inhabitant of Georgia and South Carolina who goes to the coast of Africa and, in defiance of the most sacred laws of humanity, tears away his fellow creatures from their dearest connections and damns them to the most cruel bondages, shall have more votes in a government instituted for the protection of the rights of mankind than the citizens of Pennsylvania or New Jersey who views with laudable horror so nefarious a practice. [26]

Raised in one of New York's oldest, most prosperous and most aristocratic families, with roots that went back to New York's Dutch colonial days, Morris had grown up with house slaves or "servants." But Morris, who lost a leg in a carriage accident and walked on a wooden peg leg, had become an advocate for emancipation as early as 1777. In the New York Provincial Convention, which was writing the state's constitution, Morris and his friend and colleague John Jay, future first chief justice of the Supreme Court, moved that New York abolish slavery. But this proposal did not fly. New York had the largest slave population of any northern state and strong ties to West Indies sugar plantations. Slavery was too profitable.

Like that New York convention, this Philadelphia convention a decade later was unmoved by Morris's eloquence on the subject of slaves. It was the dominant issue on which there would be a compromise, which permitted the continued existence of slavery in this new nation founded on the ideals of freedom and equality. There was also a compromise on potentially ending the foreign slave trade in 1808, as well as taxing slaves. Of course, the words "slave" and "slavery" aren't in the Constitution. But Article I: Section 9 reads: "The Migration or Importation of such Persons as any of the States now existing shall think proper to admit, shall not be prohibited by the Congress prior to the Year one thousand eight hundred and eight, but a Tax or duty may be imposed on such Importation, not exceeding ten dollars for each Person." (The tax on slaves was never imposed.)

Generous historians claim that the framers kicked this can twenty years down the road because they believed slavery would eventually die out in America. James Wilson of Pennsylvania, for instance, said, "I consider this as laying the foundation for banishing slavery out of this country."[27]

But the other piece of the grand bargain that went into the making of America's Constitution, and with it the presidency, was also related to slavery, and it was in many respects even more significant. In the census that would apportion congressional seats to the states, American slaves would be counted—as three-fifths of a person.

How did the framers come up with "electors"?

Even as those two crucial issues—ending slavery and counting slaves—dominated the debate and threatened its very existence, for much of the summer the delegates vacillated over the details of the executive. Decisions made in the first few weeks were constantly revisited and revised, as if the delegates were more uncertain about this new office than any other element of the new government they were creating.

On June 1, Madison's version of executive authority had been imprecisely defined but accepted in general. The delegates turned their attention to the issue of term length, and a single seven-year term was initially approved. On June 2, they focused on the means of election, and James Wilson, the brilliant Scotsman and attorney who had been a signer of the Declaration (eight signers were also delegates to the Constitutional Convention), proposed direct election by the people.

But Wilson's proposal was rejected in favor of an executive chosen by the national legislature—in essence a parliamentary-style system. It should be noted that in 1787, the modern British parliamentary system as we know it had not yet evolved. The British prime minister was essentially still a royal appointee, providing a poor example for the framers.

Around this point, Benjamin Franklin inserted a motion stating his belief that the executive should not be paid. But the convention politely tabled the idea, not wanting to reject the old patriot's idealistic but impractical notion out of hand.

The debate moved to the question of a single executive or an executive council. Again the question was tabled without a decisive vote. With James Wilson taking the lead on Monday, June 4, in favor of a single executive, the articulate, erudite, and influential Scotsman argued that a proposed Executive Council, or a triumvirate, would be "nothing but uncontrolled, continued and violent animosities." By the end of the day the votes were there for a single executive—although New York, Delaware, and Maryland opposed the resolution.

The least appealing plan for the executive came during a marathon, six-hour speech by Alexander Hamilton, whose idea for a "governor" called for a permanent executive, whose term was unlimited except by death, resignation, or removal (impeachment). Reeking of monarchy, Hamilton's plan was basically dismissed without discussion.

The matter of the executive was then set aside from the debates until mid-July when Pennsylvania's Gouverneur Morris moved that the citizens of the United States elect the chief executive. "If the people should elect, they will never fail to prefer some man of distinguished character, or services. . . . If the Legislature elect, it will be the work of intrigue, of cabals and of faction."

By "faction," Morris meant "party"—a reminder of the framers' disdain for the idea of political parties, as well as one of the greatest failures of their vision—the inability to see that the office they were creating and the system for choosing the executive would lead inevitably to the development of America's dominant two-party political system.

Morris reopened the question of direct election, but his motion was rejected by all but his own state of Pennsylvania, where there was a tradition of direct election of the governor.

On Thursday, July 19, the convention took up the election question once more. The accepted motion called for "electors" appointed by the legislatures of the states. The idea was accepted with more discussion to come over the precise number of electors each state would have.

On July 26, still undecided on the method of choosing the executive, the delegates took a break so a Committee of Detail could put the proposals made so far into writing.

George Washington took the opportunity to go trout fishing with Gouverneur Morris. They rode out to nearby Valley Forge, and Washington looked over the fortifications and camps his army had built in that fearful winter of 1777–78. It must have been more than poignant, as Washington noted in his diary then, that the "works were in ruins."

By August 6, the convention had a working, written draft, which drew upon a plan put forth by South Carolina's Charles Pinckney. Under Pinckney's plan, which contained more than thirty provisions that ended up in the final form of the Constitution, the executive was a single person serving a single seven-year term. But this proposal was not put to debate until August 24. The delegates were hot, tired, and seemingly despondent over their inability to settle all of the major issues they confronted.

In true congressional fashion, they eventually turned the problem of unresolved tabled motions over to a committee. Among other items, on September 4, this "Committee of Eleven" (Madison, Gouverneur Morris, and Roger Sherman, among them) reported back their recommendations for a president and vice president serving a four-year term. The committee established the qualifications for being president and gave the executive the power to make treaties and to appoint judges to the Supreme Court with the advice and consent of the Senate. At the heart of their plan was also the design of a voting system that left the method of choosing the presidential electors up to legislatures of the various states.

Summarizing these twists and turns during that Philadelphia summer as a "meandering trail," Yale historian Robert A. Dahl notes, "By now [September 4] the delegates are eager to wind up a convention that has already gone on for three months. In contradiction to the recommendation of the previous committee, however, this one recommends that the executive be chosen by electors appointed by the state legislatures. Two days later, with nine states in favor and only two opposed, the impatient delegates adopt this solution. . . . What this strange record suggests to me is a group of baffled and confused men who finally settle on a solution more out of desperation than confidence. As events were soon to show, they had little understanding of how their solution would work out in practice."[28]

What is a "natural born Citizen"?

"No Person except a natural born Citizen . . . shall be eligible to the Office of President."

What exactly does that mean? Guess what. The Constitution does not say. So much for "original intent."

The first seven presidents were all British citizens at birth, since they were born before 1776. But the Constitution covered them because it was written to include the phrase, "a Citizen of the United States, at the time of the Adoption of this Constitution." This meant that even Alexander Hamilton, born illegitimate on the Caribbean island of Nevis, was eligible to become president.

But where does that leave the modern "birther" controversy, raised several times in American presidential history and most controversially over President Barack Obama's purported birth in Kenya? No court has ever actually ruled on the issue, but Barack Obama may have still been eligible to run for president, even if he had been born in Kenya.*

That is the considered opinion of the Congressional Research Service, a nonpartisan arm of Congress, which provides legal and other scholarly research to the House and Senate. In an April 3, 2009, memorandum prepared during the Obama birther controversy, CRS reported, "The weight of scholarly legal and historical opinion appears to support the notion that 'natural born Citizen' means one who is entitled under the Constitution or laws of the United States to U.S. citizenship 'at birth' or 'by birth,' including any child born 'in' the United States (other than to foreign diplomats serving their country), the children of United States citizens born abroad, and *those born abroad of one citizen parent who has met U.S. residency requirements.*"[29] (Emphasis added.)

Why did the framers fear direct democracy?

Direct election by the people was always a no-sale to the convention delegates. The framers who feared that too much democracy was a dangerous thing opposed it. To be fair, they also feared that geography and lack of nationwide communications would keep people in one part of the country from knowing who the candidates from another part were. George Mason made this point when he said, "The extent of the Country renders it impossible that the people can have the requisite capacity to judge of the respective pretensions of the Candidates."[30]

But there is another factor to be considered and it is usually brushed under the carpet in the civics books. The issue involves the word that never appears in the Constitution. Constitutional scholar Akhil Reed Amar underscores the point: "The biggest democratic defect of Article II, a factor that is too rarely featured in standard electoral-college stories: slavery." Slaves were obviously not going to get an actual vote in a direct election—no slave state would accept that idea. But the slave

---

* The subject of Barack Obama's birth is covered in his Presidential Profile (see page 607). However, all necessary legal evidence proves that Obama was indeed born in Hawaii.

states insisted that slaves be counted for apportioning House seats and electors.

Once the three-fifths compromise on representation was settled by the Philadelphia delegates, it not only gave slave states power in Congress beyond their free population, it gave them more electors. As Reed points out, "Under America's first census and apportionment, Virginia would receive six more House seats, and thus six more electors than Pennsylvania, although the two commonwealths at that point had roughly comparable free populations. After the next census, Virginia got 20 percent more electors than did Pennsylvania, even as Old Dominion had 10 percent fewer free citizens and far fewer eligible voters. For thirty-two of the presidency's first thirty-six years, a (slaveholding, plantation-owning) Virginian would occupy the nation's highest office."[31]

The seventh president, Andrew Jackson, born in the Carolinas but elected from Tennessee, added eight more years to that string of slaveholding presidents. Of the nation's first seven presidents, only John Adams and his son John Quincy Adams, of Massachusetts, both one-termers, held no slaves. This is the hard fact of slavery and the presidency, as Clarence Lusane writes. "More than one in four U.S. presidents were involved in human trafficking and slavery. These presidents bought, sold, bred, and enslaved black people for profit. Of the twelve presidents who were enslavers, more than half kept people in bondage at the White House."[32]

In *Unruly Americans*, University of Richmond historian Woody Holton underscores that the bonus electors awarded to the slave states powerfully influenced politics in the new nation. And, he adds, "[abolitionists] denounced the Constitution for considering the enslaved American only three-fifths of a person. But they also understood that in apportioning the power to choose the president and Congress among the free and slave states, the Framers would have actually strengthened the slaveholders if they had counted slaves as equal to whites. In this one instance, the slaves' interests would have been better served if they had not been considered persons at all."[33]

For a long time to come in America, "slave power" ruled—it was the essence of presidential and political power.

PRESIDENTIAL VOICES

Whilst the members were signing it, Doctor Franklin, looking towards the president's chair, at the back of which a rising sun happened to be painted, observed to a few members near him, that painters had often found it difficult to distinguish in their art a rising from a setting sun. I have, said he, often in the course of the session, and the vicissitudes of my hopes and fears as to its issue, looked at that behind the president, without being able to tell whether it was rising or setting. But now at length I have the happiness to know that it is a rising and not a setting sun.

—RECORDED BY JAMES MADISON
September 17, 1787[34]

The Constitution was signed by thirty-nine of the fifty-five men who at various times had been in Philadelphia and participated in the secret debates. Three of the more vocal delegates who refused to sign were Elbridge Gerry, George Mason, and Edmund Randolph.

Now the men who believed in the Constitution—they would become known generally as Federalists—had to sell this idea to a somewhat skeptical nation. Groups that called themselves anti-Federalists would oppose them. James Wilson spoke to Pennsylvania's legislature and won his crucial state's approval. For his efforts, Wilson was attacked and beaten by an anti-Federalist mob.

Watching from Paris, Jefferson—who would become the third president in a controversial election—wrote to Adams of his fears of executive authority. Jefferson, who was probably the most anti of the American antimonarchists, wanted nothing resembling a king and thought one man at the head of an army was on its face a serious threat to the republic. "Once in office, and possessing the military force of the union, without the aid or the check of a council, he would not easily be dethroned, even if the people could be induced to withdraw their votes from him." Jefferson called the office a "bad edition of a Polish king."

Adams, on the other hand, approved of the proposed Constitution and thought, if anything, that the president should have had more power. Writing from his post as America's minister in London, he replied to Jefferson, "You are afraid of the one, I, the few. We agree perfectly that the many should have full, fair, and perfect representation [in the House of Representatives]. You are apprehensive of monarchy; I, of aristocracy. I would therefore have given more power to the president and less to the Senate."[35]

Politely discussed at this moment, the disagreement between these two men, allies in Philadelphia in 1776, friends through the war, would later shatter their friendship at the dawn of American political parties, when they became bitter partisan rivals as presidents.

Alexander Hamilton, James Madison, and John Jay wrote a series of essays in support of the Constitution known as the "Federalist Papers." While they remain widely studied today for their insights into the process and thinking that went into the Constitution, the influence they had in the actual ratification debate is less certain.

But just about everyone agrees that it was the endorsement of two men, Benjamin Franklin and George Washington, that really sold the country on the Constitution. Although Washington never publicly endorsed the Constitution, he privately lobbied friends and was completely in favor of ratification. As historian John Ferling notes, "Faced with defending a new constitution that would take the country into uncharted waters, the Federalists repeatedly invoked Washington's name, urging Americans to once again pin their hopes on him. . . . The new charter must be safe, they reasoned, or Washington would never have been a party to its drafting."[36]

PRESIDENTIAL VOICES

The executive power is better to be trusted when it has no screen. Sir, we have a responsibility in the person of our president; he cannot act improperly, and hide either his negligence or inattention; he cannot roll upon any other person the weight of his criminality; no appointment can take place without his nomination; and he is responsible for every nomination he makes. We secure vigor. We well know what numerous executives are. We know there is neither vigor, decision, nor responsibility, in them. Add to all this, that officer is placed high, and is possessed of power far from being contemptible; yet not a single privilege is annexed to his character; far from being above the laws, he is amenable to them in his private character as a citizen, and in his public character by impeachment.[37]

—JAMES WILSON
Address to Pennsylvania Ratification Convention
1787

PRESIDENTIAL VOICES

The public mind cannot be occupied about a nobler object than the proposed plan of government. It appears to be admirably calculated to cement all of America in affection and interest as one great nation. A result of accommodation and compromise cannot be supposed perfectly to coincide with any one's idea of perfection.

—JOHN ADAMS[38]

Are all compromises created equal?

In the current political atmosphere, in which "bipartisan compromise" has become political fantasy, Adams's laudatory note about "accommodation and compromise" seems to be describing a lost art. Of course, not everyone agreed that the compromises that went into the framing of the Constitution were such a good idea in the first place. The ardent abolitionist William Lloyd Garrison, for instance, would later call the Constitution "a covenant with Death and an agreement with Hell."

And therein lies the double-edged sword of compromise. When is it acceptable? To the framers who detested slavery, the creation of the Union was a much greater good than abolition. That bargain would ultimately lead to the Civil War.

On this question, Constitutional historian Henry May concludes, "It is hard to exaggerate the greatness of the achievement or the creativity, boldness, and good sense of the Founders. The Constitution reflects all the virtues of the Moderate Enlightenment, and also one of its faults: the belief that *everything* can be settled by compromise. One of the Convention's sets of compromises turned out to be not only immoral but unworkable."[39]

Who elected George Washington?

After the Constitution was established, Benjamin Franklin famously wrote, "Nothing can be said to be certain, except death and taxes."

He might have added one other certainty: that the man who would be elected the first president under the new Constitution was going to be George Washington.

Every man at the Constitutional debates knew that when the time came, Washington, later to be called the "Indispensable Man" by one of his biographers, would become president. But how would Washington actually win that office?

Today, Election Day and who gets to vote are matters of national standards. Back then, America hadn't quite figured out the whole election thing. The Constitution said "electors" would cast the votes. Each elector would actually get two votes. Under the original plan, the second-place finisher would become vice president, an arrangement that would quickly prove rather messy.

But how that actually happened was itself highly improvisational—like the office itself. The result was more like an old patchwork quilt, with each state deciding who would vote for president and how. Of course, African-Americans, Native Americans, and for the most part, women couldn't vote. Among the states, only New Jersey initially allowed some women to vote—a right later withdrawn.

And when the election took place in 1789—the only presidential election year to end in an odd number—there were no political parties or caucuses. Or primaries or conventions. All of the familiar machinery of modern American elections came about over time. And there was no single election day. Those details were also left to the individual states, with an official deadline of January 7, 1789, for returning the results. (Allowing states to set their own election dates would later cause problems as some states began to wait on results in other states, a glitch not fixed until 1845, when a single presidential Election Day was set by Congress.) More curious still, the first national election involved only ten of the thirteen states: Rhode Island and North Carolina had not yet ratified the Constitution and couldn't vote. And New York's legislature could not decide on how to appoint its allotment of electors and missed the deadline.

The convention also, in a modern phrase, "punted" on the exact method of choosing the electors who actually voted for the president; that decision was left up to the states. A few states had a popular vote. Most states chose their electors in the state legislature. In the end, only about 1 percent of the nearly four million Americans (as later counted in the 1790 census) at the time actually got to cast a vote directly for president in 1789. This gives new meaning to the recent controversy over the split between the wealthiest Americans and the other "99 percent," as the Occupy Wall Street movement slogans would have it.

When the electoral votes were tallied, the decision was in favor of the unanimous first choice. John Adams finished second in the voting and became the first vice president under the original rules of presidential elections. A handful of other candidates, all "favorite sons" of different states, won a sprinkling of votes.

On April 14, 1789, the secretary of Congress, Charles Thomson, formally notified Washington of his election. Washington couldn't have been too surprised by the news. His bags had already been packed. Two days later, he left for New York City, then the nation's temporary capital. The presidential election had been invented. Now Washington had to figure out how to be president.

MUST READS

Akhil Reed Amar, *America's Constitution: A Biography*; Richard Beeman, *Plain, Honest Men: The Making of the American Constitution*; Robert A. Dahl, *How Democratic Is the American Constitution?*; Woody Holton, *Unruly Americans and the Origin of the Constitution*; Edward J. Larson and Michael P. Winship, *The Constitutional Convention: A Narrative History from the Notes of James Madison.*

ONLINE RESOURCES

**"The American Constitution: A Documentary Record,"
Avalon Project, Yale Law School**

http://avalon.law.yale.edu/subject_menus/constpap.asp

"Charters of Freedom," National Archives

http://archives.gov/exhibits/charters/constitution.html

**The Founders' Constitution, University of Chicago and
the Liberty Fund**

http://press-pubs.uchicago.edu/founders/

Legal Information Institute/Cornell Law School

http://www.law.cornell.edu/constitution/overview

Library of Congress, Primary Documents of American History

http://www.loc.gov/rr/program/bib/ourdocs/Constitution.html

National Constitution Center, Philadelphia, Pennsylvania

http://constitutioncenter.org/ncc_progs_Constitution_Day.aspx

PART II

Presidential Profiles

The Life and Times of America's Chief Executives
from George Washington to Barack Obama

I do solemnly swear (or affirm) that I will faithfully execute the Office of President of the United States, and will to the best of my ability, preserve, protect and defend the Constitution of the United States.
—PRESIDENTIAL OATH OF OFFICE
Article II, Section 1
U.S. Constitution

[The Presidency] is but a splendid misery.
—THOMAS JEFFERSON
Letter to Elbridge Gerry (May 13, 1797)

No man who ever held the office of President would congratulate a friend on obtaining it.
—JOHN ADAMS
Letter following his son's election, 1825[1]

The White House is a bully pulpit!
—THEODORE ROOSEVELT[2]

No one has a right to grade a President—even poor James Buchanan—who has not sat in his chair, examined the mail and information that came across his desk, and learned why he made his decisions.
—PRESIDENT JOHN F. KENNEDY
to Lincoln biographer David H. Donald[3]

Father of Our Country
George Washington

★ ★ ★

April 30, 1789–March 4, 1797

Milestones in George Washington's Life

February 22, 1732	Born on Pope's Creek Farm, Westmoreland County, Virginia
1753	Appointed major in Virginia colonial militia
July 4, 1754	Surrendered to French troops at Fort Necessity
1754–1758	Fought in French and Indian War
1774–1775	Member of Virginia delegation to First and Second Continental Congresses
June 1775	Appointed commander of Continental Army
October 19, 1781	Victory over British at Yorktown, ending American Revolutionary War
1787	President of Constitutional Convention
1789–1797	First president
July 4, 1798	Commissioned lieutenant general and commander in chief of U.S. Army
December 14, 1799	Died at Mount Vernon, Virginia, aged sixty-seven

PRESIDENTIAL VOICES

I dwell on this prospect with every satisfaction which an ardent love for my country can inspire, since there is no truth more thoroughly established than that there exists in the economy and course of nature an indissoluble union between virtue and happiness; between duty and advantage; between the genuine maxims of an honest and magnanimous policy and the solid rewards of public prosperity and felicity; since we ought to be no less persuaded that the propitious smiles of Heaven can never be expected on a nation that disregards the eternal rules of order and right which Heaven itself has ordained; and since the preservation of the sacred fire of liberty and the destiny of the republican model of government are justly considered, perhaps, as deeply, as finally, staked on the experiment entrusted to the hands of the American people.

—George Washington
First Inaugural Address, April 30, 1789[1]

O kay. We know the cherry tree story isn't true. (We do know that, don't we?) But there is another more telling story about George Washington—also possibly apocryphal—and his carefully constructed public persona. The most familiar version is set at the Constitutional Convention in 1787. Alexander Hamilton, the ambitious, young New Yorker who had forged a close bond with Washington as his wartime aide, bet fellow delegate Gouverneur Morris a dinner that Morris didn't have the nerve to walk up to Washington, slap him on the back, and say, "My dear general, how happy I am to see you look so well."

A New Yorker by birth, Gouverneur Morris was an urbane, well-educated American aristocrat twenty years younger than Washington, but a great admirer of the general. Accepting the challenge, Morris delivered the slap on the back and won the dinner from Hamilton. But Morris would later confess that the withering look he received made this the worst moment in his life. "I have won the bet," he told Hamilton, "but paid dearly for it, and nothing could induce me to repeat it."[2]

Over his long public career, Washington carried himself with dignity, reserve, and a practiced formality. From his childhood study of a list of practical advice, *Rules of Civility & Decent Behaviour*, Washington always maintained a great public sense of decorum—"Let your Countenance be pleasant but in Serious Matters Somewhat grave"; "Rince not your Mouth in the Presence of Others." A man of few words, he counseled those who would listen to follow his example. He was ambitious, egotistical, and possessed an explosive temper but willfully moderated it.

At home on a horse. More happy as a soldier or planter than among politicians. A plainspoken frontiersman. A harsh disciplinarian who once built a gallows forty feet high. A man who liked to dance and favored pretty partners. He was all these things. But it is that cold look he gave Morris that lingers. Who *is* that man staring out so icily from an iconic painting and the dollar bill, or peering down from Mount Rushmore?

No president—with the possible exception of Lincoln—has been more mythologized than George Washington. Yet few remain so distant. And Washington probably preferred it that way. He would not want us slapping his back. We know him so well. Yet not at all.

His personality, military achievements, political ideas, religious beliefs, and views on slavery all remain shrouded in legend—and controversy. Fighter for liberty? Or unrepentant slaveholder? Brilliant commander? Or battlefield bungler? Distinguished demigod? Or, in the words of one biographer, "a monumental ego with a massive personal agenda"?[3]

It goes without saying that America exists, in large measure, because of Washington's role as a stoic revolutionary commander, the largely silent referee at the constitutional debates, the quietly assertive champion of the Constitution's ratification, and the unanimous choice as first president. But flawless he was not.

Fast Facts

RELIGION: Church of England/Episcopal (after 1776)

ASSOCIATIONS: Freemason

MILITARY SERVICE: Virginia Provincial Military (French and Indian War)
Commander of the Continental Army (American Revolution)
Lieutenant general, United States Army ("Quasi War")

CAREER BEFORE POLITICS: Planter, surveyor, soldier

POLITICAL PARTY: None (although he aligned himself with the emerging Federalist Party)

FIRST LADY: Martha Dandridge Custis Washington (June 21, 1731–May 22, 1802)

CHILDREN: Washington had no children. He adopted his wife's two children from her first marriage, John Parke "Jacky" Custis, who died from a fever following the victory at Yorktown in 1781, and Martha Parke "Patsy" Custis, who died of epilepsy as a teenager.

After Jacky's death, the Washingtons raised two of his children, Eleanor Parke "Nelly" Custis and George Washington Parke Custis, at Mount Vernon.

* A physically imposing, powerful man, Washington stood six feet, two inches tall and weighed more than two hundred pounds in his later years.

* He lost most of his teeth due to gum disease but did not have "wooden teeth." He was fitted with numerous sets of dentures made variously from lead, ivory, and teeth from animals and humans.

* On July 4, 1754, twenty-two-year-old Washington surrendered for the first and only time. Commanding a colonial Virginia militia and surrounded by a French army at Fort Necessity (near modern-day Pittsburgh), Washington had no choice but to accept terms. Among them was signing what amounted to an admission of killing a French diplomat, a "confession" that helped spark the Seven Years' War, known in America as the French and Indian War.

* On July 4, 1798, following his presidency, with the threat of war with France on the horizon, the sixty-six-year-old Washington was commissioned a lieutenant general and commander in chief of American forces, the only former president to hold such a post. (The crisis was averted.)

* Although Washington requested in his will that some of his personal slaves be emancipated, most of Mount Vernon's slaves belonged to Martha Washington.

George Washington was born on his father's Pope's Creek farm in Virginia in 1732. Known to his friends as "Gus," George's father, Augustine Washington (1694?–1743), was a modestly successful tobacco planter and iron foundry owner whose first wife, Jane Butler, bore him four children, though only two survived to maturity, Lawrence and Augustine.

When Jane died, Gus married Mary Ball in 1731. Orphaned at thirteen, George Washington's mother had been raised in the Virginia home of attorney George Eskridge and named her first-born son after her guardian.[4] A cantankerous woman who smoked a corncob pipe, she possessed a wicked temper. Although he later provided for her comfort, Washington wrote and spoke little of his mother and records show she never visited Mount Vernon after his marriage to Martha.

Little is known of Washington's early childhood. Many of the legends about him were fabricated by his so-called biographer, Mason Locke Weems, whose *Life and Memorable Actions of Washington* was published in 1800, the year after Washington's death. Weems did not know Washington and simply invented stories to underscore Washington's idealized qualities as morality tales for nineteenth-century American children.

When George was six, his father relocated the family to Ferry Farm on the east bank of the Rappahannock River. Gus died when George was eleven, and Washington would later remember him only vaguely as a tall, fair, kind man.[5] After his father's death, Gus's properties and some fifty slaves were divided. The largest share, the Little Hunting Creek property, went to George's oldest half-brother, Lawrence (he later renamed it Mount Vernon); Augustine, Jr., another half-brother, received a plantation called Wakefield; and George inherited Ferry Farm, to be shared with his mother until he turned twenty-one.

Although he received a modest amount of "grammar school," Washington never attended college. Lawrence, who had become the most influential person in Washington's life, planned to send him to England in 1746 to join the Royal Navy when he was fourteen. But that venture was squelched by his mother and an uncle, who both assumed—correctly, no doubt—that a young "provincial" American would never get far in the rigidly aristocratic British navy. George's English uncle wrote that the navy would "use him like a Negro, or rather, like a dog."[6]

Two years later, a teenaged Washington, already an athletically built six-footer, went on his first adventure into the "west," hired as a surveyor to join George Fairfax on a surveying expedition into the Shenandoah Valley. The wealthiest of Virginia's landed gentry, the Fairfax family had rights to more than five million acres of land. George's brother Lawrence had married into the Fairfax family and provided young Washington with his introduction into their world of extraordinary privilege and wealth, and he was a frequent visitor to their Belvoir Mansion estate.

On the Blue Ridge Mountain expedition in 1748, he wrote in his journal of sleeping naked on a mat of straw only to be awakened in the night by bedbugs and vowing from then on to sleep in his clothes next to the fire. He also described his first encounter with Indians who, plied with some whiskey, were encouraged to dance around the campfire.

His lack of formal education did not mean Washington was a country bumpkin. He received a surveyor's certificate from William and Mary and, like Thomas Jefferson, owned an extensive library. He was interested in the latest developments in agriculture and animal husbandry as he hoped to improve his plantation's efficiency. He loved the theater and Shakespeare. A popular play of the 1760s, *Cato*, about the hero of the Roman Republic—symbol of the young American republic—became a particular favorite. He even had it performed by officers while at Valley Forge (even though Congress had prohibited theatrical performances during the war).

Washington made a name for himself as a young man when he served in Virginia's colonial militia. Journeying from Virginia into what is now Pennsylvania, he escaped near-death, first when he and a companion fell into an icy river and then again when he was nearly shot by an Indian. Washington's report of those exploits was turned into a published account that made him a celebrity of sorts on both sides of the Atlantic.

Then he started a war. Sort of.

In his first command in 1754—a bit headstrong, cocky, and self-assured but without any real command experience—Washington led a small Virginia militia force and their Native American allies into an attack on a French detachment in a wilderness clearing. In an episode that left dozens of Frenchmen dead in a massacre, Washington disregarded orders and lost control of his men and the native warriors with him.

Making their way back to Virginia, Washington and his men were tracked down by the French, surrounded, and forced to surrender at Fort Necessity, a small, hastily built wooden outpost where the French might have simply done away with him. In the surrender papers he signed, Washington admitted to the "assassination" of a French officer; with limited understanding of French, he believed he had only acknowledged responsibility for the Frenchman's "death." This "confession" later plagued Washington. But the incident also helped spark the French and Indian War, part of a much larger world war between England and France. The French used Washington's letter of capitulation as proof that the young Virginian had murdered a French diplomat, and they cast the British as the belligerents in the French and Indian War, fought in North America, which cascaded into a much larger worldwide conflict, the Seven Years' War (1756–1763).

During the French and Indian War, Washington again escaped death in July 1755, when he witnessed one of the great military disasters in British history, the Battle of Monongahela. In a surprise attack, the French and their Indian allies nearly wiped out British General Edward Braddock's 1300 men, killing some 500 and wounding and capturing another 450 British and American colonial troops. A twenty-three-year-old volunteer aide-de-camp to Braddock, Washington survived "Braddock's Massacre," but only barely. And he would always recall the screams of the wounded as they were scalped.

For rallying survivors of the massacre, racing around the battlefield to secure reinforcements, and then carrying the dying Braddock from the field, Washington was seen as a hero of the disaster. His name was mentioned throughout the colonies, and his actions in the battle, in which he had two horses shot from under him, made Washington young America's first war hero. He had a knack, or lucky streak, for turning catastrophe into acclaim. As Ron Chernow records, "In Braddock's crushing defeat, Washington had established an indelible image of a fearless young soldier who never flinched from danger and enjoyed a special intimacy with death."[7]

Leading Virginia's militia during the rest of the war, he gained the experience, practical and political, that would, some twenty years later, help him win command of the Continental Army. But he also began to earn his reputation as a harsh disciplinarian. Desertion and drunkenness were not to be tolerated. "I have a Gallows near 40 feet high erected," Washington wrote, "and I am determined to hang two or three on it, as an example to others."[8]

As the fighting in America ended with a British victory, Washington married Martha Dandridge Custis, a wealthy young widow who brought to their marriage in 1759 a considerable fortune, more land, and more slaves. She also had two children, Patsy and Jacky, and Washington adopted them, treating them as his own.

Martha Washington has come down through history as the frumpy little lady in the Stuart painting. But modern views offer a more alluring picture that contradicts the long-held notion of a marriage of "convenience" for Washington. At twenty-six, Martha Washington was, according to biographer Patricia Brady, "very pretty, charming, entertaining and rich, she could pick and choose among her present suitors or wait for those whom the future would bring. But after George's first call on her, she invited him back. She wanted him from the beginning. Every bit of contemporary evidence shows that she adored him throughout their lives together—he knew it, their friends knew it and the general public knew it."[9] (Having surrendered so much privacy during a very public life, she did, however, protect their privacy by burning all of their letters to each other after Washington's death.)

Washington was famous, landed, well wed, and still ambitious to add to his considerable real estate holdings. When he received a land bounty promised to soldiers who fought in the French and Indian War, Washington added more than twenty-three thousand acres to his holdings. A consummate Virginia gentleman planter and a member of Virginia's elite, he ran for the Virginia legislature, providing the requisite rum punch expected by local voters to win their support.

When King George III proclaimed in 1763 that the western lands won from France would not be open to settlements, Washington and other land speculators were not happy. And as the British Crown further alienated Americans with the Stamp Act and the Townsend Acts, Washington was drawn into the growing colonial resistance. In 1769, he introduced a call to boycott British goods—no small matter for a man who ordered his suits, saddles, clothes, cheese, port, silverware, table settings, hats for Martha, and a great many other luxury and household items from London.

Washington was then chosen as a delegate to the first Continental Congress, and when the battles of Lexington and Concord took place in June 1775, he wore his old uniform to the Second Continental Congress—it was a bit tight, some tongues wagged. But his point was made. He had the experience and prestige that led to his choice as commander in chief of the ragtag bunch then bottling up the British in Boston.

Washington was no Napoléon on the battlefield; he lost more often than he won. But a master of the strategic retreat, he organized and trained an effective army and kept pressure on Congress to provide supplies for the troops. Without the support of French armies and navies, his success would have been doubtful. But he was a survivor—of battles and political intrigues. When he, and Martha, weathered the brutal winter at Valley Forge, Washington became a symbol of the new American. His character and qualities of leadership were far more important than his tactical abilities.

His personal courage was unquestioned, as he proved on the battlefield. And when a British army was trapped by a French fleet and defeated at Yorktown, the war was over and Washington was the most celebrated man in America. Then he went home to Mount Vernon. And it was there, in 1787, that he watched the growing chaos in America with a concern that would lead him back to Philadelphia to preside over the constitutional debates that created the presidency.

PRESIDENTIAL VOICES

He is polite with dignity, affable without formality, distant without haughtiness, grave without austerity, modest, wise and good. These are traits which peculiarly fit him for the exalted station he holds, and God grant that he may hold it with the same applause and universal satisfaction for many, many years, as it is my firm opinion that no other man could rule over this great people and consolidate them into one mighty empire but he who is set over us.

—ABIGAIL ADAMS (WIFE OF THE FIRST VICE PRESIDENT)
Letter dated January 5, 1790

Did Washington say "So help me God" when he took the oath of office?

Today, Inauguration Day is an iconic American spectacle, filled with traditions and rituals that have been passed down for more than two hundred years. Right?

Not exactly. It was a very different picture in 1789 when George Washington was sworn in as America's first president under the new Constitution.

Let's start with location. In 1789, there was no Washington, D.C. George Washington's inauguration took place in New York City, the temporary capital of the United States. (The plan for a national capital, the "Federal City," was first established in 1791, and the original designer of the city's plan, Pierre L'Enfant, named it Washington.)

And it wasn't on January 20, the modern Inauguration Day. Nor was it on March 4, the Inauguration Day for every other president until Franklin D. Roosevelt in 1933.

The hero of the American Revolution, Washington arrived in New York after a weeklong celebratory journey from Virginia. Departing from New Jersey on April 23, he was ferried across the Hudson River. "As the barge pulled away from the New Jersey shore, rowed by thirteen harbor pilots in sparkling white uniforms, it was surrounded by a dense mass of vessels, one of which bore musicians and a chorus whose voices were barely audible above the roar of the cannon from shore batteries and a Spanish warship in the harbor. One witness, who watched the barge pass the Battery, commented that the successive motion of the hats of cheering bystanders 'was like the rolling motion of the sea, or a field of grain.'" [10] In other words, they invented the "Wave" in New York for George Washington.

He took the oath of office on April 30, 1789, a cool, clear Thursday morning. One similarity to modern inaugurations was the big crowd. A large throng of New Yorkers filled the streets of what is now the city's financial district, then the center of a city that was much smaller than modern Manhattan.

Washington arrived by carriage to what had previously been New York's City Hall, given a "face-lift" by Pierre L'Enfant, future designer of the nation's capital city. The entire government operated out of this single building, renamed Federal Hall. Washington managed more people on his Mount Vernon plantation than worked for the new national government.

For the inauguration he was dressed in a brown suit, white silk stockings, and shoes with silver buckles, and he carried a sword. The suit cloth was made in a mill in Hartford, Connecticut, and Washington had said that he hoped it would soon be "unfashionable for a gentleman to appear in any other dress" than one of American manufacture.

Standing on the second-floor balcony, the "Father of Our Country" took the oath of office on a Masonic Bible. Legend has it that he kissed the Bible and said "So help me God"—words not required by the Constitution. But there is no contemporary report of Washington saying those words. On the contrary, one eyewitness account, by the French minister, Comte de Moustier, recounts the full text of the oath without mentioning the Bible kiss or the "So help me God" line. Washington's use of the words was not reported until late in the nineteenth century. (The demythologizing of this piece of presidential history occasioned a suit by notable atheist Michael Newdow, who sued unsuccessfully in 2009 to keep all mention of God out of the inauguration of Barack Obama.)[11]

What followed was the first Inaugural Address, written by James Madison. Here Washington spoke freely of "the propitious smiles of Heaven"—a divine hand in guiding the nation's fate. These heavenly references raise the perennial question of faith in the early republic. But, as Ron Chernow writes, "Washington refrained from endorsing any particular form of religion."[12]

There is no question that Washington was a Christian who spoke openly of Providence and called for days of prayer and fasting—even during the Revolution. But on the other side of the coin is his expressed belief that religion was a personal matter and not to be dictated or even sanctioned by government. It was a sentiment best expressed in a famous letter to America's first synagogue, in Rhode Island, shortly after he took office.

In it, Washington wrote: "All possess alike liberty of conscience and immunities of citizenship. It is now no more that toleration is spoken of, as if it was by the indulgence of one class of people, that another enjoyed the exercise of their inherent national gifts. For happily the Government of the United States, which gives to bigotry no sanction, to persecution no assistance requires only that they who live under its protection should demean themselves as good citizens, in giving it on all occasions their effectual support."*

Washington's letter is a reminder that while most of the founders and framers were Christians—Protestants, more accurately—they were devoted to the ideal of a secular democracy in which matters of conscience could not be dictated by the government.

On the night of Washington's inauguration: "Bands played, houses and ships in the harbor blazed with candles, and the skies above crackled with a two-hour long display of fireworks," Edwin G. Burrows and Mike Wallace record in *Gotham*. "Washington, who watched the show from Chancellor Livingston's house, had to get home on foot because the streets were too full of people for his carriage to pass." [13]

An inaugural ball—Washington was an enthusiastic dancer, having taken lessons since he was fifteen—was delayed a few weeks until Martha Washington arrived in New York in May.

In New York, the first "White House" was a rented property at Number 3 Cherry Street. Known as the Samuel Osgood House, it served as both private residence and executive offices, just as the White House does today. The government provided a budget to furnish the house, and while the furnishings impressed some New Yorkers, European visitors were less taken by America's "Executive Mansion" and found it "mean." (Today, the Osgood House location is the site of a housing project between the Brooklyn and Manhattan Bridges.)

---

* A number of biographers and historians suggest that the letter was actually composed by Thomas Jefferson.

When she arrived, Martha Washington found the city not to her liking, writing to a friend while Washington was touring New England, "I live a dull life here. I never go to any public place. Indeed I am more like a state prisoner than anything else."

But the first couple also set about to create a society around the presidency that projected order and civility. They went to the theater and had a regular open house—"levees" at which people bowed and curtsied in great formality to the president and first lady. They apparently also liked to play matchmaker, hoping to bring together America's new political elite in appropriate marriages.

Finding their East River neighborhood noisy, George and Martha relocated in February 1790 to a more fashionable address at 39–41 Broadway. Nearer to Federal Hall, with a view of the Hudson River from the rear windows, the house had been built by Irish-American merchant Alexander Macomb and had been used as the residence of the French minister, Comte de Moustier. George and Martha Washington bought additional furnishings from him when he left for France.[14] They also hired Samuel Fraunces, the man who had owned Fraunces Tavern, where Washington said farewell to his officers after the war, to manage the household. Here the "help" included seven slaves brought from Mount Vernon. (That residence, later converted to a hotel, is also long gone.)

In December 1790, the capital was moved to Philadelphia (where it stayed for the next ten years) and the first couple settled into a home owned by Robert Morris. That house was later torn down and once served as the location of a public restroom. Today the presidential house site is part of Philadelphia's historic district near the Liberty Bell, and its surviving cellars and foundation can be viewed from the street above.

In Philadelphia, Mount Vernon slaves were again brought in to tend to the president and the first lady. But now Washington had to play a game of "musical servants." Under Pennsylvania's emancipation laws, enacted in 1780, a slave who lived in the state continuously for six months would be freed. In a ruse designed to evade the law and deceive the public, Washington had to discreetly rotate servants in and out of Philadelphia every few months to circumvent that statute, which as

Clarence Lusane points out, was specifically amended in 1788 to close the loophole of slaveholders rotating slaves, as Washington did. "Despite this adjustment to the law," writes Lusane, "it was difficult to enforce, and Washington, while president, violated it brazenly."[15]

At least two of the household servants managed to escape while in Philadelphia. One of them was a woman named Ona "Oney" Maria Judge, a dower slave who actually belonged to the Custis estate, and heroically made her way to Portsmouth, New Hampshire. Once a slave port, Portsmouth had become an abolitionist center. Washington spent considerable time and effort trying to retrieve Oney, who rejected the promise of freedom if she returned. She remained in Portsmouth, where she died at age seventy-eight in 1845, still technically a slave but having lived free.[16]

PRESIDENTIAL VOICES

I walk on, as it were, untrodden ground, so many untoward circumstances may intervene in such a new and critical situation, that I shall feel an insuperable diffidence in my own abilities.

—GEORGE WASHINGTON
Letter following his inauguration

How did Washington stock his cabinet?

Oh, to be in New York in 1789–90. The city was filled with the heroes of the Revolution and the men who made the Constitution. A New Yorker walking down the streets near Federal Hall might have a chance encounter with Washington, Adams, Hamilton, Jefferson, or Madison. What interesting dinners they must all have had!

In creating the first presidential cabinet, Washington drew from a rich array of political talent to choose appointees for the key posts in his administration, turning to old friends and war veterans, such as the portly Quaker Henry "Ox" Knox, a holdover from the government under the Articles of Confederation, as his first secretary of war. He could, of course, draw on a veritable Who's Who of Founding Fathers for other appointments. The Supreme Court was created, and New Yorker John Jay—one of the authors of the Federalist Papers—was chosen first chief justice. Edmund Randolph, a young Virginian who had once served as Washington's lawyer and was Virginia's governor when he led the state's delegation to the Constitutional Convention, was named first attorney general. Randolph had refused to sign the Constitution, believing it lacked sufficient checks and balances. But he later lobbied for its ratification in Virginia, once passage was assured in the other states, as he did not want Virginia left out of power. Since there was not yet a Justice Department, Randolph had little power and perhaps even less to do and was encouraged to take outside clients.

But the two giants of this administration, and the men who would personify the great debates—divisions that continue in American politics today—were Thomas Jefferson and Alexander Hamilton.

America's envoy in Paris as the Bastille was stormed in 1789, Jefferson had returned to New York to lead the new State Department at Washington's request. Although a member of Virginia's aristocratic, slaveholding class, Jefferson despised the monarchy and saw Hamilton and his allies as a "British party," trying to restore a form of elected monarchy to the new nation. In this disagreement was the root of America's two-party politics.

An illegitimate child born in the West Indies, Hamilton had risen during the Revolution to become Washington's wartime secretary, aide, and chief of staff. Although they had some brief fallings-out during the war, Washington still prized Hamilton's intellect. He had become an attorney in New York, founder of the Bank of New York, and one of that state's most powerful men, first helping to frame, and then "sell," the Constitution. When Robert Morris, the Philadelphia financier, declined Washington's offer of the post in Treasury, Morris suggested Hamilton. He filled the critical role of Washington's chief adviser in money matters. Washington and Hamilton had worked together closely during the war and in the Constitutional Convention. Now Washington, unfamiliar with public finance but painfully aware of the needs of the new government, would rely on Hamilton again.

Openly ambitious, Hamilton had his work cut out for him. The nation's finances were chaotic. America owed money to foreign nations, principally France and the Netherlands, and there was massive domestic debt. The government needed revenue, and a series of tariffs was passed. Many of them were on the same items that had been taxed by the British a few years earlier.

Hamilton's plan for a new American economy and credit system, *Report on Public Credit*, was issued in January 1790 and called for assumption of the states' debts by the federal government. It was designed to create a stable credit market in which the government could put its financial house in order and regulate commerce. To Thomas Jefferson, James Madison, and the settlers and farmers who were pushing west, it was a threatening blueprint for a federally dominated economy.

Hamilton's biographer Ron Chernow summed up the anti-Hamilton view, particularly in the South: "Compounding Hamilton's problems was that his report crystallized latent divisions between north and south. . . . Still the impression persisted that crooked northern merchants were hoodwinking virtuous southern farmers. It didn't help that many New Yorkers in Hamilton's own social circle . . . had accumulated sizable positions in government debt."[17]

This was the opening of a split that crystallized the "Main Street–Wall Street" conflict that remains a powerful force in American politics and finance. From a succession of populist movements throughout American history, right up to the Tea Party and Occupy Wall Street movements of recent times, the sense that the government is too large and powerful and that the deck is stacked in favor of the well-connected, moneyed class has been a constant in American politics.

Washington discreetly took Hamilton's side in the argument, and the assumption bill passed Congress, after a deal was struck with Jefferson and Madison. In exchange for their support, Hamilton agreed that the new national capital would be located in the South. George Washington was also delighted that the new capital was going to be located on the Potomac, not far from Mount Vernon. It would be a boon for the region and increase the value of some of his real estate holdings, not a small consideration to Washington.

Late in 1790, the Hamilton-Jefferson split widened over the creation of a national bank, another part of Hamilton's grand scheme for a modern economy with federal controls. The Southerners again feared too much central power and called the bank plan unconstitutional. Washington again sided with Hamilton, after long deliberation. It was a crucial decision that had implications far beyond the bank's creation. As Ron Chernow writes, "Unlike his fellow planters, who tended to regard banks and stock exchanges as sinister devices, Washington grasped the need for these instruments of modern finance. It was also a decisive moment for Washington legally. . . . With this stroke, he endorsed an expansive view of the presidency and made the Constitution a living, open-ended document. The importance of this decision is hard to overstate for had Washington rigidly adhered to the letter of the Constitution, the federal government might have been stillborn."[18]

In essence, Washington had walked on "untrodden ground" and created the concept of "implied powers." It was a precedent that would stand.

If the founders didn't like political parties, how did they develop under Washington's administration?

The battle lines were drawn over the bank, but they did not end there. John Marshall, a Federalist and later the Supreme Court's dominant chief justice, wrote that this debate led "to the complete organization of those distinct and visible parties, which in their long and dubious conflict for power, have shaken the United States to their centre."[19]

The differences between Jefferson and Hamilton extended to other domestic policies and foreign affairs. With England and France warring again, and the French Revolution under way, Hamilton openly favored the English. Jefferson admired the French and their Revolution.

These lines were laid down most starkly over Jay's Treaty, a settlement made with the British in the midst of an Anglo-French war that threatened to involve the United States. Under its terms, British soldiers withdrew from their last outposts in the United States, but other portions of the treaty were viewed as excessively pro-British, and Jefferson's supporters attacked it. (The Senate ratified the treaty in 1795.)

As part of their ongoing feud, the two men started rival newspapers whose editors received plums from the federal pie. Jefferson's platform was the *National Gazette*, edited by Philip Freneau, James Madison's schoolmate from the College of New Jersey. And Hamilton's was the *Gazette of the United States*. There was no pretense of "fair and balanced" or objective journalism. This was bare-knuckles partisanship with mudslinging that escalated into character assassination. More important, the personal and political feuds accelerated a development seemingly disdained by Washington and the framers—the growth of political parties.

To this point, organized parties had been viewed as sinister. In the Federalist Papers, both Hamilton and Madison warned of the dangers of "faction." But a system of parties quickly evolved, and the seeds were sown in the Jefferson-Hamilton rivalry. Hamilton and his supporters coalesced in 1792 as the Federalist Party, favoring a strong central government and promoting commercial and industrial interests. Under Washington, who said he disdained any "factions," the Federalists held most of the power, dominating Congress during his two terms.

Supporters of Jefferson and James Madison, a Federalist during the ratification debate who swung to Jefferson's views after the credit and bank controversies, eventually adopted the name Democratic Republicans in 1796. (The name was shortened to Republicans, but later, during Andrew Jackson's Presidency, they became Democrats. Follow that?)

But political agendas in those days came with plenty of personal baggage. Washington's cabinet was not some early American Kiwanis Club, full of well-meaning friends. The personal in these politics would soon explode. Married to the daughter of one of New York's most powerful men, General Philip Schuyler, Hamilton was at the peak of his power as both treasury secretary and a New York state power broker. But he was about to be brought down in a scandal over money and sex.

In 1791, after the government moved to Philadelphia, Hamilton had become involved with a married woman named Maria Reynolds. Her husband, James Reynolds, had begun to blackmail Hamilton, and then began to boast that Hamilton was giving him tips—"insider information," in modern terms—that allowed him to speculate in government bonds. Accused of corruption, Hamilton actually turned over love letters from Maria Reynolds to his political enemies in order to prove that while he might have cheated on his wife, he wasn't cheating the government.

Hamilton left his Treasury post in 1795. Then, in 1797, the letters surfaced publicly through a pamphlet written by James Thomson Callender, a writer who would cause considerably more mischief before he was done. Not only was Hamilton's affair revealed, but he was also accused of speculation on Treasury policies. Hamilton confessed the affair publicly, and his political career seemed over.

PRESIDENTIAL VOICES

If ever a nation was debauched by a man, the American nation has been debauched by Washington. If ever a nation was deceived by a man, the nation has been deceived by Washington. Let his conduct, then, be an example to future ages; let it serve to be a warning that no man may be an idol.
— *Philadelphia Aurora*, 1796

(Founded in 1790 by Benjamin Franklin's grandson, Benjamin Franklin Bache, who had been trained as a printer by his grandfather, the *Aurora* became the nation's leading anti-Federalist journal. The paper was notable in its outright public attacks on Federalist policy and to a lesser, but still surprising, degree on Washington himself.)

The character with which Mr. Washington has attempted to act in this world, is a sort of non-describable, camelion-colored thing, called prudence. It is, in many cases, a substitute for principle, and is so nearly allied to hypocrisy, that it easily slides into it. . . . And as to you, sir, treacherous to private friendship (for so you have been to me, and that in the day of danger) and a hypocrite in public life, the world will be puzzled to decide whether you are an apostate or an impostor, whether you have abandoned good principles, or whether you ever had any!

— Thomas Paine
Open letter to George Washington, 1796

The great pamphleteer of the Revolution, who had once turned over his profits from *Common Sense* to help clothe Washington's army, Thomas Paine would have a catastrophic falling-out with the first president. In France during its Revolution, Paine was jailed and nearly executed. He believed that Washington had not done enough to secure his release and wrote a scathingly angry open letter denouncing him.

It might have helped Paine get things off his chest. But it did not help his reputation in America, already plunging since he had published his *Age of Reason*, an attack on religion, in 1794. In 1802, Paine returned to America at Jefferson's behest, but died, alcoholic and largely friendless, in New York City. A pariah after his assault on Washington, Paine had become an outspoken atheist and was denied burial by any church after his death in June 1809. He was buried on his farm in New Rochelle, New York. "Six mourners attended the funeral of the man who once inspired millions to think in new ways about the world," historian Eric Foner noted. "And his death passed virtually unnoticed in America."[20]

PRESIDENTIAL VOICES

Two hundred gallons of Whiskey will be ready this day for your call, and the sooner it is taken the better, as the demand for this article (in these parts) is brisk.

—GEORGE WASHINGTON

Letter to nephew William A. Washington, 1799

Why did George Washington lead troops into the field as president?
The Founding Fathers hated taxes. Right? That's why they declared their independence. Many Americans believe that modern America is unfairly and aggressively overtaxed by an unrelenting and oppressive central government—just as the thirteen colonies were.

But as the run-up to the Constitutional Convention proved, many of those rebellious founders and framers knew that they could not govern without funds to run a government and keep an army. And you can't get enough revenue without duly authorized taxes. Certainly George Washington understood that, and he would lead an army to defend that principle.

One piece of Hamilton's plan for restoring the American economy was to raise revenue through excise taxes on American-made products. (There was no income tax and there would be none until the Civil War. It was considered unconstitutional and would later be overturned by the Supreme Court.) Hamilton's first target was whiskey, most typically distilled from corn, and the Whiskey Act became law in March 1791.

Guess what? Some people didn't like it. And the ones who liked it least were farmers in the Western states and territories who used their surplus corn to make whiskey. It was cheaper to distill it than transport corn east for sale. Add to this the resentment that "Westerners" felt that the government was not doing enough to protect them from attacks by Native American nations, and there was a powerful discontent growing. That discontent had been the source of Shays' Rebellion and other backwoods revolts; it would remain a constant in American history—people who believe the government is working for the moneyed interests and not for them.

By 1794, what had been a protest of the whiskey tax was growing into larger antigovernment sentiment, with echoes of Shays' Rebellion. In July 1794, the protest grew deadly when several militiamen sent to arrest one of the Whiskey Rebellion leaders were killed. In August, some seven thousand farmers, or "rebels" to the authorities, met near Pittsburgh, planning to march on the town.

Watching with growing alarm, Washington ordered Secretary of War Henry Knox to call out more than twelve thousand militiamen. He put Virginia governor Henry Lee in command of the operation. But in late September, President Washington donned his uniform and rode to Carlisle, Pennsylvania, to review the situation. After inspecting the troops and seeing to conditions in the camps, Washington returned to Philadelphia. Although he did not actually lead any troops into battle, Washington had command of a force five times as large as the army he took into many of his Revolutionary battles.

The overwhelming show of force defused the situation with the arrest of a handful of the rebels—with very little concern for liberties, due process, or any of the other niceties supposedly guaranteed by the Bill of Rights. Two men were sentenced to hang, but were pardoned by Washington.[21]

Summarizing his actions in this crisis, Washington later wrote, "If the laws are to be so trampled upon with impunity . . . and a minority . . . is to dictate to the majority, there is an end put at one stroke to republican government."[22]

A few years after suppressing the Whiskey Rebellion, George Washington started a new enterprise back at Mount Vernon—a distillery of his own. The operation began producing whiskey in 1797, just before Washington left the presidency. Operated by six slaves under the direction of Mount Vernon's Scottish farm manager, James Anderson, it was the largest distillery in America at the time, producing eleven thousand gallons of whiskey in 1799. The distillery passed to Washington's heirs but burned to the ground in 1814. After archaeologists excavated the site in the 1990s, the distillery was rebuilt and completed in 2007. It is now in operation once more. [23]

PRESIDENTIAL VOICES

I have already intimated to you the danger of Parties in the State, with particular reference to the founding of them on Geographical discriminations. Let me now take a more comprehensive view, and warn you in the most solemn manner against the baneful effects of the Spirit of Party, generally.

This spirit, unfortunately, is inseparable from our nature, having its root in the strongest passions of the human Mind. It exists under different shapes in all Governments, more or less stifled, controuled [sic], or repressed; but, in those of the popular form it is seen in its greatest rankness and is truly their worst enemy.

The alternate domination of one faction over another, sharpened by the spirit of revenge natural to party dissention [sic], which in different ages and countries has perpetrated the most horrid enormities, is itself frightful

despotism. . . . The common and continual mischiefs of the spirit of Party are
sufficient to make it in the interest and the duty of a wise People to discourage
and restrain it.

—GEORGE WASHINGTON
Farewell Address, September 17, 1796

Final Judgment: Grade A+

He was, as one biographer called him, the "Indispensable Man." And as Virginia's Henry Lee would famously eulogize him, Washington was "first in war, first in Peace and first in the Hearts of his countrymen." In polls of presidential historians, Washington has always been ranked either number one or number two.

After his second term ended on March 4, 1797, Washington returned to Mount Vernon for good, only rousing once when war with France seemed imminent and his successor, John Adams, asked him to lead the United States Army once again. Washington made a brief trip to Washington and Philadelphia as a potential invasion of America by France was anticipated. That threat fizzled.

On December 14, 1799, Washington woke with a severe sore throat. He was bled by his doctors, treated with other typical medications of the day, and died about ten o'clock that night.

In giving the new nation a leader in whom there was nearly complete trust, in fashioning an administration that drew upon the greatest minds of the time, in stabilizing the American Experiment when it could have gone completely off the rails, Washington deserves all of the accolades.

And then he just left. There is no question that he could have run for a third term. Many of his allies hoped he would and implored him to remain. But Washington was ready to go. And his greatest achievement may be that he left when a more ambitious, ruthless, or driven man or a tyrant might have stayed and consolidated power. Consider that as Washington was dying, Napoléon was beginning his rise in France.

But Washington's enormous successes as general, constitutionalist, and president must still be balanced against the great counterweight of his life and legacy—the stain of human slavery and its tragic hold on the country's future. Around George Washington, others were emancipating their slaves. One of his dearest friends, the Marquis de Lafayette, even proposed setting up a Caribbean island refuge at his own expense to accommodate Washington's emancipated slaves.[24]

In this, Washington fell woefully short, like so many of the Founding Fathers. He might have been the man who changed America's mind, and its destiny, on this, the most fundamental contradiction to his life story.

To his credit, Washington honestly believed and hoped that slavery would end naturally in America. Beyond that, he and other founders assumed that the end of the importation of slaves in 1807, a compromise built into the Constitution, would lead to the demise of slavery in time. But as Dennis J. Pogue points out, "the compromise only postponed the ultimate resolution of the issue, while giving both sides time to bolster their forces. The slave trade was prohibited in due course, but that act had much less impact than the moderate abolitionists assumed would be the case."[25]

Apologists for Washington and the founders often cite their writings, speeches, and even legislative efforts to end slavery. But imagine for a moment if Washington, Adams, Jefferson, Madison, Hamilton, John Jay, Gouverneur Morris, George Mason, and the other giants on the stage at that glorious moment had united to speak with one voice on this critical question and then act on it.

Imagine for a moment if Washington's farewell address had not been a warning about "faction" and "foreign entanglements," but a clarion call from the leader who mattered most, to put an end to slavery. Imagine if he had not merely asked that his personal slaves be freed in his will, but spoken forcefully about freeing the nearly one million slaves in 1800 America?

Washington's greatest failure may well have been his reluctance to do anything meaningful to make that happen. And for that failure, Washington's beloved republic would pay a heavy price.

Washington Administration Milestones[26]

1789

January 7 In the eleven ratifying states, except New York, presidential electors are chosen; George Washington is elected unanimously.

July 14 The Fall of the Bastille; the French Revolution begins.

July 27 The Department of Foreign Affairs is created and renamed the State Department in September. Thomas Jefferson is the first secretary of state.

August 7 The War Department is established; Henry Knox is the first secretary of war.

September 2 The Treasury Department is established; Alexander Hamilton is the first secretary of the Treasury.

September 24 The Federal Judiciary Act is passed; a six-man Supreme Court is created; the first chief justice is New York's John Jay.

1790

March 1 The Census Act is passed. Completed on August 1, the first census shows a population of 3,929,625, including 59,557 free blacks and 697,624 enslaved blacks. Although nearly 20 percent of the population, each black is counted as three-fifths of a person for purposes of allotment of congressional seats.

March 26 The first naturalization law establishes five years as the term needed to become a naturalized citizen.

April 17 Benjamin Franklin dies at age eighty-four; twenty thousand mourners gather in Philadelphia, the largest gathering in America to that time.

May 29 Rhode Island ratifies the Constitution, the last of the original thirteen states to join the union.

December 6 Congress moves from New York to Philadelphia.

1791

February 25	The Bank of the United States is chartered.
March 3	Congress passes the Whiskey Act, an excise tax on distilled liquor and stills.
March 4	Vermont joins the Union as the fourteenth state, a free state.
December 15	The Virginia legislature ratifies the Bill of Rights; the first ten amendments to the U.S. Constitution go into effect.

1792

June 1	Kentucky becomes the fifteenth state, with slavery allowed.
October 13	The cornerstone is laid for the "Presidential Palace," designed by James Hoban.
December 5	George Washington and John Adams are reelected.

1793

February 12	The first Fugitive Slave Act passes, mandating the right of slave owners to recover runaways.
April 22	Washington issues a proclamation of neutrality in the war between the French Republic and England.
October 28	Eli Whitney files a patent for his cotton gin, granted in 1794.
December 31	Thomas Jefferson resigns as secretary of state.

1794

January 2	Attorney General Edmund Randolph becomes secretary of state.
March 27	Congress authorizes the establishment of the U.S. Navy.
July	The Whiskey Rebellion takes place; Washington leads an army to suppress it in August.
November 19	John Jay concludes Jay's Treaty with the British; it resolves border and other issues with the British but

stirs strong disagreement between the two emerging parties of the day.

1795

January 31	Alexander Hamilton resigns as secretary of the Treasury; he is replaced by Oliver Wolcott, Jr., of Connecticut, son of a signer of the Declaration of Independence.
June 24	The Senate ratifies Jay's Treaty after a fierce debate.

1796

March–April	After Congress demands that the president provide all papers relating to the Jay Treaty, Washington refuses; this establishes a precedent for the principle of executive privilege.
June 1	Tennessee becomes the sixteenth state, a slave state.
December	John Adams is elected president; Thomas Jefferson becomes vice president.

MUST READS

Richard Brookhiser, *Founding Father: Rediscovering George Washington*; Ron Chernow, *Washington: A Life*; Joseph Ellis, *His Excellency George Washington*; Henry Wiencek, *An Imperfect God: George Washington and His Slaves*.

ONLINE RESOURCES

Inaugural Addresses, Avalon Project, Yale Law School
   1789: http://avalon.law.yale.edu/18th _century/wash1.asp
   1793: http://avalon.law.yale.edu/18th_century/wash2.asp
Library of Congress Resource Guide
   http://www.loc.gov/rr/program/bib/presidents/washington/index
   .html
University of Virginia, Washington Resources
   http://etext.lib.virginia.edu/washington/
Miller Center of Public Affairs, University of Virginia
   http://millercenter.org/index.php/academic/americanpresident
   /washington

Washington's Papers

http://gwpapers.virginia.edu/project/faq/index.html

Mount Vernon Estate

http://www.mountvernon.org/

Washington Birthplace National Historic Site

http://www.nps.gov/gewa/

Ferry Farm, Washington's Boyhood Home

http://www.kenmore.org/

2

The Atlas of Independence
John Adams

★ ★ ★

March 4, 1797–March 4, 1801

Milestones in John Adams's Life

October 30, 1735	Born in Braintree (now Quincy), Massachusetts
1758	Began law practice
December 1770	Defended British soldiers in Boston Massacre
1774–1777	Attended Continental Congress as delegate from Massachusetts
1779	Wrote constitution of state of Massachusetts
1778–1788	U.S. diplomat in Europe
1789–1797	First vice president under Washington
1797–1801	Second president
December 1800	Defeated in bid for reelection
1825	John Quincy Adams, his son, elected sixth president
July 4, 1826	Died in Quincy, Massachusetts, aged ninety

PRESIDENTIAL VOICES

The history of our Revolution will be one continued lie from one end to the other. The essence of the whole will be that Dr. Franklin's electrical rod smote the earth and out sprang General Washington. That Franklin electrified him

with his rod—and thenceforward these two conducted all the policies, negotia-
tions, legislatures, and war.

—John Adams
Letter to Benjamin Rush, April 4, 1790

Pity poor John Adams. When he wrote that slightly miffed, nose-out-of-joint letter to his old friend and fellow Declaration-signer Dr. Benjamin Rush, he must have known he would play second fiddle to some of his contemporaries.

As lawyer, statesman, political theorist, and rebel leader he deserved better. Although he never led troops into battle, John Adams was one of the principal forces behind the drive for American independence, a fact some of the men who were there in Philadelphia acknowledged. Rush, the progressive Philadelphia physician and early outspoken abolition-ist, told a friend, "Every member of Congress in 1776 acknowledged him to be the first man in the House." Jefferson, with whom he would later have a sharp, ugly falling-out and then a gradual reunion, remem-bered that Adams was "the colossus of independence."[1]

He did not participate in the Constitutional debates—he was in England as America's representative in 1787—but he had written a pro-foundly influential Massachusetts state constitution in 1779 and his earlier political works were also widely read and admired.

But throughout history, Adams always seemed to be pushed to the background—as if his complaint to Dr. Rush were prophetic. When we think Declaration, we think Jefferson. When we think "president," John Adams is the only one of the first three presidents who is not carved in stone on Mount Rushmore, and it is hard to find his likeness on any American currency. As America's first vice president, an office he did not think very highly of, Adams was left out of Washington's closest circle of advisers.

Adams became president in a dawning era of hardball politics in which he would lose ground to more ambitious, and more ruthless, rivals. Adams was a politician too. He could be vain, egotistical, ambitious, and backbiting. But he was, as his modern chronicler David McCullough put it, "a great-hearted, persevering man of uncommon ability and force. He had a brilliant mind. He was honest and everyone knew it. Emphatically independent by nature, hardworking, frugal—all traits in the New England tradition—he was anything but cold or laconic as supposedly New Englanders were. . . . Ambitious to excel—to make himself known—he had nonetheless recognized at an early stage that happiness came not from fame or fortune. . . . but from 'an habitual contempt of them,' as he wrote."[2]

Adams was a man of serious convictions and deep principles, a fact he proved as a young attorney when he defended some clients who today might be equated with murderous terrorists. How many Americans would admire such a lawyer today—or elect him president?

Fast Facts

RELIGION: Congregational/Unitarian

EDUCATION: Harvard

CAREER BEFORE POLITICS: Attorney

POLITICAL PARTY: Federalist

FIRST LADY: Abigail Smith Adams (November 11, 1744–October 28, 1818)

CHILDREN: Abigail (Nabby), died of breast cancer in 1813 before her parents' deaths; John Quincy, the sixth president; Susanna, died in infancy; Charles, died of acute alcoholism in 1800; Thomas, also an alcoholic, died in deep debt a few months before his father in 1832; Elizabeth, stillborn 1777

* Adams was the first vice president of the United States under the Constitution, the first president to receive the oath of office from the chief justice, and the first president whose son became president.
* Adams cast a record twenty-nine tie-breaking votes as president of the Senate. (John C. Calhoun is second, with twenty-eight.)
* John Adams and Thomas Jefferson died on the same day, the fiftieth anniversary of the adoption of the Declaration of Independence.

PRESIDENTIAL VOICES

Facts are stubborn things and whatever may be our wishes and inclinations, or the dictums of our passions, they cannot alter the state of facts and evidence.

—JOHN ADAMS
Closing statement to jury in the "Boston Massacre" trial
December 1770

Unlike the pair of six-foot Virginians who bookmarked him as president, John Adams was short and stocky. Maybe that is one reason he was caught in their shadows.

Born into an old Massachusetts family descended on his mother's side from those famed Mayflower Pilgrims John and Priscilla Alden, and Henry Adams, who arrived in the Puritan Bay colony in 1633, John Adams was a farmer's son, born in Braintree (now Quincy), just south of Boston, on October 30, 1735. His father, also John, was a leather tanner, a Congregational deacon, a lieutenant in the militia, and a town councilman. This was the New England ideal—the honest workingman, the pillar of church and community.

As Adams told it, he once complained about school to his father, who then took him to the fields for a long day of labor, asking a mud-caked young John at day's end if he wanted to be a farmer or go to school. John told his father farming was fine, but he didn't mind school. He just didn't like his teacher. Instead of delivering a Puritanical clout on the ears, the wise father found the bright son a new teacher.

John Adams entered Harvard—then more equivalent to a modern prep school—and blossomed, at home with the Greek and Latin classics that comprised the core of a Harvard education at the time. After graduating in 1755, he contemplated becoming a minister, but his heart wasn't in it and Adams pursued a law career instead, paying for his legal education by teaching school in nearby Weymouth, while studying under a local attorney. He later read law with one of Boston's most prominent attorneys, Jeremiah Gridley, who was at the increasingly heated center of Boston's boiling political pot.

At twenty-five, Adams suffered a broken heart when a young woman he hoped to court married another man. Luckily, for him and posterity, he met the young cousin of the woman who had spurned him, Abigail Smith, daughter of a preacher from Weymouth (and also his own third cousin). Only fifteen years old when first introduced to John Adams, Abigail was nine years younger, but she caught his attention with her bookishness, love of poetry, and quick wit. Their courtship lasted several years, as John Adams began his law career, and they were married on October 25, 1764. He was almost twenty-nine. Though hardly educated in a formal sense, Abigail Adams was intelligent, well read, and full of life.

Over the course of their long marriage, extraordinary lives at the center of history, and frequent separations, they maintained a correspondence, preserved in more than twelve hundred deeply affectionate letters—a record filled with humor, literary allusion, and politics.

"His marriage to Abigail Smith was the most important decision of John Adams's life, as would become apparent with time," writes David McCullough. "She was in all respects his equal and the part she was to play would be greater than he could possibly have imagined for all his love of her and what appreciation he already had of her beneficial, steadying influence."[3]

In response to the Stamp Act of 1765, Adams was drawn deeper into Boston's patriot circle, men who believed in their birthrights as English citizens and staunchly opposed colonial Governor Thomas Hutchinson. Adams's mentor Jeremiah Gridley was the center of the group, which included Adams's second cousin Samuel Adams and attorney James Otis, the fiery orator who used the famous expression "no taxation without representation," a phrase actually coined earlier in Ireland.

When Parliament repealed the Stamp Act in 1766, tensions eased until British troops arrived in Boston in 1768 to enforce another round of taxes. That occupation provoked the next great crisis, which pulled

Adams into a white-hot spotlight. On a snowy evening on March 5, 1770, several hundred people converged on the Customs House, where a lone red-coated sentry stood guard. When some boys and unemployed dockworkers taunted the guard, the crowd grew larger. Suddenly, eight British soldiers, bayonets fixed, arrived with an officer. With rocks and snowballs raining down on the soldiers, they opened fire. Five Boston "townies" died. This was the "Boston Massacre."

John Adams was approached to defend the soldiers. Although reeling from the loss of their infant daughter Susanna in February, John and Abigail agreed that he should defend the British officer and soldiers. Staunch in his belief that no man should be denied the right to counsel and a fair trial, Adams also thought that the Sons of Liberty—and his cousin Samuel Adams in particular—had manipulated the "Massacre" for propaganda value. In the first trial, the British officer was found not guilty of ordering the deadly shots. Of the eight soldiers tried in a second case, six were acquitted and two were found guilty of the lesser charge of manslaughter.

Adams would later say that the case cost him some clients. But his advocacy of the detested British "Lobsterbacks" only bolstered Adams's reputation for honesty. He was elected to the Massachusetts legislature, moving to Boston in time to witness the Tea Party in December 1773.

In 1774, Adams was selected to represent Massachusetts at the First Continental Congress in Philadelphia. When the first shots in the War for Independence were fired on April 19, 1775, Adams was cautious about being seen as too radical in Philadelphia. Knowing that Virginia—the most populous and in many ways influential state—was needed to cement solidarity with New England, John Adams rose in June 1775 to nominate Virginian George Washington, who had arrived in Philadelphia in his militia uniform, to command the Continental Army; Samuel Adams seconded. A year later, it was John Adams who recommended the young Virginian Thomas Jefferson be included on the committee drafting the Declaration of Independence.

PRESIDENTIAL VOICES

My country has in its wisdom contrived for me the most insignificant office that ever the invention of man contrived or his imagination conceived.

—JOHN ADAMS

to Abigail Adams after his election as vice president

1789[4]

Was John Adams really a secret aristocratic monarchist?

Just as Washington had to improvise his role as president, John Adams, as first vice president, was walking on "untrodden ground"—and thinner ice. Washington essentially ignored Adams as vice president. Presiding over the Senate with no real rules established for his role, Adams made a few gaffes, including getting involved in the debates. And as partisan rancor grew, there was less room for polite disagreement.

Although it seems innocuous now, one Senate controversy boiled over. Its source was the title of the president and how Washington should be addressed when introduced. Adams took a lead in advocating for a stronger title than simply "President." One committee suggested "His Highness the President of the United States of America and Protector of the Rights of Same." The debate went on for a month, with the Senate finally deciding that Washington's title would simply be "The President of the United States." But Adams had unwittingly provided his political enemies with a charge that would haunt him—anyone in favor of such titles was a "monarchist."

The debacle over the title also served to further distance Washington from Adams. Never quite comfortable in society, the public John Adams was seemingly cold and aloof. Bookish, and not a dancer or cardplayer, he lacked the common touch, or as modern politics puts it, he was not "a guy you want to have a beer with." And his mishandling of the question of the president's title seemed to deepen the strain between Adams and other politicians. He was soon being referred to as His Rotundity, the Duke of Braintree, and His Superfluous Excellency.[5]

But in politics, then and now, perceptions matter. And as the debates grew more divisive over the next few years, that charge, along with the perception that Adams was angling for an American monarchy, was to become more than just a mild jibe. It is a truism of American politics that if you can label someone and repeat the label long enough, it will become fixed in the public mind. For Adams, a man of modest means and the furthest from an aristocrat, the label of "monarchist" stuck.

══

PRESIDENTIAL VOICES

I pray Heaven to bestow the best of blessings on this house and all that shall hereafter inhabit it. May none but honest and wise men ever rule under this roof.

—JOHN ADAMS
to Abigail Adams on arriving at the Executive Mansion
November 2, 1800
(President Franklin D. Roosevelt later had these words
inscribed on the mantel of a White House fireplace.)

══

Who elected John Adams?

Talk about tough acts to follow. Imagine filling the large boots left behind by George Washington.

That small mountain was only one that Adams would have to climb in 1796. The quest for the presidency that year became the first contested election in American history. The lines had been clearly drawn between Adams's (and Hamilton's) Federalist Party and Thomas Jefferson's Democratic-Republicans. As the system evolved, the party candidates were chosen by party leaders in a "caucus," a word possibly derived from Algonquian, meaning "counselor or adviser," and first used in America in 1773.[6]

There was no "presidential ticket," as there is today. Instead, several candidates from each party were selected. South Carolina's Thomas

Pinckney was also running as a Federalist, and up-and-coming political New York power broker Aaron Burr was a Republican. The campaign took place under the original electoral system in which the top vote-winner became president and the second-place finisher became vice president.

The two parties disputed just about everything on the table, foreign and domestic. The Federalists held to their vision of strong, centralized government, with Hamilton's plan for an economy anchored by the expansion of industry, with a powerful, national financial system and a standing army. They also tilted toward England in its disputes and conflicts with France.

Jefferson, now joined by former Federalist James Madison, wanted a weaker federal government with less financial power centered in Washington, and tilted toward the French side and a much greater reliance on militias than on a national army. To Jefferson, the Federalists were monarchists, and that was where Adams's misguided push for presidential titles came back to haunt him.

Washington stayed above the fray but let his preference for the Federalists and Adams be known. But with Washington off the scene, Jefferson and his allies knew they could take off the gloves.

The race offered little powdered-wig, debating-society civility. The candidates never went out on a campaign trail, but pamphlets, broadsides, and newspapers began to do the dirty work of presidential electioneering—including the dreaded "negative campaigning." Yes, they did it back then too.

And one of the best at it was Benjamin Franklin Bache's *Aurora*, which went after Adams with hammer and tongs, in personal as well as political terms. The vice president was "old, querulous, Bald, blind, crippled Toothless Adams" and "champion of kings, ranks and titles." And those were the genteel insults.

Adams's allies responded with attacks on Jefferson, whose sympathies for the bloody French Revolution tarred him as a "Jacobin" (modern equivalent: "radical leftist who pals around with terrorists"), an atheist, and, perhaps most damning, a coward, for having fled Monticello in the face of a British attack in 1781. (One British sally into Virginia had been led by none other than Benedict Arnold, patriot-hero-turned-traitor.)

Adams's fellow Federalist Alexander Hamilton was no ally. The ambitious, power-hungry New Yorker took a dim view of Adams, finding him lacking in comparison to Washington—and himself. Abigail Adams, wife of one president and mother of another, must have had some very profound political antennae. John's most trusted ally and adviser, she once wrote to him about Hamilton, "Beware of that spare Cassius"—her Shakespearean allusion quite clear—"I have read his Heart and his wicked Eyes many a time. The very devil is in them."[7]

Seeking control over the levers of power in the presidency, Hamilton again worked behind the scenes against Adams by advocating for South Carolina's Thomas Pinckney (brother of Charles Cotesworth Pinckney, a key member of the Constitutional Convention).

Adams was caught between Jefferson and his allies on one side and Hamilton's friendly fire on the other. But he was still able to squeak into office by a slim margin of three electoral votes. Hamilton's machinations had backfired. Some Federalists, knowing of the New Yorker's strategy, withheld their votes from Pinckney. This opened the way for Thomas Jefferson to finish second in the electoral voting. Under the original rules, that made Jefferson vice president. As president of the Senate, it was Adams's duty to read out the results of the election and proclaim that he was president.

Instead of two Federalists in office, there would be Federalist Adams and Republican Jefferson—the two men most responsible for the Declaration of Independence. But that old alliance was ancient history now, after twenty eventful, world-shaking years.

March 4, 1797, Inauguration Day in Philadelphia's Congress Hall, must have been quite a sight. The outgoing President George Washington entered, followed by Thomas Jefferson, sworn in that morning as vice president. Then came Adams in a simple broadcloth suit devoid of buckles or other finery. He had ridden to the hall in a plain coach—Adams would give his critics no ammunition to complain about his monarchist tendencies this day.

It was the last time that the three titans of the Revolution would be together.

Why did Adams sign the Alien and Sedition Acts?
Washington had warned against "entangling alliances." But it was exactly the question of where America's foreign loyalties lay that absorbed the Adams years. A single great issue—the possibility of war with France—dominated his four years. So did the related question of an alliance with England, favored by many in his own party. French privateers had begun preying on American merchant ships in 1797, seizing more than three hundred American vessels. When Adams first took office, he proposed that Jefferson and Madison—from the opposing party—take the lead in defusing the situation diplomatically. Jefferson was initially open to the idea, but Madison, who had left Washington after Adams's election and was in the Virginia legislature, rejected it. Historian Joseph Ellis notes that Madison insisted "that the Republican cause must take precedence over nostalgic bonds of brotherhood. . . . A political alliance with Adams was rooted in a merely sentimental attachment, Madison observed, and not in the abiding interests of the Republican opposition that Jefferson must now prepare himself to lead."[8] Madison allowed party loyalty to take precedence; yes, even Founding Fathers could put politics above country.

Adams then made another political blunder. He kept on some of Washington's cabinet members, all Federalists who were more loyal to Hamilton than to Adams.

When the delegation Adams later sent to France was greeted with demands for bribes, the negotiations collapsed in a crisis known as the "XYZ Affair." In April 1798, Adams released documents relating to the incident, sparking a congressional investigation. The war cries against France grew louder, and Adams was forced to prepare for an undeclared war, a "Quasi War," as it was called. A limited conflict that began in July 1798 when Congress rescinded treaties with France, this undeclared war resulted in a handful of naval engagements.

Adams asked George Washington to come out of retirement to lead the army. Adams made the appointment before Washington had actually agreed, but Washington had also made the appointment of Alexander Hamilton as his second in command a condition of the deal. Hamilton had by that time been publicly scandalized by reports of his affair with Maria Reynolds and the bribes paid to her husband, which had appeared in the anti-Federalist *Aurora*. Washington's price for agreeing to lead the army was an opportunity to rehabilitate his longtime friend and ally. Adams reluctantly agreed.

While preparing for war, Adams ordered production of new ships for the navy. At the same time, he continued to negotiate for peace, bedeviled by Federalist hawks, who were clamoring for war with France, and Republicans on the other side accusing him of an alliance with the monarchist English. By early 1799, the situation had been defused, even though there were several more naval battles fought, and George Washington hung up his sword for good.

But as part of the war fever, the Federalist majority in Congress had passed four bills known together as the Alien and Sedition Acts. Their history is instructive for modern America, as they were passed out of fear and were among the most grievous assaults on constitutional rights in American history. The bills were:

- **The Naturalization Act:** extending from five to fourteen years the requirement for residency to become a citizen.
- **The Alien Act:** allowing the president to deport any resident alien considered "dangerous to peace and safety."
- **The Alien Enemies Act:** authorizing the deportation of residents if their home country was at war with America. (Adams never signed a deportation order.)
- **The Sedition Act:** allowing the government to punish those found guilty of "printing, writing, or speaking in a scandalous or malicious way against the government of the United States." (What about the First Amendment? you might ask.)

Fear provoked these laws, but a deep-seated tradition of anti-immigrant sentiment and American religious bias was also at work. The bills were largely aimed at French people in America, but the Irish ran a close second, and anti-Catholicism was driving the anxious mood. Protestant Americans, long antagonistic towards "papists," believed that Catholics were planning to overtake the country and hand it to the pope. The legislation was also a Federalist political move designed to blunt the impact of the new urban immigrants, primarily Catholic, who were joining the opposition Republicans in large numbers.

"Party strife and the general fear among Americans at the time tell the fuller story," writes Adams biographer Edith B. Gelles. "The mood in the country, following the XYZ affair, was bellicose. War with France seemed inevitable. As Americans considered the possibility of a French invasion, stories about the bloodbath that followed the French Revolution of 1789 circulated."[9]

The excesses of the press were also part of the rationale. The Sedition Act, which enabled the government to punish those found guilty of "printing, writing, or speaking in a scandalous or malicious way against the government," was passed with the *Aurora* in mind.

In modern America, the impact of the 9/11 terrorist attacks led to the passage of the Patriot Act, which many civil libertarians claimed was an unconstitutional assault of fundamental American rights. After Pearl Harbor in 1941, as America fought a life-and-death battle with Japan, the federal policy of interning Japanese-Americans was one of the great injustices in American history. Fear is a powerful motivator in politics and policy.

Adams signed all four bills. His wife, Abigail, who had a special aversion to Bache and the *Aurora*, also urged him on. The paper's attacks on her husband were personal, scathing, and unrelenting. And the paper's editors had expanded their targets to include her son John Quincy after he was named a minister abroad. An angry mother, Abigail Adams struck back publicly and privately. Influenced to sign the laws in part by his wife, Adams later considered their passage the permanent stain on his presidential term.[10]

Among those arrested under the Sedition Act was Matthew Lyon, an Irish-born congressman from Vermont. He was jailed but reelected while serving time. Benjamin Franklin Bache, the *Aurora* editor who had called Adams "blind, crippled and toothless," was also arrested but died of yellow fever in 1798, before his trial. *Aurora* writer James Callender, the Scottish citizen expelled from Britain for his political writings and the man responsible for exposing Hamilton's affair with Maria Reynolds, was convicted and sentenced to nine months in jail.

(Jefferson, a patron at the time, pardoned Callender while president. But the muckraking journalist would later set his sights on Jefferson also.)

PRESIDENTIAL VOICES

It is habitable by fires in every part, thirteen of which we are obliged to keep daily, or sleep in wet and damp places.
—ABIGAIL ADAMS
Letter dated November 21, 1800

This was the first lady's description of the "great castle," as she called the President's House. When she arrived, it was still in a state of construction by slaves, like the rest of the new city of Washington, D.C. Abigail Adams also noted, "It is *true Republicanism* that drives the slaves half fed, and destitute of clothing . . . whilst an owner walks about idle, though one slave is all the property he can boast."[11]

During Adams's day, the "Presidential Palace" initially used outdoor "privies." One can imagine the specter of seeing President Adams stroll to the outhouse. His successor, Jefferson, would install the first indoor bathroom. As White House historian William Seale notes, "A wooden privy . . . built beside the house in 1800 was to be demolished. A presidential necessary house in full view of the public must have struck the fastidious Jefferson as ludicrous. Two water closets were to be installed upstairs."[12]

PRESIDENTIAL VOICES

The Revolution of 1776 is now, and for the first time, arrived at its completion. Till now the Republicans have indeed beaten the slaves of monarchy in the field of battle, and driven the troops of the King of Great Britain from the shores of our country; but the secret enemies of the American Revolution—her internal, insidious, and indefatigable foes, have never till now been completely discomfited. This is the true period of the triumph of Republican principle.

—*AURORA*

February 20, 1801

The controversial Alien and Sedition Acts played a key role in the election of 1800, which produced the result celebrated by the *Aurora*— the election of Thomas Jefferson. But public opposition to these assaults on basic constitutional rights was only a small piece of one of the most extraordinary elections in American history.

Much had changed since Washington's elections, uncontested both times. But the unforeseen growth of two parties had changed everything. Candidates for president were going to be put forth by the evolving party leadership. But as originally designed, electors chose two names with the top finisher becoming president and the second-place finisher elected vice president. That is how Jefferson had become vice president under Adams in 1796. The rules remained in place in 1800.

Adams once again led the Federalist campaign, which now had an official "ticket" with South Carolina's Charles Cotesworth Pinckney— brother of Thomas and a hero of the Revolution—chosen as running mate. Jefferson and Burr were again the Republican candidates, in a campaign that produced a torrent of slurs and insults from both sides. Newspapers loyal to either party were again filled with crude rumors of sexual philandering by both Adams and Jefferson. When Adams's vice presidential candidate, General Pinckney, was accused of having sent a frigate to England to procure four pretty girls as mistresses, two for Adams and two for himself, Adams had the good humor to reply that General Pinckney had kept them all for himself.

To the Federalists, Jefferson was an outright atheist who would allow the excesses of the French Revolution to come to America. There were also the first whispers of Jefferson's relationship with one of his slave women, although that rumor was not yet public. That would come later.

As the campaign of 1800 went on, John and Abigail Adams suffered the death of one of their sons, Charles, to acute alcoholism. Besides the opposition party's bashing, Adams also faced the onslaught of fellow Federalist Alexander Hamilton, whose presidential ambitions had been dashed by the Reynolds scandal. But he still hoped to pull the strings in a new Federalist administration and lashed out at Adams in a contemptuous, fifty-four-page pamphlet that assailed him for "defects of character," "disgusting egotism," and "eccentric tendencies," among other flaws. It closed with a tepid endorsement of Adams for president! But Hamilton's "endorsement" sealed the second president's fate. Supposedly a private document, it was sent to more than two hundred Federalists but found its way into Republican hands and was published in October.

When the December ballots were finally counted, Jefferson's Republicans held the day. But the problem was, which Republican?

Under the original Constitutional election scheme, there was no separate election of president and vice president; Jefferson and Aaron Burr had each collected seventy-three electoral votes. Under the existing original rules of the Constitution, the tie meant that the House of Representatives, still under Federalist control, would decide the question, with each state receiving a vote.

Faced with a choice between these two, Alexander Hamilton again tried to manipulate events and lobbied for Jefferson. While Hamilton disliked and distrusted Jefferson, he detested fellow New Yorker and political rival Burr. While Burr is remembered rather notoriously in history, he was then still considered a heroic veteran of the Revolution who had achieved some fame, particularly at the disastrous Battle of Quebec in December 1775, and in his service at Valley Forge.

Playing his hand cautiously, Burr did not campaign for himself. But he did not withdraw either—a position that did not stand the New Yorker in good stead with Jefferson. The votes of nine of the House's state delegations were needed to win, and Jefferson failed to gain them through thirty-five ballots. As the sense of crisis grew, there were calls for naming a temporary president, and some Republican leaders threatened to call out their state militias to enforce the popular will.

When Jefferson assured the Federalists that he would maintain much of the status quo, James Bayard, a Federalist from Delaware, maneuvered to elect him. The House finally chose him on Tuesday, February 17, 1801. The difficulties of selecting the president in 1800 resulted in passage of the Twelfth Amendment in 1804, which provided for separate balloting for the president and vice president. (See Appendix II.)

This "Revolution of 1800," as Jefferson later called it, was a bloodless one, but its impact was real. The Federalist Party was all but politically finished; it lost control of both the presidency and Congress. But John Adams made certain that its influence did not die with his defeat.

With little more than a month left in office, Adams nominated John Marshall to become the chief justice. It would prove to be the most important and long-lasting decision he made as president.

Final Judgment: Grade B

Adams left the presidency disappointed. And for reasons unclear, he departed Washington without attending Jefferson's inauguration. Generous apologists claim that Adams had no precedent as a defeated presidential candidate. But his early morning departure still hangs there with a faint whiff of sour presidential grapes. It would be more than a decade before Jefferson and Adams resumed a correspondence.

Adams had left the country at peace, in stable financial condition, and with a forty-nine-ship navy that would serve the country well. But his shrewdest and most long-lasting impact may have been his appointment of Federalist John Marshall as chief justice of the Supreme Court.

Adams spent the next quarter century in Quincy, writing his memoirs, corresponding with friends and colleagues from a lifetime in politics, watching as his son John Quincy rose through the government ranks, to be eventually elected president in 1825. Despite the deep fracture in their relationship, Adams and Thomas Jefferson began to correspond with each other in 1811, encouraged by Dr. Benjamin Rush. In one of his most poignant letters to his old Revolutionary comrade, Adams told Jefferson, "The dear partner of my life of fifty-four years as a wife, and for many years more as a lover now lies in extremis, forbidden to speak or be spoken to." His beloved Abigail died of typhoid fever on October 28, 1818.

Adams died on July 4, 1826, the fiftieth anniversary of the adoption of the Declaration. He did not know that Jefferson had died earlier that same day.

John Adams Administration Milestones[13]

1797

March 4	John Adams is inaugurated in Philadelphia.
May 15	Adams calls the first special session of Congress, to debate the mounting crisis in French-American relations.
September–October	The USS *Constellation* is launched in Baltimore and later the USS *Constitution* ("Old Ironsides") is launched in Boston.
October 18	In France, the Americans seeking peace are asked to pay a bribe in order to speak with French Foreign Minister Talleyrand. This episode becomes known as the "XYZ Affair."

1798

January	The Eleventh Amendment to the Constitution is ratified; it forbids suits against a state by a citizen of another state or of a foreign nation.
April 3	Adams exposes the XYZ affair, providing Congress with letters from the Peace Commission indicating French efforts to intimidate the Americans.
June 18	The Naturalization Act, first of four acts known as the Alien and Sedition Acts, is passed.
June 25	The Alien Act is passed.
July 6	The Alien Enemies Act, the third of the Alien and Sedition Acts, passes.
July 14	The Sedition Act, last of the Alien and Sedition Acts, is passed.

1800

February 1	The United States frigate *Constellation* defeats the French ship *La Vengeance* in one of the few actual engagements of the "Quasi War."

April 24	Congress establishes a Library of Congress; the purchase of books from Thomas Jefferson as the foundation of the library is authorized.
June	The new city of Washington in the District of Columbia becomes the official capital of the United States, succeeding Philadelphia.
September 30	The "Quasi War" with France ends with the signing of a treaty in Paris.
November 11	The fourth presidential election is held. Adams, the Federalist Party candidate, loses his bid for reelection, but no winner is determined.

MUST READS

Joseph Ellis, *First Family: Abigail and John Adams*; David McCullough, *John Adams*; Bernard A. Weisberger, *America Afire: Jefferson, Adams, and the First Contested Election*.

ONLINE RESOURCES

Inaugural Address, Avalon Project, Yale Law School
http://avalon.law.yale.edu/18th_century/adams.asp

Alien and Sedition Acts, Library of Congress
http://www.loc.gov/rr/program/bib/ourdocs/Alien.html

Adams Papers at Yale
http://avalon.law.yale.edu/subject_menus/adamspap.asp

Birthplace and Family Homes, Adams National Historical Park
http://www.nps.gov/adam/index.htm

John Adams Library, Boston Public Library
http://johnadamslibrary.org/

Library of Congress Resource Guide
http://www.loc.gov/rr/program/bib/presidents/adams/

Miller Center of Public Affairs, University of Virginia
http://millercenter.org/president/adams

3

The Sage of Monticello
Thomas Jefferson

★ ★ ★

March 4, 1801–March 4, 1809

Milestones in Thomas Jefferson's Life

April 13, 1743	Born at Shadwell plantation in Albemarle County, Virginia
1767	Began practicing law
1769–1779	Served in Virginia legislature
1775–1776	Member of Virginia delegation of Continental Congress
July 1776	Drafted Declaration of Independence
1779–1781	Governor of Virginia
1783–1784	Member of Virginia's delegation to Congress
1784–1785	Diplomatic commissioner of Congress in Europe
1785–1789	U.S. diplomatic minister to France
1789–1793	Secretary of state under Washington
1797–1801	Vice president under John Adams
1801–1809	Third president
July 4, 1826	Died at Monticello, Virginia, aged eighty-three

PRESIDENTIAL VOICES

We have called by different names brethren of the same principle. We are all Republicans, we are all Federalists. If there be any among us who would wish to dissolve this Union or to change its republican form, let them stand undisturbed as monuments of the safety with which error of opinion may be toler-

ated where reason is left free to combat it. I know, indeed, that some honest men fear that a republican government can not be strong, that this Government is not strong enough; but would the honest patriot, in the full tide of successful experiment, abandon a government which has so far kept us free and firm on the theoretic and visionary fear that this Government, the world's best hope, may by possibility want energy to preserve itself?

—THOMAS JEFFERSON
First Inaugural Address, March 4, 1801[1]

G athering a group of Nobel Prize winners for a White House dinner in April 1962, John F. Kennedy quipped, "I think this is the most extraordinary collection of human knowledge that has ever been gathered together here at the White House, with the possible exception of when Thomas Jefferson dined alone."[2]

And that just about says it all. Like a true Renaissance man, or the giant of the Enlightenment Age that he was, Jefferson was conversant in music, architecture, botany, meteorology, wine, mechanical engineering, philosophy. And books—"I cannot live without books," he famously wrote.

On the other hand, there is no more stunning example of the contradictions of America's founding and creation than the "Sage of Monticello." Though a tireless champion of liberty, Jefferson owned slaves all of his life, even though he considered the practice immoral and had included a condemnation of slavery in his draft of the Declaration—deleted by the Continental Congress. Like Washington, Jefferson believed that slavery would eventually die out in America. Encouraged by his friend abolitionist Benjamin Rush, he wanted to plant maple trees in the hope that maple sugar would replace the cane sugar produced by slaves and put a dent in the slave economy. But slaves, presumably, would still tend his Monticello maple trees.

As Garry Wills, a self-professed admirer of Jefferson, wrote, "I disagree with those who would diminish his great achievement, the Declaration of Independence. Or those who call him more a friend to despotism than to freedom. Or those who would reduce his whole life to one affair with a slave. My Jefferson is a giant, but a giant trammeled in a net."[3]

Lawyer, writer, scientist, philosopher, architect, visionary, Founding Father, principal author of one of the greatest documents in the history of freedom. Slaveholder. And therein lies the rub.

Fast Facts

RELIGION: No formal affiliation—Deist

EDUCATION: College of William and Mary

CAREER BEFORE POLITICS: Planter, lawyer

POLITICAL PARTY: Democratic-Republican

SPOUSE: Martha Wayles Skelton (October 30, 1748–September 6, 1782)

Jefferson's wife, Martha, first married at age eighteen and was widowed two years later. Her first son, John Skelton, died at the age of four in June 1771. In January 1772, she married Thomas Jefferson and the newlyweds set off for Monticello in a rare blizzard. Although there are no known portraits of Martha Jefferson, she was described by friends and family as small, graceful, attractive, and an accomplished musician like her husband. With Jefferson she bore six children, but only two survived to adulthood, and Martha Jefferson died four months after the birth of a daughter, Lucy (who died at the age of two). Contemporary accounts depict Jefferson as disconsolate after his wife's death, which he wrote "left him a blank." Jefferson added these lines from the *Iliad*, in Greek, to her tombstone:

> *Nay even in the house of Hades the dead forget their dead,*
> *Yet will I even there be mindful of my dear comrade.*[4]

CHILDREN: Martha ("Patsy") and Mary ("Polly")

Thomas and Martha Jefferson had six children together, but four of them did not live to maturity. Eldest daughter Martha Jefferson Randolph filled the role of first lady at times during Jefferson's White House years. Dolley Madison, the wife of Jefferson's vice president James Madison, also filled in ably as Jefferson's social hostess.

It is now widely accepted that Jefferson was also the father of six of the children of his slave Sally Hemings: Harriet (born 1795, died in infancy); Beverly (born 1798); an unnamed daughter (born 1799, died in infancy); a second Harriet (born 1801); Madison (born 1805); and Eston (born 1809). The children of Sally Hemings were emancipated by Jefferson, the only "nuclear family" of slaves so treated.[5]

* Thomas Jefferson was the first president inaugurated in Washington, D.C., on Wednesday March 4, 1801, a day described as mild and beautiful. He broke precedent by walking to and from his swearing-in ceremony.

* The *National Intelligencer*, a newly founded newspaper, printed Jefferson's entire Inaugural Address on the morning of the inauguration.

* The Marine Band played at an inauguration for the first time at Jefferson's and has played at every inauguration since.

* Jefferson did not deliver his Message to Congress, or State of the Union, in person, as Washington and Adams had done. He sent it in written form. That remained the precedent until Woodrow Wilson delivered the Annual Message to Congress in person.

* Jefferson was the third of eight Virginia-born presidents.

* With the assistance of Benjamin Latrobe, surveyor of public buildings, Jefferson expanded the Executive Mansion to include one-story east and west wings with servants' quarters, woodsheds, and a wine cellar. He also provided a well and cistern. His predecessor, John Adams, had to have water hauled from a distant spring. But water wasn't all Jefferson drank. Jefferson's wine bill as president exceeded $10,000.[6]

* In Jefferson's day, there were two public "holidays": New Year's Day and, appropriately, the Fourth of July. The public, as well as Washington officials and the diplomatic corps, was invited to visit the White House and shake hands with the president. On Independence Day, notes White House historian William Seale, the north grounds became a fair with tents and booths selling food, drinks, and merchandise. "There were horse races and tests of skill among the men. Cockfights and dogfights took place on the sidelines. . . . A

bareheaded Jefferson and his cabinet kept watch from the steps of the White House."[7]

PRESIDENTIAL VOICES

That these are our grievances which we have thus laid before his majesty, with that freedom of language and sentiment which becomes a free people claiming their rights, as derived from the laws of nature, and not as the gift of their chief magistrate: . . . [Kings] are the servants, not the proprietors of the people. Open your breast, sire, to liberal and expanded thought. Let not the name of George the third be a blot in the page of history.

—THOMAS JEFFERSON
A Summary View of the Rights of British America (1774)[8]

Born at Shadwell, his father's estate in Albermarle County, Virginia, Thomas Jefferson was the son of a planter and surveyor, Peter Jefferson, and his wife, Jane Randolph Jefferson, who came from the Randolphs, one of Virginia's wealthiest families. Thomas Jefferson's father had moved the family to the Tuckahoe Plantation, owned by William Randolph, which Peter Jefferson managed as executor. The third child in a family of ten, Thomas was a bookish boy who studied with a local clergyman and later at a school in Fredericksburg with Reverend James Maury, who taught Jefferson the classics in their original languages. The oldest son, Thomas was fourteen when his father died, leaving the boy head of an estate with about twenty-five hundred acres and thirty slaves. Always an able student, he enrolled in the College of William and Mary at Williamsburg when he was sixteen.

He came under the wing of the colonial governor Francis Fauquier and two local scholars: William Small, professor of mathematics, science, and philosophy, who Jefferson said, "probably fixed the destiny of my life," and George Wythe, a profoundly influential lawyer, judge, and future signer of the Declaration. With these three, young Jefferson later said, he "heard more good sense, more rational and philo-sophical conversation than in all my life besides." [9]

After graduating at nineteen, Jefferson continued to study law under Wythe and was admitted to the Virginia bar in 1762.

A tall, lanky redhead, with a passion for the violin, he was also caught up in Williamsburg's fashionable society, a world of fox hunts, shooting matches, and theater. But the greatest theatrical experience of the day may have consisted of going to the House of Burgesses to listen to men like Patrick Henry. Jefferson witnessed Henry's famous "Give me liberty or give me death" speech in response to the Stamp Act in 1765.

At age twenty-eight, in 1772, he married, choosing—like George Washington—a well-to-do widow, Martha Wayles Skelton, whose for-tune doubled Jefferson's estates. Four of their six children died in in-fancy, and in 1782, Martha also died, after childbirth. A publicly grief-stricken widower, Jefferson never remarried. But it has become widely accepted that he fathered the children of Monticello slave Sally Hemings, who may have been Martha's half-sister. (It is also widely believed that Martha Wayles's father, John Wayles, was Sally Hemings's father.)

After winning election to the Virginia legislature in 1769, Jefferson established his reputation as an important voice in the American pa-triot cause with *A Summary View of the Rights of British America*. That work established his literary reputation and brought him to Philadel-phia and immortality in 1776.

Jefferson's role during the Revolution was the subject of some con-troversy. As governor of Virginia for two years during the war, he was sharply criticized for his failure to raise a militia to aggressively defend the state when British forces, including armies led by General Corn-wallis, the turncoat Benedict Arnold, and the infamous British officer Banastre Tarleton, known for his cruelty, invaded Virginia. The Brit-ish forces ravaged the countryside, looting and burning towns and farms. Jefferson moved the government to Charlottesville and barely escaped capture at Monticello. His tenure as governor and his reaction to the British attacks led to an investigation by the state assembly, but

Jefferson was vindicated, although he was always prickly over this—and most other—criticism of his actions.

After the war, Jefferson represented the new United States, becoming the first minister (ambassador) to France, where he lived during the early stages of the French Revolution. His sympathies for the French would become a dividing line between his followers and the emerging Federalists, led by Adams and Hamilton.

With Washington's election, Jefferson returned to America to serve as first secretary of state under Washington and then vice president under Adams after losing to his old colleague by three electoral votes in the election of 1796.

PRESIDENTIAL VOICES

The election of Mr. Jefferson to the presidency was, upon sectional feelings, the triumph of the South over the North—of the slave representation over the purely free.

—JOHN QUINCY ADAMS[10]

Why was Thomas Jefferson called the "Negro President"?

Barack Obama has been called the first African-American president or the first "biracial" president. During his presidency, Bill Clinton was once famously described by novelist Toni Morrison, in the *New Yorker* in October 1998, as the first "black president" (to the considerable chagrin of some who thought the title undeserved). But more than two hundred years ago, Thomas Jefferson was described as the "Negro President"—the phrase attributed to Timothy Pickering, a Federalist and secretary of state under Washington and Adams.[11]

The election of 1800 in which Thomas Jefferson, and his Republican "running mate," Aaron Burr, defeated Federalists John Adams and Charles Cotesworth Pinckney of South Carolina, has always been regarded as a watershed moment in American history. It came a year after the death of George Washington in December 1799, bringing one era to a close as the nineteenth century opened and America began a new age of breathtakingly rapid expansion. It was the first truly "contested" election, in which the party divisions that had been growing for a decade burst into acrimonious campaigning, slanderous charges, and backroom dealing. It was a pivotal election, in which Aaron Burr would pioneer the new urban "machine" politics, as he brought New York State to the Republican fold, deepening the already large gulf between himself and fellow New York power broker Alexander Hamilton.

It was the first election in which a sitting president was defeated.

It was an election in which the key personalities—Adams, Jefferson, Hamilton, and Burr chief among them—demonstrated their individual capacity as politicians for scandal, personal recriminations, double-dealing, subterfuge, backbiting, and backstabbing.

And it was an election that was thrown to the House of Representatives when Jefferson and Burr managed to wind up in a tie, necessitating more than thirty votes in the House and plunging the nation into a state of near-chaos as the fate of the presidency remained unclear. It was that confusion caused by the constitutional machinery of presidential elections that led to the first "fix" of the election process with the Twelfth Amendment, separating the election of the president and the vice president. It was ratified in September 1804 in time for the next presidential election.

On its face, the 1800 presidential contest has always been presented as a success of sorts. Power changed hands peacefully at a time when places like France and Haiti, under a new regime of former slaves, were exploding in murderous upheavals. Although John Adams would not personally or graciously hand the keys to the Presidential Palace over to Jefferson, preferring to make an early morning exit from the new federal city, this "low-keyed transfer of the reins of government was a new development in the tortured, centuries-old history of dynasties violently changing hands," as Bernard A. Weisberger wrote in his history of the election. "It was a victory for the idea of popular self-government itself, which at the time was practiced almost nowhere in the world outside the United States."[12]

At the time, Margaret Bayard Smith, wife of the owner of the pro-Jefferson *National Intelligencer* newspaper and an observer of the Washington scene, wrote, "The dark and threatening cloud that had hung over the political horrison [*sic*] rolled harmlessly away, and the sunshine of prosperity and gladness broke forth."[13]

But there is another view of the election of 1800, one that has attracted more attention recently, especially since the publication of Garry Wills's 2003 book, *"Negro President": Jefferson and the Slave Power*. In it, Wills argued that Jefferson's victory was dependent on one factor above all: the three-fifths of a person compromise struck at the Constitutional Convention. This so-called "federal ratio," in which slaves were counted to determine apportionment in Congress, also affected the number of each state's electoral votes, which are of course based on the number of a state's seats in Congress, both House and Senate.

While this agreement never gave slaves an actual vote, the fact that they were counted in the census weighed in favor of the number of electors given to slave states, tipping the scales away from the popular votes of the free, white population. Wills made his case emphatically: "If real votes had been counted, Adams would have been returned to office. But, of course, the 'vote' did not depend solely on voters. Though Jefferson admittedly received eight more votes than Adams in the electoral college, at least twelve of his votes were not based on citizenry that could express its will but on the blacks owned by southern masters."[14]

Not every historian agrees with Wills—the "slave power" argument behind Jefferson's victory is still debated. Others point to such factors as Aaron Burr's success in delivering New York to Jefferson as more significant to the race's outcome.

The larger point is that many Americans still do not recognize that this compromise existed at all, or that it had such impact on national politics and American history before the Civil War. Historian Leonard Richards put it into simple numerical terms: In sixty-two years, from Washington until 1850, slaveholders controlled the presidency for fifty years and the only men reelected president were slaveholders (Washington, Jefferson, Madison, Monroe, and Jackson); the chairmanship of the powerful House Ways and Means Committee and the speaker's chair were controlled by slaveholders; and eighteen of thirty-one Supreme Court justices were slaveholders.[15]

This is not a new argument. Historian Richard Brown wrote more than fifty years ago, "From the inauguration of Washington until the Civil War, the South was in the saddle of national politics. This is the central fact in American political history to 1860."[16]

And that is why it is important to refute the notion, stated by Representative Michele Bachmann, a Republican congresswoman from Minnesota who ran for the GOP nomination in 2011, that the Founding Fathers "worked tirelessly to end slavery." The real history simply does not bear that assertion out.

Jefferson's victory over Adams was only half the battle. Since he had tied with Burr, with seventy-three electoral votes each, the victory would have to come from the House, where each state had a single vote. At the time, there were sixteen states—the original thirteen, plus Vermont, Kentucky, and Tennessee. The votes of nine states were needed to win the election. With Alexander Hamilton and others politicking and "horse-trading" for votes, the House started balloting in a howling snowstorm on February 11, 1801. At midnight on February 12, after twenty-eight failures, the balloting was adjourned, and resumed the next morning. But the deadlock continued. Federalist voters were unwilling to make Jefferson president.

As the trading behind the scenes continued, the Federalist voters finally agreed to either withdraw or cast blank votes. And on February 17, after thirty-six ballots, Thomas Jefferson was elected the third president. Aaron Burr became his vice president.

PRESIDENTIAL VOICES

Believing with you that religion is a matter which lies solely between man and his God, that he owes account to none other for his faith or his worship, that the legislative powers of government reach actions only, and not opinions, I contemplate with sovereign reverence that act of the whole American people which declared that their legislature should "make no law respecting an establishment of religion, or prohibiting the free exercise thereof," thus building a wall of separation between church and State. Adhering to this expression of the supreme will of the nation in behalf of the rights of conscience, I shall see with sincere satisfaction the progress of those sentiments which tend to restore to man all his natural rights, convinced he has no natural right in opposition to his social duties.

—Thomas Jefferson
Letter to the Danbury Baptist Association
January 1, 1802[17]

Like Washington's letter to the synagogue in Newport, RI, Jefferson's response to the Danbury Baptists is one of the most famous documents in the much-debated issue of America as a "Christian nation." Jefferson's phrase "wall of separation between church and State" was not his invention. Colonial-era freethinker Roger Williams, founder of Rhode Island, had written of a "hedge or wall of separation between the garden of the church and the wilderness of the world" in his 1644 book *The Bloudy Tenent of Persecution.*

But since Jefferson's 1802 letter, his words have been taken as a corollary to the First Amendment, although the phrase "separation of church and state" does not appear in the Constitution. It has been cited on several occasions in rulings, including several times by the Supreme Court.

In this letter, as in his earlier "Statute of Virginia for Religious Freedom," Jefferson was not arguing against religion or Christianity. He was making the very clear distinction that the government could not dictate an individual's conscience. As Jefferson wrote in a more colloquial moment: "I care not whether my neighbor believes in no god or twenty. It neither picks my pocket nor breaks my leg."

Jefferson and Madison, chiefly, but others also, including Washington and Adams, believed in a secular republic where conscience was a matter of natural rights. Not official tolerance.

PRESIDENTIAL VOICES

It is emphatically the province and duty of the judicial department to say what the law is. . . . Thus the particular phraseology of the constitution of the

United States confirms and strengthens the principle, supposed to be essential
to all written constitutions, that a law repugnant to the constitution is void.
　　　　　　　　—CHIEF JUSTICE JOHN MARSHALL
　　　　　　　　Marbury v. Madison, February 1803

Why did William Marbury sue James Madison and what did President Jefferson think of the decision?

Even before Jefferson's election was finally assured in February 1801, John Adams knew he was on his way out. Under the Judiciary Act of 1801 and working with a "lame duck" Congress still controlled by fellow Federalists, outgoing President Adams reorganized the federal judiciary, created sixteen new judgeships, and reduced the Supreme Court from six to five justices. He then appointed judges right until Jefferson was inaugurated. These so-called "midnight judges" were staunch Federalists and included John Marshall as chief justice of the United States. A Virginian and veteran of the Revolution who had served as Adams's secretary of state, Marshall—who would write the first serious biography of George Washington, five volumes published between 1804 and 1807—was also a distant cousin of Thomas Jefferson. But bloodlines meant little. They disliked each other's politics and eventually came to loathe each other. Marshall, a veteran of Valley Forge, thought Jefferson, who had not served, was a "shirker," in the words of Marshall biographer Jean Edward Smith. On the morning of Jefferson's swearing-in, which Marshall would administer, the Justice wrote, "The democrats are divided into speculative theorists and absolute terrorists: With the latter I am disposed to class Mr. Jefferson." [18]

As Jefferson tried to undo Federalist policies, Marshall often stood in his way. And he placed a stamp on the court and the young nation that is still felt today.

One of the most important decisions came in the 1803 case known as *Marbury v. Madison*, which grew out of the ongoing political fight between the Federalists and Jefferson's Republicans. William Marbury was one of the "midnight judges," named a justice of the peace in the District of Columbia by the outgoing John Adams. But as secretary of state under Adams, John Marshall had failed to deliver the necessary paperwork for some of these judges, including Marbury. When James Madison, the secretary of state for the new Jefferson administration, refused to grant Marbury's commission, Marbury sued Madison, and his appeal went to the Supreme Court—with Marshall now presiding—to order Madison to grant the commission.

But Marshall refused Marbury's request, saying that even though Marbury was theoretically entitled to the post, a section of the Judiciary Act of 1789, which had established the federal court system, was unconstitutional and void. Marshall wrote that the Constitution and the Judiciary Act were in conflict, and in such a case, the courts must follow the Constitution. For the first time the Supreme Court had overturned an act of Congress. Although Marshall's decision in this case affected only the right of the court to interpret its own powers, the concept of judicial review, a key principle in the constitutional system of checks and balances and fundamental to the idea of "separation of powers," got its first test.

"It was a judicial tour de force," writes Marshall biographer Jean Edward Smith. "Marshall had converted a no-win situation into a massive victory. The authority of the Supreme Court to declare an act of Congress unconstitutional was now the law of the land. . . . The decision itself is one of the great constitutional documents of American history. Marshall's unadorned prose evoked the spirit of constitutional balance: a government of laws, not of men."[19]

While Jefferson's secretary of state, James Madison, won the case against Marbury, Jefferson did not comment on the decision, and Jean Edward Smith argues that "the Court's authority to declare an act of Congress unconstitutional was not controversial."[20] But Jefferson later complained that if the Court could decide what the Constitution means, it would be a "mere thing of wax in the hands of the judiciary, which they may twist and shape into any form they please."

Why did Napoléon sell Louisiana to Jefferson?

While America enjoyed its bloodless "Revolution of 1800," France was still in the throes of its violent upheavals. In 1799, Napoléon Bonaparte engineered the coup that overturned the Revolutionary Directory, eventually making himself ruler of France. While most of Napoléon's grandiose plans focused on Europe, America had a place in the Napoleonic dream. With a vast possession in the center of the American continent, he had visions of recapturing the rest of America for France. His first step was to force a weak Spain to return the Louisiana Territory to France, which it did in 1800. The second step was to regain control of the Caribbean island of Saint-Domingue. (Today the island is comprised of Haiti and the Dominican Republic.)

In 1793, the island had come under control of General Toussaint L'Ouverture, a former slave and a self-taught military genius who had led a successful slave rebellion. To launch any offensive in North America, Napoléon needed the island as a base and he sent twenty thousand troops to retake it. When the French Army was practically wiped out by yellow fever and a vicious guerilla war, Napoléon wrote off North America. Lacking troops and desperate for cash, he also feared any Anglo-American alliance. In a single stroke, he ordered his foreign minister, Talleyrand, to offer to sell not only New Orleans and Florida, but all of the Louisiana Territory, to Jefferson's delegation. They dickered with the French over price, but in May 1803, the treaty turning over all of Louisiana was signed.

With the treaty, the United States would double in size for about $15 million, or approximately four cents an acre. The purchase was made with U.S. bonds, the result of Hamilton's U.S. Bank Initiative, which Jefferson had resisted as unconstitutional. Jefferson was also uncertain as to the constitutionality of a president making such a treaty. But his "Republican" ideals clearly took a backseat to his extraordinary real estate deal. And apart from a few remaining Federalists who had little power, nobody in the Congress complained about Jefferson's Louisiana coup.

PRESIDENTIAL VOICES

A Song Supposed to Have Been Written by the Sage of Monticello
> *When pressed by loads of state affairs*
> *I seek to sport and dally*
> *The sweetest solace of my cares*
> *Is in the lap of Sally,*

She's black you tell me—grant she be—
Must colour always tally?
Black is love's proper hue for me
And white's the hue for Sally
                        —JAMES THOMSON CALLENDER
                        From the *Richmond Recorder*, 1802

James Callender, the Scottish-born journalist who had revealed Alexander Hamilton's affair a few years earlier, was disappointed when he failed to win a patronage job from Jefferson following his 1801 election. He turned the tables on his former patron and charged in print that Jefferson kept a slave as his lover. This was the first public revelation of the rumored relationship. There is no evidence that Jefferson ever publicly responded to the charges.

Recent DNA evidence, along with such historical evidence as the emancipation of the Hemings children and a long oral history within the descendants of the Monticello slave community, has led many historians to accept the truth of the relationship.

And Callender? He was found floating in the James River in July 1803. A coroner ruled that he had drowned accidentally while drunk.

PRESIDENTIAL VOICES

I received intimations that designs were in agitation in the western country, unlawful and unfriendly to the peace of the Union; and that the prime mover in these was Aaron Burr, heretofore distinguished by the favor of his country. The grounds of these intimations being inconclusive, the objects uncertain, and the fidelity of that country known to be firm, the only measure taken was to urge the informants to use their best endeavors to get further insight into the designs and proceedings of the suspected persons, and to communicate them to me.

. . . In this state of the evidence, delivered sometimes too under the restriction of private confidence, neither safety nor justice will permit the exposing

of names, except that of the principal actor, whose guilt is placed beyond question.

—THOMAS JEFFERSON
Special Message on the Burr Conspiracy
to the Senate and House of Representatives of the United States
January 22, 1807[21]

Why did Thomas Jefferson accuse his first vice president of treason?
Jefferson's first term was a rousing success. He had made the historically popular move of cutting taxes, including undoing the unpopular Whiskey Tax. He did away with the Alien and Sedition Acts by allowing them to lapse. Jefferson also pardoned James Callender, the journalist, and gave him $50. (Callender, see above, was clearly expecting more.) And the purchase of the Louisiana Territory topped it all.

By election time in 1804, Jefferson's popularity was so great that the opposition Federalist Party was all but dead. Another result of that election was a new vice president, New York's first governor, George Clinton, an anti-Federalist who only accepted the Constitution after the Bill of Rights was added. Jefferson's first vice president, Aaron Burr, had not endeared himself to Jefferson in the contested election of 1800 and had been frozen out of the first administration. Burr knew he would not be vice president for the second term. Jefferson and the party leadership did not want a man they considered disloyal sharing the ticket. In February 1804, the first official nominating caucus met in Washington and Republican congressmen renominated Jefferson and chose Republican loyalist Clinton. Burr returned to New York to run for the governor's chair vacated when Clinton left to become vice president. Alexander Hamilton, Burr's longtime rival, had other ideas and criticized Burr's morals in private comments that found their way into print. Burr then challenged Hamilton to the famous duel in which the sitting vice president shot and killed the former secretary of the Treasury on July 11, 1804.

Burr was briefly a fugitive from justice, but remarkably, that case blew over. A few months later, Burr returned to Washington to preside in the Senate impeachment hearing of federal judge Samuel Chase, a signer of the Declaration from Maryland. By all accounts, Burr performed his role admirably during the unprecedented impeachment trial and left Washington following Chase's acquittal in March 1805.

But he did not disappear from the scene. In a controversial episode that still confounds historians as to Burr's ultimate designs, he envisioned a potential war with Spain and wanted to form a small army to seize parts of Spain's holdings in America, either in Florida, Mexico, or both. When "evidence" of Burr's plan was brought to Thomas Jefferson, the president announced this "conspiracy" to Congress. Without benefit of a trial and with precious little actual evidence, Jefferson publicly proclaimed Burr guilty of treason, a hanging offense. With a large reward on his head and Jefferson making promises to anyone who would witness against him, Burr was captured in rural Alabama and placed on trial in Richmond, Virginia, for treason, with Chief Justice John Marshall presiding. When Jefferson was subpoenaed to testify and provide papers to the trial, he refused, bolstering the precedent of executive privilege.

Jefferson did everything in his power to see his former political ally convicted. But Burr was acquitted, due in part to Marshall's narrow interpretation of the constitutional definition of treason. This only added to Jefferson's contempt for Marshall, who was hanged in effigy by Jefferson's supporters after the decision. Following a second acquittal, Burr jumped bail and fled to Europe, where he remained for five years, attempting to find European support for his plans. Burr returned to New York, in disguise, in 1812. Eventually he returned to his law practice, and until his death in 1836, he continued to profess his innocence.

PRESIDENTIAL VOICES

HERE WAS BURIED THOMAS JEFFERSON
AUTHOR OF THE DECLARATION OF AMERICAN INDEPENDENCE
OF THE STATUTE OF VIRGINIA FOR RELIGIOUS FREEDOM
AND FATHER OF THE UNIVERSITY OF VIRGINIA

—Epitaph of Thomas Jefferson

Final Judgment: Grade A

Maybe Jefferson's epitaph should be taken into account in evaluating his presidency. Jefferson himself did not value his years as the nation's chief executive as highly as he did writing the Declaration of Independence and the Virginia Statute for Religious Freedom and establishing his beloved University of Virginia.

The press of the ongoing Napoleonic Wars between Britain and France had weighed heavily on Jefferson during his second term. Hoping to keep America—then a weak nation with no real army and a skeleton navy—out of the upheaval in Europe had led Jefferson to sign the Embargo Acts that kept American ships out of European ports. As a means to keep America out of the Napoleonic Wars and change British policy, the law was a disaster. It mostly hurt American merchants and the economy, while annoying the British and French without influencing their actions. The failure led to the Non-Intercourse Act, a feeble measure partially lifting the embargo.

Despite the distress caused by this foreign policy failure, Jefferson left office popular. His followers hoped he would run for a third term. At sixty-six, he retired to Monticello and took up the cause of one of his passions—education—founding the University of Virginia, allowing his handpicked successor, James Madison, to follow him into the White House.

But the consequences of his presidency would roll across American politics for decades. Although one of his last acts was signing the bill ending the foreign slave trade in 1807, the purchase of Louisiana had only served to increase the demand for slaves. Whatever idealistic hopes Jefferson once held for the natural end of slavery were dashed.

"Regarding blacks, slave and free, Jefferson had abandoned the antislavery idealism of his youth as politically impractical," historian Sean Wilentz once noted. "He believed that slavery was evil and that it was doomed . . . but he had no expectation that the end would come any time soon, and was fearful that precipitate emancipation would lead to race war and economic ruin. He had also reached the conclusion that blacks and whites could never peaceably inhabit the same country."[22]

Jefferson envisioned freedom for his own slaves at Monticello. But his debts piled higher in retirement, in part because of his endless tearing down and rebuilding of the house, and his own policies as president had diminished his personal fortune. Deep in debt, he went into bankruptcy, even selling off his personal library, which became the core of the new Library of Congress. In the end, his most precious possession, Monticello, would be sold off too. In poor health, Jefferson was suffering from an enlarged prostate, bladder infections, pneumonia, and chronic diarrhea. Most of the treatments of the time, such as mercury, were either ineffective or worsened his condition.[23]

By 1812, Jefferson had renewed his correspondence with John Adams, and it would continue to the time of their mutual deaths on July 4, 1826.

Jefferson Administration Milestones[24]

1801

March 4	Thomas Jefferson is sworn in, the first president inaugurated in Washington, D.C.

1802

February 6	Congress recognizes the War with Tripoli and authorizes the arming of merchant ships to ward off attacks.
March 16	Congress establishes the United States Military Academy at West Point.
April 6	Unpopular excise taxes on commodities such as whiskey are repealed.
April 14	The naturalization laws of 1798 are repealed; the residency requirement reverts to five years.

1803

January 11	Jefferson appoints James Monroe minister to France and Spain, instructing him to purchase New Orleans and East and West Florida.
February 19	Ohio becomes the seventeenth state; it is the first state to prohibit slavery, but also excludes blacks from citizenship.

April 30	Robert R. Livingston, minister to France, and Monroe are sent to conclude a treaty for the acquisition of New Orleans, but instead arrange for the purchase of the entire Louisiana Territory.
August 31	Captain Meriwether Lewis, formerly Jefferson's personal secretary, sets out from Pittsburgh to begin an expedition of the newly acquired Louisiana Purchase territory. Captain William Clark will join as co-leader of the trip early in the next year.
December 20	The French flag is lowered in New Orleans and the U.S. flag raised.

1804

September 25	The Twelfth Amendment to the U.S. Constitution is ratified, with new rules governing the presidential election. (See Appendix II, page 641.)
December 5	Thomas Jefferson is reelected; the first governor of New York State, George Clinton, is elected vice president.

1805

March 4	In his second Inaugural Address, Jefferson proposes eliminating Federalist-passed internal taxes.
June 4	The United States and Tripoli sign a Treaty of Peace and Amity, effectively ending the Tripolitan War.
November 7	Lewis and Clark reach the Pacific Ocean.
December 3–4	Jefferson informs Congress of secret negotiations with France to buy the territory of Florida and requests $5 million to complete the deal.

1806

March 9	Congress authorizes a commission to build a national road from Cumberland, Maryland, to the Ohio River.
April 18	In protest against the seizure of American ships and sailors by Great Britain, Congress passes a law prohibiting the importation of many British products into the United States.

July 15   Zebulon Pike begins his exploration of what is now the Southwestern United States. On November 15, Pike reaches the eight-thousand-foot summit that still bears his name—Pikes Peak—in what is now Colorado.

1807

February 19   Aaron Burr is arrested on treason charges in rural Alabama.

March 12   The modified Embargo Act permits vessels to transport American goods from foreign ports.

September 1   A circuit court in Richmond acquits Aaron Burr of treason.

December 22   President Jefferson signs the Embargo Act, putting a halt to all foreign trade.

1808

January 1   The law officially banning the foreign slave trade goes into effect.

January 11   The Second Embargo Act comes into force. Commonly known as the "Ograbme Act" (embargo spelled backward), it is more stringent than the first.

December 7   James Madison is elected president, with George Clinton returning as vice president.

1809

March 1   As America's economy suffers under the embargo, Congress repeals the Embargo Act. Before leaving office, Jefferson signs the Non-Intercourse Act, closing U.S. ports only to France and England.

MUST READS

Joseph J. Ellis, *American Sphinx: The Character of Thomas Jefferson*; Thomas Fleming, *Duel: Alexander Hamilton, Aaron Burr and the Future of America*; Annette Gordon-Reed, *The Hemingses of Monticello: An American Family*; Garry Wills, *"Negro President": Jefferson and the Slave Power*.

ONLINE RESOURCES

Inaugural Addresses, Avalon Project, Yale Law School
    1801: http://avalon.law.yale.edu/19th_century/jefinau1.asp
    1805: http://avalon.law.yale.edu/19th_century/jefinau2.asp

Jefferson's Home at Monticello
    http://www.monticello.org/

Jefferson Memorial, National Park Service
    http://www.nps.gov/thje/index.htm

Jefferson Papers, University of Virginia
    http://guides.lib.virginia.edu/TJ

Library of Congress Resource Guide
    http://www.loc.gov/rr/program/bib/presidents/jefferson/index
    .html

Miller Center of Public Affairs, University of Virginia
    http://millercenter.org/president/jefferson

**"Response to Danbury Baptist Association," January 1, 1802
(the "Wall of Separation" letter)**
    http://millercenter.org/scripps/archive/speeches/detail/3473

"Instructions to Captain Lewis," June 20, 1803
    http://millercenter.org/scripps/archive/speeches/detail/3477

**"Special Message to Congress on the Burr Conspiracy,"
January 22, 1807**
    http://millercenter.org/scripps/archive/speeches/detail/3497

4

Father of the Constitution
James Madison

★ ★ ★

March 4, 1809–March 4, 1817

Milestones in James Madison's Life

March 16, 1751	Born in Port Conway, Virginia
1776	Helped write Virginia state constitution
1776–1777	Member of Virginia legislature
1780–1783	Delegate to Congress
1784–1786	Member of Virginia legislature
1787	Organizer and delegate to Constitutional Convention
	Contributed essays to the Federalist Papers
1787–1788	Member of Congress of the Confederation
1789–1797	U.S. representative in Congress
1790–1791	Wrote the amendments adopted as the Bill of Rights
1799–1800	Member of Virginia legislature
1801–1809	Secretary of state under Thomas Jefferson
1809–1817	Fourth president
1826	Succeeded Thomas Jefferson as rector of the University of Virginia
1829	Cochairman of Virginia State Constitutional Convention
June 28, 1836	Died at Montpelier, in Virginia, aged eighty-five

PRESIDENTIAL VOICES

To cherish peace and friendly intercourse with all nations having correspondent dispositions; to maintain sincere neutrality toward belligerent nations; to prefer in all cases amicable discussion and reasonable accommodation of differences to a decision of them by an appeal to arms; to exclude foreign intrigues and foreign partialities, so degrading to all countries and so baneful to free ones; . . . to avoid the slightest interference with the right of conscience or the functions of religion, so wisely exempted from civil jurisdiction; to preserve in their full energy the other salutary provisions in behalf of private and personal rights, and of the freedom of the press.

—JAMES MADISON
First Inaugural Address, March 4, 1809[1]

At five feet tall and not much more than one hundred pounds, James "Jemmy" Madison is sometimes seen as a lightweight among Founding Fathers, especially outweighed by his more statuesque Virginian friends and neighbors—Washington and Jefferson, in particular, both of whom stood more than six feet tall.

Known as the "Father of the Constitution" and considered a great champion of religious liberty, Madison is overshadowed in presidential stature by his Virginian predecessors—and to a degree by his equally statuesque wife, Dolley Madison, who carved out a new definition of the role of first lady as a celebrity in her own right. Dolley Madison was the bright light in the center of Washington, D.C., society for the first half of the nineteenth century.

While Madison is not always counted among the first rank as president, his eight years in office were significant and included America's "Second Revolution," the War of 1812—a war that should never have been fought.

Short, sickly in his youth, prone to fits similar to epilepsy, shy, bookish, with no military accomplishments, unimpressive as a speaker (the recorder of the Virginia legislature complained he couldn't hear Madison), Madison appears to be the antithesis of a great American political leader. But a great politician he was, with all the baggage that the word "politician" implies.

Of the fourth president, biographer Richard Brookhiser wrote, "He is more than the father of the Constitution, or of other intellectual constructs. He is the Father of Politics. . . . In a free country, the road to reality runs through politics. Madison spent as much time politicking as thinking, and he was equally good at both."[2]

So good, in fact, that Alexander Hamilton, his onetime collaborator and later rival, once said, "Mr. Madison, co-operating with Mr. Jefferson, is at the head of a faction . . . subversive of the principles of good government and dangerous to the Union, peace and happiness of the country."[3]

Fast Facts

RELIGION: Episcopalian (nominal)
EDUCATION: The College of New Jersey (later known as Princeton)
CAREER BEFORE POLITICS: Planter
POLITICAL PARTY: Republican
FIRST LADY: Dolley Payne Todd (May 20, 1768–July 12, 1849)
CHILDREN: John Payne Todd (stepson)

* The "Father of the Constitution" never gained admission to the bar. But Madison used a law book instead of a Bible for his swearing-in.
* Running for a second term after the War of 1812 had begun, Madison won easily. Since Madison, no incumbent wartime president has ever lost his bid for reelection.[4]
* Both of Madison's vice presidents, George Clinton (also Jefferson's second vice president and then elected in Madison's first term) and Elbridge Gerry (elected in Madison's second term) died in office. (Under the original Constitution, there was no procedure for the replacement of a vice president who died or resigned.)

* As he was nearing death in late June 1836, Madison was asked by his doctors if he wanted any medication that would help him survive until Independence Day—the illustrious date on which his predecessors Jefferson and Adams (in 1826), as well as James Monroe (in 1831), had all died. Madison chose not to attempt to extend his life.

* Like friend and neighbor Jefferson, Madison was plagued by debt in his post-presidential years. His financial difficulties included his profligate stepson John Todd's $40,000 gambling debts. Madison hoped that the sale of his secret notes from the Constitutional Convention would bring his wife Dolley a fortune sufficient to keep her comfortable after he died. She offered the notes to Congress and asked for $100,000. Congress offered $30,000 and the notes were published in 1840. They provide historians with the most detailed account of the debates at the Philadelphia Convention in 1787. But Dolley was forced to sell Montpelier and move to Washington, D.C., where the woman who once ruled the capital's social scene struggled financially until her death in 1849.

PRESIDENTIAL VOICES

Because the establishment proposed by the Bill is not requisite for the support of the Christian Religion. To say that it is, is a contradiction to the Christian Religion itself, for every page of it disavows a dependence on the powers of this world: it is a contradiction to fact; for it is known that this Religion both existed and flourished, not only without the support of human laws, but in spite of every opposition from them, and not only during the period of miraculous aid, but long after it had been left to its own evidence and the ordinary care of Providence.

—JAMES MADISON
Memorial and Remonstrance Against Religious Assessments
June 20, 1785[5]

A zeal for different opinions concerning religion, concerning government, and many other points, as well of speculation as of practice, an attachment of

different leaders, ambitiously contending for preeminence and power; or to
persons of other descriptions whose fortunes have been interesting to the hu-
man passions, have, in turn, divided mankind into parties, inflamed them
with mutual animosity, and rendered them much more disposed to vex and
oppress each other than to cooperate for their common good. . . . But the most
common and durable source of factions has been the various and unequal dis-
tribution of property.

—JAMES MADISON
The Federalist Papers, #10[6]

Born into a well-to-do planter's family at his grandparents' home in
Port Conway, Virginia, James Madison grew up on the family plantation that came to be called Montpelier. With its sweeping view west to
the Blue Ridge Mountains, the plantation was literally on the border of
the wilderness, and as a child, Madison lived in fear of Indian attack,
especially during the French and Indian War. Around 1760, his father
completed construction of the grand house at Montpelier that Madison
called home until his death. (He is buried on the grounds.)

Sickly as a boy, Madison was tutored at home, and he was not sent to
study at the College of William and Mary in Williamsburg because
its lowland climate was deemed unhealthy. Instead he went north to
the College of New Jersey (later Princeton) in 1769. Here he met
such schoolmates as Philip Freneau—later to become a poet and anti-
Federalist journalist—and William Bradford, later attorney general
under Washington. He was also friendly with Aaron Burr, son of the
school's founder. All of them were under the powerful influence of Scottish university president John Witherspoon, a future signer of the Declaration of Independence and a key voice in the American Enlightenment.

Madison returned to Virginia in 1772 and studied law but never
became a lawyer. Commissioned into Virginia's colonial militia, he
never saw service because of his health.

If time had stopped before his election to the presidency in 1808,
his résumé would still qualify him as one of the most important of the

founders. A fierce defender of religious freedom, he had been profoundly distressed as a young man when he saw Baptist ministers arrested in Virginia for preaching without a license, as required by the Anglican-dominated colony. Madison was instrumental in securing passage of the state's religious freedom statute, which Thomas Jefferson had drafted in 1776 and which Madison revised and moved through Virginia's legislature in 1786. Reacting against a bill sponsored by Patrick Henry to support churches and church schools with tax assessments, he had anonymously written *The Memorial and Remonstrance Against Religious Assessments* (June 20, 1785), one of the most influential defenses of free conscience written in American history. (Henry's Religious Assessment Bill was soundly defeated.)

After moving through a succession of state offices, Madison became the youngest member of the Continental Congress in 1780, helping to organize the government under the Articles of Confederation. Later, as a delegate from Virginia to the Constitutional Convention, he played a central role in proposing, shaping, and drafting the Constitution, having studied hundreds of histories of political systems and republics shipped to him by Jefferson. Madison had come to the Philadelphia convention in May 1787 prepared with his "Virginia Plan," and he used his ideas and skills in committee, more than his force of personality or power as a speaker, to become the center of the convention. His secret record of the convention, published in 1840, well after his death, remains the most important firsthand account of the deliberations.

Once the Constitution was drafted and ratification seemed uncertain, Madison was recruited by Hamilton to write some of the essays collected as the Federalist Papers. Although their actual influence at the time of ratification is debatable, these writings remain a key source of interpretation of national republican government. When Madison returned to Virginia, he successfully led the fight for ratification against the powerful Patrick Henry, who opposed the Constitution.

Using his influence in the Virginia legislature, which then selected U.S. senators, Henry scuttled Madison's chance for a Senate seat. Madison then ran instead for a House seat, against young James Monroe, and won by a small margin. In the first Congress under Washington, it was Madison who drafted what would become the first ten amendments to the Constitution that many states demanded as the price for ratification. While Madison had argued that these changes were unnecessary because they were natural rights that existed without being stated, he drafted them anyway. Twelve amendments were eventually passed and sent to the states, but only ten of them were ratified as the Bill of Rights.

At the same time, Madison was acting as a consultant and speechwriter for George Washington, drafting both his Inaugural Address and a Farewell Address written after Washington's first term (and later revised by Alexander Hamilton for delivery after Washington's second term).

With the election of John Adams in 1796, Madison returned to Virginia, having moved away from the Federalist camp and aligned himself more closely with Jefferson in opposition to the growing power of the federal government. He was especially opposed to the Alien and Sedition Acts and wrote a resolution declaring the acts to be unconstitutional. This resolution, along with one written by Jefferson and adopted in Kentucky, became controversial, as they supported the idea that states could nullify federal laws and suggested that secession was an option.

But with the election of Thomas Jefferson in 1800, Madison returned to national government, now in Washington, D.C., as Jefferson's secretary of state. In that role, he helped win acceptance of the Louisiana Purchase. He also pressed for the Embargo Acts as a response to the French and British attacks on American shipping and especially the British policy of "impressments," or taking sailors from American vessels and forcing them to serve in the Royal Navy.

Despite the unpopularity of the Embargo, Madison won the presidential race in 1808, easily defeating Federalist candidate Charles Cotesworth Pinckney of South Carolina. Nominated in January 1808 by a Republican caucus in Congress, Madison ran with Jefferson's second vice president, George Clinton of New York, who died in office in 1812. The system of two main parties, each led by elected congressmen who controlled the presidential nominating process, had quickly evolved and this caucus system would hold sway for decades.

Jefferson's handpicked successor, Madison, took office with war looming, with England and possibly France. Proclaiming "sincere neutrality" and pledging in his Inaugural Address to avoid "foreign intrigues," Madison hoped diplomacy would prevail. But he also pressed Congress to prepare for war.

Elected in the midterm elections of 1810, that Congress had become increasingly bent on challenging Great Britain again, with the ascent of a group of young, nationalistic "War Hawks," led by Kentucky's Henry Clay. One of the most significant Americans who failed to become president, Clay was a senator at age twenty-nine—constitutionally too young, he was appointed by the Kentucky legislature just the same. In the Senate, he had expressed the "War Hawk" attitude: "I am for resistance by the sword. . . . I prefer the troubled ocean of war to the tranquil putrescent pool of ignominious peace."[7] Clay shifted to the House, and at thirty-four years old, had become speaker, joined by other "Hawks," including South Carolina's John C. Calhoun.

That election had followed the census of 1810, which recorded an American population of 7,239,881, a 36.4 percent increase since 1800. Of that total, 1,378,110 were black—all but 186,746 of them slaves. With the admission of Ohio in 1803, there were now seventeen states and a huge American appetite to continue moving west into the lands acquired from Napoléon. But there were some very large and dangerous obstacles to that approach: the British, who were in Canada, and the Native American nations who already lived in the American West.

Why was Dolley Madison expelled by the Quakers?

Madison took office in a wave of political popularity helped significantly by the striking appearance and social celebrity of his much younger wife, Dolley. As they rode through the streets of Washington, the tall, curvaceous, blue-eyed, and black-haired Dolley Madison "outshone her husband in every way," Dolley's biographer Catherine Allgor noted. Beyond looks, adds Allgor, she possessed "an arresting combination of confidence and vulnerability that drew every eye to her."[8]

While Madison was a great champion of religious freedom and a nominal Episcopalian, his wife Dolley was raised a Quaker. Born in 1768 on a Quaker settlement in North Carolina, as a young girl she moved with her family to Philadelphia after her father freed his slaves. In 1790, she married Quaker lawyer John Todd, and they had one son, John Payne Todd. When her first husband died in Philadelphia's yellow fever epidemic of 1793, she returned to live with her mother, who ran a boardinghouse where members of Congress stayed.

It was there that Aaron Burr introduced her to Madison. Madison's Princeton schoolmate, Burr was a senator and serving as legal guardian of Dolley's son. Approval of the match came from George and Martha Washington, who had taken it upon themselves to serve as matchmakers for the next generation of America's leaders.

The Quakers, however, did not approve. For marrying Madison, a non-Quaker, Dolley was expelled from the Society of Friends.

"A buxom dame with a good word for everybody," New York writer Washington Irving once said of her. With a penchant for the newly fashionable low-cut gown, she was a beauty, who as time went by "allowed neither her years nor her weight to discourage her love for youthful fashion. Turbans, false hair, and feathers were her delights; and she created a coquettish blush with rouge and 'pearl' (powder)." Always considered elegant, Dolley Madison as first lady presiding over the White House impressed all. As one female visitor wrote, "Few of her sex at 45 look so well."[9]

What was "Mr. Madison's War"?

Whatever domestic bliss Madison enjoyed, his presidential headaches came from those "baneful" foreign intrigues he warned about at his Inauguration. While America's conflict with Great Britain was largely taking place on the high seas—as British ships stopped American vessels and American sailors were "impressed" into the British Navy—another conflict played out on land. Madison's worries included a threat from the Western wilderness where one of the most remarkable Indian leaders in American history—allied with the British—would add to the clamor for war with England.

A young Shawnee chief from the Ohio Valley, Tecumseh ("Shooting Star") envisioned a vast Indian confederacy strong enough to keep the Ohio River as a border between Indians and whites, preventing further westward expansion. A respected chief by the time he reached his twenties, Tecumseh had rejected European clothes for traditional deerskin and renounced alcohol, often used by white traders to cheat native people. He and his brother, Tenskwatawa (the "Prophet"), an Indian mystic, or shaman, who called for a revival of Indian ways and a rejection of white culture, traveled extensively among tribes from Wisconsin to Florida.

The prospect of Tecumseh uniting and leading a confederation of native nations and blocking America's westward expansion worried Americans, especially the Westerners, like Kentucky's Henry Clay, who wanted America to expand west—and north into Canada. As tensions grew with England, a potential alliance of Tecumseh with the British was also worrisome.

William Henry Harrison, governor of the Indiana Territory, was the American leader who had to confront Tecumseh. Harrison knew Tecumseh and had been dealing with the Shawnee as territorial governor for several years. Historian Colin Calloway writes that Thomas Jefferson had advised Harrison to "encourage Indians to run up debts at trading posts and then compel them to settle the bill by selling tribal lands."[10]

In July 1811, Tecumseh met Harrison and assured him that he wanted peace but would not surrender any more Indian territory to the United States. When Harrison took more than one thousand men out to Prophetstown, the Indian camp at the junction of the Tippecanoe and Wabash Rivers on November 7, 1811, Tecumseh was away on one of his organizing and recruiting trips. But his brother, the Prophet, ordered an assault on Harrison's troops.

The Prophet had assured the warriors that they would be invulnerable to American bullets. The Indians inflicted heavy losses on Harrison's men but were eventually driven back and scattered. Harrison and his troops then destroyed their food stores, burned the village, and damaged the Prophet's claim of invincible magic, shattering Indian confidence. It was a close call and Pyrrhic victory for Harrison, but a serious setback for Tecumseh's dreams of a large Indian confederacy. Tecumseh then led his warriors north to join the British in Canada.

To Henry Clay and the War Hawks and other Americans, the Indian confederation was a convenient excuse to fan anti-British sentiment in Congress. Calling Tecumseh's confederation a British scheme, land-hungry Westerners heightened the war fever, clamoring for the expulsion of the British from North America, even if it meant invading Canada to do it.

President Madison was reluctantly pushed to what Jefferson had tried to avoid, a war with England. The War of 1812 finally got under way in June, in the midst of the presidential campaign.

The War of 1812 ranks high among America's least necessary and perhaps most avoidable wars. As historian Sean Wilentz points out, "Had the British and the Americans been better informed about each other's political situation—or had communications across the Atlantic simply been speedier—war might have been averted. Misreading Madison's early caution as passivity, the British ambassador did not recognize that by the time the Americans implemented their new embargo, they fully expected war would follow. . . . Ironically, just as Madison was committing himself and the country to war . . . his peaceable coercion policies were beginning to hurt the British badly."[11]

Unaware that Great Britain was ready to make concessions, and peace, the Senate voted 19–13 in favor of war on June 18, 1812. The next day, Madison officially proclaimed the war. The New England states (except Vermont) and other states dependent on shipping and trade, like New York, New Jersey, and Delaware, voted for peace. The opponents of the war called it "Mr. Madison's War." The history books called it the War of 1812, and Americans at the time called it the "Second War of Independence."

It was a war that young America was not prepared to fight. A regular army of twelve thousand was scattered and led by political appointees rather than by experienced commanders. America's navy was still small, hardly equal in numbers or experience to England's powerful fleet.

Neither side went into this war with much enthusiasm. The results showed this, in a meandering war effort that went on for the next two and a half years, ending early in 1815. After its humbling experience in the Revolution, and preoccupied with Napoléon's armies on the continent, England fought a reluctant war. English merchants opposed the war, as they saw America as an important market and supplier. America didn't lose this war. Nor did it really win. And the greatest single American victory in the war, at the Battle of New Orleans in January 1815, came after a peace agreement had been negotiated a few weeks earlier. The news traveled slowly—much to the benefit of Andrew Jackson, the hero of New Orleans.

The War of 1812 ended with the two countries essentially occupying the same positions in North America and the issues of impressments of sailors and other conflicts unsettled. In other words, the fighting accomplished little, except that the war marked America's emergence from economic dependence on England. In 2006, a group of historians ranked Madison's failure to avoid war as the sixth worst presidential failure of all time.[12]

Among the war's most significant results was the death of Tecumseh during the Battle of Thames in Canada; the burning of York (later named Toronto) by American troops; the retaliatory burning of Washington, D.C., by British forces; and the elevation of a pair of war heroes, William Henry Harrison and Andrew Jackson, both of whom would eventually ride their military success into the White House. But the hated embargo had also actually stimulated American manufacturing, and the nation was taking its first real steps toward becoming a nation of factories instead of farms, and by battling the British to a standoff, and with Andrew Jackson's lopsided victory over a significant British army at New Orleans, America's prestige on the world stage was also greatly enhanced.

PRESIDENTIAL VOICES

Will you believe it, my sister? We have had a battle, or skirmish, near Bladensburg, and here I am still, within sound of the cannon! Mr. Madison comes not. May God protect us! . . . At this late hour a wagon has been procured, and I have filled it with plate and the most valuable portable articles, belonging to the house. . . . I insist on waiting until the large picture of General Washington is secured and it requires to be unscrewed from the wall. This process was found

*too tedious for these perilous moments; I have ordered the frame to be broken,
and the canvas taken out. It is done!*
—First Lady Dolley Madison
Letter to her sister, August 23–24, 1814

After Dolley Madison left Washington in front of the British advance, President Madison returned to the mansion from nearby Bladensburg, Maryland, where he had observed a battle. At sunset, Madison was ferried across the Potomac to Virginia.

The British entered the city at about 7:30 p.m. on August 24, 1814. Local "rabble" had already begun looting the White House. More than 150 British sailors entered the mansion and began destroying it, largely in retaliation for the burning of York—now Toronto—by Americans earlier in the war. British sailors broke windows and made piles of furniture that would be set afire.

On August 27, three days after the fall of Washington, the Madisons returned to the city. The president had been burned out of his house. The Madisons were both assailed in the press for failing to save the mansion. They lived temporarily with Dolley's sister, in view of the ruins.[13]

Known as both the "President's House"—George Washington's preference—and the "Executive Mansion," the presidential residence had always been painted white. But following the war, when the repairs were completed, it became more widely known as the "White House." By 1817, that is what most people called it. (Theodore Roosevelt issued an executive order in 1901 officially changing the building's name to the White House.)

Among those who assisted with Dolley's legendary removal of the Washington portrait was a young slave named Paul Jennings. One of the first White House servants to record a memoir, Jennings was one of very few enslaved black servants whose recollections of working in the White House were ever published.[14]

A Colored Man's Reminiscences of James Madison was published in 1865. Having witnessed the attack on Washington and been at Madison's deathbed, Paul Jennings shared close-up observations, describing his master as a frugal man who only owned one suit and was so careful with his liquor that he probably never "drank a quart of brandy in his whole life."[15]

Although Madison's last will contained no provision for freeing any of his slaves, Jennings claimed that Madison wanted to free him after his death. But Mrs. Madison refused and even loaned him out to others, keeping his earnings for herself. Financially pressed in her later years, Dolley Madison finally sold Jennings to an insurance agent who in turn sold him to Senator Daniel Webster. The Massachusetts senator allowed Jennings to work off his debt as a household servant. Jennings finally secured his freedom in 1836. He died in 1874 at age seventy-five.

Final Judgment: Grade B

Following the War of 1812, Madison made a number of shifts in policy that have been interpreted by many historians as abandoning Jefferson's Republican ideals in favor of a more typically Federalist approach. For instance, he seemed to favor a Hamiltonian-style national bank, effective taxation, and a standing professional army and navy—each of these policy shifts based, no doubt, on his largely disastrous experience as a wartime president with an empty treasury and poorly trained and equipped troops who were often led by incompetent officers.

Some historians see this not so much as an abandonment of pure Jeffersonian Republicanism, but as the simple recognition of reality and changing times. America was entering a new and different era in the nineteenth century. "What Madison was forced unconsciously to adopt was not an ideology but a historical phenomenon—modernity," writes Garry Wills.[16]

As America entered its next phase, a so-called "Era of Good Feelings" that flourished under James Monroe, Madison's successor and next in the Virginia Dynasty, the country was undergoing a fundamental transformation. The cotton gin and the looms of New England were remaking both the South and the North. Politicians spoke of "internal improvements"—what today would be called "public works projects"—to build roads and canals to open up the way west and speed commerce and communication. The practical age of steamships had begun during Madison's first term. And a new class of soldiers who were engineering graduates from the military academy at West Point was going to help change the face of America as it looked less toward Europe and more toward its own Western lands.

Struggling with rheumatism in his retirement, Madison enjoyed little of the "Good Feelings" he had helped foster. He also suffered increasing financial difficulties as crop failures struck Montpelier. He would be forced to battle controversy when his and Jefferson's Virginia and Kentucky Resolutions dating from the Washington administration were later cited to justify the idea of nullification of federal laws and secession over tariffs. In retirement, Madison had to respond that the states could not nullify federal laws or secede.

After Jefferson's death, Madison became rector (president) of the University of Virginia. And in 1833, he accepted a post as honorary president of the American Colonization Society, which was attempting to solve America's slavery problem by establishing an African homeland for emancipated slaves—who were not consulted on the matter, needless to say. This was the best political "solution" to slavery that politicians like Madison could produce. Yet Madison did not free any of his own slaves, and deeply in debt, he had to sell sixteen of them to a relative in Louisiana in 1834.

Madison died at Montpelier on June 28, 1836.

In assessing Madison, Garry Wills commented, "Among the nation's founders only two were more important—Washington and Franklin. As a framer and defender of the Constitution he had no peer. . . . The finest part of Madison's performance as president was his concern for preserving the Constitution. As a champion of religious liberty, he is equal, perhaps superior, to Jefferson—and no one else is in the running. . . . No man could do everything for the country—not even Washington. Madison did more than most, and did some things better than any. That is quite enough."[17]

Madison Administration Milestones[18]

1809

February 8	Republican James Madison easily defeats Federalist opponent Charles C. Pinckney.

| June | The *Phoenix*, a seagoing steamboat, makes an ocean voyage out of Hoboken, New Jersey, to Philadelphia. It was designed by John Stevens, who also patents such improvements as the screw propeller and a plow and develops an early steam railroad in New Jersey. |

1810

May 1	To replace the Non-Intercourse Act, Congress passes Macon's Bill Number 2, which allows American ships to carry French or English goods while barring warring powers from American ports.
June 23	John Jacob Astor founds the Pacific Fur Trading Company and becomes America's first millionaire. Later this year, Cornelius Vanderbilt starts regular ferry service between Staten Island and Manhattan, founding one of the most powerful shipping and later railroad empires in America.
October 27	Madison issues a proclamation authorizing occupation of West Florida, also claimed by Spain.

1811

February	In California, still Spanish territory, a group of Russians establishes Fort Ross, north of San Francisco; it is an agricultural colony and fur trading post.
March 11	The Bank of the United States closes when its charter expires; the closure of the bank will make it difficult to finance the war effort.
July 6	The British foreign minister warns Madison that if non-intercourse remains the policy of the United States, Britain will retaliate against American commerce.
November 7	General William Henry Harrison's militia wins a narrow victory at the Battle of Tippecanoe in Indiana Territory.

1812

| April 15 | Louisiana is admitted to the nation as the eighteenth state, a slave state. |

June 1	In a message to Congress, Madison asks for a declaration of war. The House supports the declaration; a closely divided Senate also votes narrowly for war.
June 19	Madison proclaims war against Britain.
August 11	Michigan governor and general William Hull, in charge of the American offensive into Upper Canada, surrenders Detroit without firing a shot.
November/ December	Madison wins reelection over Federalist DeWitt Clinton.

1813

September 10	Captain Oliver Perry wins control of Lake Erie. Perry sends word to General Harrison, stating, "We have met the enemy and they are ours."
October 5	General Harrison wins the Battle of the Thames River, in which Shawnee chief Tecumseh is killed.
December 9	Madison calls for a total embargo on exports and a ban on all imports of British origin, believing that Britain depends on trade with the United States.

1814

March 27	The Battle of Horseshoe Bend: Under Andrew Jackson, two thousand troops defeat the Creek Confederation in Alabama. Jackson forces the Creeks to cede two-thirds of their lands to the United States.
March 31	Napoleon's European empire collapses.
August 24	In retaliation for the torching of Canadian parliament buildings in York (now Toronto), British forces attack and burn Washington, D.C., setting fire to the White House, the Capitol, and other federal buildings.
September 14	Following the sack of Washington, U.S. general Samuel Smith turns back a British attack on Fort McHenry at Baltimore. Negotiating a prisoner release with the British, attorney Francis Scott Key observes the British bombardment of the fort while detained on a British ship and writes the words to "The Star-Spangled Banner."

September 27	Madison nominates James Monroe as secretary of war to replace John Armstrong. Monroe will serve as secretary of both war and state until the war's end.
October 5	Alexander J. Dallas is appointed secretary of the Treasury; to finance the war Dallas calls for Congress to establish a national bank and to increase taxes.
December 24	Ending the war, the United States and Britain sign the Treaty of Ghent (in modern-day Belgium), but news of the peace treaty will not reach the United States until February 1815.

1815

| January 8 | Andrew Jackson, leading four thousand militiamen and regular soldiers, wins a resounding victory over six thousand British forces in the Battle of New Orleans. Jackson becomes a national hero. |
| December | Madison presents his seventh Annual Message; he calls for building up the military, a new national bank, and protective tariffs to promote industry. |

1816

April 10	Madison signs a bill reestablishing a national bank in Philadelphia, with a twenty-one-year charter.
November/December	Secretary of State James Monroe is elected president, easily defeating Federalist Rufus King of New York.
December 11	Indiana, the nineteenth state, is admitted as a free state.

MUST READS

Catherine Allgor, *A Perfect Union: Dolley Madison and the Creation of the American Nation*; Richard Brookhiser, *James Madison*; Sean Wilentz, *The Rise of American Democracy: Jefferson to Lincoln*; Garry Wills, *James Madison*.

ONLINE RESOURCES

Papers of James Madison, Avalon Project, Yale Law School
    http://avalon.law.yale.edu/subject_menus/madispap.asp

Library of Congress Resource Guide

http://www.loc.gov/rr/program/bib/presidents/madison/memory
.html

Madison Papers, Library of Congress

http://lcweb2.loc.gov/ammem/collections/madison_papers/

The Founders' Constitution, University of Chicago Press

http://press-pubs.uchicago.edu/founders/help/about.html

Montpelier (Virginia home)

http://www.montpelier.org/

Madison Museum, Orange, Virginia

http://thejamesmadisonmuseum.org/

Miller Center of Public Affairs, University of Virginia

http://millercenter.org/index.php/academic/americanpresident
/madison

"Dolley Madison," *The American Experience*, PBS

http://www.pbs.org/wgbh/americanexperience/films/dolley/

Dolley Madison Digital Edition, University of Virginia

http://rotunda.upress.virginia.edu/dmde/

5

The Last Cocked Hat

James Monroe

★ ★ ★

March 4, 1817–March 4, 1825

Milestones in James Monroe's Life

April 28, 1758	Born in Westmoreland County, Virginia
1776–1780	Fought in Revolutionary War
1782	Member of Virginia legislature
1783–1786	Member of Virginia's delegation to Congress
1786–1790	Member of Virginia legislature
1790–1794	U.S. senator from Virginia
1794–1796	U.S. minister to France
1799–1802	Governor of Virginia
1803	Helped negotiate the Louisiana Purchase
1803–1807	U.S. minister to Great Britain
1811	Governor of Virginia
1811–1817	U.S. secretary of state under Madison
1814–1815	U.S. secretary of war under Madison
1817–1825	Fifth president
1829	Cochairman of Virginia State Constitutional Convention
July 4, 1831	Died in New York City, aged seventy-three

PRESIDENTIAL VOICES

Never did a government commence under auspices so favorable, nor ever was success so complete. If we look to the history of other nations, ancient or modern, we find no example of a growth so rapid, so gigantic, of a people so prosperous and happy. In contemplating what we still have to perform, the heart of every citizen must expand with joy when he reflects how near our Government has approached to perfection.

—JAMES MONROE
First Inaugural Address, March 4, 1817[1]

Washington has his grand monument, his Mount Vernon home, an entire city, and all that money bearing his image. Jefferson has a memorial, a historic plantation home that is a Mecca for tourists, the two-dollar bill, and the nickel. Madison is "Father of the Constitution" and got a few cities and a famous avenue named after him.

But James Monroe is best remembered for a "doctrine" he didn't write; a city named in his honor as the capital of Liberia, which was part of the failed attempt to send emancipated slaves back to Africa; and the iconic Emanuel Leutze painting, *The Crossing of the Delaware*, where he occupies the boat with General Washington. But unbeknownst to millions, the future fifth president was not in the boat on that Christmas night—and the flag he is shown holding is also historically inaccurate.

James Monroe was the last of the "Virginia Dynasty," those four of five first presidents who were born in Virginia. He came to office in a time remembered as the "Era of Good Feelings," as a war ended and the bitter partisanship of recent years had drained away. Tremendously popular when reelected in 1821, he essentially ran unopposed for a second term. But not everyone enjoyed the "Good Feelings." And the feelings did not last long.

A soldier before he was a successful diplomat and politician, Monroe was a man of action whose popularity in office was impressive. But in posterity, he has slipped in esteem. He is overshadowed by his more famous fellow Virginians, just as his modest Virginia house is largely overlooked by most visitors making the pilgrimage to its more famous nearby neighbor up the road, Thomas Jefferson's Monticello.

Fast Facts

RELIGION: Anglican (Episcopal after 1776)
ASSOCIATIONS: Freemason
MILITARY SERVICE: Continental Army in the American Revolution
CAREER BEFORE POLITICS: Planter, lawyer
POLITICAL PARTY: Republican
FIRST LADY: Elizabeth Kortright Monroe (June 30, 1768–September 23, 1830)
CHILDREN: Eliza and Maria Hester

* Monroe's wife, Elizabeth Kortright, ten years younger than he, was the daughter of a British army officer and New York merchant who had a made a fortune as a privateer during the French and Indian Wars. Described as a statuesque beauty, she met and married Monroe while he was in Congress in New York in 1786. Later, while Monroe served as America's minister in Paris during the Reign of Terror, Elizabeth Monroe helped rescue the Marquis de Lafayette's wife from prison, possibly saving her from execution. A popular figure while in France, Elizabeth Monroe was known as "la belle Americaine." [2]

* Chronically ill from an unidentified illness, Elizabeth Monroe would be criticized by Washington society for her lack of socializing, especially in comparison with her notable predecessor, Dolley Madison.

* Monroe's younger daughter, Maria, was married in the first wedding performed in the White House, on March 9, 1820. Due to her mother's poor health, the guest list was kept small and the first lady was criticized in Washington's social circles and the diplomatic corps.

* Monroe was the last veteran of the Revolution to be president, the

reason for his nickname "Last of the Cocked Hats." He was also the last to wear the powdered wig and queue, knee breeches, and tricorne hat typical of men's eighteenth-century style. A new age was dawning and fashion would change as well.

* Monroe was the first president to both take the oath of office and deliver the Inaugural Address outdoors, in 1817; in 1821, March 4 fell on Sunday for the first time. After consulting with the justices of the Supreme Court, Monroe took the oath on Monday, March 5, instead of a Sunday; however, under the rules of the Constitution he was already president on March 4.

* As the war-damaged White House was being rebuilt, the Monroes bought furniture and silverware in France at an auction of possessions of the executed queen Marie Antoinette.[3]

The rebuilt White House opened to the public on New Year's Day in 1818, although work continued long afterward. The construction went over budget.

Monroe also expanded the White House with the addition of the south portico and colonnade designed by Benjamin Latrobe, based on James Hoban's original plan, in 1824 (the north portico was added in 1829). [4]

* After leaving the White House in 1825, Monroe's wife fell into a fire after suffering a seizure. She died in 1830, and Monroe left Virginia to live with his daughter in New York, at 63 Prince Street, where he died on July 4, 1831.

* Like Washington, Monroe was a Freemason, but unlike his predecessors he spoke and wrote very little about religious matters. Historian David Holmes notes, "The surviving evidence indicates that Monroe was not a Christian in the traditional sense. . . . No evidence exists to show that he was an active or emotionally engaged Christian. . . . Like Washington, Monroe was neither a philosophical nor a highly intellectual man. A practical, problem-solving person, he was highly effective when he worked on practical matters. Unlike Franklin, Adams, Jefferson, and Madison, he did not seem to spend extensive time considering why the universe was so."[5]

PRESIDENTIAL VOICES

I find by your letter . . . that you think Sierra Leone, on the coast of Africa, a suitable place for establishment of our insurgent slaves, that it may also become so for those who are or may hereafter be emancipated. . . . It appears that slavery is prohibited in that settlement, hence it follows that we cannot expect permission to send any who are not free to it. . . . I do not know that such an arrangement would be practicable in any country, but it would certainly be a very fortunate attainment if we could make these people instrumental in their own emancipation, by a process gradual and certain, on principles consistent with humanity, without expense or inconvenience to ourselves.

—JAMES MONROE

Letter to Thomas Jefferson, June 11, 1802[6]

Another of the imposing Virginia six-footers who became president, James Monroe was born on April 28, 1758, into the moderately prosperous family of Spence Monroe, a planter who boycotted British goods to protest England's colonial policies. The young Monroe studied at Campbelltown Academy in Washington Parish, where George Washington was first briefly schooled. When his father died, the sixteen-year-old James Monroe inherited the estate and then entered the College of William and Mary.

But for a young man of action this was no time for books. Following the battles of Lexington and Concord in April 1775, Monroe joined a few dozen older men in raiding the governor's arsenal in Williamsburg, taking two hundred muskets and three hundred swords to arm the Williamsburg militia. In 1776, he left William and Mary without taking a degree and joined the Continental Army.

Monroe's first notable action came on Christmas Day 1776 when he took part in Washington's crucial attack on Trenton, New Jersey. Leading a raid during the assault on the Hessian troops, Monroe was severely wounded and might have died if a doctor from Trenton had not been there to attend him quickly. He fought in the battles at Germantown and Brandywine and served through the brutal winter of 1777–1778 at Valley Forge, sharing a cabin with John Marshall, his boyhood schoolmate and the future chief justice.[7] Never one for hyperbole, Marshall later wrote, "At no period of the war had the situation of the American army been more perilous than at Valley Forge. Even when the troops were not entirely destitute of food, their stock of provisions was so scanty that a quantity sufficient for one week was scarcely in store. . . . Even among those capable of doing duty, many were so badly clad, that exposure to the cold of the season must have destroyed them."[8]

Closely allied with then governor Thomas Jefferson, Monroe was appointed military commissioner of the state in 1780 and admitted to the Virginia bar in 1786. Although he opposed the Constitution in Virginia's Ratification Convention, Monroe supported the new national government under Washington and was elected to the Senate in 1790. When he replaced Gouverneur Morris as George Washington's minister to France, Monroe eventually secured the release of Thomas Paine from a French prison. Washington later recalled him from France as he disagreed with Washington over the Jay Treaty with England, which had become one of the sharp dividing lines between Federalists and Jefferson's Republicans, who—like Monroe—opposed it.

After returning to America, Monroe was elected governor of Virginia in 1799 and faced the crisis of Virginia's first major slave revolt, an 1800 uprising known as "Gabriel's Rebellion," so-called after a slave named Gabriel (sometimes called Gabriel Prosser, for his owner Thomas Prosser). Inspired by Haiti's slave rebellion in 1791, Gabriel planned to strike Richmond in August with an army of slaves recruited from nearby plantations, capture James Monroe as a hostage, and begin a general slave revolution. Alerted to the plot, Governor Monroe called out the state militia to protect Richmond and recapture the rebellious slaves. Gabriel eluded capture for a month, until slave patrols caught him and more than twenty other rebels; they were tried quickly and hanged.

Coming on the heels of the revolution in Haiti, Gabriel's Rebellion sparked harsh new slave laws in Virginia. Monroe toughened existing slave codes, especially with regard to the prohibition on teaching slaves to read. The Virginia legislature also passed a law requiring free blacks to leave the state.*

Having worked to secure his friend and neighbor Thomas Jefferson's controversial 1800 presidential victory, Monroe was rewarded with a post in the new administration. He first negotiated with France for the Louisiana Purchase and then spent four years as Jefferson's minister in London. Although he had initially opposed Madison's election in 1808, Monroe was then appointed the fourth president's secretary of state in 1811, and he hoped, like Madison, to find a peaceful resolution to the rising tensions with England. After the War of 1812 began, Madison named Monroe his secretary of war in 1814, and Monroe filled both posts, winning acclaim for his performance in those dual roles.

Who felt good about the "Era of Good Feelings"?

The death of the Federalist Party, which had opposed the otherwise popular War of 1812, was evident in 1816, when they barely mounted any opposition to James Madison's chosen successor, James Monroe, who was easily elected and named John Quincy Adams, son of the Federalist president John Adams, his secretary of state.

With the country having made peace with England, and with one-party rule bringing a sense of domestic peace, Monroe's years were almost immediately dubbed the "Era of Good Feelings." Monroe set off on a victory lap around the nation, touring New England and heading as far west as Detroit. The end of the war brought a period of rapid economic expansion, especially in the Northeast, as manufacturing began to replace shipbuilding as America's leading industry; the nation was moving headlong into the first stages of its Industrial Revolution.

It may have been the Era of Good Feelings for Monroe, but not everyone felt so good about it. Certainly not the native nations, which

---

* In 2007, Virginia governor Tim Kaine gave Gabriel and his followers an informal pardon. Kaine noted that "Gabriel's cause—the end of slavery and the furtherance of equality of all people—has prevailed in the light of history." "Gov 'Pardons' Gabriel's Rebellion," *Washington Post*, August 31, 2007.

were being decimated by war in places like Florida. Under Monroe, the policy of removing native nations from their traditional lands to territory in the West was first proposed and put into effect. The Native Americans were not going easily.

Where and what was the "Negro Fort"?

During the War of 1812, British officers had established a small, fortified stronghold on the Apalachicola River in Florida's western panhandle. For years, escaped slaves had been coming to this territory, which was still in Spanish control. By 1814, more than three hundred escaped slaves had taken refuge in the fort, welcomed by the British. Joining the fugitive slaves were Creek and Seminole Indians escaping from American territory, who had made the fort a base to continue battling white American settlers.

An offshoot of the Creek, the Muskogee-speaking Seminoles had begun to emigrate into northern Florida beginning in the early 1700s. Their name was derived from the Spanish *cimarrón*, which means "wild" or "runaway." The Spanish had continued to encourage Indians from neighboring territories and runaway slaves to move south, hoping that they would provide a buffer against English (and later American) expansion.

The British had learned that escaped slaves and Native Americans lived and worked reasonably well together—united by their common enemies, the U.S. government and American settlers. During the War of 1812, the Seminoles, Creek, and their free black allies, also known as "Maroons," fought beside the British. When the British evacuated Florida in the spring of 1815, they turned over a well-constructed fortification to the freed blacks who had fought with them. As word of this refuge outside American borders spread, the enclave eventually attracted more than eight hundred fugitive slaves and became known as the "Negro Fort."

Pressured by slaveholding Georgia planters to do something about the fort, which had become a haven for runaways, President Monroe directed Andrew Jackson, now known as the Hero of New Orleans, to act. With friendly Creek warriors as allies, Jackson ordered an attack on the Negro Fort. The two sides exchanged cannon fire, but the inexperienced gunners inside the fort failed to hit their targets. When a shot from the American forces hit the fort's powder magazine, the explosion practically leveled the Negro Fort, killing all but thirty of an estimated three hundred people inside the stockade. The black survivors were returned to slavery.

The resistance of the Seminoles and free blacks in Florida eventually spurred President Monroe to order Jackson to lead a wider campaign against the Creek and Seminoles in Georgia and cut off Spanish Florida as a haven for runaway slaves. With the tacit approval of the Monroe administration, and under the pretext of having been attacked by Seminoles, Jackson invaded Florida and captured Pensacola, a Spanish outpost, with barely a shot fired.

Jackson then arrested two British citizens, Robert Ambrister, an ex–British Marine, and a seventy-year-old Scottish trader, Alexander Arbuthnot. Under a hastily assembled military tribunal, the two were convicted of "aiding and abetting the enemy." At the time, Jackson said, "The laws of war did not apply to conflicts with savages." British nationals, both men were executed on Jackson's orders in late April 1818.[9]

The episode set off a brief diplomatic furor with the British. And in Congress, Henry Clay excoriated Jackson in a two-hour House speech that compared the military hero to a military dictator. It was the beginning of a long, mutual antagonism. But Jackson's star as a conqueror had never shone brighter. He had accomplished exactly what the Monroe administration expected. After a treaty with Spain was signed, Florida was turned over to the United States. And Andrew Jackson was named the first military governor of the territory.

Shortly after America acquired Florida, Monroe made it clear that the Seminoles had to leave, saying that they "should be removed . . . or concentrated within narrower limits."[10]

For Jackson, it was the culmination of a series of brief but brutal wars that he had commenced against the Creek nation in 1813 and continued against the Seminoles. But these wars against America's native people had an impact far beyond simply adding Florida to America's holdings. Assessing Jackson's role, historian Sean Michael O'Brien wrote, "The conflicts shattered the power of the once mighty

Muscogee nation forever and paved the way for the removal of all the southeastern tribes from their lands east of the Mississippi. . . . The removal of the southeastern tribes opened the door to millions of acres destined for cotton. By selling the land cheaply to settlers and speculators, the United States in effect financed the Cotton Kingdom, and with it slavery."[11]

What "momentous question" faced America in the Monroe years?

The future of Florida and portions of Alabama and Louisiana, as well as renunciation of Spanish claims to other territory, was now part of the greater issue facing Monroe. It would confront every president and candidate for president for the next three decades: What was the future of slavery in these new territories that were now part of the rapidly expanding American nation?

The earlier compromises made over slavery in both the Declaration and the Constitution were beginning to show their age. Even though the foreign slave trade had been outlawed in 1808, the illicit trade of imported slaves continued. And trading slaves within the United States was completely legal. But the central question had become whether new states would be admitted to the Union as free or slave states.

Even though abolition movements were beginning to gather strength in early nineteenth-century America, the essence of the slavery debate was less about its morality and contradiction to American ideals than it was about politics and economics. The three-fifths compromise continued to give slave states a political advantage over free states. Every new state meant two more Senate votes and a proportional number of House votes—as well as additional presidential electors. Slaveholding states obviously wanted more of those votes to maintain their political power.

Of course, there was a powerful economic dimension to the argument. Wage-paying Northerners were forced to compete against slave labor in the South. And with the advent of Eli Whitney's cotton gin (the word "gin" is short for "engine") and many versions of similar machines allowing for huge increases of efficiency in production, the factories of Great Britain and Lowell in New England were demanding more cotton. As demand for cotton boomed, demand for the land and slaves to work it also exploded. If gaining new land to plant meant creating new states, slaveholders wanted them to be slave states.

The free state/slave state issue was brought to a head when Missouri petitioned for statehood in 1817. With Kentucky's Henry Clay taking the lead, Congress agreed on another compromise, which would be known as the Missouri Compromise of 1820. Under Clay's bill, Missouri would be admitted as a slave state, but slavery would not be allowed in any Western territories above Missouri's southern border.

Monroe was largely uninvolved in the congressional debates and dealings that led to the Missouri Compromise, the most significant piece of legislation passed during his years in office. Reelected handily in 1820, in an election that left the Federalist Party all but dead, Monroe considered vetoing the Missouri Compromise, as he thought Congress lacked the constitutional power to ban slavery in any territories. But he favored Missouri's admission as a slave state and feared that a veto might lead to civil war. Other politicians and observers could see the strict sectional lines being drawn over the question.

As historian Sean Wilentz points out, "Clay's brokered bargain bought national peace, but the Missouri crisis hardened northern and southern positions on slavery, in and out of Congress. What occurred in 1820 and 1821 was not genuine compromise so much as it was a cleverly managed political deal, patched together by moderate leaders frightened by the depth of sectional antagonisms, yet unable to achieve genuine sectional accord."[12]

An aging Thomas Jefferson worried, "This momentous question, like a fire bell in the night, awakened and filled me with terror." In this 1820 letter, Jefferson wrote, "I considered it at once as the knell of the Union."[13]

In 1822, an alarm of a different sort rang when Monroe was confronted by another slave insurrection, reminiscent of Gabriel's Rebellion, which Monroe had dealt with as Virginia's governor. This time, in June 1822, Charleston, South Carolina, was the target. The region was gripped in fear over rumors of another slave rebellion. Authorities rounded up slaves and in secret court sessions uncovered what they said was a massive slave plot led by a carpenter named Denmark Vesey, who had been able to purchase his own freedom. Vesey and five others were hanged in July on evidence obtained under coercion. The reality of the size of the plot has been questioned, but once again, the slaveholding states were thrown into panic, and slaveholders blamed the rhetoric and politics of abolitionists for stirring up the slaves.

Monroe's own favored solution to slavery was gradual emancipation and repatriating the freed slaves to Africa. He had written to Jefferson about this idea much earlier. In 1816, the American Colonization Society was formed and the Monroe administration provided federal grants to purchase land in Africa, in what is now Liberia, whose capital, Monrovia, was named after him.

According to the census of 1820, the U.S. population was 9,638,453. New York had become the most populous state with 1.3 million people, followed by Pennsylvania with a little more than a million. The population in the Northern free states and territories was 5,152,635; the total for the Southern states was 4,485,818. The slave population had risen to 1,538,022.[14]

PRESIDENTIAL VOICES

It is impossible that the allied powers should extend their political system to any portion of either continent without endangering our peace and happiness; nor can anyone believe that our southern brethren, if left to themselves, would adopt it of their own accord. It is equally impossible, therefore, that we should behold such interposition in any form with indifference. If we look to the comparative strength and resources of Spain and those new Governments, and their distance from each other, it must be obvious that she can never subdue them. It is still the true policy of the United States to leave the parties to themselves, in hope that other powers will pursue the same course.

—James Monroe
December 2, 1823

Who wrote the Monroe Doctrine?

Only a handful of presidents get their name on an important law or piece of policy. In James Monroe's case, he didn't even write the one that bears his name.

After a series of treaties with the British following the War of 1812, the nation's boundaries were secure and the threat of another war with England eliminated. But the most notable foreign policy milestone in Monroe's administration came in an address he delivered to Congress in December 1823. The speech was the work of Monroe's secretary of state, John Quincy Adams, son of the second president. Decades later, it came to be called the "Monroe Doctrine."

In it, Monroe essentially declared that the United States would not tolerate intervention in the Americas by European nations. Monroe also promised that the United States wouldn't interfere with already established colonies or with governments in Europe. In one sense, this declaration was an act of isolationism, with America withdrawing from the political tempests of Europe. But it was also recognition of a changing world order. Part of this new reality was the crumbling of the old Spanish Empire in the New World, and the rebellions that were sweeping through South America, creating republics under such leaders as Simon Bolívar, José de San Martín, and—the most unlikely name in South American history—Bernardo O'Higgins, the son of an Irish army officer and leader of the new republic of Chile. By 1822, America recognized the independent republics of Mexico, Brazil, Chile, Argentina, and La Plata (comprising present-day Colombia, Ecuador, Venezuela, and Panama).

The Monroe Doctrine marked what might be called the last step in America's march to independence—a declaration that America was now one of the main players on the world stage.

Final Judgment: Grade B

James Monroe led the nation through eight relatively placid years, the nation's growing prosperity broken only by the Panic of 1819, the first severe depression in American history, brought about by postwar inflation, land speculation, and a credit crisis.

The only serious fighting that took place during his administration was the short and swift victory that brought Florida into the union. And Monroe's negotiations with the British over border disputes, and later with Spain to purchase Florida, expanded the nation.

After he left office, Monroe was personally staggered by debt, as Jefferson and Madison had been. He was forced to sell off his Highland plantation (now called Ash Lawn-Highland), from which Monticello can be seen a few miles away.

But his most profound immediate legacy was his unwillingness to anoint an heir apparent. In 1824, five powerful men would vie for the presidency in a bitterly fought campaign that would eventually remake American politics and history.

Monroe Administration Milestones [15]

1817

March 4	James Monroe is sworn in; New York's Daniel Tompkins is vice president.
June–September	Monroe begins a sixteen-week "victory" tour of New England. The tour leads the *Columbian Sentinel*, a Boston newspaper, to anoint Monroe's administration as the "Era of Good Feelings."
November	The first Seminole War begins in Florida.
December 10	Mississippi becomes the twentieth state, a slave state.
December 26	Secretary of war John C. Calhoun orders General Andrew Jackson to put down Seminole uprisings in Florida and southern Georgia.

1818

May 24	Andrew Jackson seizes Pensacola, effectively ending the first Seminole War.
June 18	Though conceding that Jackson's actions in Pensacola amount to acts of war, Monroe knows that by securing Pensacola and suppressing the Seminole threat, Jackson has provided him with a favorable position to negotiate the acquisition of Florida.

| December 3 | Illinois is admitted as the twenty-first state, a free state. |
| December 14 | Alabama becomes the twenty-second state, a slave state. |

1819

January	The Panic of 1819.
February 15	A debate over Missouri's statehood begins when a New York congressman introduces an amendment to the Missouri statehood bill prohibiting further introduction of slavery in Missouri.
February 22	A treaty transfers the Florida territories from Spain to the United States for $5 million.
March 6	In *McCulloch v. Maryland*, the Supreme Court rules that states cannot tax federal agencies. The ruling also allows Congress to create a national bank and establishes a precedent of broad federal powers.

1820

March 3	Congress agrees to the first Missouri Compromise, addressing congressional jurisdiction over the conditions of statehood.
March 15	As part of the Compromise, Maine is admitted as the twenty-third state of the Union, a free state.
December 6	Monroe is reelected, receiving 231 electoral votes to John Quincy Adams's 1. Vice President Tompkins (for whom New York City's Tompkins Square Park is named) also wins a second term.

1821

| August 10 | Missouri is admitted as the twenty-fourth state, a slave state. Liberia is founded by the American Colonization Society as a haven for free slaves. |

1823

| December 2 | In his annual message to Congress, Monroe announces the "Monroe Doctrine." |

1824

April 30	Monroe signs the General Survey Bill; the United States Army Corps of Engineers will survey and plan road and canal routes.
May 22	The Tariff of 1824 becomes law; it is promoted to protect American industries but is seen as more favorable to the North.
November	Monroe, age sixty-seven, decides not to seek reelection. Five men, Henry Clay, William Crawford, John Quincy Adams, Andrew Jackson, and John C. Calhoun initially vie for the office.

1825

January	Monroe determines that the solution to the controversy over Native American lands is to force them west, a change from his earlier recognition of Cherokee claims.

MUST READS

Gary Hart, *James Monroe*; Jean Edward Smith, *John Marshall: Definer of a Nation*; Harlow Giles Unger, *The Last Founding Father: James Monroe and a Nation's Call to Greatness*.

ONLINE RESOURCES

Ash Lawn-Highland (Monroe home adjacent to Monticello)
 http://www.ashlawnhighland.org/
Library of Congress Resource Guide
 http://www.loc.gov/rr/program/bib/presidents/monroe/
Library of Congress, Monroe Doctrine
 http://www.loc.gov/rr/program/bib/ourdocs/Monroe.html
Inaugural Addresses, Avalon Project, Yale Law School
 1817: http://avalon.law.yale.edu/19th_century/monroe1.asp
 1821: http://avalon.law.yale.edu/19th_century/monroe2.asp
"The Religion of James Monroe," *Virginia Quarterly Review*
 http://www.vqronline.org/articles/2003/autumn/holmes-religion
 -james-monroe/

Monroe Doctrine Text, Avalon Project, Yale Law School
http://avalon.law.yale.edu/19th_century/monroe.asp
Miller Center of Public Affairs, University of Virginia
http://millercenter.org/president/monroe
James Monroe Museum and Memorial Library
http://jamesmonroemuseum.umw.edu/about-the-museum/mission
-statement/

6

Old Man Eloquent
John Quincy Adams

★ ★ ★

March 4, 1825–March 4, 1829

Milestones in John Quincy Adams's Life

July 11, 1767	Born in Braintree (now Quincy), Massachusetts
1790	Admitted to the Massachusetts bar
1794–1801	U.S. minister in several European countries under Washington and his father, John Adams
1803–1808	U.S. senator from Massachusetts
1806–1809	Taught oratory and rhetoric at Harvard
1809–1814	Served as first U.S. minister to Russia under Madison
1814	Led negotiations that drew up Treaty of Ghent, ending the War of 1812
1815–1817	U.S. minister to England under Madison
1817–1825	U.S. secretary of state under Monroe
1825–1829	Sixth president
1830–1848	U.S. representative from Massachusetts
February 23, 1848	Died in Washington, D.C., aged eighty

PRESIDENTIAL VOICES

Fellow-citizens, you are acquainted with the peculiar circumstances of the recent election, which have resulted in affording me the opportunity of addressing you at this time. You have heard the exposition of the principles which will direct me in the fulfillment of the high and solemn trust imposed upon me in

this station. Less possessed of your confidence in advance than any of my prede-
cessors, I am deeply conscious of the prospect that I shall stand more and oftener
in need of your indulgence. Intentions upright and pure, a heart devoted to the
welfare of our country, and the unceasing application of all the faculties allot-
ted to me to her service are all the pledges that I can give for the faithful per-
formance of the arduous duties I am to undertake.

—JOHN QUINCY ADAMS
Inaugural Address, March 4, 1825[1]

The "peculiar circumstances" referred to by President John Quincy Adams hinged on the fact that the younger Adams gained office in a political maneuver from which his presidential administration never recovered. For the second time since the Constitution was adopted, the election of the president would be left to the House of Representatives—and the results in 1824 would not be as satisfying to most people as they had been the first time around, when Jefferson became president in 1800.

Much like his father, John Quincy (pronounced "Quinzy") Adams has been consigned to the minor leagues of presidential history—a one-term president from Massachusetts caught between a towering two-term titan of the "Virginia Dynasty" and the larger-than-life Andrew Jackson, who followed. The two campaigns in which John Quincy Adams seriously competed, however—1824, when he won, and 1828, when he lost—are milestones in American political history.

John Quincy Adams, by virtue of education, experience, intelligence, and a sense of history was well equipped to become one of the all-time great presidents. Unfortunately for him, the presidency sometimes requires a different "tool kit." His controversial victory in 1824 essentially doomed his four years in office before they even began. But his greatest legacy may rest with what he accomplished after he left the White House—a unique post-presidential career in the

House of Representatives, where he became an outspoken opponent of slavery.

Fast Facts

RELIGION: Congregationalist—Unitarian branch
EDUCATION: Harvard
CAREER BEFORE POLITICS: Attorney, diplomat
POLITICAL PARTY: Republican
FIRST LADY: Louisa Johnson Adams (February 12, 1775–May 15, 1852)
CHILDREN: Louisa Catherine, died in infancy; George; John; Charles Francis, a diplomat in the Lincoln and Andrew Johnson administrations and also a member of the House of Representatives.

* At age ten, John Quincy Adams accompanied his father on a diplomatic mission to France and attended schools in France and the Netherlands. At fourteen, he was permitted to serve as secretary to Francis Dana, the first American diplomat assigned to the Russian court.[2]
* He met his future wife, Louisa Catherine Johnson, in London, where she was born. She is, to date, the only foreign-born first lady.
* John Quincy Adams was the first man to win the presidency with fewer electoral votes and fewer popular votes than his chief opponent, Andrew Jackson.
* He wore the pants—literally. Adams was the first president to be inaugurated in long pants rather than breeches.
* John Quincy Adams is the subject of the oldest known photograph of a sitting president, taken in 1843. (The original daguerreotype is in the National Portrait Gallery of the Smithsonian.)
* For installing the first billiards table in the White House and purchasing a chessboard with public funds, Adams would be accused of bringing "gaming tables" to the "President's House."
* His early morning naked swims in the Potomac were legendary, and he was said to swim the width of the river in an hour at age fifty-eight. He continued the practice when he returned to Congress and swam for the last time at age seventy-nine.[3]

* John Quincy Adams was the first and, to date, only former president to join the House of Representatives. He was elected from Massachusetts in the 1830 midterm election.

* As ex-president and while a member of the House, Adams argued before the Supreme Court in the 1841 *Amistad* case, which he won in a major victory for the cause of abolition.

* He served in Congress until he collapsed after voting on the House floor on February 21, 1848, when he suffered a cerebral hemorrhage. He died two days later.

* Including his congressional career, John Quincy Adams served in public office during the administrations of the first eleven presidents.

PRESIDENTIAL VOICES

Expired at Washington on the ninth of February, of poison administered by the assassin's hands of John Quincy Adams, the usurper, and Henry Clay, the virtue, liberty, and independence of the United States.

—MOCK OBITUARY
Newspaper allied with Andrew Jackson
February 1825

So you see, the Judas of the West has closed the contract and will now receive his thirty pieces of silver. His end will be the same.

—ANDREW JACKSON
Following the appointment of Henry Clay as secretary of state
by President-elect John Quincy Adams, February 1825[4]

How did a "corrupt bargain" ruin the presidency of John Quincy Adams?

If America needed any evidence that Monroe's "Era of Good Feelings" was over, it came with the election of 1824. For a second time, the choice of a president would be sent to the House of Representatives, after a ruthlessly bitter campaign demonstrated how clearly sectionalism, or the division of the country into geographic areas with their own agendas, had replaced party loyalties.

The leading candidates for president in 1824 were all from one party, the Democratic-Republicans of Jefferson, Madison, and Monroe. Even John Quincy Adams, son of the last Federalist president, had joined. As Monroe's secretary of state, he was a leading contender for president in a field of candidates, all from the South or West, that included General Andrew Jackson, senator from Tennessee; speaker of the House Henry Clay of Kentucky; and Georgia's William H. Crawford, Monroe's treasury secretary. Jackson had been nominated for president by Tennessee's legislature, the first break with the established system in which a "caucus" of party leaders in Congress made the choices. But this system was about to be overhauled, as Paul Boller writes. "Arguments for and against 'King Caucus' filled the columns of newspapers and resounded in resolutions passed by state legislatures and local party conventions. But the bent of the people was strongly anti-caucus."[5] This was the slow and agonizing birth of a new era of American democracy in which power would begin to shift away from the few in Washington and into the local levels of party organization.

Modern voters who continue to wish for the good old days of polite presidential contests should get a good whiff of the stench in this race. Issues became negligible in the campaign; personalities were the only subject of debate, and all threw about slanderous charges. The old charge of "monarchist," and worse, was raised against Adams. It was now compounded because he was charged with having an English wife. Henry Clay was called a drunkard; Jackson, a murderer whose military successes had been inflated. Georgian William H. Crawford, Monroe's secretary of the Treasury, escaped the worst of the slander but was ridiculed as the choice of the "undemocratic" caucus system and was merely accused of malfeasance in office. After he suffered a stroke in September 1828, Crawford's fortunes tumbled.

While Adams and Jackson took the lead as popular favorites, the election was inconclusive, with neither winning a majority of electoral votes, and the decision, as it had been in 1800, was given over to the House, which would choose between the top three finishers: Jackson, Adams, and Crawford. With 43.1 percent of the popular vote and ninety-nine electoral votes, Jackson had a legitimate claim to the office. But in 1824, many states still chose their presidential electors—and consequently the president—in the state legislature and not by direct popular election, so popular votes had even less meaning. Having finished fourth in the electoral tally, Clay would not be eligible in the House vote. The powerful Clay had only disdain for Jackson; he legitimately believed Adams was the more experienced candidate. "I cannot believe," said Clay, "that killing 2,500 Englishmen at New Orleans qualifies for the various, difficult and complicated duties of the Chief Magistracy." [6]

Clay also believed that an Adams election would benefit his own political future. The two men met the night before the vote. Throwing his considerable influence in the House behind Adams, Clay helped Adams win on the first ballot. Adams then named Clay to be his secretary of state, prompting Jackson supporters to scream that a "corrupt bargain" had been made between the two men in their meeting. (The controversy led to a later duel between Clay and Jackson supporter Senator John Randolph. Pistol shots were exchanged, without harm.)

Whether or not a deal had been struck did not matter. The damage was done. Jackson, the people's choice, had had the election "stolen" from him. Adams never recovered from the controversy. The Tennessee legislature immediately designated Jackson its choice for the next election, and the campaign of 1828 actually began in 1825.

With the steadfast opposition of Jackson's allies in Congress, little was accomplished during Adams's presidency, in which he championed Clay's "American system," an ambitious national program of road and canal building. Outlined in Adams's first Message to Congress, the plan also called for astronomical observatories—"lighthouses to the sky"—as he called them. It was a moment that recalled the Enlightenment-era vision that would have been shared by such science-minded founders as his father, Jefferson, and Franklin. But as John Quincy Adams called for such nationally funded "improvements," he was seen to be advocating a larger federal role in promoting advances in education, science, and the arts. In other words, the "big government" controversy of modern-day America is nothing new. Adams's speech was immediately denounced as an assault on states' rights. Adams would lose his reelection bid to the man he had defeated four years earlier.

Final Judgment: Grade C

For all his education, world travels, and diplomatic and political experience, John Quincy Adams may have never spent enough time getting to know Americans. There is something to be said for the "common touch," which he lacked and which summons comparison to the contemporary "elitist" charge in American politics.

The issue was summarized in a quip about Adams's contest with military hero Jackson, describing it as a campaign between "one who can write and one who can fight." Though Adams had been born and lived on a small plot of New England land and came from a family of farmers, it was Andrew Jackson, the plantation owner with more than one hundred slaves, who would be touted as the simple farmer and "man of the people." Adams was cast as the cold, aloof "monarchist," like his father. Having an English wife didn't help his cause. In many ways John Quincy Adams, like his father, wasn't a "guy you'd want to have a beer with," in modern political parlance. Image has always mattered.

"John Quincy Adams represented another man of talent and virtue, a worthy son of his father. His intellectual ability and courage were above reproach, and his wisdom in perceiving the national interest has stood the test of time," historian Daniel Walker Howe wrote. "The limitations of his effectiveness lay partly beyond his control, but some responsibilities rested with contradictions in Adams's own conception of his presidential role."[7]

Adams did not let his 1828 defeat, or his depression over it, end his long life of public service. Without campaigning, John Quincy Adams was returned to Washington by the people of Massachusetts in 1830 as a member of the House. This is where he truly worked "tirelessly to end slavery." Although not a radical abolitionist, Adams was completely opposed to slavery. In 1839, he won a landmark court battle as defense counsel to the Africans who revolted aboard the *Amistad*, a Spanish slave ship. (For further reference on the *Amistad* case, see Chapter 8, "Martin Van Buren.") During his years in Congress, Adams fought to eliminate the "gag rule" that prevented discussion of slavery in Congress. The gag rule was finally abolished in 1845.

In late February 1848, Adams was casting a vote in the House when he became ill and lapsed into a coma, dying two days later, of a cerebral hemorrhage, on February 23.

PRESIDENTIAL VOICES

The slave has lost a champion who gained a new ardor and new strength the longer he fought; America has lost a man who loved her with his heart; religion has lost a supporter; Freedom an unfailing friend, and mankind a noble vindicator of our inalienable rights.

—THEODORE PARKER
Massachusetts Unitarian clergyman and abolitionist leader
1848

John Quincy Adams Administration Milestones[8]

1825

February 5	The House of Representatives elects John Quincy Adams; John C. Calhoun is elected vice president.
October	Balking at the established caucus system, the Tennessee legislature nominates Andrew Jackson as their presidential challenger for the 1828 election. Other states will follow suit.

October 26   The first passage of the 363-mile-long Erie Canal is completed; the canal links Lake Erie to New York City and its completion will lead to an economic boom for New York and other cities along the canal route. The Erie Canal's success spurs a surge in canal-building projects.

1826

July 4   On the fiftieth anniversary of the adoption of the Declaration of Independence, Thomas Jefferson and John Adams both die.

September 12   A Freemason named William Morgan disappears after disclosing some of the society's secrets; the case arouses suspicions over the Masons and leads to the creation of the Anti-Masonic Party, America's first "third party."

In midterm elections, supporters of Andrew Jackson win a majority in both houses of Congress.

1827

February 28   The Baltimore & Ohio Railroad is chartered. The surviving signer of the Declaration of Independence, Charles Carroll, breaks ground for the railroad on July 4, 1828.

1828

November   Andrew Jackson defeats John Quincy Adams with 56 percent of the popular vote and 178 electoral votes to Adams's 83.

MUST READS

Daniel Walker Howe, *What Hath God Wrought: The Transformation of America, 1815–1848*; Paul C. Nagel, *John Quincy Adams: A Public Life, a Private Life*; Lynn Hudson Parsons, *The Birth of Modern Politics: Andrew Jackson, John Quincy Adams and the Election of 1828.*

ONLINE RESOURCES

Adams Birthplace and Family Homes, Adams National Historical Park
http://www.nps.gov/adam/index.htm

Inaugural Address, Avalon Project, Yale Law School
http://avalon.law.yale.edu/19th_century/qadams.asp

John Quincy Adams Diaries, Massachusetts Historical Society
http://www.masshist.org/jqadiaries/

Miller Center of Public Affairs, University of Virginia
http://millercenter.org/president/jqadams

Library of Congress Resource Guide
http://www.loc.gov/rr/program/bib/presidents/jqadams/memory.html

Arguments Before the Supreme Court in the *Amistad* Case
http://avalon.law.yale.edu/19th_century/amistad_002.asp

7

Old Hickory
Andrew Jackson

* * *

March 4, 1829–March 4, 1837

Milestones in Andrew Jackson's Life

March 15, 1767	Born in Waxhaw, South Carolina (North Carolina border)
1780–1781	Teenaged member of militia in Revolutionary War
1787	Admitted to the North Carolina bar
1795	Member of Tennessee State Constitutional Convention
1797	U.S. representative from Tennessee
1797–1798	U.S. senator from Tennessee
1798–1804	Judge of Tennessee Superior Court
1812–1815	Major general in the War of 1812
1817–1818	Commanded U.S. troops in Seminole War in Florida
1821	Provisional governor of Territory of Florida
1823–1825	U.S. senator from Tennessee
1829–1837	Seventh president
June 8, 1845	Died at the Hermitage near Nashville, Tennessee, aged seventy-eight

PRESIDENTIAL VOICES

As long as our Government is administered for the good of the people, and is regulated by their will; as long as it secures to us the rights of person and of property, liberty of conscience and of the press, it will be worth defending; and so long as it is worth defending a patriotic militia will cover it with an impenetrable aegis. Partial injuries and occasional mortifications we may be subjected to, but a million of armed freemen, possessed of the means of war, can never be conquered by a foreign foe.

It will be my sincere and constant desire to observe toward the Indian tribes within our limits a just and liberal policy, and to give that humane and considerate attention to their rights and their wants which is consistent with the habits of our Government and the feelings of our people.

—ANDREW JACKSON
First Inaugural Address, March 4, 1829[1]

Does Andrew Jackson deserve his place on the twenty-dollar bill? There are quite a few people who would quickly answer in the negative.

Part of the reason might be found in the depiction of the war hero turned politician in *Bloody, Bloody Andrew Jackson*, to date the only "emo hard rock" musical about an American president, which opened in New York City in 2010. With catchy numbers like "Populism Yea, Yea" and "Ten Little Indians," the musical underscored Jackson's reputation as "a land-snatching, Indian-slaughtering general and president."[2]

That description also leaves out the slaves he owned and sold, the British citizens he illegally executed, and his numerous dueling victims. But it is mostly for Jackson's treatment of Native Americans—who called him "Sharp Knife"—and his slaveholding ways that a quixotic movement was born to replace him on the bills.[3]

In our day and ever since his own, Andrew Jackson has inspired high emotions and sharp opinions. Aaron Burr, who met him when they served together in the Senate and tried to recruit him for his Western "adventure," thought Jackson was "a man of intelligence, and one of those prompt, frank, ardent souls who I love to meet."[4]

To Thomas Jefferson, however, Jackson was "a dangerous man." His predecessor and chief rival, John Quincy Adams, went even further—Jackson was "a barbarian who could not write a sentence of grammar and hardly could spell his own name." One bitter antagonist, Henry Clay, thought Jackson was "ignorant, passionate, hypocritical, corrupt and easily swayed by the base men who surround him."[5]

But Jackson also transformed American politics and the presidency as few other men have. Love him or hate him, he certainly ranks among the most influential figures in the presidential pantheon.

Fast Facts

RELIGION: Presbyterian

ASSOCIATIONS: Freemason

MILITARY SERVICE: Tennessee Militia (courier in the Revolutionary War) United States Army—major general (Creek War, War of 1812, Seminole War)

CAREER BEFORE POLITICS: Planter, attorney

POLITICAL PARTY: Democratic

SPOUSE: Rachel Donelson Robards Jackson (June 15, 1767–December 22, 1828)

CHILDREN: Jackson had no biological children. He and Rachel adopted one of Mrs. Jackson's nephews and named him Andrew Jackson, Jr. He later managed the Hermitage.

Another nephew, Andrew Jackson Donelson, became Jackson's protégé and later was his private secretary during Jackson's presidency.

* Jackson was the first president to take the oath of office on the east front of the U.S. Capitol.
* John Quincy Adams, the outgoing president, did not attend Jackson's inauguration, just as his father had not attended the inauguration of his successor, Thomas Jefferson.
* Andrew Jackson Donelson's wife, Emily, served as first social hostess and unofficial "first lady" during Jackson's presidency until 1834, when she left the White House over the "Peggy Eaton Affair," a

social scandal that caused a rift and crisis in Jackson's cabinet. (See below: *How did Jackson's cabinet crumble over the "Petticoat Affair"?*) Sarah Yorke Jackson, wife of Andrew Jackson, Jr., later served as White House hostess.

* Jackson took his second oath of office on March 4, 1833, in the House chamber because a deep snow had fallen three days before. It was the last time the oath was administered by Chief Justice Marshall, who presided over nine inaugurations from Jefferson to Jackson.

* Jackson escaped the first attempted assassination of a sitting president, on January 30, 1835. Richard Lawrence, described as a mentally disturbed housepainter, shot at Jackson with a derringer, which misfired. Lawrence was confined to a mental institution until his death in 1861.

* Andrew Jackson used his veto twelve times, more than all his predecessors combined.[6]

* Running cold water was brought to the White House during Jackson's presidency. By early 1834, a "bathing room" in the East Wing followed. It had a hot bath, a cold bath, and a shower bath, with water heated by coal-fired copper boilers.[7] Running hot water would not appear upstairs at the White House for many years.

* In 1804, when Jackson bought the Hermitage, the plantation he called his "farm," he owned 9 slaves. By 1829, he owned more than 100, and at the time of his death, more than 150 slaves worked the plantation.[8]

* Jackson's portrait replaced that of Grover Cleveland on the twenty-dollar bill in 1929. Jackson was violently opposed to paper money.

When he arrived in Washington, D.C., for his inauguration on March 4, 1829, the seventh president was "a tall gaunt man, his face wrinkled with pain and age, his thick gray hair turning snow-white. His eyes were sad and heart empty from the recent death of his wife."[9]

There was more reason for pain and sadness in Andrew Jackson's hardened face than just the death of his wife. Unlike his predecessors from the "Virginia Dynasty," he was not the son of a well-to-do planter.

Nor was Jackson reared in the more refined world of Boston and experienced in Europe's royal court, as the Adamses were. Andrew Jackson was the orphaned son of immigrant pioneers, and he had known a hard-knocks childhood of death, war, and hardship.

Born on March 15, 1767, in a rough cabin near Waxhaw Creek, in the border area between North and South Carolina (Jackson claimed he was born in South Carolina, but the records are unclear), Jackson was the son of Irish immigrants who had arrived in America two years earlier. Weeks before Jackson was born, his father died, leaving his mother to care for three boys, one an infant. Jackson's mother earned a living tending the eight children of nearby relatives, the Crawford family.

Although he lacked much formal education, Jackson learned to read early, and he later recalled that he read the Declaration of Independence aloud in public in the summer of 1776.

When the Revolution began, he and brother Robert joined the militia company of their uncle as couriers and were captured in 1781. A possibly apocryphal story has a British officer ordering Andrew to clean his boots, which he refused to do. For his insolence, young Andrew was struck by the officer with a saber, perhaps helping explain Andrew Jackson's vitriolic, lifelong hatred of the British, whom he already blamed for the death of his oldest brother, Hugh, at the battle of Stono Ferry in 1779. After his mother won her sons' release from the British, Jackson watched Robert die of smallpox in the spring of 1781. Shortly after that, his mother fell victim to a cholera epidemic in November 1781 as she nursed the sick. For these deaths, Jackson would always despise the English.

The orphaned Andrew Jackson went to live with his Crawford relatives, and when he unexpectedly came into a small inheritance at sixteen, Jackson showed a hint of his devil-may-care attitude, squandering the money on horse racing, dice, and the taverns of Charleston, South Carolina. In 1784, he moved to Salisbury, North Carolina, and began to read law, although he seemed to spend more time raising hell with a group of rowdy friends. One contemporary called him "the most roaring, rollicking, game-cocking, card-playing, mischievous fellow that ever lived in Salisbury."[10] When a town dance was planned, Jackson hired a well-known pair of prostitutes—a mother and daughter—to attend the ball. The locals were not amused by the six-foot-tall Jackson, with his penchant for strong language, gambling on cards, cockfights, and racehorses. But those were attributes that wore much better when he moved to America's frontier. As biographer Jon Meacham wrote, Jackson possessed "charm that made other men like him and want to join him in exploits that crossed the line of respectability, but never so dramatically that they could not stumble back into the good graces of their wives and neighbors by the next morning. . . . His ability to lead was already evident in North Carolina."[11]

Admitted to the bar in 1787, Jackson moved in October 1788 to Nashville, where he established himself as an attorney willing to barter his services for land. For a time, he lived in the boardinghouse of Mrs. John Donelson, where he was captivated by Rachel Robards, the landlady's dark-haired, pipe-smoking daughter. When Rachel's estranged husband, Lewis Robards, later suggested that there was an illicit relationship between Jackson and Rachel, Jackson threatened to cut off his ears. Jackson had a butcher knife in hand when he made the threat. Lewis Robards agreed to a divorce.

Although recent evidence suggests that Andrew Jackson and Rachel Robards were living together before they ever married,[12] Rachel believed she had been granted a legal divorce. The couple went to Natchez, Mississippi, where they wed in August 1791. When they later learned that Lewis Robards had petitioned for the divorce but it had not been legally granted at the time, the couple was remarried in Nashville on January 7, 1794, after the divorce was finalized. Their "unmarried" years together would come back to haunt them.

Jackson earned money selling to speculators some of the land he had acquired, and when Tennessee was admitted to the Union, he began his political climb, serving as the state's first congressman and then briefly in the Senate. As his standing in Tennessee grew, the slurs and gossip about Rachel began to surface, and Jackson made his wife's honor a matter of life and death. He attacked the governor of Tennessee over the matter and, in 1806, killed Nashville attorney Charles Dickinson in a duel, after Dickinson had insulted Rachel. Before he died, Dickinson shot Jackson in the chest—a bullet that Jackson carried for the rest of his life and which would cause serious complications later. In another notorious gun battle, in September 1813, Jackson and his companions traded shots with the Benton brothers, one of whom—Thomas Hart Benton—was the future senator from Missouri. With blood streaming from his wounds, Jackson refused an amputation in the aftermath of the fight.

That Nashville brawl had come just after the war with England broke out in 1812. When war was first declared, Jackson had been appointed a Tennessee militia commander and ordered to prepare an attack on Florida. He marched a contingent of Tennessee militia to Florida, and during this initial campaign, Jackson won the admiration of his men when he refused to leave some of his sick soldiers behind when ordered to return to Tennessee. Leading his men back to Nashville, sometimes on foot himself, Jackson earned his famous nickname "Old Hickory" because his men thought that he was tough, ramrod-straight, and immovable, like an iron-hard hickory tree.

After his return to Nashville, the street fight with the Bentons only burnished Jackson's reputation as fearless and a fighter. The war soon added to that reputation for ruthless bravery as he won the signature triumphs that made him a national military hero. In 1813, still weak from the blood lost in the Benton fight, Jackson led his Tennessee militia in a brutal campaign against Creek warriors under Chief Red Eagle, also called William Weatherford, a half-Scot and half-Creek leader inspired by Tecumseh. After the Creek massacred hundreds of settlers and slaves in a frontier outpost called Fort Mims, Jackson led a scorched-earth war against Weatherford. He saw the war with the Creek as a piece of the larger war against England and Spain, believing that the two countries were arming Indians to massacre American women and children. On March 27, 1814, Jackson commanded two thousand men, including Cherokee who had been promised government favor, against eight hundred Creek in the Battle of Horseshoe Bend, one of the most destructive battles between whites and Indians in North American history. It was a complete rout, and in the aftermath, the Tennesseans under Jackson sliced off the tips of the dead Creek's noses. Some soldiers mutilated the Creek corpses, cutting long strips of skin to make horse bridles.[13] Jackson then forced the vanquished Creek and Red Eagle to surrender more than twenty-three million acres of Creek land.

Given command of a regular army by President Madison, Jackson went on to his greatest victory on January 8, 1815, when he defeated veteran British troops at the Battle of New Orleans with a small force composed of local militiamen, free blacks, and regular soldiers. The forty-seven-year-old Jackson was hailed as the hero of a war that had already ended when the battle was fought. That fact mattered little to adoring Americans.

In 1818, with deliberately ambiguous instructions from President Monroe that allowed the Monroe administration to deny ordering an attack, Jackson embarked on a war against the remaining Creek and Seminoles of Florida. Claiming that Florida, still in Spanish hands, was a sanctuary for escaped slaves and marauding Seminoles, Jackson invaded the territory, unleashing a bloody campaign that left native villages and Spanish forts smoldering. Jackson's incursion set off a diplomatic crisis when he executed two British citizens, but his actions eventually forced Spain to sell Florida to the United States in 1819 on favorable terms, under the Adams-Onis Treaty, negotiated by Secretary of State John Quincy Adams. Jackson became territorial governor of the newly conquered territory.

After his defeat in the 1824 election and the bitterness of the "corrupt bargain," Jackson immediately began running for president and would handily win the election of 1828, arguably one of the most mean-spirited in American history. One notorious piece of campaign literature, featuring a row of coffins and known as the "Coffin Handbill," called Jackson a murderer for his duels, the deaths of militiamen under his command, and the two British citizens he had executed in Florida. The supporters of Adams also accused Jackson's mother of being a prostitute and claimed he was a "mulatto." And his wife, Rachel, would once again be the target of vicious slanders. A congressional candidate from Jackson's own state of Tennessee put out a handbill that said Jackson was a man who thought that if he took a fancy to his neighbor's wife, he only had to "take pistol in one hand and a horsewhip in another and . . . possess her."[14] An Adams supporter asked, "Ought an

adulteress and her paramour husband be placed in the highest offices?"
And one popular campaign ditty went:

> *Oh Andy! Oh Andy!*
> *How many men have you hanged in your life?*
> *How many weddings make a wife?*

These attacks were devastating to Rachel Jackson, who felt that her
name was being dragged through the mud. In December 1828, before
Jackson's inauguration in March 1829, Rachel died while readying to
move to the White House. Before her death, she is quoted as saying, "I
had rather be a door-keeper in the house of God than to live in that
place."

Rachel Jackson was buried in the garden at the Hermitage, in the
white dress she had planned to wear to the inauguration. Jackson
blamed his political opponents for her death and vowed revenge. At
Rachel's burial, he said, "I can and do forgive all my enemies. But
those vile wretches who have slandered her must look to God for
mercy."[15]

And the man Jackson chiefly blamed was his political antagonist,
the man he had once called the "Judas of the West," Henry Clay.

PRESIDENTIAL VOICES

*But what a scene did we witness! The majesty of the people had disappeared,
and a rabble, a mob, of boys, Negroes, women, children, scrambling, fighting,
romping. What a pity, what a pity! No arrangements had been made, no police officers placed on duty, and the whole house had been inundated by the
rabble mob. We came too late. The president, after having been literally nearly
pressed to death and almost suffocated and torn to pieces by the people in their
eagerness to shake hands with Old Hickory, had retreated through the back
way or south front and had escaped to his lodgings at Gadsby's.*

—MARGARET BAYARD SMITH,
Account of Andrew Jackson's inauguration[16]

Did Andrew Jackson invent the "spoils system"?

In the rerun election of 1828, Jackson avenged the "corrupt bargain" of four years earlier, sweeping to victory in the popular vote, which had grown in importance as more states began allowing voters to choose presidential electors by direct vote instead of leaving the choice of the electors to the state legislatures. It was still a far cry from direct election of the president, but the process of choosing the electors who would ultimately cast the vote for president was becoming more openly democratic.

Money had also become more important in elections, and funds collected from supporters were disbursed by New York's Martin Van Buren, who was Jackson's de facto national treasurer, with money spent on newspapers, campaign badges, books, and pamphlets, some mailed courtesy of the government under the so-called "franking" privilege given to congressmen.

As Sean Wilentz records, Jackson's popular totals came from a vastly larger number of voters. "More than a million white men voted in 1828, roughly four times the total of 1824."[17] With 56 percent of that vote, Jackson took 178 electoral votes to Adams's 83. For the first time in America's brief history, the country had a president who was not a Virginian or an Adams.

That a new American era was born became apparent with Jackson's victory and inaugural. A large crowd of Old Hickory's supporters, mostly rough-hewn Western frontiersmen with little regard for niceties, crowded into Washington, flush with the excitement of defeating what they saw as the aristocratic power brokers of the Northeast and Tidewater Virginia. When Jackson finished his inaugural address, hundreds of well-wishers stormed into the White House, where tables had been laid with cakes, ice cream, and punch. Supreme Court Justice Joseph Story would famously comment on the dawn of the new administration, "The reign of King 'Mob' seemed triumphant."

Part of this new order—the so-called "Jacksonian Democracy"—came from the reformed voting rules in states where property ownership was no longer a qualification to vote. And this new democracy was, in modern political language, more of a grassroots movement. Jackson, an orphan, a frontiersman, a horse-racing man, a hard-fighting war hero, and the bane of "savages," was its symbol. Tough and uncompromising, Old Hickory embodied the new American spirit and became the idol of the ambitious men who now called themselves Democrats. With men like Martin Van Buren, who recognized the importance of party discipline and organization, the nature of politics itself was changing. It was the dawn of "machine politics," an art that Van Buren, a senator about to move up the ladder, quickly mastered.

As in every new administration, many of those celebrating Jackson's victory and overturning the tables filled with inaugural ice cream at the White House had come to Washington for a job. It was expected that Jackson would sweep out holdovers from the hated Adams administration. When New York's other senator, William T. Marcy, a lieutenant of Martin Van Buren who had helped build Jackson's victory, declared in Congress, "To the victor belong the spoils," the practice had a new name: the "spoils system."

There was nothing new about this "spoils system"; it had been practiced by every administration from the beginning of the republic. And Jackson only replaced about 10 percent of appointed office holders. But the widespread and loud calls for patronage that swept Washington in the wake of Jackson's election have attached Jackson's name to the spoils system ever since, in part because of the excessive levels of corruption that followed. In one of the most notorious cases of the day, Samuel Swartwout, a veteran New York City politician with ties going back to Aaron Burr (he was a codefendant in Burr's treason trial), was named collector of Customs in the New York Port and embezzled more than $1 million.[18]

PRESIDENTIAL VOICES

Our Union—it must be preserved!
—ANDREW JACKSON
April 13, 1830

Offering a toast at the Jefferson Day Dinner in Washington, D.C., Jackson aimed his words at his vice president, Calhoun, and his theory of nullification. Calhoun responded:

The Union, next to our liberty most dear!

The following month, Jackson learned that in 1818, Calhoun had supported a measure to discipline Jackson for his military involvement in Florida. The discovery deepened the mistrust between the two.

How did Jackson's cabinet crumble over the "Petticoat Affair"?

Margaret "Peggy" O'Neale was the daughter of a Washington, D.C., barkeep and boardinghouse owner. At the age of twelve, she had danced for Dolley Madison, and her father's tavern had become a popular watering hole for Washington's politicians. Peggy married a naval officer, John Timberlake, and bore him three children. But during his long absences at sea, there were whispers that Margaret was "friendly" with her father's famous guests. After her husband died at sea in an apparent suicide in 1828, Peggy married John Eaton, at the urging of Andrew Jackson, who had made Eaton his secretary of war. He was a senator with whom Peggy had often been spotted while still married.

Now Mrs. Eaton, Peggy created a White House palace revolt. Unwilling to befriend an allegedly "loose woman of low origins," several cabinet wives, led by the wife of Vice President Calhoun, snubbed

Peggy, refusing to attend any White House functions she was attending. Even Jackson's niece (the wife of Andrew Jackson Donelson) refused to socialize with Peggy. The White House social world came to a screeching halt. And so did Jackson's cabinet. As Sean Wilentz notes, "The Eaton matter had direct political implications, as most of Eaton's critics were either southerners or close friends of the Calhouns, or both."[19]

Jackson liked Peggy, and her treatment at the hands of "proper" Washington must have reminded him of Rachel's experience with "society." He sided with the Eatons. But the "Petticoat Affair," or the "Eaton Malaria," as it was dubbed, was bigger than a social tempest. Currying favor with Jackson, Martin Van Buren—now secretary of state—saw a political opening and organized receptions for the Eatons. With this act of loyalty, Van Buren rose in Jackson's esteem.

Eventually Jackson elevated Van Buren as his favorite, and he replaced Calhoun as vice presidential running mate in his reelection campaign. Van Buren became Jackson's de facto heir. Calhoun and his wife returned to South Carolina, where he won a Senate seat in 1832 and became the most prominent advocate of states' rights, slavery, and economic issues affecting the South, eventually including secession.

PRESIDENTIAL VOICES

On this subject I do not wish to think, or speak, or write, with moderation. No! No! Tell a man whose house is on fire, to give a moderate alarm; tell him to moderately rescue his wife from the hands of the ravisher; tell the mother to gradually extricate her babe from the fire into which it has fallen; but urge me not to use moderation in a cause like the present. I am in earnest—I will not equivocate—I will not excuse—I will not retreat a single inch—AND I WILL BE HEARD.

—WILLIAM LLOYD GARRISON
First issue of the abolitionist journal the *Liberator*
1831

How did a slave force Andrew Jackson to censor the mail?

Nothing struck deeper fear into the hearts of Southerners, whether they held slaves or not, than the idea of a slave revolt. Long years of American slaveholding propaganda arguing that slavery was beneficial to slaves had been paired alongside popular imagery of docile slaves working in peaceful servitude under paternalistic masters. But those sanitized impressions were contradicted by the reality of the many rebellions and uprisings by slaves, sometimes in union with Indians or disaffected whites, that had taken place over the long history of slavery in the Americas, going back to the time of Spanish arrival. These were not limited to the South; there had been violent uprisings in colonial Connecticut, Massachusetts, and New York City, where slaves made up one-fifth of the population at the time of a suspected 1741 slave conspiracy, according to historian Jill Lepore's *New York Burning.*[20]

In 1829, the year Jackson took office, David Walker, son of a slave, published *Appeal to the Coloured Citizens of the World*, a pamphlet that advocated violent rebellion. According to Walker, slaves were more than justified to take up arms. "It is no more harm for you to kill a man, who is trying to kill you, than it is for you to take a drink of water."

Walker's call was set against the greatest horror and threat to slaveholding America—a republic of former slaves that had emerged in the Caribbean. Toussaint L'Ouverture, a former carriage driver, led the slaves of Saint-Domingue (modern Haiti and the Dominican Republic) in a successful rebellion during the 1790s. Spurred on by the revolutions in America and France, Toussaint's rebellion resulted in some sixty thousand deaths and a republic of freed slaves on the island.

The Haitian uprising directly inspired several significant American slave rebellions in the early nineteenth century, including the one during Jackson's term, in 1831, that frightened white Americans most. Led by Nat Turner, a charismatic preacher, the rebellion ultimately failed, but it transformed the South. To whites and slaves alike, Turner was larger than life; he and his followers had killed more than a dozen whites in Southampton, Virginia. Turner then eluded capture for two months, becoming a sort of bogeyman to the people of the South.

Even after his hanging, slave owners feared Nat Turner's influence. Across the slaveholding South, stringent new slave laws were passed, making it illegal to teach slaves to read. Strict censorship laws aimed at abolitionist materials or pamphlets like David Walker's were also passed. With Andrew Jackson's blessing, postal inspectors were instructed to seize abolitionist pamphlets and other materials in the mails.

What was the "Bank War"?

When Andrew Jackson didn't like something, there were few half measures. He built his military career by attacking, with little restraint, such enemies as the British, Spanish, Creek, and Seminoles. His political enemies were no different. And in 1829, he made clear his hatred of the national bank, centerpiece of Alexander Hamilton's federal economic system. Jackson thought that the Second Bank of the United States, then centered in Philadelphia, was one of the roots of evil in America. He believed that the bank, which held public money but was a privately managed institution, exerted too much control over the nation's economy. He thought it should be under the people's or the president's control. But Jackson also viewed the bank as a political adversary, which made loans to influence reelections and paid retainers to favored lawmakers—much the way Fannie Mae, the mortgage agency, has in recent years been criticized for its relationships with current and former legislators.

When the bank's charter came up for renewal in 1832, Jackson vetoed the bill. When Jackson's opponents, chiefly Henry Clay, his longtime rival, tried to make the bank an issue in the election of 1832, Jackson campaigned on the bank veto, making it a class issue and arguing that what he called the "Monster Bank" benefited the few at the expense of the people. The bank was headed by Nicholas Biddle, a perfect foil to Jackson, as he was, in the words of business historian Steve Fraser, "an unapologetic patrician . . . politically tactless enough to advertise his disdain for the popular will."[21] Jackson made the bank the defining campaign issue, and it was a successful political argument. The result was a landslide in favor of Jackson's repudiation of the bank and a mandate to kill the Second Bank of the United States.

In 1833, Jackson ordered all federal deposits in the bank withdrawn and deposited in state banks. Two treasury officials refused, so Jackson sacked them and placed his attorney general, Maryland's Roger Taney, in charge of the Treasury. Despite the Senate's refusal to confirm his appointment, during his nine months as acting secretary, Taney carried out Jackson's orders.

Then Jackson announced that effective October 1, 1833, surplus federal funds would no longer be deposited in the national bank and would be moved instead into smaller state banks known as "pet banks." Initially this helped fuel a boom, but when Jackson issued the "Specie Circular," an executive order that required all payments for land purchased from the federal government be made in specie (gold) instead of paper money, the policy helped lead to a panic, or depression, during his successor Van Buren's first year. (The third central bank, the Federal Reserve, was created in 1913 to rein in speculation and create a measure of federal control over the economy, as a solution to a long series of nineteenth-century boom-and-bust panics.)

Jackson's bank moves precipitated a political crisis as his nemesis, Henry Clay, sought to reverse the withdrawals and even impeach and remove Jackson. That effort failed, but in an unprecedented move, the Senate censured President Jackson in 1834 for claiming unprecedented powers. Clay's allies derided Jackson as "Caesar." But a later Senate vote overturned the censure. And in 1836, Jackson appointed Roger Taney to be chief justice of the Supreme Court, replacing the legendary John Marshall.

Assessing the bank controversy and Jackson's power, biographer Jon Meacham wrote, "On balance, it seems most reasonable to say that the nation's interests would have been best served had the Bank been reformed rather than altogether crushed, but balance was not the order of the day once Jackson decided . . . that the Bank was a competing power center beyond his control. The history of banking and finance in the nineteenth century would have been different had the Bank survived."[22]

Final Judgment: Grade A

Modern critics decry his attitudes toward slaves and Native Americans, but Jackson goes into the top ranks of presidents because of his extraordinary impact. He helped create the aura of presidential power in ways that even his predecessors had not. That does not mean his policies were flawless. His attack on the U.S. Bank probably weakened the American economy and damaged the nation's financial strength, and his policies toward Native Americans—certainly popular at the time—were practically genocidal.

Andrew Jackson's Democratic Party was an outgrowth largely of Jackson's personality and individual opinions rather than of the strict party line or platform associated with modern politics. His popularity was undeniable; it resulted in his overwhelming reelection in 1832 (55 percent of the popular vote; 77 percent of the electoral vote), which also brought in New York politico Martin Van Buren as the new vice president.

Jackson's appeal was simple: suspicion of the upper classes and big business, typified by the Second Bank of the United States, which Jackson had eliminated; freedom of economic opportunity, including the removal of native nations to open up Indian lands for white expansion; increased voting rights (for white men, at least); and a general opening of the political process to the middle and lower classes, which had been closed out by the earlier, gentry-based administrations.

On the increasingly heated question of the Union versus states' rights, Jackson tiptoed cautiously, proclaiming a strong Unionist position but tending to limit the powers the federal government held over the states, the ostensible reason behind his opposition to the national bank.

Jackson's general popularity almost completely stifled opposition, but not entirely. Out of the ashes of the old Federalists came heirs of Hamilton who believed in a national approach to economic problems. Jackson also found himself up against more extremist states' rights advocates and those who simply disliked him and feared his unchecked power. From this loose coalition a new party started to take life with two congressional giants, Daniel Webster (1782–1852) and Henry Clay (1777–1852), as its most prominent leaders. In 1834, they took the name Whigs, recalling the pre-Revolution days when patriots adopted that name to contrast themselves with Tories loyal to the British Crown. For this new generation of Whigs, the tyrant was not a foreign monarch but "King Andrew," as Jackson was called by friend and foe alike.

Jackson continued to dominate American politics in some respects after leaving the White House. For the next eight years, he wrote frequent letters on policy matters and became a forceful advocate of the annexation of Texas. Suffering from tuberculosis, dropsy, and chronic diarrhea, Jackson spent his last years in great discomfort, eased by opiates. He died at the Hermitage and is buried in the gardens there, beside his wife, with one of his former slaves, Alfred Jackson, nearby. Alfred Jackson had remained at the Hermitage, working there after it became a museum, until his death in 1901.

Jackson Administration Milestones[23]

1829

March 4	Andrew Jackson is sworn in as the seventh president.
August 25	Mexico rejects Jackson's offer to buy Texas.

1830

April 13	Vice President John C. Calhoun suggests that his state of South Carolina annul the federally imposed protective tariff. Jackson threatens to deploy federal troops to occupy the state in the event of nullification.
May 26	Congress passes the Indian Removal Act, sanctioning the forcible relocation of Creek, Chickasaw, Cherokee, Choctaw, and Seminole tribes to land allotments west of the Mississippi River.

1831

January 1	In Boston, William Lloyd Garrison begins publication of the abolitionist journal the *Liberator*.
April	Jackson reshuffles his cabinet following the divisive "Petticoat Affair."

1832

July 10	Jackson vetoes a bill that would have extended the charter of the Second Bank of the United States.

December 5	Jackson is reelected, with 219 electoral votes to Henry Clay's 49. The election marks the first entrance of a third party onto the national scene, with William Wirt running on the Anti-Masonic ticket. (The Anti-Masonic Party will merge with the Whigs four years later.)
December 10	Jackson issues a Proclamation that forbids states and municipalities from nullifying federal laws and warns that no state can secede.
December 12	Vice President Calhoun resigns and takes a Senate seat from South Carolina instead.

1833

March 1	Jackson pushes through the Force Bill, authorizing the army to enforce all federal laws. It is a threat aimed directly at Calhoun in South Carolina.

1834

March 28	Viewing his reelection as a mandate to continue his war against the Second Bank of the United States, Jackson orders the Treasury Department to withdraw federal deposits from the Bank of the United States and place them in state banks.
November 24	In South Carolina, a state convention adopts the Ordinance of Nullification, a decree that says a state does not have to respect congressional acts involving tariffs or any duties on imported foreign commodities.

1835

December 28	A group of U.S. soldiers is ambushed and wiped out in Florida; the "Dade Massacre" sets off the Second Seminole War.

1836

December 7	Handpicked by Jackson to be his successor, Martin Van Buren wins the presidential election, running against three Whigs. The Whig Party hoped to split

the popular vote so that the House of Representatives would decide the election's outcome. Van Buren, however, emerged with more votes than all his opponents combined. Also for the first time, the vice presidential election is decided in the Senate and Richard Johnson is elected.

1837

March 3   Jackson recognizes the independence of the Lone Star Republic of Texas but does not address the question of annexing Texas into the Union.

MUST READS

H. W. Brands, *Andrew Jackson: His Life and Times*; Andrew Burstein, *The Passions of Andrew Jackson*; Jon Meacham, *American Lion: Andrew Jackson in the White House*; Sean Michael O'Brien, *In Bitterness and in Tears: Andrew Jackson's Destruction of the Creeks and Seminoles*; David S. Reynolds, *Waking Giant: America in the Age of Jackson*; Arthur M. Schlesinger, Jr., *The Age of Jackson*.

ONLINE RESOURCES

The Hermitage (Jackson home)
http://www.thehermitage.com/
The Jackson Cottage in Ireland (ancestral home)
http://www.carrickfergus.org/tourism/museum/andrew-jackson
-cottage/
Inaugural Addresses, Avalon Project, Yale Law School
1829: http://avalon.law.yale.edu/19th_century/jackson1.asp
1833: http://avalon.law.yale.edu/19th_century/jackson2.asp
Library of Congress Resource Guide
http://www.loc.gov/rr/program/bib/presidents/jackson/related.html
Miller Center of Public Affairs, University of Virginia
http://millercenter.org/president/jackson

8

The Little Magician
Martin Van Buren

★ ★ ★

March 4, 1837–March 4, 1841

Milestones in Martin Van Buren's Life

December 5, 1782	Born in Kinderhook, New York
1803	Admitted to the New York bar
1812–1820	Member of New York State Senate
1816–1819	Attorney general of New York
1821–1828	U.S. senator from New York
January 1– March 12, 1829	Governor of New York (resigned to become secretary of state)
1829–1831	Secretary of state under Andrew Jackson
1833–1837	Vice president under Andrew Jackson
1837–1841	Eighth president
July 24, 1862	Died in Kinderhook, New York, aged seventy-nine

---

PRESIDENTIAL VOICES

The last, perhaps the greatest, of the prominent sources of discord and disaster supposed to lurk in our political condition was the institution of domestic slavery. Our forefathers were deeply impressed with the delicacy of this subject, and they treated it with a forbearance so evidently wise that in spite of every sinister foreboding it never until the present period disturbed the tranquility of our common country.

. . . I must go into the Presidential chair the inflexible and uncompromis-

ing opponent of every attempt on the part of Congress to abolish slavery in the District of Columbia against the wishes of the slaveholding States, and also with a determination equally decided to resist the slightest interference with it in the States where it exists.

—MARTIN VAN BUREN
Inaugural Address, March 4, 1837[1]

M artin Van Buren may be best known for his birthplace of Old Kinderhook, New York, because the town's initials, OK, became part of the political language and the source of the word "okay." But Van Buren's legacy deserves more than a mere nod from America's idiomatic dictionary. Although a single-term president, he was a master politician whose influence in shaping the nineteenth-century Democratic Party makes him a far more significant player. A loyal Jackson man, Van Buren's ability to bring together the planter tradition of Jefferson's time with the emerging urban vote created a powerful national political force.

Whether that alliance of the urban machine Democrats with the slaveholding South was "OK" is an entirely different question.

Fast Facts

RELIGION: Dutch Reformed
CAREER BEFORE POLITICS: Attorney
POLITICAL PARTY: Democratic
Free Soil (1848–1854)
SPOUSE: Van Buren married Hannah Hoes (1783–1819), apparently a childhood sweetheart and distant cousin. Hannah died of tuberculosis and he never remarried, one of the few presidents unmarried while in office. He did not mention his wife in some eight hundred pages of autobiography.

CHILDREN: Abraham, John, Martin, and Smith. The eldest, Abraham, became a career military officer, taking a leave to serve as his father's secretary in the White House, where he met and later married Angelica Singleton, cousin of Dolley Madison, who still lived near the White House and remained a central character in Washington society. Angelica served as White House hostess during Van Buren's term.

The second son, John, went into politics and was an organizer of the Free Soil Party, which promoted the rights of the free, white workingman.

* Van Buren was the first president who was born an American citizen. His predecessors were all British citizens at birth, having been born before 1776.
* He was also the first president who was not of British descent. Growing up in a Dutch-speaking household, Van Buren was also the only president who spoke English as a second language.
* Van Buren was the first of four presidents born in New York. (The others are Millard Fillmore, Theodore Roosevelt, and Franklin D. Roosevelt.)
* As a young attorney in New York City, Van Buren became a protégé of power broker Aaron Burr, then planning his 1804 run for governor of New York. Because of a passing resemblance and because of their political and professional connections, there was gossip that Burr was Van Buren's father. The rumor was given fresh life in Gore Vidal's fictional *Burr* (1976), but most biographers and historians totally dismiss it.
* Elected governor of New York in November 1828, Van Buren took office on January 1, 1829, but resigned on March 12, 1829, to become Andrew Jackson's secretary of state, making him the shortest tenured governor in New York history.
* Van Buren and President Jackson rode to Van Buren's inauguration together in a carriage, the first time the president-elect and the outgoing president rode together.
* Van Buren was the first president sworn in by Chief Justice Roger B. Taney.

* After the 1835 assassination attempt on Andrew Jackson, Van Buren began to carry two pistols with him to the Senate.

* When President George H. W. Bush was elected forty-first president in 1988, he was presented with a portrait of Van Buren, since Bush became the first vice president since Van Buren to be elected in his own right. And like Van Buren, the senior Bush was a one-term president.

PRESIDENTIAL VOICES

I believe him not only deserving of my *confidence but the confidence of the Nation. . . . He is not only well qualified, but desires to fill the highest office in the gift of the people, who in him, will find a friend and safe repository of their rights and liberty.*

—PRESIDENT ANDREW JACKSON, 1829

Van Buren is as opposite to General Jackson as dung is to a diamond.

—REPRESENTATIVE DAVY CROCKETT, 1832

The dread modern epithet "Career politician" might have been a term coined for Van Buren.

A founding member of what was called the "Albany Regency," a political machine he created in the region surrounding New York's capital, Van Buren dominated New York politics in his time, just as Aaron Burr had earlier. For his role in helping secure Jackson's 1828 victory by bringing New York's electors to the Democratic fold, Van Buren was rewarded with a cabinet post and then the vice presidency, easing his path to the White House in 1837.

A short, portly man who liked dandified dress and muttonchop whiskers, Van Buren was born into modest circumstances, the son of a tavern keeper in the upstate New York town of Kinderhook, an old

Dutch settlement near Albany. He studied law first in Troy, New York, where he reportedly summed up a case at age fifteen, and then in New York City, under the tutelage of William Van Ness, an Aaron Burr lieutenant. In 1803, he was admitted to the bar and opened a successful law practice. But by age twenty-nine, Van Buren had turned his full attention to politics, winning a seat in the New York Senate.

Rising through a succession of state posts and a term as New York's senator (1821–1828), he had come to dominate New York politics by 1828, earning the nickname the "Magician" or "Sly Fox." Devoted to Jeffersonian Democratic principles, Van Buren was a sharp, experienced politician and adept tactician who had begun to master the new politics of group voting, or "machine politics," first engineered by Aaron Burr. He delivered New York's electoral votes to Andrew Jackson and the Democrats in the rough-and-tumble race of 1828 and was the chief dispenser of campaign funds. He was rewarded by being named Jackson's secretary of state and became one of the president's closest allies, a member of the so-called "Kitchen Cabinet" of Jackson advisers and a chief ally in the "Petticoat Affair."

As Jackson's differences with his first vice president, Calhoun, grew larger, and Calhoun departed for the Senate, Jackson added the wily New Yorker to his 1832 ticket as his second vice president.

Running on Jackson's coattails in 1836—political cartoons showed Jackson carrying the little New Yorker into the White House on his back—Van Buren was elected president when the Whig opposition, not yet a cohesive national party, fielded three regional candidates, hoping to split the electorate, deny Van Buren sufficient electoral votes, and throw the decision to the House once more. But that stratagem failed and Van Buren won a narrow victory, though he clearly lacked Jackson's "people's president" touch.

How did a federal policy called "removal" turn into a "Trail of Tears"?

The harsh treatment of America's native nations had been a constant since Europeans arrived in North America. But under Andrew Jackson, the nation's popular anti-Indian sentiment and the sporadic conflicts with various Native American nations were transformed into official federal policy. Although some of this had been first encouraged by

Thomas Jefferson and practiced by the Monroe administration, Van Buren continued the more aggressive policy of Jackson in taking Native American lands.

The tidy word given this policy was "removal," suggesting a sanitary resolution of a messy problem. But some of the native people who were actually removed would later call the policy by a different name. In the language of the Cherokee nation, the trek west was called *Nunna dual Isunyi*—the "Trail Where We Cried," better known as the Trail of Tears.[2]

Jackson's policy dictated the wholesale forced migration of native people from their homelands to unsettled lands across the Mississippi. He professed to have a humane motive, according to some historians. Better to move the natives, Jackson argued, than to slaughter them, which was already happening and had been since the arrival of Europeans in America. As historian Sean Wilentz pointed out, "Jackson was a benevolent if realistic paternalist who believed that the Indians would be far better protected under federal jurisdiction than under state law."[3]

In 1831, for instance, Sac and Fox people, forcibly removed from lands near Rock River in Illinois, initially balked at leaving their ancestral lands and returned across the Mississippi under Black Hawk. A group of Black Hawk's warriors killed twelve militiamen in May 1832, starting the Black Hawk War. The fighting ended when hundreds of Sac, including women and children, were killed at the Battle of Bad Axe in August 1832, many drowning as they tried to escape across the Mississippi. (Abraham Lincoln served very briefly in the Black Hawk War.)

Like others that had been forced out, the Cherokee were among the "civilized" tribes who attempted to coexist with white, Euro-American culture. The Cherokee had built roads, schools, and churches, had a system of representational government, and were becoming farmers and cattle ranchers. The Cherokee even attempted to fight removal legally by challenging the removal laws in the Supreme Court and by establishing an independent Cherokee nation. Some of the Cherokee adopted another white American practice: They owned more than two thousand black slaves.

But they were fighting the tide of history. Continuing Jackson's Indian policies, in 1838, Martin Van Buren forced more than seventeen thousand Cherokee out of Georgia. The policy was Jackson's, but Van Buren was now president. Rounded up at bayonet point, about four thousand Cherokee people died along the route, which took them through Tennessee and Kentucky, across the Ohio and Missouri Rivers, and into what would later become Oklahoma. It was this removal that specifically became known as the Trail of Tears. But it is an appropriate name for this entire episode in U.S.-Indian relations.

Van Buren also maintained pressure on the native nations by continuing the Seminole War, one of the longest and most costly in American history, against Chief Osceola in Florida. On Christmas Day in 1837, General Zachary Taylor, a future president, defeated a Seminole force in Okeechobee Swamp, in one of the few pitched battles of what was a long guerilla war. But it was only when Chief Osceola was captured, after being tricked by a flag of truce, that Seminole resistance was broken. Even then, the costly war in Florida continued throughout Van Buren's years and well beyond. (Although it is often said that no wartime president has ever been turned out of office, Van Buren may be an exception to the rule. However, the Seminole conflict was never officially declared a war, the only extenuating circumstance in this case. Harry Truman and Lyndon B. Johnson also both chose not to test this old saw, by deciding not to run while fighting unpopular wars.)

How does Congress gag itself?

As a defender of slavery and the rights of slaveholders, Martin Van Buren—whose father owned six slaves but who did not own slaves himself—was the ideal Northerner to every states' rights Democrat. Believing he could "moderate the prejudices between free and slaveholding states," he promised when he took the oath of office that he planned to follow in the "footsteps of his illustrious predecessor"[4] and continue Jackson's pro-slavery policies. But in Van Buren's time, public attitudes and the makeup of Congress were shifting. Van Buren did not use slaves in the White House; his daughter-in-law Angelica Van Buren apparently did, but they were not considered part of the White House staff.

With a growing abolitionist movement that was becoming more vocal and aggressive, matched by increasingly violent responses to those abolitionists, the House of Representatives thought it could tamp down the slavery controversy by not talking about it. While freedom of speech is pretty much a given—a fundamental right enshrined in the First Amendment—it wasn't so when it came to Congress and slavery in Van Buren's time. In 1836, the first so-called "gag rule" had been introduced in the House of Representatives to "table," or postpone, any discussion of petitions relating to slavery, especially banning it in Washington, D.C.

But when the Congress reconvened in 1837, after Van Buren's election, the "gag rule" had lapsed and had to be reintroduced in the new Congress. Former President John Quincy Adams took advantage of this temporary opening to present antislavery petitions to the House. In 1837 alone, abolitionists sent more than 130,000 petitions to Congress requesting the abolition of slavery in Washington, D.C.

But by the end of December 1837, Congress had reinstituted an even stricter "gag rule," which was then renewed every year until 1844, despite the protests of Adams and other Northern representatives, including Joshua Giddings of Ohio, the first abolitionist elected to Congress.[5]

The second issue underscoring the deepening rifts over slavery was the capture of the Spanish slave ship *Amistad* by the U.S. Navy. In July 1839, while sailing between Cuban ports, a group of kidnapped Africans held aboard the *Amistad* had rebelled and taken over the ship, which then was sailed into American waters and captured by the navy. Van Buren supported the Spanish demand that the ship and its cargo of Africans be returned—Spain claimed they were legal slaves born in Cuba. With Representative John Quincy Adams arguing for the Africans, the Supreme Court heard the case in 1840, and the *Amistad* controversy exploded into a proxy for the abolitionist cause. In a major victory for the antislavery forces, in 1841 the Supreme Court rejected the Van Buren administration and Spanish arguments and ruled that the Africans had been illegally transported and held as slaves. They were freed and the survivors returned to Africa. The case only deepened the growing American political rift over slavery's future.

Final Judgment: Grade C

Van Buren earns the "Gentleman's C" because he stands as the perfect example of how a very good politician does not necessarily make a good president. The backroom deals that win elections don't always win popularity. Nor do they add up to effective leadership or legislation.

He also may be the first president to exemplify Bill Clinton's famous campaign dictum: "It's the economy, stupid."

A severe economic depression—the Panic of 1837—lasted for years and ruined Van Buren's chance for a second term. Staunch opposition in Congress also blocked his efforts to stimulate the economy—a familiar theme in modern American politics.

But Van Buren was also undone by a new Whig strategy that turned the tables on Andrew Jackson's earlier campaign against John Quincy Adams, which had cast Adams as a remote aristocrat.

Called "Martin Van Ruin," Van Buren was painted as an effete snob, a haughty and somewhat effeminate aristocrat. The famous Davy Crockett, then a congressman from Tennessee, said of Van Buren, "He is what the English call a dandy. When he enters the Senate-chamber in the morning, he struts and swaggers like a crow in the gutter. He is laced up in corsets, such as women in town wear, and if possible, tighter than the rest of them. It would be difficult to say, from his personal appearance, whether he was a man or woman."[6]

The personal attacks amounted to a form of "class warfare," and it worked. Cursed with a president's worst enemy, a bad economy, Martin Van Buren lost the election of 1840 to the Whig candidate, sixty-eight-year-old William Henry Harrison, whose military career was highlighted by his narrow victory over the Shawnee at Tippecanoe in 1811 and victory at the Battle of Thames in 1812. Hailed as the "hero of Tippecanoe," in a campaign extolling his virtues as a simple man of the people—a pioneer born in a log cabin, in the mold of Andrew Jackson—Harrison was in fact born on a Virginia plantation, the son of a wealthy planter and signer of the Declaration of Independence.

William Henry Harrison secured a large electoral victory, although the popular margin was slimmer.

Van Buren attempted to gain the Democratic nomination again in

1844, but failed when he opposed the annexation of Texas favored by Andrew Jackson. Despite his earlier support for slavery, Van Buren became the first former president to run as a third-party candidate in 1848 when he joined the antislavery Free Soil Party. Avoiding the moral issue of abolition, its members presented the party as a proponent of free white laborers, opposed to slavery as inefficient and undemocratic. William Lloyd Garrison, the abolitionist, dismissed the party as "white manism." But the emphasis on the white workingman opening up free territory and not on emancipation was the position that formed the core of what would later become the Republican Party.

Van Buren Administration Milestones[7]

1837

March 4	Martin Van Buren is sworn in as the eighth president.
May 10	The Panic of 1837 begins in New York, as banks can no longer redeem currency notes for gold and silver. A depression in England causes the price of cotton to drop, and the British cut off loans to the United States. More than nine hundred state banks fail and there are food riots in some cities. This severe downturn lasts seven years.
August 5	Van Buren announces his opposition to the annexation of Texas, a politically unpopular move.
November 7	Abolitionist publisher Elijah Lovejoy is killed by a mob in Illinois.

1838

May 17	In Philadelphia, a mob burns Pennsylvania Hall to the ground when it hosts an antislavery meeting.
October–November	Van Buren loses control of both houses of Congress.
December 3	Joshua Giddings becomes the first professed abolitionist elected to Congress. The Underground Railroad is first organized.

1839

August 26   The USS *Washington* seizes the *Amistad*, a Spanish slave ship sailing between Cuban ports. The Van Buren administration agrees to return the *Amistad* and its "cargo" to Havana.

December 4   The Whigs nominate William Henry Harrison for president and John Tyler for vice president.

1840

September 19   The *Amistad* hearings begin in a Hartford, Connecticut, courtroom. The Supreme Court rewards compensation for the ship only. The slaves will be returned to Africa in January 1842.

November   Whig William Henry Harrison soundly defeats Van Buren in the largest turnout of any election to that point.

MUST READS

Ted Widmer, *Martin Van Buren: The 8th President, 1837–1841*; Sean Wilentz, *The Rise of American Democracy*.

ONLINE RESOURCES

Inaugural Address, American Presidency Project, University of California, Santa Barbara

http://www.presidency.ucsb.edu/ws/index.php?pid=25812#axzz1bSfThOFK

Van Buren National Historic Site, National Park Service

http://www.nps.gov/mava/

Library of Congress Resource Guide

http://www.loc.gov/rr/program/bib/presidents/vanburen/memory.html

Miller Center of Public Affairs, University of Virginia

http://millercenter.org/president/vanburen

9

Old Tippecanoe

William Henry Harrison

★ ★ ★

March 4, 1841–April 4, 1841

Milestones in William Henry Harrison's Life

February 9, 1773	Born in Charles City County, Virginia
1791–1798	Served in U.S. Army, rising to rank of captain
1799–1800	Delegate to Congress from Northwest Territory
1800–1812	Governor of Indiana Territory
November 7, 1811	Defeated Shawnee at Battle of Tippecanoe
1812–1814	General in War of 1812
1817–1819	U.S. representative from Ohio
1819–1825	Member of Ohio State Senate
1825–1828	U.S. senator from Ohio
1828–1829	U.S. minister to Colombia
1841	Ninth president
April 4, 1841	Died in the White House, aged sixty-eight

PRESIDENTIAL VOICES

[It] is the part of wisdom for a republic to limit the service of that officer at least to whom she has intrusted [sic] the management of her foreign relations, the execution of her laws, and the command of her armies and navies to a period so short as to prevent his forgetting that he is the accountable agent, not the principal; the servant, not the master. Until an amendment of the Constitution can be effected public opinion may secure the desired object. I give my

aid to it by renewing the pledge heretofore given that under no circumstances
will I consent to serve a second term.
       WILLIAM HENRY HARRISON
      Inaugural Address, March 4, 1841

H arrison kept his promise. He was elected. He gave a very long inaugural address in which he pledged not to serve a second term. He died a month later.

Like Andrew Jackson, Harrison was largely elected on the strength of his heroics as a military leader and Indian fighter. As the governor of Indiana territory, he was given by Thomas Jefferson the power to negotiate for native lands and earned the nickname "Jefferson's Hammer" for his dealings with native nations, including the Sauk and Shawnee. He had been a tough bargainer who acquired native lands for pennies an acre, but his policies were partly responsible for driving these native nations to join the British in 1812. He had also tried to undo the prohibition against slavery in Indiana under the Northwest Ordinance. But he was best known as the "Tippecanoe" of the famed campaign slogan "Tippecanoe and Tyler too," which celebrated Harrison's victory over the Shawnee on November 7, 1811, at the Battle of Tippecanoe.

His electoral victory, unlike his military glory, was short-lived. And Harrison is largely remembered today for the brevity of his presidency and being the first president to die in office. The other notable aspect of his election was the "log cabin" campaign—one of the earliest attempts to "market" a presidential candidate. His Whig party depicted Harrison as a simple man who lived in a log cabin and drank hard cider—an attempt to make him appear more like Andrew Jackson, while casting President Van Buren as an "elitist." As part of that campaign, a Philadelphia distiller named E.C. Booz began selling whiskey in log cabin–shaped bottles called "Old Cabin Whiskey." And that is how liquor became "booze."[1]

Fast Facts

RELIGION: Episcopalian

MILITARY SERVICE: United States Army (Indian Wars, War of 1812)

CAREER BEFORE PRESIDENCY: Soldier, planter

POLITICAL PARTY: Whig

FIRST LADY: Anna Symmes Harrison (July 25, 1775–February 25, 1864)

CHILDREN: Nine of Harrison's children lived to maturity: Elizabeth; John Cleves Symmes; Lucy; William Henry; John Scott, the only man who was both son and father of a president—Benjamin Harrison; Benjamin; Mary; Carter Bassett; and Anna Tuthill. However, five of them died before he was inaugurated, so only four of his children lived to see their father reach the White House.

* Harrison was the last president born a British subject. He was the oldest president elected until Ronald Reagan in 1980.

* His father, Benjamin Harrison V (1726–1791), was a signer of the Declaration of Independence and is known as the "Signer" to distinguish him from his great-grandson.

* Harrison was the fifth of eight Virginia-born presidents.

* When he attended college in Philadelphia, Harrison boarded in the home of Declaration signer Robert Morris, who became his guardian after his father died.

* In Philadelphia, Harrison studied medicine under yet another Declaration signer, Benjamin Rush, but did not complete his medical studies and lacked funds for school after his father's death. He joined the army, instead, with the assistance of Virginia governor Henry "Light Horse Harry" Lee, father of Robert E. Lee.

* Harrison was the first president to arrive in Washington, D.C., by train for his inauguration.

* His inaugural address was the longest recorded in history (8,455 words), taking him nearly two hours to read on a cold, rainy day. On March 26, just weeks after the inaugural, he developed a cold, which soon turned into pneumonia and pleurisy. He was treated with opium, castor oil, leeches, and Virginia snakeweed—none of which helped and which may have worsened his illness.

* The first American president to die in office, Harrison also served the shortest term: thirty-one days, twelve hours, and thirty minutes.

* While his wife was officially first lady, she had been ill when he was inaugurated and was packing for the move to Washington when Harrison died. Mrs. Harrison never set foot in the White House. In June 1841, President Tyler signed a bill providing a $25,000 grant as a pension for the president's widow. (Pensions are not routinely granted to first ladies, although Congress has since provided a pension for a number of first ladies whose husbands also died in office.)[2]

* Harrison's grandson, Benjamin, became the twenty-third president.

What is the "Curse of Tippecanoe"?

Back in 1931, the popular Ripley's *Believe It or Not!* noted a curiosity of presidential history. Since Harrison, every president elected in a year that ended in zero (every twenty years) had died in office: Lincoln, 1860; Garfield, 1880; McKinley, 1900; and Warren G. Harding, 1920. Since Harrison was the first in this line, a popular legend sprang up claiming that Harrison was cursed by the chief Tecumseh, or his brother Tenskwatawa, also known as the "Prophet," after Harrison defeated Tenskwatawa and the Shawnee at the Battle of Tippecanoe in 1811 (see Chapter 4, "James Madison").

Tecumseh later allied his confederacy with the British as the War of 1812 began and Harrison defeated the Shawnee-British troops in the 1812 Battle of Thames River near what is now Toronto. Tecumseh, a great threat to America's continued settlement of the West, was killed in that battle, after which Harrison emerged as a war hero second only to Andrew Jackson.

Whether it was "Tecumseh's Curse" or the "Curse of Tippecanoe," the string continued after being noted in the 1931 Ripley's book, with Franklin D. Roosevelt in 1940 and John F. Kennedy in 1960. It was broken in 1980 with the election of Ronald Reagan. George W. Bush, elected in 2000, also beat the "Curse."

Final Judgment: I (for Incomplete)

Due to his abbreviated term, Harrison went unranked in most of the major historical surveys.

MUST READS

Colin G. Calloway, *The Shawnees and the War for America*; Robert M. Owens, *Mr. Jefferson's Hammer: William Henry Harrison and the Origins of American Indian Policy*; John Sugden, *Tecumseh: A Life*.

ONLINE RESOURCES

Inaugural Address, Avalon Project, Yale Law School
http://avalon.law.yale.edu/19th_century/harrison.asp
Berkeley Plantation Birthplace
http://www.berkeleyplantation.com/index.html
Grouseland Home, Vincennes, Indiana
http://www.grouselandfoundation.org/Grouseland/The_Mansion
.html
Library of Congress Resource Guide
http://www.loc.gov/rr/program/bib/presidents/wharrison/external
.html
Miller Center of Public Affairs, University of Virginia
http://millercenter.org/index.php/academic/americanpresident
/harrison

10

His Accidency

John Tyler

★ ★ ★

April 6, 1841–March 4, 1845

Milestones in John Tyler's Life

March 29, 1790	Born in Charles City County, Virginia
1809	Admitted to the Virginia bar
1811–1816	Member of Virginia legislature
1816–1821	U.S. representative from Virginia
1823–1825	Member of Virginia legislature
1825–1827	Governor of Virginia
1827–1836	U.S. senator from Virginia
1838–1840	Member of Virginia legislature
1841	Vice president under Harrison
1841–1845	Tenth president
1861	President of Peace Conference in Washington, D.C.
1862	Member of Congress of the Confederate States
January 18, 1862	Died in Richmond, Virginia, aged seventy-one

PRESIDENTIAL VOICES

The United States can not but take a deep interest in whatever relates to this young but growing Republic [Texas]. Settled principally by emigrants from the United States, we have the happiness to know that the great principles of civil liberty are there destined to flourish under wise institutions and wholesome laws, and that through its example another evidence is to be afforded of the capacity of popular institutions to advance the prosperity, happiness, and permanent glory of the human race. The great truth that government was made for the people and not the people for government has already been established in the practice and by the example of these United States, and we can do no other than contemplate its further exemplification by a sister republic with the deepest interest.

JOHN TYLER
First Message to Congress
December 7, 1841[1]

Sworn in at Brown's Hotel on Sixth Street and Pennsylvania Avenue, two days after President William Henry Harrison died, John Tyler would be known immediately as the "Acting President." Detractors called him "His Accidency." From the outset, Tyler had to struggle for legitimacy in rough-and-tumble political times.

He took office with no precedent and ambiguous constitutional authority. There were many who believed he could not act with presidential authority and should step aside following a special election for president. But Tyler moved quickly and decisively to establish his legitimacy—symbolically returning any mail addressed to him as "Acting President." And for establishing that precedent alone, he is usually lauded. His actual presidency is considerably less distinguished.

PRESIDENTIAL VOICES

If the tide of defamation and abuse shall turn, and my administration come to be praised, future Vice-Presidents who may succeed to the Presidency may feel some slight encouragement to pursue an independent course.
—JOHN TYLER, 1848[2]

Fast Facts

RELIGION: Episcopal

EDUCATION: College of William and Mary

MILITARY SERVICE: Organized a militia unit in Virginia to defend Richmond during the War of 1812, but dissolved the unit without seeing action

CAREER BEFORE POLITICS: Attorney

POLITICAL PARTY: Democratic (1825–1834)

Whig (1834–1842)

FIRST LADIES: Letitia Christian Tyler (November 12, 1790–September 10, 1842). Since suffering a stroke in 1839, Letitia remained upstairs at the White House, except to attend the wedding of her daughter Elizabeth in January 1842. When she suffered another stroke later that year and died on September 10, she became the first first lady to die in the White House and, at age fifty-one, the youngest first lady to die.

Julia Gardiner Tyler (May 4, 1820–July 10, 1889)

CHILDREN: With his first wife, Tyler had nine children, seven of whom lived to maturity: Mary; Robert; John Tyler III; Letitia; Elizabeth, who was married in a White House wedding in 1842; Alice; and Tazewell.

Second wife Julia Gardiner Tyler gave birth to seven more Tyler children: David, John, Julia, Lachlan, Lyon, Robert, and Pearl.

* Tyler had more children than any other president. In 2012, many people may have been surprised by news reports that two of Tyler's grandchildren were still alive, in their eighties.
* Tyler was the first president born after the adoption of the U.S. Constitution and the sixth of eight Virginia-born presidents.
* He was first to succeed to the office on the death of his predecessor.
* Julia Gardiner, thirty years younger than Tyler, was the daughter of Senator David Gardiner of New York, a wealthy landowner. When a naval gun exploded on the new steam frigate *Princeton* on February 28, 1844, Julia's father was killed along with Secretary of State Abel B. Upshur, Secretary of the Navy Thomas W. Gilmer, and

Tyler's black valet, Armistead. Unharmed, Tyler carried the twenty-four-year-old Julia off the gunship himself. [3] They were married in a discreet New York ceremony on June 26, 1844. On his sixty-second birthday, she wrote to him, "Wit I prefer to youth."[4]

* Tyler was the first of three sitting presidents to marry while in office (the others were Grover Cleveland and Woodrow Wilson).

* The first president to have a veto overridden by Congress, Tyler was contested on a rather obscure bill—related to revenue ships—in 1845.

* Tyler was the only former president elected to office in the Confederacy (he died before he took the office).

* For having joined the Confederacy, Tyler is the only president who was not officially mourned in Washington after his death, in 1862.

Born into the landed gentry of Virginia's aristocracy, John Tyler was the son of a governor of Virginia—a slaveholder who was also Thomas Jefferson's friend and roommate at the College of William and Mary. Tyler was a promising student, studying law with his father after his graduation in 1807 and later in the Richmond office of Edmund Randolph, the first U.S. attorney general.

Tall and courtly, the perfect picture of a Southern "gentleman" planter, Tyler married Letitia Christian, the daughter of another wealthy planter family, on his twenty-third birthday in 1813. The considerable fortune Letitia inherited freed Tyler to focus on his political career.

Tyler moved through a succession of political posts, including three terms in the House, where he opposed the Missouri Compromise of 1820. As Virginia's governor from 1825 to 1827, he delivered Thomas Jefferson's funeral oration in 1826 and was chosen senator from Virginia in 1827, joining the forces loyal to Andrew Jackson in the campaigns of 1828 and 1832.

During the nullification controversy that began in 1832 over South Carolina's threat to declare a federal tariff unconstitutional and not obey it, Tyler turned against Jackson. He allied himself with the states' rights position and secessionist threats of South Carolina's John Calhoun (formerly Jackson's vice president, who had resigned and moved to the Senate) and shifted his allegiance to the newly formed Whigs, led by Henry Clay, Jackson's chief antagonist. When Virginia ordered its senators to expunge the censure of President Jackson, which Tyler had favored, he refused and resigned his Senate seat.

In 1840, after backing Henry Clay's failed attempt at another Whig presidential nomination, Tyler was added to William Henry Harrison's ticket to gain Southern support, and their campaign gave birth to the memorable slogan, "Tippecanoe and Tyler too."

Never part of Harrison's inner circle, Tyler might have simply become one more obscure American vice president. When he received word of Harrison's death on April 5, he returned to Washington and took the oath of office in his hotel on April 6. (Vice presidents historically lived in their own homes; it was not until 1974 that the mansion at the U.S. Naval Observatory became the official residence of the vice president.)

PRESIDENTIAL VOICES

I am very glad to have in my Cabinet such able statesmen as you. But I can never consent to being dictated to as to what I shall or shall not do. I am the President. . . . When you think otherwise, your resignations will be accepted.

JOHN TYLER
to his first cabinet meeting

What was John Tyler's greatest contribution as president?

Given the ambiguity of the Constitution on the matter of succession, the most important thing Tyler did may have been to establish the precedent that he *was* the president after Harrison's death. On June 1, when both houses of Congress passed resolutions declaring that Tyler was the tenth president, his assumption of the title and powers of the presidency established the precedent followed by every vice president who succeeded to the presidency after him. The rules of succession were eventually codified under the Twenty-fifth Amendment in 1967. (See Appendix II.)

Tyler later asserted this authority when he vetoed a bank bill drafted with his cabinet's approval. The entire cabinet resigned, except for Daniel Webster, secretary of state. In the face of Tyler's defiance, congressional Whigs called for his resignation, to be followed by a special election. But the steely Tyler did not oblige. Enraged by Tyler's actions, Henry Clay, still the most powerful Whig politician in Washington, attempted to have him impeached and even moved to change the Constitution to allow a simple majority to override a presidential veto, but the Whigs lacked the votes to pass such an amendment or to override Tyler. Staying on, Tyler vetoed ten bills in all, only one of which was overridden by Congress—an otherwise obscure bill relating to revenue cutters, which became the first congressional override of a veto in history.

In another show of independence, Tyler appointed a new cabinet of Democrats, including former vice president John C. Calhoun, the fiery advocate of states' rights, as secretary of state.

But his most important battle with Congress came over Texas, which Tyler proposed to annex. When the Senate rejected the Texas Annexation Treaty he offered, Tyler—now a lame-duck president after the election of his successor, Polk, in 1844—interpreted the election of pro-annexation Polk as a mandate for the policy and circumvented the constitutional requirements for treaty ratification. Between the election and Polk's inauguration, he used a joint resolution of Congress, requiring only a simple majority instead of the usual two-thirds majority needed for a treaty ratification. And with this sly maneuvering, Tyler accomplished his most significant presidential act—the annexation of Texas.

PRESIDENTIAL VOICES

Tyler is a political sectarian, of the slave-driving, Virginia, Jeffersonian school principled against all improvement, with all the interests and passions and vices of slavery rooted in his moral and political constitution—with talents not above mediocrity.

—John Quincy Adams, 1841

Final Judgment: Grade C

Drummed out of the Whig Party, Tyler was denied the Democratic nomination as well in 1844. He contemplated a third-party run, but was dissuaded when Andrew Jackson supported fellow Democrat James K. Polk, a pro-annexation slaveholder, over former President Martin Van Buren, an opponent of annexation. Dropping out of the race, Tyler supported Polk.

Tyler returned to his Virginia plantation, renamed "Sherwood Forest" because he believed his party had "outlawed" him, like the legendary Robin Hood. In 1852, he rejoined the Whigs, and as the nation moved toward Civil War in 1861, Tyler attempted to use his influence at the Virginia Peace Convention, which was meant to broker a compromise between North and South in February 1861.

The convention's proposal for a constitutional amendment that extended the old Missouri Compromise lines all the way to the Pacific Coast failed to meet Republican demands to halt the expansion of slavery and went nowhere. After President-elect Lincoln met with him, and after Congress rejected the convention's proposals, Tyler joined other prominent Virginians who called for secession. Elected to the newly formed Confederate House of Representatives in November 1861, Tyler died, most likely of a stroke, in a Richmond hotel room on January 18, 1862, before taking his seat.

He has consistently ranked at the bottom of most historical assessments, but his C grade as president is due in part to his significance in securing the legitimacy of presidential succession.

Tyler Administration Milestones[5]

1841

March 9   Ruling in the *Amistad* case, the Supreme Court frees fifty-three Africans who took control of the slave ship and allows them to return to Africa.

April 4   President William Henry Harrison dies; Vice President John Tyler assumes the presidency.

September 11   Tyler's entire cabinet, with the exception of Secretary of State Daniel Webster, resigns after Tyler vetoes a second bill for the establishment of a National Bank of the United States.

November 7   A group of slaves who mutiny aboard the *Creole* while being legally transported from Virginia to New Orleans, sail to Nassau, where they are freed by British authorities. Like the *Amistad* case, the *Creole* case inflames the slavery debate.

1842

May   Beginning a career that will make him famous as the "Pathfinder" and open the West to settlement, Colonel John C. Frémont leads an expedition to explore and map the Rocky Mountains.

1843

May   One thousand people leave from Independence, Missouri, to settle in Oregon Territory. This marks the beginnings of the large westward migration.

July 12   Mormon leader Joseph Smith announces a divine prophecy sanctioning polygamy.

August 14   The Second Seminole War ends after years of costly fighting. The Seminoles have been reduced to a few hundred in number.

August 23   Mexican President Santa Anna warns that annexing Texas will be considered a declaration of war.

1844

May 24	The first telegraph line in the United States is completed between Washington, D.C., and Baltimore.
June 8	The Texas Annexation Treaty fails to gain the required two-thirds majority in the Senate.
June 27	Mormon leader Joseph Smith and his brother Hiram Smith are murdered by a mob in Carthage, Illinois.
December 3	The House rescinds the gag rule of 1836 that prohibited discussion of antislavery petitions.
December 4	James K. Polk is elected as the eleventh president of the United States on promises to "re-annex" Texas and "re-occupy" Oregon.

1845

February 28	Congress passes the joint resolution (which only requires a simple majority by both houses) submitted by Tyler to annex Texas, which will become a state in December 1845.
March 3	Florida admitted as the twenty-seventh state, a slave state.

MUST READS

Edward P. Crapol, *John Tyler: The Accidental President*; T. R. Fehrenbach, *Lone Star: A History of Texas and the Texans*; Gary May, *John Tyler.*

ONLINE RESOURCES

Library of Congress Resource Guide
   http://www.loc.gov/rr/program/bib/presidents/tyler/index.html
Miller Center of Public Affairs, University of Virginia
   http://millercenter.org/index.php/academic/americanpresident
   /tyler
Sherwood Forest/Tyler Home (National Historic Site)
   http://www.sherwoodforest.org/
Annexation of Texas, Avalon Project, Yale Law School
   http://avalon.law.yale.edu/19th_century/texan01.asp

11

Young Hickory
James K. Polk

★ ★ ★

March 4, 1845–March 4, 1849

Milestones in James K. Polk's Life

November 2, 1795	Born in Mecklenburg County, North Carolina
1820	Admitted to the North Carolina bar
1823–1825	Member of Tennessee state legislature
1825–1839	Representative from Tennessee
1835–1839	Speaker of the House of Representatives
1839–1841	Governor of Tennessee
1845–1849	Eleventh president
June 15, 1849	Died in Nashville, Tennessee, aged fifty-three

PRESIDENTIAL VOICES

The world has nothing to fear from military ambition in our Government. While the Chief Magistrate and the popular branch of Congress are elected for short terms by the suffrages of those millions who must in their own persons bear all the burdens and miseries of war, our Government can not be otherwise than pacific. Foreign powers should therefore look on the annexation of Texas to the United States not as the conquest of a nation seeking to extend her dominions by arms and violence, but as the peaceful acquisition of a territory once her own, by adding another member to our confederation,

with the consent of that member, thereby diminishing the chances of war and
opening to them new and ever-increasing markets for their products.
—JAMES K. POLK
Inaugural Address, March 4, 1845[1]

W hen Jimmy Carter, then a rather obscure governor from Georgia, began his campaign to become president in 1976, many Americans asked, "Jimmy Who?"

It was not a first. In the election of 1844, candidate Henry Clay's campaign literature asked, "Who is James K. Polk?"

Clay did not get off as easily. A popular Democratic pamphlet issued by Polk's campaign presented "Twenty-one Reasons Why Clay Should Not Be Elected"; Reason Two was "Clay spends his days at the gaming table and his nights in a brothel."[2]

That should help put to rest the notion of the "good old days" of high-minded American politics when there was no such thing as a negative campaign.

In a turning-point election, Americans found out exactly who Polk was. The young, relatively obscure protégé of Andrew Jackson defeated the far more famous Henry Clay, a giant of both houses of Congress. If résumé was all that mattered in elections, this should have been a slam dunk for the "Great Compromiser" Clay.

Recognized by many historians as the most effective president between Jackson and Lincoln, James Knox Polk led America as it grew by more than a million square miles—an area that now includes the states of Arizona, Utah, Nevada, California, Oregon, Idaho, Washington, much of New Mexico, and portions of Wyoming, Montana, and Colorado. More than any other president, Polk pursued "Manifest Destiny," a phrase attributed to journalist John L. O'Sullivan, expressing the conviction that the United States was divinely ordained to spread across North America. The acquisition of this vast territory would set the stage for a decisive next decade that would determine the fate of the Union.

Fast Facts

RELIGION: Presbyterian and Methodist
ASSOCIATIONS: Freemason
EDUCATION: University of North Carolina-Chapel Hill
MILITARY SERVICE: Captain in militia
CAREER BEFORE POLITICS: Attorney
POLITICAL PARTY: Democratic
FIRST LADY: Sarah Childress Polk (September 4, 1803–August 14, 1891)

* Forty-nine-years old when elected, Polk was the youngest president elected to that date.
* Polk is the only speaker of the House of Representatives to be elected president.
* His inauguration was the first to be reported by telegraph.
* Polk and his wife, Sarah, were childless. Closely involved in all of his campaigns, she was one of the first acknowledged "political wives." A strict Presbyterian, Sarah Polk limited dancing, drinking, card-playing, and other forms of entertainment at the White House. The Polks opened their home twice a week, shaking visitors' hands for hours.
* The first gaslights were installed in the White House in 1848. Someone forgot to tell the gas company, which shut its plant down nightly at nine, to keep the gas flowing to the president's house. During a reception, the White House went dark, except for a single chandelier that first lady Sarah Polk had insisted remain candle-lit.
* The White House also received its first central heating system under Polk. Plaster-lined ducts carried warm air from furnaces to the principal rooms and second floor. "By today's standards of heating the rooms were barely warmed," notes White House historian William Seale. "But in 1846 they must have seemed supremely comfortable." [3]

* In his will, Polk asked his wife to have their slaves emancipated upon her death. But slavery ended in America long before she died in 1891.

Born in North Carolina, the eldest of ten children, James K. Polk was the son of Samuel Polk, a prosperous farmer, surveyor, and land speculator who moved his family to Tennessee in 1806, when James was ten. Samuel Polk came to own thousands of acres and, as a staunch Jeffersonian Republican, soon became a supporter and friend of Tennessee's first citizen, Andrew Jackson.

In poor health for much of his childhood, young James suffered from gallstones. At the age of seventeen, in a grisly frontier procedure eased only by brandy, a doctor pushed forceps through an incision behind Polk's scrotum to remove the stones. That he survived this ghastly procedure is a small miracle and may explain why he had no children.[4]

Polk graduated with honors from the University of North Carolina in three years but later returned to Tennessee, studying law under Andrew Jackson's friend Felix Grundy. At age twenty-seven, Polk was supposedly told by Jackson to settle down and find a wife. When asked if he had anyone in mind, Old Hickory told him, "The one who will never give you trouble. Her wealth, family, education, health, and appearance are all superior. You know her well."

He meant Sarah Childress, seven years younger than Polk and the daughter of a family that Rachel and Andrew Jackson also knew well. For the ambitious young politician, Sarah Childress would become, as one Polk biographer put it, "the only person to hold more sway over him than Old Hickory."[5] She told Polk that she would accept his marriage offer only if he ran for the state legislature. He did, winning a seat in 1823, and they married on January 1, 1824. She remained a powerful influence in Polk's political career, offering advice at a time when women, including first ladies, were expected not to express any views on political matters, and were in fact not deemed capable of even having opinions.

With Jackson's estimable support, Polk continued his climb in Tennessee politics, earning the nickname "Napoleon of the Stump" for his slight stature. He won Jackson's old Tennessee House seat in 1825—and with it the title of "Young Hickory." Ten years later, he was the powerful speaker of the House during the last two years of Jackson's presidency and the first two of Van Buren's, a period in which the gag rule was instituted and the House was the scene of battles between John Quincy Adams and the Southern Democrats who despised him.

In 1839, Polk left the House and was elected governor of Tennessee. After two failed reelection bids for the state house, "Young Hickory" seemed to be finished in politics. But in 1844, the Democrats were deadlocked between former President Van Buren and Lewis Cass of Michigan. When Polk received the blessing of an aging Andrew Jackson, who still loomed over the political landscape as few ex-presidents ever have, he became a dark horse candidate and even President John Tyler, contemplating a third-party run, stepped aside. Word of Polk's nomination was flashed out of Baltimore on the telegraph—the first time Samuel Morse's invention had been officially used.

PRESIDENTIAL VOICES

Other nations have undertaken to intrude themselves into it, between us and the proper parties to the case, in a spirit of hostile interference against us, for the avowed object of thwarting our policy and hampering our power, limiting our greatness and checking the fulfillment of our manifest destiny to overspread the continent allotted by Providence for the free development of our yearly multiplying millions.

—JOHN L. O'SULLIVAN
"Annexation"
United States Magazine and Democratic Review
July-August 1845

Who elected James K. Polk?

With the enthusiastic backing of his mentor Andrew Jackson, Polk was a compromise candidate who had slipped by former President Van

Buren in a sharply divided Democratic Convention and was narrowly elected president in 1844 over Whig candidate Henry Clay. A swing of about two thousand of the nearly one-half million votes cast in New York State, which Polk barely carried, would have given the White House to Clay.

Although Polk lost his home state of Tennessee, the New York vote was considered crucial because a third-party candidate, James G. Birney of the antislavery Liberty Party, ran well there. A onetime Kentucky slaveholder who had become an outspoken abolitionist publisher, Birney siphoned off enough votes that he likely cost Henry Clay the election. Voting irregularities were also notable, as Mississippi in particular delivered Polk a sizable number of votes that would not be equaled for years.

It was a "Manifest Destiny" election, although that phrase was actually coined well after Polk's victory. But the question of American expansion dominated the contest, spotlighting the Texas issue on the southern border and, in the north, a dispute with England over the Oregon Territory, then jointly occupied by the two nations. Polk and the Democrats wanted an area much larger than present-day Oregon. That territory included a northern boundary for Oregon at 54°40', then the border with Russian Alaska. Although widely thought to be Polk's campaign slogan, the memorable phrase "Fifty-four-forty or fight" was not used in the election.[6] (It is attributed to Senator William Allen.) Neither Polk nor the British really wanted another war over the issue, and it was resolved diplomatically with secretary of state—and future president—James Buchanan negotiating terms with the British. But far more significant was the annexation of Texas (which Clay had opposed) or, in Polk's words, the "reannexation," implying that Texas was part of the original Louisiana Purchase.

After President Tyler annexed Texas, it would be Polk's job to secure this large new piece of American real estate from the country that thought it belonged to them: Mexico.

What was the centerpiece of the Polk administration?

There was only one real issue confronting Americans during the presidency of James K. Polk: war with Mexico.

When Mexico heard the news of annexation in March 1845, it severed diplomatic relations with the United States and war became more certain. After taking office, Polk dispatched General Zachary Taylor into the territory with about fifteen hundred troops in May 1845, to guard the undefined border against a Mexican "invasion." Although Mexico had officially severed relations with the United States, Polk sent an emissary to secretly negotiate with Mexico to purchase Texas. When that effort failed, Polk ordered General Taylor to move to the bank of the Rio Grande. This "army of observation" numbered some thirty-five hundred men by January 1846, about half the entire U.S. Army. Escalating the provocations, Polk next had Taylor cross the river. When a U.S. soldier was found dead and some Mexicans attacked an American patrol on April 25, President Polk had the perfect pretext he needed to announce to Congress, "War exists."

An agreeable Democratic majority in the House and Senate quickly voted—with little dissent from the Whig opposition—to expand the army by an additional fifty thousand men.

Although a few in Congress opposed the war, it was popular across America. Not among the supporters was a fairly unknown writer from Massachusetts who went to jail rather than pay taxes to fund the war. His name was Thoreau, and he put his ideas into an essay called "Civil Disobedience." Also opposing the war was a somewhat obscure freshman congressman, a Whig from Illinois, who spoke against the Mexican War and challenged Polk to name the "spot" where the Mexicans had allegedly spilled American blood. Polk ignored Abraham Lincoln's "Spot Resolution." Afterward, Lincoln was counseled to amend his antiwar views, which essentially cost him a second term in Congress.

In February 1848, the Treaty of Guadalupe Hidalgo ended the war. Under its terms, the United States received more than five hundred thousand square miles of Mexican territory. The border with Mexico was set at the Rio Grande. In return, Mexico was paid $15 million and the United States absorbed the claims made against Mexico by Americans, totaling another $3.25 million. One Whig newspaper announced, "We take nothing by conquest. . . . Thank God." The war cost more than $100 million (a billion dollars in today's money).[7]

More than twelve thousand Americans died in Mexico, one of the highest casualty rates in American wartime history. While the war was popular among the people, soldiers—many of them newly arrived immigrants—were far less enthusiastic, and there were many desertions. According to historian Daniel Howe, the desertion rate in the Mexican War was more than 8 percent—highest for any foreign war in United States history and double the desertion rate in Vietnam.[8]

The Mexican War also provided a cadre of young American army commanders with hands-on combat experience they would later put to use—often against one another—in the Civil War. Among them was one young officer who fought in Mexico and later called the war "one of the most unjust ever waged by a stronger against a weaker nation." He was Lieutenant Ulysses S. Grant.

Won quickly, the Mexican War completed the dream of Manifest Destiny. With California and Oregon, the United States went "from sea to shining sea." Then on the morning of January 24, 1848, James Marshall, a New Jersey mechanic building a sawmill for Johann Sutter on California's American River, which originates in the Sierra Nevada Mountains and runs through Sacramento, spotted what proved to be gold, sparking the mad gold rush of 1849. That year, more than one hundred thousand people went racing west.

Polk added more territory to America than any president since Thomas Jefferson. But the addition of these enormous parcels of new territory just made the future of slavery a bigger question; there was now that much more land to fight about.

Final Judgment: Grade A

Polk has consistently ranked among the top ten best presidents because he stated what he was going to do and accomplished his goals. He also promised he wouldn't run again and kept his word. In terms of influencing the course of American history, he made America the undisputed continental power in North America. Bolstered by the California gold discovery, it was also a new economic power.

But many historians also regard him as a president who tragically missed a critical opportunity. A slaveholding Tennessean, like his mentor Andrew Jackson, Polk failed to understand the depth of popular

emotion over the westward expansion of slavery. The nation was changing, and free, white workers did not want to compete with slave labor.
While there was a growing and powerful moral element to the abolition
movement, antislavery feelings in the country had more to do with encouraging free labor than promoting idealistic notions of emancipation.

After attending his successor General Zachary Taylor's inauguration, Polk went back to Nashville. Three months later, he was dead of
cholera, an early death attributed, in part, to how intensely he'd worked
while in office.

Polk Administration Milestones[9]

1845

March 4	James K. Polk is inaugurated.
May	Frederick Douglass publishes *Narrative of the Life of Frederick Douglass, An American Slave.* The book's success, despite critics who doubted that a former slave could write such a book, propel Douglass to international fame as an abolitionist speaker and writer.
June 25	Polk orders General Zachary Taylor to move troops to a position "on or near the Rio Grande" in Texas to discourage a Mexican invasion.
August–September	The great Irish potato famine begins; from 1845 to 1852, great waves of immigrants leave Ireland for the United States, Canada, Australia, and England. In the United States, this great migration increases America's existing sharp anti-Catholic, anti-immigrant senti-ment. Earlier, in 1844, this antagonism had resulted in the "Bible Riots" in Philadelphia where dozens were killed in waves of sectarian street fighting. During these years, an estimated five hundred thousand Irish came to America and soon made up as much as a quarter of the population in such cities as Boston, New York, and Philadelphia.
October 10	The naval academy opens at Annapolis, Maryland.
December 29	Texas is admitted as the twenty-eighth state, a slave state.

1846

February 4	Led by Brigham Young, the Mormon migration to Utah begins.
May 13	Congress declares war on Mexico.
June 14	In the Bear Flag Revolt, about thirty American settlers take over a small Mexican garrison in Sonoma, California, and declare California an independent republic.
August 8	In Congress, David Wilmot proposes that slavery be banned in any territory acquired from Mexico as part of a bill to fund the war. The "Wilmot Proviso" does not pass Congress but becomes a sharp dividing line in the slavery debate.
December 28	Iowa is admitted as the twenty-ninth state, a free state.

1847

February 22–23	General Zachary Taylor defeats the Mexicans under General Santa Anna at the Battle of Buena Vista. Taylor's victory propels him to the 1848 Whig nomination.
September 14	General Winfield Scott captures Mexico City.

1848

January 24	Gold is discovered near Sacramento, California.
February 2	The Treaty of Guadalupe Hidalgo ends the Mexican War and brings vast territory to the United States, which will become the battleground over the future of slavery.
May 29	Wisconsin is admitted as the thirtieth state, a free state.
July 12–20	Elizabeth Cady Stanton and Lucretia Mott hold a women's rights convention in Seneca Falls, New York, calling for women's suffrage.
November	Zachary Taylor is elected.

1849

| March 3 | The United States Department of the Interior is created, combining into a single department the General Land Office, the Bureau of Indian Affairs, the Pension Office, the Bureau of the Census, and the Patent Office. |

MUST READS

Walter R. Borneman, *Polk: The Man Who Transformed the Presidency and America*; John S. D. Eisenhower, *So Far From God: The U.S. War with Mexico, 1846–1848*; Robert W. Merry, *A Country of Vast Designs: James K. Polk, the Mexican War, and the Conquest of the American Continent.*

ONLINE RESOURCES

James K. Polk Home site, North Carolina
  http://www.nchistoricsites.org/polk/main.htm
Inaugural Address, Avalon Project, Yale Law School
  http://avalon.law.yale.edu/19th_century/polk.asp
Library of Congress Resource Guide
  http://www.loc.gov/rr/program/bib/presidents/polk/memory.html
Miller Center of Public Affairs, University of Virginia
  http://millercenter.org/president/polk

12

Old Rough and Ready
Zachary Taylor

★ ★ ★

March 4, 1849–July 9, 1850

Milestones in Zachary Taylor's Life

November 24, 1784	Born in Orange County, Virginia
1808–1848	Served in U.S. Army; promoted to major general
1832	Commanded troops in the Black Hawk War
1837	Commanded troops in the Seminole War
1845–1847	Commanded troops in the Mexican War
1849–1850	Twelfth president
July 9, 1850	Died in Washington, D.C., aged sixty-five

PRESIDENTIAL VOICES

For more than half a century, during which kingdoms and empires have fallen, this Union has stood unshaken. The patriots who formed it have long since descended to the grave; yet it still remains, the proudest monument to their memory and the object of affection and admiration with everyone worthy to bear the American name. In my judgment its dissolution would be the greatest of calamities, and to avert that should be the study of every American. Upon its preservation must depend our own happiness and that of countless generations to come. Whatever dangers may threaten it, I shall stand by it and maintain it in its integrity to the full extent of the obligations imposed and the power conferred upon me by the Constitution.

ZACHARY TAYLOR
Annual Message, December 4, 1849[1]

Fast Facts

RELIGION: Episcopal

CAREER BEFORE POLITICS: Soldier

MILITARY SERVICE: Promoted to major general in the U.S. Army; served in War of 1812, Black Hawk War, Second Seminole War, Mexican-American War

POLITICAL PARTY: Whig

FIRST LADY: Margaret Smith Taylor (September 21, 1788–August 14, 1852)

CHILDREN: The Taylors had six children, four of whom lived to maturity: Ann; Sarah; Mary; and one son, Richard, who served as a Confederate general during the Civil War. (President Taylor's brother, Joseph Pannell Taylor, a career officer, served as a Union general in the Civil War, a perfect example of how that war split American families.)

* Taylor's daughter, Sarah Knox Taylor, married Jefferson Davis, the future president of the Confederacy, in 1835, against her father's wishes. She died three months later of malaria.

* Taylor was the seventh of eight Virginia-born presidents.

* The last American president to own slaves while holding office, Taylor brought at least fifteen of his own slaves to the White House, but they were mostly kept from sight. "By 1850, northerners in Washington were increasingly uncomfortable about the presence of slaves," historian William Seale notes. "Allowing them to move about in public view in the White House might have invited incident."[2]

* Taylor was the second president to die in office. After long speculation that he might have been killed by poisoning, his remains were exhumed in 1991 and subjected to testing. The tests revealed he had not been poisoned by arsenic and had died of natural causes.[3]

PRESIDENTIAL VOICES

The Mormons are, at present, eliciting considerable interest and inquiry in reference to the organization of a new State in the far West under the cognomen, State of Deseret.... Ought they be admitted without strict inquiry? For starting point, Congress might appoint a committee to inquire into and report the facts ... relative to polygamy and, if the facts are unfavorable, that they be not ... styled "the State of Deseret" but the "State of Whoredom." ... And further to inquire whether the whole movement be more or less a mere Mormon church maneuver to create a Mormon church State, designed to be under Mormon church jurisdiction exclusively.

—*NATIONAL ERA*, JANUARY 24, 1850

(A weekly abolitionist Washington, D.C., newspaper, the *National Era* would later publish the serialized installments of what became *Uncle Tom's Cabin*.)

Although born into a prominent Virginia family related to James Madison and Robert E. Lee, Zachary Taylor was mostly raised in Kentucky. His father, Richard, had been given land in Louisville in return for his service during the American Revolution, and Taylor was born, en route to Kentucky, in Virginia, near James Madison's Montpelier home. Leaving behind his wife and three children, Taylor's father proceeded to Kentucky to build a farm. He returned to Virginia and brought his family to what was then the Kentucky frontier. Zachary Taylor grew up there, with seven brothers and sisters, in a small cabin. As his father prospered, the Taylors later moved into a brick house, and by 1800, Taylor senior owned ten thousand acres, town lots in Louisville, and twenty-six slaves.[4]

With little formal education, Taylor was on track to remain a planter, but at age twenty-three he received a commission in the army through the intervention of his distant cousin James Madison, then secretary of state. Fighting under William Henry Harrison in the Ohio Valley Indian campaigns during the War of 1812, Taylor rose through the ranks of the regular army in a series of frontier posts. In 1837, he won one of the few major battles of the Second Seminole War, on Christmas Day, adding further luster to his career.

When President Polk ordered him to deploy troops in territory claimed by Mexico in 1846, Taylor led a series of quick victories over the poorly trained and equipped Mexican Army. As newspapers reported his exploits, Taylor emerged as a national hero. However, with his political fortunes rising, he had offered terms to the defeated Mexican Army that were deemed too generous by an irate Polk. Taylor was ordered to take command of a much smaller force while General Winfield Scott commanded the more glamorous assault on Mexico City. But Taylor and his troops routed a large Mexican army at Buena Vista in February 1847, catapulting him to greater heights in the press. He soon occupied a place on the pedestal near Washington and Andrew Jackson as an American war hero.

How did ice water, cherries, and cold milk change history?

With his hero's laurels but no political experience—he had never even voted—Taylor was anointed the Whig candidate—even though the Whigs had objected to the war that made Taylor famous—and defeated Democrat Lewis Cass, a veteran of the War of 1812, in a very close election. (It was the first time Election Day for presidential electors fell on a single day, November 7, following an 1845 act of Congress.)

Once again, an ostensible abolitionist third party helped decide the outcome. Former President Martin Van Buren had entered the race only three months earlier on the Free Soil ticket, and won about 10 percent of the popular vote. Just as the Liberty Party had helped Polk in New York in 1844, Taylor benefited from antislavery votes going to Van Buren instead of Cass.

The Free Soil platform was gaining strength in Northern states. But its success was more an indication of the growing resistance to expanding slavery in the new territories rather than moral opposition to the practice. The Free Soilers, for instance, demanded that the new lands be opened to "the hardy pioneers of our own land, and the oppressed and banished of other lands." They made no mention of blacks, free or slave. Even David Wilmot, who had attached a famous proviso to keep slavery out of new territory taken from Mexico, said, "I would preserve for free white labor a fair country, a rich inheritance, where the sons of toil, my own race and color can live without the disgrace which association with Negro slavery brings upon free labor."[5]

Although a slaveholder, Taylor was fairly moderate about extending slavery in the new Western territories. Moving to quickly bring California and New Mexico into the Union as free states, he squelched any secessionist rhetoric with the threat of hanging for anyone who talked about disunion. John Calhoun took the challenge and said if California was admitted as a free state, the Southern states could not stay in the Union. He was not strung up.

When the aging Senator Henry Clay, frustrated by his every effort to become president, offered a series of resolutions to deal with slavery and expansion that would come to be known as the Compromise of 1850, Taylor opposed the measures, leaving their future uncertain.

Then, on an extremely hot July 4, 1850, President Taylor attended the laying of the cornerstone for the Washington Monument in Washington, D.C. After spending much of the afternoon listening to patriotic speeches, he supposedly gorged himself on cold water, ice milk, and copious amounts of cherries and raw vegetables. The next day he fell severely ill, with acute gastroenteritis. As Taylor biographer John S. D. Eisenhower notes, "The fact is that Washington's water and sewer systems were still primitive and unsanitary; other prominent people . . . were all sick with something like Taylor's condition at the very moment. In no case was anyone sure of the nature of the disease."[6]

Whatever it was, it killed the president. Taylor died on July 9, most likely from food poisoning or cholera.

Vice President Millard Fillmore succeeded him. He had different ideas about the compromise measures.

Final Judgment: Grade I (Incomplete)

Although generally graded among the lower ranks of presidents by most historians, Taylor deserves some consideration for the brevity of his term. Had he served longer, he might have grown in office. But as a nonpolitical soldier, Taylor won the office on the strength of his military skills and war-hero status. His appointments were sometimes disastrous—three cabinet officers were charged with corruption—and before his death he offered no real policies as a solution to the slavery problem.

As a slaveholder, Taylor voiced fairly moderate views on the slavery issue and was totally committed to the Union. Whether his opposition to what became the Compromise of 1850 would have produced a result other than a set of bills that further divided the country is pure speculation. Whether he had the political skills to avert the Civil War if he had survived his Fourth of July splurge is a different question.

Taylor Administration Milestones[7]

1849

March 5	Zachary Taylor is inaugurated.
May	Henry David Thoreau publishes the text of a speech, "Resistance to Civil Government" (better known as "Civil Disobedience"), which grew out of his refusal to pay taxes in support of the Mexican War.

1850

May–September	As Congress debates the solutions to the issue of slavery in the territories won in the Mexican War, Henry Clay proposes the Compromise of 1850.
July 9	Zachary Taylor dies of "cholera morbus"; Vice President Fillmore assumes office.

MUST READS

H. W. Brands, *The Age of Gold: The California Gold Rush and the New American Dream*; David S. Heidler and Jeanne T. Heidler, *Henry Clay: The Essential American*; John S. D. Eisenhower, *Zachary Taylor*.

ONLINE RESOURCES

Inaugural Address

http://www.presidency.ucsb.edu/ws/index.php?pid=25815#axzz1cSEydBwa

Library of Congress Resource Guide

http://www.loc.gov/rr/program/bib/presidents/tyler/index.html

Miller Center of Public Affairs, University of Virginia

http://millercenter.org/president/taylor

Message to Congress (State of the Union Address)

http://www.presidency.ucsb.edu/ws/index.php?pid=29490#axzz1cSoI0LZV

13

Millard Fillmore

★ ★ ★

July 9, 1850–March 4, 1853

Milestones in Millard Fillmore's Life

January 7, 1800	Born in Cayuga County, New York
1815–1819	Served as cloth-maker's apprentice
1823	Admitted to the New York bar
1828–1831	Member of New York State legislature
1833–1835; 1837–1843	U.S. representative from New York
1846	Founded the University of Buffalo
1848	Comptroller of the State of New York
1849–1850	Vice president under Taylor
1850–1853	Thirteenth president of the United States
1856	Defeated as presidential candidate of American and Whig Parties
March 8, 1874	Died in Buffalo, New York, aged seventy-four

PRESIDENTIAL VOICES

The Government of the United States is a limited Government. It is confined to the exercise of powers expressly granted and such others as may be necessary for carrying those powers into effect; and it is at all times an especial duty to guard against any infringement on the just rights of the States.

MILLARD FILLMORE

First Annual Message, December 2, 1850[1]

Maybe there is something unlucky about thirteen after all.

And maybe the only thing you know about Millard Fillmore is that the White House bathtub was installed during his presidency. Sorry, that's a hoax. Noted journalist H. L. Mencken made that story up in 1917—and like Washington's cherry tree, it stuck.[2]

The poor guy didn't even get a presidential nickname of note. Maybe if Millard Fillmore had been an effective president instead of one of those consigned to the bottom of the presidential barrel, his remarkable personal story might be better known. As a rags-to-riches, "make-it-in-America" tale, Fillmore's life has few equals among presidents.

Born into squalid poverty on a farm in Upstate New York, he was apprenticed at age fourteen to a local cloth-maker. Although he lacked a formal education, Fillmore possessed a Lincoln-like love of reading and managed to buy his way out of his apprenticeship—indentured servitude by another name—and make his way back home.

There he met a teacher who helped satisfy his enormous appetite for books and self-improvement. Just two years older, Abigail Powers was the daughter of a Baptist minister, and she taught at the school where Fillmore enrolled. Their mutual love of literature and reading grew into a romance, as Fillmore studied law and later passed the bar. After their marriage, Abigail Fillmore continued to teach, giving her the distinction of being the first professional woman to become first lady.

Fillmore, meanwhile, found his way into New York politics, beginning his career with the Anti-Masons, a group that coalesced in Upstate New York over fears of a Freemason conspiracy involving powerful men who wanted to control the government. The group's targets included Andrew Jackson, a Mason, and his New York ally Martin Van Buren. Later, as a founding member of New York's Whig Party, which absorbed the Anti-Mason contingent, Fillmore rose steadily through the ranks until he was named Zachary Taylor's running mate to give the ticket a non-slaveholding Northerner to balance Taylor, a slaveholding Westerner. While Taylor did no campaigning, the tall, silver-haired, impeccably dressed Fillmore was an enthusiastic stump speaker.

As president, Taylor essentially ignored Fillmore. Fillmore had already told Taylor that if given the opportunity to break a tie in the Senate, he would vote for the Compromise. And then, on July 9, Fillmore learned that Taylor was dead. On the tenth, Fillmore was administered the oath of office in the House chamber—the cloth-maker's apprentice was now the thirteenth president.

Fast Facts

RELIGION: Unitarian

CAREER BEFORE POLITICS: Attorney

POLITICAL PARTY: Anti-Masonic (to 1832)

Whig (1832–1856)

American (Know-Nothing) (1856–1860)

FIRST LADY: Abigail Powers Fillmore (March 13, 1798–March 30, 1853)

Five years after his first wife's death, Fillmore married Caroline McIntosh (1813–1881), a wealthy widow, on February 10, 1858.

CHILDREN: Fillmore had two children with his first wife: Millard and Mary, who served as White Houses hostess when her mother fell ill; Mary died of cholera at age twenty-two.

* Fillmore was the second vice president to succeed to the presidency.

* Six feet tall with striking blue eyes, Fillmore made an impressive appearance, but as an "accidental president," he never commanded the power of the office—he was a modest, unassuming man usually described as merely "amiable."

* During Fillmore's tenancy, the White House was modernized with a cast-iron cooking stove (replacing an open-hearth fireplace) and the first White House library, established by Abigail Fillmore, a voracious reader like her husband, who requested congressional funding for the project.

* Fillmore gave the order for Commodore Matthew C. Perry to sail to Japan and open its ports to foreign trade.

* The last Whig president, Fillmore failed to win his party's nomination in the 1852 election.

* Fillmore, who began his political career with the Anti-Masons, ended it in 1856 as the third-party candidate of the American (Know-Nothing) Party, a rabidly anti-immigrant, anti-Catholic party.

PRESIDENTIAL VOICES

Eliza made her desperate retreat across the river just in the dusk of twilight. The gray mist of evening, rising slowly from the river, enveloped her as she disappeared up the bank, and the swollen current and floundering masses of ice presented a hopeless barrier between her and her pursuer.

—HARRIET BEECHER STOWE
Uncle Tom's Cabin, 1852

What happened when Fillmore agreed to the Compromise of 1850?
As the sectional tensions increased over the question of extending slavery into America's vast new territories, another compromise temporarily saved the Union. Hotly debated—and as distasteful to abolitionists as many of the other American compromises over slavery had been—the series of five bills known as the Compromise of 1850 was passed only after Zachary Taylor's death in office. Taylor had favored California's quick admission as a free state and threatened to hang anyone who discussed secession. Fillmore had other ideas.

An enthusiastic supporter of Henry Clay, architect of the Compromise of 1850, Fillmore signed its five bills, believing that these measures would save the Union. Instead, they would more deeply divide the country. In response to their new president's decision, Zachary Taylor's entire cabinet resigned.

Under the bills:

- California was admitted as a free state.
- The territories of New Mexico and Utah were organized without restrictions on slavery.
- Texas, which would enter the union without restrictions on its existing slaves, had its boundaries set and received $10 million for the land that would become New Mexico.
- The slave trade (but not slavery itself) was abolished in the District of Columbia.
- A new Fugitive Slave Act provided federal jurisdiction to assist slaveholders in the recovery of escaped slaves.

The last of these bills was too much for opponents of slavery—even the more accommodating and moderate abolitionists. As the Fugitive Slave Act granted slaveholders federal assistance in recovering escaped slaves, with only a sworn affidavit needed to prove ownership, it also authorized fugitive slave commissioners with extraordinary legal powers to make arrests and determine whether a black person was a slave or free. Commissioners were paid a bounty for every "fugitive" they returned to slavery. Even the expenses of capturing and returning a fugitive slave were to be borne by the federal government. The difficult burden of proving their free status was shouldered by the accused "fugitives"— there was no presumption of freedom. And citizens who concealed, aided, or rescued fugitives were subject to fines and jail.

Suddenly free blacks, thinking they had found safety in Northern towns, were subject to seizure. Violent protests began to break out as mobs in several cities balked at the law. When federal marshals snatched a fugitive named Shadrach Minkins, who was working as a waiter in a Boston coffeehouse, a large crowd of angry black abolitionists overwhelmed the marshals and sent Shadrach to Montreal along the Underground Railroad. An outraged Fillmore ordered the arrest of nine of the abolitionists; all had their charges dismissed or were acquitted by juries.[3] Fillmore often had to call on the military to enforce the act: he sent troops to Boston to remove a seventeen-year-old captured slave named Thomas Sims and dispatched marines after other slaves who had killed their owners before escaping to Canada. (Canada refused to extradite them.)

The number of blacks actually captured and sent south under the Fugitive Slave Act was relatively small, perhaps three hundred. But the law created new and more vocal opponents to slavery. Ralph Waldo Emerson called it a "filthy enactment" and vowed he would not obey it. The former slave Frederick Douglass, who had emerged as the most forceful voice in the abolitionist camp, went further. In 1852, he told the Free Soil Convention in Pittsburgh, "The only way to make the Fugitive Slave Law a dead letter is to make half a dozen or more dead kidnappers. There is more protection there for a horse, for a donkey, or anything, rather a colored man—who is therefore justified in the eye of God in maintaining his right with his arm."[4]

Calling the law a "nightmare abomination," a young woman decided to write stories that shook the conscience of America and the world.

Harriet Beecher Stowe was the daughter, sister, and wife of Protestant clergymen. Her father, the Reverend Lyman Beecher, was a Calvinist minister and leading anti-Catholic, anti-immigrant Nativist who took the family to Cincinnati, where he headed a new seminary. There, Harriet Beecher met and married Calvin Stowe, and in 1850, she moved with him to Maine when he took a teaching post at Bowdoin College. After putting their children to bed at night, Stowe followed her family's urgings to write about the evils of slavery. Her fictionalized tale, *Uncle Tom's Cabin, or Life Among the Lowly*, first appeared in serial form in the *National Era*, an abolitionist journal edited by poet and ardent abolitionist John Greenleaf Whittier, and was an immediate sensation, leaving readers clamoring for more. In 1852, a Boston publisher released the tale of slave life in book form, conveying unforgettable images and scenes, perhaps the most famous of which was the picture of the barefoot slave Eliza, her child in her arms, leaping from one ice floe to another across the frozen Ohio River to escape a ruthless slave trader. Beecher Stowe also depicted the vicious plantation overseer, Simon Legree—deliberately a transplanted Yankee—trying to break the will and spirit of the hero, Tom; and Uncle Tom himself, resilient and saintly, beaten by Legree but refusing to submit to overseeing the other slaves.

The reaction of the public—North, South, and worldwide—was astonishing. Sales reached three hundred thousand copies within a year, making Stowe a rich woman. As Debby Applegate wrote in her biography of Harriet's famous brother, Henry Ward Beecher, "This quiet parson's wife had accomplished the impossible. She took the most unpopular subject in the country and turned it into the most popular book in American history."[5]

In a time when slavery was discussed with euphemistic code words like "states' rights" and "popular sovereignty," this book personalized the question of slavery as no abolitionist literature or congressional debate had. For the first time, thousands of whites got an admittedly melodramatic inkling of the grotesque human suffering caused by slavery. Harriet Beecher Stowe put a human face on the "peculiar institution."

PRESIDENTIAL VOICES

It must always be regretted that such a man as Millard Fillmore had not a mind comprehensive enough to properly meet a great crisis. . . . It was moreover, his misfortune to see in slavery a political not a moral question. Upon this issue, which, it is true, was one of transcendent importance, he was a politician, not a statesman.

—*New York Times*, March 10, 1874

Final Judgment: Grade F

Hoping that the Compromise measures would solve the slavery problem, Fillmore left office having failed to win his party's nomination in 1852. To some in the North, he was the "perfidious Fillmore," and his acceptance and enforcement of the Fugitive Slave Act, in particular, doomed his chances with the Whigs—now a party deeply divided over the future of slavery and how to respond to it.

Fillmore retired to New York but remained active in politics. In 1856, he tried for a comeback with the third-party American, or "Know-Nothing," Party, whose organizing principle was a rabidly anti-Catholic, anti-immigrant stance. Their nickname came from their secretiveness—when asked about the party, members would routinely answer that they "knew nothing" about it.

With a platform proclaiming, "Americans must rule America," Fillmore and running mate Andrew Jackson Donelson—Andrew Jackson's nephew and private secretary—won 25 percent of the popular vote and carried one state, Maryland.

Once the Civil War broke out, Fillmore organized a group of older men as a local militia in Buffalo. After meeting Lincoln in Buffalo in February 1861, Fillmore later called him a "tyrant" who "makes my blood boil."[6] Discredited for his stance, he faded from the national scene until his death in 1874.

His failure to assert presidential authority and be a more forceful leader in resolving the slavery issue not only doomed his presidential aspirations, but helped push the country to Civil War. His "accidental" tenure has consigned Fillmore consistently to the lowest ranks of presidents.

Fillmore Administration Milestones[7]

1850

July 10	Millard Fillmore is sworn in as the nation's thirteenth president. Zachary Taylor's entire cabinet resigns, and Fillmore appoints a new cabinet with pro-Union, pro-Compromise Whigs, including Daniel Webster as secretary of state.
September 9	California enters the Union as the thirty-first state, a free state, giving non-slaveholding states a majority in the Senate.
September 18	The Fugitive Slave Act is passed.

1851

June 5	*Uncle Tom's Cabin* begins to appear in serialized form.
September 18	The first issue of the *New York Daily Times* is published. In 1857, it becomes the *New York Times*.

| December 1 | Congressional elections reveal the political division over the Compromise of 1850. Abolitionist senator Charles Sumner is elected in Massachusetts. |

1852

June 1–6	The Democratic National Convention nominates Franklin Pierce of New Hampshire; his party confirms its support for the Compromise of 1850.
June 16–21	The Whig National Convention rejects Fillmore and nominates Mexican War hero General Winfield Scott; the Whigs also confirm their belief that the Compromise is the best solution to slavery, but the party is more divided on the issue.
June 29	Whig leader Henry Clay dies. In October, Senator Daniel Webster dies. The two men were the key architects of the 1850 Compromise and had, along with John Calhoun, dominated congressional politics in their era.
August 11	The Free Soil Party holds its convention, condemning slavery and the Compromise; they also favor easing immigration rules and opening up new territory to homesteaders.
November 2	Democrat Franklin Pierce is elected with William R. King as his vice president. The Free Soil Party fares poorly and the Whigs are losing strength as a national party.

1853

| March 3 | On Fillmore's last day in office, Congress authorizes the transcontinental railroad survey. |

MUST READS

Paul Finkelman, *Millard Fillmore*; James M. McPherson, *Battle Cry of Freedom: The Civil War Era*; Sean Wilentz, *The Rise of American Democracy: Jefferson to Lincoln*.

ONLINE RESOURCES

Library of Congress Resource Guide

http://www.loc.gov/rr/program/bib/presidents/fillmore/index.html

Millard Fillmore House (National Parks Service)

http://www.nps.gov/nr/travel/presidents/millard_fillmore_house
.html

First Annual Message to Congress

http://millercenter.org/president/speeches/detail/3552

Miller Center of Public Affairs, University of Virginia

http://millercenter.org/president/fillmore

14

Young Hickory of the Granite Hills
Franklin Pierce

* * *

March 4, 1853–March 4, 1857

Milestones in Franklin Pierce's Life

November 23, 1804	Born in Hillsborough, New Hampshire
1827	Admitted to the New Hampshire bar
1829–1833	Member of New Hampshire state legislature
1833–1837	U.S. representative from New Hampshire
1837–1842	U.S. senator from New Hampshire
1846–1848	Served in Mexican War
1853–1857	Fourteenth president
October 8, 1869	Died in Concord, New Hampshire, aged sixty-four

PRESIDENTIAL VOICES

I hold that the laws of 1850, commonly called the "compromise measures," are strictly constitutional and to be unhesitatingly carried into effect. I believe that the constituted authorities of this Republic are bound to regard the rights of the South in this respect as they would view any other legal and constitutional right, and that the laws to enforce them should be respected and obeyed, not with a reluctance encouraged by abstract opinions as to their propriety in a different state of society, but cheerfully and according to the decisions of the tribunal to which their exposition belongs. Such have been, and are, my convictions, and upon them I shall act. I fervently hope that the question is at rest,

*and that no sectional or ambitious or fanatical excitement may again threaten
the durability of our institutions or obscure the light of our prosperity.*

FRANKLIN PIERCE
Inaugural Address, March 4, 1853[1]

G ood looks, breeding, brains, and piety do not a good president
make. Franklin Pierce offers proof of that. Widely agreed to be
among the most handsome men ever elected to the White House,
Pierce was the son of a bona fide hero of American Independence, who
left his plow and rose to brigadier general in the Revolution. Franklin
Pierce coasted through college, his intelligence deemed extraordinary.
He impressed everyone by reciting his entire 3,929-word inaugural address from memory. Both Pierce and his wife, Jane, daughter of a
preacher, were extremely devout Christians. Attempting to carry on his
family's military tradition, Pierce was eventually promoted to brigadier
general during the Mexican War. His service almost derailed his ambition when a cannon shot made his horse jump, driving his groin into
the pommel of his saddle and causing him to pass out. Opposition
newspapers ridiculed him for fainting on the battlefield.

But his less than heroic military stature is not what doomed Pierce's
place in history. He was among the trio of prewar presidents whose un-
inspired, shortsighted, and even cowardly administrations did nothing to
avert the Civil War.

Fast Facts

RELIGION: Episcopal
EDUCATION: Bowdoin College
MILITARY SERVICE: U.S. Army, Mexican War
CAREER BEFORE POLITICS: Attorney
PARTY: Democratic

FIRST LADY: Jane Appleton Pierce (March 12, 1806–December 2, 1863)
CHILDREN: The Pierces had three children, all of whom died in childhood.

* When he was president-elect, Pierce and his family were on a train that derailed, decapitating their eleven-year-old son Benny before their eyes. Pierce was devastated by the loss, as was his wife, who had already lost two other children in infancy. Jane Pierce became a recluse in Washington known as the "Shadow of the White House."

* Among Pierce's fellow students at Bowdoin College were Nathaniel Hawthorne, a lifelong friend who later wrote his campaign biography, and poet Henry Wadsworth Longfellow.

* At age forty-eight when inaugurated, Pierce was the youngest president to that date.

* Pierce, as permitted by the Constitution, "affirmed" the oath of office rather than swore it.

* Reflecting the violent tenor of the times, Pierce was the first president to have a full-time bodyguard—a federal employee whose job was to protect the president.[2] (The Secret Service was created as part of the treasury department in 1865 by Abraham Lincoln to suppress counterfeit currency. In 1894, the Secret Service began to informally protect President Cleveland and took over formal protection of the President in 1902 after the assassination of William McKinley.)

* Under Pierce, the White House got a new bathroom on the second floor. The new bathroom was luxurious in having both hot and cold water piped in.[3]

* Pierce's vice president was William Rufus King, who died of tuberculosis in April 1853 without actually assuming his duties. At the time, there was no constitutional mechanism for replacing a vice president who died or resigned and no vice president was named, leaving the office unfilled. This constitutional shortfall went uncorrected until the Twenty-fifth Amendment was ratified in 1967; before that, the vice presidency was left unfilled sixteen times until a new president was inaugurated (William Rufus King had also been the longtime housemate of James Buchanan, Pierce's successor as president.)

Why was there a civil war in Kansas?

For nearly half a century, from the Louisiana Purchase in 1803 through the Mexican War in 1846, America's politics was absorbed by a single overwhelming issue: the place of slavery in territories being opened up by America's frenzied westward expansion.

To slaveholding Southerners in Congress, who saw America's immigration boom tilting the political scales North and West, allowing slavery into those new states—and with it the three-fifths compromise that gave them extra votes and electors—was crucial to their political survival.

In 1854, Illinois Democratic senator Stephen Douglas, who had helped engineer the Compromise of 1850, wanted to organize new territory in the West that would become the states of Kansas and Nebraska. Vermont-born and transplanted to Illinois, the five-foot political dynamo was known as the "Little Giant." As a director of the Illinois Central Railroad and a land speculator, Douglas wanted to open the way for America's railroad development, with Chicago as its terminus. Because Kansas would lie above the line marking slavery's boundary under the Missouri Compromise of 1820, Kansas would be free if admitted as a state.

Railroads, in the mid-nineteenth century, were the Internet and Interstate Highway System rolled into one. Now that America went from sea to shining sea, and California had become the fortune hunter's Paradise, connecting East to West was critically important. The hundreds of thousands of immigrants flooding into Eastern cities simply aggravated demand for the heartland territory to be open and accessible for development. The railroad was the answer. But the railroad needed capital, land, and labor. Lots of it. And it needed a route—a decision that Congress would make because most of the land was still held by the federal government.

Stephen Douglas wanted to make sure that the railroads had the land and government support they needed. And he wanted to make sure that the route of the railroad ran through his adopted state of Illinois and the city of Chicago. Knowing that Southern Democrats would not vote for any new free territory, and hoping to make a presidential run in 1856, for which he would need Southern Democratic support,

Douglas proposed a solution. To win over the Southerners, who were more interested in plantations and growing cotton than in building a railroad across the South, he agreed to support repeal of the 1820 Missouri Compromise, which had governed the admission of new territories for thirty-four years.

Joining forces with President Pierce, Douglas and his Southern Democratic allies overturned the Missouri Compromise in May 1854 with the Kansas-Nebraska Act. A key to this compromise was Douglas's idea of "popular sovereignty"—which meant the slavery decision would be left up to the people in the territories.

Instead of resolving the slavery questions, Douglas had let the genie out of the bottle. "His Kansas-Nebraska Act unleashed the frenzied wrath of many who had never before joined in antislavery agitation," writes historian Richard Kluger. "And the sad spectacle of Kansas turned into a bloody cockpit of free-soilers battling slaveholders for control of their territory spawned a new northern political party, the Republicans."[4]

Growing out of the former Whigs, Free Soilers, antislavery activists (including some Democrats), and modernizers who wanted the national government to aid Western development, they chose the name at the suggestion of newspaperman Horace Greeley, who wrote in a June 1854 editorial, "Though we think some simple name like 'Republican' would more fitly designate those who had united to restore the Union to its true mission of champion and promulgator of Liberty rather than propagandist of slavery." The name was chosen in homage to Jefferson's republican ideals and his original Republican Party—which had, in fact, evolved into the Democratic Party under Jackson.

Pierce—a former congressman and senator from New Hampshire—had already weakened his standing among abolitionists and driven the wedge between North and South deeper when an escaped slave named Anthony Burns was arrested in Boston two days after the Kansas-Nebraska Act was passed. Armed with hatchets and a battering ram, an antislavery crowd of blacks and whites tried to free Burns from a federal courthouse. When a deputy was killed in the chaos, Pierce ordered Secretary of War Jefferson Davis to dispatch Marines, cavalry, artillery, and a ship to Boston. On June 2, the troops marched Burns in irons to the Boston wharf, where he was put on a ship and returned south. This turn of events, witnessed by thousands of angry Bostonians, provoked another sensation when abolitionist William Lloyd Garrison publicly burned a copy of the Constitution a few weeks later, on the Fourth of July.

With the Kansas-Nebraska Act's allowance for "popular sovereignty" to decide the future of slavery, Kansas was flooded with groups from both sides of the slavery issue. Northerners opposed to slavery's expansion attempted to transport antislavery settlers to Kansas to ensure that the territory would eventually vote against slavery. Enraged by this interference from the New England "foreigners," thousands of Missourians who called themselves Border Ruffians poured across the line into Kansas to tip the balance in favor of slavery in the territory. In an illegal and rigged election, the pro-slave Ruffians won, but antislavery forces refused to concede defeat and set up a provisional free state government in Topeka.

President Pierce denounced this government, giving the pro-slave forces justification for an offensive. Soon Kansas was bleeding, with some of the most vicious fighting between Americans before the Civil War actually began in 1861. What might be called the first true blows in the Civil War were struck in May 1856 when the town of Lawrence, established as an antislavery center, was sacked by pro-slave forces. Three days later, in retaliation, fanatical abolitionist John Brown attacked a pro-slavery town on Pottawatomie Creek, slaughtering five settlers in the night. These attacks brought Kansas to a state of chaos. By October 1856, more than two hundred people had died in "Bloody Kansas" and Pierce's mishandling of the Kansas fighting left him without support. He was denied renomination. As historian James Rawley summarized, "His personal traits of accommodation and deference to the powerful southern wing of his party made for an inept president who piloted the ship of state to the shoals of secession and civil war."[5]

Retiring to New Hampshire, Pierce resumed his law practice but was finished in politics. Following his wife's death of tuberculosis in 1863, he sunk into depression and alcoholism. In time, he came to be regarded as a traitor, and when Lincoln was assassinated in April 1865, an angry crowd stormed Pierce's home.

Final Judgment: Grade F

In the years before the Civil War, America was seemingly cursed because the greatest political advantage generally went to those men who offended the fewest people. Pierce fit that mold, which also places him in the ranks of the worst presidents—three feckless, overmatched men who were in the White House in the decade before the Civil War: Fillmore, Pierce, and his successor, James Buchanan.

"An indecisive chief executive prone to adopt the views of the last advisor he consulted,"[6] as historian Richard Kluger described him, Pierce was inflexible and seemingly more devoted to his Democratic Party than to the nation. Abolitionists denounced him, especially after he had attacked Lincoln and his policies, but his old friend Nathaniel Hawthorne, loyal to the end, generously wrote of him, "There is a certain steadfastness and integrity with regard to a man's own nature (when it is such a peculiar nature as that of Pierce) which seems to me more sacred and valuable than the faculty of adapting one's self to new ideas, however true they may turn out to be."[7]

Following Pierce's death in 1869, the former president went largely unmourned and it took more than fifty years for his home state of New Hampshire to erect a statue in his honor.

Pierce Administration Milestones[8]

1853

January 6	Two months before Pierce takes office, his eleven-year-old son Benjamin is killed in a train wreck.
March 4	Franklin Pierce is inaugurated.
December 30	The Gadsden Purchase, negotiated by James Gadsden, U.S. minister to Mexico, is signed. At the renegotiated cost of $10 million, the United States acquires more than 29,600 square miles of additional territory in southwest Arizona and New Mexico. Gadsden hopes to build a transcontinental railroad along a southern route through this territory.

1854

February 28 Antislavery opponents of the Kansas-Nebraska Act meet in Ripon, Wisconsin, and begin to form a new political party, the Republicans.

March 31 Commodore Matthew Perry—ordered to Japan by President Fillmore—signs the Treaty of Kanagawa, opening Japanese ports to trade.

April 26 The Massachusetts Emigrant Aid Society is founded by Eli Thayer to encourage opponents of slavery to move to Kansas.

May 30 The Kansas-Nebraska Act is signed into law.

July 6 Coinciding with the further disintegration of the Whig Party, the Republican Party is officially founded in Jackson, Michigan. The party is composed of former Whigs, Free Soilers, and antislavery Democrats.

1854–1856

In "Bleeding Kansas," a guerilla war begins between pro-slavery and antislavery settlers as they attempt to establish "popular sovereignty."

1855

May Former slave Frederick Douglass publishes his second work of autobiography, *My Bondage and My Freedom.* He has become a world-renowned speaker, author, publisher, and fiery advocate of abolition.

September 5 Antislavery settlers in Kansas form the Free State forces with guns provided by Northern abolitionists.

October 23 In response to a pro-slavery territorial government, the Topeka Constitution, written by Free State forces and outlawing slavery, creates a second government in Kansas.

1856

February 11 The Know-Nothing Party nominates Millard Fillmore for president; they want to exclude Catholics and

foreigners from office and call for a twenty-one-year-
residency requirement for citizenship. Renaming
themselves the "American Party," they call the "Black
Republicans" a threat to the Union.

May 21
Pro-slavery forces attack Lawrence, Kansas, a Free
State stronghold.

May 22
A cane-wielding Representative Preston Brooks
(D-SC) attacks abolitionist Senator Charles Sumner
(R-MA) on the Senate floor. The fight is provoked by
derogatory remarks made by Sumner as the Senate
debates the admission of Kansas.

May 24
John Brown and his followers massacre five pro-slavery
Kansans along the Pottawatomie Creek, retaliating for
the deadly raid on Lawrence.

June 2–5
The Democratic National Convention nominates
James Buchanan for president and John Breckinridge
of Kentucky for vice president.

June 17–19
The Republican National Convention nominates
California Senator John C. Frémont, the famed
explorer of the West, for president.

November 4
James Buchanan is elected president, with John
Breckinridge his vice president.

1857

January 15
The State of Disunion Convention, contemplating
the peaceful separation of North and South, is held
in Worcester, Massachusetts. William Lloyd Garrison delivers a speech avowing "No union with
slaveholders."

MUST READS

Michael Holt, *Franklin Pierce*; Henry Mayer, *All on Fire: William Lloyd
Garrison and the Abolition of Slavery*; David S. Reynolds, *John Brown,
Abolitionist: The Man Who Killed Slavery, Sparked the Civil War, and
Seeded Civil Rights*.

ONLINE RESOURCES

Library of Congress Resource Guide
   http://www.loc.gov/rr/program/bib/presidents/pierce/index.html
Pierce Manse, Concord, New Hampshire
   http://www.piercemanse.org/
Inaugural Address, Avalon Project, Yale Law School
   http://avalon.law.yale.edu/19th_century/pierce.asp
Miller Center of Public Affairs, University of Virginia
   http://millercenter.org/president/pierce
Jane Pierce: Letter to Dead Son, New Hampshire Historical Society
   http://nhhistory.org/libraryexhibits/manuscriptcollection/mom/5
   -01janepierce/janepierce.html

Old Buck
James Buchanan

* * *

March 4, 1857–March 4, 1861

Milestones in James Buchanan's Life

April 23, 1791	Born in Cove Gap, near Harrisburg, Pennsylvania
1812	Began law practice in Lancaster, Pennsylvania
1814–1816	Member of Pennsylvania legislature
1821–1831	U.S. representative from Pennsylvania
1832–1833	Minister to Russia under Jackson
1834–1845	U.S. senator from Pennsylvania
1845–1849	Secretary of state under Polk
1853–1856	U.S. minister to England under Pierce
1857–1861	Fifteenth president
June 1, 1868	Died at home in Lancaster County, Pennsylvania, aged seventy-seven

PRESIDENTIAL VOICES

If you are as happy in entering the White House as I shall feel on returning to Wheatland, you are a happy man indeed.

—JAMES BUCHANAN
to Abraham Lincoln, March 4, 1861

J ames Buchanan cut a tall, handsome, imposing figure. Professing his moral opposition to slavery while devoted to the cause of Union and the Constitution, he was intelligent, well educated, held many positions of prominence in government, and, like his predecessor Franklin Pierce, seemed well equipped for the presidency.

But as the leader of a nation on the verge of a civil war, James Buchanan is counted an abject failure. He not only failed to avert the war but may have actually hastened its coming.

Fast Facts

RELIGION: Presbyterian

ASSOCIATIONS: Freemason

EDUCATION: Dickinson College

MILITARY SERVICE: Pennsylvania Militia, War of 1812

CAREER BEFORE POLITICS: Attorney

POLITICAL PARTY: Democratic

* Buchanan was the last president born in the eighteenth century.
* He was the last secretary of state to become president.
* Buchanan's is the first known photographed inaugural.
* The only president who was a lifelong bachelor, for fifteen years of his political career Buchanan lived in Washington, D.C., with Rufus King, an Alabama senator who became Franklin Pierce's vice president. (King died before assuming office.) Their relationship was the source of rumor and cutting remarks—Andrew Jackson called King "Aunt Fancy" or "Miss Nancy," while another politician referred to the men as "Buchanan and his wife."[1] And there are letters suggesting more than male friendship. Both men's relatives, however, burned their private correspondence, and there is no conclusive evidence of Buchanan's sexual preference.

Buchanan's orphaned niece, Harriet Lane, then in her twenties, served as official White House hostess for Buchanan.

* In 1866, Buchanan wrote a book defending his actions, *Mr. Buchanan's Administration on the Eve of the Rebellion*; it was the first published presidential memoir.

PRESIDENTIAL VOICES

All agree that under the Constitution slavery in the States is beyond the reach of any human power except that of the respective States themselves wherein it exists. May we not hope, then, that the long agitation on this subject is approaching its end, and the geographical parties to which it has given birth, so much dreaded by the Father of his Country, will speedily become extinct?

—JAMES BUCHANAN

Inaugural Address, March 4, 1857[2]

In many ways, it is a classic American success story—the perfect example of the "anyone can become president" idea. Born in a log cabin, the eldest of eleven children, James Buchanan was the son of an Irish immigrant who parlayed a small frontier trading post in the Blue Mountains of Pennsylvania into a thriving business. Buchanan's father prospered sufficiently to build a brick house, a sign of affluence, in Mercersburg, Pennsylvania.

By the time Buchanan was a teenager, his father was successful enough to send him to Dickinson College, from which he was expelled for an unspecified "youthful indiscretion." Buchanan settled down, returned to school, graduated, and studied law, beginning his practice in 1812. When the War of 1812 began, he volunteered for the militia that helped defend Baltimore from British attack. Returning to Pennsylvania, Buchanan built a successful law practice, then commenced a lifelong career in politics, rising in the Pennsylvania legislature.

While he would be known as the only "bachelor president," James Buchanan had one romantic interest as a young man that ended in tragedy and scandal. He was courting Ann Coleman, the daughter of a wealthy mill owner in Lancaster, Pennsylvania, when her parents decided that Buchanan was a "fortune hunter" and the engagement was broken off in 1819. When Ann died in circumstances suggesting suicide, her parents refused to allow Buchanan to attend the young woman's funeral.

In 1820, Buchanan was elected to Congress as a Federalist, but he soon began to follow the Democratic line of Andrew Jackson. Rewarded with a diplomatic post in Russia in 1832, Buchanan negotiated the first trade treaty between the two countries, then returned to America and was elected to the Senate in 1834, representing Pennsylvania for the next eleven years.

After turning down a post as attorney general and a Supreme Court seat, Buchanan became President Polk's secretary of state in 1845. When he failed to win a presidential nomination in 1848, he returned to his law practice but was appointed minister to England by President Pierce in 1853.

Who was the first Republican to run for president?

Passing over the ineffectual and unpopular Pierce in 1856 in the conflict over the Kansas-Nebraska Act, the Democrats settled on Buchanan as their candidate. A party loyalist, always sympathetic to Southerners and slave interests, Buchanan was perfectly positioned to take the Democratic nomination in 1856, largely because he was minister to England during the Kansas furor. In other words, his chief political asset was that he had been out of the country amid the fray over Kansas-Nebraska.

During the campaign, Buchanan said little, prompting opposition senator Thaddeus Stevens to say that there was no such person as Buchanan—that "he was dead of lockjaw."[3]

The newly formed Republican Party, gaining popular strength as blood was spilled in Kansas, took a page from the old Whig playbook in 1856 and chose a hero in uniform—the Pathfinder, John C. Frémont—as its first standard-bearer. The most celebrated Western explorer, Frémont had led the way to California, fomented the "Bear Flag" rebellion against Mexico, and then aided it with a small force of American soldiers. He went on to become California's first senator. He had also become very wealthy when gold was found on his California property.

Like the Whig generals before him, Frémont was a military man with no real political experience, although his father-in-law, Senator Thomas Hart Benton of Missouri, was one of the most powerful men in Congress. The Pathfinder's campaign slogan was simple: "Free Soil, Free Speech, Free Men, Frémont."

The Nativist anti-Catholic, anti-immigrant Know-Nothing, or American, Party was also bolstered by the Kansas-Nebraska debacle, which brought to its ranks free, white workingmen who had no interest in abolition. But they were ultimately as divided over slavery as the Democrats were, and the Know-Nothings sent up former President Millard Fillmore as their candidate.

What sort of high-minded campaign was it in 1856? In Indiana, Democrats organized a parade featuring young girls in white dresses holding banners that read, "Fathers, save us from nigger husbands."[4]

Frémont was also attacked as a Catholic and—in the first presidential "birther" controversy—a foreigner, though he was neither. His father was French Canadian and his mother was American, but Frémont was born in Virginia, out of wedlock. Prominent abolitionist preacher Henry Ward Beecher, brother of Harriet Beecher Stowe, stumped for Frémont and assured voters that the first Republican presidential candidate was no "Papist." So did Abraham Lincoln, who made some fifty speeches for the Republican candidate.

Having prominent abolitionist Beecher on his side helped Frémont in the North but not in the Southern states. Pledging secession if Frémont was elected, Southern Democrats forced preservation of the Union to the forefront of the election—a threat that carried weight. But the increasingly intense sectionalism of the country was clear in the results. With only 45 percent of the popular vote, Buchanan was elected as Frémont (with 33 percent) and Fillmore (with 22 percent) split the rest.

The electoral vote was not as close. Buchanan won every Southern state except Maryland. He also carried the free states of New Jersey, Indiana, Illinois, his home state of Pennsylvania, and perhaps surprisingly, California. For a new party, the Republicans did exceptionally well, as Frémont carried eleven free states, the rest of the North. Nativist

Fillmore took only Maryland, still a slave state. In these returns, Abraham Lincoln saw a coalition of Republicans and Fillmore voters as the way to victory in 1860.

The last of the Democratic heirs to Andrew Jackson, Buchanan was the weakest, most ineffectual of the prewar presidents. A conservative Democrat known as a "Doughface," he stocked his cabinet with Southern Democrats, pledged noninterference and popular sovereignty when inaugurated in 1857, and took office professing a hope that the Supreme Court would solve America's slavery problem.

PRESIDENTIAL VOICES

The right of property in a slave is distinctly and expressly affirmed in the Constitution. The right to traffic in it, like an ordinary article of merchandise and property, was guaranteed to the citizens of the United States, in every State that might desire it, for twenty years. And the Government in express terms is pledged to protect it in all future time, if the slave escapes from his owner. . . . And no word can be found in the Constitution which gives Congress a greater power over slave property, or which entitles property of that kind to less protection than property of any other description. The only power conferred is the power coupled with the duty of guarding and protecting the owner in his rights.

—CHIEF JUSTICE ROGER B. TANEY
Dred Scott v. Sandford, March 6, 1857

Why did Chief Justice Roger Taney compare a man to a mule?
President Buchanan hoped that the Supreme Court would settle the burning question of slavery in the territories. In his inaugural address on March 4, 1857, he said the slavery question "belongs to the Supreme Court of the United States, before whom it is now pending, and will, it is understood, be speedily and finally settled."

Two days later, the Supreme Court altered the future of the debate and of the nation when eighty-year-old Chief Justice Taney delivered his majority opinion—a two-hour reading in the Dred Scott case that threw gasoline on a smoldering fire.

The case came out of a legal odyssey that began in 1834 when Dr. John Emerson joined the army as a surgeon and moved through a succession of army posts accompanied by Dred Scott, a slave. When Emerson died in 1846, a sympathetic lawyer assisted Scott in suing for his freedom, claiming that because he had lived in territories where slavery was illegal, he was legally free.

A St. Louis county court accepted Scott's position, but a higher court overturned it, and Dred Scott, his wife, and their child were returned to slavery. On appeal, the case went to the U.S. Supreme Court, where the chief justice was Roger Taney, the former slave owner and states' rights advocate who had been appointed by President Andrew Jackson after serving as Jackson's attorney general and secretary of the treasury.

The court split along regional and party lines, although Justice Robert Grier of Pennsylvania joined the majority. Letters from Buchanan to Grier later revealed that the justice did so at the request of President Buchanan, who interfered to prevent a purely sectional decision. Taney's ruling, which stood as the majority decision, contained three central points:

- Free or slave, blacks were not citizens; Negroes, Taney wrote, "are so inferior that they had no rights which a white man was bound to respect."
- Scott had never ceased to be a slave and therefore was not a citizen, but property of his owner, no different from a mule or a horse.
- Slaves were property, and property was protected by the Fifth Amendment in the Bill of Rights. Taney ruled that Congress had no right to deprive citizens of their property—including slaves—anywhere within the United States.

With this sweeping decision, Taney obliterated the entire legislative history of compromises that restricted slavery, from the Northwest Ordinance of 1787 to the Missouri Compromise of 1820 and the Compromise of 1850.

Overjoyed Southerners wanted to use the decision to question the constitutionality of the 1807 law prohibiting the slave trade itself and any laws that proscribed slavery.

But instead of giving slavery a new lease on life and destroying the Republican Party, the decision worsened the split between Northern and Southern Democrats, while strengthening the Republicans, politically and morally. Rather than accepting Taney's decision as a defeat, Republicans were emboldened by it. Many people who had been fence sitters on the slavery question were pulled into the Republican camp. The situation got uglier when prominent Republicans charged that President Buchanan knew of the court's ruling in advance and had conspired with Taney to extend slavery by this decision. History proved them correct.

"Well before inauguration day, Buchanan was fully apprised of how the Court would rule," writes historian Sean Wilentz. "He disingenuously undertook an advance campaign to get the nation to accept it."[5]

Buchanan's standing was not helped when the nation experienced yet another economic depression, the relatively brief Panic of 1857, shortly after the Dred Scott decision came down.

PRESIDENTIAL VOICES

Had I so interfered in behalf of the rich, the powerful, the intelligent, the so-called great, or in behalf of any of their friends. . . . every man in this court would have deemed it an act worthy of reward rather than punishment.

—JOHN BROWN

Last speech to the court, November 2, 1859

Why did John Brown place a bounty on President Buchanan's head?
All of the talk about ending slavery had failed. Some said action was needed. And the man calling loudest for action was John Brown (1800–1859). Viewed throughout history as a lunatic, psychotic, fa-

natic, visionary, terrorist, and martyr, Brown came from a New England abolitionist family and had been an obscure failure until he went to Kansas with some of his twenty-two children to fight for the antislavery cause and gained notoriety for an attack that left five proslavery settlers hacked to pieces.

Following that slaughter, known as the "Pottawatomie Massacre," Brown had gone into hiding, then returned east to raise money and cultivate wealthy New England friends who believed in his violent rhetoric. A group known as the Secret Six formed to fund Brown's audacious plan to march south, arm slaves, and establish a black "republic" in the Appalachians to wage war against the slaveholding South. Brown had announced that he was appointed by God to free their slaves by "a violent and decisive move." When President Buchanan added $250 to a $3,000 bounty already on his head, Brown responded with a bounty of $20.50 on Buchanan's.

On October 16, 1859, Brown, with three of his sons and fifteen followers, white and black, attacked the federal arsenal at Harpers Ferry, Virginia, on the Potomac River. Taking several hostages, including one descendant of George Washington, Brown's brigade was trapped inside the arsenal by local militia until federal soldiers commanded by Colonel Robert E. Lee captured Brown and the eight men who survived the assault.

Within six weeks Brown was indicted, tried, convicted, and hanged by the state of Virginia, with the full approval of President Buchanan. Before his execution, this wild-eyed fanatic underwent a transformation, emerging as a forceful, eloquent spokesman for abolition. At his sentencing, Brown told the court, "Now if it is deemed necessary that I should forfeit my life for the furtherance of the ends of justice, and mingle my blood with the blood of my children, and with the blood of millions in this slave country whose rights are disregarded by the wicked, cruel and unjust enactments, I submit: so let it be done." In a note before he was executed, he wrote, "The crimes of this guilty land can never be purged away but with blood."[6]

While disavowing violence and condemning Brown, many in the North, as well as in Europe and Haiti, the republic of former slaves where he was hailed as a hero, came to the conclusion that John Brown was a martyr in a just cause. Even peaceable abolitionists who disdained violence, such as Henry David Thoreau and Ralph Waldo Emerson, overlooked Brown's homicidal tendencies and glorified him. Thoreau and Ralph Waldo Emerson both likened Brown to Christ. But as Northerners began to glorify Brown while disavowing his tactics, it was one more blow forcing the wedge deeper and deeper between North and South.

PRESIDENTIAL VOICES

In 1860 the rebels were encouraged by the contempt they felt for the incumbent of the presidency. . . . Mr. Buchanan's policy had, I think, rendered collision inevitable, and a continuance of that policy will not only bring it about. But will go far to produce a permanent division of the Union.

POSTMASTER GENERAL MONTGOMERY BLAIR, 1861[7]

Final Judgment: Grade F

Following Lincoln's election, but before Buchanan left office, seven states had left the Union and nearly all of the federal forts and arsenals in the seceding states had been lost. A large number of federal soldiers surrendered to troops in the newly seceded states. And Buchanan waited.

Then in January 1861, Buchanan uncharacteristically ordered a ship to carry reinforcements and supplies to Fort Sumter, the federal garrison in the Charleston harbor of the recently seceded South Carolina. Buchanan had dispatched the ship even though federal commander Robert Anderson, who held the fort, had not requested any reinforcements. The ship was fired on by South Carolina forces on January 9 and left the harbor undamaged. In response to this assault on federal power and authority, Buchanan did nothing.[8]

He did too little, too late. Believing that secession was illegal, Buchanan also thought that he could not use force against the seceding states—an argument that left the crisis for Lincoln. Buchanan's only strong desire, history suggests, was to get out of office before the shooting really began, so he would not be blamed for starting the war.

In attempting to answer the question of why Buchanan was such a catastrophically poor president, biographer Jean H. Baker concludes, "The answer speaks to one of the palpable characteristics of failed presidencies—the arrogant, wrongheaded, uncompromising use of power. . . . He assumed—and assumptions are always the heart of arrogance—that he would achieve his goals and would return to Wheatland a national hero."[9]

Buchanan retired to his home, Wheatland, in Lancaster, Pennsylvania, where he died on June 1, 1868, of pneumonia. For doing so little to stop that war, Buchanan is counted among the worst presidents in history, and his response to the Fort Sumter crisis and secession are deemed the greatest single failure of any American president.

Buchanan Administration Milestones[10]

1857

March 4	James Buchanan is inaugurated.
March 6	The *Dred Scott* decision is handed down.
September 7–11	The Mountain Meadow Massacre in Utah results in the deaths of roughly 140 people. Mormon militiamen kill emigrants heading for California in retaliation for Buchanan's order to remove Mormon leader Brigham Young as Utah's governor. Buchanan later asks Congress for troops to suppress the Mormon uprising.

1858

February	After months of voting by rival camps in Kansas, Buchanan asks Congress to admit Kansas as a slave state.
May 11	A Republican-controlled Congress admits Minnesota as the thirty-second state, a free state.

August–October   The Lincoln-Douglas debates take place. Senator Stephen Douglas attempts to reconcile "popular sovereignty" with the *Dred Scott* decision by arguing that territorial governments can refuse to pass laws necessary to support slavery. Abraham Lincoln denounces the *Dred Scott* decision as opening the way for Congress to permit slavery to expand without restraint and voices his moral opposition to slavery while carefully distancing himself from radical abolitionists. Lincoln loses the Illinois Senate race but emerges with an enhanced national reputation for his antislavery position.

1859

February 14   Oregon is admitted as the thirty-third state, a free state.

October 4   The Kansas Constitution is ratified as an antislavery document by an overwhelming popular vote.

October 16   John Brown's band raids Harpers Ferry. Brown is captured and hanged at Charles Town, Virginia, on December 2.

1860

April 23   The national Democratic Party, led by Stephen Douglas, meets at Charleston, South Carolina. They're divided over a pro-slavery stance among Southern delegates, and no nominations are made.

May 9   The Constitutional Union Party, composed of remnants from the Whig and American Parties, nominates John Bell for president.

May 18   The Republican National Convention in Chicago nominates Abraham Lincoln.

June 18   The Democratic Party meets again in Baltimore and nominates Stephen Douglas.

June 28   The delegations of Southern Democrats that abandoned the April convention nominate John C. Breckinridge for president; their platform supports slavery in the territories.

November 6   Abraham Lincoln is elected, winning roughly 39 percent of the popular vote.

December 18	The Crittenden Compromise is proposed, allowing slavery south of the old Missouri Compromise line. Lincoln opposes the plan, affirming that he will not compromise on the issue of slavery.
December 20	In South Carolina, a convention votes unanimously for an Ordinance of Secession and secedes.

1861

January 8	In his final message to Congress, Buchanan calls the Union "a sacred trust."
January 9	Mississippi becomes the second state to secede.
January 10	Florida secedes from the Union.
January 11	Alabama secedes from the Union.
January 19	Georgia secedes from the Union.
January 26	Louisiana secedes from the Union.
January 29	Kansas is admitted to the Union as the thirty-fourth state, a free state.
February 1	Texas secedes from the Union.
February 4	The seven states that have seceded form the Confederate States of America (CSA) in Montgomery, Alabama.
February 9	Jefferson Davis is elected president of the CSA, with Alexander Stephens as vice president.

MUST READS

Jean Baker, *James Buchanan*; Hampton Sides, *Blood and Thunder: The Epic Story of Kit Carson and the Conquest of the American West.*

ONLINE RESOURCES

Inaugural Address, The American Presidency Project, University of California, Santa Barbara

    http://www.presidency.ucsb.edu/ws/index.php?pid=25817#axzz1cw bgF5v3

Buchanan Resource Center, Dickinson College

    http://deila.dickinson.edu/buchanan/

Library of Congress Resource Guide

http://www.loc.gov/rr/program/bib/presidents/buchanan/index
.html

Miller Center of Public Affairs, University of Virginia

http://millercenter.org/president/buchanan

Wheatland Home

http://www.lancasterhistory.org/index.php?option=com_content
&view=article&id=1304&Itemid=278

Buchanan Papers, Historical Society of Pennsylvania

http://www2.hsp.org/collections/manuscripts/b/Buchanan0091
.html

16

The Great Emancipator
Abraham Lincoln

★ ★ ★

March 4, 1861–April 15, 1865

Milestones in Abraham Lincoln's Life

February 12, 1809	Born near Hodgenville, Kentucky
1816	Family moved to Indiana
1830	Family moved to Illinois; Lincoln became a clerk in New Salem, Illinois
1834–1842	Member of Illinois legislature
1836	Admitted to the Illinois bar
1847–1849	U.S. representative from Illinois
1858	Lincoln-Douglas debates; defeated in campaign for U.S. Senate
1861–1865	Sixteenth president
April 15, 1865	Died in Washington, D.C., aged fifty-six

PRESIDENTIAL VOICES

In your hands, my dissatisfied fellow-countrymen, and not in mine, is the momentous issue of civil war. The Government will not assail you. You can have no conflict without being yourselves the aggressors. You have no oath registered in heaven to destroy the Government, while I shall have the most solemn one to "preserve, protect, and defend it."

I am loath to close. We are not enemies, but friends. We must not be enemies. Though passion may have strained it must not break our bonds of affection. The mystic chords of memory, stretching from every battlefield and

*patriot grave to every living heart and hearthstone all over this broad land,
will yet swell the chorus of the Union, when again touched, as surely they will
be, by the better angels of our nature.*

—ABRAHAM LINCOLN

First Inaugural Address, March 4, 1861[1]

From worst to first. By most measures, James Buchanan possessed all the requirements to make a good president, including a college education and a lifetime of experience in politics and diplomacy. His successor, Abraham Lincoln, had next to none of the "right stuff." Poor, self-taught, he had come from hardscrabble beginnings and was dismissed as uncouth and uncultured.

After George Washington, no American president—or American historical figure of any kind—has been draped in more mythic splendor than Abraham Lincoln. The Railsplitter. The Great Emancipator. Honest Abe. Assailed in office, nearly denied the nomination to a second term, vilified throughout the South as well as by Northern opponents, and martyred in death, Lincoln eventually came to be considered this country's finest president. Was he?

Fast Facts

RELIGION: Christian (no professed denomination)
CAREER BEFORE POLITICS: Attorney
POLITICAL PARTY: Whig (to 1854)
    Republican (1854–1865)
    National Union Party (1864)
FIRST LADY: Mary Todd Lincoln (December 13, 1818–July 16, 1882)
CHILDREN: Robert Todd, Edward Baker, William Wallace (Willie), and Thomas (Tad)

* Of Lincoln's four boys, Edward died in Springfield just before turning four; William ("Willie") died in 1862 of typhoid fever (he is the only child of a president to die in the White House); and Tad survived his father but died at age eighteen of what is thought to have been congestive heart failure.

  Eldest son Robert Todd Lincoln was a Harvard graduate who served on Ulysses Grant's Civil War staff late in the Civil War and was present at Robert E. Lee's surrender to Grant. He later became a lawyer, served as war secretary under Presidents Garfield and Arthur, was appointed minister to Great Britain by President Harrison, and was president of the Pullman Car Company, then one of America's largest companies, from 1897 to 1911. While not present at his father's assassination, Robert Todd Lincoln was an eyewitness to the assassination of President Garfield in 1881 and was in Buffalo when President McKinley was shot and killed in 1901.

* Few first ladies before or since have been as harshly criticized as Mary Todd Lincoln. Born into a wealthy slaveholding family, she was publicly accused of being a Confederate sympathizer because some family members fought for the Confederacy. She was also excoriated in the press for what were considered extravagant clothing and furniture purchases. Her actual purchases were made worse by false reports of thousand-dollar shawls. "The stories traveled from paper to paper," notes White House historian William Seale. "Shots had been fired, and blood had been shed; America was at war, and the president's wife was on a shopping spree. . . . Mrs. Lincoln was branded as extravagant and insensitive to the national upheaval."[2] Even more hostile treatment and greater tragedy lay ahead. With the enormity of her losses and the public scorn she endured, it is small wonder that Mary Todd Lincoln was deeply depressed, as many contemporary accounts describe her.

* At six feet, four inches, Lincoln is still the tallest president on record.

* There has been considerable speculation over Lincoln's health, physical and mental, as well as his sexuality. One prominent theory was that Lincoln suffered from Marfan's Syndrome, a hereditary

disease that affects growth and is typical of people with Lincoln's long, bony frame; that idea has been largely dismissed, but no DNA tests have ever been performed on Lincoln's remains.

Similarly, Lincoln has been called "bipolar," or clinically depressed, as is frequently speculated about Mrs. Lincoln as well. In his early life, Lincoln clearly suffered from severe bouts of depression, melancholy, and anxiety. But he always said he got over the "hypo," as he called it, by reading. And biographers routinely note that Lincoln never suffered the "hypo" during the Civil War years, when he certainly had the most reason to be depressed, between the travails of the war, his relentless critics and opponents, the grievous losses he saw, and the death of his son Willie in the White House.

In 2004, C. A. Tripp's controversial book, *The Intimate World of Abraham Lincoln*, claimed that Lincoln was homosexual and had a sexual relationship with, among others, Joshua Speed, his closest friend in Springfield. Lincoln sublet a room above Speed's store before his marriage to Mary Todd Lincoln. Tripp offered circumstantial evidence of Lincoln having slept with men on many occasions and cited passages of "purple" poetry Lincoln had written that suggested homosexuality.

Many historians note that such sleeping arrangements were commonplace in the nineteenth century, as men like Lincoln often shared small rooms in boardinghouses and taverns. Doris Kearns Goodwin, for instance, dismisses the notion in *Team of Rivals*. "Their intimacy," wrote Goodwin of Lincoln and Speed, "is more an index to an era when close male friendships, accompanied by open expressions of affection and passion, were familiar and socially acceptable. Nor can sharing a bed be considered evidence of an erotic involvement. It was common practice in an era when private quarters were a rare luxury."[3]

Others, including Jean H. Baker, a biographer of Mary Todd Lincoln, accept the possibility of Lincoln's homosexuality, which remains in the realm of speculation.

* Cavalrymen surrounded Lincoln as he rode to his first inauguration, unprecedented security as the nation was on the brink of war.

* For his second inauguration in 1865, African-Americans marched in the Inaugural Parade for the first time.
* Lincoln was the first of four presidents to be assassinated.

Unlike some other self-proclaimed "log cabin" presidents who tried to give themselves an aura of common touch humility, Abraham Lincoln was the "real deal."

Born in Kentucky in 1809, at the family's Sinking Spring farm, Lincoln was the son of Thomas Lincoln, an illiterate pioneer farmer who moved several times before relocating his family to Indiana when Lincoln was seven, dogged by land title controversies and looking to get away from slavery. When Abraham was nine, his mother, Nancy Hanks Lincoln, died at age thirty-four of a common pioneer illness called the "milk sickness" that came from drinking milk from cows who had eaten poisonous "snakeweed." The boy had to help fashion her coffin from cherrywood and pull it by sled to a hill where she was buried in an unmarked grave. Lincoln's father left Abraham and a cousin, Dennis Hanks, in the charge of Lincoln's twelve-year-old sister, Sarah, as he went back to Kentucky to find a new wife. When he returned with the widowed Sarah Bush Johnston, she found Abraham and the other children were "wild, ragged and dirty."[4] (Lincoln's sister Sarah died in childbirth at age nineteen, another in a series of sharp tragedies for Lincoln.)

Though herself uneducated, his stepmother recognized Abraham's "uncommon natural Talents"[5] and encouraged young Lincoln's famous bookishness. He read *Arabian Nights* and Parson Weems's *Life of Washington* by firelight and would walk long distances to borrow a book. Lincoln's stepmother is also credited with introducing him to the Bible, and biblical phrases would color some of his greatest speeches, among the best written by (or for) any president. Without self-righteousness, false piety, or ever joining any particular church, Lincoln was a deeply spiritual man. But he had another side, the cracker barrel, storytelling side that he got from his father. "His jokes were as raw and pungent as the frontier he lived in," biographer Stephen Oates records. "Raunchy ballads about one Barbara Allen or about the silk merchant's daughter that had [his comrades] howling in delight."[6]

In April 1828, Lincoln went by riverboat as a deckhand delivering farm produce to New Orleans. That is when he got his first real taste of seeing slaves in chains. In 1830, the Lincoln family moved again, this time to southern Illinois, trying to escape another outbreak of "milk sickness" and looking for land to homestead. After helping build a new cabin, with little more than a year of any sort of formal schooling, the twenty-two-year-old Lincoln set out on his own, leaving his family to make another voyage to New Orleans and then manage a general store in the small but booming pioneer town of New Salem. During the Black Hawk War of 1832, Lincoln briefly led a detachment of Illinois militia. But, as he liked to say of his military experience, he "had a good many bloody struggles with mosquitoes."

At twenty-five, while studying for the bar, Lincoln won a seat in the Illinois legislature. He became a lawyer in 1836 and moved to Springfield, where he later met Mary Todd, the daughter of a well-to-do Louisville, Kentucky, slaveholding family. Mary Todd had already been courted by Lincoln's future political rival, Stephen Douglas. After an initial engagement with Mary, Lincoln got "cold feet" and broke it off. But he returned to Springfield in 1842 and resumed the courtship, and in November of that year, they were married.

With his law practice blossoming, Lincoln won a seat in Congress in 1846 as a Whig, or "Clay Man," as he put it. Lincoln's views in opposition to "Polk's War" in Mexico were unpopular and marked his single term. After returning to Springfield to refocus on his legal practice with partner William Herndon, he joined the new Republican Party in 1856 and was sufficiently well known to win 110 votes for a vice presidential nomination at the first Republican National Convention. Lincoln then campaigned for Republican candidate John C. Frémont, earning high marks as a stump speaker and loyal Republican.

In 1858, Lincoln ran for the U.S. Senate in Illinois and gave his famous "House Divided" speech. Following this were the famous Lincoln-Douglas debates, a series of statewide confrontations over the future of slavery in America, in which Lincoln challenged Democratic incumbent Stephen Douglas for the Illinois Senate seat. (Senators were still chosen by the state legislature at the time.) Though he lost to Douglas narrowly, Lincoln had established himself as a national figure.

PRESIDENTIAL VOICES

"A house divided against itself cannot stand." I believe this government cannot endure, permanently, half slave and half free. I do not expect the Union to be dissolved; I do not expect the house to fall; but I do expect it will cease to be divided.

—ABRAHAM LINCOLN

"House Divided" Speech, June 16, 1858[7]

Who elected Abraham Lincoln?

Without question, the election of 1860 stands as the most momentous in American history. The campaign followed John Brown's attack on Harpers Ferry by a few months. And there was only one question at hand—the future of slavery and the Union. Fresh from their strong showing in 1856, and bolstered by the unpopularity of the *Dred Scott* ruling, the Republican platform did not call for abolition, but the end of extending slavery into new territories, and for preservation of the Union. The Republicans also called for construction of a transcontinental railroad and making other "internal improvements"—the nineteenth century's answer to "infrastructure."

Another key policy goal was passage of the Homestead Act, which opened up the American West to settlement by giving white pioneers free public land. Though painted in the South as wild-eyed abolitionists who wanted to "mix the races," the Republicans were more accurately the party of the free, white workingman. While they were miles ahead of Southern Democrats and many other Americans in their racial attitudes, Republicans, including Lincoln, were not advocating citizenship or voting rights for emancipated slaves. Even at this late date, they hoped to return most freed slaves to Africa under President Monroe's policy of colonization that had created Liberia as a refuge for returning American slaves.

Meeting in Chicago, the Republicans had a front runner in New York senator William Seward, viewed by some as too extreme on abolition. The Republicans wanted someone who could deliver the newly important Western states, and on the third ballot, they turned to Lincoln, a "Westerner." Maine's Hannibal Hamlin was chosen as his running mate to strengthen appeal to Northern states.

Although well known to many Republicans for his role in the 1856 election, a series of noteworthy speeches he had made around the country, and the debates with Douglas, Lincoln was still a mystery to many Americans. "Lincoln seemed to have come from nowhere," Doris Kearns Goodwin points out. "A backwoods lawyer who had served one undistinguished term in the House of Representatives and lost two consecutive contests for the U.S. Senate. . . . When viewed against the failed efforts of his rivals, it is clear that Lincoln won the nomination because he was the shrewdest and canniest of them all. More accustomed to relying upon himself to shape events, he took the greatest control of the process leading up to the nomination, displaying a fierce ambition, an exceptional political acumen, and a wide range of emotional strengths, forged in the crucible of personal hardship."[8]

Opposing Lincoln and the Republicans were three different parties. Former Whigs whose sole goal was preservation of the Union had formed the Constitutional Union Party. They nominated John Bell, a former speaker of the House and Whig from Tennessee, and were largely dismissed as an old man's party, hopelessly stuck in the past. The Democrats had split into Northern and Southern wings. The Northern Democrats nominated Stephen Douglas, Lincoln's debate opponent, while disaffected Southern Democrats put up John C. Breckenridge, who had been vice president under James Buchanan.

Lincoln won the popular vote with about 40 percent of the total cast, even though he wasn't on the ballot in Southern states. The combined votes of Douglas, Breckenridge, and Bell were greater by a million. But Lincoln had taken the key elector-rich states in the North and West. Lincoln carried eighteen free states, Breckenridge eleven slave states, Bell three Border States, and Douglas won Missouri and three votes from New Jersey.

Following his victory, Lincoln began a train ride from Springfield to Washington, D.C.—growing his famous beard along the way at the urging of a child named Grace Bedell, who had written the suggestion to Lincoln and met the president-elect in Buffalo, New York.[9] As he approached the nation's capital, Lincoln was warned of a plot against his life. He left his special train in Philadelphia and secretly made his way to Washington for his inauguration.

The mixture of his homespun folksiness—dismissed by many as the uncouth, unsophisticated ways of a "Westerner"—the notoriety of accepting the beard advice from a child's letter, and his surreptitious arrival in the capital meant Lincoln was seen widely as an innocent "hick" who would be at the mercy of the more erudite and experienced Cabinet members and Congress.

Why did Lincoln suspend a basic constitutional right?

Between Lincoln's election and inauguration, secession was no longer a mere threat; it had become reality. As lame-duck President Buchanan dithered, seven Southern states left the Union, took control of federal forts, and formed a new "nation," the Confederate States of America, with Jefferson Davis selected president in February 1861.

On April 12, 1861, Confederate forces fired on Fort Sumter in the harbor of Charleston, South Carolina, and the Civil War was truly under way. On April 15, 1861, Lincoln called for seventy-five thousand militia troops to join the regular army to "repossess the forts, places, and property which had been seized from the Union."

The first years of the war brought mostly disaster and dissent as poorly trained and led Union forces lost a series of battles to more competently led Confederate armies in Virginia. Practically under siege, Washington, D.C, was nearly surrounded by hostile territory, leading Lincoln to one of his most controversial decisions, to suspend the writ of habeas corpus in a limited area in late April 1861. A basic constitutional right, habeas corpus—literally *to have the body*—protects the accused from arbitrary arrest and imprisonment. With Maryland threatening secession and Congress not in session, Lincoln issued the order suspending the writ so his military commanders could arrest potential secessionists who might take Maryland out of the Union. He believed such a suspension was provided for in the Constitution in the case of invasion or rebellion. Among those first arrested were the mayor of Baltimore, the city's police chief, and nine members of the Maryland legislature.

Supreme Court Chief Justice Roger Taney, author of the *Dred Scott* ruling and a Marylander himself, issued a writ of habeas corpus in 1861 following the arrest of John Merryman, an otherwise obscure secessionist from Maryland. Taney said that the suspension clause appears in Article I—which describes the legislature—and contains "not the slightest reference to the executive department." Lincoln ignored the order. In February 1862, he ordered most of the prisoners released.

Lincoln suspended habeas corpus twice more during the war, first in September 1862 on his own authority and then in March 1863 when the Republican-dominated Congress went along with him, authorizing the suspension anywhere in the country under the Habeas Corpus Suspension Act. Although the records are somewhat obscure, more than thirteen thousand Americans were arrested (and some estimates range as high as eighteen thousand), most of them opposition Democrats known as "Copperheads," so named for a poisonous snake.

(Since the Civil War, Seth Lipsky notes, Congress has only suspended habeas corpus three other times: in 1871 to suppress the Ku Klux Klan, during the Philippine Insurrection from 1899 to 1902, and in Hawaii after Pearl Harbor in 1941.[10])

How did the Emancipation Proclamation affect the war?

After a decisive Union victory at the Battle of Antietam in Maryland, Lincoln announced that he would issue a proclamation freeing their slaves unless the rebelling states returned to the Union by January 1, 1863. The day came with no changes, and on January 1, 1863, Lincoln released the formal Emancipation Proclamation, freeing those slaves in the rebellious states not under federal control.

If the Civil War was not "about" slavery before, it surely was now. Until that proclamation was made, many loyal Unionists believed that the war was being fought to end the secessionist rebellion, an unconstitutional insurrection. While slavery's role in the coming of the war was clear for political and economic reasons, many Northerners were not interested in abolition and certainly weren't interested in fighting and dying for the emancipation of black slaves.

ABRAHAM LINCOLN 257

Lincoln had made this case himself many times as he said he was fighting to save the Union. But with the Emancipation Proclamation, and a few months later in the Gettysburg Address, the war's aims and rationale became clear. America was no longer going to be "half-slave, half-free." The "house divided" would be one.

It was not a popular decision, and the draft riots in many cities soon proved that many Americans were not willing to be drafted into a war that was now about fighting to free the slaves.

How did Lincoln win a second term?

There were dark days as Lincoln looked toward the election of 1864. Three years of savage fighting, bloody standoffs, newspapers filled with casualty lists—many Republicans were looking for a new candidate.

Uncertain that the Republicans would choose him, Lincoln famously cautioned, "It is not best to swap horses while crossing the river," arguing in his homespun style that the surest way to end the conflict was to stay the course. He added, "I am not so poor a horse that they might not make a botch of it in trying to swap." It was a line he would trot out during the campaign as well.

In June 1864, just after Grant hurled tens of thousands of Union troops at Robert E. Lee's Confederate Army in the ferocious battle at Cold Harbor, Virginia, the Republicans gathered in Baltimore. Under the banner of the "National Union Party"—the national Republican ticket in all but name; state Republican parties kept the name Republican—they did select Lincoln and added Tennessee's Andrew Johnson, a slaveholding senator from Tennessee who remained loyal to the Union, as running mate. The change in party name was meant to attract Northern Democrats who would not vote Republican. But by any name, the party's chances looked poor, with popular sentiment turning against the war, and when the losses were tallied at Cold Harbor, Union casualties were more than sixty thousand dead and wounded. The carnage was being called "not war but murder."

These losses enabled Lincoln's opponents to throttle him in the 1864 wartime campaign as a "Monster" and "Butcher." But one of the most damaging assaults was a pamphlet called *Miscegenation*—a new word that meant race mixing. Attributed to the Republican Party, the pamphlet advised New York's Irishmen to take black wives. This was a year after the 1863 draft riots in which more than a hundred blacks were lynched by mostly Irish mobs in New York angry over the Enrollment (or Conscription) Act, a wartime draft law that required males between twenty and forty-five to register for the draft but allowed men to hire a substitute. The *Miscegenation* pamphlet, it turned out, was a campaign "dirty trick" hatched by opposition Democratic journalists to discredit the Republicans.

As late as August 1864, Lincoln thought his prospects were doomed.

It took several Union victories, including Admiral Farragut's capture of Mobile in August and the fiery fall of Atlanta in September, to save Lincoln's presidency. It did not hurt Lincoln's chances that his Democratic opponent, George B. McClellan, was a general that Lincoln had dismissed for a case of the "slows," meaning he didn't fight hard enough. McClellan proved as poor a candidate as a general.

Lincoln rolled to a convincing electoral victory, as Union armies started to roll up battlefield victories—although at a tremendous cost. There was no horse swap in 1864—and the conventional wisdom first born in the War of 1812 prevailed: America reelects its wartime presidents.

PRESIDENTIAL VOICES

One-eighth of the whole population were colored slaves, not distributed generally over the Union, but localized in the southern part of it. These slaves constituted a peculiar and powerful interest. All knew that this interest was somehow the cause of the war. To strengthen, perpetuate, and extend this interest was the object for which the insurgents would rend the Union even by war, while the Government claimed no right to do more than to restrict the territorial enlargement of it.

Both read the same Bible and pray to the same God, and each invokes His aid against the other. It may seem strange that any men should dare to ask a just God's assistance in wringing their bread from the sweat of other men's faces, but let us judge not, that we be not judged. The prayers of both could not be answered. That of neither has been answered fully.

Fondly do we hope, fervently do we pray, that this mighty scourge of war may speedily pass away. Yet, if God wills that it continue until all the wealth piled by the bondsman's two hundred and fifty years of unrequited toil shall be sunk, and until every drop of blood drawn with the lash shall be paid by another drawn with the sword, as was said three thousand years ago, so still it must be said "the judgments of the Lord are true and righteous altogether."

—ABRAHAM LINCOLN
Second Inaugural Address, March 4, 1865[11]

Who was behind the conspiracy to kill Lincoln?

On April 3, 1865, Abraham Lincoln toured the defeated capital of the crippled Confederacy and sat in Jefferson Davis's Richmond office. On April 9, 1865, Robert E. Lee surrendered to Ulysses S. Grant, effectively bringing the Civil War to a close. More than 600,000 Americans were dead, an astonishing 2 percent of the population. (That number, widely cited since 1900, is being questioned. Based on new Census information, the estimates range from 750,000 to as high as 850,000, according to historian J. David Hacker.[12])

On Friday, April 14, 1865—Good Friday—Lincoln met with his cabinet and lifted the blockade of the South. His mood was high and he was preaching moderation and reconciliation to all around him, preparing a plan of reconstruction that would bring the rebellious states back into the Union fold with a minimum of recriminations and punishment.

That evening he took his wife and a young couple they knew to see a play called *Our American Cousin* at Ford's Theatre in downtown Washington. The Washington policeman guarding the president left his post, either for a drink or to get a better view of the play. There was a pistol shot. Lincoln slumped over. A man jumped from the president's box to the stage, in the process catching his spur on the bunting that draped the box and breaking his shin. He brandished his gun and shouted, "*Sic semper tyrannis,*" the state motto of Virginia, "Thus always to tyrants." Then he escaped through a back exit to a waiting horse.

Lincoln was taken to a lodging house across the street from the theater, where he died the next morning, throwing the shocked nation into a profound grief of a kind it had never experienced before. Hated and derided during the war years by the Copperheads, "Radical Republicans" who thought him too moderate, and a host of other groups who found fault with him for one reason or another, Abraham Lincoln had become, in death, a hero of the entire nation. Even leaders of the Confederacy spoke of his death with regret.

Even as Lincoln was shot, a second assassin had assaulted Secretary of State William Seward at home with a knife. Attacks on General Grant and Vice President Johnson were planned but never carried out.

Secretary of War Stanton took charge, and martial law was declared in Washington. The assassin, it was soon discovered, was John Wilkes Booth, an actor like his more famous father, Junius Brutus Booth, and his brother Edwin Booth. A fanatical supporter of the South—he had watched John Brown hang but never joined the Confederate Army— Booth first plotted with a small group of conspirators in a Washington boardinghouse to kidnap Lincoln. With Lee's surrender and the war's end, they planned instead to assassinate the president, along with other key government figures, including Vice President Andrew Johnson and Secretary of State Seward.

An intensive, unprecedented manhunt followed, in which a $50,000 reward was placed on Booth's head and hundreds of people with any connection to the actor were initially arrested. Booth was finally trapped in a Bowling Green, Virginia, tobacco-drying barn on April 26, after the Union Army was tipped off to his whereabouts. After Booth refused to surrender, a Union officer set the barn afire. Limping from his broken leg, Booth moved toward the barn door and was shot; he died two and a half hours later. His body was secretly returned to Washington for burial in an undisclosed location to avoid it becoming a symbolic site for sympathizers.

Eight suspects ultimately faced a military tribunal for the assassination conspiracy: seven men and Mary Surratt, owner of the boardinghouse where the plot was hatched and mother of suspect John Surratt, who had escaped capture and evaded arrest until 1866. The tribunal sentenced four of the conspirators, including Mary Surratt, Lewis Powell, David Herold, and George Azterodt, to be hanged; all four were executed by hanging on July 7, 1865. Mary Surratt became the first woman executed by the U.S. government.

Three others were tried and received life sentences, including Dr. Samuel Mudd, who treated Booth after the assassination but whose role in the plot remain controversial. Edman Spangler, the Ford's stagehand who held Booth's horse, but likely had nothing to do with the plot, received a six-year prison sentence. John Surratt, a plotter and son of the boardinghouse owner, escaped to Europe, was eventually captured in Egypt in 1866, and was tried but acquitted by a civil, not military, trial. He planned a lecture tour that was canceled, but Surratt lived until 1916.[13]

Although conspiracy theories involving Jefferson Davis and most other prominent leaders of the Confederacy abounded in the press, they were all largely dismissed. Davis was captured and held for two years without trial, but he was eventually released to go home to write his version of events in the war.

On Tuesday, April 18, thousands of mourners viewed Lincoln's corpse in the White House. The funeral on April 19 was for several hundred invited guests and Ulysses S. Grant sat alone, his face glistening with tears. Lincoln's casket and that of his son Willie, whose remains had initially been buried in a Georgetown cemetery, were taken back to Springfield by train.

During the public opening of the White House, people stole anything they could lay their hands on as White House souvenirs, including the silver and china. Adding to Mary Todd Lincoln's distress, some newspapers accused her of ransacking the White House. She was, in fact, absorbed by grief, howling in hysterics for days. Lincoln's bereft widow finally departed the White House on May 22, a day before the Grand Review of the Armies of the Republic, the official celebration of the end of the Civil War.

Final Judgment: Grade A+

A melancholy man who suffered greatly, for both public and private reasons, Lincoln confronted a hornets' nest of problems graver than those faced by any other president. He did things that modern presidents might not attempt—creating a national army out of state militias, calling up tens of thousands of volunteers, blocking ports, and, in what may be the most controversial decision of all, suspending the writ of habeas corpus in order to detain thousands of opponents without firm charges or due process of law.

During the war, Lincoln faced opposition from all sides, including so-called "Radical Republicans" and hard-line abolitionists, for his seeming moderation toward slavery. More dangerous opposition came from the Peace Democrats, or "Copperheads," who were remnants of the Northern Democratic Party and sympathetic to the South. Copperheads wanted to stop the war, viewing Lincoln as a dictator for his suspension of the writ of habeas corpus, the widely scorned draft under the Enrollment Act of 1863, and the Emancipation Proclamation, among other actions.

With great personal courage, a native intelligence, the writing skills of a poet, a self-deprecating sense of humor, and a central core of humility and humanity, Lincoln surmounted these challenges, winning reelection and managing the most costly war in American history, but losing his life. By the time of his assassination, Lincoln had moved from resolute commander in chief, prosecuting the war at horrendous costs, to healing unifier. While some called him a dictator, there is little doubt that a weaker president might have failed in the most basic test of Lincoln's presidency—preserving the Union from potential destruction.

History can never be about speculation, but there can be little doubt that the nation's course would have been greatly different if Lincoln had lived and not been succeeded by his vice president, Andrew Johnson.

Lincoln Administration Milestones[14]

1861

March 4	Abraham Lincoln is inaugurated.
March 11	The Confederate Congress unanimously adopts the Confederate Constitution, which forbids the passage of any bill outlawing slavery.
April 12	South Carolina's Confederate batteries, under the command of General P. G. T. Beauregard, open fire

on Fort Sumter, in the Charleston harbor, at 4:30 a.m. After thirty-three hours under attack, Major Robert Anderson surrenders the fort.

April 15 Lincoln calls for seventy-five thousand volunteers to put down the "rebellion."

April 17 Virginia secedes, followed by North Carolina, Tennessee, and Arkansas.

April 19 Lincoln orders a blockade of Confederate ports.

May 21 After Virginia secedes, the capital of the confederacy moves to Richmond.

July 21 The Battle of Bull Run is fought near Manassas, Virginia, with a humiliating rout of Union forces.

October 31 General Winfield Scott retires as commander in chief of the Union Army at age seventy-five. Following General Scott's retirement, President Lincoln names George McClellan, a West Point graduate, as the new commander.

1862

February 20 Willie Lincoln dies from typhoid fever.

April 16 Slavery is abolished in the District of Columbia.

June 1 General Robert E. Lee is appointed commander of the Confederate Army of Northern Virginia.

August 29–30 The Second Battle of Bull Run. Union troops suffer another defeat and retreat to Washington, D.C.

September 17 The Battle of Antietam Creek near Sharpsburg, Maryland, ends in a Confederate defeat: the bloodiest one-day engagement of the Civil War—nearly five thousand men are killed and eighteen thousand wounded. A frustrated Lincoln removes McClellan from command. His replacements will include Generals Burnside, Hooker, and Meade, who are also eventually removed.

September 22 After the victory at Antietam, Lincoln announces the Emancipation Proclamation, to go into effect on January 1, 1863.

1863

January 1	The Emancipation Proclamation goes into effect. The document frees all slaves in Confederate or contested areas of the South. Slaves in non-Confederate border states and in parts of the Confederacy under Union control are not included.
March 3	Congress passes a conscription law; for $300, a draftee can hire a substitute.
May 1–4	The Battle of Chancellorsville, Virginia, is fought. General Lee wins a brilliant victory and commences another invasion into the North. Union general Hooker is replaced by George Meade.
May 2	Confederate general Stonewall Jackson is accidentally wounded by his own troops in the Battle of Chancellorsville; Jackson dies of pneumonia on May 10.
June 20	Carved out of Virginia, West Virginia is admitted as the thirty-fifth state, a free state.
July 1–5	The Battle of Gettysburg ends in a Confederate defeat. Lee takes his troops across the Potomac, with nearly thirty thousand killed, wounded, or missing; Union forces suffer twenty-three thousand casualties.
July 4	General Ulysses S. Grant captures Vicksburg, Mississippi, giving the Union control over the Mississippi River.
July 13	Draft riots in New York and other Northern cities protest the Conscription Act. In New York, more than one hundred people, many African-American, are killed by angry mobs who object to fighting to free slaves.
November 19	Lincoln delivers the Gettysburg Address at the dedication of a national cemetery on the bloody battlefield.
November 25	The Battle of Chattanooga, a Union victory under Ulysses S. Grant, opens the way for an invasion of Georgia.

1864

March 9
Lincoln gives Ulysses S. Grant command of the entire United States Army; he is promoted to lieutenant general, a position held before only by George Washington.

June 7
The Republican National Convention nominates President Lincoln for a second term; Democrat Andrew Johnson is chosen as his new running mate.

August 29
The Democratic National Convention nominates General George B. McClellan, the Union commander Lincoln had fired; the Democrats call for a cease-fire and peace conference.

September 1–2
Atlanta falls to Union forces led by General William Tecumseh Sherman.

October 31
Nevada becomes the thirty-sixth state, a free state whose statehood was rushed to give Republicans additional votes in the upcoming presidential election.

November 8
Abraham Lincoln is reelected, with 55 percent of the popular vote; Lincoln wins 212 electoral votes to McClellan's 21.

December 15
Salmon P. Chase is appointed chief justice of the Supreme Court. Secretary of the Treasury under Lincoln, Chase is credited with keeping the nation out of financial ruin. The men had disagreed over policy, and his appointment was seen as a conciliatory move by Lincoln.

1865

March 3
Congress creates the Freedmen's Bureau to help Southern blacks affected by the war. It will supply newly emancipated blacks with food, clothing, and medical care, and will orchestrate the placement of freedmen on abandoned lands.

March 4
Abraham Lincoln is inaugurated for his second term.

April 3
The Confederate government evacuates Richmond.

April 9	Robert E. Lee surrenders to General Grant, marking the end of the Civil War.
April 14	Actor and Confederate sympathizer John Wilkes Booth shoots President Lincoln at around 10:15 p.m.
April 15	Abraham Lincoln dies at 7:22 a.m. in the home of William Petersen. Vice President Andrew Johnson is sworn in as the seventeenth president.

MUST READS

Doris Kearns Goodwin, *Team of Rivals: The Political Genius of Abraham Lincoln*; Philip B. Kunhardt, Jr., Philip B. Kunhardt III, and Peter W. Kunhardt, *Lincoln: An Illustrated Biography*; Abraham Lincoln, *Abraham Lincoln: Speeches and Writings* (two volumes); Stephen B. Oates, *With Malice Toward None: The Life of Abraham Lincoln*; James L. Swanson, *Manhunt: The Twelve-Day Chase for Lincoln's Killer*; Jay Winik, *April 1865: The Month That Saved America*.

ONLINE RESOURCES

Inaugural Addresses, Avalon Project, Yale Law School
  1861: http://avalon.law.yale.edu/19th_century/lincoln1.asp
  1865: http://avalon.law.yale.edu/19th_century/lincoln2.asp
First Message to Congress
  http://www.presidency.ucsb.edu/ws/index.php?pid=29502
  #axzz1JcPYWVyq
Emancipation Proclamation, National Archives
  http://www.ourdocuments.gov/doc.php?flash=true&doc=34
Emancipation Proclamation, Library of Congress
  http://memory.loc.gov/ammem/alhtml/almintr.html
Lincoln Birthplace
  http://www.nps.gov/abli/
Abraham Lincoln Library and Museum
  http://www.alplm.org/home.html
Lincoln Home, National Park Service
  http://www.nps.gov/history/nr/twhp/wwwlps/lessons/127liho/
Lincoln Cottage
  http://www.lincolncottage.org/visit/index.htm

Lincoln Memorial, National Park Service
http://www.nps.gov/linc/index.htm

Miller Center of Public Affairs, University of Virginia
http://millercenter.org/index.php/academic/americanpresident
/lincoln

"Times Topics," *New York Times*: Abraham Lincoln
http://topics.nytimes.com/top/reference/timestopics/people/l
/abraham_lincoln/index.html

"Abraham and Mary Lincoln—A House Divided," *The American Experience*, PBS
http://www.pbs.org/wgbh/americanexperience/films/lincolns
/player/

Dinitia Smith, "Finding Homosexual Threads in Lincoln's Legend," *New York Times*, December 16, 2004
http://www.nytimes.com/2004/12/16/books/16linc.html?scp=1
&sq=c%20a%20tripp&st=cse

17

Andrew Johnson

* * *

April 15, 1865–March 4, 1869

Milestones in Andrew Johnson's Life

December 29, 1808	Born in Raleigh, North Carolina
1822–1824	Worked as tailor's apprentice
1828–1830	Alderman of Greeneville, Tennessee
1830–1833	Mayor of Greeneville, Tennessee
1835–1837/ 1839–1841	Member of Tennessee House
1841–1843	Member of Tennessee Senate
1843–1853	U.S. representative from Tennessee
1853–1857	Governor of Tennessee
1857–1862	U.S. senator from Tennessee
1862–1864	Military governor of Tennessee
1865	Vice president under Lincoln
1865–1869	Seventeenth president
1874–1875	U.S. senator from Tennessee
July 31, 1875	Died at Carter Station, Tennessee, aged sixty-six

PRESIDENTIAL VOICES

This is a country for white men and, by God, as long as I am president it shall be a government for white men.

—ANDREW JOHNSON[1]

James Buchanan, Lincoln's predecessor, is routinely ranked among the worst presidents. He is often saved from the ignominy of "last place" by Lincoln's successor, Andrew Johnson.

Of course, Andrew Johnson—the first president to succeed to the office following an assassination and the first to be impeached—is immediately cast in a poor light just for following the martyred Lincoln. If Johnson had been merely adequate or competent, he might have avoided such a regrettable legacy.

But the stakes for the country have rarely been so high as they were when he came to office: a nation scarred by a brutal war that had taken some 2 percent of the population; an embittered, defeated Confederacy; many in the Union states angry with the "rebels" who brought on the war and were seen as responsible for Lincoln's murder; and some four million formerly enslaved Americans whose rightful place in the nation was a great, unanswered question.

Had Johnson possessed the temperament to provide solutions to some of these problems, he might have joined the presidential pantheon. He did not. And for that, the country—and Johnson—paid a steep price.

Fast Facts

RELIGION: Christian (no formal affiliation)
ASSOCIATIONS: Freemason
CAREER BEFORE POLITICS: Tailor
POLITICAL PARTY: Democratic
> National Union (Johnson ran with Lincoln on this ticket but was a Democrat for most of his career.)

FIRST LADY: Eliza McCardle Johnson (October 4, 1810–January 15, 1876)
CHILDREN: Martha, Charles, Mary, Robert, and Andrew Jr.

* Sixteen when she married Andrew Johnson—himself then eighteen—Eliza McCardle was wed at a younger age than any other first lady. In

poor health after Johnson succeeded Lincoln, she remained on the second floor of the White House, appearing only two times publicly: at a reception for the queen of Hawaii in 1866 and her husband's birthday party in 1867. Daughter Martha served as Johnson's White House hostess in place of her ailing mother.

* Son Charles Johnson joined the Tennessee Union Infantry and died during the war after being thrown from his horse.

* Like Andrew Jackson, an adopted son of Tennessee, Johnson admired Jackson and, when he moved into the White House, kept some movers from taking Jackson's old desk to auction. "Whatever was Old Hickory's I revere," said Johnson. "It is about the only thing that is a memento of bygone years, when the Constitution of the United States was worth more than the paper on which it is printed."[2]

* Congress overrode fifteen of Johnson's twenty-nine vetoes of legislation, the most overrides of any president.

* When Johnson considered trying Robert E. Lee for treason, he was stopped short by the angry objection of Ulysses S. Grant. Grant's intervention probably saved Lee from trial and possible execution.[3] After his election, Grant would not ride to the inaugural with the outgoing president, so Johnson did not attend his successor's swearing in.

* Andrew Johnson was the first president to be impeached. He was acquitted in the Senate by one vote.

* Johnson is the only president to join the U.S. Senate following his presidency.

* Before his death, Johnson requested that his body be wrapped in an American flag and that his head rest on his personal copy of the Constitution.

On the face of it, Andrew Johnson's life would count as an incredible American success story. Born in Raleigh, North Carolina, then a small town of some one thousand people, including more than three hundred slaves, Johnson was even poorer than Lincoln. He came into a hard-

scrabble life, the second of two sons (a sister died in childhood). His father, Jacob Johnson, was a landless, illiterate workingman who made a living doing odd jobs—a porter, constable, captain of the town watch, and bell-ringer, he died shortly after rescuing some men from drowning. Andrew was three at the time, and his mother struggled as a seamstress and laundress to support him and his brother. (When Andrew Johnson later became more prominent, there would be town smirks and gossip that the young boy did not look like his father. But there was never any proof of these rumors.[4])

Consigned to the world of "poor, white trash," Johnson did not attend school but instead was indentured to a tailor at the age of fourteen, with the understanding that he must remain with the tailor until he was twenty-one, little more than a slave. During this period, Johnson developed his lifelong aversion to the wealthy, planter-society elite of the South. Still, as biographer Hans L. Trefousse makes clear, Johnson was not at the bottom of the social pecking order. "After all, he was white, a fact that gave him a standing immeasurably higher than that of Raleigh's numerous blacks. . . . He certainly could never escape the ingrained racism so prevalent in Southern society. . . . Exposed to these attitudes at an early age, Johnson was never able to shake them off."[5]

While in the tailor's shop, Johnson began to teach himself to read and listened as others read from collections of great speeches. When Johnson and his brother, also an apprentice, ran away from the shop, the tailor posted a reward for the boys' return that read like a runaway slave notice. Eventually returning home to his mother, who had since remarried, Johnson then moved west with her and his stepfather, crossing the mountains into Tennessee with a two-wheeled cart drawn by a blind pony. They settled in Greeneville, where at age seventeen, Johnson set up his own tailoring shop.

At eighteen, he married sixteen-year-old Eliza, and she later helped teach him to read, write, and do mathematics. By nineteen, Johnson had entered politics on a local level and devoted his energy to promoting the interests of the "mechanics"—the free, white working class.

A Jackson Democrat who continued to sew his own suits, Johnson later served as a U.S. representative, Tennessee's governor, and a senator from Tennessee, where he was one of the architects of the Homestead Act, which granted free public land to settlers—one of his few significant legislative accomplishments. Campaigning for the Democratic presidential nomination in 1860, Johnson lost, but he stayed loyal to the Union after Lincoln's election, the only senator from a seceding state to remain in Congress. He proclaimed in 1861, "Show me the man who makes war on the government, and fires on its vessels, and I will show you a traitor."

In 1862, Johnson was appointed military governor of Tennessee, and in 1864, Lincoln saw Johnson as a loyal "War Democrat," a Southerner who would help win votes in the border states with the newly formed Union Party. The choice was not widely applauded by Northern Republicans or the press. "To think that one frail life stands between this insolent, clownish creature and the presidency! May God bless and spare Abraham Lincoln," said the *New York World* in 1865.

Johnson did not help his cause when he had a few too many whiskeys with Hannibal Hamlin, Lincoln's outgoing first vice president, before he was sworn into office. He gave a rambling, slurred drunken speech to the Senate chamber.

One of the co-conspirators in the Lincoln assassination, George Atzerodt, had been assigned to target Johnson, and he stalked the vice president, trailing him to his Washington hotel room, but lost his nerve at the last minute. Atzerodt got drunk at the hotel bar instead. Caught and tried, he was executed with the other conspirators.

PRESIDENTIAL VOICES

There are moments in the lives of most men, when the doors of their souls are open, and unconsciously to themselves, their true characters may be read by the observant eye. It was at such an instant when I caught a glimpse of the real nature of this man, which all subsequent developments proved true. I was standing in the crowd by the side of Mrs. Thomas Dorsey, when Mr. Lincoln touched Mr. Johnson and pointed me out to him. The first expression which came to his face, and which I think was the true index of his heart, was one of bitter contempt and aversion. Seeing that I had observed him, he tried

to assume a more friendly appearance, but it was too late. . . . I turned to
Mrs. Dorsey and said, "Whatever Andrew Johnson may be, he is not friend
to our race."

—FREDERICK DOUGLASS[6]

(Here is what Johnson thought of Douglass and the other African-
Americans who later came to the White House to urge suffrage for
emancipated Negroes: "Those damned sons of bitches thought they
had me in a trap. I know that damned Douglass; he's just like any
nigger, and he would sooner cut a white man's throat than not."[7])

What did Reconstruction fix?

In the aftermath of the war, the Southern states were devastated. Provisional military governors were established in the rebellious states, but
Lincoln's emerging plans for restoring the seceded states to full membership in the Union were moderate and reconciliatory. Southerners
could become citizens once more by taking a simple loyalty oath. When
10 percent of the citizens of a state had taken the oath, the state could
set up a government. "Radical Republicans," led by Thaddeus Stevens
of Pennsylvania, Ben Wade of Ohio, and Charles Sumner of Massachusetts, wanted stricter terms, but when Lincoln died and was succeeded
by Andrew Johnson, that situation was at a standstill.

As president after Lincoln's assassination, Johnson favored Lincoln's
moderate approach to what Lincoln called "restoration," which would
readmit states after they had ratified the slavery-abolishing Thirteenth
Amendment, which had been passed in December 1865.

Johnson, who maintained a hatred of the Southern planter society
that had scorned him, had spoken out during the war for harsh punitive
measures toward the Confederates. But his approach as president softened, and he began to butt heads with the Radical Republicans, who
wanted not only retribution, but also to maintain the control of Congress they had enjoyed during the war years, when Democrats, mostly
Southerners, were absent. As the Southern states gradually returned to

the fold, politicians from the former Confederacy returned to Congress and antagonized Northerners by passing restrictive laws meant to control emancipated slaves. Obviously designed to circumvent the Thirteenth Amendment, these "Black Codes" outraged the Republicans, who formed a Committee of Reconstruction that heard tales of violence and cruelty toward freed slaves.

The Republican-dominated Congress also established the Freedmen's Bureau, aimed at helping the approximately four million freed slaves. And although Johnson vetoed the Civil Rights Act of 1866, which declared blacks citizens and denied states the power to restrict their rights, the Republicans had the votes to override him and the bill was passed.

Under the congressional plan of Reconstruction, passed in July 1867, former Confederate states were required to grant the vote to black men in their states and to ratify the Fourteenth Amendment, which extended citizenship to blacks and everyone born in the United States (with some exceptions, including Indians) and guaranteed equal protection and due process under law. (The constitutional guarantee of black male suffrage came about with ratification of the Fifteenth Amendment in 1869.)

The plan also placed Confederate states under military control, with twenty thousand federal troops maintaining the peace in five military districts. White Republicans joined newly franchised black voters to create biracial legislatures; public schools were built, and some of the first all-black colleges were founded. Under U.S. Army control, ten former Confederate states were readmitted by the end of 1870. (Tennessee had previously been readmitted in 1866.)

Despite its successes, including the shocking idea that black men were voting and holding office in the South, Reconstruction was bitterly opposed by most white Southerners. The result was a revived Democratic party dedicated to the end of Reconstruction, and the emergence of the Ku Klux Klan to promote white supremacy. With beatings, lynches, cross burnings, and other forms of violent intimidation, combined with the "Black Codes," the political aims of congressional Reconstruction faced a monumental challenge.

Final Judgment: Grade F

In 1867, Congress passed—over Johnson's veto—the Tenure of Office Act that prohibited the president from removing certain officials from office without Senate consent. When Johnson dismissed Secretary of War Stanton in February 1868, the House voted to impeach the president, lodging eleven articles of impeachment against him, most of the charges related to his breach of the Tenure of Office Act.

In May, the Senate acquitted Johnson by a vote of 35–19, one less than the two-thirds majority required for conviction. A few days later, the Republicans nominated General Ulysses S. Grant for president.

History has treated Johnson's struggle with Congress favorably in the sense that his impeachment and subsequent acquittal were a victory for the separation of powers. But that is about as far as the laudatory notes go. Andrew Johnson was stubborn to the point of inflexibility, outright racist in his public and private comments, and unbending.

Describing Johnson's legacy, historian Lewis L. Gould wrote, "Andrew Johnson was a major disruptive force in the history of the Republican Party. As president he made the least of the historic opportunity afforded him, and his racism has tainted his reputation. . . . Johnson encouraged the South to believe that it could escape the consequences of the war. In so doing the President made the task of Reconstruction divisive and bitter."[8]

Although he shared a life story with Lincoln, he lacked all of Lincoln's saving graces. In so many ways, he was the wrong man at the wrong time.

Andrew Johnson Administration Milestones[9]

1865

April 15	Vice President Andrew Johnson takes the presidential oath in his hotel room at the Kirkwood House.
April 21	Lincoln's funeral train departs Washington, D.C., on its journey to Springfield, Illinois.
May 23–24	The end of the Civil War is celebrated in Washington, D.C., as Union armies parade through the streets.

May 29	Johnson announces his plan for restoring Confederate states to the Union: He grants amnesty to all white Southerners who take a loyalty oath and proposes to appoint to the defeated states provisional governors who can direct new constitutions abolishing slavery and renouncing secession. Once these constitutions are authorized, the states will be readmitted.
June 13	Johnson appoints a provisional governor of Mississippi and, over the next few weeks, appoints provisional governors for Georgia, Texas, Alabama, South Carolina, and Florida.
December 2	Mississippi passes the first "Black Code," which restricts the newly won rights of African-Americans; other ex–Confederate states follow suit.
December 12	Johnson orders the provisional governors of Mississippi, Alabama, Georgia, South Carolina, and Florida to hand power over to newly elected governments populated with numerous ex–Confederate officials.

1866

February 19	Johnson vetoes a bill calling for the extension of the Freedmen's Bureau. Congress overrides the veto.
March 27	Johnson vetoes the Civil Rights Act, a second attempt by Congress to provide freedmen with federal citizenship. Congress overrides the veto.
June 19	Congress sends the Fourteenth Amendment to the states for ratification. The amendment seeks to prevent ex-Confederates from holding office; it also establishes the citizenship of African-Americans: "All persons born or naturalized in the United States, and subject to the jurisdiction thereof, are citizens of the United States and of the State wherein they reside."
July 24	Tennessee is readmitted to the Union after it ratifies the Fourteenth Amendment, the first state to do so.
November	Radical Republicans score major victories in congressional elections. The Republican-dominated Congress

will try to take the upper hand in national policy, including Reconstruction.

1867

March 1	Nebraska, the thirty-seventh state, joins the Union.
March 2	Congress passes, over a Johnson veto, the First Reconstruction Act, setting up five military districts in the South, each under a military commander appointed by the president. Congress also passes—over another Johnson veto—the Tenure of Office Act, prohibiting President Johnson from removing cabinet officers without the Senate's consent.
March 23	Johnson vetoes the Second Reconstruction Act, which orders military commanders to call elections in the South. Congress overrides Johnson's veto that day.
March 30	Secretary of State William H. Seward acquires Alaska from Russia for $7.2 million—the land is referred to as "Seward's Icebox" and "Seward's Folly."
July 19	Johnson vetoes the Third Reconstruction Act, which spells out election procedures in the South and reasserts congressional control over Reconstruction. Congress overrides.
August 5	Johnson asks Secretary of War (and Radical Republican) Edwin Stanton to resign after Stanton says the military governors must answer to both Congress and the president. Stanton refuses to step down.
August 12	Johnson suspends Secretary Stanton from his position.

1868

February 21	Johnson formally removes Stanton and gives control of the War Department to General Lorenzo Thomas. Stanton barricades himself in his cabinet office for roughly two months.
February 24	The House of Representatives votes to impeach Johnson, focusing on his breach of the Tenure of Office Act. The 126–47 vote is along party lines.

March 5	The Senate begins its impeachment trial.
May 16	The Senate votes 35–19 to convict President Johnson, but falls one vote short of the necessary two-thirds majority. Seven Republicans, including Edmund Ross of Kansas, vote against impeachment and are denounced as traitors.
May 20–21	The Republican National Convention meets in Chicago and nominates war hero General Ulysses S. Grant for president.
November 3	Republican Ulysses S. Grant defeats Democrat Horatio Seymour by only 300,000 votes of 5,715,000 cast. The large numbers of black Republican votes are decisive, and the party becomes convinced that black suffrage is a political necessity.
December 8	Johnson delivers his final Annual Message to Congress, again requesting the repeal of the Reconstruction Acts.

MUST READS

Eric Foner, *A Short History of Reconstruction*; Annette Gordon-Reed, *Andrew Johnson*.

ONLINE RESOURCES

Library of Congress Resource Guide
　　http://www.nps.gov/anjo///www.loc.gov/rr/program/bib/presidents
　　/ajohnson/

Miller Center of Public Affairs, University of Virginia
　　http://millercenter.org/president/johnson

Andrew Johnson National Historic Site, National Park Service
　　http://www.nps.gov/anjo/

"Impeachment of Andrew Johnson," *Harper's Weekly*
　　http://www.andrewjohnson.com/

Obituary, *New York Times*
　　http://www.nytimes.com/learning/general/onthisday/bday/1229
　　.html?scp=4&sq=%22Andrew%20Johnson%22%20book%20review
　　&st=cse

18

Unconditional Surrender
Ulysses S. Grant

★ ★ ★

March 4, 1869–March 4, 1877

Milestones in Ulysses S. Grant's Life

April 27, 1822	Born in Point Pleasant, Ohio
1839–1843	Attended West Point
1843–1853	Served in the Mexican War
1854–1858	Farmed near St. Louis, Missouri
1860–1861	Clerked in tannery store at Galena, Illinois
1861–1865	Served in Civil War; commanded all Union armies
1869–1877	Eighteenth president
1880	Unsuccessful candidate for Republican presidential nomination
July 23, 1885	Died at Mount McGregor, New York, aged sixty-three

PRESIDENTIAL VOICES

The country having just emerged from a great rebellion, many questions will come before it for settlement in the next four years which preceding Administrations have never had to deal with. In meeting these it is desirable that they should be approached calmly, without prejudice, hate, or sectional pride, remembering that the greatest good to the greatest number is the object to be attained.

This requires security of person, property, and free religious and political

opinion in every part of our common country, without regard to local prejudice.
All laws to secure these ends will receive my best efforts for their enforcement.

ULYSSES S. GRANT

First Inaugural Address, March 4, 1869[1]

T he conquering hero of the Union, Ulysses S. Grant did not look the part. He was short, scruffy, favored enlisted men's uniforms, and was dogged by reports of his fondness for drink—a slightly undeserved reputation. Grant clearly was a drinker at times in his life, but the image of him as a stumbling drunk is a caricature. One successor, Theodore Roosevelt, later called him the "Hammer of the North" and wrote, "Grant's supreme virtue was his doggedness. . . . He was master of strategy and tactics, but he was also a master of hard-hitting. . . . His name is among the greatest in our history."[2]

There is no question that he was a dogged, determined general whose command skills helped win the war for the Union. Unfortunately, those strengths did not translate into the complexities of leading the large, swiftly growing, and rapidly changing nation. Another of his successors, James A. Garfield, who served on the battlefield under Grant, once said, "He has done more than any other President to degrade the character of Cabinet officers by choosing them on the model of the military staff, because of their pleasant personal relationship to him and not because of their national reputation and public needs."

Garfield was right. Personally honest, Grant was notoriously inept when it came to surrounding himself with men who were corrupt, both in private and as president. Some of them blackened his presidency; others would reduce Grant to bankruptcy. Finally, a third later successor, Woodrow Wilson, once wrote of him, "The honest, simple-hearted soldier had not added prestige to the presidential office. He himself knew he had failed . . . that he ought never to have been made president."[3]

Fast Facts

RELIGION: Methodist (Although raised Methodist, Grant never officially joined a church.)

EDUCATION: United States Military Academy (West Point)

MILITARY SERVICE: U.S. Army, Mexican War and Civil War

CAREER BEFORE POLITICS: Soldier, farmer, leather shop clerk

POLITICAL PARTY: Republican

FIRST LADY: Julia Boggs Dent Grant (January 26, 1826–December 14, 1902)

CHILDREN: Frederick, Ulysses S. Grant, Jr. ("Buck"), Ellen ("Nellie"), and Jesse Root Grant

* Grant was the first of seven presidents born in Ohio (second most from one state after Virginia).
* At age forty-six, Grant was the youngest president elected up to that time.
* After Grant's death in 1885, more than sixty thousand people marched in and one million spectators watched the funeral procession to his burial on New York City's Upper West Side.

  Twelve years later, Grant's Tomb was dedicated. Built with $600,000 donated by more than ninety thousand people, it is the largest mausoleum in North America. Once again, more than one million people attended the parade and dedication ceremony when Grant was interred in the tomb on April 27, 1897. Grant's wife, Julia, was also interred—not buried—in Grant's Tomb, after her death in 1902.[4]

PRESIDENTIAL VOICES

Our noble army of the Mississippi is being wasted by the foolish, drunken, stupid Grant. He can't organize or control or fight an army. . . . There is not among the whole list of retired major-generals a man who is not Grant's superior.

—*CINCINNATI GAZETTE,* 1863

*Grant has treated me badly; but he was the right man in the right place dur-
ing the war, and no matter what his faults were or are, the whole world can
never write him down.*

—PRESIDENT ANDREW JOHNSON[5]

Hiram Ulysses Grant (Hiram for his grandfather, Ulysses for the
Greek hero) was born on April 27, 1822, in Point Pleasant, about twenty-
five miles upstream from Cincinnati on the Ohio River. The future
general and president was the son of a modestly successful tanner, Jesse
Grant, who moved his family to neighboring Georgetown, where
Ulysses Grant grew up. A middling student with an aptitude for mathematics and a gift for handling horses, Grant was surprised when his
father arranged his appointment to West Point. Founded in 1802 under
President Jefferson, the academy had become the nation's first, and for
many years leading, engineering school.

The congressman who had secured his place had listed his name
erroneously as Ulysses Simpson Grant, his mother's maiden name being Simpson. Since he preferred not to have a trunk bearing the initials H.U.G. (for Hiram Ulysses Grant), the cadet let the mistake
stand. His classmates started calling him "Uncle Sam" Grant and later
just Sam.

Although he requested a cavalry post after graduation in 1843,
Grant was assigned to the infantry and posted in Missouri. Unhappy
there, he applied for a teaching post at West Point. But in 1844, he met
Julia Dent, the sister of a West Point classmate, who came from a well-
to-do St. Louis slaveholding family. Before Grant's unit was ordered to
Texas in preparation for war with Mexico, he and Julia were secretly
engaged.

In Mexico, in a war Grant personally opposed, he began his combat
career, serving first under Zachary Taylor, who would later be elected
president and whom Grant admired and emulated. Grant liked Taylor's

rough-hewn style, his disdain for fancy military dress, his simple language, and his strict demands for order and discipline in the ranks. Grant would write of Taylor, "No soldier could face either danger or responsibility more calmly than he. These qualities are more rarely found than genius or physical courage."[6] Grant later wore his general's stars on a private's uniform.

After the war was over, Grant and Julia were married in 1848. His best man was West Point classmate James Longstreet, who would, along with Robert E. Lee, surrender to Grant at Appomattox Court House in April 1865. (Longstreet was one of the few former Confederate generals to become a Republican. He endorsed his old friend Grant for president in 1868 and was given a patronage job in New Orleans.)

Assigned to a succession of dreary army outposts, and separated from Julia, Grant began to drink heavily. Disillusioned by army life, he resigned his commission and returned in 1854 to a family farm near St. Louis, where he struggled when the Panic of 1857 drove crop prices to depression levels. Grant went on to a string of unsuccessful jobs before doing what he had promised himself he would never do—work in one of his father's leather goods stores in Galena, Illinois—in 1860. At thirty-eight, U.S. Grant had been a failure at just about every profession he had attempted.

How did the "U.S." in U.S. Grant come to mean "Unconditional Surrender"?

In April 1861, when Lincoln issued his call for volunteers, Grant left the tannery to help raise a company of militia in Galena. With his West Point training and Mexican War experience, Grant was given the job of drilling and organizing a regiment of Illinois volunteers. His talents for command emerged immediately, and Grant was commissioned a brigadier general in August 1861.

Working in concert with ironclad gunboats, Grant won one of the Union's first—and much needed—victories when he captured two forts in Tennessee, taking more than twenty thousand Confederate troops prisoner. His nickname was solidified when the press learned of the terms offered to the surrendering Confederate general, another West Point classmate: "No terms except an Unconditional Surrender."

As Lincoln suffered through a succession of failed and flawed generals in the war's early years, Grant rose through the ranks, sometimes with grim victories, including the one at Shiloh in Tennessee, one of the war's bloodiest battles. Grant would be accused of drinking on the day of the battle, but Lincoln investigated the reports and stood by the general. On July 4, 1863, Grant captured the crucial Mississippi River city of Vicksburg, a day after the battle at Gettysburg in Pennsylvania.

The Union's fortunes were turning, and Grant's would turn with them, but not without great cost. In March 1864, he was summoned to Washington and given command of all the Union armies. Lincoln had found his general.

Ignoring grievous losses for which critics on both sides would call him a butcher and murderer, Grant pressed Confederate Robert E. Lee in Virginia as William T. Sherman made his way to Atlanta and then across Georgia to the sea. On April 9, 1865, Grant forced Lee's surrender at Appomattox Court House. The Civil War was over.

With Andrew Johnson's presidency unhinged, Grant was the unquestioned favorite to lead the Republican Party in 1868. He faced former New York governor Horatio Seymour and won a large electoral victory, although the popular vote was somewhat closer. The Republicans were undoubtedly aided by the new black voters who had been registered under the congressional Reconstruction plan. (The Fifteenth Amendment was not yet in effect.)

Without some half a million black votes, Grant would not have won the popular majority. To safeguard that advantage, the Republican-dominated Congress moved quickly to pass the Fifteenth Amendment, which guaranteed black men the vote, and sent it to the states where Republicans controlled the majority of legislatures. It was ratified in February 1870.

PRESIDENTIAL VOICES

The belief is common in America that the day is at hand when corporations . . . swaying power such as has never in the world's history been trusted in the hands of mere private citizens, controlled by single men like Vanderbilt, or by combinations of men like Fisk, Gould and Lane, after having created a system of quiet but irresistible corruption—will ultimately succeed in directing government itself. Under the American form of society, there is now no authority capable of effective resistance.

—HENRY ADAMS
"The New York Gold Conspiracy"[7]

What scandals marred Grant's presidency?

Though Grant's personal honesty was never questioned, his two terms would be marked by major scandals. Some of them grew out of his inability to select competent appointees. Others grew out of greed and corruption that flourished on a monumental scale—much of it related to the boom in the railroad business and America's extraordinary postwar expansion.

Here is a scorecard of Grant's scandals:

- **Black Friday:** In 1869, Jay Gould, who had built a large empire with small local railroad lines that were integrated into a regional monopoly in the Southwest, attempted to manipulate the gold market with his partner James Fisk. Since President Grant's brother-in-law worked for them, Gould and Fisk were able to use an unwitting Grant for their purposes. According to historian John Steele Gordon, "Gould lobbied Grant hard not to authorize any sale of gold, citing the need of American farmers to export their crops at good prices. Meanwhile, he and his allies began accumulating the metal on Wall Street."[8]

    Grant stopped federal gold sales for a time, forcing up gold prices. When he realized that he had been fooled, Grant ordered the release of $4 million in gold, sharply driving prices down on "Black Friday," September 24, 1869. The sudden dislocation in the gold market caused a stock market panic that ruined businesses and investors and devastated the American economy for months. American agriculture went into a steep decline from which it did not recover for years.

"The mess," concludes Gordon, "was more swept under the rug than straightened out."[9] Gould had broken no existing laws and he remained a major player on Wall Street until he died in 1892, leaving a fortune of more than $70 million. Fisk was less lucky. He was shot and killed by the jealous lover of a woman with whom he was involved.

- **Credit Mobilier:** The plan to link East and West Coasts by railroad provided massive opportunities for schemes to bilk the Treasury. Corruption came to the fore with the exposure of the Credit Mobilier scandal in 1872, which broke in the midst of the campaign for Grant's second term.

  Credit Mobilier was a company founded by Oakes Ames, a Massachusetts congressman and one of the directors of the Union Pacific Railroad, the company taking the line westward from Nebraska. Ames had spread Credit Mobilier shares to friendly congressmen in exchange for votes on inflated construction contracts. The scandal ensnared congressional leaders and President Grant's first- and second-term vice presidents Schuyler Colfax—dropped from the ticket in 1872 and never formally charged—and Henry Wilson, who died in office and was not replaced.

  Among those later tainted by the scandal was future President James A. Garfield, who publicly revealed that he had turned down the stock, and was eventually absolved of wrongdoing.[10] Congress censured Ames and Representative James Brooks of New York. Ames dropped dead a few months later.

- **The Whiskey Ring:** During the Grant administration, hundreds of distillers and federal officials were caught diverting liquor taxes into their own pockets. Grant was shocked to learn that the government had been defrauded of millions in tax dollars with the assistance of his personal secretary, Orville Babcock, a man with his proverbial finger in every pie.

• **Belknap Bribery**: In the Office (later Bureau) of Indian Affairs— originally created to administer Native American lands held in trust by the federal government—corruption was also widespread, with millions in kickbacks paid to administration officials all the way down the line, ending up with Indians on the reservations getting rotten food. Accused of receiving kickbacks, Secretary of War William W. Belknap resigned before his Senate impeachment trial, in which he was acquitted.

The scandals and corruption were followed by the Panic of 1873, which began when one of America's most prominent bankers, Jay Cooke, who had devised a bond drive to help pay for the Civil War, suddenly announced he was insolvent. Panic swept Wall Street, and banks and brokerage houses failed by the dozens as the New York Stock Exchange closed down for ten days.

Does all this sound familiar? Corruption, scandal, banks closing, the economy in a tailspin—America has been there, done that. More than once.

The panic led to a sharp, ugly, and painful depression that lasted for six years. America's disgust with Washington led to a sweeping change of Congress, the Democrats winning a majority in the House for the first time since the Civil War.

Final Judgment: Grade D

Surprisingly popular after his second term ended in 1876, despite the scandals, Grant briefly considered running for a third term. His wife, Julia, who had gloried in the splendor of her role as first lady, was sharply disappointed when Grant told her that he had committed not to run again without consulting her. "I do not want to be here another four years," he told her. [11]

When the Grants left America for a Grand Tour of Europe,

Rutherford B. Hayes had taken office, already tainted by the election controversy in 1876 that would prevent him from winning nomination for a second term. In 1880, despite a checkered history as president, Grant nearly became the first president to be nominated for a third term. But the Republicans instead turned to James A. Garfield that year.

Grant moved to New York and put all his money into Grant and Ward, a brokerage house owned by his son Ulysses Jr. (known as Buck) and partner Ferdinand Ward, who was jailed after the firm went bankrupt in 1881. Virtually penniless, the savior of the Union began to sell some of his Civil War memorabilia and to write magazine articles about the Civil War to raise cash to pay his debts. Mark Twain then offered Grant an advance to write his memoirs.

Diagnosed with throat cancer, Grant raced to complete the book before he died. It was sold by Twain's firm on a door-to door subscription basis, by salesmen dressed in Civil War uniforms, and went on to become one of the greatest successes in American publishing history. Grant's *Personal Memoirs* is still regarded among the finest military memoirs ever written. The book's success, along with his restoration to general's rank by Congress, allowed Grant to go to his death assured that his wife had been provided for.

President Grant did not fare well among many twentieth-century historians, some of whom rank him among the worst, largely because of the significant corruption scandals that damaged his presidency. Other recent assessments have become more generous. In particular, some contemporary historians credit Grant for his enlightened efforts to bring African-Americans into the mainstream of the nation with his lobbying for ratification of the Fifteenth Amendment and such legislation as the Civil Rights Act of 1875, which assured "full enjoyment of" inns, public conveyances, theaters, and other "places of amusement" to African-Americans. Grant also used his presidential powers to aggressively counteract the growing terrorism of the Ku Klux Klan.

As Grant himself noted, he lacked political training, and it showed as he ignored some of those in his party who might have kept him from his worst errors. As an admiring Michael Korda noted, "The corruption that marked Grant's administration was brought about by his innocence and his trust in other people, not by any desire for personal gain, and was in any case, endemic to what came to be called the 'Gilded Age.' The United States was growing too fast, in too many directions at once, and the inevitable consequence was corruption and an unstable economy, and it would have taken a more astute man than Grant to slow things down or clean them up."[12]

Grant Administration Milestones[13]

1869

March 4	Ulysses S. Grant is inaugurated.
May 10	The first transcontinental railroad is completed at Promontory Point, Utah.
September 24	"Black Friday"—a financial panic sweeps Wall Street and New York's banks, growing from the efforts of two men—Jay Gould and James Fisk, Jr.—to corner the gold market.

1870

January 26	Virginia is readmitted to the Union.
February 23	Mississippi is readmitted to the Union.
March 30	Texas is readmitted to the Union.
	The Fifteenth Amendment—no state shall deprive any citizen of the right to vote because of "race, color, or previous condition of servitude"—is declared in effect.

1871

February 28	The Federal Election Law passes; its purpose is to ensure fair treatment of black voters in the South.
March 3	An Indian Appropriation Act is passed with an amendment ending tribal recognition and the treaty system. All Indians are made wards of the state.

March 4	Grant establishes the first Civil Service Commission. Without additional appropriations from Congress, however, the commission is rendered ineffective.
April 20	The Ku Klux Klan Act is passed to enforce the Fourteenth Amendment in the South. It outlaws activities such as wearing disguises, forming conspiracies, and intimidating officials.
September 4	A citizen's commission is formed to investigate corruption, bribery, and fraud at New York's Tammany Hall, the notorious political organization.
October 8–11	The Great Fire of Chicago destroys much of the city.
October 12	Grant issues a proclamation against the Ku Klux Klan in South Carolina.

1872

June 5–6	The Republican National Convention nominates Grant for reelection; Vice President Schuyler Colfax is dropped in favor of Senator Henry Wilson.
July 9	The Democrats nominate *New York Tribune* editor Horace Greeley for president. A leading abolitionist and reformer, Greeley is first approved by Liberal Republicans. The Democratic Party then endorses Greeley as the only candidate who can possibly defeat Grant and the Radical Republicans.
November 5	Grant is reelected in the largest popular-majority victory for a Republican in the nineteenth century. He wins 55.6 percent of the popular vote and 214 electoral votes to Greeley's 80. Greeley dies before the electoral votes are counted.

1873

January 6	An investigation of the Credit Mobilier scandal is launched, revealing that Union Pacific Railroad directors used the dummy corporation to pay themselves from the railroad treasury; additionally they had bribed congressmen to avoid an investigation.
February 27	A House resolution censures Oakes Ames of Massa-

chusetts and James Brooks of New York in connection
with the Credit Mobilier scandal.

March 4   Grant is inaugurated for his second term.

September 18   "The Panic of 1873" hits America. The failure of the
prominent brokerage firm Jay Cooke & Company
leads to six years of depression.

November 19   Tammany Hall's William M. "Boss" Tweed is
convicted on 204 charges of fraud. Tweed escapes from
prison in 1875 and flees to Cuba and then Spain before
being recaptured.

1874

November 4   Samuel Tilden becomes governor of New York; he is
largely responsible for breaking up the Tweed Ring of
Tammany Hall, which has corruptly controlled New
York politics for decades.

November 18–20   The Women's Christian Temperance Union (WCTU)
is established in Cleveland, Ohio. It is the beginning of
a growing national movement for the prohibition of
alcohol.

1875

March 1   The Civil Rights Act of 1875 passes, guaranteeing
blacks equal rights in public places and prohibiting the
exclusion of blacks from jury duty. (The Supreme
Court will declare the act unconstitutional in 1883.)

May 10   Two hundred thirty-eight people are indicted in
connection with the "Whiskey Ring Scandal," in
which distillers conspired with Treasury Department
officials to defraud the government of millions of
dollars in liquor taxes. Orville E. Babcock, Grant's
private secretary, will be indicted later in the year.

November 22   Vice President Henry Wilson dies.

1876

April 4   Impeachment articles are adopted against Secretary of
War William W. Belknap, who is accused together

with his late wife in a scandal involving bribes from traders at Indian trading posts. Belknap resigns before his trial and the Senate acquits him.

June 14–16   The Republican National Convention nominates Ohio's Rutherford B. Hayes.

June 25   "Custer's Last Stand": The nation is shocked by news that Custer and 265 men of the Seventh Cavalry have been killed in a battle with the Sioux at Little Bighorn.

June 27–29   The Democrats nominate reformer Samuel J. Tilden.

August 1   Colorado, the thirty-eighth state, is admitted.

November 7   The presidential election results are inconclusive. Tilden appears to have a slight edge in the popular vote, as well as 184 electoral votes to Hayes's 165. But the returns from Florida, Louisiana, and South Carolina, representing 19 electoral votes, are contested.

1877

January 29   A congressional commission is created to determine the results of the contested presidential election.

February 26   Ohio Republicans and Southern Democrats meet in Washington, D.C., and forge the Compromise of 1877. The Democrats promise to withdraw opposition to Hayes, who will in turn remove federal troops from Louisiana and South Carolina. It marks the end of congressional Reconstruction.

MUST READS

Ulysses S. Grant, *Personal Memoirs*; William S.McFeely, *Grant: A Biography*; Jean Edward Smith, *Grant*.

ONLINE RESOURCES

Inaugural Addresses, Avalon Project, Yale Law School
   1869: http://avalon.law.yale.edu/19th_century/grant1.asp
   1873: http://avalon.law.yale.edu/19th_century/grant2.asp

Library of Congress Resource Guide

    http://www.loc.gov/rr/program/bib/presidents/grant/index.html

Miller Center of Public Affairs, University of Virginia

    http://millercenter.org/president/grant

Ulysses S. Grant Association, Mississippi State University

    http://library.msstate.edu/usgrant/collection_description.asp

Ulysses S. Grant Historic Site, National Park Service

    http://www.nps.gov/ulsg/index.htm

Ulysses S. Grant Cottage, New York State (site of Grant's last days and death)

    http://grantcottage.org/index.html

General Grant National Memorial ("Grant's Tomb"), National Park Service

    http://www.nps.gov/gegr/historyculture/index.htm

19

Dark-Horse President
Rutherford Birchard Hayes

★ ★ ★

March 4, 1877–March 4, 1881

Milestones in Rutherford B. Hayes's Life

October 4, 1822	Born in Delaware, Ohio
1845	Began law practice in Ohio
1858–1861	City solicitor in Cincinnati
1861–1865	Served in Union Army in Civil War
1865–1867	U.S. representative from Ohio
1868–1872 and 1876–1877	Governor of Ohio
1877–1881	Nineteenth president
January 17, 1893	Died in Fremont, Ohio, aged seventy

PRESIDENTIAL VOICES

But at the basis of all prosperity, for that as well as for every other part of the country, lies the improvement of the intellectual and moral condition of the people. Universal suffrage should rest upon universal education. . . .

Let me assure my countrymen of the Southern States that it is my earnest desire to regard and promote their truest interest—the interests of the white and of the colored people both and equally—and to put forth my best efforts in behalf of a civil policy which will forever wipe out in our political affairs the color line and the distinction between North and South, to the end that we may have not merely a united North or a united South, but a united country.

—RUTHERFORD B. HAYES

Inaugural Address, March 5, 1877[1]

(March 4, 1877, fell on a Sunday, so Hayes was privately inaugurated on March 3, in the White House. The public ceremony fell on March 5, 1877.)

L ike America's sixth president, John Quincy Adams, Rutherford B. Hayes took office under the cloud of a tainted election from which his administration never recovered. For the second of four times in presidential history, the victor in the popular vote—Samuel Tilden, Democrat of New York, in this case—was not elected president.

Republican Hayes lost the popular vote in a close and controversial race that came during America's centennial year and ended in a compromise that elevated him to the White House. Immediately, his opponents referred to him as "Rutherfraud" or "His Fradulency." The Democrats soon took control of Congress, and Hayes was essentially crippled, a lame duck from his first day in office.

Fast Facts

RELIGION: Raised Presbyterian. He attended Methodist church with his very devout wife (although he never joined a church).

EDUCATION: Kenyon College, Harvard Law School

MILITARY SERVICE: Union Army, Civil War

CAREER BEFORE POLITICS: Attorney

POLITICAL PARTY: Republican

FIRST LADY: Lucy Ware Webb Hayes (August 28, 1831–June 25, 1889)

CHILDREN: Five of their eight children lived to maturity: Sardis, James, Rutherford, Frances ("Fanny"), and Scott.

* Hayes joined the Ohio militia after Lincoln's call for volunteers. He was wounded five times in battle, eventually being promoted to major general.

* A devout Methodist, First Lady Lucy Hayes believed in temperance, and President Hayes banned alcohol at the White House with her full support. For that she was later known as "Lemonade Lucy."
* Educated at Wesleyan Women's College, Lucy Hayes was the first first lady to have graduated from college.
* Lucy Hayes is also credited with beginning the tradition of the White House Easter Egg Roll. The practice had actually been going on for years at the Capitol, but in 1879, the Capitol prohibited the Easter Monday morning tradition in which children rolled colored eggs down Capitol Hill. Mrs. Hayes allowed the children to use the White House lawn instead.
* The first telephone in the White House was installed for Hayes in 1879; the next year brought the first typewriters.

Born in Delaware, Ohio, on October 4, 1822, Rutherford Hayes was the son of a fairly prosperous merchant who died a few weeks before his birth. Raised by his mother and an uncle, Hayes attended a preparatory school in Connecticut, then Ohio's Kenyon College, and later studied law with a local attorney before going to Harvard Law School in 1843. In 1852, he married Lucy Ware Webb, a well-educated young woman and devout Methodist who held strong views about both temperance and abolition. She helped convince Hayes to leave the Whigs for the antislavery Republicans.

When the Civil War began, Hayes enlisted, joining an Ohio infantry regiment. Despite his lack of military experience, he proved a more than able citizen-soldier, rising through the ranks as he fought in several major engagements, including Antietam in 1862 and serving under John C. Frémont, the former presidential candidate and controversial general who was relieved by Lincoln when he announced a policy of emancipating slaves in the territory he controlled. Popular in the ranks, Hayes once stood up to a general who chastised his soldiers for taking straw for bedding. His men cheered Hayes on, to the general's displeasure.

Eventually Hayes took part in some fifty major battles and was wounded several times. He would later write in his diary that his Civil War experiences gave him much more satisfaction than being president. Before leaving the army in June 1865, he was promoted to brigadier general of volunteers. While still in uniform, he was nominated for one of Ohio's seats in Congress and was then elected governor of Ohio in 1868 for the first of two nonconsecutive terms. In 1876, he won the presidential nomination of the Republicans.

Why isn't there a President Tilden?

Struggling to come out from under the cloud of corruption created by the otherwise popular and honest Grant, the Republicans had turned to Hayes, another Civil War veteran from Ohio. As his chief assets were simply his honesty and an all-important Civil War service record, Rutherford Hayes was touted for his scrupulous character. And the Democrats would be cast as the party of treason.

There was no soft sell in 1876. One Republican campaign slogan was "The man that assassinated Lincoln was a Democrat." Another was "Soldiers, every scar you have on your heroic bodies was given you by a Democrat."

The Democrats, choosing Samuel Tilden as their candidate, lashed out at the widespread corruption and scandals of the Grant years, as well as the depressed American economy. The campaign was distinguished by the fact that Hayes and Tilden agreed on many things, including civil service reform and withdrawing federal troops from the South.

When all was said and done after the election, Tilden had apparently won the popular vote but come up one short in the electoral contest. Twenty-one votes from South Carolina, Louisiana, and Florida and one of Oregon's three electoral votes were in doubt. The struggle over the contested ballots lasted from November 8 until March 2, 1877, just two days before the scheduled inauguration.

There was clearly fraud involved in the three Southern states, where forgery, bribery, violence, and ballot box stuffing had accompanied the voting. Blacks, who had voted overwhelmingly Republican when permitted to vote, had been intimidated and kept away from the polls, and multiple sets of returns were sent to Washington to be counted.

There was no clear Constitutional solution to the dispute. To bring the election to a close, Congress created a commission with ten members from the Congress (five senators and five House members) and five from the Supreme Court. The plan was for an even number of Democrats and Republicans and one independent member. But Supreme Court justice Joseph Bradley was a late addition to the commission. Professing nonpartisanship, he was a loyal Republican and tipped the balance; the Republicans ended up with the upper hand, and after three votes, the commission declared Hayes the winner with 185 electoral votes.

It was clear that the Democrats had cut a deal with the Republicans. Hayes would win the election, but he would promise to remove federal troops from the South.

What did it all mean?

For African-Americans, it meant the end of Reconstruction. As Lewis Gould writes in his history of the Republican Party, "Although the outcome in 1876 did not signify complete Republican abandonment of black Americans, it did mark an important turning point in the nation's approach to race. Over the next quarter of a century the South became less Republican and more segregated. Civil rights would not return to the region for seventy-five years. . . . After a generation of trying to build a freer and more open society for all its citizens, the United States lapsed back into the customs and prejudices of old."[2]

PRESIDENTIAL VOICES

In church it occurred to me that it is time for the public to hear that the giant evil and danger in this country, the danger which transcends all others, is the vast wealth owned or controlled by a few persons. Money is power. In Congress, in state legislatures, in city councils, in the courts, in the political conventions, in the press, in the pulpit, in the circles of the educated and the talented, its influence is growing greater and greater. Excessive wealth in the hands of the few means extreme poverty, ignorance, vice, and wretchedness as the lot of the many.

—RUTHERFORD B. HAYES,
Diary and Letters.[3]

Final Judgment: Grade C

Viewed as personally honest and honorable, Hayes had pledged both to reform the corrupt civil service and serve only a single term. He ran into heavy opposition on the reform plans he put forth, but he did not run again, as promised. Hayes did suggest amending the Constitution to shift to a single six-year term for president, but the proposal went nowhere.

After leaving the White House, he wrote an assessment of his term that many historians accept: "The Southern question; the money question; the hard times and riots; the Indian question; the Chinese question; the reform of the civil service; the partisan bitterness growing out of a disputed election; a hostile Congress; and a party long in power on the verge of defeat. Is there any one of these which was not left in a better condition than it was found? I have often said that, leaving out of the question Lincoln's Administration, it would be difficult to find one which began with so rough a situation, and few which closed with so smooth a sea."[4]

Hayes would never escape the taint of his contrived and controversial election, along with the agreement he honored to withdraw federal troops from the South. But he proved true to his word on many counts. And in spite of the circumstances of his election, he garners high marks for his personal honesty and ability to restore some of the luster to the presidency following the ravages of the Civil War, Lincoln's assassination, the impeachment of Andrew Johnson, and the Grant-era corruption.

A reform-minded—if paternalistic—Christian, Hayes had a remarkably progressive attitude toward Native Americans, particularly coming on the heels of the 1876 disaster of Custer at the Little Bighorn. He also batted back the racist anti-Chinese sentiment that was building in the nation and vetoed a measure restricting Chinese immigration. (In 1882, the Chinese Exclusion Act would be passed.) His civil service reforms were a remarkable attempt to wrest power away from an increasingly corrupt Congress, which had dominated American political appointments and patronage since the Civil War. He also pushed back on Southern Democratic attempts to weaken the protection of African-American voters.

As for the "hard times and riots," Hayes favored, like most Republican presidents of this era, "hard money" policies that were meant to limit inflation but also failed to stimulate a weak economy. And he would also dispatch federal troops to stop riots that broke out in response to a railroad strike—the beginning of a new era in corporate and labor relations and an issue that would increasingly bedevil a generation of presidents.

Hayes Administration Milestones[5]

1877

March 5	Rutherford B. Hayes is publicly sworn in as the nineteenth president.
April 24	Hayes officially withdraws soldiers from Louisiana.
June 14	The first Flag Day marks the one hundredth anniversary of the American flag.
June 21	Ten members of the Molly Maguires, a secret Irish coal miner's society in Pennsylvania, are hanged for murder after a trial widely questioned by historians for its fairness. The Pinkertons, private detectives known for their anti-union violence, had infiltrated the Molly Maguires.
July 14	The Great Railroad Strike of 1877 begins as workers walk out on the Baltimore & Ohio (B&O) Railroad, another indication of rising worker anger. Other unions strike in sympathy. Hayes sends in federal troops to protect the mails and quell riots in several cities.

1878

January 1	The Knights of Labor is established as a national organization, the first labor union to attempt to organize all workers.
July 11	Striking a blow at the "Boss System" in his quest for civil service reform, Hayes removes Chester A. Arthur as collector of customs in New York—one of the most

prized patronage plums. Hayes wants to institute a "merit system" as part of his reform plan.

November Following congressional midterm elections, the Democratic Party controls both houses of Congress for the first time since the Civil War.

1879

January 1 The country returns to the "gold standard," as Hayes allows the resumption of gold payments for Civil War "greenbacks," the paper money first issued during the Civil War to pay for war. During the Hayes administration, as the government's gold supply grows and the issuance of silver coins increases, the economy begins to recover. By the spring of 1879, the government has retired all Civil War bonds.

1880

June 7 The Republicans meet in Chicago. Hayes had already pledged not to run again, and after thirty-six ballots, James A. Garfield, the speaker of the House of Representatives and a friend of Hayes from Ohio, wins the nomination.

June 24 The Democrats meet in Ohio and nominate Winfield S. Hancock, a Civil War general and hero of Gettysburg, for president.

November 2 James A. Garfield is elected president by a narrow popular margin (with only 48.5 percent of the vote) but with a comfortable majority of electoral votes, 214–155.

MUST READS

Hans Trefousse, *Rutherford B. Hayes.*

ONLINE RESOURCES

Inaugural Address, Avalon Project, Yale Law School
http://avalon.law.yale.edu/19th_century/hayes.asp

Library of Congress Resource Guide

http://www.loc.gov/rr/program/bib/presidents/hayes/index.html

Miller Center of Public Affairs, University of Virginia

http://millercenter.org/index.php/academic/americanpresident/hayes

Hayes Presidential Center

http://www.rbhayes.org/hayes/

20

James Abram Garfield

* * *

March 4, 1881–September 19, 1881

Milestones in James A. Garfield's Life

November 19, 1831	Born in Orange, Ohio
1857–1861	President of Hiram Eclectic Institute (now Hiram College)
1859–1861	Member of Ohio State Senate
1861–1863	Served in U.S. Army in the Civil War
1863–1880	U.S. representative from Ohio
1880	Elected to U.S. Senate
1881	Twentieth president
July 2, 1881	Shot in Washington, D.C.
September 19, 1881	Died at Elberon (Long Branch), New Jersey, aged forty-nine

PRESIDENTIAL VOICES

The elevation of the negro race from slavery to the full rights of citizenship is the most important political change we have known since the adoption of the Constitution of 1787. . . . There was no middle ground for the negro race between slavery and equal citizenship. There can be no permanent disenfranchised peasantry in the United States. Freedom can never yield its fullness of blessings so long as the law or its administration places the smallest obstacle in the pathway of any virtuous citizen.

—INAUGURAL ADDRESS, MARCH 4, 1881[1]

The last "log cabin" president, James A. Garfield was born into extreme poverty in rural Ohio and, with the perseverance and resourcefulness usually associated with Lincoln, became a self-made teacher, lawyer, college president at age twenty-six, army general at age thirty, powerful politician, and, finally, president. He accomplished these things while battling powerful men in his own party and being an outspoken champion of the emancipated slaves. Six feet tall with a full beard, he was considered a spellbinding speaker.

Then a mentally ill office seeker's gunshots cut him down.

Fast Facts

RELIGION: Disciples of Christ
ASSOCIATIONS: Freemason
EDUCATION: Western Reserve Eclectic Institute, Williams College
MILITARY SERVICE: Union Army, Civil War
CAREER BEFORE POLITICS: Teacher, attorney
POLITICAL PARTY: Republican
FIRST LADY: Lucretia Rudolph Garfield (April 19, 1832–March 14, 1918)
CHILDREN: Four sons and a daughter lived to maturity: Harry, who later became president of Williams College; James; Mary ("Mollie"); Irvin McDowell; and Abram.

* While at Williams College, Garfield taught school in North Pownal, Vermont, in the school where the previous teacher had been Chester A. Arthur—his future vice president and successor.
* Garfield was the youngest general in the Union Army at age thirty.
* He was the only sitting member of the House of Representatives to be elected president. Having run successfully for the Senate at the same time he ran for president, Garfield was simultaneously a sitting representative, a senator-elect, and president-elect.
* Garfield was the first left-handed president.
* The second of four presidents to be assassinated, Garfield's presi-

dency lasted 199 days—the second shortest, after Harrison's. For eighty of those days, he lay near death.

* Robert Todd Lincoln, Abraham Lincoln's son, was Garfield's secretary of war.

* Garfield's son, James R. Garfield, who witnessed his father's shooting when he was fifteen, served as the secretary of the interior under President Theodore Roosevelt.

* Garfield's only executive order gave government workers the day off on May 30, 1881, to place flowers on the graves of Civil War soldiers—the beginning of the official federal recognition of "Decoration Day" (later Memorial Day).

PRESIDENTIAL VOICES

The people are responsible for the character of their Congress. If that body be ignorant, reckless and corrupt, it is because the people tolerate ignorance, recklessness and corruption.

—JAMES A. GARFIELD
"A Century of Congress," *Atlantic*, July 1877

The son of Abram Garfield, a struggling farmer who had also worked on construction of the Ohio and Erie Canal, James A. Garfield was born in November 1831 in a cabin built by his father near Cleveland, Ohio. In 1833, a forest fire threatened the home and Abram Garfield worked all day fighting back the flames. Afterward, he fell sick from exhaustion and a fever, dying within days and leaving his wife with four children, including James, not yet two. The boy's mother sold off pieces of the farm to keep them all together and with incredible determination raised her family in the Ohio wilderness.

Setting off at age sixteen to work on the Erie and Ohio Canal that his father had helped build, Garfield caught malaria and returned home, where, at his mother's insistence, he enrolled in a small preparatory school called Western Reserve Eclectic Institute, founded by the Disciples of Christ as a secular school (later Hiram Eclectic and then Hiram College). He worked there as a school janitor to pay his tuition.

A naturally gifted student, Garfield took classics and math and proved so proficient that he soon rose from janitor to assistant teacher at the school. In 1854, Garfield was accepted at Williams College in Massachusetts, graduating there with honors two years later. He returned to teach at Eclectic Institute in Hiram, Ohio, and by the time he was twenty-six, he was the school's president.

When an Ohio state senator died, Garfield was asked to take his place, beginning his long political rise. In 1859, he joined the antislavery contingent in the Ohio State Senate, and after Fort Sumter, he volunteered for the Ohio militia and was made a lieutenant colonel. Despite his inexperience, Garfield won one of the first battles he commanded, earning instant fame and a promotion to brigadier general. Although totally committed to the war effort and aims, Garfield would later say that after seeing the battlefield dead, "something went out of him . . . that never came back; the sense of the sacredness of life and the impossibility of destroying it."[2]

Eventually promoted to major general, after fighting at Shiloh and being wounded at the battle of Chickamauga, Garfield was rewarded at home with election to the House from Ohio in 1863. He became one of the most radical of Radical Republicans, only reluctantly endorsing Lincoln for a second term. Though implicated and investigated in the Credit Mobilier scandal during Grant's administration, Garfield was exonerated, but the taint of the scandal would cost him some support.

Garfield served as a member of the controversial electoral commission that decided the 1876 election in favor of fellow Ohio Republican Rutherford B. Hayes. When Hayes announced he would leave office after one term, the Republicans met in Chicago in 1880, the "cow town" that had emerged as a modern metropolis since recovering from the Great Fire of 1871. That year, the Republican Party, which had dominated the presidency since 1860, was divided. The rift was over reform of government corruption under the increasingly outrageous patronage and nepotism of the "Boss System," in which powerful politicians controlled patronage jobs and with them large blocs of votes.

Who were the "Stalwarts" and the "Half-Breeds"?

With their near-total dominance of American politics since the end of the Civil War, the Republican Party had begun to split over issues, personalities, and, most important, patronage. A near monopoly on control of the federal government for so long had left power entrenched in the hands of a few men—"bosses" in the political vernacular of the day.

By the late nineteenth century, there were two Republican camps—the Stalwarts, mostly the "bosses" who were determined to defend the spoils system in Washington, and a group of reformers known as "Half-Breeds." The division between the two wings was over more than policy—it was also personal, as men who hated each other led the two sides. New York power broker Senator Roscoe Conkling, known as Boss Conkling, headed up the Stalwarts. The highly popular and charismatic Senator James Blaine, the "Magnetic Man from Maine," led the Half-Breeds.

The leading candidate to win the party's nomination in 1880 was Boss Conkling's choice, Ulysses S. Grant, who had returned from his post-presidency world tour. Despite the controversies and scandals of his two terms, Grant still enjoyed enormous personal popularity. And he was prepared for the controversial notion of breaking the two-term precedent that dated to George Washington.

The convention balloting went on for days. It was heated, noisy, occasionally bordering on violent, and seemingly deadlocked. There was also plenty of behind-the-scenes negotiating and bribery. And somehow momentum built for the darkest of dark horses, James A. Garfield. He didn't seek the nomination but he had placed the name of Senator John Sherman before the party in a speech that shook the convention.

When it was over, Garfield had emerged as a surprising compromise candidate acceptable to both Stalwarts and Half-Breeds. The price of that compromise was rewarding the Stalwarts with the nomination of Chester A. Arthur as Garfield's running mate. A "spoilsman" protégé of Boss Conkling, Arthur had never been elected to office. His biggest job had been serving as collector of customs for the Port of New York, the country's most politically significant and lucrative patronage job—a job arranged by Conkling.

In the campaign against another Civil War veteran, Democrat Winfield S. Hancock, a hero of Gettysburg, there were few differences between the two men on policy. In an election with a huge 78 percent turnout—spurred by interest in the race after the tainted election of 1876—Garfield barely won the popular vote but won the electoral majority, 214–155.

Final Judgment: Grade I (Incomplete)

Garfield is not included in most historical rankings because his term was so abbreviated.

When he came to office, Garfield wrangled with Boss Conkling over patronage—and won. Conkling resigned his Senate seat to protest a Garfield decision, but the New York State Legislature did not return him to the office. Boss Conkling's power was broken and he departed the scene.

On the morning of July 2, 1881, Garfield was leaving Washington by train for a visit to his alma mater Williams College when Charles Guiteau fired two shots, hitting Garfield in the arm and back. Guiteau shouted, "I am a Stalwart! Arthur is now president!"

Physicians were not able to find the bullet lodged near Garfield's spine. There were no X-rays yet. But telephone inventor Alexander Graham Bell had devised what he called an "induction balance," a primitive metal detector that was specifically designed by Bell to locate the bullet. Unfortunately, Bell was unaware that President Garfield was lying on a sickbed with metal bedsprings, which threw off the machine's results. At the same time, Garfield's doctors had been probing his wound with their bare hands. They were unmindful of the then-controversial ideas of British physician Joseph Lister, who was trying to convince American doctors to clean their hands and instruments with carbolic acid to prevent infection. Lister was basically treated as a crank.[3] The president died of sepsis, or blood poisoning—introduced by his treatment.

Garfield's assassin had been to the White House several times hoping for a diplomatic post in Europe despite his lack of credentials. Executed in June 1882, Charles Guiteau may have spurred Congress to act on one of Garfield's key goals—civil service reform. In 1883, Congress passed the Pendleton Act, which was intended to do away with the "spoils system" of awarding jobs in return for contributions of political service. Although it initially covered only a small number of federal positions, the act led to civil service exams and the creation of a Civil Service Commission to manage the civil service (now the Office of Personnel Management).

Garfield Administration Milestones[4]

1881

March 4	Republican James A. Garfield is sworn in.
May 21	Clara Barton organizes the American Red Cross.
July 2	Charles J. Guiteau shoots Garfield in a Washington, D.C., railroad station.
July 4	The Tuskegee Normal and Industrial Institute—now Tuskegee University—officially opens in Alabama. Dr. Booker T. Washington is the school's first president.
September 19	James Garfield dies from blood poisoning and complications from his wounds. Vice President Chester A. Arthur becomes the twenty-first president. The assassin, Guiteau, will be hanged on June 30, 1882.

MUST READS

Candice Millard, *Destiny of the Republic: A Tale of Madness, Medicine and the Murder of a President.*

ONLINE RESOURCES

Inaugural Address, American Presidency Project, University of California, Santa Barbara

http://www.presidency.ucsb.edu/ws/index.php?pid=25823#axzz1dnknVrqK

James A. Garfield National Historic Site, National Park Service
http://www.nps.gov/jaga/index.htm
Library of Congress Resource Guide
http://www.loc.gov/rr/program/bib/presidents/garfield/index.html
Miller Center of Public Affairs, University of Virginia
http://millercenter.org/index.php/academic/americanpresident
/garfield

21

The Gentleman Boss
Chester A. Arthur

★ ★ ★

September 19, 1881–March 4, 1885

Milestones in Chester A. Arthur's Life

October 5, 1829	Born in Fairfield, Vermont
1853	Admitted to the New York bar
1861–1862	Served as quartermaster in New York Militia during Civil War
1871–1879	Served as collector of customs for the Port of New York
1881	Vice president under Garfield
1881–1885	Twenty-first president
November 18, 1886	Died in New York City, aged fifty-seven

PRESIDENTIAL VOICES

The fact that adherents of the Mormon Church, which rests upon polygamy as its corner stone, have recently been peopling in large numbers Idaho, Arizona, and other of our Western Territories is well calculated to excite the liveliest interest and apprehension. It imposes upon Congress and the Executive the duty of arraying against this barbarous system all the power which under the Constitution and the law they can wield for its destruction.

—CHESTER A. ARTHUR

First Annual Message to Congress, December 6, 1881[1]

C ollector of the Ports? Party hack? "Spoilsman"? As the second president to come to office following an assassination, Chester A. Arthur—Chet to his friends—may have been the least suited presidential successor in history.

Never elected to office before becoming Garfield's vice president, Arthur owed his place to one of the great political "machines" of the nineteenth century—Senator Roscoe Conkling, New York's Republican boss. Arthur surprised both his friends and critics by picking up the mantle of reform that his fallen predecessor Garfield had carried to the White House, chiefly by signing the Pendleton Act of 1883, the first serious legislative attempt to reform the "boss" system then in operation and create a modern civil service based on competitive exams and not patronage.

An urbane dandy with large, extravagant, and fastidious tastes, Arthur brought in New York's leading young society designer, Louis Comfort Tiffany, to redo the Executive Mansion and turn it into a Gilded Age showplace. The thirty-four-year-old Louis was the son of Arthur's friend New York jeweler Charles Tiffany, who made a fortune manufacturing medals for the Union Army in the Civil War.

Fast Facts

RELIGION: Raised Baptist, Arthur attended Episcopal churches (although he never formally joined a church).

EDUCATION: Union College

MILITARY SERVICE: New York State Guard, Civil War

CAREER BEFORE POLITICS: Attorney

POLITICAL PARTY: Republican

SPOUSE: Ellen Herndon Arthur (August 30, 1837–January 12, 1880)
Ellen Arthur died of pneumonia before Arthur became vice president.

CHILDREN: Two children lived to maturity: Chester Alan and Ellen ("Nell"); another son died in infancy.

* The son of an abolitionist, Arthur defended fugitive slaves as an attorney and once obtained the freedom of six slaves when their owner transported them through New York.

* Arthur was the target of a "birther" inquiry, the second since Frémont in 1856. During the 1880 campaign, Democrats questioned whether Arthur was actually born across the border from Vermont in Canada, an unproven allegation. A Democratic attorney looking into the question even claimed that Arthur was born in Ireland, his father's native country. But Vermont claims Arthur as a native son, the first of its two presidents.

* Although born poor, Arthur became a true dandy by the time he was in college. After his marriage and considerable success as a New York attorney and the well-paid collector of customs for the Port of New York, Arthur and his wife, Ellen, were renowned for lavish New York parties at the Lexington Avenue town house they owned. Arthur was said to own eighty pairs of pants, which he supposedly changed several times a day.[2]

PRESIDENTIAL VOICES

Mr. Arthur's temperament is sluggish. He is indolent. It requires a great deal for him to get to his desk and begin the dispatch of business. Great questions of public policy bore him. No President was ever so much given to procrastination as he is.

—*Chicago Tribune, 1882*[3]

The son of an itinerant Baptist minister, Chester Alan Arthur was born in a cabin, a temporary parsonage in rural Vermont near the Canadian border, in 1829. His father, an Irish immigrant and outspoken abolitionist, moved from church to church around Vermont and upstate New York, and as a boy, Chester attended local schools in the towns where his father preached. His mother was a native Vermonter and quite devout, expressing disappointment that her son never chose to be baptized or join a church.[4] At fifteen, he went to Union College in Schenectady, New York, graduating in three years, and was admitted into Phi Beta Kappa, the honor society.

In 1853, Arthur went to New York City, studied law, and was admitted to the New York bar that year. With strong abolitionist sympathies learned from his father, Arthur joined the new Republican Party and campaigned for John C. Frémont in his failed bid for president as the first Republican standard-bearer in 1856. Working up through the Republican ranks, Arthur was, in 1860, given the post of acting quartermaster to supply New York's militia troops, a job he performed efficiently and without scandal, eventually winning the rank of brigadier general.

A loyal soldier in Boss Conkling's powerful New York Republican machine, Arthur was rewarded with a major plum in 1871, when President Grant appointed him the collector of customs for the Port of New York. At the time, the job was a "position of greater influence than all but a handful of federal appointments. . . . The New York Customhouse remained the pinnacle," generating more than a third of the government's revenues.[5] The collector had the power to appoint one thousand employees, and Arthur made as much as $40,000 a year in the office. Holding the position for eight years, he also built a loyal political machine, doling out jobs in exchange for party fealty.

But in 1879, President Hayes removed Arthur from the job as part of his reform effort. That was one reason that the nomination of 1880 was so crucial to Boss Conkling and his men. A victory by his Stalwarts would mean the return of the collector's job and a good many other federal posts to parcel out.

When President Garfield was shot, and the assassin shouted that he wanted Arthur to be president, suspicions were raised and Arthur kept a low profile, never moving to assume any presidential duties during the months the president lay dying. When he got news of Garfield's death, Arthur took the oath of office in New York City before a local judge. Two days later, the oath was administered again in Washington, D.C., by a federal judge—just to be sure.

PRESIDENTIAL VOICES

Why not discriminate? Why aid in the increase and distribution over our domain of a degraded and inferior race, and the progenitors of an inferior sort of men?

—SENATOR JOHN F MILLER, FEBRUARY 1881[6]

What piece of legislation passed under President Arthur still reverberates in modern America?

In 1882, Congress passed the Chinese Exclusion Act, suspending Chinese immigration to America for twenty years. President Arthur vetoed that measure but signed a subsequent act, which shortened the suspension to ten years. The law also forbade U.S. courts to grant citizenship to Chinese already residing in the United States. (The law was renewed in 1892 and 1902 and not repealed until 1943.)

The law was a reaction to the large number of Chinese who had been welcomed to the country, especially in California, during the Gold Rush years and construction of the transcontinental railroad—built largely with immigrant labor.

But after the Civil War, as panics set in and wages fell along with prices, American workers and some politicians began to blame the Chinese for the problems in the American economy. In 1871, the anti-Asian anger had exploded in Los Angeles, where a mob burned shacks in "Chinatown," killing at least twenty-eight people. Federal troops were called in to quell the violence. In 1880, a stone-throwing crowd in New York attacked the Chinese minister to America as policemen laughed. Part of the resentment was that the Chinese tended to work harder and longer than other Americans.

When California Senator John F. Miller introduced the exclusion bill in February 1881, he compared Chinese to "inhabitants of another planet" and implored Americans to protect "American Anglo-Saxon civilization without contamination or adulteration."

While economics motivated the law, racism played a big role as well. No other group was singled out by the act. Once, the Irish had had to endure the same sort of derision and complaints that were being leveled at the Chinese in postwar America. But now some of the loudest complaints about the Chinese came from Irish-Americans, newly powerful as an urban Democratic voting bloc and ready to flex their political muscle.

The Exclusion Act had two major consequences. Urban America was never a "melting pot," but rather had always been a collection of ethnic enclaves. For the Chinese, the Exclusion Act worsened that reality, forcing them into "ghettos" routinely called "Chinatowns" that limited their ability to assimilate into American culture as many European groups had slowly done.

And the law also gave rise to the first great wave of human smuggling in America, bringing in illegal workers to meet the demand for cheap labor. And sex. According to historian H. W. Brands, "At the stroke of Chester Arthur's pen, a phenomenon that was previously unknown in America but that would grow in size and complexity ever afterward: illegal immigration. . . . Employers discovered merit—that is, profit—in the existence of a class of workers beyond the protection of the American legal system, who could be mistreated at will."[7] Many of those illegally smuggled—then, as now—were young women who ended up in brothels.

Final Judgment: Grade C

With the bar of expectations set very low, Arthur compiled a reasonably good record in seeing through the first meaningful civil service reforms, especially passage of the Pendleton Civil Service Reform Act, perhaps his most surprising accomplishment given his personal history as a creation of the "Boss System." He may have felt morally obligated to continue Garfield's reform crusade after his predecessor's murder, especially since the assassin had invoked Arthur's name at the time of the shooting. But his commitment to reform certainly set back his old friends in the party who'd expected Arthur to keep the lucrative flow of patronage jobs going. He disappointed them.

Handicapped as an "Accidental President," Arthur was also up against a Congress that was far more powerful after the Civil War. And wealthier. By Arthur's time, the Senate had become known as the "Millionaire's Club" as the rich increasingly bought seats in Congress.

But he pressed ahead, beginning a long overdue upgrade of the U.S. Navy, which had been allowed to fall into disrepair through neglect and corruption. He used a budget surplus to reduce the national debt. And as the election drew near, Arthur began to entertain hopes of winning the Republican nomination in his own right, even though his kidney disease was worsening.

It was not to be. Having disappointed his Stalwart friends and never a favorite of the party's Half-Breeds, Arthur also suffered from the seeming "illegitimacy" of an "Accidental President." And with his health already failing, he did not press hard for a second term. His party instead chose James G. Blaine, the charismatic and popular senator who led the opposition to Conkling's Stalwarts.

Among Chester Arthur's last public acts was dedicating the Washington Monument on February 21, 1885. He returned to his New York law practice and died of kidney disease in November 1886.

Not usually known for his good words directed at politicians, Mark Twain said of Arthur as president: "I am but one in fifty-five million. Still in the opinion of this one-fifty-five-millionth of the country's population, it would be hard to better President Arthur's administration."[8]

Arthur Administration Milestones[9]

1881

September 20	Chester A. Arthur is sworn in.
November 14	The murder trial of assassin Charles Guiteau begins. Convicted on January 25, 1882, he will be executed on June 30, 1882.
December 15	Secretary of State James G. Blaine resigns due to political differences between himself and President Arthur.

1882

March 4	Nine men are indicted for defrauding the government in a widespread postal scam known as the Star-Route Scandal.
March 16	The Senate ratifies the Geneva Convention of 1864.
March 22	Aimed at Mormons, the Edmunds Act prohibits bigamists and polygamists from voting and holding office.
April 4	Arthur vetoes the first Chinese Exclusion Act.
May 6	Arthur signs a revised version of the Chinese Exclusion Act, reducing the period of non-immigration to ten years but maintaining the ban on Chinese citizenship.
August 1	Arthur is diagnosed with Bright's disease, a fatal kidney ailment; his health deteriorates rapidly.
September 4	Thomas Edison's Pearl Street Station begins providing electricity to New York City.
September 5	New York trade unions organize the first "Labor Day" parade to promote the right to organize and demand decent working conditions, an eight-hour day, and fair wages.

1883

January 16	The Pendleton Civil Service Reform Act passes; it establishes a three-man Civil Service Commission and specifies a merit system for filling jobs. The law covers about 12 percent of federal employees.
March 3	Arthur signs a bill appropriating funds for the navy's first steel vessels to rebuild a deteriorating fleet that has been plagued by corruption.
May 24	The Brooklyn Bridge opens. President Arthur and New York governor Grover Cleveland attend the ceremony.

1884

March 13	The United States participates in an international conference making Greenwich, England, the prime meridian and creating standard time.

June 6	In Chicago, former secretary of state James G. Blaine defeats Arthur for the Republican nomination.
June 27	The United States Bureau of Labor is created within the Interior Department.
July 11	The Democrats meet in Chicago and nominate New York governor Grover Cleveland.
November 4	Grover Cleveland defeats James G. Blaine.

MUST READS

Zachary Karabell, *Chester Alan Arthur.*

ONLINE RESOURCES

Library of Congress Resource Guide
http://www.loc.gov/rr/program/bib/presidents/arthur/index.html
Miller Center of Public Affairs, University of Virginia
http://millercenter.org/president/arthur
Chester A. Arthur House (Vermont State Historic Site)
http://www.historicvermont.org/sites/html/arthur.html

22

Big Steve or Uncle Jumbo
Grover Cleveland

* * *

March 4, 1885–March 4, 1889*

Milestones in Grover Cleveland's Life

March 18, 1837	Born in Caldwell, New Jersey
1859	Admitted to the New York bar
1863–1865	Assistant district attorney, Erie County, New York
1871–1873	Sheriff of Erie County
1882	Mayor of Buffalo, New York
1883–1884	Governor of New York
1885–1889	Twenty-second president
1893–1897	Twenty-fourth president
June 24, 1908	Died in Princeton, New Jersey, aged seventy-one

PRESIDENTIAL VOICES

At this hour the animosities of political strife, the bitterness of partisan defeat, and the exultation of partisan triumph should be supplanted by an ungrudging acquiescence in the popular will and a sober, conscientious concern for the general weal.

---

* Grover Cleveland is the only president to serve nonconsecutive terms and so he is usually counted as both the twenty-second and twenty-fourth president. See page 339 for the entry on Cleveland as twenty-fourth president.

Your every voter, as surely as your chief magistrate, exercises a public trust.

—GROVER CLEVELAND
First Inaugural, March 4, 1885[1]

W ould modern America elect a president with what the tabloids call a "love child"? Certainly Americans would not have been expected to do so in the straitlaced Victorian days of 1884. But they did.

In fact, they did it twice in electing Grover Cleveland. When New York's Governor Cleveland first campaigned for president in 1884, he was greeted by a headline from his hometown *Buffalo Evening Telegraph*: A TERRIBLE TALE—DARK CHAPTER IN A PUBLIC MAN'S HISTORY.

The newspaper exposed Cleveland's earlier relationship with a woman named Maria C. Halpin, a thirty-three-year-old widow. In 1874, eleven years earlier, Maria Halpin had given birth to a boy she named Oscar Folsom Cleveland, claiming that Grover Cleveland was the father. A bachelor at that time, Cleveland was still unmarried when he ran for president. Complicating the story was the fact that the child's first and middle names were those of Cleveland's law partner, Oscar Folsom—who was also the father of the young woman Cleveland later married. Uncertain of the child's paternity, Cleveland had accepted responsibility and agreed to support the child but would not marry Maria Halpin. According to the newspaper account, the tale of Halpin and the child took many more twists as Halpin ended up an alcoholic in and out of hospitals.

But in 1884, the question for candidate Cleveland was simple: how to respond to the story. Cleveland told his campaign managers to tell the truth, which led to one of the most memorable jingles in presidential campaign history. Pushing baby carriages as they marched, Republicans chanted:

Ma, Ma, where's my Pa?
Gone to the White House, Ha, Ha, Ha![2]

That is, in fact, where Cleveland went, becoming the first Democrat elected president since James Buchanan in 1856, following one of the meanest, nastiest campaigns in history.

After Cleveland's victory, his supporters offered a triumphant reply to the Republican ditty:

Hurrah for Maria,
Hurrah for the kid,
We voted for Grover
And we're damn glad we did.[3]

Fast Facts

RELIGION: Presbyterian

MILITARY SERVICE: Cleveland was drafted during the Civil War but purchased a substitute, then permitted under the 1863 Conscription Act.

CAREER BEFORE POLITICS: Attorney

POLITICAL PARTY: Democratic

FIRST LADY: Frances Folsom Cleveland (July 21, 1864–October 29, 1947)

CHILDREN: Ruth, Esther, Marion, Richard, and Francis.

* "Baby Ruth"? Ruth Cleveland, born in New York between Cleveland's two terms, died of diphtheria in 1904 at age twelve. She had been referred to as "Baby Ruth" in the press. This led a candy bar company to claim that their "Baby Ruth" bar was named in honor of the child when the candy bar was introduced in the 1920s, long after Ruth Cleveland's death. It seems more likely that the child's name was used so the company did not have to pay for the right to use the name of baseball's legendary George Herman "Babe" Ruth, then at the peak of his popularity.[4]

* Esther Cleveland, born during Cleveland's second term, in 1893, was the first and—to date in 2011—only child of a president born in the White House itself.

* The city of Cleveland, Ohio, is named for a distant relative, General
  Moses Cleaveland, a Revolutionary War–era soldier, lawyer, and
  politician who founded the city. A newspaper dropped the "a" in
  Cleaveland for space and it stuck.
* Cleveland was the second president to marry in office (John Tyler
  was first), but the first and only one to be married in the White
  House. His wife, Frances, called "Frank," was twenty-seven years
  younger than Cleveland, the daughter of his law partner, Oscar Folsom, who had died in an accident, and Cleveland's own ward. Twenty-
  one years old at the time of the wedding, Frances Folsom was the
  youngest first lady in history.
* A large, hulking man weighing more than 250 pounds, Cleveland
  was the heaviest president up to that time. His bulk inspired his
  nicknames, dating to his years in office in Buffalo as "Big Steve" and
  "Uncle Jumbo."
* As sheriff of Erie County, New York, Cleveland also served as public executioner and personally sprang the trap on two convicted
  murderers.

PRESIDENTIAL VOICES

This office seeking is a disease—I am entirely satisfied of that. It is even catch-
ing. Men get it and they lose the proper balance of their minds. I've known
men who come here to Washington on other business, with no thought of office,
but when they had been here a couple of weeks they had caught it.
            —GROVER CLEVELAND, 1885[5]

The fifth of nine children of a Yale-educated Presbyterian minister,
Steven Grover Cleveland was born in New Jersey into a family that
moved to Clinton, New York, when the boy was four. After his father
died, sixteen-year-old Cleveland began to pick up odd jobs to help
support the family. His father's death ended his hopes for a college
education, and instead he became an assistant teacher in the New York

Institute for the Blind. Later, an uncle offered him a job editing a cattle breeders' newsletter, and while doing that, Cleveland began to study law and was admitted to the bar in New York in 1859.

He became involved in local Buffalo politics and was elected sheriff of Erie County, where he quickly earned a reputation as a reformer who battled graft and corruption. In 1882, Cleveland went on to become mayor of Buffalo, then a booming town on Lake Erie, and his success as a reformer led to his election as governor of New York in 1883. As governor, he built his reputation by standing up to the most powerful machine of all—New York's Tammany Hall. In 1883, he signed into law a bill for civil service reform that had been pushed by an aggressive young assemblyman of the opposition Republican Party named Theodore Roosevelt, who commented about Cleveland that he was "much impressed by his high standard of official conduct and his rugged strength of character."[6] That reform bill went far in ensuring Cleveland's election.

Cleveland took the presidential nomination as the candidate of the reformers and, despite the scandalous revelation of his earlier affair, won a close election with 49 percent of the popular vote. The key to his electoral victory was carrying New York, which he did by 1,149 votes out of a million cast. One reason was that his opponent had said nothing when a prominent Protestant minister called the Democrats the party of "Rum, Romanism and Rebellion," raising the old specter of hateful Nativist Catholic-bashing and lumping Catholics in with the despised Confederacy. Usually reliable Democratic voters, Irish Catholics had been leaning toward Republican Blaine. But the remark, and Blaine's failure to disavow it, were widely reported and may have tipped the balance in Cleveland's favor.

How did President Cleveland deal with America's growing labor pains?

If slavery had dominated politics before the Civil War, and Reconstruction and government reform had emerged as the great issues afterward, the landscape was shifting once more. The battle lines were being drawn between labor and business—and the government would have to take sides.

By the time Cleveland took office, the great disparity in income between the working class and America's wealthy class had grown enormous. It was an era known for its Gilded Age excess, as railroad barons and corporate tycoons lived lavishly while workers were near poverty. Although not new in America, that disparity was growing, coupled with the harsh, dangerous, and unsanitary working conditions then prevalent in America's factories and mines as the postwar Industrial Era boom gathered steam and barreled down the rails toward modernity. As it did, America's new "class struggle" came to a head in a series of violent labor battles that eventually took thousands of lives in this Victorian era that was anything but genteel.

In 1877, a nationwide railroad strike was triggered by wage cuts imposed on workers typically putting in twelve-hour shifts six days a week. The strike turned violent and left more than one hundred people dead and a thousand strikers in jail. An organized labor movement had begun to take root as the first generation of national trade unions began to emerge. The first was the Noble Order of the Knights of Labor, begun in 1869. By 1884, the Knights had more than seven hundred thousand members and had acquired a measure of political and negotiating clout.

In early 1886, the Knights called a strike against Jay Gould's Missouri-Pacific Railroad System. The strike was broken by May, but the labor battles were getting larger and more violent. In an April 1886 speech President Cleveland made a slight concession to labor, suggesting the government serve as arbitrator in labor disputes. That was near heresy at the time, as the government existed to put down strikes, not settle them.

The violent atmosphere worsened in May 1886 when the Knights of Labor tried to force an eight-hour workday at Chicago's McCormick Reaper Company. On May 3, police fired on a crowd of striking workers, killing six and wounding dozens more. On May 4, several thousand people gathered at Haymarket Square to protest the police action. As the police arrived to break up the rally, a bomb was thrown, killing seven officers.

There was no hard evidence, but blame fell on anarchist labor leaders, some of whom were tried and quickly convicted. Some were hanged, and others received life sentences. Tarred with the anarchist brush after the Haymarket Square riot, the Knights of Labor were badly discredited. By 1890, their membership had fallen to a hundred thousand.

Although the Knights' organizing efforts failed in the wake of Haymarket Square, and the labor movement was sharply set back by its association with anarchists, the cause of labor was just beginning to intensify. Having struck a mildly conciliatory note in his first term by proposing to arbitrate between labor and business, Cleveland would confront much worse labor pains in his second term and hold fast to the view that government existed to create conditions for business to flourish. That was pretty much the view from both parties. But that was beginning to change as new progressive voices and a more vocal Populist movement began to emerge in the waning days of the nineteenth century.

Commenting on the riots and death in Chicago, future President Theodore Roosevelt professed no sympathy with the "Haymarket bomb throwers," but recognized that the company hit by the strikers was a "very wicked corporation."

Voicing what would become his Populist tone while not actually becoming a Populist himself, Roosevelt criticized Cleveland as "completely controlled by corporations." Wrote Roosevelt, "Cleveland . . . represents to the Wall Street type of men almost the ideal president. Some of the big banks paid the expenses of Cleveland's campaign in 1892. . . . Cleveland has never been brought into contact from the philanthropic side with wage workers, with poor people. He knows nothing of sweatshops on the East Side. All the people around him are the big corporation people and lawyers."[7]

Theodore Roosevelt's comments also underscored a new reality in late nineteenth-century American politics. It had increasingly become a big money affair. The Senate was already called the "Millionaire's Club." But as the country grew, as candidates had to reach more voters, the role of money in presidential politics was only going to increase— and there were no laws yet to control campaign finance. For a very long time, it would be anything goes.

PRESIDENTIAL VOICES

*I want you to take good care of all the furniture and ornaments in the house
for I want to find everything just as it is now when we come back again. We
are coming back in four years.*

—FIRST LADY FRANCES CLEVELAND
on leaving the White House, March 1889[8]

Final Judgment:

See assessment under Cleveland's second term, as the twenty-fourth
president.

First Cleveland Administration Milestones[9]

1885

March 4	Former New York governor Grover Cleveland is sworn in.

1886

January 19	The Presidential Succession Act is passed. It specifies that in the absence of a president and vice president, heads of executive departments will succeed to the presidency in the order in which the departments were created. The act remains unmodified until 1947.
April 22	In the first presidential message relating to labor, Cleveland suggests government arbitrate industrial disputes.
May 3–4	In Chicago, the Haymarket Square Riot takes place.
May 25	Cleveland announces his plans to marry twenty-one-year-old Frances Folsom, setting off a newspaper frenzy.
June 2	Cleveland and Frances Folsom marry in the White House, a month before her twenty-second birthday.

| October 28 | The Statue of Liberty is dedicated. |
| December 8 | Samuel Gompers, a Russian immigrant cigar maker turned union organizer, forms the American Federation of Labor (AFL). |

1887

| February 4 | The Interstate Commerce Commission (ICC), the first independent regulatory agency, is created to ensure fairness in the management of interstate railroads. |

1888

June 13	A Department of Labor, while not yet given full cabinet status, is established by Congress in recognition of the growing importance of workers' issues.
June 25	Republicans nominate Indiana senator Benjamin Harrison, the grandson of President William Henry Harrison.
September 8	Cleveland accepts the Democratic nomination.
November 6	Cleveland wins the popular vote in the presidential election; he loses to Harrison in the electoral vote, 233 to 168.

1889

| February 11 | The Department of Agriculture is created. |
| February 22 | The Omnibus Bill turns the territories of North Dakota, South Dakota, Montana, and Washington into states. |

MUST READS

H. W. Brands, *American Colossus: The Triumph of Capitalism*; Henry F. Graff, *Grover Cleveland*.

ONLINE RESOURCES

Inaugural Address, Avalon Project, Yale Law School
http://avalon.law.yale.edu/19th_century/cleve1.asp

Library of Congress Resource Guide

http://www.loc.gov/rr/program/bib/presidents/cleveland/index
.html

Miller Center of Public Affairs, University of Virginia

http://millercenter.org/index.php/academic/americanpresident
/cleveland

**Grover Cleveland Library (library planned—currently
Web site only)**

http://groverclevelandlibrary.org/

23

Little Ben
Benjamin Harrison

★ ★ ★

March 4, 1889–March 4, 1893

Milestones in Benjamin Harrison's Life

August 20, 1833	Born in North Bend, Ohio
1854	Began law practice in Indianapolis, Indiana
1862–1865	Served in Civil War, commanding Seventieth Indiana Regiment
1876	Defeated as Republican candidate for governor of Indiana
1881–1887	U.S. senator from Indiana
1889–1893	Twenty-third president
1893–1894	Lectured in law at Leland Stanford University
March 13, 1901	Died in Indianapolis, Indiana, aged sixty-seven

---

PRESIDENTIAL VOICES

Is it not quite possible that the farmers and the promoters of the great mining and manufacturing enterprises which have recently been established in the South may yet find that the free ballot of the workingman, without distinction of race, is needed for their defense as well as for his own?

—Benjamin Harrison
First Inaugural, March 4, 1889[1]

L argely distinguished by the fact that he was the grandson of a president, Benjamin Harrison was a rock-solid Republican and Civil War veteran. Victor in a controversial election tainted by accusations of fraud and ballot box stuffing, Harrison was also a transitional figure as America moved toward the twentieth century. He was dealing with nineteenth-century problems, such as the continuing war against Native Americans, at the same time he had to confront a modern problem—labor unions. He also came to office when the American economy was swinging through booms and busts at a dizzying rate as the country barreled toward a twentieth-century future with a government designed for a horse-and-buggy age.

Fast Facts

RELIGION: Presbyterian

EDUCATION: Miami University (of Ohio)

MILITARY SERVICE: Civil War (He rose from second lieutenant to brigadier general.)

CAREER BEFORE POLITICS: Attorney

POLITICAL PARTY: Republican

FIRST LADY: Caroline Scott Harrison (October 1, 1832–October 25, 1892) Caroline Harrison died of tuberculosis in the White House just weeks before Harrison lost his bid for a second term in the 1892 election.

A little more than three years later, Benjamin Harrison married Mary Dimmick (April 30, 1858–January 5, 1948), the niece of his first wife. A widow whose first husband died when she was twenty-three, Mary Harrison was twenty-five years younger than Harrison.

CHILDREN: Harrison had two children with his first wife, Russell and Mary ("Mamie"). They were estranged from their father after he remarried.

* Harrison won the presidency despite losing the popular vote to Grover Cleveland in 1888.
* Harrison is the only president to date who was grandson of another president (William Henry Harrison, the ninth president). His great-grandfather, Benjamin Harrison V, was a signer of the Declaration of Independence.
* More states were admitted under Harrison than under any president since Washington: North Dakota, South Dakota, Montana, and Washington in 1889; Idaho and Wyoming in 1890.
* Electric lights were installed in the White House during Harrison's term. At the time, the Harrisons did not yet fully trust them and used gas as well, like many other people. As long as they remained in the White House, the Harrisons feared electric shocks, which were much more common with early wiring, and refused to operate the lights themselves.[2]
* In 1891, the first Christmas tree was brought into the White House. Benjamin Harrison also dressed as Santa Claus to entertain his grandchildren.

PRESIDENTIAL VOICES

I could not name my own Cabinet. They had sold out every place to pay the election expenses.

—BENJAMIN HARRISON, FOLLOWING HIS ELECTION[3]

Descended from a signer of the Declaration of Independence and the ninth U.S. president, Benjamin Harrison grew up on an Ohio farm that his grandfather had given to his father.

Homeschooled with his eight siblings in a one-room log schoolhouse that his father, John Scott Harrison, had built, Benjamin later attended a preparatory school, then transferred to Miami College in Oxford, Ohio. After graduating, he studied law and married his school sweetheart Caroline Lavinia Scott before moving to Indiana in 1854 and working in the courts.

When the war broke out, Harrison commanded a regiment of volunteers that saw heavy fighting in Georgia and earned him a promotion to brigadier general. With his famous bloodlines and distinguished war record, Harrison made a run for governor of Indiana but lost. He was, however, elected U.S. senator by the state legislature five years later. When the Republicans convened in Chicago in June 1888, Harrison was given the presidential nomination with the blessing of party power broker Senator James Blaine. His lackluster campaign failed to win the nation's popular vote, which went to President Cleveland by some one hundred thousand votes. But he won the key states of New York and Indiana, where voting irregularities were widely reported. According to presidential campaign historian Paul Boller, the Republicans raised $400,000 to buy votes in the Hoosier state.[4] When the very devout Harrison remarked that "Providence" had helped provide the victory, one of the Republican bosses remarked that Harrison would never know "how close a number of men were compelled to approach . . . the penitentiary to make him President."[5]

One of the leading Republican fund-raisers was famed Philadelphia department store magnate John Wanamaker, whom Theodore Roosevelt—soon to be appointed a civil service commissioner—called a "hypocritical haberdasher." After Harrison won, Wanamaker became postmaster general and actually introduced three innovations: parcel post, rural free delivery, and the postal savings bank.

Since his grandfather was a famous Indian fighter, what were Harrison's policies toward Native Americans?

By the time Harrison took office, most of the great wars against the native nations had been fought. Harrison, after all, was the grandson of "Old Tippecanoe," and undoubtedly tales of fighting Tecumseh and his Shawnee braves had been a regular part of the family lore.

But the fighting against the native nations was not quite over. A group of Sioux who had been confined to a reservation in South Dakota grew belligerent under the influence of a shaman named Wovoka, who was spurring a native religious revival movement called the Ghost Dance. The Ghost Dancers wanted to reject white ways, including alcohol, and return to a pure traditional Sioux lifestyle. Some of the younger men also believed that they could wear "Ghost Shirts" that would protect them from the white man's bullets. Alarmed by the movement, the army tried to arrest some of its leaders, including the great but aging chief Sitting Bull. When tribal police in the government's employ captured Sitting Bull, he was killed during a scuffle.

On December 29, 1890, a group of Sioux—some 350 men, women, and children—were traveling to the Pine Ridge Reservation when they were intercepted by the Seventh Cavalry and escorted to a camp near Wounded Knee Creek in South Dakota. When the Sioux were ordered to surrender their weapons, a gun went off. The cavalrymen panicked and opened fire with repeating guns and rifles. At least 150, and possibly as many as 300, Sioux were killed in the massacre known as Wounded Knee.

Harrison's official policy toward Indians was influenced by a piece of legislation called the Dawes Act (passed during his predecessor's term in 1887), which was intended to provide Native Americans with private land instead of tribal lands, in the hopes that they would assimilate more easily if they owned property. Instead, the Dawes Act was abused and simply became another way in which Indians were cheated out of their land, which was taken and then resold to speculators.

In 1889, Harrison completed the Indian Appropriation Act that opened up millions of acres of prime territory, once Indian land but now governed by less stringent laws, in the Oklahoma Land Rushes of 1889 and 1892, and later opened up land in the Dakotas as well.

PRESIDENTIAL VOICES

I pledge allegiance to the flag of the United States of America, and to the republic for which it stands, one nation indivisible, with liberty and justice for all.

—THE ORIGINAL PLEDGE OF ALLEGIANCE

Written in 1892 by Francis Bellamy, a minister and "Christian socialist," the pledge was meant to mark the four hundredth anniversary of the arrival of Columbus in the Americas. President Harrison issued a proclamation making the pledge a part of the public school ceremony honoring Columbus Day. The words "under God" were not added to the pledge until June 14, 1954.

PRESIDENTIAL VOICES

The indiscriminate denunciation of the rich is mischievous. It perverts the mind, poisons the heart and furnishes an excuse to crime. No poor man was ever made richer or happier by it. It is quite as illogical to despise a man because he is rich as because he is poor. Not what a man has, but what he is, settles his class. We can not right matters by taking from one what he has honestly acquired to bestow upon another what he has not earned.

—BENJAMIN HARRISON[6]

Final Judgment: Grade C

In a rematch with Cleveland in 1892, Harrison had several shortcomings. He was seen as cold and aloof and was even known as the "White House Iceberg." His wife, Caroline, was seriously ill and died two weeks before the election, and her illness muted the campaign. The McKinley Tariff of 1890, passed with Harrison's blessing, was an extremely high tariff on foreign goods and was meant to protect domestic industry. Popular with businesses, the tariff drove up prices on consumer goods and hurt average, working Americans. And another violent labor episode, at the Andrew Carnegie Steel Company in Homestead, Pennsylvania, in July 1892 damaged the Republican Party with working voters. They saw tariffs going up to protect business but nothing being done by government to help American workers.

A Populist, or People's, Party also sprang up, presenting the plight of farmers and workers who felt ignored by both main parties. One of their famous organizers was Mary Lease, who declared, "Wall Street owns the country," a cry that echoed through the "Occupy Wall Street" movement that emerged in 2011. In a surprising show of strength, the Populist candidate, James B. Weaver, won more than one million popular votes and twenty-two electoral votes.

In this rematch, Grover Cleveland easily won a second term, and Mrs. Cleveland's bold prediction of returning proved right.

In retirement, Harrison remarried, wrote two memoirs, taught law, and did international legal work before he died at home in Indianapolis at the age of sixty-seven.

A colorless, one-term president, Harrison was mostly regarded by history as one more of the rather faceless presidents who failed to put a stamp on the country or the presidency. His most far-reaching policy decision—the McKinley Tariff—pushed the country toward another panic. And the other piece of significant legislation during his term, the Sherman Antitrust Act, meant to rein in corporations, was rarely used until one of his successors, Theodore Roosevelt, found it a bully "big stick."

Harrison Administration Milestones[7]

1889

March 4	Benjamin Harrison is inaugurated.
April 22	The Oklahoma Land Rush: Nearly two million acres in central Oklahoma, land formerly ceded to Indians, are opened to white settlers.
May 13	Harrison appoints Theodore Roosevelt to be civil service commissioner.
May 31	The Great Johnstown Flood kills nearly twenty-three hundred people in Pennsylvania.
November 2	North and South Dakota are admitted as the thirty-ninth and fortieth states.
November 8	Montana becomes the forty-first state.
November 11	Washington is admitted as the forty-second state.

1890

July 2	The Sherman Antitrust Act is passed; it is designed to limit business practices that restrain trade and commerce or attempt to create monopolies.
July 3	Idaho is admitted as the forty-third state.
July 10	Wyoming is admitted as the forty-fourth state, the first with suffrage for women.
October 1	Congress passes the McKinley Tariff; meant to protect U.S. businesses by applying high tariffs to foreign products, the bill drives up prices for many Americans.
November 7	In midterm elections, Democrats sweep the House, while the Republican majority in the Senate is reduced. Senator William McKinley loses his Senate seat, and the Democratic victory reflects the unpopularity of the tariff bearing his name.

1891

May 19	The Populist Party is formed mostly by workers and farmers; it backs an eight-hour day, an income tax, popular election of senators, and secret ballots, among other reforms.

1892

April 19	The first American automobile is perfected by the Duryea brothers in Springfield, Massachusetts.
	Harrison opens to settlers another three million acres of Oklahoma land that had belonged to the Cheyenne and Arapaho.
June 7–10	Harrison is nominated on the first ballot at the Republican National Convention.
June 23	The Democrats nominate Grover Cleveland.
July 6	Steelworkers at the Homestead plant in Pennsylvania fight with strikebreakers from the Pinkerton Detective Agency. Seven Pinkerton men and nine workers die in the fighting. Six days later, eight thousand militiamen accompany the Pinkerton men to break the strike.

July 11	Silver miners at Coeur d'Alene, Idaho, begin a violent strike. Thirty men are killed as they fight non-union help. Harrison sends in federal troops to restore order.
July 30	Harrison privately supports mediation in the Homestead Steel strike, which lasts five months, breaks the union, and deals a major blow to organized labor.
November 8	Grover Cleveland defeats Harrison.

1893

January 17	Queen Liliuokalani of Hawaii is deposed on January 17, with a provisional government established under Sanford B. Dole. Harrison deploys 150 Marines to Hawaii to protect the new government.

MUST READS

Dee Brown, *Bury My Heart at Wounded Knee: An Indian History of the American West*; Charles W. Calhoun, *Benjamin Harrison*.

ONLINE RESOURCES

Inaugural Address, Avalon Project, Yale Law School
 http://avalon.law.yale.edu/19th_century/harris.asp

Library of Congress Resource Guide
 http://www.loc.gov/rr/program/bib/presidents/bharrison/index
 .html

Miller Center of Public Affairs, University of Virginia
 http://millercenter.org/president/bharrison

Benjamin Harrison Presidential Home, Indianapolis, Indiana
 http://www.presidentbenjaminharrison.org/

24

Grover Cleveland

★ ★ ★

March 4, 1893–March 4, 1897*

PRESIDENTIAL VOICES

Under our scheme of government the waste of public money is a crime against the citizen, and the contempt of our people for economy and frugality in their personal affairs deplorably saps the strength and sturdiness of our national character.

It is a plain dictate of honesty and good government that public expenditures should be limited by public necessity, and that this should be measured by the rules of strict economy; and it is equally clear that frugality among the people is the best guaranty of a contented and strong support of free institutions.

—GROVER CLEVELAND
Second Inaugural Address, March 4, 1893[1]

Fast Facts

* In 1893, at the beginning of Cleveland's second term, a malignant tumor was removed from the president's mouth during a secret operation performed aboard a yacht as it cruised New York City's East

---

* Grover Cleveland is the only president to serve nonconsecutive terms and so he is usually counted as both the twenty-second and twenty-fourth president. See page 320 for the entry on Cleveland as twenty-second president and for general biographical material.

River. Cleveland was fitted with a rubber prosthesis to replace part of his jaw and palate, and kept this operation and a follow-up procedure secret. The nation was in the midst of an economic crisis, and it was thought that word of the president's illness might lead to an even bigger panic. The public did not learn about the operation until 1917, when one of the doctors revealed it in the *Saturday Evening Post.*

* Cleveland signed the first Labor Day holiday into law in June 1894, in an era of violent labor struggles in which Cleveland, like his predecessors, used federal troops to help suppress strikes.

* Cleveland vetoed more bills in his two terms than all other presidents to that date combined. His 414 first-term vetoes are still a single-term record. Most of them were vetoes of what he considered "pork barrel" spending; others vetoed bills granting private pensions and one granting grain to drought-stricken farmers. His first-term veto of a bill that would grant a pension to a disabled veteran was a factor in his 1888 loss. Cleveland's two-term total was 584 vetoed bills, only two of which were overridden. That record stood until Franklin D. Roosevelt vetoed 635 pieces of legislation in his four terms.

Cleveland's aggressive use of the veto represented a pendulum swing toward greater presidential power over Congress, a swing from earlier Republican presidents who had largely acquiesced to congressional wishes.

Who helped Cleveland bail out America in 1895?

One reason that many American presidents of the later nineteenth century have been somewhat obscured is that the office had lost its central role as the most powerful post in America. After Lincoln, Congress had begun to exert itself more forcefully, beginning with the Radical Republicans and their impeachment of Andrew Johnson. Political power in Washington swung toward Capitol Hill, where wealthy congressmen—the "bosses"—held more clout than presidents.

But even more significant was the postwar emergence of the genera-

tion of extremely wealthy and successful business giants who dominated the landscape of the American economy and politics during this
period, largely dwarfing the parade of post–Civil War presidents.

The names are now legendary. Rockefeller. Vanderbilt. Carnegie.
Astor. Known for their excesses as well as their successes, many would
be described as "robber barons."

Of them, few were wealthier or more powerful than J. P. Morgan,
the banker's banker. Today, when the phrase "bailout" refers to the
federal government assisting banks and businesses deemed "too big to
fail," it is worth recalling that in 1896, it was banker Morgan who
bailed out a nearly bankrupt United States government.

Right after Cleveland's second inaugural, the nation was sinking
into another of its periodic postwar depressions. Wall Street historian
Steve Fraser records, "Fourteen of the twenty-five years between 1873
and 1897 were years of depression or recession." Despite the era's incredible industrial and technological growth, there were, as Fraser puts
it, "ferocious acts of creation and destruction."[2]

Recall that this was a time when there was no national or central
bank, very little—if any—federal regulation of banking or business,
and no income taxes (the Civil War era income tax had ended in 1872).
There was no "invisible hand" of government. In other words, this was
about as "free" as a free market gets. Yet it was clearly a highly inefficient one.

The reasons for a panic, or depression, in 1893 sound all too familiar. A failed bank in England, bankruptcies in a few major American
industries, poor crop prices, and foreclosures of farm mortgages all
stressed the banking system that had grown out of the horse-and-carriage
era and was ill-suited to the needs of a rapidly modernizing, dynamic
industrial economy, best symbolized by the growth of railroads and steel
mills. Unemployment was high in a country that was now more dependent on factory and industrial jobs. The nation was still on the gold standard, which meant that people could redeem their "greenbacks" for gold
from the United States reserves. As banks in England cashed in their
holdings in American paper money for gold—"hard money"—the U.S.
gold reserves slipped to a frighteningly low level.

Having spent time on Wall Street as a lawyer, Cleveland knew J. P. Morgan, and turned to him. Morgan traveled by private train car to Washington to meet with the president. The banker told Cleveland that the nation's gold reserves might be gone by that afternoon. Morgan then offered to put together a syndicate that included the London Rothschild banks to buy American bonds with gold, in essence bailing out a government on the verge of insolvency. Morgan even cited an obscure Civil War–era law that permitted Cleveland to do all of this without congressional approval. As Ron Chernow explains in his biography of Morgan, "This was the showstopper that mystified the financial world—a promise to rig, temporarily, the gold market. . . . When the deal was concluded, Cleveland gave Pierpont a fresh cigar to replace the one he had nervously ground up."[3]

In this moment of supreme brinksmanship, Cleveland agreed to the deal with Morgan with little more than a handshake. Morgan merely gave his word that he would make good. That was enough for the banking world, as H. W. Brands writes. "News of the bargain brought immediate relief. Morgan's syndicate included European bankers who now returned to the Treasury vaults much of the gold they had been withdrawing during the previous months. More important was the psychological support the government drew from its association with Morgan. The word of Cleveland . . . meant nothing to investors at this stage; the word of Morgan meant everything."[4]

Morgan's bonds-for-gold exchange was repeated several times over the next few years, until America's gold reserves were once again healthy. Populists didn't like it, and there was plenty of anti-Semitism voiced over the role of the Rothschild bank in this rescue. But Morgan had essentially filled the role of the Federal Reserve, which was not created until 1913.

At the other end of the economic spectrum, in the midst of this 1893 Panic, a militant Eugene V. Debs was organizing the American Railway Union, which absorbed remnants of the Knights of Labor and called for a strike in 1894 against the Pullman Car Company. Since Pullman cars were found on almost every train in the country, the strike soon became national in scope.

The strike peaked when sixty thousand rail workers went out around the country, and the federal government, at the railways' behest, stepped in. Attorney General Richard Olney, a former railroad lawyer, declared that the strike interfered with federal mails; the Supreme Court agreed, and President Cleveland called out troops to suppress the strike. After a pitched battle in Chicago, in which strikers were killed, Debs was arrested and jailed for contempt of court. He later joined the Socialist Party and ran for president five times.

Final Judgment: Grade B

Cleveland was asked to run for another term by a third party, conservative Democrats who favored a gold standard and called themselves Gold-Democrats. He refused and was happy to see the Republican McKinley—a "sound money man"—defeat Democrat William Jennings Bryan in 1896. On leaving the White House, Cleveland settled in Princeton, New Jersey, and was regarded with increasing respect as time went by. Suffering from heart and kidney ailments, he died at home in his bed in 1908, at age seventy-one.

Honest and able, Grover Cleveland stands above most of the other mediocre or worse presidents of the latter half of the nineteenth century, although some historians view him as a ponderous, unimaginative man, lacking in statesmanship. That is what helps place him solidly in the middle ranks of presidents, according to the majority of historian surveys.

Apart from several decisions that continued civil service reform and the repeal of the tariff that had hurt American workers, his legislative agenda and vision for the country were slight. He has been compared to a small-town mayor, and he was, after all, mayor of Buffalo—no small town, but not a great city then, either. His other significant achievement may have been standing up to Congress, especially through his aggressive use of the veto. He was far from an imperial president, but he helped restore some of the balance of power lost by his presidential predecessors during the post–Civil War era.

There has also been a perception that when he left office, Cleveland was unpopular with the average American. But as biographer Henry Graff points out: "He was once revered by millions of his contemporaries for genuine merits, especially integrity. They had seen virtue enough in him to accord him popular majorities in three presidential elections. He had the ill luck to be president in a time of rampant political corruption. . . . The public understood that what the nation required, above all, was not brilliance but the cleansing honesty and straightforwardness he provided."[5]

Second Cleveland Administration Milestones[6]

1893

March 4	Grover Cleveland is inaugurated, becoming the only president to serve two nonconsecutive terms.
April 22	For the first time, U.S. Treasury gold reserves fall below $100 million.
May 4–5	The Panic of 1893 begins after the National Cordage Company and the Philadelphia and Reading Railroads go bankrupt.

1894

March 25	Led by Populist Jacob Coxey, four hundred members of the "Army of the Commonwealth of Christ," or "Coxey's Army," leave Ohio to march on Washington. Later joined by a West Coast contingent that includes a young writer named Jack London, they demand that the government provide worthwhile jobs for the unemployed during the depression.
May–July	The Pullman Car strike, organized by Eugene Debs, president of the American Railway Union, begins in Pullman, Illinois. When the walkout turns violent, Cleveland sends federal troops to Chicago on July 3. Debs and others are arrested, and the strike is broken.
July 4	Hawaii's provisional government declares the Republic of Hawaii. On August 8, the U.S. government recognizes the Republic of Hawaii.

1895

February 8–20	A third Treasury bond sale to a syndicate headed by J. P. Morgan restores gold reserves.
May 20	The Supreme Court nullifies the income tax law in *Pollock v. Farmers' Loan and Trust Company.*

1896

January 4	Utah is admitted as the forty-fifth state.
January 6	A fourth bond sale of $100 million is announced; gold reserves are restored to a generally safe level of $124 million. The four bond sales between 1894 and 1896 have created $262 million in federal debt.
June 16–18	The Republican National Convention chooses William McKinley as its candidate.
July 7–11	The Democratic Convention nominates William Jennings Bryan, a Nebraska congressman and champion of silver. The move signals the party's abandonment of the gold standard, upsetting many party members. Populists decide to back Bryan.
November 3	William McKinley is elected president, carrying 51 percent of the popular vote and 271 electoral votes to Bryan's 176.

1897

February 9	Cleveland vetoes a bill that would prohibit illiterate immigrants from entering the country.

MUST READS

Ron Chernow, *The House of Morgan: An American Banking Dynasty and the Rise of Modern Finance;* Henry F. Graff, *Grover Cleveland: The American Presidents Series: the 22nd and 24th President, 1885–1889 and 1893–1897.*

ONLINE RESOURCES

Inaugural Address, Avalon Project, Yale Law School
   http://avalon.law.yale.edu/19th_century/cleve2.asp

Library of Congress Resource Guide

http://www.loc.gov/rr/program/bib/presidents/cleveland/index
.html

Miller Center of Public Affairs, University of Virginia

http://millercenter.org/index.php/academic/americanpresident
/cleveland

Grover Cleveland Library (library planned—currently
Web site only)

http://groverclevelandlibrary.org/

25

Idol of Ohio
William McKinley

* * *

March 4, 1897–September 14, 1901

Milestones in William McKinley's Life

January 29, 1843	Born in Niles, Ohio
1860	Taught school and clerked in post office
1861–1865	Served in Civil War, promoted to major
1867	Admitted to the Ohio bar
1869–1871	Prosecuting attorney of Stark County, Ohio
1877–1892	U.S. representative from Ohio
1892–1896	Governor of Ohio
1897–1901	Twenty-fifth president
September 6, 1901	Shot by assassin in Buffalo, New York
September 14, 1901	Died in Buffalo, aged fifty-eight

PRESIDENTIAL VOICES

Military service under a common flag and for a righteous cause has strengthened the national spirit and served to cement more closely than ever the fraternal bonds between every section of the country.

—William McKinley
First Message to Congress, December 6, 1897[1]

He was the last president of the nineteenth century and the first of the twentieth. As he came to office, Americans were buying packaged pancake mix, Ivory soap, mass-produced bicycles from the Montgomery Ward catalog, and a host of new consumer products that would help make them the envy of the new age.[2]

In spite of this shift in American consumers' tastes and buying habits, William McKinley entered the White House with the nation in the midst of another of its periodic economic calamities, the worst to that date. By the time he ran for a second term, the economy was humming and America had just won a "splendid little war" with Spain. The victory expanded America's reach into the Caribbean and across the Pacific. America no longer ended at its shoreline. And in his last public speech, McKinley himself said, "Isolation is no longer possible or desirable."

America was on the verge of becoming a global empire, just as the era that would be called the "American Century" was set to open. Unfortunately, McKinley didn't get to see it. With a record-setting plurality of votes, he was elected to a second term with a new vice president, Theodore Roosevelt. But a few months later, McKinley was dead at the hands of an assassin.

Fast Facts

RELIGION: Methodist

ASSOCIATIONS: Freemason

EDUCATION: Attended Allegheny College but dropped out. McKinley also did not complete law school, but he was admitted to the Ohio bar.

MILITARY SERVICE: Captain, U.S. Army Twenty-third Ohio Volunteers

CAREER BEFORE POLITICS: Attorney

POLITICAL PARTY: Republican

FIRST LADY: Ida Saxton McKinley (June 8, 1847–May 26, 1907)

CHILDREN: Two daughters, both of whom died in childhood

* Following the loss of her two daughters and mother in a short space of time, Ida McKinley became increasingly depressed, nervous, and sick. She suffered seizures and was nearly an invalid. Devoted to his wife, McKinley broke with protocol by having her seated next to him at state dinners so he could tend to her if she suffered a seizure. McKinley would gently cover her contorted face with a napkin until the seizure had passed.

* McKinley was the last veteran of the Civil War to serve as president.

* He enlisted in the Ohio Volunteers in June 1861. Among the officers in his regiment was Rutherford B. Hayes, the future president, who praised and promoted the young officer.

* The first president to appear extensively on film, McKinley was also the first to ride in an automobile, in 1899.

* McKinley was the third of four presidents killed by an assassin.

PRESIDENTIAL VOICES

McKinley is an upright and honorable man, of very considerable ability and good record as a soldier and in Congress. He is not a strong man, however. . . . I should feel rather uneasy about him in a serious crisis. I do hope he will take a strong stand about Hawaii and Cuba. I do not think a war with Spain would be serious enough to cause much strain on the country.
—THEODORE ROOSEVELT[3]

William McKinley was the seventh of nine children born to a second-generation pig iron miner and manufacturer in what was then still the wilderness in Niles, Ohio. It was a childhood of simple nineteenth-century American virtues—Methodist church, the importance of a good education, and a strict work ethic.

When the war came in 1861, McKinley did what was expected and volunteered; a commissary sergeant, he delivered hot meals by wagon to men under fire. His bravery at Antietam caught the attention of Rutherford B. Hayes, a senior officer, and McKinley was promoted, becoming a member of Hayes's staff. The two future presidents would remain close friends and political allies.

By 1877, having begun his law career, McKinley went to Washington as a freshman congressman from Ohio and served in Congress for fifteen years before moving to the Ohio statehouse as governor. When the depression of 1893 hit Ohio, he sent carloads of provisions to unemployed miners, paying for them out of his modest personal savings.

McKinley won the 1896 Republican nomination with the help of Mark Hanna, a wealthy businessman and friend who had become a power in Ohio's Republican circles and who would pioneer modern advertising techniques in political campaigns. McKinley's opponent was the silver-tongued William Jennings Bryan, one of the most famous orators of his day, who favored "free silver" and was considered dangerous by "corporate America," which feared his currency plans.

So did Theodore Roosevelt: "Bryan is a personally honest and rather attractive man, a real orator and born demagogue," Roosevelt wrote. "Every crank, fool, and putative criminal in the country is behind him, and a large portion of the ignorant honest class. . . . The combination of all the lunatics, all the idiots, all the knaves, all the cowards, and all the honest people who are hopelessly slow-witted is a formidable one to overcome when backed by the solid South."[4]

Pouring money into Mark Hanna's pockets, big businesses bankrolled the McKinley campaign. Some companies went beyond that, placing notes in the pay envelopes they handed out, warning their employees that the business would close and they would lose their jobs unless McKinley was elected.

This combination of soft sell and hard sell worked. McKinley easily defeated Bryan in both the popular and electoral votes. The two men would run again in 1900 with the result even more lopsided in McKinley's favor. Campaign money—combined with changing marketing techniques—was making its presence felt in the way America picked its presidents.

Who remembers the Maine?

On February 15, 1898, the battleship *Maine*, in the harbor of Havana, Cuba, mysteriously exploded. The ship had been dispatched to "protect" American citizens in Cuba, where a rebellion against Spain was under way. America's sympathies and interests were with the rebels, but both Grover Cleveland and his successor, McKinley, sought a peaceful solution to gaining the island's independence.

But they were in the minority. Watching England, Germany, France, and Belgium spread their global empires in Asia and Africa, many Americans hoped that this war would help expand trade markets overseas, capture valuable mineral deposits, and acquire land that was good for growing fruit, tobacco, and sugar. It was a war wanted by banks and brokers, steelmakers and oilmen, manufacturers and missionaries.

And it was a war the newspapers wanted. War, after all, was good for circulation. When a naval board of inquiry decided that a mine had destroyed the *Maine*, the press and the public were in full war cry. "Remember the *Maine*! To Hell with Spain!" was their battle call. The actual cause of the explosion was disputed both then and later.*

The ostensible reason for going to war with Spain was to "liberate" Cuba, a Spanish colony. A fading world power with holdings in the Caribbean, along with the Philippine Islands and other Pacific areas, that would be useful as naval bases, Spain was trying to maintain control over a Cuban population that demanded its freedom. When Spain sent a military governor to throw rebels into concentration camps, America acted the part of the outraged sympathizer.

Powerful men inside the government who wanted war with Spain matched forces with those outside the government. Chief among them was Henry Cabot Lodge (1850–1924), the influential senator from Massachusetts. An outspoken booster of American imperialism, Lodge said, "In the interests of our commerce and our fullest development, we should build the Nicaraguan canal, and for the protection of that canal

---

* According to the U.S. Navy: "Technical experts at the time of both investigations disagreed with the findings, believing that spontaneous combustion of coal in the bunker adjacent to the reserve six-inch magazine was the most likely cause of the explosion on board the ship. . . . Using documentation gathered from the two official inquiries, as well as information on the construction and ammunition of *Maine*, the experts concluded [in 1976] that the damage caused to the ship was inconsistent with the external explosion of a mine. The most likely cause, they speculated, was spontaneous combustion of coal in the bunker next to the magazine."

and for the sake of our commercial supremacy in the Pacific we should control the Hawaiian Islands and maintain our influence in Samoa. . . . Commerce follows the flag, and we should build up a navy strong enough to give protection to Americans in every quarter of the globe."

That was music to the ears of Theodore Roosevelt, then assistant secretary of the navy. The aggressive young reformer from New York had been profoundly influenced by Captain Alfred Mahan's book *The Influence of Sea Power Upon History, 1660–1783*, a work of history calling for the aggressive expansion of American naval power to bases around the world, especially in the Pacific.

Adding pressure for war were the two most powerful newspaper barons in American history, William Randolph Hearst (1863–1951) and Joseph Pulitzer (1847–1911). Both men knew that headlines sold newspapers. Tabloid front pages screeching about Spanish atrocities against Cubans became commonplace. Hearst and Pulitzer were not afraid of sensationalizing to heighten the war fever.

Against the urging of party and press, as well as businessmen and also missionaries who wanted to bring Anglo-Saxon Christianity to the world, McKinley tried to avert war. "I have been through one war," he said, "I have seen the dead pile up and I do not want to see another."[5]

But the finding that the *Maine* had been sunk gave the country all the justification it needed. Congress declared war on Spain in late April 1898, and with sabers rattling loudly across the country and jingoistic slogans splashed across the front pages, volunteers eagerly set off.

The brief war produced 5,462 American deaths, only 379 of which were battle casualties. Yellow fever, malaria, and other diseases were primarily responsible for the losses.

In the aftermath, America now held Cuba and Puerto Rico, as well as Wake Island, Guam, and the Philippines—all of them former Spanish colonies. President McKinley was somewhat uncertain about what should be done with these far-flung territories. But he kept them for America. With the annexation of Hawaii in 1898, America had in place its "stepping-stones" to a new Pacific world of trade and opportunity.

The people in the Philippines were less enthusiastic. Emiliano Aguinaldo, a rebel leader who had been assisted in his struggles against Spain by American Admiral Dewey, was no more interested in American rule than he had been in Spanish rule. What followed was a violent conflict more bloody than the one with Spain: the Philippine Insurrection. The Philippines would be an unhappy "protectorate" in the American Pacific for years to come. Five thousand Americans died fighting there.

PRESIDENTIAL VOICES

There was nothing left for us to do but to take them all, and to educate Filipinos, and uplift and civilize and Christianize them, and by God's grace do the very best we could for them, as our fellowmen for whom Christ also died.
—WILLIAM MCKINLEY
on his decision to claim the Philippine Islands, 1899[6]

Cuba also provided America with a real, live war hero in Colonel Theodore Roosevelt. Outfitting his own volunteer regiment, he had been a star of news reports as he led charges with reckless abandon. Unashamedly, he rode his Rough Rider fame into the statehouse of New York in 1898, where his reform-minded ideas unsettled some Republicans. A number of New York Republicans felt it would be an eminently prudent idea to move the ambitious Rough Rider Roosevelt out of New York. They wanted to put him on McKinley's ticket, where he could do them no harm. Mark Hanna, now a senator as well as chairman of the Republican Party, did not join in this thinking. Hanna commented, "Don't any of you realize there's only one life between this madman and the presidency?"[7]

Roosevelt, whose view of McKinley to this point was that he lacked backbone, initially balked at running with him in 1900. Young and ambitious, Roosevelt thought being vice president was a political dead end. The bullets fired by anarchist Leon Czolgosz in Buffalo in September 1901 changed all that. McKinley, the most traveled president to that time, was in Buffalo, New York, for the Pan-American Exposition, the equivalent of a World's Fair, which had opened in May 1901 and would continue through November. McKinley was greeting well-wishers in front of the Temple of Music, a grand Italian Renaissance–inspired "wedding cake" of a building with extensive electric lights. It was designed to be a marvel of the new world. At a little after four in the afternoon, he reached out to greet a young man. Instead of shaking hands, the man took out a concealed revolver and put two bullets in McKinley's chest at point-blank range. The assassin was an unemployed steelworker from Detroit, twenty-eight-year-old Leon F. Czolgosz, a self-avowed anarchist who reflected the class hatred that was then growing in urban, industrial America. As Morton Keller noted, "McKinley was a transitional man straddling the Americas of the late nineteenth and early twentieth centuries. He was felled by a product of the social anomie that came with mass, industrialized urban society: the world of the century to come."[8]

McKinley reportedly told his Secret Service agents not to hurt the shooter and whispered to his private secretary to be careful how Mrs. McKinley was told. He was rushed to a hospital, but gangrene set in and McKinley died on September 14.

At age forty-two, Theodore Roosevelt became the youngest president in American history.

PRESIDENTIAL VOICES

Four more years of the full dinner pail.
—McKinley campaign slogan, 1900

Final Judgment: Grade B

One of the most remarkable facts about McKinley is the universal respect and admiration he seems to have enjoyed. People genuinely liked him. He was considered gentle and generous and was spoken of in his life as graciously as he was in death.

But for a long time after his death, McKinley was also seen as less than successful. The tariffs he reintroduced as president were higher than those under the McKinley Tariff he sponsored in the Senate—part of his Republican, pro-business creed. But they were policies viewed as antiquated. Although the war was popular and greatly expanded the power and prestige of the presidency—the White House clerical staff under McKinley grew from six to eighty—he was also criticized for allowing the nation to be taken into an unnecessary conflict. He was viewed as too slow to accept the progressive changes that the country was demanding. And his paternalistic view of nonwhites, including those who had come under American control in an increasingly far-flung empire, sound racist to modern ears.

More recent assessments, however, paint a picture of McKinley as a key transitional figure, beginning to lead America's transition into the twentieth century. While he was not a jingoistic war hawk, he understood the axiom that "commerce follows the flag." That new reality forced McKinley to back off the isolationist, protectionist line he had always toed. "The expansion of our trade and commerce is the pressing problem," he said after the war.

Political commentator Kevin Phillips notes: "McKinley's was the administration during which the United States made its diplomatic and military debut as a world power. He was one of eight Presidents who, either in the White House or on the battlefield, stood as principals in successful wars, and he was among the six or seven to take office in what became recognized as major realignment of the U.S. party system. No other Republican nominee could have made of the 1896 election what McKinley did—and no other Republican would have had the stature and self-assuredness to take Theodore Roosevelt as his ticket mate in 1900."[9]

Perhaps he was later diminished when he fell into the outsized shadow cast by his successor, Theodore Roosevelt. Time has since raised McKinley's standing in some historians' estimates. In his final public speech, McKinley was pointing toward a transition, turning away from the economic ideas of the past and engaging very differently with the world.

His successor would completely change the rules of engagement.

McKinley Administration Milestones[10]

1897

March 4	William McKinley is inaugurated.
May 24	Congress appropriates $50,000 for the relief of Americans in Cuba.
July 14	The first shipment of Alaskan gold, totaling $750,000, arrives in San Francisco. With new gold supplies from the Alaska gold fields, the controversial "gold standard" loses steam as a passionate controversy.
December 6	In McKinley's first Annual Message to Congress, the president states that Spain should be given time to reform its behavior in Cuba.

1898

January 25	The U.S. battleship *Maine* arrives in Havana on a nominally "friendly visit."
February 15	The *Maine* explodes and sinks in the Havana harbor, killing 266 Americans aboard. The sinking of the *Maine* fans public outrage, already sympathetic to the cause of Cuban independence.
March 17	The U.S. Navy reports that the *Maine* explosion was the result of external factors, possibly a mine.
April 21	President McKinley orders a blockade of northern Cuban ports.
April 22	Congress passes the Volunteer Army Act, which authorizes the organization of the First Volunteer Cavalry, or Rough Riders, under the command of Colonel Leonard Wood and Lieutenant Colonel Theodore Roosevelt.
April 25	Congress declares war on Spain.
May 1	Commodore George Dewey, commanding an American squadron of six ships, defeats a large but antiquated Spanish fleet in the Philippines.
June 10	Roughly six hundred U.S. Marines land at Guantánamo, Cuba.

July 1	After heavy fighting, American forces in Cuba take the Spanish garrisons at El Caney and San Juan Hill. Roosevelt leads the assault.
July 25	American forces invade Puerto Rico.
August 13	Spain and the United States sign an armistice, ending hostilities.
December 10	Under the Treaty of Paris, Spain agrees to grant Cuba its independence and cede the Philippines, Puerto Rico, and Guam to the United States.

1899

February 4	Philippine guerrillas, led by Emilio Aguinaldo, attack U.S. forces in Manila, beginning the Philippine Insurrection.
February 14	Congress approves voting machines but their use is left to the discretion of the states.
November 21	Vice President Garret Hobart dies; he is not replaced.

1900

February 5	Britain and the United States sign a treaty to provide for a canal in Central America.
March 7	President McKinley signs the Gold Standard Act, which fixes the standard of value for all money issued or coined by the United States.
April 30	Hawaii is granted territorial status by Congress.
June 6	In Kansas, Carrie Nation leads her anti-liquor forces on a campaign to destroy saloons. The Prohibition movement is gaining steam.
June 19–21	The Republicans select McKinley for the 1900 campaign. New York governor Theodore Roosevelt is nominated for vice president.
July 5	The Democratic National Convention nominates William Jennings Bryan for president and Adlai E. Stevenson for vice president.
November 6	William McKinley is easily reelected.

1901

January 10	The first great Texas oil strike is made near Beaumont.
March 4	William McKinley is inaugurated for a second term.
April 19	The Philippine Insurgency ends.
September 6	Anarchist Leon Czolgosz shoots McKinley at the Pan-American Exposition in Buffalo, New York. After confessing, Czolgosz will die in the electric chair on October 29, 1901.
September 14	President McKinley dies from his wounds. Vice President Theodore Roosevelt becomes the twenty-sixth president.

MUST READS

Scott Miller, *The President and the Assassin: McKinley, Terror and Empire at the Dawn of the American Century*; Kevin Phillips, *William McKinley*.

ONLINE RESOURCES

Inaugural Addresses, Avalon Project, Yale Law School
  1897: http://avalon.law.yale.edu/19th_century/mckin1.asp
  1901: http://avalon.law.yale.edu/19th_century/mckin2.asp
Library of Congress Resource Guide
  http://www.loc.gov/rr/program/bib/presidents/mckinley/index
  .html
Library of Congress, "Last Days of McKinley"
  http://rs6.loc.gov/papr/mckhome.html
McKinley Museum, Canton, Ohio
  http://www.mckinleymuseum.org/
Miller Center of Public Affairs, University of Virginia
  http://millercenter.org/president/mckinley
McKinley Birthplace Museum and Library
  http://www.mckinley.lib.oh.us/

26

"TR" The Trust Buster
Theodore Roosevelt

★ ★ ★

September 14, 1901–March 4, 1909

Milestones in Theodore Roosevelt's Life

October 27, 1858	Born in New York City
1882–1884	Representative to New York State legislature
1889–1895	Member of U.S. Civil Service Commission
1895–1897	President of New York City Board of Police Commissioners
1897–1898	Served in Spanish-American War
1899–1900	Governor of New York
1901	Vice president under McKinley
1901–1909	Twenty-sixth president
1912	Defeated as third-party candidate in presidential election
January 6, 1919	Died in Oyster Bay, New York, aged sixty-nine

PRESIDENTIAL VOICES

In life, as in a football game, the principle to follow is: Hit the line hard.
—THEODORE ROOSEVELT, 1900[1]

Vice President Theodore Roosevelt was—what else?—descending from a mountain climb when he was met by a messenger carrying the news: President McKinley was dying. By the time he got to Buffalo, McKinley was dead, and Theodore Roosevelt took the oath of office—at forty-two, the youngest president in American history to date.

His youth was only part of the energy, excitement, and profound sense of change that Roosevelt brought to the White House. Whatever his particular policies were, it was his exuberant approach to the presidency that transformed the office from its staid past. It's unlikely that when Alexander Hamilton wrote of the presidency needing an "energetic" man with "vigor," he could have remotely imagined Theodore Roosevelt.

He climbed mountains, hunted in Africa, led cavalry charges, herded cattle in the Wild West, boxed, and practiced judo. He filled the White House with children who were as exuberant as he was. He welcomed the press into the White House, giving birth to the press conference. And he elevated the presidency to the center stage as no other president had done before.

Fast Facts

RELIGION: Dutch Reformed

ASSOCIATIONS: Freemason, Sons of the American Revolution

EDUCATION: Harvard

MILITARY SERVICE: Colonel in First U.S. Volunteers, Spanish-American War

CAREER BEFORE POLITICS: Author, historian, explorer, conservationist, police commissioner

POLITICAL PARTY: Republican

FIRST SPOUSE: Alice Lee Roosevelt (July 29, 1861–February 14, 1884)

Roosevelt's first wife died from Bright's disease and childbirth complications on February 14, 1884, the same day Roosevelt's mother died. After this double tragedy, Roosevelt left New York to live on a ranch in the Badlands of North Dakota. Crushed by the loss, he never spoke of his first wife again. They had one child, Alice Roosevelt Longworth.

FIRST LADY: Edith Carow Roosevelt (August 6, 1861–September 30, 1948) Edith Carow had grown up next door to the Roosevelt family in Manhattan, and she and young "Teedie," as he was called, were childhood friends. A year after his first wife's death, Roosevelt asked Edith if he could see her. They were married in London on December 2, 1886.

CHILDREN: With his second wife, Roosevelt had five children: Theodore Jr., Kermit, Ethel, Archibald, and Quentin.

Theodore Roosevelt, Jr., went on to serve with distinction in both world wars. He was part of the first assault force to land on Normandy Beach on D-Day in June 1944 and died soon after. He was awarded the Congressional Medal of Honor posthumously.

Archie also served in both world wars. He was severely wounded in France in World War I and was discharged as disabled. During World War II, however, he still went to the Pacific and was again severely wounded there.

Quentin was an army air corps pilot in World War I and was shot down and killed during an air fight over France in 1918.

* With McKinley's assassination, Theodore Roosevelt became, at forty-two, the youngest president in the nation's history, just shy of his forty-third birthday.

* Although the "Teddy Bear" was inspired by a 1902 political cartoon about Roosevelt, he disliked being called "Teddy" because he found it "vulgar." He preferred "Colonel." The German toy company Stieff produced a version of plush bears with button eyes that sold by the thousand at the FAO Schwarz store in New York, while another "Teddy Bear" came from a Brooklyn manufacturer, eventually becoming an iconic toy.

* Roosevelt was the first president to win the Nobel Prize for Peace for mediating the end of a war between Russia and Japan.

* Roosevelt was posthumously awarded the Congressional Medal of Honor for his bravery in the Spanish-American War, the only president to have won the award. His son Theodore Jr. was also given the

award posthumously—making them one of only two father-son winners with that distinction. The other father-son winners of the Medal of Honor were Arthur MacArthur, who won it during the Civil War, and his son, the controversial General Douglas MacArthur.

* Theodore Roosevelt was the fifth cousin of Franklin D. Roosevelt, the thirty-second president. He was also the uncle of Eleanor Roosevelt, Franklin D. Roosevelt's wife.

* It's official. In 1901, President Roosevelt issued an executive order changing the name of the "Executive Mansion" to the "White House." Under Roosevelt, the White House also underwent a major architectural transformation under the architect Charles McKim of the prominent New York architectural firm McKim, Mead and White. The West Wing was added at that time.

* Though personally devout, Roosevelt tried to have the words "In God We Trust" removed from the currency because he thought it was a sacrilege to combine God and money.

* The vigorous exercise regimen of President Roosevelt included horseback riding, brisk walks with his cabinet in tow, tennis, shooting, hiking, and in the winter—shades of John Quincy Adams—skinny-dipping in the Potomac.

PRESIDENTIAL VOICES

A man who is good enough to shed his blood for his country is good enough to be given a square deal afterwards. More than that no man is entitled to, and less than that no man shall have.

—THEODORE ROOSEVELT, JULY 4, 1903

The second of four children born to a New York banker, Theodore Roosevelt was raised in a town house on New York City's East 20th Street and grew up in Gilded Age Manhattan's Knickerbocker Society, in the midst of great wealth. When the Civil War broke out, his father, a loyal Lincoln Republican, hired a substitute, as was legal practice, but also set up a plan under which Union soldiers could set aside pay for their families. Theodore's mother, from a slaveholding Southern family, supposedly once hung a Confederate flag from her New York window. According to biographer Edmund Morris, his father's failure to fight for the Union cause led to the suggestion that guilt drove the "future Rough Rider's almost desperate desire to wage war."[2]

Sickly and asthmatic as a boy, Theodore later recalled his father rushing him out at night for carriage rides, hoping that the air would fill his lungs. He did everything possible to build himself up, and his father had a gymnasium installed on a floor of their brownstone. Studies at home and family wilderness adventures led to his lifelong passion for natural science, and he once surprised streetcar passengers when he lifted his hat and frogs came leaping out. The house in New York became Roosevelt's personal Museum of Natural History.

An adolescence spent traveling Europe and the world with his father gave way to Harvard, where he pursued boxing—but couldn't see his opponents without his glasses. He was always striving. After graduating from Harvard, and marrying for the first time in 1880, he tried law school but found it dull. Instead he wrote, completing an influential work called *The Naval War of 1812*, begun while he was at Harvard.

At twenty-three, Roosevelt joined New York's state legislature in 1882 and made a name for himself by investigating corruption involving railroad tycoon Jay Gould. He was proving himself fearless in his adventures—and in choosing his enemies.

In 1884, two days after delivering her first child, Roosevelt's beloved young wife Alice and his mother died on the same day—February 14, Valentine's Day—and he wrote in his diary, "The light has gone out of my life."[3]

Roosevelt went to North Dakota and tried his hand at cattle ranching in his "cowboy period," only to return to New York and politics when his cattle herd was wiped out in the blizzard of 1886. Marrying his second wife, childhood friend Edith Carow, in 1886, Roosevelt wrote several more works of biography and history. In 1888, he campaigned enthusiastically for Benjamin Harrison, with Edmund Morris noting, "His performance was good enough to establish him, within a week, as one of the campaign's more effective speakers."[4] The Republicans won not only the White House but majorities in the Senate and House as well. Roosevelt was rewarded with a position on the new Civil Service Commission.

In 1895, he brought his reformist zeal and corruption-fighting idealism back to New York to join the New York City Police Commission. As a police commissioner, Roosevelt was known for prowling the streets of the city to check on policemen doing their duty. He also met social reformer Jacob Riis, whose 1890 documentary book, *How the Other Half Lives*, had exposed the harsh tenement life of New York's immigrants. They toured the Lower East Side together, and Riis, along with Lincoln Steffens, another ambitious reporter, pricked Roosevelt's social conscience. While his campaign to shut New York's saloons on Sunday did not win popularity in New York, it made the young Roosevelt a national figure. It was around this time that Bram Stoker, the author of *Dracula*, met and observed Roosevelt. He recorded in his diary, "Must be President some day. A man you can't cajole, can't frighten, can't buy."[5]

When McKinley was first elected, Roosevelt went to Washington as an assistant secretary of the navy and became one of the loudest voices for war with Spain. Acting above his "pay grade," Roosevelt directed Admiral Dewey to move his fleet to the Philippines, in anticipation of the war. Once war was declared, Roosevelt immediately enlisted, outfitting his own regiment—the Rough Riders. His success in the war—he always made good newspaper copy—elevated him further, making Roosevelt the most famous man in America. When he returned to New York, he won the governor's race in 1899. He then took aim at the most entrenched bastion of corruption in America, Tammany Hall.

When his corruption fighting got too overbearing, "Boss" Thomas Platt, one of New York's powerful political leaders, "kicked him upstairs," to become McKinley's vice president.

Only months after Roosevelt was sworn in, McKinley was dead and he was now President Theodore Roosevelt.

His first storm of controversy as president came over a dinner invitation. On October 16, 1901, educator and scientist Booker T. Washington was invited to dinner at the White House, the first African-American in history to dine with a president. The dinner unleashed a storm of racist controversy. The *Memphis Scimitar* reported, "The most damnable outrage which has ever been perpetrated by any citizen of the United States was committed yesterday by the President, when he invited a nigger to dine with him at the White House." That was soon joined by headlines across the former Confederacy screaming: ROOSEVELT DINES A DARKEY and OUR COON-FLAVORED PRESIDENT.[6]

Though Roosevelt had not deliberately set out to create a racial incident, the episode reverberated through his administration, as many Southerners were unforgiving at what they considered an outrage. Black Americans cheered what they thought was another great step forward. Roosevelt's racial views, perhaps influenced by his mother's Southern heritage, were typical of the day—Edmund Morris writes that TR believed that "blacks were better suited for service than suffrage; on the whole they were 'altogether inferior to whites.'"[7] He saw Washington as an example of a black man who had risen through Roosevelt's cherished values of hard work and individual perseverance. While he regretted the controversy the invitation had caused, he never backed down from doing what he thought was right.

What was the "big stick"?

Theodore Roosevelt's favorite saying was an old African proverb: "Speak softly, and carry a big stick; you will go far."

Although he rarely spoke softly himself, he was always ready to use a big stick, abroad and at home. His first chance to use one came when 140,000 mine workers went on strike in May 1902. Underpaid and forced to buy overpriced supplies in company stores and to live in company-owned houses, the miners were kept in perpetual debt.

When they organized into the United Mine Workers, the mine companies, owned almost exclusively by the railroads (meaning, for the most part, J. P. Morgan), refused to recognize the union or to negotiate.

As the work stoppage would soon cripple an economy largely run on coal power, Roosevelt stepped in and threatened to use troops. But unlike in the past, when they had been used as deadly strikebreakers to force workers back into the mines, these troops would operate the mines in the "public interest."

With this "big stick" over their heads, the mine owners agreed to accept the decision of a Coal Strike Commission, which ruled in favor of the miners. "Theodore Roosevelt's mediation between capital and labor," concludes biographer Edmund Morris, "earned him fame as the first head of state to confront the largest problem of the twentieth century. . . . At home Roosevelt basked in a popular outpouring of admiration. That boded well for 1904."[8]

Using powers under a strengthened antitrust law, Roosevelt went after other selected targets, subjectively labeled "bad trusts," such as the "beef trust" (*Swift & Co. v. United States*, 1905) and the American Tobacco Company. Roosevelt was hardly a radical; he believed that monopoly was fine as long as it could be regulated, and that there were benevolent trusts, such as International Harvester.

His tenure produced some reforms that were significant and long-lasting, such as the strengthening of the Interstate Commerce Commission, the creation of a cabinet-level Department of Labor and Commerce (later separated into two departments), and the passage of the Pure Food and Drug Act.

PRESIDENTIAL VOICES

It is not the critic who counts: not the man who points out how the strong man stumbles or where the doer of deeds could have done better. The credit belongs to the man who is actually in the arena, whose face is marred by dust and sweat and blood, who strives valiantly, who errs and comes up short again and again, because there is no effort without error or shortcoming, but who knows the great enthusiasms, the great devotions, who spends himself for a worthy cause; who, at the best, knows, in the end, the triumph of high achievement, and who, at the worst, if he fails, at least he fails while daring greatly, so that his place shall never be with those cold and timid souls who knew neither victory nor defeat.

—Theodore Roosevelt,
"Citizenship in the Arena," April 23, 1910[9]

How did Teddy Roosevelt help save college football?

In 1905, before the NCAA and the NFL existed, a sensational two-part article by journalist Henry Beach Needham in the June and July 1905 issues of muckraking *McClure's Magazine* exposed the violence and corruption then dominating collegiate football. At the turn of the century, the game was brutal, with star players targeted for intentional injury. Needham revealed how a black Dartmouth player had his collarbone broken on a vicious play against Princeton. "We didn't put him out because he was a black man," Needham's article quoted one of the Princeton players as saying. "We're coached to pick out the most dangerous man on the opposing side and put him out in the first five minutes."[10]

The competition among powerhouse schools also meant plenty of money was changing hands. Players were paid to compete, and Needham told of athletes who played for pay on different school teams in the space of a few days.

The rash of football injuries and deaths at the time that Needham's article appeared had some of the collegiate football powers—then mostly in the Ivy League—questioning whether the game should be outlawed.

Into the arena came Theodore Roosevelt, Harvard fan number one and America's champion of all things manly and vigorous. Roosevelt loved the game. But at a generous five feet, eight inches and weighing 124 pounds, he had been a scrawny teenager too small to play at Harvard. (A Cambridge-era photograph of him in rowing gear shows a sinewy, more wiry Roosevelt than the bearish 200-pounder of the presidential years.) But he addressed football's problem in his June 1905 Harvard commencement speech.

"I do not mind in the least that they are rough games, or that those who take part in them are occasionally injured. . . . I have a hearty contempt for him if he counts a broken arm or collar bone as of serious consequence," said Roosevelt. "But when these injuries are inflicted wantonly or of set design, we are confronted by the question, not of damage to one man's body, but of damage to the other man's character. Brutality in playing a game should awaken the heartiest and most plainly shown contempt for the player guilty of it, especially if this brutality is coupled with a low cunning in committing it without getting caught by the umpire."[11]

The following fall, with a fresh rash of injuries, some fatal, Harvard's president threatened to abolish the sport. Columbia's president agreed, and back then, those two Ivy League schools carried enormous weight in college athletics. In response, Roosevelt brought six leading coaches to the White House in October 1905 for a signature "big stick" moment.

The group later issued a statement condemning brutality and disregard for the rules. As the injuries and fatalities grew, the crisis led to the establishment of a reform committee that changed many of the game's fundamental rules and became the nucleus of the National Collegiate Athletic Association (NCAA). The notion that Roosevelt saved football, or even invented the modern game, is overblown, but he deserves credit for helping rescue the sport from an uncertain future.

Sports were a metaphor for Roosevelt and his worldview. He prized fair play, by the rules, whether it was on the field or in big business. He had only contempt for corporations or teams that bent those rules, just as he had contempt for those who expected to be coddled or for government to provide for them.

Who built the Panama Canal?

A man, a plan, a canal, Panama.

There were few things that Theodore Roosevelt wanted more than a canal across Central America. Back in 1898, when America was preparing for war with Spain over Cuba, the American battleship *Oregon* was ordered to the Caribbean. Stationed off the coast of California, the *Oregon* steamed around South America and arrived in time to take part in the Battle of Santiago Harbor. The fourteen-thousand-mile voyage, tracked in the national press, took sixty-six days. But it was clear that America needed a faster way to move its warships from ocean to ocean.

The dream of connecting the Atlantic and the Pacific had been held almost since the Spanish conquistador Balboa first spotted the Pacific from the cliffs of Darien (in modern Panama) in 1513. During the 1849 Gold Rush, thousands of Americans had struggled across the Isthmus of Panama by canoe and mule train to reach the Pacific and from there move on to California. After the Civil War, President Grant sent a survey team to look for the best route to dig a canal across Central America.

After a brief revolution in 1903—with the U.S. Navy standing off-shore to provide the "big stick"—Panama was freed from Colombia's control. The new regime in Panama was swiftly recognized, received $10 million, a yearly fee of $250,000, and guaranteed "independence." In return, the United States got rights to a ten-mile swath across the country—the Canal Zone—"in perpetuity." Since the zone comprised most of Panama and would be guarded by American troops, the United States effectively controlled the country.

A few months later, Americans took over the remnants of an earlier French canal-building project. And in 1904, the first Americans were in Panama. From day one, the work was plagued by the same problems the French had encountered: tropical heat, the jungle, and the mosquitoes. And according to David McCullough's epic account of the creation of the canal, *The Path Between the Seas*, the death rate by accident and disease for blacks was about five times that of whites in Panama.

But the canal was completed ahead of schedule and under budget, despite the challenges. More remarkably, according to McCullough, it was completed without suspicion of corruption, graft, kickbacks, or bribery. Roosevelt would not see its opening as president. The work was carried on by TR's successor, Taft, and the Panama Canal was completed and opened in 1914, under Woodrow Wilson—just in time for another war.

Final Judgment: Grade A+

Building a canal that people had been discussing for centuries. Stopping a war and winning a Peace Prize. Busting trusts and taking on the most powerful men and business interests in the country. Passing a Pure Food and Drug Act. Creating the Conservation Movement and some of the nation's first great national parks. And having fun while he did it.

About the only thing Roosevelt couldn't do well was exit gracefully. Following his 1904 victory, a landslide, he had vowed to maintain precedent and not run again for what would have been considered a third term. Although he later regretted the decision, Roosevelt somewhat reluctantly chose William Howard Taft, the lumbering three-hundred-pounder who had served as his secretary of war, to be his handpicked successor. Then he went off to Africa to hunt.

But Theodore Roosevelt was not a man to sit on the sidelines during the big game. After a few years away from the arena, Colonel Roosevelt, as he preferred to be called, was ready for a comeback in 1912.

Theodore Roosevelt Administration Milestones[12]

1901

September 14	Vice President Theodore Roosevelt takes the oath of office in Buffalo, New York.
October 16	Roosevelt dines with Booker T. Washington at the White House, sparking racist outrage across the country, especially in the South.

1902

April 29	Congress extends the Chinese Exclusion Act, prohibiting the immigration of Chinese laborers from the Philippines.
October	Roosevelt settles the Anthracite Coal strike, which threatened to shut down businesses, schools, factories, and other buildings dependent on coal; he suggests he will use troops to mine the coal. The companies settle with the miners.

1903

February 14	The Department of Commerce and Labor, the ninth cabinet office, is created.
February 19	The Department of Justice announces that the federal government will prosecute the Northern Securities Company (a subsidiary of J. P. Morgan) for violating the Sherman Antitrust Act.
November 3	A revolt breaks out in Panama against Colombian rule. The American Navy's presence prevents Colombia

from crushing the rebellion. Three days later, the
United States recognizes Panama.

December 17   The Wright Brothers successfully test their airplane at
Kitty Hawk.

1904

March 14   The Supreme Court, in *Northern Securities Company v.
United States*, orders the dissolution of the Northern
Securities Company. The decision is a major victory
for Roosevelt and his belief in the necessity of "trust
busting."

June 21–23   The Republican Party nominates Roosevelt.

July 6–9   The Democrats nominate Alton B. Parker of
New York.

November 8   Roosevelt wins the election, trouncing Parker, 336
electoral votes to 140. With the exception of Maryland, Roosevelt wins every state north of Washington,
D.C., including all Midwestern and Western states;
Parker sweeps the South and Texas. Southerners were
unforgiving about Booker T. Washington dining with
Roosevelt.

1905

February 1   Roosevelt establishes the National Forest Service.

March 4   Roosevelt is inaugurated.

April 17   In *Lochner v. New York*, the Supreme Court rules that
state laws limiting working hours are illegal.

July 7   The Industrial Workers of the World (IWW), known
as the "Wobblies," forms in Chicago; this union is
more radical and aggressive than the more conservative American Federation of Labor.

September 2   Ending the Russo-Japanese War, Russia and Japan sign
the Portsmouth Treaty, mediated by Roosevelt.

1906

April 18   The San Francisco Earthquake kills 452 people and
levels much of the city.

June 8	Roosevelt signs the National Monuments Act, establishing the first eighteen national monuments, including Devils Tower, Muir Woods, and Mount Olympus.
June 30	Roosevelt signs the Meat Inspection Act and the Pure Food and Drug Act. The legislation was inspired by *The Jungle*, writer Upton Sinclair's scathing indictment of meatpacking plants.
November 9–26	The president and Mrs. Roosevelt go to Panama to inspect the building of the Panama Canal; it is the first trip abroad by a sitting American president.
December 10	Roosevelt is awarded the Nobel Peace Prize for his role in ending the Russo-Japanese War.
December 12	Roosevelt appoints Oscar Straus to head the Commerce and Labor Department; he is the first Jewish cabinet member.

1907

January 26	Congress passes the first law prohibiting campaign contributions to candidates for national office.
October 22	The Panic of 1907 begins when shares of the United Copper Company fluctuate wildly. America's banking and financial systems are again shaken. Wall Street blames the panic on Roosevelt's reforms.
November 16	Oklahoma is admitted as the forty-sixth state.
December 16	One of Roosevelt's signature accomplishments, the "Great White Fleet" of new American warships, embarks on a voyage around the world emphasizing America's naval strength.

1908

February	In *Loewe v. Lawlor*, the Supreme Court rules that antitrust law applies to labor unions.
May 28	Congress passes a child labor law for the District of Columbia.
June 8	Roosevelt establishes the National Commission for the Conservation of Natural Resources.

June 16–20	The Republican Party nominates William Howard Taft.
July 7–10	William Jennings Bryan wins the Democratic nomination.
September 16	General Motors incorporates in New Jersey.
October 1	Ford introduces the "Model T" automobile, which costs $850, a price that puts the automobile within reach of average workers.
November 3	William Howard Taft is elected president.

1909

| February 12 | On the centennial of Lincoln's birth, black leaders, including W. E. B. DuBois, and white progressives, led by Oswald Garrison Villard, form the National Association for the Advancement of Colored People (NAACP). |

MUST READS

David McCullough, *Mornings on Horseback: The Story of an Extraordinary Family, a Vanished Way of Life and the Unique Child Who Became Theodore Roosevelt* and *The Path Between the Seas: The Creation of the Panama Canal, 1870–1914*; Candice Millard, *The River of Doubt: Theodore Roosevelt's Darkest Journey*; Edmund Morris, *The Rise of Theodore Roosevelt, Theodore Rex*, and *Colonel Roosevelt*.

ONLINE RESOURCES

Inaugural Address, Avalon Project, Yale Law School
  http://avalon.law.yale.edu/20th_century/troos.asp
Library of Congress Resource Guide
  http://www.loc.gov/rr/program/bib/presidents/troosevelt/index.html
Theodore Roosevelt Birthplace, New York, National Park Service
  http://www.nps.gov/thrb/
Sagamore Hill, Theodore Roosevelt Home, National Park Service
  http://www.nps.gov/sahi/
Obituary, *New York Times*
  http://www.nytimes.com/learning/general/onthisday/big/0106
  .html#article

New York Times **archive**

http://topics.nytimes.com/top/reference/timestopics/people/r/theodore_roosevelt/index.html

Congressional Medal of Honor

http://www.cmohs.org/recipient-detail/2178/roosevelt-theodore.php

Nobel Prize

http://nobelprize.org/nobel_prizes/peace/laureates/1906/index.html

Miller Center of Public Affairs, University of Virginia

http://millercenter.org/president/roosevelt

"TR," *The American Experience,* **PBS**

http://www.pbs.org/wgbh/americanexperience/features/general-article/tr-legacy/

Theodore Roosevelt Association

http://www.theodoreroosevelt.org/

27

William Howard Taft

* * *

March 4, 1909–March 4, 1913

Milestones in William H. Taft's Life

September 15, 1857	Born in Cincinnati, Ohio
1880	Admitted to the Ohio bar
1887–1890	Judge of Superior Court, Cincinnati
1890–1892	Appointed solicitor general (under President Harrison)
1892–1900	U.S. circuit judge
1900	President of the U.S. Philippine Commission
1901–1904	First civil governor of Philippine Islands under President McKinley
1904–1908	Secretary of war under Roosevelt
1909–1913	Twenty-seventh president
1913	Professor of Law, Yale University
1921–1930	Chief Justice of the U.S. Supreme Court
March 8, 1930	Died in Washington, D.C., aged seventy-two

PRESIDENTIAL VOICES

The negroes are now Americans. Their ancestors came here years ago against their will, and this is their only country and their only flag. They have shown themselves anxious to live for it and to die for it. Encountering the race feeling against them, subjected at times to cruel injustice growing out of it, they may well have our profound sympathy and aid in the struggle they are making.

—WILLIAM HOWARD TAFT
Inaugural Address, March 4, 1909[1]

Taft. It was an unfortunate name in one respect. Everyone agreed it meant "Take Advice From Teddy."

Fast Facts

RELIGION: Unitarian
"I believe in God," Taft wrote in an 1899 letter not made public until after he left office. "I do not believe in the divinity of Christ, and there are many other of the postulates of the orthodox creed to which I cannot subscribe."[2]

ASSOCIATIONS: Freemason

EDUCATION: Yale, University of Cincinnati Law School

CAREER BEFORE POLITICS: Attorney, judge

POLITICAL PARTY: Republican

FIRST LADY: Helen Herron Taft (June 2, 1861–May 22, 1943)

CHILDREN: Robert, Helen, and Charles
Oldest son Robert went into politics and became the leader of the conservative wing of the Republican Party, known as "Mr. Republican." Later generations of Tafts continued the tradition with another senator, Robert Taft, and his son, Ohio governor Bob Taft.

* Taft was the only president to date to become a Supreme Court justice. President Harding appointed him chief justice in 1921.
* Taft's inauguration was forced into the Senate chamber due to a heavy snowfall. Afterward his wife, Helen, accompanied him from

the Capitol to the White House, the beginning of what is now a regular tradition. At the time, it was taken as a sign of support for women's suffrage. Mrs. Taft also broke with the existing policy of only white ushers at the White House, introducing uniformed black ushers to White House service.[3]

* On Taft's Inauguration Day, Congress raised the annual presidential salary for only the third time since George Washington took office. Set at $25,000 in 1789, it had been doubled for Grant's second term in 1873; it was then increased to $75,000 on March 4, 1909.

* In 1909, Taft added the White House Oval Office next to the Executive Wing ("West Wing") that had been built under Roosevelt, though it would not be called the "Oval Office" until half a century later.[4]

* Weighing more than three hundred pounds, Taft was the heaviest president.

* Taft is known as the "first golfing president" as he was the first to publicly admit playing the game. Despite his size, Taft had been an athletic young man. He was an excellent wrestler and baseball player. He also began the annual rite of throwing out the first ball to open the baseball season.

* When Arizona was admitted as a state in 1912, Taft became the first president of all forty-eight contiguous states.

* Taft is one of two presidents buried in Arlington National Cemetery. John F. Kennedy is the other.

PRESIDENTIAL VOICES

I do not believe there can be found in the whole country a man so well fitted to be president. He is not only absolutely fearless . . . but he has the widest acquaintance with the nation's needs.

—PRESIDENT THEODORE ROOSEVELT ON TAFT, 1908

He once set about undoing all my administration had done. He is a flubdub with a streak of the second-rate and the common in him, and he has not the slightest idea of what is necessary if this country is to make social and industrial progress.

—Former President Theodore Roosevelt on Taft, 1911[5]

With roots in colonial New England, William Howard Taft was born into the long-established and politically well-connected family of Alphonso Taft, Ulysses Grant's secretary of war and attorney general. Among his ancestors was Lydia Chapin Taft, credited as the first woman to cast a vote in America, in colonial Massachusetts in 1756, and Revolutionary War soldier Samuel Taft, a Massachusetts tavernkeeper who once welcomed President George Washington as a guest during his inaugural trip to New England.

An excellent student, William Taft attended Yale and went to law school in Cincinnati. He moved smoothly through a succession of appointed jobs and judgeships and was asked in 1900 by President McKinley to establish a civil government on the newly won Philippine Islands. Hoping to be made a Supreme Court justice, Taft agreed, with the understanding that a court appointment would later follow. He successfully organized the Filipino court system and improved the roads and schools there. In 1904, he accepted Theodore Roosevelt's offer to become secretary of war.

Although he was not eager to run when offered the White House by the departing Roosevelt, Taft was persuaded. Continuing Roosevelt's antitrust policies, he brought ninety suits in four years and broke up, most significantly, the Standard Oil and American Tobacco monopolies. Taft also backed passage of the Sixteenth Amendment, which authorized the federal income tax.

Never an instinctive politician, and laboring in the wake of Roosevelt's extraordinary presidency, Taft had a bigger problem: He fell way short in the eyes of the man who mattered most—his former boss.

Why did Roosevelt ruin Taft's reelection?

A year of bagging big game didn't quench Theodore Roosevelt's political hunting instincts. He came back to America, intent on recapturing the White House from Taft, who had disappointed him.

It was to be an election fought to prove who appeared most progressive. And it was Roosevelt who presented himself as the champion reformer. The election of 1912 was significant because it was the first time that state primary elections, usually a pro forma confirmation of what party bosses wanted, were contested. Roosevelt won nine state Republican primaries to Taft's one; TR even won Ohio, Taft's home state. But the delegates he won in these primaries were not enough to give Roosevelt the nomination. He showed up at the convention, where Taft's men won the support of the delegates from non-primary states in return for favors or cash—deals made in the proverbial "smoke-filled rooms." Rejected by the Republicans, Roosevelt said the nomination had been stolen and led a group of dissatisfied liberal Republicans out of the fold and into the Progressive Party.

Afterward, Roosevelt wrote, in typically grandiose terms, "It was very bitter for me to see the Republican Party, when I had put it back on the Abraham Lincoln basis, in three years turned over to a combination of big financiers and unscrupulous political bosses. . . . My nomination would have meant putting the Republican Party definitely on an antiboss and progressive basis. This was why the bosses preferred my defeat to Republican victory."[6]

During this memorable and historic three-way campaign, Roosevelt survived an assassination attempt when he was shot in Milwaukee. With a bullet in his chest, he pulled a bloodied paper from his pocket, delivered his speech, and went to the hospital. He was, as promised, "as strong as a bull moose," giving this third party its memorable name.

The Democrats struggled through forty-six ballots before turning to Woodrow Wilson (1856–1924), born and raised in the Deep South but then New Jersey's governor. He was a surprise choice and, for his times, progressive in at least some respects. The Democratic Party solidified behind Wilson, especially in the South, where Roosevelt was never forgiven for welcoming Booker T. Washington to the White House.

Taft essentially threw in the towel and stayed out of the campaign—later to head the Supreme Court, the job he really always wanted. In spite of the unsuccessful assassination attempt that seemed to confirm his invincibility, Roosevelt campaigned hard, and Wilson's popular vote was less than the combined Taft-Roosevelt vote. Socialist candidate Eugene V. Debs polled 6 percent of the vote—nearly a million votes, and an indication that the political winds had clearly shifted to the left.

But Wilson's electoral victory was sweeping. Taft won only two states and Roosevelt six. The rest of the country was solidly Democratic behind Wilson. And once again, a third-party candidacy had changed the course of American politics.

Final Judgment: Grade C

Although Taft failed to win personal popularity, the outsized president was okay with that. He left Washington and went back to Yale to teach. When Harding was elected, Taft got what he wanted most—an appointment to the Supreme Court, becoming Chief Justice in 1921. He spent what he viewed as the happiest nine years of his life on the high bench.

Consistently rated an average president, Taft has to simply be counted as one of history's most notable "second bananas." However, his record of progressivism in pursuing antitrust matters in particular and continuing TR's conservation policies is better than his mentor-turned-rival Theodore Roosevelt gave him credit for.

Taft Administration Milestones[7]

1909

March 4	William Howard Taft takes the oath of office.
April 6	Robert E. Peary reaches the North Pole.
September 27	Following Roosevelt's conservation policy, Taft sets aside three million acres of oil-rich Western lands.

1910

| February 6 | The Boy Scouts are chartered in Washington, D.C. |

May 16 The Bureau of Mines is set up; at least twenty-five hundred miners have been killed in disasters and accidents over the previous five years.

June 25 The Mann Act, also known as the "white slave traffic act," is passed; it outlaws the interstate or international transport of women for "immoral purposes."

August 31 Theodore Roosevelt delivers the most radical speech of his career, in Ossawatomie, Kansas. Calling for a "New Nationalism," he outlines a progressive agenda—endorsing conservation, greater control of trusts, labor protections, and a graduated income tax.

1911

January 21 The Progressive League is founded by reformer Senator Robert La Follette (R-WI) to promote more responsive government at all levels. La Follette champions direct primary elections, federal regulatory commissions, and an income tax—many of the issues Theodore Roosevelt had addressed.

March 25 The Triangle Shirtwaist Company tragedy takes place in Lower Manhattan, one of the great disasters of the sweatshop era. A factory fire breaks out, and women working in the cramped and unsafe conditions stampede toward inadequate exits, some of which are locked; 146 women die, most of them young immigrants. The gruesome death toll highlights the need for decent working conditions in American factories.

May 15 The U.S. Supreme Court orders the dissolution of the Standard Oil Company under the Sherman Antitrust Act.

May 29 The Supreme Court finds the American Tobacco Company in violation of the Sherman Antitrust Act.

November 10 Industrialist Andrew Carnegie founds the Carnegie Corporation with an initial endowment of $125 million.

1912

January 6	New Mexico is admitted as the forty-seventh state.
February 14	Arizona, the forty-eighth state, is admitted.
February 22	Theodore Roosevelt announces that his "hat is in the ring" as a candidate for president.
March 27	First Lady Helen Taft plants the first of the cherry trees, given to the United States by Japan, along the Tidal Basin.
April 14	The British luxury liner *Titanic* sinks off the coast of Newfoundland.
June 18–22	Taft wins the Republican presidential nomination over Theodore Roosevelt.
June 19	Congress passes a labor law authorizing an eight-hour working day for all workers with federal contracts.
June 25–July 2	The Democratic Party nominates Woodrow Wilson.
August 5	Breaking from the Republicans, Roosevelt is nominated by the Progressive (Bull Moose) Party.
October 30	Vice President John Sherman dies, and Nicholas Butler, the president of Columbia University, replaces him on the Republican ticket.
November 5	Woodrow Wilson defeats Taft and Roosevelt.

1913

February 14	Taft vetoes a bill calling for literacy tests for immigrants.
February 25	The Sixteenth Amendment is adopted, providing for a legal graduated income tax.
March 4	The Departments of Labor and Commerce are split into two separate departments, both with cabinet status.

MUST READS

James Chace, *1912: Wilson, Roosevelt, Taft and Debs—the Election That Changed the Country.*

ONLINE RESOURCES

Inaugural Address, Avalon Project, Yale Law School
http://avalon.law.yale.edu/20th_century/taft.asp

Library of Congress Resource Guide
http://www.loc.gov/rr/program/bib/presidents/taft/index.html

Taft Historic Site, National Park Service
http://www.nps.gov/wiho

Miller Center of Public Affairs, University of Virginia
http://millercenter.org/index.php/academic/americanpresident/taft

28

Schoolmaster in Politics
Woodrow Wilson

★ ★ ★

March 4, 1913–March 4, 1921

Milestones in Woodrow Wilson's Life

December 29, 1856	Born in Staunton, Virginia
1882–1883	Practiced law in Atlanta, Georgia
1885–1888	Associate professor of history, Bryn Mawr College
1888–1890	Professor of history and politics, Wesleyan University
1890–1902	Professor of jurisprudence and politics, Princeton University
1902–1910	President of Princeton University
1911–1913	Governor of New Jersey
1913–1921	Twenty-eighth president
October 2, 1919	Suffered stroke and was incapacitated for months
February 3, 1924	Died in Washington, D.C., aged sixty-seven

PRESIDENTIAL VOICES

But the evil has come with the good, and much fine gold has been corroded. With riches has come inexcusable waste. We have squandered a great part of what we might have used, and have not stopped to conserve the exceeding bounty of nature, without which our genius for enterprise would have been worthless and impotent. . . .

We have been proud of our industrial achievements, but we have not hitherto stopped thoughtfully enough to count the human cost . . . the fearful physical and spiritual cost to the men and women and children upon whom the dead weight and burden of it all has fallen pitilessly the years through. . . . The great Government we loved has too often been made use of for private and selfish purposes, and those who used it had forgotten the people.

—WOODROW WILSON

First Inaugural, March 4, 1913[1]

H is slogan claimed, "He kept us out of war." But then he didn't. He had a Utopian idea for creating a more peaceful world. He was a reform-minded progressive when it came to workers' rights. But his vision for a better world didn't seem to have room for "Negroes" and Socialists. Woodrow Wilson was a president, like many others, whose White House years were marked by contradictions.

Yet few presidents can claim the intellectual breadth and depth of Woodrow Wilson. Few had a more scholarly grasp of American history. The only president with a Ph.D., he was one of the most intellectually brilliant of America's chief executives.

Reluctantly leading the nation into wartime, Wilson helped transform America's place in the world.

Fast Facts

RELIGION: Presbyterian

EDUCATION: Princeton, Johns Hopkins (Ph.D.)

CAREER BEFORE POLITICS: Teacher, author, university president

POLITICAL PARTY: Democratic

FIRST LADIES: Ellen Louise Wilson (May 15, 1860–August 6, 1914)

Ellen Wilson died in the White House of Bright's disease (kidney failure).

Edith Galt Wilson (October 15, 1872–December 28, 1961)

This engagement caused some Washington gossip coming only a little more than a year after the death of Wilson's first wife. The couple was married in the home of the bride, in Washington.

CHILDREN: Three daughters by his first wife: Margaret, Jessie, and Eleanor

* Wilson was born in Virginia, the last of eight presidents born in that state.

* Wilson was the last president born during the Civil War and the last born into a slaveholding household. His family did not actually own slaves; they were the property of the church Wilson's father led.

* At Wilson's second inaugural in 1917, Edith Galt Wilson accompanied the president both to and from the Capitol, going a step farther than Mrs. Taft, who had joined her husband on the walk to the White House; it was also the first Inaugural Parade in which women participated as marchers.

* As president, Wilson began the tradition of regularly scheduled press conferences. He was also the first president to address the joint sessions of Congress for the Message to Congress and other special sessions since Jefferson had abandoned the practice of personally addressing Congress. (Although Article II of the Constitution requires the president to provide "information of the State of the Union," the annual Message to Congress did not become popularly known as the State of the Union Address until Franklin D. Roosevelt used the term in 1934.[2])

* Wilson collapsed on September 25, 1919, and then suffered a stroke, leaving him partially paralyzed on his left side. His wife, Edith, kept him sequestered in the White House for five weeks, in one of the most serious cases of presidential disability in history. It would be November 1 before he made a public appearance, and weeks more before he was more fully involved in presidential affairs. (The Twenty-fifth Amendment, which deals with presidential succession, vacancies, and disabilities, was not passed until 1967.)

During this time, Edith Wilson served as his "steward," as she described it, selecting business Wilson could tend to, and she made decisions for him—biographer John Milton Cooper asserts she made at least one important policy decision by authorizing a presidential veto of the Volstead Act enforcing Prohibition, which was quickly overridden. While Wilson's closest aides considered the possibility of Vice President Thomas Riley Marshall taking over, the idea was rebuffed by Marshall himself.

While newspaper reports and rumors suggested Wilson was disabled, the public largely did not know about the severity of Wilson's disability until after his death. When a suspicious delegation from the Senate came to visit in December, Wilson was propped in bed, his useless left arm tucked under the bedcovers. After an interview, a senator shook Wilson's hand and remarked, "We've been praying for you." To which Wilson reportedly replied, "Which way, Senator?" (Wilson biographer Cooper disputes the witticism but not the fact that Wilson had performed beautifully.[3])

* Wilson was awarded the Nobel Peace Prize in 1919 for his role in ending what would become known as World War I.
* Wilson is the only president buried in Washington, D.C.

PRESIDENTIAL VOICES

I come from the South and I know what war is, for I have seen its terrible wreckage and ruin. It is easy for me as President to declare war. I do not have to fight, and neither do the gentlemen on the Hill who now clamor for it. It is some poor farmer's boy, or the son of some poor widow—who will have to do the fighting and dying.

—Woodrow Wilson[4]

Born into the manse, or Presbyterian minister's residence, in Staunton, Virginia, Thomas Woodrow Wilson grew up in the Deep South during the Civil War. (He later dropped the first name.) A secessionist, his father organized the Presbyterian Church of the Confederate States, and Wilson had a recollection of seeing Robert E. Lee and wounded Confederate soldiers being brought to his father's church.

With schools disrupted by the war, Wilson took much of his early education at home. In 1875, however, he went north to the Presbyterian College of New Jersey—now known as Princeton. He was a brilliant student and later studied law, passing the Georgia bar without having finished law school.

At twenty-six Wilson earned his Ph.D. in political science from Johns Hopkins and began writing scholarly works about government and history—including a five-volume *History of the American People*, completed after he joined the Princeton faculty. In 1902, he was named president of the University.

With the backing of powerful Democrats, he was offered the chance to run for governor of New Jersey and won easily in 1911. It proved to be his stepping-stone to the White House. When former President Roosevelt announced his third-party run in 1912, Wilson was all but assured of victory.

Was Wilson really a progressive?

Like his opponents, Roosevelt and Taft, Wilson ran on a fairly progressive reform platform, which he called the "New Freedom." He also dismissed Roosevelt and Taft as "Tweedledum and Tweedledee." And with the president and former president splitting the Republican vote, Wilson won, easily taking the electoral vote, but only 42 percent of the popular vote.

During his first administration, Wilson's legislative success was remarkable. Duties on foreign goods, the almost sacred weapon held by big business to keep out foreign competition, were reduced for the first time since the Civil War. The Seventeenth Amendment, providing for election of U.S. senators by popular direct vote, was ratified. (Previously, U.S. senators had been chosen by state legislatures.) And a Federal Reserve Act gave the country its first central bank since Andrew Jackson's time. Antitrust laws were strengthened, and the first attempts to regulate child labor were passed (though they were struck down as unconstitutional in 1922). In another key reform, the Federal Trade

Commission was created to control unfair and restrictive trade practices. Wilson also pushed passage of a bill that fixed the eight-hour day for railroad trainmen, heralding eventual wider acceptance of the eight-hour workday standard.

The shame of Wilson's "progressive" administration was his abysmal record on civil rights. Under Wilson, Jim Crow became the policy of the U.S. government, with segregated federal offices, and blacks losing some of the few government jobs they held. But his handling of racial issues was of little concern to a nation that was warily watching the approach of a European war.

If Wilson "kept us out of war," why did Americans fight in World War I?

When that war came in August 1914, Wilson and America wanted no part of it. While sympathetic to the Allies—England and France principally—Wilson wanted to remain neutral. There was also a large German-American population that did not want to see America enter the fight. With four years of prosperity and peace, Wilson campaigned in 1916 on the proud slogan "He Kept Us out of War."

But with increased German submarine attacks on American shipping, pressure built. When British spies uncovered a secret German plot to start a war between Mexico and America and promise Mexico help from Germany in recovering lands lost to America (revealed in what is known as the "Zimmerman Telegram"), public opinion turned against Germany. The Bolshevik Revolution, which took Russia out of the Alliance, was also a factor.

PRESIDENTIAL VOICES

It is a fearful thing to lead this great peaceful people into war, into the most terrible and disastrous of all wars, civilization itself seeming to be in the balance. But the right is more precious than peace, and we shall fight for the things which we have carried nearest to our hearts—for democracy, for the right of those who submit to authority to have a voice in their own Governments, for the rights and liberties of small nations, for a universal dominion of right by such a concert of free people as shall ring peace and safety to all nations and make the world itself at last free.

—WOODROW WILSON

War Message to Congress, April 2, 1917[5]

Wilson's speech was greeted with wild applause, and Congress overwhelmingly approved war a few days later. Wilson told an aide afterward, "My message today was a message of death for our young men. How strange it seems to applaud that."

More than one hundred thousand Americans died in the trench warfare of Europe between America's entry into the war in 1917 and the Armistice on November 11, 1918. Of course, Europe suffered much more grievously, with as many as twenty million dead soldiers and civilians.

In 1919 Wilson attempted to use the war's catastrophic losses to propose establishment of a League of Nations that would prevent such wars, and he put all of his presidential weight behind it. But a Republican Congress that wanted nothing to do with Europe rebuffed him. The Senate rejected the Treaty of Versailles, which Wilson helped negotiate. Whether or not such a League could have prevented the next Great War in Europe is speculation. But the defeat of his plan was Wilson's greatest personal failure.

The debate over the League also came while Wilson was recovering from his October stroke. As John Milton Cooper wrote, "Wilson played no role in the League fight during October and the first part of November. He was in such bad physical shape . . . that he could not pay attention to public business. There is never a good time to suffer a stroke, and Wilson's came at a particularly bad time in the League fight."[6] The isolationist Republican Party, led by Senator Henry Lodge, won a sweeping victory. The United States would never ratify the Treaty of Versailles and never join the League of Nations.

Final Judgment: Grade A

Generally viewed as a progressive Democrat who tried mightily to keep the nation out of war but was eventually forced into it, Wilson has consistently been ranked among America's top ten presidents. But like any admired or successful president, he did not have a blotless record.

Despite many impressive accomplishments, Wilson had flaws and shortcomings that remain troubling. In one recent assessment, biographer John Milton Cooper, Jr., fairly summed them up: "Two things will always mar his place in history: race and civil liberties. He turned a stone face and deaf ear to the struggle and tribulations of African Americans. . . . During the war, Wilson presided over an administration that committed egregious violations of civil liberties. . . . It remains a mystery why such a farseeing, thoughtful person as Wilson would let any of that occur."[7] The first answer is his upbringing. Although not a fire-breathing white supremacist, he was a product of his birth into a slaveholding household with Confederate loyalty. His heritage, and the times, played a role. The second is politics. Keeping a Democratic Southern Congress quiescent required Wilson—and many of his successors in the White House—to tread lightly on matters of race. On the question of cracking down on leftists and radical unionists, political reality also must have prevailed over progressive principle.

Wilson Administration Milestones[8]

1913

March 4	Woodrow Wilson is inaugurated.
	Congress divides the Department of Commerce and Labor into two departments, with each having cabinet status.
May 2	President Wilson recognizes the new Republic of China.
May 31	The Seventeenth Amendment is ratified, providing for direct popular election of U.S. senators.
June	Adapting a meat processor's conveyor belt system, the Ford Motor Company sets up the first automobile assembly line to produce the Model T. Henry Ford

also begins paying workers $5 a day, believing that higher wages will lead to greater worker productivity and loyalty. The efficiency of the assembly line reduces the car's price from $850 in 1908 to $265 by 1920.[9]

December 23   The Federal Reserve Act is signed into law, creating a central bank.

1914

June 28   A Serbian nationalist assassinates Archduke Francis Ferdinand of Austria in Sarajevo, Serbia.

August 4   Germany launches war on Belgium, France, and Great Britain. The United States declares its official neutrality.

August 6   Ellen Louise Wilson, Woodrow Wilson's first wife, dies of Bright's disease.

August 15   The Panama Canal officially opens.

September 26   The Federal Trade Commission is established, designed to regulate business conglomeration.

1915

January 2   Congress approves a bill requiring literacy tests for all immigrants; Wilson vetoes the bill.

May 7   A German U-boat torpedoes the British passenger liner *Lusitania* off the coast of Ireland, with the loss of 1,198 civilians, including 114 Americans. Wilson resists pressure to join the war against Germany.

June 7   Secretary of State William Jennings Bryan resigns in protest over Wilson's handling of the *Lusitania* sinking.

July 29   U.S. Marines land in Haiti to restore order after the Haitian president is assassinated; U.S. forces will remain in Haiti until 1934.

December 18   President Wilson marries Edith Bolling Galt.

1916

January 28	Wilson appoints the first Jewish justice, Louis B. Brandeis, to the Supreme Court.
March 15	General John Pershing begins an expedition into Mexico to capture Pancho Villa and his bandit force.
May	U.S. Marines land in the Dominican Republic to restore political stability; this occupation continues until 1924.
June 7–10	New York governor Charles Evans Hughes wins the Republican nomination. Theodore Roosevelt has withdrawn from consideration.
June 14–16	Democrats renominate Woodrow Wilson.
August 25	The National Park Service is established.
October 16	Margaret Sanger and colleagues open the nation's first birth control clinic in Brooklyn, New York.
November 7	Woodrow Wilson is reelected with the slogan "He kept us out of war."

1917

February 5	Congress overrides President Wilson's veto of the Immigration Act, which requires a literacy test for immigrants and restricts the entry of Asian laborers.
February 24	British officials reveal a coded message from German foreign minister Alfred Zimmerman to the German ambassador to Mexico. The note reveals a German plot to support Mexico in a war against the United States. Once revealed, the controversy fuels America's war fever.
March 4	President Woodrow Wilson is inaugurated for second term.
April 2	The first woman in the House of Representatives, Jeannette Rankin, a Republican from Montana, is seated.

April 2	President Wilson asks for a declaration of war against Germany.
April 4–6	Congress declares war against Germany.
May 18	The Selective Service Act requires all men between the ages of twenty-one and thirty to register with local draft boards. It is the first draft law since the Civil War.
June 26	The first U.S. troops arrive in France.

1918

January 26	To promote wartime food conservation, food administrator Herbert Hoover calls for one meatless day, two wheatless days, and two porkless days each week.
May 16	The Sedition Act is passed; it gives the postmaster general the right to ban publications deemed subversive, and calls for penalties for critics of the government or the war effort.
September 14	For giving an antiwar speech, Eugene V. Debs is sentenced to ten years in jail under the Espionage Act.
September 30	Wilson tells the Senate that women's suffrage is a "vitally necessary war measure." Previously he had stated that women's suffrage should be left to the states.
October	A worldwide influenza epidemic reaches its height in the United States, with more than six hundred thousand deaths in America and as many as twenty million around the globe.
November 11	An armistice ends the fighting in Europe.

1919

| January 29 | The Eighteenth Amendment is ratified. A nationwide ban on the sale, distribution, and production of alcoholic beverages will go into effect on January 16, 1920. The Prohibition era begins. |
| October 2 | While on a national speaking tour, Wilson suffers a stroke in Wichita, Kansas. |

October 28	The Volstead Act providing enforcement power to the Eighteenth Amendment is passed over Wilson's veto.
November 19	The Senate rejects the Treaty of Versailles, which Wilson had urged them to ratify.
December 22	The Department of Justice deports foreign-born "radicals" to Russia in the "Red Scare of 1919."

1920

January	In a series of raids during the "Red Scare," nearly twenty-seven hundred people are arrested.
April 1	U.S. forces sent to Siberia to support Russian counter-revolutionary forces are withdrawn.
June 8–12	Breaking a convention deadlock in what one attendee calls a deal "in a smoke-filled room," Republican leaders choose Ohio Senator Warren G. Harding.
June 28	Ohio governor James M. Cox and assistant secretary of the navy Franklin Delano Roosevelt of New York become the Democratic candidates for president and vice president.
August 26	The Nineteenth Amendment takes effect, granting women the right to vote.
November 2	Warren G. Harding is elected. Socialist Eugene V. Debs wins nearly one million popular votes from his jail cell.
November 20	Woodrow Wilson wins the Nobel Peace Prize.

MUST READS

Cooper, John Milton, Jr., *Woodrow Wilson*; Daniel Okrent, *Last Call: The Rise and Fall of Prohibition*.

ONLINE RESOURCES

Inaugural Addresses, Avalon Project, Yale Law School
  1913: http://avalon.law.yale.edu/20th_century/wilson1.asp
  1917: http://avalon.law.yale.edu/20th_century/wilson2.asp
Library of Congress Resource Guide
  http://www.loc.gov/rr/program/bib/presidents/wilson/index.html

Miller Center of Public Affairs, University of Virginia
  http://millercenter.org/index.php/academic/americanpresident
  /wilson
Presidential Library and Museum, Boyhood Home, Staunton,
Virginia
  http://www.woodrowwilson.org/
  http://www.wilsonboyhoodhome.org/
Wilson Center for Scholars
  http://www.wilsoncenter.org/
Woodrow Wilson House, Washington, D.C.
  http://www.woodrowwilsonhouse.org/
"Times Topics," *New York Times*: **Woodrow Wilson**
  http://topics.nytimes.com/top/reference/timestopics/people/w
  /woodrow_wilson/index.html

29

Warren Gamaliel Harding

* * *

March 4, 1921–August 2, 1923

Milestones in Warren G. Harding's Life

November 2, 1865	Born in Blooming Grove, Ohio
1884	Became editor-publisher of the daily *Marion Star*
1900–1904	Ohio state senator
1904–1906	Lieutenant governor of Ohio
1915–1920	U.S. senator from Ohio
1921–1923	Twenty-ninth president
August 2, 1923	Died in San Francisco, California, aged fifty-seven

PRESIDENTIAL VOICES

America's present need is not heroics but healing; not nostrums but normalcy; not revolution but restoration . . . not surgery but serenity.
—WARREN G. HARDING
Campaign Speech, May 1920[1]

A self-made publisher, Warren G. Harding, the first president elected after women got the vote, was a handsome, poker-playing, whiskey-drinking, all-around nice guy and "man's man." He is also routinely classed among the worst presidents. One reason is the epidemic of graft scandals that rocked his administration—easily the most corrupt since Grant's and among the most controversy-ridden ever—before and after his death in office.

Fast Facts

RELIGION: Baptist
ASSOCIATIONS: Freemason
EDUCATION: Ohio Central College
CAREER BEFORE POLITICS: Newspaper editor-publisher
POLITICAL PARTY: Republican
FIRST LADY: Florence Kling Harding (August 15, 1860–November 2, 1924)

* Harding was the first incumbent U.S. senator to be elected president.
* On Armistice Day, November 11, 1921, Harding dedicated the Tomb of the Unknown Soldier in Arlington Cemetery.
* Harding was the first president to ride to his inauguration in an automobile.

Often described as a great-looking president with movie-star qualities, Warren G. Harding possessed an "all-American," small-town appeal that won over crowds. A dynamic speaker with superb delivery, he looked the part of president to a nation shocked by the Great War. They wanted "normal," and Harding was sent from Central Casting to provide it.

Harding was born in Corsica (now Blooming Grove), Ohio, a farmer's son. After attending a local college, he taught school, sold insurance, and worked as a reporter. With a couple of partners, he brought a bankrupt newspaper, the *Marion Star*, back to life in 1884. By 1886, Harding was complete owner and the paper had begun to challenge other dailies as the "official" Marion newspaper, which published government notices. At the same time, Harding made an enemy of local real estate speculator and banker Amos Hall Kling, the richest man in Marion.

But in 1891, Harding married Florence ("Flossie") Kling DeWolf, five years his senior and the daughter of Amos Kling. Previously married, with a ten-year-old child, she was an astute businesswoman who had sharp political instincts. But her wealthy father objected to the marriage because of local talk that Harding had some black ancestors, a rumor that would resurface during his presidential campaign. Kling wouldn't let his wife attend the wedding and didn't speak to his daughter and son-in-law for years.

But Flossie Harding was credited with astutely managing the business side of the newspaper and liked to claim credit for her husband's success. According to White House historian William Seale, after they arrived in Washington, she was overheard to say, "Well, Warren Harding. I have got you the Presidency; what are you going to do with it?"[2]

Harding began his political career with a seat in the Ohio State Senate, serving two terms before becoming U.S. senator from Ohio in 1914. During his term as senator, Harding gained a reputation for missing more sessions than he attended, including votes on both the Prohibition and suffrage amendments. But that also meant he had avoided controversy. At a deadlocked 1920 Republican Convention, he became the dark horse candidate apparently based on his looks, amiability, winning personality, and willingness to take orders from party bosses.

Worn by the war and Woodrow Wilson's aggressive reform agenda, America wanted to catch its breath. With famous entertainer Al Jolson touring the nation for him, and running on the slogan "A Return to Normalcy," Harding provided the recipe and beat progressive Democrat James M. Cox, also an Ohio newspaperman, who was Ohio's governor, in an electoral landslide.

PRESIDENTIAL VOICES

It would be folly to ignore that we live in a motor age. The motorcar reflects our standard of living and gauges the speed of our present-day life. It long ago ran down Simple Living, and never halted to inquire about the prostrate

figure which fell as its victim. With full recognition of motorcar transportation we must turn it to the most practical use. It can not supersede the railway lines, no matter how generously we afford it highways out of the Public Treasury.
—WARREN G. HARDING
Second Message to Congress, December 8, 1922[3]

What was Teapot Dome and how did it boil over in the Harding Administration?

Sick of the war, frightened of the Bolshevik threat that came from Russia's revolution, weary of eight years with Democrat Woodrow Wilson, the nation welcomed the affable Warren G. Harding. Opposed by James M. Cox—who ran with President Wilson's young assistant secretary of the navy, Franklin D. Roosevelt—Harding and his running mate, Calvin Coolidge, the governor of Massachusetts, easily won in a fairly low-turnout election. (Socialist Eugene V. Debs garnered 3.5 percent of the vote.) Cox won only the "Solid South."

Harding's victory was genuinely more about the outgoing President Wilson than about him. America was turning inward, rejecting the internationalism of the League of Nations and the rationing and sacrifice the war effort had demanded. A professed "Dry"—meaning he favored Prohibition—Harding was privately quite "Wet," preferring Scotch and soda by most accounts. But in his Senate campaigns and presidential race, he had the considerable support of the Anti-Saloon League (ASL).[4] Nonetheless, Alice Roosevelt Longworth—Theodore Roosevelt's daughter, who shared her father's outspoken candor—once described the Harding White House as a kind of "frat house: air heavy with tobacco smoke, trays with bottles containing every imaginable brand of whisky. . . . cards and poker chips ready at hand—a general atmosphere of the waistcoat unbuttoned, feet on the desk, and the spittoon alongside."[5]

Under Harding, the old standby of Republican nineteenth-century politics, stiff tariffs, returned to protect American industry. But mostly his administration is remembered for a series of what were called the "Harding scandals." Like those under Grant, they require a scorecard:

- **The Veterans Hospitals:** With three hundred thousand wounded American war veterans, the Harding administration created the Veterans Bureau. Unfortunately, director Charles Forbes, a close friend of Harding, was convicted of taking in kickbacks millions of dollars allocated for hospital construction and veterans' care. Over the next few months, two officials—one of them, Charles Cramer, was legal counsel to Forbes at the Veterans Bureau—committed suicide because of this scandal engulfing the administration.

- **Alien Property:** Harry Daugherty, attorney general and Harding's former campaign manager, was implicated in a fraud charge related to the return of German assets seized during the war. Although indicted in 1926 and tried twice on this charge, Daugherty was never convicted.

- **Bootlegger Bribes:** Daugherty was also implicated in taking bribes from bootleggers during Prohibition. It was said that Daugherty provided the White House with liquor confiscated by the Justice Department. He resigned but wasn't formally charged. (He was also implicated in yet another scandal, related to overcharges on war contracts.)

- **Teapot Dome:** Two federal oil reserves—one in Elk Hills, California, and the other in Teapot Dome, Wyoming—were marked for the future use of the U.S. Navy. But the interior secretary, Albert B. Fall, formerly senator from New Mexico, contrived to have these lands turned over to his department. He then sold off drilling leases to two oil companies without competitive bidding, in return for more than $400,000 in bribes and kickbacks in the form of cash, stock, and cattle. While the leases were technically legal, Fall was convicted of conspiracy and accepting a bribe, achieving the distinction of becoming the first cabinet officer in American history to go to jail.

As this and other Harding administration scandals were beginning to come to light through a series of Senate investigations and newspaper reports, Harding set out on a "Voyage of Understanding," in an attempt to reconnect with the public. While in San Francisco, after having made the first presidential visit to Alaska, he suffered a fatal heart attack, dying in his hotel room on August 2, 1923.

Final Judgment: Grade F

Indecisive. Surrounded by corrupt cronies. Affable but lazy. Intellectually weak—his predecessor Woodrow Wilson once told a journalist that Harding "has nothing to think with,"[6] and one of his successors, Herbert Hoover, said, "He was not a man with either the experience or the intellectual quality that the position needed."[7] Harding has routinely been ranked near or at last among presidents—dead last in three famous polls of historians and second to last by the *Wall Street Journal*'s 2005 survey. Like Grant, he was apparently unaware of the corruption swirling around him. Nobody ever said Harding was corrupt, just incompetent.

But, like every president, he made contributions of some note. Chief among these was reversing Wilson's segregationist policies in federal jobs and commuting the sentence of the imprisoned Eugene V. Debs and greeting him at the White House.

Harding's life and death left some unanswered questions. The immediate cause of death was a heart attack, but he was not autopsied. He was also suspected of having food poisoning and was under extreme stress. The later revelations of additional scandals, as well as the public revelation of extramarital affairs, led to continued speculation that Harding had committed suicide or been murdered, possibly by his wife. Although she refused to permit an autopsy, no evidence of unnatural death exists.

Vice President Calvin Coolidge, untainted by the administration's scandals, took Harding's place.

Harding Administration Milestones[8]

1921

| March 4 | Warren G. Harding is inaugurated. |
| May 19 | Harding signs into law the Emergency Quota Act, limiting the number of immigrants from any given |

country to 3 percent of that nationality already in the United States by 1910. The law signals America's growing nativism and increasing fear of Bolshevism, motivated, in part, by the massive influx of south and east European immigrants into the United States following World War I.

June 10	Harding signs the Budget and Accounting Act, establishing the Bureau of the Budget and the General Accounting Office under the Treasury Department.
June 20	Alice Robertson of Oklahoma becomes the first woman to preside over the House of Representatives.
June 30	Harding appoints former President Taft chief justice of the Supreme Court.
November 23	Harding signs the Maternity and Infancy Act, granting federal funds to states for maternal and child care. The legislation also recognizes the emergent political power of women, a constituency that gained the right to vote during the previous year.
December 23	Harding commutes the sentence of Eugene Debs along with others found guilty under the Espionage Act.

1922

April 7	Interior Secretary Albert B. Fall leases the Teapot Dome oil reserves to Harry Sinclair, setting in motion what becomes known as the Teapot Dome scandals.
June 5	In *United Mine Workers v. Coronado Coal Co.*, the Supreme Court rules, under the Sherman Act, that striking miners are liable for damage inflicted upon company property. The ruling is part of a federal effort to control organized labor.

1923

January 2	As the Teapot Dome scandal unfolds, Harding accepts the resignation of Interior Secretary Fall.
January 29	Charles Forbes, head of the Veterans Bureau, resigns in anticipation of the Senate investigation of his

department. He is later indicted and convicted on charges of fraud, conspiracy, and bribery.

June 20 Harding and his wife leave for a cross-country speaking tour designed to bolster faith in the administration as the corruption scandals widen.

August 2 Harding suffers an attack of ptomaine poisoning and develops pneumonia. He dies, most likely of a heart attack, with his wife by his side in a San Francisco hotel room on the evening of August 2. (Harding was never autopsied and an exact cause of death was not determined, although congestive heart failure is now believed to have been the cause.)

August 3 In a simple 2:30 a.m. ceremony, presided over by his father, a notary, at his home in Plymouth, Vermont, Calvin Coolidge is sworn in.

MUST READS
David Pietrusza, *1920: The Year of Six Presidents.*

ONLINE RESOURCES
Inaugural Address, Avalon Project, Yale Law School
http://avalon.law.yale.edu/20th_century/harding.asp
Library of Congress Resource Guide
http://www.loc.gov/rr/program/bib/presidents/harding/bibliography.html
Miller Center of Public Affairs, University of Virginia
http://millercenter.org/index.php/academic/americanpresident/harding

30

Silent Cal
Calvin Coolidge
★ ★ ★
August 2, 1923–March 4, 1929

Milestones in Calvin Coolidge's Life

July 4, 1872	Born in Plymouth Notch, Vermont
1897	Admitted to the Massachusetts bar
1899–1900	Member of the Northampton, Massachusetts, City Council
1905	Mayor of Northampton
1912–1915	Member of Massachusetts State Senate
1919–1920	Governor of Massachusetts
1921–1923	Vice president under Harding
1923–1929	Thirtieth president
January 5, 1933	Died in Northampton, Massachusetts, aged sixty

PRESIDENTIAL VOICES

I favor the policy of economy, not because I wish to save money, but because I wish to save people. The men and women of this country who toil are the ones who bear the cost of the Government. Every dollar that we carelessly waste means that their life will be so much the more meager. Every dollar that we prudently save means that their life will be so much the more abundant. Economy is idealism in its most practical form.

—CALVIN COOLIDGE
Inaugural Address, March 4, 1925[1]

Notoriously laconic, Calvin Coolidge once said he couldn't recall that any presidential candidate hurt himself much by not talking. When a woman bet a friend that she could pry more than two words out of Coolidge, he told her, "You lose."[2]

Once relegated to second-rate presidential stature by some historians who viewed him as the straitlaced, terse New Englander who replaced Warren G. Harding and his corrupt cabinet, Calvin Coolidge has enjoyed a resurgence of late. There is no question that he revived the image of a White House left in tatters after the disastrous revelations of the Harding-era misdoings.

But Coolidge's recently elevated status also stems from the fact that another Republican president, Ronald Reagan, announced his admiration for Coolidge, prominently displaying his portrait in the White House. As President Reagan put it in 1981, "You hear a lot of jokes every once in a while about 'Silent Cal Coolidge.' The joke is on the people who make the jokes. Look at his record. He cut the taxes four times. We had probably the greatest growth and prosperity that we've ever known."[3] What President Reagan did not address was what responsibility Coolidge bears for the looming disaster of the Great Depression. And that is where the debate over his place in the presidential pantheon begins and ends.

Fast Facts

RELIGION: Congregationalist

EDUCATION: Amherst (Massachusetts) College

CAREER BEFORE POLITICS: Attorney

POLITICAL PARTY: Republican

FIRST LADY: Grace Anne Goodhue Coolidge (January 3, 1879–July 8, 1957). Born in Burlington, Vermont, Grace Coolidge worked as a lip reading instructor at a school for the deaf in Northampton, Massachusetts. She later told of looking out her window and seeing Calvin

Coolidge in a neighboring house, wearing a hat while shaving in his long underwear. The two met and fell in love.

CHILDREN: The Coolidges had two sons, John and Calvin. While playing tennis at the White House with his brother, Calvin Jr. developed a blister on his right foot. It rapidly advanced to blood poisoning, and he died a few days later, on July 7, 1924, leaving Coolidge deeply depressed. (Firstborn son, John, later became a railroad executive and donated the buildings that became the President Coolidge Historic Site in Plymouth, Vermont.)

* After receiving a telegram advising him of President Harding's death, Coolidge was administered the oath of office on August 3, 1923, by his seventy-eight-year-old father, a notary, in the family farmhouse by the light of a kerosene lamp.

* Coolidge's 1923 State of the Union was the first broadcast over radio. Despite his notorious reputation for silence, Coolidge used the radio frequently, and many of his speeches, including his 1925 Inaugural Address, were broadcast live. Chief Justice William Howard Taft administered Coolidge's second presidential oath, the first time a former president administered the oath of office.

PRESIDENTIAL VOICES

Mr. Coolidge belongs rather in the class of Presidents who were distinguished for character more than for heroic achievement. His great task was to restore the dignity and prestige of the Presidency when it had reached the lowest ebb in our history, and to afford, in a time of extravagance and waste, a shining public example of the simple and homely virtues which came down to him from his New England ancestors.

—NEW YORK GOVERNOR ALFRED SMITH, 1933[4]

The only president born on the Fourth of July, Calvin Coolidge was born in 1872 in Plymouth Notch, a tiny hamlet in rural Vermont. The

Coolidges were an old New England farming family, with roots in the colonial era. Calvin's father, John Coolidge, held a variety of local offices, from tax collector to constable, and also kept a general store. While the family was far from wealthy, Coolidge did not grow up in rural poverty. Coolidge professed that he had learned from his father Yankee frugality and a sense of commitment to public service that was part of small-town New England tradition. His mother died when he was twelve, possibly from tuberculosis; his younger sister Abigail died when she was fifteen.

Coolidge went to Amherst College in neighboring Massachusetts and at his father's urging settled in Northampton, not far from Amherst, to study and practice law. There he began to slowly climb the long ladder of local politics in Massachusetts. He went from city council in 1900 to city solicitor, then clerk of court, and finally mayor in 1905.

After serving in the state legislature, Coolidge ran unopposed for governor of Massachusetts in 1918 and then garnered national attention when he called in the militia to break the Boston police strike. "There is no right to strike against the public safety by anybody, anywhere, anytime," said Coolidge, winning Republican admirers around the country for this decisive stand at a time when unionizing was largely considered a short step from Bolshevism.

That boldness was enough to put him on the Republican ticket as the vice presidential nominee with Warren Harding. As vice president, Coolidge lived up to his nickname, sitting silently during cabinet meetings and seldom speaking as presiding officer of the U.S. Senate.

Coolidge emerged unscathed from the scandals that plagued the Harding administration, earning a reputation for being honest, direct, and hardworking. The eminently quotable Alice Roosevelt Longworth said Coolidge's White House was as different from Harding's as "a New England parlor is from the backroom of a speakeasy."[5] Journalist William Allen White once called him "a Puritan in Babylon."

With a rebounding economy, Coolidge won another Republican landslide in 1924 with the slogan "Keep Cool With Coolidge." In his elected term, Coolidge swept out some of Harding's cabinet, and the new members included his Amherst classmate Harlan Fiske Stone as attorney general, to replace the disgraced Harry M. Daugherty, whom Coolidge dismissed. (Coolidge later elevated Harlan Stone to the Supreme Court, where he surprisingly joined the liberals on the bench; he became chief justice under Franklin D. Roosevelt.) Among the Harding holdovers was Secretary of the Treasury Andrew W. Mellon, a Pittsburgh banker and one of the wealthiest men in America. Mellon was the chief proponent of the sharply reduced tax rates on wealthy Americans. He continued to serve in the same post under Coolidge's successor Herbert Hoover, another Coolidge holdover from the Harding administration as commerce secretary.

How did Silent Cal make the twenties roar?

It was the era of the speakeasy. The box office rang up sales for Chaplin and Keaton, Valentino and Clara Bow. And soon the movies would all be talking and singing. A guy named Walt Disney drew a mouse he first called "Oswald" and only later Mickey. The Babe was hitting home runs. The flappers started to Charleston and jazz started to swing.

This was the Roaring Twenties, a rambunctious decade in America's economic and social history that stands so completely at odds with the man who then occupied the White House.

It was a period of tremendous economic boom times, as a combination of technological innovation and a transition to production of consumer goods, like automobiles, radios, the first commercially produced airplanes, and washing machines, transformed society, and the rapid growth of industry sparked a boom in middle-class wealth. With the war over, Americans wanted to dance the Charleston.

That party was spurred in large measure by the Coolidge administration's tax-cutting programs, urged by Treasury Secretary Andrew Mellon, that reduced the wartime tax level of 77 percent on the wealthiest Americans to 7 percent. Coolidge also blocked almost every attempt to increase government control over business. Even when it came to Prohibition, which he publicly supported, Coolidge didn't like "big government," as Daniel Okrent records in his history of Prohibition: "He

[Coolidge] believed that government should keep its nose out of the lives of citizens. He so hated to spend federal money that in 1926, with the economy in the midst of spectacular boom, he whacked the Prohibition Bureau's budget by 3.5 percent."[6]

In his first State of the Union address in December 1923, Coolidge expressed his support for Prohibition and U.S. involvement in the World Court. He also made it clear he opposed government interference with business and called for lowering taxes, thereby extending Harding's policies, which would become known as "trickle down" economics. His annual message was the first radio broadcast of a presidential address, made possible by the more than 2.5 million radios in U.S. homes; in 1920 there had been fewer than 5,000.

Coolidge's prescription for America proved a frothy mix, and the postwar economic good times were matched by social changes—in America and the rest of the world. Women who could vote had new freedoms. Cities were booming, as if to confirm the popular World War I song, "How Ya Gonna Keep 'Em Down on the Farm (After They've Seen Paree)?"

But possibly the most roaring place of all in the 1920s was Wall Street, where Coolidge's economic policies and the low interest rates set by the Federal Reserve—created in 1913—combined to set off the "Coolidge bull market." With new companies like General Motors growing wildly and leading the way, the stock market ballooned. It was an era, writes economic historian Steve Fraser, in which "crony capitalism implied more than mere corruption; or rather it raised corruption to the level of state policy, to a form of extra-legal mercantilism in which one could no longer easily tell the difference between the representation of a political constituency and the servicing of a corporate client." Fraser concludes that, although free from Harding-style corruption, the Coolidge administration perfected this "crony capitalism." One example was the United Corporation, which controlled public utilities across twelve states, generating 20 percent of the country's electrical power. Shares of its stock were offered privately to members of both parties, including Coolidge after he left the presidency.[7] This was, of course, in a time before there was a Securities and Exchange Commission (created in 1933) "regulating" Wall Street.

A real estate boom, in such places as Florida, accompanied the Wall Street boom. Sound familiar?

But as many economic historians have noted, the Roaring Twenties were also creating a speculative bubble. One of those worried about such a bubble was the head of the Federal Reserve, Benjamin Strong, who recognized that America's inherent optimism, so wildly alive in the exuberance of the Roaring Twenties, carried the potential for dangerous speculative fads. "It seems a shame that the best sort of plans can be handicapped by a speculative orgy," he said in 1925. "And yet the temper of the country is such that these situations cannot be avoided."[8]

PRESIDENTIAL VOICES

In what manner he would have performed himself if the holy angels had shoved the Depression forward a couple of years—this we can only guess, and one man's hazard is as good as another's. My own is that he would have responded to bad times precisely as he responded to good ones—that is by pulling down the blinds, stretching his legs upon his desk, and snoozing away the lazy afternoons.

JOURNALIST H. L. MENCKEN, 1933[9]

Final Judgment: Grade C

As America's mood and attitudes swing from one end of the political spectrum to the other, presidential fortunes sometimes change. Long relegated to the lower rungs of the presidential ladder, Coolidge has had a recent makeover. He is now seen as a hero to the modern tax-cutting, small-government side of the political aisle. His policies put more money in the hands of people; he kept the government small; and he retired the national debt. On the other hand, critics say his hands-off policies allowed the excesses of speculation that ultimately contributed to the stock market bubble of the 1920s and finally the Great Crash and subsequent Great Depression.

Coolidge Administration Milestones[10]

1923

August 3   At a 2:30 a.m. ceremony in Plymouth Notch, Vermont, Calvin Coolidge's father administers the oath of office.

September 15   Oklahoma is placed under martial law in order to suppress the increasing terrorism of the Ku Klux Klan, which has reemerged in the South and Midwest.

1924

March 18   Congress passes the Soldiers' Bonus Bill, providing twenty-year annuities for veterans. Coolidge vetoes it; Congress overrides the veto.

May 26   In the nation's postwar nativist, isolationist mood, Congress passes a restrictive immigration law with tough new quotas, banning Japanese immigrants completely.

June 2   The Indian Citizenship Act is passed, granting full citizenship to all American Indians.

                   The Revenue Act of 1924 cuts federal taxes.

November 4   Coolidge easily wins reelection; third-party Populist candidate Robert La Follette wins a surprisingly large 4,823,000 popular votes, but only 13 electoral votes.

1925

March 4   Coolidge is inaugurated for his first elected term.

May 5   The "Scopes Monkey Trial" takes place in Tennessee, after public school teacher John T. Scopes is arrested for teaching Darwin's theory of evolution. Scopes ultimately loses and pays a $100 fine, but the trial serves as the focus of a national debate between science and religion.

August 8   A massive Ku Klux Klan demonstration takes place in Washington, D.C., as some forty thousand people march down Pennsylvania Avenue in white Klan robes; the Klan's numbers have surged with America's postwar anti-foreign mood.

1926

May 9   Rear Admiral Richard E. Byrd and Floyd Bennett make the first successful flight over the North Pole.

May 10   The U.S. Marines land in Nicaragua to suppress a revolt and maintain a presence there until 1933.

1927

March 7   The Supreme Court rules that a Texas law prohibiting blacks from voting in Democratic primaries is unconstitutional.

May 21   Charles A. Lindbergh completes the first transatlantic flight, in his monoplane, the *Spirit of St. Louis*. A year later, Amelia Earhart becomes the first woman to make the flight.

August 2   Coolidge ends any talk of his candidacy for the 1928 election, stating, "I do not choose to run."

October 6   The first "talkie," *The Jazz Singer*, starring Al Jolson, debuts.

1928

June 29   The Democratic Party nominates New York governor Alfred E. Smith. Smith is Catholic and anti-Catholic prejudice plays a large role in the election.

November 6   Herbert Hoover wins the election in a landslide, 444 electoral votes to Smith's 87.

MUST READS

Liaquat Ahamed, *Lords of Finance: The Bankers Who Broke the World*; David Greenberg, *Calvin Coolidge*; Amity Shlaes, *The Forgotten Man: A New History of the Great Depression*.

ONLINE RESOURCES

Inaugural Address, Miller Center of Public Affairs, University of Virginia

http://millercenter.org/scripps/archive/speeches/detail/3569

Library of Congress Resource Guide
http://www.loc.gov/rr/program/bib/presidents/coolidge/index.html

Library of Congress Online Collection—"Prosperity and Thrift"
http://memory.loc.gov/ammem/coolhtml/coolhome.html

President Coolidge Historic Site, Vermont
http://www.historicvermont.org/coolidge/

Coolidge Library and Museum, Northampton, Massachusetts
http://www.forbeslibrary.org/coolidge/coolidge.shtml
http://www.calvincoolidge.blogspot.com/

Miller Center of Public Affairs, University of Virginia
http://millercenter.org/index.php/academic/americanpresident
/coolidge

"Times Topics," *New York Times*: Calvin Coolidge
http://topics.nytimes.com/top/reference/timestopics/people/c
/calvin_coolidge/index.html

31

Herbert Clark Hoover

★ ★ ★

March 4, 1929–March 4, 1933

Milestones in Herbert C. Hoover's Life

August 10, 1874	Born in West Branch, Iowa
1884	Moved to live with relatives in Oregon after the death of his parents
1897–1898	Managed gold mining operations in Australia
1899–1908	Managed coal, zinc, and silver mines in Asia
1908–1914	Formed global engineering company
1914–1917	Chairman of Commission of Relief for Belgium
1917–1919	United States food administrator during World War I
1921–1928	Secretary of commerce under Harding and Coolidge
1929–1933	Thirty-first president
October 20, 1964	Died in New York City, aged ninety

PRESIDENTIAL VOICES

We are challenged with a peace-time choice between the American system of rugged individualism and a European philosophy of diametrically opposed doctrines—doctrines of paternalism and state socialism.

. . . Our American experiment in human welfare has yielded a degree of well-being unparalleled in all the world. It has come nearer to the abolition of poverty, to the abolition of fear of want than humanity has ever reached before.

—Herbert Hoover, October 22, 1928[1]

Fast Facts

RELIGION: Quaker

EDUCATION: Stanford

CAREER BEFORE POLITICS: Mining engineer, businessman

POLITICAL PARTY: Republican

FIRST LADY: Lou Henry Hoover (March 29, 1874–January 7, 1944)

CHILDREN: Herbert Charles and Allen Henry

* Hoover was the first president born west of the Mississippi.

* His wife, Lou, was the only female geology major at Stanford when they met. They later collaborated on a translation from Latin of a mining and metallurgy text, *De Re Metallica*, published in 1912. While they lived in China, the Hoovers lived through the 1900 Boxer Rebellion and both learned Chinese, and they sometimes spoke to each other in Chinese at the White House.

* Hoover's inaugural in 1929 was the first to be recorded on talking newsreel.

* Hoover was the first of two Quaker presidents. (The other was Richard M. Nixon.)

Born in Iowa in 1874, Herbert Hoover was the son of a blacksmith who died when he was six. When his mother, a women's rights advocate and schoolteacher who also took in sewing after her husband's death, died of pneumonia two years later, the nine-year-old orphan was sent to Oregon to live with relatives and attend a Friends (Quaker) school. Although he never graduated high school, he excelled in math and won admission to Stanford University's first freshman class. Hoover studied geology and engineering, graduating and moving through a succession of jobs in the mining field in Australia, China, and Russia. In 1908, he formed an engineering company that opened up oil reserves in Russia. By 1914, he was worth an estimated $4 million—the orphaned blacksmith's son from Iowa had made an impressive fortune in the oil and mining business. But he also identified with the progressive wing of the Republican Party and supported Theodore Roosevelt's 1912 bid for the presidency, contributing $1,000 to the third-party campaign.

Steeped in Quaker philosophy but a successful businessman and engineer, Hoover emerged on the world stage during World War I, when he helped organize the evacuation of 120,000 Americans trapped in Europe. Without direct government support, he then started a Committee for the Relief of Belgium, which raised millions of dollars in food relief for starving Europeans, and he was hailed as a hero for his efforts. When Hoover returned to the United States from wartime London, Woodrow Wilson asked him to oversee the U.S. Food Administration, which rationed wheat, pork, and other goods during the war—introducing the word "hooverize," meaning to ration food and other household goods, into the language. After the war, President Wilson asked him to head a relief organization that again helped feed and clothe war-torn Europe.

Although an internationalist and supporter of the League of Nations, Hoover was loyal to the Republican Party, and his support of Warren G. Harding was rewarded with the post of commerce secretary. Avoiding any taint of the scandals that took down others in the Harding cabinet, he remained in the job under Coolidge. His practical and business expertise raised the commerce post to new heights as Hoover saw that there was a need for government involvement in setting industrial standards and expanding American trade overseas.

A vigorous defender of Prohibition (although a discreet drinker himself), Hoover won the Republican nomination in 1928 when Prohibition was really the only issue. His opponent, New York Governor Al Smith, opposed Prohibition. Since Smith was the first Catholic nominee for president, it was also a campaign featuring some of the most vitriolic anti-Catholic propaganda seen in America since the Know-Nothing days of the early nineteenth century. "A Vote for Smith is a vote for the Pope" was one of the milder slogans. The largely Protestant "Dries" also linked Catholicism and opposition to Prohibition—Smith would bring "Rum, Romanism and Ruin." The famous evangelist Reverend Bob Jones, founder of the university bearing his name, campaigned for Hoover in the South and said, "I would rather see a saloon on every corner than a Catholic in the White House." A segregationist, Jones also said he would prefer "a nigger president" to the Catholic Smith.[2]

Hoover won a huge victory, sweeping most of the country. Then a few months after his inauguration, the stock market crashed on "Black Friday" and the walls came tumbling down around him.

How did Herbert Hoover handle the Great Depression?

America had suffered depressions or, in the nineteenth-century parlance, "panics" before. But none of them had been capitalized like the Depression of the 1930s. None had ever lasted so long, and none had ever touched so many Americans so devastatingly.

When the stock market crashed in October 1929, the economy was paralyzed. In one year, thirteen hundred banks failed at a time when there was no federal deposit insurance guaranteeing the savings of working people. As five thousand banks closed during the next three years, millions of Americans saw their savings disappear.

Without banks to extend credit and capital, businesses and factories closed, forcing more workers onto unemployment lines. Statistics are virtually meaningless when it comes to the magnitude of joblessness then. Official numbers said 25 percent of the workforce was unemployed. Other historians of the period put the number at 40 to 50 percent.

Through his last three desperate years in office, Herbert Hoover continued to voice optimism. Like most economists of his day, Hoover believed that such depressions were part of the business cycle. But despite his stream of hopeful pronouncements—"Business and industry have turned the corner," he said in January 1930—the situation turned bleaker.

For years after the Depression, Hoover came down in history as a do-nothing. But the characterization is unfair and simplistic. The problem was that just about everything Hoover tried either backfired or was too little, too late. One thing is widely agreed upon: The Tariff Act of 1930, also known as the Smoot-Hawley Tariff—which threw up trade barriers around the United States—was a devastating mistake.

Passed in 1930, this law was meant to protect American manufacturers, but it set off an international trade war as European nations simply did the same thing. By 1931, the Depression had spread throughout Europe, where the scars of the war were still not healed and the crush of wartime debt contributed to the crisis. Austria, England, France, and, most ominously, Germany were all sucked into a violent whirlpool of massive unemployment and staggering inflation.

Bedrock conservative Republican principles kept Hoover from seeking to enact government relief programs, which he viewed as Socialism. But with Hoover unable or unwilling to help restore the flow of credit, the economy ground to a halt. Falling prices led to bankruptcies, shuttered factories, and an almost complete deep freeze of America's economic activity. Fearful consumers stopped buying, and the economy went into a death spiral.

In 1932, Hoover reluctantly created the Reconstruction Finance Corporation, which loaned money to railroads and banks. In an echo of modern American complaints that the government bails out banks and big business, Hoover was seen as willing to aid corporations while showing little concern for the poor. In spite of the lengthening breadlines and the "Hoovervilles" of cardboard shacks being set up in America's large cities, Hoover refused to allow the government to issue direct aid. When a belated public works program was passed, it was woefully inadequate.

In her history of the Depression era, *The Forgotten Man*, Amity Shlaes characterizes the response of Hoover by noting: "Hoover ordered wages up when they wanted to go down. He allowed a disastrous tariff, Smoot-Hawley, to become law when he should have had the sense to block it. He raised taxes when neither citizens individually nor the economy as a whole could afford the change."[3]

While Americans at every level suffered in the Depression, some bankers and brokers walked away with large fortunes even as the market was destroyed.

In 2007 and 2008, as Americans watched another crisis unfurl in the Great Recession, comparisons to the 1930s were commonplace as a rescue effort was patched together. But 1929 was different. As Liaquat Ahamed summarizes in *Lords of Finance*, "The collapse of the world economy from 1929 to 1933 . . . was the seminal economic event of the 20th century. No country escaped its clutches; for more than ten years the malaise brought in its wake hung over the world, poisoning every aspect of social and material life and crippling the future of generations. From it flowed the turmoil of Europe in the 'low dishonest decade' of the 1930s, the rise of Hitler and Nazism, and the eventual slide of much of the globe into a Second World War even more terrible than the first."[4]

Final Judgment: Grade C

A nation desperate for relief from the increasing despair of the Depression turned away from Hoover and the Republicans in 1932, choosing in a landslide Franklin D. Roosevelt and his promise of a "New Deal." Unfortunately, America had to wait some time for the new president. In the midst of the most devastating economic crisis in history, there was the traditional long lag between the election and Inauguration Day in March. The Depression crisis changed that. The Twentieth Amendment was ratified a year later, shifting Inauguration Day to January 20 to speed the future transitions between administrations.

Hoover gets hard knocks for the hard times. But others assess him more generously. Historian Richard Norton Smith, director of the Hoover Presidential Library, notes, "Herbert Hoover saved more lives through his various relief efforts than all the dictators of the 20th century together could snuff out. Seventy years before politicians discovered children, he founded the American Child Health Association. The problem is, Hoover defies easy labeling. How can you categorize a 'rugged individualist' who once said, 'The trouble with capitalism is capitalists; they're too damn greedy.'"[5]

Hoover Administration Milestones[6]

1929

March 4	Herbert Hoover is inaugurated.
April 15	New York City police raid the Birth Control Clinical Research Center established by Margaret Sanger, arresting two doctors and three nurses and confiscating numerous records.
May 16	The first annual Academy Awards are presented.
May 27	The U.S. Supreme Court upholds the use of the pocket veto by the president for the purpose of blocking legislation.
June 15	The Agricultural Marketing Act is passed to revitalize the increasingly poor market for farm products.
September 3	The index of common stock prices reaches an average of 216, more than double what it was three years earlier. At the same time, national income statistics indicate that roughly 60 percent of Americans have annual incomes below the poverty line, estimated at $2,000.
September 22	The construction contract for the Empire State Building is awarded. It will be completed in 1931.
October 24	"Black Thursday" strikes the New York Stock Exchange with a collapse in stock prices as 13 million shares are sold. Wealthy investors J. P. Morgan and John D. Rockefeller step in to save the market by furiously buying stock, but they cannot check the fall.
October 29	On "Black Tuesday" a record 16.4 million shares of stock are traded on the New York Stock Exchange as large blocks of equities are sold at extremely low prices. The trading continues the sharp slide of the previous week.

1930

January	The U.S. Census reports a population of nearly 123 million.

February 10	A major bootlegging operation in Chicago is shut down with the arrest of 158 people from 31 organizations. Together, these groups were estimated to have distributed more than seven million gallons of whiskey nationwide, with an estimated worth of around $50 million.
June 17	The Smoot-Hawley Tariff Act is signed; it raises duties on many imports. As other countries follow suit, an international trade war worsens the Depression.
September	A bank panic begins; 305 banks across the country close before the end of the month; more than 500 close in October.
December 2	Hoover asks Congress to fund public works projects in order to stem the growing tide of unemployment.
December 11	The Bank of the United States in New York City, with sixty branches and four hundred thousand depositors, closes; the largest of more than thirteen hundred bank failures.

1931

February 27	Congress passes the Bonus Loan Bill over Hoover's veto. The act allows veterans to obtain cash loans of up to 50 percent of their bonus certificates issued in 1924.
March 3	"The Star Spangled Banner" officially becomes the national anthem.
September 21	Britain goes off the gold standard in an effort to solve the continuing economic crisis. Fearing that the United States will soon do the same, Americans begin to withdraw their money from banks and hoard gold. Over the next month, 827 more banks will close.
October 17	Notorious gangster Al Capone is convicted of income tax evasion and sentenced to eleven years in prison and a $50,000 fine.
December 7	Hundreds of "hunger marchers" arrive in Washington hoping to present a petition to Hoover asking for jobs. They are turned away from the White House.

1932

January 22	Hoover establishes the Reconstruction Finance Corporation, designed to lend money to banks, insurance companies, and other institutions to stimulate the economy.
March 1	The Lindbergh kidnapping case: The nation is transfixed when the twenty-month-old son of famed aviator Charles Lindbergh is kidnapped. After a $50,000 ransom is paid, the boy is found dead on May 12.
May 20	Amelia Earhart becomes the first woman to complete a solo flight across the Atlantic Ocean.
May 29	The first of nearly twenty thousand World War I veterans arrive in Washington, D.C., setting up camps near the Capitol. Known as the "Bonus Army," they hope Congress will grant them the full value of their bonus certificates, which were not to mature until 1944. The army later forces these veterans out of the city.
July 2	Accepting the Democratic nomination, Franklin D. Roosevelt pledges "a new deal for the American people."
November 8	Roosevelt wins the presidential election in dramatic fashion, capturing 472 electoral votes to Hoover's 59.

MUST READS

Steve Fraser, *Every Man a Speculator: A History of Wall Street in American Life*; John Steele Gordon, *An Empire of Wealth: The Epic History of American Economic Power*; William E. Leuchtenberg, *Herbert Hoover*.

ONLINE RESOURCES

Inaugural Address, Avalon Project, Yale Law School
   http://avalon.law.yale.edu/20th_century/hoover.asp
Library of Congress
   http://www.loc.gov/rr/program/bib/presidents/hoover/memory
   .html

Herbert Hoover National Historic Site, National Park Service
http://www.nps.gov/heho/
Hoover Library and Museum
http://www.hoover.archives.gov/
Miller Center of Public Affairs, University of Virginia
http://millercenter.org/academic/americanpresident/hoover
Obituary, *New York Times*
http://www.nytimes.com/learning/general/onthisday/bday/0810
.html
"Times Topics," *New York Times*: **Herbert Hoover**
http://topics.nytimes.com/top/reference/timestopics/people/h
/herbert_clark_hoover/index.html

32

FDR
Franklin Delano Roosevelt

★ ★ ★

March 4, 1933–April 12, 1945

Milestones in Franklin D. Roosevelt's Life

January 30, 1882	Born in Hyde Park, New York
1907	Admitted to the New York bar
1911–1912	Senator, New York state legislature
1913–1920	Assistant secretary of the navy under Wilson
1929–1932	Governor of New York
1933–1945	Thirty-second president
April 12, 1945	Died at Warm Springs, Georgia, aged sixty-three

PRESIDENTIAL VOICES

The money changers have fled from their high seats in the temple of our civilization. We may now restore that temple to the ancient truths. The measure of the restoration lies in the extent to which we apply social values more noble than mere monetary profit.

—Franklin D. Roosevelt
First Inaugural Address, March 4, 1933[1]

One man was born in the Midwest, orphaned young, and became a self-made success. The other was born in the lap of luxury, to America's aristocracy, scion of one of the wealthiest families in America, and was dispatched to all the "right" schools. But the second one, the "gifted" one, became the greatest hero in history to America's poor and downtrodden and was eventually called a "traitor to his class."

While Herbert Hoover crashed in presidential esteem along with the stock market of 1929, Franklin D. Roosevelt is routinely ranked among the greatest, shoulder-to-shoulder with Lincoln and Washington.

For most of the last half of the twentieth century, FDR was placed on a pedestal. He was elected at the moment of America's gravest crisis since Lincoln confronted secession, with the nation crippled by an economic disaster so severe that millions had simply lost hope. When the full fury of the Great Depression was unleashed on the country—closing banks and businesses, forcing people from their jobs and homes, leaving millions starving—the idea that the government should actually do something about it was still heresy, especially to the Republican Party and the business class. Government was supposed to stay out of the way and let the markets fix things. To do otherwise was Socialism. Bolshevism. And certainly un-American.

Franklin D. Roosevelt had other ideas.

Fast Facts

RELIGION: Episcopal
ASSOCIATIONS: Freemason, Sons of the American Revolution
EDUCATION: Harvard
CAREER BEFORE POLITICS: Attorney
POLITICAL PARTY: Democratic
FIRST LADY: Anna Eleanor Roosevelt (October 11, 1884–November 7, 1962)
CHILDREN: Anna, James, Elliott, Franklin Jr., and John

* FDR was the only president elected to more than two terms and became the longest-serving president in history. The Twenty-

second Amendment limiting the president to two terms was passed after Roosevelt's four terms.

* As a reward for backing Woodrow Wilson in 1912, FDR was named an assistant secretary of the navy, a position once held—it was widely noted—by his cousin Theodore Roosevelt.

* FDR used the same family Bible in all four of his inaugurations; the oldest Inaugural Bible, it was printed in 1686 and is the only Inaugural Bible written in a modern foreign language—Dutch.[2]

* Roosevelt's second Inaugural in 1937 was the first on January 20, a change made by the Twentieth Amendment, which moved Inauguration Day from March 4.

* There was no Inaugural Parade for FDR's fourth inauguration due to wartime gas rationing and a lumber shortage.

* Buried in the Rose Garden at Hyde Park along with Franklin and Eleanor Roosevelt is their famous Scottie dog, Fala, perhaps the most famous presidential pet in history. In 1944, Roosevelt answered Republican charges that Fala had been left behind on the Aleutian Islands and a navy destroyer had been sent to collect the dog at a cost of millions. The story proved false and the speech was among FDR's most famous and winning: "I am accustomed to hearing malicious falsehoods about myself—such as that old, worm-eaten chestnut that I have represented myself as indispensable. But I think I have a right to resent, to object, to libelous statements about my dog!"

* Roosevelt appointed eight justices to the Supreme Court, more than any other president except Washington, who appointed ten.

PRESIDENTIAL VOICES

This country needs, and unless I mistake its temper, demands bold, persistent experimentation. It is common sense to take a method and try it. If it fails, admit it frankly and try another. But above all, try something.

—FRANKLIN D. ROOSEVELT,
May 22, 1932

Franklin Delano Roosevelt was born in 1882 in Hyde Park, just north of New York City, to James Roosevelt, a lawyer and financier, and Sara Delano Roosevelt, the daughter of a merchant who made a fortune in the China trade. Sara doted on Franklin and was, in most biographical accounts of FDR, an overbearing and overly controlling force in his life. The Roosevelts were wealthy enough to own their own railroad car and look down their noses at dining with the Vanderbilts. Franklin's parents had him schooled at home with tutors and took him to Europe for extended trips.

Finally, at age fourteen, Franklin was sent to the Groton School, a Massachusetts boarding school, going from there to Harvard, where he spent most of his time on the college newspaper and with the Hasty Pudding theatrical group. While at Harvard, FDR declared himself a Democrat and began courting his distant cousin, Eleanor Roosevelt.

Niece of the patriarch Theodore Roosevelt, Eleanor (named Anna Eleanor at birth, she preferred to use her middle name) had also been born into a world of wealth and privilege. Her maternal grandmother raised her after her mother died when she was eight, and her alcoholic father died in a sanitarium less than two years later. Eleanor was tutored privately and then sent to a school near London where the headmistress was a pioneering progressive feminist. After returning to New York and her "debut" in New York society, she began doing charitable work as a volunteer with the newly formed Junior League of New York. That was where Eleanor Roosevelt got her first glimpse of what reformer Jacob Riis called the "other half."

She saw the slums of New York firsthand and became completely committed to improving the life of America's poor. When she met her distant cousin Franklin Roosevelt, a Harvard student, for the first time that year, she would introduce him to the world of New York's squalid immigrant quarters and she is credited with profoundly awakening FDR's ideas of social and economic justice. After a New Year's Day reception and dinner at her uncle Theodore's White House, she began her formal courtship with FDR.

Despite strenuous objections from Franklin's mother, Franklin and

Eleanor were married in New York City in 1905, a few months after FDR began law school at Columbia. Like distant cousin Theodore—Eleanor's uncle—Franklin left law school, but he still passed the bar. He then worked in some prestigious "white shoe" law firms but was clearly more interested in politics.

He ran successfully for the New York State Senate in 1910 and was reelected in 1912. The following year, President Wilson brought him and his famous name into the administration as assistant secretary of the navy, and he played a key role in readying the United States for entry into the world war.

It was during this time that FDR began an affair with Eleanor's secretary Lucy Mercer. Although Eleanor offered him a divorce, FDR's mother was adamant—doing so would ruin his political career. He promised to end the relationship. (While he did cut off the affair, it was rekindled after he became president, and Lucy Mercer—later Rutherford—was with FDR at his death in April 1945.)

The marriage survived the crisis, and as a rising star in Democratic circles in 1920, FDR was named the party's candidate for vice president. Although the ticket of James Cox and FDR lost, Roosevelt's future seemed bright.

But then his seemingly charmed life came crashing down. The crisis point came in August 1921 when he went for a swim at his family's summer home in Campobello in New Brunswick. A sailor, swimmer, tennis player, and golfer, he had always been physically active, and one of his children, Jimmy, would say that his father was "the handsomest, strongest, most glamorous, vigorous father in the world."[3]

That afternoon, he had a high fever, and by the end of the day he was paralyzed from the waist down. In the 1920s, FDR invested a considerable part of his fortune in building a spa in Warm Springs, Georgia, whose curative waters he thought aided his own rehabilitation. The effects of his disease led to a long, painful period spent attempting to regain use of his legs. Over the next few years, he exercised daily for hours, drenched in sweat, trying to move his legs without crutches. But by 1929, when he was running for governor of New York, he finally had abandoned the effort, knowing he was permanently crippled by polio. And he would spend his political life deceiving the public about his condition. Few would know that the man with the jaunty smile and the cigarette holder clenched rakishly in his teeth was in excruciating pain.

Astonishingly, few Americans ever knew that Franklin D. Roosevelt was virtually wheelchair-bound and used canes to drag his legs and appear to "walk." Only three photographs of him in a wheelchair even exist. But as Anthony Badger points out, "Polio revealed great depths of resilience on the part of a privileged young man who had rarely been denied whatever he wanted. If Roosevelt felt sorry for himself, he never allowed self-pity to show."[4]

Biographer H. W. Brands shares that view: "Crushed by despair, he had clawed his way back to hope; struck down physically, he gradually regained his feet. He reentered the political arena, a fuller man for what he had lost, a deeper soul for what he had suffered. His touch with the people seemed surer, his voice more convincing."[5]

As Eleanor Roosevelt later said, "Anyone who has gone through a great suffering is bound to have a greater sympathy and understanding of the problems of mankind."[6]

His return to politics came with his election as governor of New York in 1929, and he used the office to establish his progressive credentials by easing credit for farmers and creating a Temporary Emergency Relief Administration to provide jobs for the growing numbers of unemployed. He also began to use the radio to make regular, informal addresses—the precursor to his famous presidential "fireside chats." As the economy crashed around America, the Democrats turned to Roosevelt in June 1932. With the Depression in full force, he cruised to a definitive victory over Herbert Hoover, with 57 percent of the popular vote and winning the electoral contest by a margin of 472–59, forty-two states to Hoover's six.

PRESIDENTIAL VOICES

This great Nation will endure as it has endured, will revive and will prosper. So, first of all, let me assert my firm belief that the only thing we have to fear is fear itself—nameless, unreasoning, unjustified terror which paralyzes needed efforts to convert retreat into advance.

—FRANKLIN D. ROOSEVELT,
First Inaugural, March 4, 1933[7]

What were the New Deal and the Hundred Days?

When he accepted the Democratic nomination with a ringing acceptance speech, Roosevelt promised the people a "New Deal." After his election, in his first inaugural, he told Americans they had "nothing to fear but fear itself," and he promised a special session of Congress to deal with the national economic emergency. He came through on both promises.

The centerpiece of Roosevelt's response to the Great Depression, the New Deal was a complete revolution in the American way of life. It was an unprecedented legislative agenda demanded by the rapidly sinking American economy. Between Election Day and the inauguration, the country scraped bottom. Bank closings continued as long lines of panicky depositors lined up to get at their savings. Governors around the country began to declare "bank holidays" in their states. On March 5, his first day in the White House, Roosevelt did the same thing, calling for a nationwide four-day bank holiday. That night he talked to Americans about how banking worked in the first of his "fireside chats"—radio addresses aimed at educating the public, soothing fears, and restoring the confidence and optimism of a nation that had little left.

Then he called Congress to a special emergency session. From March through June, known as the Hundred Days, the U.S. Congress passed an extraordinary series of measures, sometimes without even reading them. Roosevelt's approach was "Take a method and try it. If it fails, try another."

The result was the "alphabet soup" of new federal agencies, some of them successful, some not. The array of agencies was extraordinary:

- **The Civilian Conservation Corps (CCC)** provided jobs for young men from eighteen to twenty-five years old, in works of reforestation and other conservation.

- **The Agricultural Adjustment Administration (AAA)** was created to raise farm prices by paying farmers to take land out of production. This plan had two major drawbacks. While there were so many people starving, the nation was outraged to see pigs slaughtered and corn plowed under by government decree to push up farm prices. And thousands of mostly black sharecroppers and tenant farmers, lowest on the economic pecking order, were thrown off the land when farmers took their land out of production.

- **The Tennessee Valley Authority (TVA),** a federally run hydroelectric power program, was one of FDR's most radical departures and controversial undertakings as it introduced a new level of government-run enterprise in direct competition with private industry. The TVA produced hydroelectric power, but also built dams, produced and sold fertilizer, reforested the area, and developed recreational lands. (The TVA also created the Oak Ridge facility, which later provided much of the research and development of the atomic bomb.) At the time, most power companies were in private hands, but Roosevelt thought they were monopolies and overcharging; the TVA became one of the largest power companies in the country, and the Supreme Court upheld its constitutionality in 1936. (One man who did not like the TVA was future president Ronald Reagan. A spokesman for General Electric, Reagan was fired by GE in 1962 when he complained that the TVA was "big government." The authority was also one of GE's biggest customers.[8])

- **The Federal Deposit Insurance Corporation (FDIC),** designed to protect savings.

- **The Home Owners Loan Corporation,** which refinanced mortgages and prevented foreclosures.

- **The Federal Securities Act,** which began policing the activities of Wall Street.

- **The Securities and Exchange Commission (SEC)** was created in 1934, to regulate the stock market, and Roosevelt appointed Joseph Kennedy, a notorious speculator in his day, to be its first chief.

- **The Federal Emergency Relief Administration (FERA)** was created and given $500 million in federal relief funds for the most seriously destitute, the beginning of a federal welfare program.

- **The National Industrial Recovery Act (NIRA),** one of the final acts of the Hundred Days and the most controversial New Deal bill, aimed at stimulating industrial production and a sweeping attempt to establish government control over production, labor, and costs. With such divisive and unprecedented aims, the bill contained goodies for both business and labor organizations in order to win their support. It allowed manufacturers to create "business codes," a legal form of price-fixing that would have been forbidden under antitrust laws, while giving workers minimum wages, maximum hours, and collective bargaining rights.

When the Hundred Days came to an end with passage of the NIRA bill, the Great Depression was still far from over. But in a short time, Roosevelt had not just created a series of programs designed to prop up the economy, his New Deal marked a turning point in America as decisive as that in 1776 or 1860. It was nothing less than a revolutionary transformation of the federal government from a smallish body that had limited impact on the average American into a powerful machine that left few Americans untouched. For better or worse, Roosevelt had begun to inject the federal government into American life on an unprecedented scale, establishing a previously unthinkable reliance on government to accomplish tasks that individuals and the private economy were unwilling or unable to do. From the vantage point of the twenty-first century, there is little in modern America that is now unaffected by the decisions made in Washington. But when Franklin Roosevelt created the federal machinery to carry the country out of crisis, he was viewed by some, especially the many Republicans who deeply despised him, as a Communist leading America down the road to Moscow.

PRESIDENTIAL VOICES

*Franklin D. Roosevelt proposes to destroy the right to elect your own represen-
tatives, to talk politics on street corners, to march in political parades, to attend
the church of your faith, to be tried by jury, and to own property.*

—REPUBLICAN CANDIDATE ALF LANDON, 1936[9]

PRESIDENTIAL VOICES

*In the future days, which we seek to make secure, we look forward to a world
founded upon four essential human freedoms.*

   The first is freedom of speech and expression—*everywhere in the
   world.*

   **The second is freedom of every person to worship God in his own
   way**—*everywhere in the world.*

   The third is freedom from want—*which, translated into world
   terms, means economic understandings which will secure to every
   nation a healthy peacetime life for its inhabitants—everywhere
   in the world.*

   The fourth is freedom from fear—*which, translated into world
   terms, means a world-wide reduction of armaments to such a
   point and in such a thorough fashion that no nation will be in a
   position to commit an act of physical aggression against any
   neighbor—anywhere in the world.*

   *That is no vision of a distant millennium. It is a definite basis for a kind of
world attainable in our own time and generation. That kind of world is the
very antithesis of the so-called new order of tyranny which the dictators seek to
create with the crash of a bomb.*

                    —FRANKLIN D. ROOSEVELT
            "Four Freedoms" speech, January 6, 1941[10]

(Roosevelt delivered this State of the Union Address as America remained on the sidelines of the war against Germany and with negotiations under way to avert war with Japan. A little less than a year later, Pearl Harbor was attacked, on December 7, 1941, and the United States was fully engaged in World War II.)

How did Eleanor Roosevelt become the most influential first lady in history?

To this day, every president's wife is still measured against the standard set by Eleanor Roosevelt. While many first ladies had been influential forces in their husbands' lives before her, none had been such a visible and powerful force of change in her own right—not only in America but also on the world stage.

After a youthful life of privilege and loss—both parents and a brother died when she was very young—Eleanor Roosevelt became a social crusader. Inspired by her friend Mary Harriman, daughter of a railroad tycoon, she had become involved in the Junior League in New York City, working among New York's desperately squalid tenements.

After their marriage and his paralysis, Eleanor began to stand in as a surrogate for Franklin, making public appearances, despite the near breakup of their marriage. She became an outspoken advocate of union rights and the unions' goals of a forty-hour workweek and an end to child labor. She was also politically active, campaigning for New York governor Al Smith and then promoting Franklin's bid to replace him as governor in 1928.

In the White House years, Eleanor only increased her visibility and public role, in a way no first lady had before. As she became part of the human face of Roosevelt's New Deal programs, she began to hold press conferences, wrote a regular newspaper column, and had a daunting speaking schedule.

She was also crucial in connecting FDR to the African-American community, which since after the Civil War had been loyal to the

Republican Party as the "Party of Lincoln." While FDR had to carefully negotiate his way around the powerful Southern congressmen whose votes he needed, Eleanor could be outspoken in support of civil rights. Most famously, she invited opera singer Marian Anderson to give a concert on the steps of the Lincoln Memorial in 1939 when the conservative Daughters of the American Revolution refused to allow the African-American star the use of their Constitution Hall.

"At a time when her husband was preoccupied with winning the war, Eleanor insisted that the struggle would not be worth winning if the old order of things prevailed," wrote historian Doris Kearns Goodwin. "Unless democracy were renewed at home, she repeatedly said, there was little merit in fighting for democracy abroad. . . . Without her consistent voice at the upper levels of decision, the tendency to put first things first, to focus on winning the war before exerting effort on anything else, might well have prevailed."[11]

After the war, she became a delegate to the United Nations General Assembly and was first chairperson of the UN Commission on Human Rights, helping draft the Universal Declaration of Human Rights.

Although she was often viciously attacked and vilified by Republican opponents and was the object of hateful mail and media attacks, she remained one of the most admired and beloved people in America long after her death in 1962. And in 1999, Eleanor Roosevelt was ranked among the top ten in a Gallup poll of "Most Widely Admired People of the 20th Century."[12]

Final Judgment: Grade A+

Roosevelt's Hundred Days and the New Deal did not, as many economists and historians fairly point out, end the Great Depression. That was solved, frankly, by the other great crisis that Franklin D. Roosevelt led the nation through—the war against Germany and Japan for the survival of democracy.

There is no question that when the war came, with the attack on Pearl Harbor on December 7, 1941, it propelled America to become, in Roosevelt's words, the "arsenal of democracy." And the mobilization of millions of men to fight a world war on two fronts finally ended the Depression—of course, at enormous human cost.

Roosevelt saw the nation through the war years as he had through the economic crisis—with endless reserves of public hope and confidence.

And because of that, for much of the last half of the twentieth century, Roosevelt's place in the pantheon of greatest presidents has been secure.

But more recently, the question of Roosevelt having created a "welfare state" has had more conservative critics chipping away at that image. As questions about the size and scope of the federal government have grown in recent years, "small government" critics increasingly disdain Roosevelt's try-anything approach. From the "Reagan Revolution" of the 1980s through the recent "Tea Party" surge in Republican ranks and the increasing popularity of Ayn Rand–influenced "libertarian" philosophy that balks at big government, FDR's once-lustrous legacy has lost some of its glimmer.

But that criticism seriously overlooks how desperate times were when FDR came to office. The Depression wasn't an inconvenience in which people had to simply pull themselves up by the bootstraps. "The desperate plight of ordinary Americans exposes the wishful thinking that lies behind the criticism of the economic historians and the lamentations of the right," Anthony Badger concludes in his assessment of the Hundred Days. "Angry farmers were taking the law into their own hands to halt foreclosures. Charities and the local and state government simply could not look out after the more than a quarter of the workforce that was out of work. . . . Roosevelt and Congress did not have the luxury of such a hands-off policy."[13]

Roosevelt's solutions to the economic problems and his management of the war effort were not perfect. The lead-up to Pearl Harbor involved bureaucratic mismanagement and shortsightedness. In hindsight, it is simple, and simplistic, to overlook the crushing dangers Roosevelt and the nation faced. But there is little question that FDR's unique qualities led the nation through this period of unprecedented twin crises.

"His leadership of the home front was the essential condition of military victory," Doris Kearns Goodwin writes. "Through four years of war, despite strikes and riots, overcrowding and confusion, profiteering, black markets, prejudice, and racism, he kept the American people united in a single cause. . . . It seemed that he could truly see it all."[14]

In the decades since, other administrations of both parties have added layers of bureaucracy to what was at its inception a much less complex means to deal with America's emergency. But beneath the arguments over FDR's policies lies the fundamental question of how the government can best serve the people it supposedly exists to serve. Roosevelt believed that the cynical attitudes of the wealthiest were not the answer when Americans were on their knees.

As historian H. W. Brands eloquently summarized, "Beyond everything else he provided hope. . . . A president who speaks to the hopes and dreams of the people can change the nation. Roosevelt did speak to the people's hopes and dreams, and together they changed America. They changed the world as well. Just as he trusted democracy to reach the right decisions regarding America, so he trusted democracy to reach the right decisions about the rest of the planet."[15]

Franklin D. Roosevelt Administration Milestones[16]

1933

March 4	Roosevelt is inaugurated.
March 5	Roosevelt declares a four-day "bank holiday" to halt the panic "run" on banks.
March 9–June 16	Congress meets in what is later known as the Hundred Days.
March 31	Congress creates the Civilian Conservation Corps (CCC).
April 19	FDR takes the United States off the gold standard. The value of the dollar declines internationally, but the policy also allows more money to become available to Americans, stimulating the economy.
May 12	Congress passes the Federal Emergency Relief Act (FERA).
May 18	The Tennessee Valley Authority (TVA) is created to control flooding in the Tennessee River Valley as well

as provide electric power for rural areas which commercial power companies would not serve.

May 27 The Federal Securities Act requires all issues of stocks and bonds to be registered and approved by the federal government.

June 16 On the final day of the Hundred Days, Congress passes the National Industrial Recovery Act (NIRA), the centerpiece of Roosevelt's efforts to revive American industry. It establishes two of the early key agencies of the New Deal: the Public Works Administration (PWA) and the National Recovery Administration (NRA).

November 8 By executive order, FDR establishes the Civil Works Administration to provide work for four million unemployed Americans.

December 5 Utah becomes the thirty-sixth state to ratify the Twenty-First Amendment, bringing Prohibition to an end.

1934

June 6 The Securities and Exchange Commission is created to license stock exchanges and determine the legality of certain speculative market practices. Joseph Kennedy becomes its first chairman.

June 19 The Federal Communications Commission is created to regulate radio, telegraph, and telephone communications.

1935

May 6 FDR issues an executive order establishing the Works Progress Administration (WPA), which provides work and income for millions of Americans through the construction and repair of roads, bridges, public schools, post offices, parks, and airfields. The WPA also establishes projects to employ artists and scholars.

May 27	The Supreme Court rules that the National Industrial Recovery Act of 1933 is unconstitutional.
July 5	Under the Wagner-Connery Act, the National Labor Relations Board (NLRB) is created to ensure the right of workers to organize unions with supervised elections and to collective bargaining; its constitutionality will be upheld in 1937.
August 14	The Social Security Act is passed. It guarantees pensions to Americans over the age of sixty-five, establishes a system of unemployment insurance, and assists states in aiding dependent children, the blind, and the aged who do not already qualify for Social Security.

1936

January 6	The Supreme Court rules the Agricultural Adjustment Act is unconstitutional.
June	The Republicans nominate Kansas governor Alfred M. Landon. The Democrats renominate Roosevelt and Vice President John Nance Garner for a second term.
August	The Summer Olympics in Berlin are used by Hitler to demonstrate Nazi Germany's racial superiority. African-American sprinter Jesse Owens steals the spotlight, winning a historic four gold medals.
November 3	Roosevelt wins reelection in stunning fashion, gaining 523 electoral votes to Alf Landon's 8. FDR loses only the states of Maine and Vermont.

1937

| January 20 | In his second Inaugural Address, FDR promises to continue his fight to return the nation to economic health, stating, "I see one-third of a nation ill-housed, ill-clad, ill-nourished."[17] |
| February 5 | Following his landslide win, FDR sends a "court packing" plan to Congress. FDR wants to add as many as six justices to the Supreme Court should any of the current members over age seventy refuse to retire. But even Roosevelt's supporters balk at the legislation, which is |

seen as an attempt to interfere with the independence of
the judiciary. A watered-down measure passes.

April 12   By a narrow 5–4 majority, the Supreme Court upholds
            the National Labor Relations Act. The following
            month, the court upholds the Social Security Act,
            another victory for FDR in his battles with the court.

June 22   Joe Louis becomes World Heavyweight Champion,
            the second African-American to win the title. He will
            remain the champ until he retires in 1949.

July 2   American aviator Amelia Earhart vanishes over the
            Pacific Ocean during her round-the-world flight.

August 12   FDR appoints liberal Hugo L. Black of Alabama to the
            Supreme Court.

1938

March 13   German troops move into Austria.

June 25   The Fair Labor Standards Act raises the minimum
            wage and sets the maximum workweek at forty hours
            for businesses engaged in interstate commerce.

September 30 At the Munich Conference, the British and French
            prime ministers agree to allow Germany to annex the
            Sudetenland.

1939

March 15   The German Army invades Czechoslovakia, five and a
            half months after gaining the Sudetenland peacefully
            through the Munich pact.

June 28   Transatlantic passenger air service begins with a Pan
            American Airways flight from Long Island, New York,
            to Lisbon, Portugal.

August 23   Germany and the USSR sign a non-aggression pact in
            Moscow.

September 1 Germany launches a major invasion of Poland, starting
            the Second World War.

September 3 France and Britain declare war on Germany; FDR
            declares U.S. neutrality.

1940

April 9	The German Army invades Norway and Denmark.
May 10	Germany invades Luxembourg, the Netherlands, and Belgium. Winston Churchill also becomes the prime minister of Britain on this day, replacing the discredited Neville Chamberlain.
May 26–June 4	As the German Army sweeps across France, thousands of British and French troops converge on Dunkirk, a French coastal town, in preparation for evacuation of the country. By the time the Germans reach the beach to stop the operation, more than 330,000 troops have been evacuated.
June–July	The Republicans nominate Wendell L. Willkie for president; a popular candidate despite having never held elective office, he supports most of FDR's policies. The Democrats nominate Roosevelt in an unprecedented bid for a third term.
July 10	The Battle of Britain begins with the first bombing raids by the German Air Force.
September 16	FDR signs the Selective Training and Service Act, authorizing the first peacetime military draft in U.S. history and requiring all men between the ages of twenty-one and thirty-five to register for military training.
November 5	In a closer than expected election, FDR wins an unprecedented third term.
December 29	In a fireside chat, FDR declares that the United States must be the "arsenal of democracy."

1941

March 11	The Lend-Lease Act gives FDR power to lend arms and other war material to any country deemed vital to U.S. interests.
June 22	Germany breaks the Nazi-Soviet Non-Aggression Pact of 1939 when it invades the USSR.

| December 7 | Japanese bombers attack Pearl Harbor, the U.S. naval base in Hawaii. The attack kills twenty-four hundred soldiers, sailors, and civilians, and wounds nearly twelve hundred others. That evening, Japan will officially declare war on the United States. The next day, Roosevelt appears before a special joint session of Congress, calling December 7 a "date which will live in infamy" and asking for a declaration of war against Japan. The Senate immediately approves the declaration 82–0; the House vote is 388–1, with only Jeannette Rankin, the first woman elected to the House, opposing. The declaration of war sets FDR to directing the war effort with the full force of the American government. |
| December 11 | Germany and Italy declare war on the United States; Congress, in turn, declares war on Germany and Italy. |

1942

January 14	FDR orders all aliens in the United States to register with the federal government.
February 20	FDR formally authorizes a program to move Japanese-Americans living in the Pacific Coast states to internment camps in Colorado, Utah, and Arkansas.
June 3–6	At the Battle of Midway, the U.S. Navy establishes U.S. naval superiority as the Japanese lose a significant number of their best pilots.
June 19	FDR meets with Winston Churchill in Washington, D.C., to plan the invasion of North Africa. On November 8, four hundred thousand Allied troops will land in Morocco and Algeria, under the command of General Dwight D. Eisenhower, the newly appointed commander of U.S. forces in the European theater.
August 7	U.S. Marines land on Guadalcanal in the Solomon Islands in the Pacific.
December 2	Scientists at the University of Chicago demonstrate the first sustained nuclear chain reaction.

1943

February 7	Shoe rationing begins in the United States; each civilian is limited to three pairs of leather shoes per year.
March I	The rationing of canned goods begins; one month later, meats, fats, and cheese will also be rationed in this way.
May 16	In Poland, German troops finally subdue an uprising by Jews in Warsaw. The Germans will move the Warsaw Jews to concentration camps and level the ghetto.
June 14	The Supreme Court rules that it is unconstitutional to require children to salute the flag if doing so runs counter to their religious beliefs.
July 10	Allied forces invade Sicily.
July 25	King Victor Emmanuel of Italy forces Benito Mussolini to resign, ending Italy's role as Germany's ally in the war. Italy surrenders unconditionally on September 8.

1944

June 6	On D-Day, Operation Overlord, the invasion of Normandy, begins just after midnight, with some 4,000 invasion ships, 600 warships, 10,000 planes, and about 176,000 Allied troops; commanding the operation is American general Dwight D. Eisenhower.
June 22	The Servicemen's Readjustment Act is passed; it is better known as the "G.I. Bill of Rights."
June–July	The Republicans nominate New York Governor Thomas E. Dewey for president. FDR is nominated for an unprecedented fourth term, despite insider concerns about his failing health. Senator Harry S. Truman of Missouri is nominated for vice president.
July 1–22	At Bretton Woods, New Hampshire, delegates from forty-four nations meet for a monetary and financial conference. They establish an International Monetary

Fund (IMF) and an International Bank for Reconstruction and Development, also known as the World Bank.

August 10   The island of Guam, a U.S. territory captured by the Japanese after the attack on Pearl Harbor, falls to U.S. forces.

August 25   Allied forces liberate Paris.

November 7   FDR wins an unprecedented fourth term.

December 16   Germany launches its final offensive in what is known as the Battle of the Bulge.

1945

January 20   FDR is inaugurated for his fourth term.

February 4–11   The Yalta Conference: FDR, Churchill, and Stalin meet to discuss the final assault on Germany and the treatment of that country following the war.

February 19– March 16   U.S. Marines capture the island of Iwo Jima.

April 1–June   The U.S. Army captures Okinawa after fierce fighting.

April 12   While vacationing in Warm Springs, Georgia, President Franklin D. Roosevelt dies after suffering a massive cerebral hemorrhage. Vice President Harry Truman is sworn in as president.

MUST READS

Anthony J. Badger, *FDR: The First Hundred Days*; H. W. Brands, *Traitor to His Class: The Privileged Life and Radical Presidency of Franklin Delano Roosevelt*; Blanche Wiesen Cook, *Eleanor Roosevelt* (two volumes); Timothy Egan, *The Worst Hard Time: The Untold Story of Those Who Survived the Great American Dust Bowl*; Doris Kearns Goodwin, *No Ordinary Time: Franklin and Eleanor Roosevelt: The Home Front in World War II*.

ONLINE RESOURCES

Inaugural Addresses, Avalon Project, Yale Law School
    1933: http://avalon.law.yale.edu/20th_century/froos1.asp
    1937: http://avalon.law.yale.edu/20th_century/froos2.asp

1941: http://avalon.law.yale.edu/20th_century/froos3.asp

1945: http://avalon.law.yale.edu/20th_century/froos4.asp

Library of Congress Resource Guide

http://www.loc.gov/rr/program/bib/presidents/fdroosevelt/index
.html

Miller Center of Public Affairs, University of Virginia

http://millercenter.org/academic/americanpresident/fdroosevelt

Eleanor Roosevelt Center at Val-Kill

http://www.ervk.org/index.html

33

Give 'Em Hell Harry

Harry S. Truman

★ ★ ★

April 12, 1945–January 20, 1953

Milestones in the Life of Harry S. Truman

May 8, 1884	Born in Lamar, Missouri
1906–1917	Farmed near Grandview, Missouri
1917–1919	Commanded artillery battery in World War I
1919–1922	Owned men's clothing store in Kansas City
1923–1924	County judge of Jackson County, Missouri
1927–1934	Presiding judge of Jackson County
1935–1945	U.S. senator from Missouri
1945	Vice president under Roosevelt
1945–1953	Thirty-third president
December 26, 1972	Died in Kansas City, Missouri, aged eighty-eight

PRESIDENTIAL VOICES

Boys, if you ever pray, pray for me now. I don't know whether you fellows had a load of hay fall on you, but when they told me yesterday what had happened, I felt like the moon, the stars, and all the planets had fallen on me.

—HARRY S. TRUMAN
Remarks to reporters, April 13, 1945

Thus could not be a greater contrast between two men's backgrounds and personalities than between those of Franklin D. Roosevelt and his successor Harry S. Truman. Roosevelt was the patrician son of wealth. Harry S. Truman was the plainspoken son of a Missouri mule trader who never went to college and, like Ulysses S. Grant, had struggled to make a living. White House historian William Seale commented, "Even more than most vice presidents, he had been overshadowed by the man in the White House. At first glance, he seemed unequal to the job before him. The antithesis of the Olympian Roosevelt, he was striking for his ordinariness."[1]

When Truman took office, most Americans were in a state of shock. FDR was the only president they could remember. Despite their enormous personal differences, however, Truman pledged to carry out FDR's policies. He would just do it in his own style. It was a style famously summed up in the sign on his desk, "The buck stops here."

Fast Facts

RELIGION: Southern Baptist

ASSOCIATIONS: Freemason, Sons of the Revolution, Sons of Confederate Veterans

MILITARY SERVICE: Major; commander of an artillery battery in the Thirty-fifth Infantry Division, World War I

CAREER BEFORE POLITICS: Farmer, bank clerk, insurance salesman, haberdasher

POLITICAL PARTY: Democratic

FIRST LADY: Elizabeth "Bess" Truman (February 13, 1885–October 18, 1982)

CHILDREN: Margaret

At the age of twenty-one, when she moved into the White House, Truman's daughter first came to prominence when her father threatened to punch the nose of a music critic who had given her debut singing recital a poor notice. She went on to greater fame for a series of successful mystery novels set in and around Washington, D.C., beginning with *Murder in the White House* in 1980. Margaret Truman Daniel died in 2008.

* Truman is the only president with combat experience in World War I.
* After Grover Cleveland, Truman is the only other president who did not attend college. He attended law school briefly but dropped out.
* The Twenty-second Amendment, limiting the president to two terms, was ratified in 1951. Its terms did not apply to Truman, who could have run for a third term but was extremely unpopular in the last days of his presidency.

In 1960, Truman gave a series of lectures, later published as *Truman Speaks*, in which he denounced the Twenty-second Amendment because it made a "lame duck" out of every president serving a second term. He recalled that the amendment did not apply to him and jokingly announced, "I'm going to run again when I'm ninety."[2]

* In 1948, Truman ordered an addition built on the White House's second floor. It is known as the "Truman Balcony." Shortly after that, a floor in the White House collapsed and engineers determined that massive renovations needed to be made. The Truman family moved to nearby Blair House as the interior of the original White House was demolished and excavated for a new foundation and complete renovation, a process that took more than two years. The Trumans returned to the White House in March 1952.
* Truman's 1949 Inaugural was the first to be televised.
* A pair of Puerto Rican nationalists made an unsuccessful assassination attempt against Truman in November 1950. One of the assassins was killed, and a Secret Service agent died in the gun battle outside Blair House. The second gunman, Oscar Callazo, was sentenced to death, which was commuted to a life sentence by Truman in 1952, one week before the scheduled execution. Callazo's sentence was commuted to time served by Jimmy Carter in 1979, and he returned to Puerto Rico, where he died in 1994 at the age of eighty.[3]

PRESIDENTIAL VOICES

Within the first few months, I discovered that being a President is like riding a tiger. A man has to keep on riding or be swallowed.

Three things can ruin a man—money, power and women. I never had any money, I never wanted power, and the only woman in my life is up at the house right now.

—HARRY TRUMAN[4]

Born in Missouri on May 8, 1884, Truman grew up near Independence, outside Kansas City, the son of a mule trader. A lover of history as a boy, he dreamed of going to West Point, but his poor eyesight kept him out.

After a series of small-time clerking jobs, Truman worked on the family farm between 1906 and 1914, when, after his father's death, he tried to run a small mining company and oil business. When the nation entered the war in 1917, he went to France as part of the American Expeditionary Force and turned his Missouri artillery command into a top-notch unit. They fought at the Argonne Forest in northwest France, in one of the war's last major battles; American casualties during the fighting totaled more than one hundred thousand dead and wounded, making it one of the bloodiest battles in American history. Truman's war experience is largely credited with developing his leadership skills and a loyal following of war buddies who would support his political career.

After his return from Europe's frightful trench war, Truman went into business with one of those army buddies and opened a men's furnishings store. Although it failed after a few years, the business had made Truman a respected and well-liked local leader. Then in 1922, Thomas Pendergast, the Democratic boss and patronage king of Kansas City, who had connections to gambling and Prohibition-era bootlegging, approached him to run for a county judgeship. Uncle of one of Truman's war buddies, Pendergast wanted Truman to run precisely because of the reputation for honesty he had built as a local business-man and his strong ties to veterans' groups. Although it sounds like it required a legal background, the judgeship was more like a county commissioner job, with responsibility for roadwork and local budgets—which of course meant patronage jobs for Pendergast to dole out. Despite his association with the rather notorious Pendergast, Truman established a reputation for personal integrity, honesty, and efficiency. But he could not escape being seen as a Pendergast puppet when elected to the U.S. Senate in 1934. (Pendergast was convicted of tax evasion in 1940 and died five years later. Despite his notoriety, Truman, then vice president, attended his funeral.)

From the Senate, Truman was later selected as FDR's running mate in 1942, and eighty-two days after FDR's historical fourth inaugura-tion, Harry S. Truman was president. A few weeks later, the end of the war with Germany came in May. But the war with Japan continued. And one of Truman's first decisions was going to be whether or not Ameri-cans would invade Japan. That decision meant he had to choose whether or not to use the atomic bomb—a bomb he had not known existed until he became president.

PRESIDENTIAL VOICES

We have discovered the most terrible bomb in the history of the world. It may be the fire destruction prophesied in the Euphrates valley Ersa, after Noah and his fabulous Ark.

This weapon is to be used against Japan between now and August 10th. I have told the Sec. of War, Mr. Stimson, to use it so that military objectives and soldiers and sailors are the target and not women and children. Even if the Japs are savages, ruthless, merciless and fanatic, we as the leaders of the world for the common welfare cannot drop this terrible bomb on the old Capital or the new.

He & I are in accord. The target will be a purely military one and we will

*issue a warning statement asking the Japs to surrender and save lives. I'm
sure they will not do that, but we will give them the chance. It is certainly a
good thing for the world that Hitler's crowd or Stalin's did not discover this
atomic bomb. It seems to be the most terrible thing ever discovered, but it can
be made to be the most useful.*

—HARRY S. TRUMAN
Diary entry, June 1945[5]

What great threat did Truman face after World War II?

May 7, 1945. The War in Europe was over. Twenty million Soviet soldiers and civilians were dead. Eight million British and Europeans had
been killed, along with another five million Germans. The Nazis had
murdered six million Jews in ghettoes or concentration camps. For the
second time in a generation, Europe had become what historian Richard Rhodes once called "a charnel house."[6]

By June 1, Truman had apparently made his decision to use the
atomic bomb to end the war with Japan. But the bomb had not yet been
tested. Once the bomb had been successfully detonated in the New
Mexico desert, the decision to use it moved forward, a fateful choice
that was set against the recent American experience on Okinawa, where
more than 12,500 Americans and more than 100,000 Japanese had died
in brutal combat. When the Japanese said they would fight to the death
rather than make an unconditional surrender, the final decision was
cast. Winston Churchill later summarized the decision: "To avert a
vast, indefinite butchery."

PRESIDENTIAL VOICES

*Sixteen hours ago an American airplane dropped one bomb on Hiroshima. . . .
It is an atomic bomb. It is a harnessing of the basic power of the universe. . . .
We are now prepared to obliterate more rapidly and completely every produc-
tive enterprise the Japanese have above ground in any city. We shall destroy*

their docks, their factories, and their communications. Let there be no mistake;
we shall completely destroy Japan's power to make war.
—HARRY S. TRUMAN
White House release, Monday, August 6, 1945, 11 a.m.

Early reports indicated that 60 percent of the city of Hiroshima had been leveled. The estimated death toll was eighty thousand people killed instantly and another sixty thousand who died in the next few months. Of those, ten thousand were Japanese soldiers.[7] As many as 90 percent of Hiroshima's nurses and doctors also died instantly in the bombing. (By 1950, according to a U.S. Energy Department estimate, as many as two hundred thousand people had died as a result of cancer and other long-terms effects of radiation, little understood at the time.)

On August 9, a second atomic bomb—a plutonium bomb—was dropped on the city of Nagasaki, a southern Japanese seaport. The decision had been made earlier and was never questioned after the dropping of the first bomb. Estimates of deaths there reached eighty thousand by the end of 1945.

On August 14, Japan announced its surrender to the Allies.

When World War II ended, the victory over Germany and Japan was tempered for Americans by a new threat. Communism was on the march around the globe. In one of the first tests of U.S. resolve, the Soviets had tried to close off Berlin, forcing the United States to conduct a massive airlift in 1948 that finally cracked the Russian hold on the city. In China, Mao's Communist forces crushed the Nationalists in 1949. Around that time, it was also revealed that the Soviets had the atomic bomb. The world seemed to be in the grasp of a Communist conspiracy for international domination, and the president responded with what became known as the "Truman Doctrine," the beginning of America's all-out postwar efforts to "contain" Communism, usually with the support of a bipartisan Congress.

The fear of Communism in America was not new to this postwar period. Americans had been battling the "Red Menace" for years, and the first wave of Communist hysteria had followed World War I. But it seemed as if the fears were much more real now, heightened by the threat of atomic war. Communism was the cutting issue on which people voted. To be "soft" on Communism was political suicide. Responding to pressure, Truman had set up loyalty boards in 1947 to check on reports of Communist sympathizers in the federal government. Thousands were investigated, but there was no meaningful trace of subversion.

PRESIDENTIAL VOICES

The very existence of the Greek state is today threatened by the terrorist activities of several thousand armed men, led by Communists, who defy the government's authority at a number of points, particularly along the northern boundaries. . . . Meanwhile, the Greek Government is unable to cope with the situation. The Greek army is small and poorly equipped. It needs supplies and equipment if it is to restore authority to the government throughout Greek territory.

Greece must have assistance if it is to become a self-supporting and self-respecting democracy.

The United States must supply this assistance. . . . There is no other country to which democratic Greece can turn.

—HARRY TRUMAN, MARCH 12, 1947[8]

Truman's speech about the threat to democracy in Greece and Turkey marked the unofficial beginnings of the Cold War—a phrase first used in a Senate hearing in October 1948—during which the United States was going to contain Communism through a combination of diplomacy, economic measures, and military strategies. This policy would be used instead of a direct attempt to "roll back" Communism with outright warfare. Congress appropriated the money Truman requested then and again in 1948 for the Marshall Plan, designed to restore postwar Europe's economies. Containment also led to the creation of the North Atlantic Treaty Organization (NATO) in April 1949, a military alliance established as a counterforce to the Soviet armies stationed in Eastern Europe.

Who was Alger Hiss and what were the "Pumpkin Papers"?

The fear of Communism came home in 1949, when Whittaker Chambers (1901–1961), a repentant Communist Party member and later a senior editor at *Time* magazine, charged that Alger Hiss, a Roosevelt New Dealer with impeccable credentials and a long, distinguished public career, was a member of the Communist Party and part of a high-reaching Soviet spy ring. The charge was shocking to those who knew Hiss. Beginning as a law clerk under Supreme Court Justice Oliver Wendell Holmes, Hiss was known as a well-educated progressive. But to conservatives, Hiss carried a taint because he was secretary general of the United Nations organizing conference in 1945–46, increasingly viewed as part of the Communist scheme for weakening America.

Chambers claimed that Hiss was a Communist who had given him classified documents to be passed on to Moscow in the 1930s. Pressed on this issue by Congressman Richard Nixon in a 1948 hearing before the House Un-American Activities Committee (HUAC), Hiss denied the allegations.

But Chambers then produced microfilm copies of stolen State Department documents that he testified Hiss had given him. Chambers had hidden the material inside a hollowed-out pumpkin on his Maryland farm. Overnight, these became the "Pumpkin Papers."

Claiming that he didn't know Chambers and that his reputation had been damaged, Hiss sued Chambers for slander. But in the courtroom, Chambers proved he knew Hiss, and in the wake of the failed suit, Hiss was indicted for perjury, for lying to a congressional committee. (The statute of limitations protected Hiss from espionage charges.) Tried and convicted for perjury in January 1950, Hiss was sentenced to five years in prison and served three years before his release in 1954.

Hiss's downfall elevated Richard Nixon. As Sam Tanenhaus wrote in his monumental biography of Chambers, "Nixon was motivated by more than dislike of Hiss. He also saw a political opportunity. . . . Since his arrival in Washington [Nixon] had been diligently throwing out lines to its dense network of Red hunters. . . . With brilliant clarity, Nixon grasped that the emerging Chambers-Hiss mystery could yield great political dividends for the man who solved it. And so he pitched himself into the case with methodical intensity few in Washington—or anywhere—could match."[9]

The Hiss case was followed by revelations of spying in the trial of the Rosenbergs, a couple accused of turning over atomic secrets to the Soviets. The couple was tried and then executed in 1953. By then, Wisconsin Senator Joseph McCarthy had heightened the fear, anxiety, and paranoia about Communism in the United States with his charges that Truman's State Department was riddled with Communists and that even Secretary of State George Marshall was guilty of treason. McCarthy's charges were eagerly abetted by a press that either agreed wholeheartedly with McCarthy or simply enjoyed the spectacle he presented, which was selling newspapers. In his social and political chronicle of the 1950s, David Halberstam wrote of the much-feared and loathed senator, "He had a talent for imagining conspiracy and subversion. . . . He knew instinctively how to brush aside the protests of his witnesses, how to humiliate vulnerable, scared people. In the end, he produced little beyond fear and headlines."[10]

Truman and McCarthy battled privately and publicly. But the Republicans had a visceral issue in the Communist fear, although Truman branded McCarthy and other isolationist Republicans as "animals." Believing that McCarthy's charges were spreading fear and division, Truman told a March 1948 press conference, "I think the greatest asset that the Kremlin has is Senator McCarthy."[11]

Truman thought that the Senate he had served in for so long would rein McCarthy in, but nothing he said diminished McCarthy and other Republicans who eagerly seized the issue, keeping Truman constantly on the defensive.[12]

When is a "police action" like a war?

As if Hiss, the Rosenbergs, and McCarthyism weren't enough to strike fear into 1950s America, ninety thousand North Koreans did the trick. In June 1950, after a large-scale artillery barrage, the sound of bugles signaled the massed charge of North Koreans, armed and trained by the

Soviets, who came down from the mountains to roll over an American-sponsored government in South Korea.

This was the onset of the Korean War, a "hot war" in the midst of the Cold War maneuvering, and one that cost more than two million Korean lives as well as one hundred thousand American casualties. But it wasn't a war, as Harry Truman told reporters repeatedly in a June 1950 press conference. Asked several times by reporters if it was a "police action," Truman replied that it was.

Whatever Truman labeled it, for Americans at home in the 1950s, Korea was not like the "good war." Korea was a far-off mystery, and fighting for containment lacked the moral urgency that had been behind the crusade against the Nazi scourge and the "murderers" of Pearl Harbor.

The Asian Communists were assumed in 1950 to be part of a worldwide Communist conspiracy that reached right into the heart of America's government—as Senator McCarthy was setting out to prove in dramatic televised hearings. The United States actually fought in Korea under a United Nations flag. The fighting started out against the North Koreans, but it quickly escalated into a much deadlier and more dangerous war against the massive armies of Red China.

At home, "hawks" supported total commitment to the effort and were led by General Douglas MacArthur and the powerful "China lobby" of senators, and media moguls like Henry Luce, who wanted all-out war against Communism—including an assault on Mao's China. In one of the most dramatic moments of the Korean War, Truman fired General MacArthur, a World War II hero, a presidential aspirant, and then one of the most popular men in America, for insubordination. MacArthur wanted Truman to drop thirty to fifty atomic bombs on Manchuria and mainland China. A great general and World War II icon in most Americans' eyes, MacArthur publicly rebuked Truman's decision not to commit air power to attacking China and the president's war strategy in general. The fired general came home to a hero's welcome, and Truman's approval ratings plummeted.

With his popularity at around 22 percent, Truman was done in by reports of corruption in his administration and the increasingly unpopular "war" in Korea. His departure opened the way for a Republican—Dwight D. Eisenhower.

Final Judgment: Grade A

Harry S. Truman's very low popularity when he left office also dogged his legacy for years. He was, first of all, seen in relation to his predecessor, FDR, who was routinely viewed as one of the three greatest presidents in American history. Truman was also criticized for "allowing" Communism to flourish, "losing China," and letting Communists have free rein in America. The lack of a clear-cut victory in Korea also weighed on his reputation.

But in recent years, Truman's reputation and legacy have been revived. One reason was an acclaimed 1992 biography by David McCullough in which the historian wrote, "In just three months in office Harry Truman had been faced with a greater surge of history, with larger, more difficult, more far-reaching decisions than any President before him. Neither Lincoln after first taking office, nor Franklin Roosevelt in his tumultuous first hundred days, had had to contend with issues of such magnitude and coming all at once."[13]

And as journalist David Halberstam wrote in assessing Truman, "Unprepared he may have been, but he turned out to have the right qualities: the ability to take considerable pressure, and, if need be, to wave aside the momentary political advantage to do what he thought was right in the long run. In a way, his early failures helped him to empathize with his fellow Americans and allowed him to arrive in the White House without the overweening ambition and distorted values that often distinguish those who devote themselves to the singular pursuit of success."[14]

His common sense and plainspoken honesty—he hated "stuffed shirts," "two-dollar words," and "weasel words"—have all added to Truman's presidential stature. His controversial decision to desegregate the armed forces is seen as one of the most important steps in American racial progress of the last century. His recognition of Israel immediately after it declared its independence is also praised. And the Marshall Plan to rebuild Europe is credited as one of the greatest foreign policy successes in American history.

But it was his approach to fighting the Cold War that has received the greatest recalculation now that the Soviet Union no longer exists. As presidential historian Robert Dallek concluded in assessing Truman:

"By 1991, the collapse of the Soviet Union had vindicated Truman's judgment on the wisdom of containing rather than fighting an all-out war with the Communists, as MacArthur had urged. His contribution to victory in the cold war without a devastating nuclear conflict elevated him to the stature of a great or near-great president."[15]

Truman Administration Milestones[16]

1945

April 12	President Franklin D. Roosevelt dies in Warm Springs, Georgia; Harry S. Truman becomes the thirty-third president.
May 8	Germany surrenders, ending World War II in Europe.
August 6	The United States drops an atomic bomb on Hiroshima, Japan.
August 9	The United States drops an atomic bomb on Nagasaki, Japan.
August 14	Japan surrenders, ending World War II in Asia.

1946

March 5	In a speech at Westminster College in Fulton, Missouri, Winston Churchill says an "Iron Curtain" has fallen across Eastern Europe.

1947

March 12	Truman delivers his "Truman Doctrine" speech.
March 21	Truman creates the Federal Employee Loyalty Program via Executive Order 9835. Designed to root out Communist influence in the federal government, it gives the FBI wide freedom to investigate federal employees or applicants.
April 15	Jackie Robinson plays his first game with the Brooklyn Dodgers and integrates major-league baseball.
June 5	George Marshall proposes economic aid to Europe in an address at Harvard University; the package becomes known as the Marshall Plan.

June 20	Truman vetoes the Taft-Hartley Act, which places limits on union activities and rights. Congress overrides Truman's veto.
June 29	Truman becomes the first president to address the NAACP.
July 26	The National Security Act passes: it creates the National Security Council, the Central Intelligence Agency, the Department of Defense, and the National Security Resources Board.

1948

April 2	Congress passes the European Recovery Program known as the Marshall Plan.
May 14	The United States recognizes the state of Israel.
June 24	The Soviet Union blockades overland access into West Berlin.
	The Republicans nominate Governor Thomas Dewey of New York.
June 26	In a joint operation with the British, Truman orders an airlift of supplies into West Berlin.
July 15	Truman accepts the Democratic Party nomination.
July 17	The States Rights Party—former Democrats who object to a civil rights plank in the Democratic platform—nominates segregationist Strom Thurmond of South Carolina for president. They are known as "Dixiecrats."
July 26	At the opening of a special session of the eightieth Congress, Truman asks for legislation on housing, civil rights, and price controls. The same day, the president signs Executive Order 9981, which desegregates the armed forces.
August	Whittaker Chambers testifies to the House Un-American Activities Committee that Alger Hiss, a former high-ranking official in the State Department, is a Soviet spy. Hiss sues Chambers for slander.

September 6– October 30	Trailing Dewey in the polls, Truman attacks the "do-nothing" Republican-controlled Congress with a ten-thousand-mile "Whistle Stop" tour across the United States.
November 2	In one of the most surprising finishes in presidential history, Truman defeats Dewey and the Democrats retake both the Senate and the House of Representatives.

1949

January 5	Truman proposes the basics of what will be called the "Fair Deal": It includes extension of Social Security benefits, an increase in the minimum wage, aid to education, housing projects for the poor, and national health insurance. He also pushes hard for civil rights laws to protect blacks from discrimination. Combined Republican and Southern Democrat opposition blocks most of these proposals from becoming law.
April 4	Twelve nations from Europe and North America sign the North Atlantic Treaty.
May 12	The Soviet Union lifts the Berlin blockade.
September 23	Truman announces that the Soviet Union has detonated an atomic bomb.
October 1	Mao Zedong announces the establishment of the People's Republic of China.

1950

January 21	Alger Hiss is convicted on two counts of perjury for lying to a congressional committee.
February 9	Republican Senator Joseph McCarthy of Wisconsin charges that the State Department employs 205 known Communists.
February 14	Chairman Mao and Stalin sign the Sino-Soviet Alliance.
June 25	North Korea invades South Korea.
June 30	Truman announces that he has ordered American ground forces stationed in Japan to Korea. General

Douglas MacArthur commands the U.S. (and United Nations) troops.

September 15   U.S. forces launch a successful counterattack at Inchon, South Korea.

September 23   Congress passes the Internal Security Act over Truman's veto. It requires Communists to register with the government.

November 26   China launches a massive counteroffensive against American advances in North Korea.

December 16   Proclaiming a state of national emergency, Truman imposes wage and price controls.

1951

April 5   Julius and Ethel Rosenberg are sentenced to death following their convictions on conspiring to provide secret information to the Soviet Union.

April 11   Truman relieves General Douglas MacArthur from his command of both U.S. and U.N. forces in Korea.

June 25   The first color television program is broadcast, but no color sets are available for sale.

1952

March 29   Truman declares that he will not run for another term.

April 8   Truman signs an executive order directing the secretary of commerce to seize steel mills in order to prevent a strike by steelworkers.

June 2   The Supreme Court declares the seizure of steel mills unconstitutional.

July 11   General Dwight D. Eisenhower receives the Republican nomination.

July 26   Illinois governor Adlai Stevenson receives the Democratic nomination.

November 1   The United States detonates the first hydrogen bomb.

November 4   Dwight D. Eisenhower is elected president.

MUST READS
Robert Dallek, *Harry S. Truman*; David McCullough, *Truman*; Sam
Tanenhaus, *Whittaker Chambers: A Biography*.

ONLINE RESOURCES
Inaugural Address, Avalon Project, Yale Law School
    http://avalon.law.yale.edu/20th_century/truman.asp
Library of Congress Resource Guide
    http://www.loc.gov/rr/program/bib/presidents/truman/index.html
Truman National Historic Site, National Park Service
    http://www.nps.gov/hstr/
Truman Library and Museum
    http://www.trumanlibrary.org/
Miller Center of Public Affairs, University of Virginia
    http://millercenter.org/academic/americanpresident/truman
"Times Topics," *New York Times*: Harry S. Truman
    http://topics.nytimes.com/top/reference/timestopics/people/t
    /harry_s_truman/index.html
Alger Hiss Case, University of Missouri Famous Trials Site
    http://law2.umkc.edu/faculty/projects/ftrials/hiss/hisschronology
    .html

34

Ike

Dwight David Eisenhower

* * *

January 20, 1953–January 20, 1961

Milestones in Dwight D. Eisenhower's Life

October 14, 1890	Born in Denison, Texas
1917–1918	Commander, U.S. Army Tank Training School
1932–1935	Senior military assistant to General Douglas MacArthur, U.S. Army chief of staff
1935–1939	Senior military assistant to General MacArthur in the Philippines
1941	Chief of Staff, Third Army
1942	Commanding general, U.S. Forces in Europe
1943–1945	Supreme commander, Allied Expeditionary Forces in Europe
1945–1948	Chief of staff, U.S. Army
1948–1950	President of Columbia University
1951–1952	Supreme commander of NATO Forces in Europe
1953–1961	Thirty-fourth president
March 28, 1969	Died at Walter Reed Army Hospital in Washington, D.C., aged seventy-eight

PRESIDENTIAL VOICES

What can the world, or any nation in it, hope for if no turning is found on this dread road? The worst to be feared and the best to be expected can be simply stated.

The worst is atomic war. . . .

Every gun that is made, every warship launched, every rocket fired signifies, in the final sense, a theft from those who hunger and are not fed, those who are cold and are not clothed. This world in arms is not spending money alone. . . .

The cost of one modern heavy bomber is this: a modern brick school in more than 30 cities. It is two electric power plants, each serving a town of 60,000 population. It is two fine, fully equipped hospitals. It is some 50 miles of concrete highway. We pay for a single fighter plane with a half million bushels of wheat. We pay for a single destroyer with new homes that could have housed more than 8,000 people.

This is not a way of life at all, in any true sense. Under the cloud of threatening war, it is humanity hanging from a cross of iron.

—DWIGHT D. EISENHOWER
"Chance for Peace" speech, April 16, 1953[1]

Three simple words said it all. "I like Ike."

His presidential campaign slogan that adorned millions of buttons summed up how America felt about this genial father-figure president who was a revered hero to a generation. Ike was one of the most admired men not only in America, but in the whole world for his role in the Allied victory in World War II. To the so-called Greatest Generation, Ike was the greatest of all.

His easygoing amiability caused some to complain that he slept through eight years of America's rapid postwar expansion. But historians now give him higher marks for guiding the country through some of the most dangerous early years of the Cold War.

Coming to office on a promise of bringing American troops home from Korea, the former general who once ordered hundreds of thousands of men into battle committed American troops overseas only once. And when he left office, he would famously warn about the dangers of a "military-industrial complex."

Fast Facts

RELIGION: Presbyterian

EDUCATION: U.S. Military Academy, West Point

MILITARY SERVICE: Supreme commander, Allied Forces in Europe, World War II

CAREER BEFORE POLITICS: Soldier, university president

POLITICAL PARTY: Republican

FIRST LADY: Mamie Geneva Doud Eisenhower (November 14, 1896–November 1, 1979)

CHILDREN: Doud ("Icky"), their firstborn son, died of scarlet fever at three. Like his father, John Sheldon Doud Eisenhower attended West Point, and he is a prominent military historian. He made headlines in 2004 when he announced he would vote for Democrat John Kerry instead of George W. Bush for president.

* Eisenhower was the last president born in the nineteenth century.
* Ike played army football, but his career was cut short by a broken leg, and so he became a cheerleader instead. No pom-poms.
* Eisenhower was the first president to be constitutionally prevented from standing for reelection following ratification of the Twenty-second Amendment; the amendment originated, according to journalist Tom Wicker, "in the Republican Eighty-second Congress as partisan, posthumous revenge against a hated Democrat, Franklin D. Roosevelt, and his four terms."[2]
* The last two of the fifty states were admitted under Eisenhower: Alaska (January 1959) and Hawaii (August 1959).
* At seventy, Eisenhower was the oldest president at that time; the youngest elected president, John F. Kennedy, succeeded him.
* During his presidency, Eisenhower suffered both a heart attack and a stroke, and was temporarily incapacitated. However, news of both health problems was made public, unlike Woodrow Wilson's stroke. The Twenty-fifth Amendment, which revised and clarified the rules of presidential succession and allowed for temporary disabilities, was not ratified until 1967, and while Vice President

Nixon was acting as executive, he lacked real constitutional authority to do so.

PRESIDENTIAL VOICES

A landing was made this morning on the coast of France by troops of the Allied Expeditionary Force. This landing is part of the concentrated United Nations plans for the liberation of Europe, made in conjunction with our great Russian allies. . . . I call upon all who love freedom to stand with us now. Together we shall achieve victory.

—DWIGHT D. EISENHOWER,
Radio broadcast on D-Day, June 6, 1944

Born in Texas but raised in Kansas, Dwight D. Eisenhower grew up on a hardscrabble farm where all the boys worked to make ends meet. His father had moved the family to Texas after a failed business venture, and there cleaned locomotives, before returning the family to Kansas when an in-law offered him a job at a creamery. Although he was raised by a pacifist mother, Ike decided to take the service academy exams when a good friend was accepted into the U.S. Naval Academy. Eisenhower won an appointment to the U.S. Military Academy.

After graduating from West Point, Eisenhower experienced several years of frustration as World War I had ended a week before he was scheduled to go to Europe. Clearly attracting the attention of superiors with his organizational and leadership skills, he gradually won assignments and promotions, serving as a military aide to General John J. Pershing, a World War I hero, and then to General Douglas MacArthur in the Philippines. One of the most controversial generals in history, MacArthur taught Eisenhower mastery of details. He also gave Eisenhower a determination to avoid politics.

What followed was a meteoric rise through the ranks. Given his first star and promoted to brigadier general shortly before the United

States entered World War II, Eisenhower went to Washington, D.C., to work as a planning officer for army chief of staff General George C. Marshall. After working on several important command assignments, he was tasked with planning and overseeing the invasion of North Africa—Operation Torch—as a prelude to the invasion of Normandy.

By 1944, Ike was supreme commander of Operation Overlord, the Allied assault on Nazi-occupied Europe. In only five years, he had risen from a lowly lieutenant colonel in the Philippines to commander of the greatest invasion force in history. When he returned home in 1945 to serve as chief of staff of the army, Eisenhower was an international hero. He was, as Tom Wicker wrote, "simply the conqueror of Hitler, the man who had brought victory in World War II—a typical American who had risen to a demanding occasion by hard work and high merit."[3]

Both parties hoped that Eisenhower would join their ticket. Truman even offered to run in second place if Eisenhower wanted to join him on the Democratic ticket in 1948.[4] Eisenhower refused and instead became president of Columbia University and then, after the outbreak of the Korean War, the first supreme commander of NATO Forces in Europe. In 1952, he declared that he was a Republican and returned home to win his party's presidential nomination, with Richard M. Nixon as his running mate. "Ike" endeared himself to the American people with his plain talk, charming smile, and sense of confidence. He easily beat Democrat Adlai Stevenson in 1952 and again in 1956.

His eight years were dominated by the Cold War. Few policy decisions, foreign or domestic, were made without taking the competition with the Soviet Union into account. Although tensions eased slightly in 1953 when the murderous Soviet dictator Josef Stalin died and was replaced by Nikita Khrushchev, every international hot spot was now infused with Cold War tensions, heightened by the fact that there was also a nuclear arms race, as well as a space race. That reality came home when the Soviets shocked America by launching *Sputnik*, the first man-made satellite, in 1957. Suddenly, the Soviets, who seemed backward and technologically inept, had taken a great leap in front of the United States.

PRESIDENTIAL VOICES

This unwarranted exercise of power by the Court, contrary to the Constitution, is creating chaos and confusion in the States principally affected. It is destroying the amicable relations between the white and Negro races that have been created through 90 years of patient effort by the good people of both races. It has planted hatred and suspicion where there has been heretofore friendship and understanding.

FROM THE "SOUTHERN MANIFESTO"
Signed by ninety-nine Democratic senators and representatives
March 1956

Why did Eisenhower send troops to Little Rock?

While Eisenhower's eight years were largely dominated by the tension and conflicts that emerged from the Cold War competition with the Soviet Union, the long-deferred question of meaningful civil rights for black Americans was coming to a boiling point.

First came the landmark *Brown v. Board of Education* decision, announced by Chief Justice Earl Warren, an Eisenhower appointee, in May 1954. That ruling ordered schools to desegregate. (A second Supreme Court ruling related to Brown ordered desegregation "with all deliberate speed.") The Brown decision was followed by the 1955 arrest of Rosa Parks for refusing to give up her bus seat to a white person in Montgomery, Alabama, and the yearlong bus boycott led by the rising young civil rights leader Martin Luther King, Jr.

But as the Supreme Court decisions and Martin Luther King made history, the Eisenhower White House stood on the sidelines.

Ike was fearful of alienating the powerful bloc of "Dixiecrats," the Southern Democratic congressmen who had signed the "Southern Manifesto" protesting the Brown decision and whose votes Eisenhower needed. He was ambiguous in his public comments, promising to uphold the laws of the land but refraining from endorsing the court's rulings. At the time, a more authoritative stance, decisive stroke, or even an expression of moral outrage at Jim Crow conditions from this popular president might have given the Civil Rights Movement additional vigor and force. Instead, Eisenhower was ultimately forced to act, with great reluctance, in a showdown that was more about presidential power than about the rights of black children.

In September 1957, nine black students were going to enter previously all-white Little Rock Central High under court order. On American television and all over the world, people watched as the first group of children walked toward the school and were turned away under orders from Arkansas governor Orval Faubus. When a federal district court order forced Faubus to allow the children into the school, the governor withdrew the Arkansas state guard, leaving the protection of the black children to a small contingent of resentful local policemen, some of whom refused to carry out the order. Again, as the press watched and television cameras rolled, the children walked to the school, only to be screamed at and spat on.

To defend the sovereignty of the federal court, Eisenhower ordered eleven hundred paratroopers from the 101st Airborne to Little Rock and placed the state national guard under his direct orders. For the first time since Reconstruction, U.S. troops were in the South to protect the rights of blacks. Eisenhower had not acted out of concern for the students' rights or safety, but because he believed that he couldn't allow the force of federal law to be ignored.

"Ike was very much in conflict within himself whether integration was right or wrong," wrote David Halberstam. "His essential sympathies were with neither the nine children nor the mob in the street but primarily with his new and extremely wealthy and conservative Southern golfing and hunting friends who found integration objectionable. As such the President remained silent on the issue and continued to dally. . . . He saw even the smallest change in the existing racial order as radical and upsetting."[5]

Ike's admirers see the dispatch of the Airborne as proof of his resolve. Other critics say he moved too slowly. But the troops remained at Little Rock Central High for the rest of the school year, and eight of the black students stayed through the year despite curses, harassment, and abuse. Whatever else it proved, Little Rock showed that the Civil

Rights Movement was going to need the full force of the federal government to enforce the new racial reality that the Supreme Court had created.

PRESIDENTIAL VOICES

In the councils of government, we must guard against the acquisition of unwarranted influence, whether sought or unsought, by the military-industrial complex. The potential for the disastrous rise of misplaced power exists and will persist.

We must never let the weight of this combination endanger our liberties or democratic processes. We should take nothing for granted. Only an alert and knowledgeable citizenry can compel the proper meshing of the huge industrial and military machinery of defense with our peaceful methods and goals, so that security and liberty may prosper together.

—DWIGHT D. EISENHOWER
Farewell Address, January 17, 1961[6]

Final Judgment: Grade A

Initially dismissed by historians as a complacent, "do-nothing" president who slept through eight years in office, Eisenhower has moved up the ranks in more recent historical judgments. Reflecting the revision of Ike's presidential status in a laudatory biography, Michael Korda writes, "It is hard to think of any other political figure who was so immersed in every detail of foreign defense and domestic policies, or who went to such lengths to ensure what was done in his name represented exactly what he wanted done. . . . He was briefed on every detail of the CIA's buildup of a Cuban anti-Castro force, and fully approved of the intention; but he insisted that no landing should take place until the Cuban exiles had produced a viable and popular government in exile."[7]

Eisenhower saw the nation through eight years of relative prosperity and peace, and kept the Cold War from going hot. When the French were losing battles in Vietnam, he saw Vietnam for what it was and did not want to commit American troops there. His successors were not as wise.

One of his more "concrete" accomplishments might be one of his greatest legacies: the Interstate highway system. It is difficult to imagine an America before these roads created tremendous opportunity for economic expansion. The success of the highway system is also a reminder that there are things big government does do well.

On the other side of the ledger stand some missteps. Under Eisenhower, the CIA was allowed to run roughshod with covert operations, flush with its "success" after toppling Iran's elected government and installing the pro-American shah in 1953. Though deemed an initial victory, that CIA-led coup ultimately helped lay the groundwork for the Iranian Revolution twenty-five years later.

Near the end of his term, Ike also wanted to defuse tensions with the Soviet Union with a 1959 summit meeting. But the plans were dropped when an American U-2 spy plane was shot down by the Soviets.

Although recent documents reveal Eisenhower working behind the scenes to blunt Joseph McCarthy, Ike never publicly challenged the senator as he began his vitriolic and dangerous campaign against Communist subversion in America. The "Great Fear" that gripped the country in the 1950s would ruin lives and careers with "guilt by association." The mere suggestion or allegation of complicity with a Communist Party member meant "blacklisting" for at least three hundred people in Hollywood. The accusations flew with little regard for due process or other Constitutional rights. Only when McCarthy threatened the army, and even then belatedly, was Eisenhower willing to risk a collision with the anti-Communist wing of his party—and then hardly with the full force of his authority. After the "Army-McCarthy" Senate hearings were televised live, McCarthy's fortunes turned. He was censured by the Senate in 1954 and died in Bethesda Naval Hospital in 1957.

Eisenhower was also deemed less than heroic when it came to leadership on civil rights—the great moral issue of his day. As Tom Wicker wrote, "Eisenhower enforced the law in Little Rock, but never found it within himself to speak for the equality of the races."[8]

Before leaving office, Eisenhower gave a halfhearted blessing to Vice President Richard M. Nixon as he ran against John F. Kennedy in 1960. Then he retired to his farm near Gettysburg, Pennsylvania, to write and play golf. Having suffered heart trouble throughout his presidency, Ike died of heart failure in 1969.

Eisenhower Administration Milestones[9]

1953

January 20	Dwight D. Eisenhower is inaugurated.
March 5	The Soviet Union announces the death of Josef Stalin.
March 17	All price controls officially ended by the Office of Price Stabilization.
April 1	The Department of Health, Education, and Welfare is created.
June 19	Julius and Ethel Rosenberg are executed.
July 26	Eisenhower announces an armistice in Korea.
August 1	Eisenhower proposes broadening the provisions of the Social Security Act to cover more than ten million additional Americans.
August 7	Eisenhower signs the Refugee Relief Act of 1953, admitting 214,000 more immigrants than permitted under existing immigration quotas.
August 19	With CIA support, Iranians overthrow the government of Prime Minister Mohammad Mossadegh, bringing the shah to power.
September 30	Eisenhower appoints Earl Warren chief justice.
October 8	Eisenhower announces that the Soviet Union has tested a hydrogen bomb.

1954

April 23–June 17	The televised Army-McCarthy hearings begin.
May 7	France surrenders its garrison at Dien Bien Phu to the Vietminh.

May 17	*Brown v. Topeka Board of Education*: The Supreme Court overturns racial segregation in public schools.
June 18	A CIA-sponsored coup overthrows the government of Guatemala.
December 2	The Senate votes to censure Senator Joseph McCarthy.

1955

March 16	Eisenhower announces that the United States would use atomic weapons in the event of war with Communist China.
May 31	In *Brown II*, the Supreme Court orders schools integrated "with all deliberate speed."
November 25	The Interstate Commerce Commission bans racial segregation on interstate trains and buses.
December 1	Rosa Parks is arrested in Montgomery, Alabama, for refusing to give up her seat on a bus to a white man. Led by Reverend Martin Luther King, Jr., the African-American community organizes a boycott of the city's buses that lasts for more than a year.
December 5	The merger of the American Federation of Labor (AFL) and the Congress of Industrial Organizations (CIO) is ratified.

1956

March 12	Nineteen senators and eighty-one representatives sign the "Southern Manifesto," promising to use "all lawful means" to reverse the two *Brown* decisions.
May 31	Eisenhower approves U-2 spy flights over the Soviet Union.
June 4	A three-judge district court rules that bus segregation in Montgomery, Alabama, is unconstitutional.
June 29	Eisenhower signs the Federal Aid Highway Act, providing federal funding for the construction of the interstate highway system.
August 1	The Salk polio vaccine is sold on the open market.

August 13– August 17	The Democrats nominate Adlai Stevenson for president.
August 21	Eisenhower accepts nomination as the Republican candidate.
November 4	The Soviet Union crushes the Hungarian Revolution.
November 6	Eisenhower defeats Stevenson to win a second term.

1957

January 6	Elvis Presley makes his third appearance on *The Ed Sullivan Show*; network executives decide to show him only from the waist up.
January 20	Eisenhower is inaugurated for a second term.
February 14	The Southern Christian Leadership Conference (SCLC) is organized in New Orleans. Martin Luther King, Jr., is elected president.
July 12	The surgeon general reports that a link has been established between cigarette smoking and lung cancer.
August 30	South Carolina senator Strom Thurmond filibusters against civil rights legislation for a record twenty-four hours, twenty-seven minutes.
September 24	Eisenhower orders federal troops to Little Rock, Arkansas, to enforce a federal desegregation ruling.
October 4	The Soviet Union launches *Sputnik*.

1958

May 13	Eisenhower orders one thousand troops from Caribbean bases to rescue Nixon, if necessary, after the vice president was threatened during a tour of Latin America.

1959

January 1	Fidel Castro leads the overthrow of Cuban dictator Batista.
March 18	Eisenhower signs a bill admitting Hawaii as the fiftieth state.

1960

February 1	Civil rights sit-ins begin in Greensboro, North Carolina.
March 17	Eisenhower authorizes the CIA to start training exiles to invade Cuba.
April 15–April 17	The Student Nonviolent Coordinating Committee (SNCC), a civil rights group born out of the sit-in demonstrations, organizes in Raleigh, North Carolina.
May 5	The Soviet Union announces that it has shot down an American U-2 spy plane.
July 13	Senator John F. Kennedy receives the Democratic nomination.
July 27	Nixon receives the Republican nomination.
November 8	Kennedy narrowly defeats Nixon.

1961

January 3	Eisenhower severs diplomatic relations with Cuba.
January 17	Eisenhower's Farewell Address warns the nation of the growing power of the "military-industrial complex."

MUST READS

David Halberstam, *The Fifties*; Michael Korda, *Ike: An American Hero*; Tim Weiner, *Legacy of Ashes: The History of the CIA*; Tom Wicker, *Dwight D. Eisenhower.*

ONLINE RESOURCES

Inaugural Addresses, Avalon Project, Yale University
    1953: http://avalon.law.yale.edu/20th_century/eisen1.asp
    1957: http://avalon.law.yale.edu/20th_century/eisen2.asp
Library of Congress Resource Guide
    http://www.loc.gov/rr/program/bib/presidents/eisenhower/index.html

Eisenhower Library and Museum, Abilene, Kansas
  http://www.eisenhower.archives.gov/
**Eisenhower National Historic Site, Gettysburg, Pennsylvania,
National Park Service**
  http://www.nps.gov/eise/
Miller Center of Public Affairs, University of Virginia
  http://millercenter.org/academic/americanpresident/eisenhower
"Times Topics," *New York Times*: **Dwight D. Eisenhower**
  http://topics.nytimes.com/top/reference/timestopics/people/e
  /dwight_david_eisenhower/index.html

35

JFK
John Fitzgerald Kennedy

★ ★ ★

January 20, 1961–November 22, 1963

Milestones in John F. Kennedy's Life

May 29, 1917	Born in Brookline, Massachusetts
1940	Published *Why England Slept*
1941–1945	Served in U.S. Navy, World War II
1945	Worked as newspaper reporter
1947–1952	U.S. representative from Massachusetts
1953–1960	U.S. senator from Massachusetts
1955	Published *Profiles in Courage*, which won the Pulitzer Prize
1961–1963	Thirty-fifth president
November 22, 1963	Assassinated in Dallas, Texas, aged forty-six

---

PRESIDENTIAL VOICES

We dare not forget today that we are the heirs of that first revolution. Let the word go forth from this time and place, to friend and foe alike, that the torch has been passed to a new generation of Americans—born in this century, tempered by war, disciplined by a hard and bitter peace, proud of our ancient heritage—and unwilling to witness or permit the slow undoing of those human rights to which this Nation has always been committed, and to which we are committed today at home and around the world. . . .

And so, my fellow Americans: ask not what your country can do for you—
ask what you can do for your country.

—John F. Kennedy
Inaugural Address, January 20, 1961[1]

Fifty years after John F. Kennedy was inaugurated, the public remains fascinated with the man, his family, and his times. In 2011,
two best-selling books—one based on a collection of audiotapes made
by his widow, Jacqueline, in 1964, the other a mostly laudatory evalua-
tion by political commentator Chris Matthews—attested to the ongoing near-obsession with the assassinated president. A 2012 book by a
woman claiming an affair with JFK began when she was a nineteen-
year-old White House intern underscored the dark side of the Kennedy legend. His life and loves, his controversial death, and the legacy
of his brief presidency and extended family continue to exert a hold on
the American imagination as nothing about any other politician in
American memory has.

When John F. Kennedy was assassinated on November 22, 1963,
the modern mythmaking machine was set in motion. It transformed a
president who had committed serious mistakes while also conjuring
brilliant successes into a sun-dappled, all-American legend—a modern young King Arthur from *Camelot,* the popular musical of the day,
which became the enduring image of his abbreviated life and presidency.

Elected at forty-two—still the youngest elected president—and
dead at forty-six, John F. Kennedy had, in the lyrics of *Camelot,* a "brief,
shining moment" that remains one of the most extraordinary passages
in American history, shaping the course of modern presidential politics
and history.

Fast Facts

RELIGION: Catholic

EDUCATION: Harvard

MILITARY SERVICE: Lieutenant in the U.S. Navy commanding a torpedo boat in World War II

CAREER BEFORE POLITICS: Newspaper correspondent, author

POLITICAL PARTY: Democratic

FIRST LADY: Jacqueline Bouvier Kennedy (July 28, 1929–May 19, 1994)

CHILDREN: Caroline and John Jr.

Another child was stillborn and still another died in infancy. In July 1999, John F. Kennedy, Jr., died in the crash of a plane he was piloting off Martha's Vineyard.

* Kennedy was the first president born in the twentieth century.
* He was the first, and so far only, Roman Catholic to be elected president.
* The 1960 campaign was highlighted by four televised debates between Kennedy and Vice President Richard Nixon—for the first time most Americans were able to see and hear both candidates face-to-face, in what would become one of the most radical transformations of the presidential election process.
* To date, Kennedy is the only president to win a Pulitzer Prize, for *Profiles in Courage.* Before his death in 2010, former Kennedy speechwriter Theodore Sorensen confirmed that he had written the book with Kennedy.
* Kennedy was the first president to have a poet take part in his inaugural. Robert Frost recited from memory an older poem, "The Gift Outright"; he was unable to read the poem "Dedication," which he had written for the occasion, because of the glare of the bright sun on the snow that had fallen the day before.
* While there had been gardens at the White House since the time of John Adams, and presidents such as Jefferson and John Quincy Adams had been enthusiastic gardeners, the iconic "Rose Garden," outside the president's office, was formalized by Kennedy. Eisenhower had used the Rose Garden for announcements and bill sign-

ings. But after his 1961 trip to Europe, Kennedy wanted a more formal setting for official use. He enlisted a family friend, Rachel "Bunny" Mellon, to redesign the Rose Garden. "He wanted a garden to appeal to the most discriminating taste," she later recalled. "Yet a garden that would hold a thousand people for a ceremony. . . . What gardener could resist?"[2]

* John F. Kennedy and William Taft are the only presidents buried at Arlington National Cemetery.

Born into a wealthy Boston Irish Catholic family with a long political history, including a maternal grandfather who had been mayor of the city, John F. Kennedy was one of nine children, the second son of Joseph P. Kennedy. One of the richest men in America, Joseph Kennedy had made his fortune on Wall Street and in the entertainment business, managing to take his money out of the market just before the crash of 1929. An FDR backer, Kennedy had been named the first head of the Securities and Exchange Commission. In 1938, on the eve of the Second World War, President Roosevelt appointed him to the key post of ambassador to the United Kingdom. Joseph Kennedy took JFK with him to London.

Having observed the miscalculations made by the British as Hitler came to power, JFK wrote his senior thesis at Harvard University on England's lack of preparation for the coming war. With the help of his father's friend, a member of the *New York Times* editorial board, who also suggested the title, his thesis was successfully published as *Why England Slept*.

After Pearl Harbor, JFK and his older brother, Joe, who was being groomed for a political career by his father, both enlisted in the military. The handsome and outgoing Joe Kennedy, Jr., became a pilot but was killed on a bombing mission in Europe. Initially rejected from service for health issues, JFK was accepted into the navy with his father's intervention. An accomplished sailor since his youth, he was assigned to serve in the South Pacific, commanding a small motor-torpedo, or "PT," boat.

In August 1943, as his men were sleeping without posting a watch as required, Kennedy's PT-109 was rammed by a Japanese destroyer. Towing a badly burned crewmate by a life-jacket strap clenched in his teeth, Kennedy led the crew's ten survivors on a three-mile swim to refuge on a tiny island. Widely credited with the rescue of his crew, Kennedy returned home to a hero's welcome.

After the war, JFK worked briefly as a reporter. Then, in 1946, the twenty-nine-year-old Kennedy won election to the U.S. Congress representing a working-class Boston district, with more than a quarter million dollars spent on electioneering in the district by his father—subway and radio ads, billboards, direct mailings, even cash dispensed discreetly in pay toilets by one of Joe Kennedy's aides.[3] (The amount dwarfed the cost of other House races of the time.)

But Jack Kennedy also proved to be a tireless, relentless, and very good campaigner, working factories and trolley cars by day and small groups of women organized by two of his sisters at night. As historian Robert Dallek records, "Jack was at his best with these small groups, flashing his disarming smile, answering questions with a leg draped over an armchair, combining serious discussion with boyish informality. Within days, the campaign would issue invitations to all the young women to become volunteers for Kennedy. The technique created a corps of workers who expanded Jack's ability to reach out to hundreds and possibly thousands of other voters."[4]

After serving three terms in the House, he ran for the U.S. Senate in 1952, again bankrolled by his father, defeating the Republican incumbent, Henry Cabot Lodge, Jr., in a year that the country went mostly Republican. That same year, JFK met Jacqueline Bouvier at a dinner party, and they were married a year later.

Due to his continuing poor health—Addison's disease, severe back pain, malaria contracted during the war—Kennedy had one of the worst attendance records in Congress. Laid up in the hospital during the censure of Senator Joseph McCarthy, Kennedy, an avowed anti-Communist, didn't vote on the issue. (A Catholic, like the Kennedys, McCarthy also happened to be a friend of JFK's father, and Jack's younger brother Robert F. Kennedy worked for McCarthy's committee.)

Despite few achievements in the Senate, JFK returned from his convalescence after back surgery and almost immediately began looking for higher office. In 1956, he mounted a serious quest for the vice presidential nomination as running mate to Democratic candidate Adlai Stevenson. He narrowly lost the spot, and Stevenson lost the election. But Kennedy was reelected to the Senate in 1958 and became a member of its influential Foreign Relations Committee. From there, he began to attack President Eisenhower's policies, claiming that the United States was on the wrong side of a "missile gap" with the Soviet Union. And it was as a Cold Warrior, not a liberal Northerner, that JFK made his pursuit of the presidency in 1960.

What media moment defined the 1960 campaign for president?
"If you give me a week, I might think of one."

That's what President Eisenhower told a reporter who asked what major decisions Vice President Richard Nixon had participated in during their eight years together. Although Ike later said he was joking, the cutting remark hurt Nixon personally and politically. That was in August 1960, as Nixon and John F. Kennedy ran neck-and-neck in the polls.

How many votes did Ike's quip cost? It would have taken a shift of only about a hundred thousand votes out of the record 68,832,818 cast to change the .2 percent margin of popular victory JFK won and alter the course of contemporary events.

Ike's comment is cited as an example of the strained relationship between the men, but whether it altered the outcome is questionable. The true turning point may have come in another defining moment— the face-off between the contenders in the first televised debates in presidential campaign history.

More than seventy million people watched the first of these meetings between the candidates. Hospitalized for two weeks before the debate, Nixon was underweight, pale, and haggard. Despite his own ailments, Senator Kennedy was the picture of youth and athletic vigor. While radio listeners thought there was no clear winner in the debates, television viewers were riveted by Kennedy's presence. If FDR had mastered radio in an earlier generation, JFK was the first "telegenic" candidate, custom-tailored for the instant image-making of the television age. Running for president would never be the same.

The audience fell off for the three subsequent debates, and the impression made by the first debate seemed to be most lasting. Kennedy got a boost in the pre-election polling, but the decision was still too close to call. On the sidelines through most of the contest, Eisenhower did some last-minute campaigning for Nixon, but it was too little, too late.

The other key factor throughout the Democratic primaries and the general election was Kennedy's religion. America in 1960 was still conservative and Protestant. The old anti-Catholic animus was barely concealed. The idea that Kennedy, a Catholic, was loyal to the Vatican would not go away. Prominent Protestant leaders including Billy Graham and Norman Vincent Peale organized religious leaders to stop Kennedy. On September 12, 1960, Kennedy delivered a speech on religion to the Ministerial Association, a group of evangelical leaders, in Houston. "I believe in an America where the separation of church and state is absolute," said Kennedy.[5] The speech, widely hailed at the time, was credited with defusing the issue for Kennedy.

The debate, Joe Kennedy's sizable campaign war chest, JFK's appeal to women, the newly important black vote, and vice presidential candidate Lyndon B. Johnson's role in delivering Texas and the rest of the South all played a part in what was the closest presidential election in modern history to that time.

PRESIDENTIAL VOICES

I think it's so unfair for people to be against Jack because he's Catholic. He's such a poor Catholic.

JACQUELINE KENNEDY DURING THE 1960 CAMPAIGN[6]

What happened at the Bay of Pigs?

During his first hundred days in office, Kennedy announced a program that perfectly demonstrated his inaugural appeal to "ask what you can do for your country." The newly created Peace Corps would dispatch the energy of American youth and know-how to assist developing nations. Directed by another Kennedy extended family member, brother-in-law Sargent Shriver (husband of John's sister Eunice), the Peace Corps was the new generation's answer to Communism, promoting democracy with education, technology, and idealism. The Peace Corps was one visible symbol of the vigorous activism and youthful exuberance that Kennedy hoped to bring to American policy.

What the Peace Corps idealism masked was a continuing policy of aggressive anti-Communism that factored into all decision-making and would lead to some of the great disasters in American foreign policy. One failure in particular would bring the nation to its most dangerous moment since the conflict in Korea had America on the brink of atomic warfare.

It took its unlikely name from an obscure spot on the Cuban coast: the Bay of Pigs. The plan behind the Bay of Pigs invasion was hatched by the CIA and brought to the new president by Allen Dulles, the legendary CIA director and a holdover from the Eisenhower era. During the waning days of the Eisenhower administration, Dulles's CIA conceived a plan that called for landing in Cuba a force of anti-Castro Cuban exiles called Brigade 2506 or "La Brigada" to launch a counter-revolution. It was part of a larger CIA venture called the "Cuba Project," aimed at overthrowing and, if necessary, assassinating Fidel Castro. Eisenhower nominally approved the operation but insisted on some very careful restrictions before it could be put in motion. He left office without giving it the go-ahead.

Eager to prove himself as a Cold Warrior, Kennedy signed off on the plan, almost every step of which was flawed or misguided. The CIA had underestimated Castro and the popular support he enjoyed, relying on sketchy information, making erroneous assumptions, and misrepresenting the plot to the newcomer in the White House.

On April 17, 1961, some fourteen hundred Cubans set down on the beach at the Bay of Pigs where Castro had begun building a resort, including a seaside cabin for himself. The operation was a fiasco. While the invasion force fought bravely, they lacked sufficient ammunition and air support except for a group of B-26 bombers flown by National

Guardsmen, which arrived late over confusion about time zones. Those planes were shot down. Six unmarked fighter planes promised by the CIA to provide cover for the bombers never arrived.

In a short time, the invading force was pinned down on the beaches by more than twenty thousand Cuban troops. In Washington, Kennedy feared that any direct U.S. combat involvement might send the Russians into West Berlin, precipitating World War III and an all-out nuclear exchange.

The sad toll was 114 Cuban invaders and many more defenders killed in the fighting; 1,189 others from La Brigada were captured and held prisoner until Attorney General Robert Kennedy ransomed them from Cuba for $53 million worth of food and medical supplies in December 1962. The four American fliers, members of the Alabama Air National Guard in CIA employ, also died in the invasion, but the American government did not acknowledge their existence or their connection to the operation.

The disastrous invasion led the administration to initiate Operation Mongoose, a plan to destabilize and sabotage Castro's Cuba, which had become a CIA obsession.[7] "They [John and Robert Kennedy] wanted swift, silent sabotage to overthrow Castro," Tim Weiner records in a history of the CIA. The agency created "the largest peacetime intelligence operation to date, with some six hundred CIA officers in and around Miami, almost five thousand CIA contractors, and the third largest navy in the Caribbean, including submarine, patrol boats, coast guard cutters, seaplanes and Guantánamo Bay for a base. The plans included blowing up an American ship in Guantánamo harbor and faking a terrorist attack against an American airliner." Other plots directed at Castro included poison pills to be dropped in his coffee, delivered by mobsters linked to the Mafia.[8]

What happened during thirteen days in October 1962?

Soviet leader Nikita Khrushchev (1894–1971) immediately saw the Americans' Bay of Pigs defeat as the opening to start arming Cuba more heavily, precipitating the most dangerous moment in Cold War history, the missile crisis of October 1962.

When American spy flights produced evidence of Soviet missile sites in Cuba, America and the Soviet Union were brought to the brink of war. For thirteen tense days, the United States and the Soviet Union stood toe-to-toe as Kennedy, forced to prove himself after the Bay of Pigs, demanded that the missile sites be dismantled and removed from Cuba. To back up his ultimatum, Kennedy ordered a naval blockade to "quarantine" Cuba and readied a full-scale American invasion of the island. With Soviet ships steaming toward Cuba, Premier Khrushchev warned that his country would not accept the quarantine.

On day five, the president was campaigning for congressional candidates in Chicago and suddenly returned to Washington, "due to a cold," it was reported. But the crisis had reached an urgent point. On day seven, Kennedy addressed the nation, explaining the crisis. As the Soviet ships carrying military supplies steamed closer toward Cuba, the world tracked their progress, nervously awaiting a confrontation. Only later was it learned that Castro had actually asked the Kremlin to launch a missile attack on the United States.

Senior members of the Kennedy administration and their families were evacuated from Washington. Well past the "eleventh hour," a back-channel deal was struck that the Soviets would dismantle the missiles in exchange for a U.S. promise not to invade Cuba. On Sunday, October 28, Radio Moscow announced that the arms would be crated and returned to Moscow. In exchange, American missiles, it was secretly agreed, would be removed from Turkey. That part of the deal remained a secret for twenty-five years.[9]

Nuclear disaster was averted.

One immediate result of the crisis was the creation of a Moscow-Washington "hotline," a system that allowed direct communication between the White House and the Kremlin. But there would be no "Hello Nikita" calls between JFK and the Soviets; the "hotline" was actually an encrypted teletype machine (later upgraded as technology changed). It was not used until the 1967 Six Day War between Israel and the Arab countries.

How did Mrs. John F. Kennedy become the cultural icon "Jackie O"?
With Kennedy's election, America had its youngest elected president, its youngest attorney general in JFK's brother Robert F. Kennedy, and

a new national obsession with a photogenic family that appeared in constant pictures of sailboats and touch football. America also fell in love with the president's beautiful young wife.

No small part of John F. Kennedy's charismatic allure as he came to the White House was his remarkably active and attractive family. Two and a half weeks after the election, Jacqueline Bouvier Kennedy gave birth to their second child, John Jr., and at thirty-one, she was the third youngest first lady in history. She was coquettish, stylish, and lively—as complete a contrast as could be imagined from her two much-admired predecessors, Bess Truman and Mamie Eisenhower. While they were beloved, it was in the way you love a kindly aunt. "Jackie," as the press and public quickly came to call her, was different.

She was born to a wealthy family in Southampton, New York, and had gone to all the "right schools." Despite what was then the stigma of the divorce of her parents, she continued to live in the stylish upper crust of New York society when her mother remarried, later attending Vassar College. In 1951, she was at work as the "Inquiring Camera Girl" for a Washington newspaper—an ironic beginning for a woman who would have lifelong battles with aggressive paparazzi. It was at that time she met JFK, and they were married in 1953.

When she came to the White House, Jackie Kennedy set about turning it into a home for her family but also restoring a sense of stylish history to an Executive Mansion that had seen many presidents and decorating trends come and go. Under her eye, the White House was restored and refurnished. Then she opened the residence to cameras, and her televised tour of the White House captivated the nation.

Jackie Kennedy added to her worldwide allure during a trip to Europe in which she impressed Parisians with her fashion sense and ability to speak French. After that trip, JFK famously quipped, "I am the man who accompanied Jackie Kennedy to Paris—and I enjoyed myself."[10]

While she was not quite the social reformer that Eleanor Roosevelt had been, Jackie Kennedy was keenly aware of her image and the responsibility that came with it. While JFK was cautious about pushing civil rights too far, Jackie Kennedy used her power to advance the cause. When she started her own White House kindergarten for daughter Caroline and included the children of White House staff in this very select school, she made a point of including the son of a black press aide and made sure he was featured in the photographs. While it might seem like a small thing in modern America, this was daring for a first lady in 1961. And she knew exactly what she was doing.

In 1963, another child was born to the Kennedys but died on August 9. More tragedy was soon to come, with images that would be seared in the American memory. Jackie standing beside Lyndon Johnson, still wearing her bloodstained Chanel suit as he took the oath of office on Air Force One. Jackie leaning and whispering to a young John Jr. during JFK's funeral, which she had meticulously planned. John Jr. snapping an unforgettably poignant salute as his slain father's coffin rolled by.

In 1968, after the assassination of her brother-in-law Senator Robert F. Kennedy, Jackie Kennedy left the country, fearing for her children's lives. She then married Greek shipping tycoon Aristotle Onassis, becoming internationally famous in this phase of her life as "Jackie O," an era in which she would be relentlessly tracked by photographers and serve as fodder for tabloid newspapers. She later returned to New York City, became a book editor, and was intensely involved in the preservation of New York City architectural landmarks that were threatened by development, including Grand Central Terminal.

Final Judgment: Grade B

"Before he came along, politics mostly meant gray men in three-piece suits, indoor types, sexless: Truman, Taft, Dewey, Kefauver, Eisenhower, Nixon. What he did was grip the country, quickening us," wrote political commentator Chris Matthews in an admiring biography. "From the black-and-white world in which we suddenly opened our eyes, feeling alive and energized, and saw Technicolor, JFK was wired into our central nervous system and juiced us. He sent us around the planet in the Peace Corps, and then rocketing beyond to the moon. Most of all . . . he saved us from the perilous fate toward which we were headed."[11]

The Cuban episodes—first the Bay of Pigs and then the missile crisis—highlighted the fact that Kennedy's administration was focused on foreign affairs.

It was that focus that led JFK to begin sending thousands of advisers to Vietnam, the next scene for a proxy battle between the United States and the Soviet Union. Weeks before JFK's death, a CIA-sponsored coup in November 1963 heightened American involvement in the civil war between North and South Vietnam. A generation of historians has debated whether Kennedy would have continued the buildup in Vietnam that was tragically carried out by his successor, Lyndon B. Johnson.

On the domestic front, the great issue of the day was civil rights. The growing nonviolent movement led by Martin Luther King, Jr., and a series of court decisions pushed civil rights to the front burner. But Kennedy moved cautiously in this area, fearful of losing the segregationist South that was still mostly Democratic. He was in Dallas in November 1963 to shore up support in the Southern states.

The Kennedy assassination on November 22, 1963, devastated and shocked the nation to its core. With the threat of the Soviet Union and questions of Cuban involvement in Kennedy's death, the assassination had many in the country fearful of atomic confrontation again. As Gerald Posner writes, "There was even a possibility of war if either Cuba or the Soviet Union was found to have sponsored JFK's death, and Johnson appointed a seven-man panel of distinguished public servants he thought had unimpeachable credentials." When Chief Justice Earl Warren initially balked at heading the commission, Johnson argued, "the only way to dispel these rumors . . . was to have an independent and responsible commission." Johnson told Warren, "If the public became aroused, there might be war."[12]

In the half century since that extraordinary event, investigated first by what was known as the Warren Commission, many Americans have felt that there were still too many unanswered questions. Appointed by President Johnson five days after the assassination, the President's Commission on the Assassination of President Kennedy was headed by the chief justice of the Supreme Court, Earl Warren. Its members included CIA director Allen Dulles and future president Gerald Ford, then House minority leader.

Almost from the time its conclusions were published, the commission was criticized for its methods, omissions, and conclusions, although several authoritative follow-up investigations confirmed the conclusion that the two bullets fired by Lee Harvey Oswald killed JFK. A House Select Committee report in 1979 professed the possibility of a conspiracy and another shooter, but it relied on acoustic evidence, which was later deemed faulty. Yet by 1992, less than one-third of Americans accepted that the Warren Commission was correct in finding that Oswald acted alone in killing John F. Kennedy. Two other notable journalistic investigations of the assassination—Gerald Posner's *Case Closed* (1993) and Vincent Bugliosi's *Reclaiming History* (2007)—upheld the Warren Commission's findings.

As some of the golden glow of the Kennedy era has been tarnished in the half century since, JFK's legacy remains mixed. However, presidential historian Robert Dallek recently concluded, "Kennedy's greatest achievements were his management of Soviet-American relations and his effectiveness in discouraging a U.S. military mind-set that accepted the possibility—indeed even likelihood—of a nuclear war with Moscow. As with Cuba and Vietnam, no one can say with any certainty that two full Kennedy terms would have eased the Cold War between the United States and the USSR. But it is certainly imaginable." [13]

PRESIDENTIAL VOICES

It should be clear now that a nation can be no stronger abroad than she is at home. Only an America which practices what it preaches about equal rights and social justice will be respected by those whose choice affects our future.

—JOHN F. KENNEDY
Undelivered speech, Dallas, 1963[14]

Kennedy Administration Milestones[15]

1961

January 20	John F. Kennedy is inaugurated.
March 1	JFK issues an executive order creating a temporary Peace Corps.
April 12	Soviet cosmonaut Yuri Gagarin becomes the first man in space.
April 15–20	The Bay of Pigs invasion fails. Kennedy takes full responsibility for the disaster.
May 4	Supported by the Congress of Racial Equality (CORE), young people set out by bus on the "Freedom Rides" that test the enforcement of rules against discrimination in interstate travel.
May 5	Alan Shepard, Jr., becomes the first American in space.
May 25	Kennedy pledges that the United States will land a man on the moon by the end of the decade.
June 3	Kennedy meets with Soviet premier Nikita Khrushchev in Vienna. The conference fails to resolve conflict over the status of Berlin.
August 13	The East Germans, supported by the Soviet Union, begin construction of the Berlin Wall.

1962

February 3	Kennedy halts virtually all trade with Cuba.
February 20	John Glenn becomes the first American to orbit the earth.
February 26	The U.S. Supreme Court rules that segregation in transportation facilities is unconstitutional.
September 30	The U.S. Supreme Court orders the University of Mississippi to admit James H. Meredith, its first African-American student. U.S. marshals escort Meredith to campus while federalized National Guardsmen maintain order.
October 16	Kennedy is informed of Soviet missile installations in Cuba.

October 22	Cuban Missile Crisis: Kennedy addresses the American people about Cuba and orders a naval quarantine of the island to prevent further shipments of weapons.
October 28	After thirteen days, the Cuban Missile Crisis is resolved. The United States pledges not to invade Cuba and agrees to remove missiles from Turkey, in exchange for the removal of the Soviet weapons.
November 20	Kennedy lifts the naval blockade of Cuba.

1963

March 18	The Supreme Court rules in *Gideon v. Wainwright* that states must supply counsel in criminal cases for individuals who cannot afford it.
April 3	Martin Luther King, Jr., leads a civil rights drive in Birmingham, Alabama. Police use fire hoses and dogs on demonstrators.
June 12	Medgar W. Evers, NAACP field secretary for Mississippi, is assassinated outside his home in Jackson.
June 26	Speaking in West Berlin, Kennedy demonstrates his solidarity with the city, declaring in German, *"Ich bin ein Berliner."* ("I am a Berliner.")
August 28	The March on Washington for Jobs and Freedom attracts 250,000 demonstrators to the nation's capital, where Martin Luther King, Jr., delivers his "I Have a Dream" speech.
September	Four young African-American girls are killed in the bombing of a church in Birmingham, Alabama.
October	Kennedy signs a limited nuclear test-ban treaty with the Soviet Union and the United Kingdom.
November 1	South Vietnamese President Ngo Dinh Diem is assassinated in a U.S.-supported coup.
November 22	Kennedy is assassinated while riding in a motorcade in Dallas, Texas. Lee Harvey Oswald is arrested and accused of the crime. Vice President Lyndon Baines Johnson is sworn in on Air Force One.

November 24   Jack Ruby shoots and kills Lee Harvey Oswald.

November 25   Kennedy is buried at Arlington National Cemetery.

MUST READS

Robert Dallek, *An Unfinished Life: John Kennedy 1917–1963*; Chris Matthews, *Jack Kennedy: Elusive Hero*; Gerald M. Posner, *Case Closed: Lee Harvey Oswald and the Assassination of JFK*; Richard Reeves, *President Kennedy: Profile of Power*; Peter Wyden, *Bay of Pigs*.

ONLINE RESOURCES

Inaugural Address, Avalon Project, Yale Law School
  http://avalon.law.yale.edu/20th_century/kennedy.asp
Library of Congress Resource Guide
  http://www.loc.gov/rr/program/bib/presidents/kennedy/index.html
Miller Center of Public Affairs, University of Virginia
  http://millercenter.org/academic/americanpresident/kennedy
White House Recordings
  http://millercenter.org/scripps/archive/presidentialrecordings/kennedy/index
JFK Library and Museum
  http://www.jfklibrary.org/

36

LBJ
Lyndon Baines Johnson

★ ★ ★

November 22, 1963–January 20, 1969

Milestones in Lyndon B. Johnson's Life

August 27, 1908	Born near Stonewall, Texas
1930–1931	Taught public speaking and debate at Sam Houston High School
1932–1935	Secretary to U.S. representative Richard M. Kleberg (Texas)
1935–1937	Director of National Youth Administration in Texas
1941–1942	Served in U.S. Navy, World War II
1949–1960	U.S. senator from Texas
1955–1960	Majority leader of the Senate
1961–1963	Vice president under Kennedy
1963–1969	Thirty-sixth president
January 22, 1973	Died in Stonewall, Texas, aged sixty-four

PRESIDENTIAL VOICES

All I have I would have given gladly not to be standing here today. This nation will keep its commitments from South Viet-Nam to West Berlin. We have talked long enough in this country about equal rights. We have talked for one hundred years or more. It is time now to write the next chapter, and to write it in the books of law.

—LYNDON B. JOHNSON
Address to joint session of Congress
November 27, 1963[1]

I n some ways, history has been kinder to Lyndon B. Johnson than his tortured presidency—and certainly the vociferous critics of his day—would have suggested. A power broker extraordinaire during his days in Congress, especially during more than a decade in the Senate, Lyndon B. Johnson challenged John F. Kennedy for the Democratic nomination in the 1960 primaries and then, in a surprise move, accepted Kennedy's offer to become his vice presidential running mate.

Johnson was credited with helping Kennedy win Southern votes and ultimately the election. As vice president, he was clearly not a member of JFK's inner circle and would always have a tense relationship with Robert F. Kennedy, the president's younger brother, attorney general, and closest adviser.

On November 22, 1963, everything changed and Johnson became president, taking the oath of office aboard Air Force One with Jacqueline Kennedy, the dead president's widow, standing beside him.

Driven by an unwavering sense of social justice, born out of his youth and upbringing in hardscrabble, Depression-era Texas, Johnson had become one of Franklin D. Roosevelt's most loyal New Dealers, first in a federal job, then in Congress, and later as "Master of the Senate." As president, Johnson set the country on a quest for what he called the "Great Society," looking for ways to end the great economic injustice and bitter racial disparity that existed in America in 1963. But his vision for that "Great Society" was counterbalanced and ultimately overshadowed by his doomed course in pursuing the war in Vietnam.

Fast Facts

RELIGION: Disciples of Christ

EDUCATION: Southwest Texas State Teachers College

MILITARY SERVICE: Lieutenant commander, United States Navy, World War II

CAREER BEFORE POLITICS: Schoolteacher

POLITICAL PARTY: Democratic

FIRST LADY: Claudia "Lady Bird" Taylor Johnson (December 22, 1912– July 11, 2007)

CHILDREN: Two daughters, Lynda and Luci

Lynda Bird Johnson Robb was married in the White House in 1967. Her husband, Charles Robb, later became governor of and senator from Virginia. Luci was married in a Catholic Church ceremony in 1966, also while her father was president; she later divorced and remarried.

* LBJ was the first congressman to enlist for active duty after Pearl Harbor.
* Johnson was the fourth president to come into office upon the death of a president by assassination.
* The oath of office was administered to Johnson aboard Air Force One, a first; it was also the first time a woman, U.S. district judge Sarah T. Hughes, administered the oath.
* In 1965 Johnson rode to his second inauguration in a bulletproof limousine, reflecting new security concerns after the Kennedy assassination.
* Johnson is one of four presidents to serve in all four elected federal offices: representative, senator, vice president, and president. (The others were John Tyler, Andrew Johnson, and Richard Nixon.)

* Johnson appointed the first black Supreme Court justice, Thurgood Marshall.
* Johnson was the first incumbent president to welcome a reigning pontiff to the United States; he met with Pope Paul VI in October 1965 in New York. (Woodrow Wilson was the first president to meet, in 1919, with a reigning pope.)

PRESIDENTIAL VOICES

The inspiration and commitment of the Great Society have disappeared. In concrete terms, the President simply cannot think about implementing the Great Society at home while he is supervising bombing missions over North Vietnam. There is a kind of madness in the facile assumption that we can raise the billions of dollars necessary to rebuild our schools and cities and public transport and eliminate the pollution of air and water while also spending tens of billions to finance an "open-ended" war in Asia.

—SENATOR WILLIAM FULBRIGHT, 1966[2]

Lyndon Baines Johnson was the oldest of five children born to Samuel Ealy Johnson, Jr., and Rebekah Baines Johnson, both schoolteachers. Both his father and grandfather had been members of the Texas legislature, and politics was like "mother's milk" to Johnson.

When he was five, the family moved to Johnson City—named for his grandfather—and he attended public school there, graduating from Johnson City High School in 1924 at age fifteen. Uninterested in more school, Johnson and a few friends bummed their way to California, where he lived a hobo's life—picking crops, washing dishes, and realizing firsthand the difficulties of making a living with the Dust Bowl and the Great Depression around the corner.

Johnson returned to Johnson City and took work on a road crew. Finally, he followed the urging of his parents and returned to school, borrowing $75 to enroll in Southwest Texas State Teachers College. Taking jobs as a janitor and then an office helper to the school's president, Johnson worked his way through college, dropping out one year to teach Mexican children in a tiny school in the poverty-ridden town of Cotulla.

After graduating, Johnson taught school for another year before he got an opportunity to enter the Texas political world as a secretary to Representative Richard Kleberg. From 1932 to 1935, as the country entered the worst of the Depression and Herbert Hoover was replaced by Franklin D. Roosevelt, Johnson watched Congress at work in the midst of America's greatest economic crisis.

During a trip home, he also met twenty-one-year-old Claudia Alta Taylor, known to her family and friends since childhood as "Lady Bird." Wasting no time, Johnson asked her to marry him, and they wed on November 17, 1934—just two months after they met. A few years later, using some of her inheritance, Lady Bird Johnson bought a radio station in Austin. With considerable skill, she managed the investment into a media empire eventually worth more than $150 million. According to the *Dallas Morning News*, Lady Bird Johnson was the first president's wife to become a millionaire in her own right.

In 1935, President Roosevelt had established the National Youth Administration (NYA) as one of the many New Deal "alphabet soup" agencies designed to combat joblessness. At age twenty-six, Johnson was appointed the Texas state director, the youngest of the state directors, and he soon began to organize projects that put thousands of unemployed young people to work. Two years later, he won a special election for a House seat, and two powerful men singled him out: President Franklin D. Roosevelt and House majority leader Sam Rayburn, a fellow Texan. After Pearl Harbor, Johnson enlisted and served briefly in the South Pacific, until Roosevelt ordered all members of Congress in the military to return to Washington.

In 1949 Johnson moved on to the Senate, where his skills of cajoling, flattering, coercing, and compromising made him one of the most skilled legislative leaders in history. Tall and physically imposing, he was ambitious, fiercely competitive, at times gentle and solicitous, sometimes ruthless. Biographers like Robert Dallek describe the full complement of LBJ's abilities to intimidate: "Outlandish comments and behavior were parts of Johnson's political calculations. Urinating in a sink, inviting people into the bathroom, showing off a scar, exposing his private parts—after a while nothing surprises the biographer. For Johnson, they were meant to shock and confuse and leave him in control."[3]

Although he hoped to win the 1960 Democratic nomination, Johnson finished behind the well-financed John F. Kennedy, who then sought out the Texan to help bring Southern votes to the young Northern Democrat.

PRESIDENTIAL VOICES

Will you join in the battle to give every citizen an escape from the crushing weight of poverty?

Will you join in the battle to make it possible for all nations to live in enduring peace—as neighbors and not as mortal enemies?

Will you join in the battle to build the Great Society, to prove that our material progress is only the foundation on which we will build a richer life of mind and spirit?

There are those timid souls who say this battle cannot be won; that we are condemned to a soulless wealth. I do not agree. We have the power to shape the civilization that we want. But we need your will, your labor, your hearts, if we are to build that kind of society.

—LYNDON B. JOHNSON, MAY 22, 1964[4]

What was the "Great Society"?

In May 1964, less than a year after he took office, Johnson gave one of the signature speeches of his presidency at the University of Michigan. In it he laid out a course toward not only the "rich society and the powerful society, but upward to the Great Society." America could be, he told the students, a society that would "end poverty and racial injustice." The phrase "Great Society" has been credited to speechwriter Richard N. Goodwin.

The speech set the stage for an ambitious legislative agenda that was begun as Johnson completed Kennedy's term, with passage of the Civil Rights Act of 1964, and then continued after his landslide victory over Republican Barry Goldwater in 1964. It would eventually amount to the largest expansion of the role of the federal government since the New Deal.

The laws passed and departments created could be divided over several broad categories:

- **Civil Rights:** The Civil Rights Act of 1964 attacked discrimination in jobs and public accommodations; the Voting Rights Act of 1965 protected minority voting rights; the Immigration and Nationality Act abolished national origin quotas; and the Civil Rights Act of 1968 banned housing discrimination.

- **Poverty:** What Johnson called a "War on Poverty" began with the Economic Opportunity Act of 1963 and continued with such programs as VISTA (a domestic Peace Corps), Upward Bound, Head Start (for early childhood education), and the Food Stamp Act of 1964.

- **Education:** The Elementary and Secondary Education Act began providing significant federal aid to public schools. In the related areas of arts and humanities, the National Endowment for the Arts and the National Endowment for the Humanities were created, as was the Corporation for Public Broadcasting.

- **Health:** Medicare was created in 1965 to provide funds for medical costs of older Americans. Medicaid was created in 1965 to aid welfare recipients with health care. Health was also addressed in the first consumer protection laws, including the Cigarette Labeling Act, which required cigarette packages to carry the first warning about the health risks of tobacco, and creation of the National Highway Safety Administration in response to warnings about unsafe automobiles, an issue raised by Ralph Nader in his landmark 1965 book, *Unsafe at Any Speed*, which put him and automobile safety on the national radar.

- **Environment:** The beginning of government involvement in environmental protection and a greater conservation effort came through a series of bills passed, among them the Wilderness Act, the National Historic Preservation Act, and the Motor Vehicle Air Pollution Control Act.

These are a handful of the more than two hundred significant pieces of legislation passed under Johnson during the "Great Society" rush.

And as a quick glance at these laws and Johnson-legacy agencies makes clear, it amounts to a veritable "hit list" of federal departments and regulations that many conservatives have been committed to abolishing ever since.

What was the Gulf of Tonkin Resolution and why did LBJ ask for it?
Vietnam was not Lyndon Johnson's war of choice. When he inherited it with the presidency, America was already more than ten years into its commitment. Since the French withdrawal from Indochina and the partition of Vietnam in 1954, the United States had committed money, materials, advice, and, by the end of 1963, some fifteen thousand military advisers in support of the anti-Communist Saigon government. The CIA was also in the thick of things, having helped foster the coup that toppled Prime Minister Ngo Dinh Diem in 1963. When Lyndon Johnson took office, he sought a glimmer of legitimacy to ramp up America's involvement, in hopes of ending the war decisively.

It came in August 1964 with a brief encounter in the Gulf of Tonkin, the waters off the coast of North Vietnam. To support assaults on the North by CIA-trained Vietnamese, the U.S. Navy posted warships in the gulf, loaded with electronic eavesdropping equipment enabling them to monitor North Vietnamese military operations and provide intelligence to the South Vietnamese commandos.

Two of these ships were reportedly fired on. But there was never any confirmation that either ship had actually been attacked. Later, the radar blips would be attributed to weather conditions and jittery nerves among the crew.

According to Stanley Karnow's *Vietnam: A History*, "Even Johnson privately expressed doubts only a few days after the second attack supposedly took place, confiding to an aide, 'Hell, those dumb stupid sailors were just shooting at flying fish.' "[5]

But that didn't stop Johnson. He ordered an air strike against North Vietnam in retaliation for the "attacks" on the U.S. ships. American jets flew more than sixty sorties against targets in North Vietnam.

President Johnson followed up the air strike by calling for passage of the Gulf of Tonkin Resolution. This proposal gave the president the authority to "take all necessary measures" to repel attacks against U.S. forces and to "prevent further aggression." The resolution not only gave Johnson the powers he needed to increase American commitment to South Vietnam, but also allowed him to blunt Goldwater's accusations that he was "timid before Communism." The Gulf of Tonkin Resolution passed the House unanimously after only forty minutes of debate. In the Senate, there were only two voices in opposition. What Congress did not know was that the resolution had been drafted several months before the Tonkin incident took place.

Congress, which alone possesses the constitutional authority to declare war, had handed that power over to a man who was not a bit reluctant to use it. One of the two senators who voted against the Tonkin Resolution, Oregon's Wayne Morse, later said the resolution's supporters "would live to regret it." But Johnson's advisers were pleased with the outcome. Said one about the incident in the gulf, "We don't know what happened but it had the desired result." [6]

PRESIDENTIAL VOICES

With America's sons in the fields far away, with America's future under challenge right here at home, with our hopes and the world's hopes for peace in the balance every day, I do not believe that I should devote an hour or a day of my time to any personal partisan causes or to any duties other than the awesome duties of this office—the Presidency of your country.

Accordingly, I shall not seek, and I will not accept, the nomination of my party for another term as your President.

—LYNDON B. JOHNSON, MARCH 31, 1968[7]

Final Judgment: Grade B

In 1964, Johnson ran against conservative Republican Barry Goldwater and defeated him in an electoral landslide. Johnson counted on the reserve of goodwill toward him that came out of the post-assassination mood. Americans believed that Goldwater's conservative positions were too extreme and Johnson's campaign created a memorable television ad, with a child shown holding a daisy and plucking petals until a mushroom cloud appears in the background. Though it aired only once, the ad powerfully suggested that Goldwater would use nuclear weapons if elected.

Johnson used this smashing victory as evidence of a mandate to enact his stream of "Great Society" social programs. The federal government was going to move aggressively into funding for housing, medical care, education, welfare, urban renewal. Johnson believed that America owed more to its least powerful citizens. And he spearheaded the most ambitious set of social programs since the New Deal days of FDR. Many of them, like Medicare and Medicaid, are part of the so-called "entitlements" that have grown over the decades and are currently at the heart of the debate over the future of the federal government in America.

Johnson was also dedicated to improving civil rights in America and pushed landmark legislation through Congress including several Civil Rights Acts and a voting act. But all of his domestic success soon collapsed under the groaning weight of Vietnam. There were no battlefield victories, and the surging American casualties that eventually reached more than fifty-eight thousand and the billions of dollars spent began to take a greater toll on the country's appetite for a war it considered a "quagmire."

By early 1968, public opinion had largely swung against Johnson. Sequestered in the White House, he could hear protestors outside the White House chanting, "Hey, Hey LBJ/How many kids did you kill today?" Whatever hopes he once held for bringing his vision of a "Great Society" to reality were dashed by the rising anger of the antiwar opposition that was beginning to fracture the country.

When antiwar senator Eugene McCarthy challenged LBJ in the 1968 Democratic New Hampshire primary election, McCarthy finished a close second with 42 percent of the vote. A few days later, Robert F. Kennedy, who had moved to New York and won a Senate seat there, announced that he too would challenge for the nomination. Then, on March 31, Johnson stunned America by announcing he was withdrawing from the race.

Physically and emotionally shattered by the war, the once indomitable LBJ, with his prowess as master of the legislative deal, seemed a shell of himself. He left Washington for Texas, largely viewed as a failed president, with the Vietnam War the albatross he would wear to his death by heart attack in January 1973, the same month a peace treaty was negotiated with North Vietnam.

While every president carries with him the weight of his contradictions, those contradictions are rarely so pronounced as they were in Lyndon B. Johnson. He was, as Robert Dallek once wrote, "Driven, tyrannical, crude, insensitive, humorless and petty, he was also empathic, shy, sophisticated, self-critical, uproariously funny, and magnanimous."[8]

He had tremendous compassion for America's neediest and a sense of social justice. But his hopes for ending poverty in America were ultimately crushed by reality and his great albatross of Vietnam. Says Dallek, "The war brought out Johnson's propensities for overbearing, high-handed control and imperiousness, which is often displayed by insecure characters threatened by any challenge to their power and stature. Though the public did not know the full story of LBJ's erratic behavior during his presidency, it did become increasingly aware of his manipulativeness and morbid determination to sustain a questionable war in Vietnam."[9]

Balancing Johnson's high hopes for social and economic justice against his Ahab-like pursuit of a disastrous war is what kept Lyndon Johnson from becoming the great president he might have been.

Johnson Administration Milestones[10]

1963

November 22	Lyndon Johnson takes the oath of office aboard Air Force One. Two days later, Lee Harvey Oswald, the accused assassin of President Kennedy, is fatally shot

by Jack Ruby. On November 29, Johnson appoints a commission, led by Chief Justice Earl Warren, to investigate the Kennedy assassination.

1964

January 11	The surgeon general announces proof that cigarette smoking causes lung disease.
January 23	The Twenty-fourth Amendment is ratified, banning the poll tax in federal elections.
July 2	The Civil Rights Act of 1964 is signed into law.
July 15–16	Senator Barry Goldwater of Arizona wins the nomination to become the Republican candidate for president.
August 7	The Gulf of Tonkin Resolution is passed, authorizing Johnson to "repel any army attacks in Vietnam," following the alleged attack on two U.S. destroyers patrolling the gulf. In a televised speech on the resolution, a few days earlier, Johnson had said, "We still seek no wider war."
August 11	The War on Poverty Bill passes.
August 26	The Democrats nominate Johnson; his running mate is Minnesota Senator Hubert Humphrey.
September 27	The Warren Commission Report concludes that Lee Harvey Oswald acted as a lone gunman.
October 14	The Reverend Dr. Martin Luther King, Jr., wins the Nobel Peace Prize.
October 21	In remarks at Akron University in Ohio, Johnson says, "We are not about to send American boys nine or ten thousand miles away from home to do what Asian boys ought to be doing for themselves."
November 3	Lyndon Johnson is elected President in a landslide.

1965

January 4	LBJ describes his legislative goals for the "Great Society" in his State of the Union message.

February 7	Continuous bombing of North Vietnam begins after a Vietcong guerilla attack on a U.S. military base in South Vietnam.
July 30	Medicare is signed into law; it provides limited health care insurance for the elderly and disabled.
August 6	The Voting Rights Act is signed into law; it allows the federal government to suspend all literacy, knowledge, and character tests for voting in areas where less than 50 percent of the voting age population is registered.
August 11	The Watts Riots: A major race riot breaks out in the southwest Los Angeles neighborhood. It is the first of several major deadly urban race riots.
September 9	The Department of Housing and Urban Development, a new cabinet-level agency, is created. Robert C. Weaver, the first black cabinet member, heads the department.

1966

March 26	Antiwar demonstrations are staged in many large cities.
June 13	In its *Miranda* decision, the Supreme Court rules that an accused must be informed of his or her rights before interrogation.
July 12	Rioting erupts in Chicago's black neighborhoods and six other cities in this "long, hot summer," continuing an escalation in race-related violence in American cities.

1967

June 12	In the case of *Loving v. Virginia*, the Supreme Court unanimously strikes down state laws that prohibit interracial marriages.
July	Urban rioting erupts in Detroit and Newark, New Jersey. In Detroit, the death toll reaches forty-one; in Newark, twenty-six people die.
August 30	Thurgood Marshall is confirmed by the Senate, becoming the first African-American justice of the Supreme Court.

December 8	After four days of antiwar demonstrations in New York City, 585 protestors are arrested. They include famed "baby doctor" Benjamin Spock and poet Allen Ginsberg.

1968

January 30	In Vietnam, the North launches a major offensive on the eve of Tet (a celebration of the lunar New Year). Expecting a holiday truce, U.S. forces are caught off-guard.
March 12	Antiwar candidate Senator Eugene McCarthy wins 42 percent of the vote in the New Hampshire primary, embarrassing President Johnson. Four days later, Senator Robert F. Kennedy announces he will run for the Democratic nomination.
March 31	Johnson stuns the political world when he announces that he will not run for reelection.
April 4	Martin Luther King, Jr., is assassinated in Memphis by James Earl Ray.
May 10	Peace talks with North Vietnam open in Paris.
June 5	Campaigning for president in Los Angeles, Senator Robert F. Kennedy is shot by Sirhan Sirhan. RFK dies the next day.
June 26	Chief Justice Earl Warren announces his decision to retire; Johnson nominates Justice Abe Fortas to replace him.
August 8	Completing a stunning political comeback, Richard Nixon is nominated in Miami by the Republicans, with Maryland governor Spiro Agnew chosen as his running mate.
August 26	The Democratic National Convention is disrupted by antiwar protests and riots in the streets. The Democrats nominate Hubert Humphrey. A later review of the riots blames the Chicago police for inciting the violence.
October 13	U.S. bombing in Vietnam is halted.
November 5	Republican Richard Nixon is elected president, defeating Johnson's vice president, Hubert Humphrey.

MUST READS

Robert A. Caro, *The Years of Lyndon Johnson: The Path to Power*; *Means of Ascent*; *Master of the Senate*; Robert Dallek, *Flawed Giant: Lyndon Johnson and His Times, 1961–1973*; Doris Kearns Goodwin, *Lyndon Johnson and the American Dream*.

ONLINE RESOURCES

Inaugural Address, Avalon Project, Yale Law School
  http://avalon.law.yale.edu/20th_century/johnson.asp
Library of Congress Resource Guide
  http://www.loc.gov/rr/program/bib/presidents/lbjohnson/index.html
Lyndon B. Johnson Library and Museum
  http://www.lbjlibrary.org/
Miller Center of Public Affairs, University of Virginia
  http://millercenter.org/academic/americanpresident/lbjohnson
Secret White House recordings
  http://millercenter.org/scripps/archive/presidentialrecordings/johnson/index

37

Tricky Dick
Richard Milhous Nixon

★ ★ ★

January 20, 1969–August 9, 1974

Milestones in Richard M. Nixon's Life

January 9, 1913	Born in Yorba Linda, California
1937–1941	Practiced law in Whittier, California
1942–1946	Served in U.S. Navy during World War II
1947–1950	U.S. representative from California
1950–1953	U.S. senator from California
1953–1961	Vice president under Eisenhower
1960	Lost presidential race to John F. Kennedy
1962	Lost race for governor of California
1963–1968	Practiced law in New York City
1963	Published *Six Crises*, detailing his career to date
1969–1974	Thirty-seventh president
August 9, 1974	Resigned as president
April 22, 1994	Died in New York City, aged eighty-one

PRESIDENTIAL VOICES

I have never been a quitter. To leave office before my term is completed is abhorrent to every instinct in my body. But as President, I must put the interests of America first. America needs a full-time President and a full-time Congress, particularly at this time with problems we face at home and abroad.

To continue to fight through the months ahead for my personal vindication would almost totally absorb the time and attention of both the President and the Congress in a period when our entire focus should be on the great issues of peace abroad and prosperity without inflation at home.

Therefore, I shall resign the Presidency effective at noon tomorrow. Vice President Ford will be sworn in as President at that hour in this office.
        —RICHARD M. NIXON, AUGUST 8, 1974[1]

There have arguably been better presidents and worse presidents. But there is probably no more complex president than Richard M. Nixon. Journalist Elizabeth Drew once described Nixon as "insecure, self-pitying, vindictive, suspicious—even literally paranoid—and filled with long-nursed anger and resentments, which burst forth from time to time. He never seemed the happy warrior."[2]

But for three decades Richard Nixon was one of the central players on the world stage. He made decisions, especially in the arena of relations with the Soviet Union and by reaching out to Communist China as only a committed Cold Warrior could do, that altered the arc of history. As journalist David Halberstam put it, "He became the man who opened the door to normalized relations with China (perhaps, thought some critics, he was the only politician in America who could do that without being attacked by Richard Nixon)."[3]

His extraordinary career in the American political spotlight flamed out in the Watergate scandals that overshadowed all else that Richard Nixon did—or didn't do.

Fast Facts

RELIGION: Quaker

The second of two presidents raised as Quakers—the other being Hoover—Nixon attended various church services as president. He clearly rejected Quaker pacifism, in World War II and as president. He also rejected the Society of Friends ban on swearing an oath, although the Constitution offers the choice to "affirm" rather than swear the oath.

EDUCATION: Whittier College, Duke University Law School

MILITARY SERVICE: Lieutenant commander, U.S. Navy (World War II)

CAREER BEFORE POLITICS: Attorney

POLITICAL PARTY: Republican

FIRST LADY: Thelma Catherine "Pat" Ryan Nixon (March 16, 1912–June 22, 1993)

CHILDREN: Tricia, Julie

* Nixon was the first former vice president to win the White House by election rather than succession in 132 years (Martin Van Buren was the last).
* His comeback from his loss to JFK in 1960 was the first of its kind since Grover Cleveland. (Other defeated candidates who came back to win were Thomas Jefferson, Andrew Jackson, and William Henry Harrison.)
* Nixon was the first and, to date, only president to resign from office.

PRESIDENTIAL VOICES

Nixon is a man of great reading, a man of great intelligence and a man of great decisiveness.

—FORMER PRESIDENT EISENHOWER, 1968

Richard Nixon is a no-good lying bastard. He can lie out of both sides of his mouth at the same time, and if he ever caught himself telling the truth, he'd lie just to keep his hand in it.

—HARRY S. TRUMAN[4]

Born into a struggling family in Whittier, California, Richard Nixon was the second of five boys whose father ran a roadside gas station, grocery, and small farm stand. Nixon's mother, Hannah, was from one of the wealthier families in Whittier, the large Milhous clan, and she had married Frank Nixon, a non-Quaker, against her family's wishes. Frank failed in a misguided attempt to start a lemon grove, eventually selling his land at a loss. As a teen, Richard Nixon had to rise at 4 a.m., drive a truck to Los Angeles, buy vegetables, and return to wash them for display. He later said he listened to the trains pass and dreamed of becoming a railroad engineer.

Hardworking and always serious as a student, Nixon did well enough in local public school to be accepted into Harvard. But a brother's illness forced him to remain at home. Attending nearby Whittier College, a Quaker institution, Nixon earned a full scholarship to the newly opened Duke University Law School, where he was class president and graduated third in his class in 1937. Nixon applied to work for the FBI—but according to one account was rejected because he was not considered aggressive enough.[5] He was also rejected by the New York "Establishment" law firms to which he applied. That failure to find acceptance was a continuation of a pattern from Nixon's childhood that has led many biographers and commentators to suggest that he harbored a deep grudge against those he viewed as "Eastern elites" who kept him out of their exclusive club.

Nixon returned to a small law office in Whittier and, after Pearl Harbor, enlisted and served in the Navy during World War II, resigning his commission in 1946. That was the year he upset a five-term incumbent California congressman, and in a short time, he went from obscurity to national prominence for his role in the Alger Hiss case in 1948, which propelled him to a Senate seat two years later. (See Chapter 33, "Harry S. Truman.")

When Eisenhower became the Republican nominee for president, he was advised to take Nixon as a running mate by the more conservative wing of the party, for Nixon's staunch anti-Communist reputation. Nixon's somewhat frosty eight years with Eisenhower ended with his loss to Kennedy in 1960, a return to California, and a failed race for governor in 1962, after which he held his "last press conference," telling reporters they would not have Richard Nixon to "kick around anymore."

In 1964, Nixon campaigned hard for Republican presidential candidate Barry Goldwater at a time when other prominent Republicans were keeping their distance from the leader of the budding conservative movement. After Goldwater lost to LBJ in a landslide, Nixon had won the gratitude of conservatives, the growing power within the party. In 1968, promising to end the war in Vietnam, just as Eisenhower had promised to get the United States out of Korea, Nixon won a presidential election almost as narrow as the one he had lost in 1960. He defeated Vice President Hubert Humphrey—who was carrying the weight of LBJ's Vietnam policies and targeted by angry hecklers protesting the war—by a small popular margin, and there has always been conjecture that if Johnson had announced an end to bombing in Vietnam a little sooner than he did, the result in 1968 might have been different.

Nixon won by a little more than half a million votes of some seventy-three million cast in 1968. Although the electoral margin was wider, Nixon won with 43.3 percent of the popular vote to Humphrey's 42.7 percent. Third-party candidate George Wallace, the segregationist former governor of Alabama, won nearly ten million votes (and five states, with forty-five electoral votes between them). In the future, Nixon and other GOP strategists would attempt to draw from Wallace's success in winning white Southern votes—once the Democratic "Solid South"— with the use of slogans promising "states' rights" and "law and order," seemingly innocuous words but always racially loaded. This "Southern Strategy," as it has been called, was key to several Republican victories, at the expense of an almost total abandonment of the African-American vote to the Democrats. (The strategy elicited an apology from the head of the Republican National Committee to the NAACP in 2005.[6])

Nixon was reelected in 1972 in a landslide over liberal antiwar Democrat George McGovern.

Why did Richard Nixon and Henry Kissinger try to stop the* New York Times *from publishing the Pentagon Papers?
In June 1971, the *New York Times* ran a headline that hardly seemed sensational: VIETNAM ARCHIVE: PENTAGON STUDY TRACES 3 DECADES OF

GROWING U.S. INVOLVEMENT. What the headline did not say was that the study also traced thirty years of deceit and ineptitude on the part of the United States government.

In page after numbingly detailed page, the *Times* reprinted thousands of documents, cables, position papers, and memos, all referring to the American effort in Vietnam. Officially titled *The History of the U.S. Decision Making Process in Vietnam*, the material quickly became known as the "Pentagon Papers."

Ordered by Robert McNamara, one of Kennedy's "best and brightest" prior to his resignation as defense secretary in 1968, this massive compilation had involved the work of large teams of scholars and analysts. The avalanche of paper ran to some two million words. Richard Nixon was not aware of its existence. But it would shake his administration and the military establishment in America to the core.

Among the men who had helped put it together was Daniel Ellsberg, a Rand Corporation analyst and onetime hawk who had become disillusioned by the war. Working at MIT after his resignation from Rand, which was involved in collecting and analyzing the papers, Ellsberg decided to go public with the information. He turned a copy over to *Times* reporter Neil Sheehan.

When the story broke, the country soon learned how it had been duped. The Pentagon Papers revealed a history of deceptions and policy disagreements within several White House administrations, as far back as Truman's. Among the most damaging revelations were cables from the American embassy in Saigon, dated weeks before Prime Minister Diem was ousted in a military coup and then executed with CIA encouragement and funding. The records showed the depth of the American involvement in this coup. There was the discovery that the Tonkin Resolution had been drafted months before the incident occurred from which it took its name. And there were memos showing Lyndon Johnson committing infantry to Vietnam at the same time he was telling the country that he had no long-range plans for a strategy there.

The papers did not cover the Nixon years, and White House reaction was at first muted, even gleeful at the prospect of the embarrassment it would create for the Democrats. But Nixon and his national security adviser, Henry Kissinger, soon realized that if something this highly classified could be leaked, so could other secrets. Both men were already troubled by leaks within the administration. How could they carry on the business of national security if documents this sensitive could be photocopied and handed out to the nation's newspapers like press releases? There was a second concern. The revelations in the Pentagon Papers had fueled the antiwar sentiment that was growing louder and moving off the campuses and into the halls of Congress.

Nixon's administration tried to halt publication. Attorney General John Mitchell threatened the newspaper with espionage charges. These were ignored. The brushfire started by the *Times* was growing into a forest fire as the *Washington Post* and the *Boston Globe* were also publishing the documents. A federal court ordered the *Post* to halt publication, and the question went to the Supreme Court. On June 30, the court ruled six to three in favor of the newspapers on First Amendment grounds.

Having lost in the courts, Nixon also turned his attention to the source of the leaked papers. When Ellsberg was revealed as the culprit, a new White House unit was formed to investigate him. Officially the Special Investigation Unit (SIU), their job was to stop leaks, so they were jokingly called the "plumbers."

One of the SIU's first jobs was to break into the office of Daniel Ellsberg's psychiatrist. As a burglary, it was only marginally more successful than the next break-in planned by the group, at an office complex called Watergate.

Apart from setting into motion some of the events that would become the Watergate affair, the publication of the Pentagon Papers had other important repercussions. From the government's standpoint, American security credibility had been crippled, severely damaging intelligence operations around the world. On the other side, the antiwar movement gained new strength and respectability, increasing the pressure on Nixon to end the U.S. involvement in Vietnam. And the Supreme Court's action in protecting the newspapers from prior restraint established and strengthened First Amendment principles.

But the Pentagon Papers case also reinforced a "bunker mentality" that already existed within the White House "palace guard." There was an us-against-them defensiveness emanating from the Oval Office. Publication of the Pentagon Papers made the Nixon administration far more aggressive in its defense of "national security," an idea that was expanded to include the protection and reelection of Richard Nixon by any means and at any cost.

How did a botched burglary become a crisis called Watergate?

When news of a break-in at the offices of the Democratic National Committee first surfaced, Nixon press secretary Ron Ziegler dismissed it as "a third-rate burglary." It would slowly emerge as a nationally televised revelation of corruption, conspiracy, and criminality that brought down a powerful president.

When a group of men were arrested trying to break into the DNC offices in the Watergate complex, on June 17, 1972, a few eyebrows were raised. But the news of this curious break-in had no impact on the Nixon victory over McGovern in November.

But as reporters continued to work the story, the threads of a conspiracy leading back to the White House all came together. The men arrested had connections to the Committee to Reelect the President (CRP or CREEP), and when one of them revealed that he had been given the orders by CRP chairman (and former attorney general) John Mitchell, the investigation snowballed. FBI director Patrick Gray then admitted to destroying evidence in the case.

Eventually, White House lawyer John Dean told a Senate investigating committee that Nixon had authorized a cover-up of the break-in and payments of "hush money" to the men involved.

When the committee learned that the White House had taped all of these conversations, it demanded the tapes and Nixon resisted, claiming executive privilege. By the spring of 1974, the Watergate investigation had absorbed all of the government. When the Supreme Court ordered Nixon to turn over the tapes, and their contents were revealed, the House Judiciary Committee prepared three articles of impeachment.

That bungled burglary was only a tiny strand in the web of domestic spying, criminal acts, illegal campaign funds, enemies lists, and obstruction of justice that emerged as "Watergate." As the evidence of the conspiracies emanating from the Oval Office was revealed in a series of news stories and Senate testimony, it became clear that Richard Nixon could not survive. He resigned from the presidency in disgrace, only a few steps ahead of impeachment and probable removal from office.

PRESIDENTIAL VOICES

Dean: I think that there's no doubt about the seriousness of the problem we've got. We have a cancer within—close to the presidency, that's growing. It's growing daily. It's compounding. It grows geometrically now, because it compounds itself. That'll be clear as I explain, you know, some of the details of why it is, and it basically is because 1) we're being blackmailed; 2) people are going to start perjuring themselves very quickly that have not had to perjure themselves to protect other people and the like. And that is just . . . and there is no assurance—

President Nixon: That it won't bust.

—WHITE HOUSE COUNSEL JOHN DEAN
AND PRESIDENT NIXON
March 12, 1973[7]

In two hundred years of history, he's the most dishonest president we've ever had. I think he's disgraced the presidency.

—GEORGIA GOVERNOR JIMMY CARTER, 1974[8]

Final Judgment: Grade D

In a history of America in the 1950s, journalist David Halberstam summed up Richard Nixon's complex character. "He was a very private man, a true loner, who lacked the instinctive affability and gregariousness of most successful politicians. One thought of him more easily as a strategist than a candidate. He hated meeting ordinary people, shaking hands and making small talk with them. He was always awkward at the clubby male bonding of Congress. When he succeeded it was because he worked harder and thought something out more shrewdly than an opponent had, and above all, because he wanted it more. Nixon had to win."[9]

The preeminent Cold Warrior of his day, Richard Nixon came to office promising to end America's involvement in Vietnam. He did that in part by secretly widening the war into neighboring Laos and Cambodia.

When this secret and unauthorized escalation of the war was revealed, it only increased the growing antiwar sentiment on the streets and campuses of America, leading most dramatically to a shooting at Kent State University in Ohio, where National Guardsmen killed four protestors in May 1971. Ten days later, two more students were killed, in a protest at Mississippi's Jackson State University.

The shootings and deaths of antiwar protestors were the culmination of the increasingly divisive, angry, and often violent student unrest in America, driven by the increasingly unpopular war. Anti-draft protests featuring draft card burnings, takeovers of university buildings, and violence at the 1968 Democratic Convention in Chicago had the country feeling like it was on the edge of anarchy. Another turning point came after the massacre of Vietnamese civilians at a hamlet called My Lai, along with the army's attempted cover-up of the incident, was revealed in 1969.

As protests grew, Nixon called on the "Silent Majority" who supported him and his policies. But in 1970, more than 480 campuses across the country were shut down by strikes over the deaths of student antiwar protestors. With the June 29 announcement of a withdrawal from Cambodia and the front lines, the campus unrest began to settle down.

After protracted negotiations between Henry Kissinger and North Vietnam's Le Duc Tho, a cease-fire was put in place. The Paris Peace Accords in early 1973 allowed America to gradually withdraw its combat forces from Vietnam and welcome home its prisoners of war from Hanoi. But the wounds of Vietnam were deep, and the crimes and deceptions of the wartime period were only made worse in the cynicism spawned by Watergate and related controversies, as the Nixon administration unraveled. The mood of mistrust sharpened when Vice President Spiro Agnew, one of the most vocal critics of the antiwar movement, was forced to resign in 1973 after revelations of corruption while he was governor of Maryland, leading to the appointment of Gerald Ford as the first unelected vice president, late in 1973.

Vietnam and Watergate overshadowed Nixon's accomplishments, at least for some time. The most dramatic of these was his approach to open relations with Communist China, which had been America's most implacable foe for a generation. The opening had come through Ping-Pong. As the Cold War and the Vietnam War both continued, a group of American table tennis players in Japan were invited to China in April 1971, becoming the first American group to set foot in China since the revolution in 1949. Their visit opened up secret negotiations between Henry Kissinger and the Chinese, and after a reciprocal visit to the United States by a Chinese table tennis team, Richard Nixon announced that in 1972 he would become the first American president to visit China.[10]

Richard Nixon's chief interest was always in the arena of foreign affairs, and his domestic policies took a backseat. While he was a conservative at heart, a number of progressive milestones were achieved during his years, including the creation of the Environmental Protection Agency (EPA) and the Occupational Safety and Health Administration (OSHA), although both of these agencies represent the anathema of government regulation to many modern GOP conservatives.

Another foreign issue that had great impact on America at the time was the continuing strife in the Middle East. When Israel was attacked in the Yom Kippur War in October 1973, the shock waves registered in America as Arab oil producers called for an oil embargo, hitting Americans in the pocketbook and gas tank. It was the first of a wave of energy shocks that continued through most of the decade, wreaking havoc on the American economy. For a period, as oil shortages grew, there was mandatory rationing of gasoline in America, where gas had always been cheap and abundant. Americans now had to line up at gas stations and were only able to fill their tanks if they were below half-full and only on certain days, based on whether their license plate ended in an odd or even number.

After Watergate exploded, most of Nixon's policy initiatives were placed on hold as the Watergate hearings brought the nation to a near standstill and forced him to resign in August 1974.

Assessing Nixon five years after his death, journalist Bob Woodward—one of the men most responsible for bringing Nixon down with his relentless investigation of Watergate for the *Washington Post* with fellow journalist Carl Bernstein—wrote, "Although Nixon's responsibility for Vietnam is large and for Watergate central, he could be forgiven for not entirely understanding the convulsions he had visited upon politics and the presidency. . . . Nixon's tapes of his office and telephone conversations left an irrefutable historical record that the president abused government power for political purposes, obstructed justice and ordered his aides to do so as well. . . . But after more than 25 years of covering presidents, I am still surprised that his successors did not fully comprehend the depth of distrust left by Nixon."[11]

Nixon Administration Milestones[12]

1969

January 20	Nixon is inaugurated.
March 4	Nixon warns that the United States will take action in the event of a new Vietcong offensive.
May 14	Nixon proposes a plan whereby the United States and North Vietnam would agree to withdraw forces from South Vietnam.
June 8	Nixon announces a plan to withdraw twenty-five thousand U.S. troops from South Vietnam by August 31.
July 20	Neil Armstrong steps onto the moon.
July 25	Nixon affirms his desire to withdraw U.S. troops from Southeast Asia and declares that individual nations will bear a larger responsibility for their own security; the statement later becomes known as the "Nixon Doctrine."
August 15–18	Woodstock: The four-day music festival draws five hundred thousand people to a farm in Bethel, New York.

November 3	Nixon reveals that North Vietnam has rejected his secret peace offers.
November 15	The largest antiwar rally takes place in Washington, where 250,000 gather to protest Vietnam.
November 24	The army charges William L. Calley in connection with a March 1968 massacre in the Vietnam hamlet of My Lai. (Calley will be convicted of murder in March 1971; Nixon will order his sentence reduced to house arrest. Later Nixon will order a tacit pardon of Calley.)
November 26	Nixon signs the Selective Service Reform Bill, ensuring that draftees are selected by a lottery system.

1970

April 23	An executive order ends occupational and parental deferments for the draft.
July 23	Nixon approves a plan for an Interagency Committee on Intelligence to conduct operations against domestic targets.
October 7	Nixon proposes a five-point peace plan for Indochina; the plan includes a "cease-fire in place" and the negotiated withdrawal of U.S. troops from Vietnam.
December 29	Nixon signs the Occupational Health and Safety Act of 1970, which gives the secretary of labor the responsibility of setting workplace safety standards in the United States.
December 31	A Clean Air Bill mandates that car manufacturers reduce certain pollutants by 90 percent.

1971

May 18	A Wage-Price Controls Bill extends Nixon's authority to impose restraints on wages, prices, salaries, and rents for another year.
June 13	The publication of the "Pentagon Papers" begins.
July 15	Nixon shocks the nation with the news that he plans to visit China.

1972

February 21–27	President and Mrs. Nixon visit China.
May 8	Nixon tells the nation that he has ordered the mining of North Vietnamese ports and the bombing of military targets in North Vietnam.
May 22	Nixon arrives in the Soviet Union for a summit meeting. He is the first sitting president to visit the Soviet Union.
June 17	The Watergate break-in is discovered when police arrest five men inside Democratic headquarters in Washington, D.C.'s Watergate Hotel. They are Republican operatives and possess cameras, wire-tapping materials, and $2,300 in cash.
June 23	Nixon orders chief of staff H. R. Haldeman to tell the FBI not to go any further with its Watergate investigation, justifying his actions on national security grounds.
August 23	Nixon is nominated for a second term.
October 21	Nixon expands the power of the Environmental Protection Agency to regulate pesticides.
November 7	Nixon wins the presidential election in a landslide over Democrat George McGovern.

1973

January 20	Nixon is inaugurated for his second term.
January 22	In a 7–2 vote, the Supreme Court issues the *Roe v. Wade* decision, legalizing abortion.
January 27	The Paris Peace Accords are signed by the parties at war in Vietnam.
April 30	Nixon accepts ultimate responsibility for the Watergate affair but continues to assert no prior knowledge of it.
June 13	Nixon declares a freeze on all prices for sixty days, with the exception of raw agricultural products and rents.

July 16	Testifying before the Senate Watergate Committee, Alexander Butterfield confirms the existence of an Oval Office taping system.
July 23	Claiming executive privilege, Nixon refuses to turn over subpoenaed tapes to the Senate Watergate Committee, chaired by Senator Sam Ervin (D-NC).
August 7–8	Vice President Spiro Agnew comes under scrutiny for charges stemming from campaign contributions he received while governor of Maryland.
August 15	In a televised address, Nixon denies involvement in the Watergate cover-up.
October 10	Vice President Agnew resigns and pleads "no contest" to charges stemming from a kickback scheme he ran while governor of Maryland.
October 12	Gerald Ford is appointed vice president.
December 8	Nixon discloses his personal finances, which indicate he paid less than $1,000 in taxes in 1970 and 1971.

1974

January 4	The Senate Watergate Committee subpoenas more than five hundred tapes, which Nixon refuses to hand over, stating that presidential communications must remain confidential.
January 30	In his State of the Union address, Nixon refuses to resign and demands an end to the Watergate investigation.
April 3	As a result of an IRS investigation into Nixon's finances, the president is forced to pay $432,787 in back taxes and $33,000 interest.
April 29	Nixon addresses the nation before disclosing more than twelve hundred pages of his conversations regarding Watergate.
May 23	Nixon again refuses to hand over Watergate-related tapes.
July 24	In an 8–0 ruling, the Supreme Court orders Nixon to turn over sixty-four tapes to the Senate Watergate

Committee. The tapes disclose Nixon's knowledge and participation in the cover-up of the Watergate burglary.

July 27-30   Three articles of impeachment are brought against Nixon by the House Judiciary Committee.

August 5   Three new transcripts are released, showing that Nixon ordered a cover-up less than a week after the break-in.

August 8   Told he will lose in an impeachment trial, Nixon resigns the presidency, effective at noon the next day.

August 9   Nixon leaves for California. His letter of resignation makes Gerald Ford the thirty-eighth president of the United States.

MUST READS

Elizabeth Drew, *Richard M. Nixon*; Stanley Karnow, *Vietnam: A History*; Joe McGinniss, *The Selling of the President*; Richard M. Nixon, *Six Crises*; Richard Reeves, *President Nixon*; Bob Woodward and Carl Bernstein, *All the President's Men* and *The Final Days*; Bob Woodward, *Shadow: Five Presidents and the Legacy of Watergate*.

ONLINE RESOURCES

Inaugural Addresses, Avalon Project, Yale University
   1969: http://avalon.law.yale.edu/20th_century/nixon1.asp
   1973: http://avalon.law.yale.edu/20th_century/nixon2.asp
Library of Congress Resource Guide
   http://www.loc.gov/rr/program/bib/presidents/nixon/index.html
Miller Center of Public Affairs, University of Virginia
   http://millercenter.org/academic/americanpresident/nixon
Watergate Tapes, University of California, Berkeley
   http://www.lib.berkeley.edu/MRC/watergate.html
Nixon Foundation, Birthplace
   http://library.nixonfoundation.org/
Nixon Presidential Library and Museum
   http://www.nixonlibrary.gov/

Obituary, *New York Times*

http://www.nytimes.com/1994/04/23/obituaries/37th-president
-richard-nixon-81-dies-master-politics-undone-watergate.html

"Times Topics," *New York Times*: **Richard M. Nixon**

http://topics.nytimes.com/top/reference/timestopics/people/n
/richard_milhous_nixon/index.html

38

Gerald Rudolph Ford

★ ★ ★

August 9, 1974–January 20, 1977

Milestones in Gerald R. Ford's Life

July 14, 1913	Born in Omaha, Nebraska.
1941–1942	Practiced law, Grand Rapids, Michigan
1942–1946	Served in U.S. Navy, World War II
1946–1948	Returned to law practice
1949–1973	U.S. representative from Michigan
1965–1973	Minority leader of the House
December 6, 1973	Appointed vice president under Nixon
1974–1977	Thirty-eighth president
December 26, 2006	Died in Rancho Mirage, California, aged ninety-three

PRESIDENTIAL VOICES

If you have not chosen me by secret ballot, neither have I gained office by any secret promises. I have not campaigned either for the Presidency or the Vice Presidency. I have not subscribed to any partisan platform. I am indebted to no man, and only to one woman—my dear wife—as I begin this very difficult job. . . .

My fellow Americans, our long national nightmare is over. Our constitution works. Our great republic is a government of laws and not of men. Here, the people rule. But there is a higher power, by whatever name we honor Him,

who ordains not only righteousness but love, not only justice, but mercy. . . .
Let us restore the golden rule to our political process and let brotherly love
purge our hearts of suspicion and hate.

—ADDRESS TO THE NATION, AUGUST 9, 1974[1]

America's first unelected President, Gerald R. Ford was one of the presidency's true "nice guys." First appointed to be vice president when Spiro Agnew resigned, he then had to take the Oval Office when Nixon was forced to resign in the wake of Watergate.

He faced incredible challenges on a wide series of fronts: a nation still at war, an economic crisis brought on by the new Arab oil power OPEC, and an ugly, sour mood in the country brought on by Nixon's "high crimes and misdemeanors." He did not succeed in solving all those problems. But Gerald Ford won high praise both in his day and afterward for providing a soothing balm desperately needed by a broken nation.

Fast Facts

RELIGION: Episcopal
ASSOCIATIONS: Freemason
EDUCATION: University of Michigan, Yale Law School
MILITARY SERVICE: Lieutenant commander, U.S. Navy, World War II
CAREER BEFORE POLITICS: Attorney
POLITICAL PARTY: Republican
FIRST LADY: Elizabeth "Betty" Ann Bloomer Ford (April 8, 1918–July 8, 2011)
CHILDREN: Michael, John ("Jack"), Steven, and Susan

* At birth, Ford was named Leslie Lynch King, Jr. Sixteen days after his birth, his mother, Dorothy Ayer Gardner, separated from his

birth father, eventually moving to Grand Rapids, Michigan, and obtaining a divorce in 1913. In 1916, she married Gerald Rudolff Ford and they renamed her son Gerald Rudolff Ford, Jr. He was never formally adopted by his stepfather and did not legally change his name until December 1935. Gerald Ford also changed the spelling of his middle name to "Rudolph."

* While a Yale law student, Ford displayed an all-American style that won him modeling jobs in a 1940 issue of *Look* and a 1942 issue of *Cosmopolitan.*

* Ford was a member of the Warren Commission that investigated the Kennedy assassination.

* He was the first president appointed under the terms of the Twenty-fifth Amendment (ratified in 1967).

* Ford was the first president who was not elected either president or vice president.

* There are two famous phrases associated with Ford; one he said, the other he didn't. When he was sworn in as vice president, he told Congress he was "A Ford, not a Lincoln."

    And as president, Ford refused to give federal economic aid to New York City during a financial crisis in October 1975. Instead he advised the city to use financial restraint, leading to a memorable *New York Daily News* headline: FORD TO CITY—DROP DEAD.

* Gerald Ford survived a pair of assassination attempts. The first was in September 1975 when Lynette "Squeaky" Fromme, a follower of Charles Manson, attempted to shoot him in Sacramento. Later that month, a woman named Sara Jane Moore also tried to shoot Ford, in San Francisco. Although he said these incidents would not alter his planned appearances, Ford began to wear a bulletproof vest at Secret Service insistence. (Since that time, presidents have occasionally but not always worn protective vests in public.)

* As first lady, Betty Ford won the nation's admiration for her candor about her health and politics. She spoke openly to *60 Minutes* about how she would counsel a daughter who might have an extra-marital affair and her children's possible use of marijuana—subjects that landed her in hot water with GOP conservatives. She also admitted to strongly favoring the Supreme Court ruling

making abortion legal. She was not only pro-choice, but favored the Equal Rights Amendment then being considered by the states for ratification.

Once divorced before her marriage to Ford, the former Martha Graham dancer did not accept the image of dutiful Midwestern, conservative Republican "homemaker." She freely stated her admiration for Eleanor Roosevelt—then heresy in GOP circles; she courageously discussed her breast cancer, at that time still considered somewhat taboo to talk about in public; and, after leaving the White House, Betty Ford acknowledged a dependence on painkillers and alcohol—a startling admission that made her one of the most admired first ladies in history. The admiration only deepened when she cofounded the Betty Ford Center in 1982, a Rancho Mirage, California, clinic specializing in the treatment of drug and alcohol dependency.

* Gerald Ford lived longer than any other president (93 years, 165 days).

PRESIDENTIAL VOICES

He's a nice fellow but he spent too much time playing football without a helmet.
—President Lyndon B. Johnson[2]

Born in Omaha, Nebraska, on July 14, 1913, Ford grew up in Grand Rapids, Michigan, with his mother and stepfather. An all-American football player as first-string center for Michigan, he entertained offers from the NFL, but in those days, pay was low and the pro-football game, in its pre–Super Bowl days, was far less glamorous and lucrative. The Bears and the Green Bay Packers offered Ford a contract paying $200 a game. "It was hard to walk away from the NFL," Ford later recalled. "But my ambition was to go to law school."[3]

Ford graduated from Yale Law School in 1941. After the Japanese attack on Pearl Harbor, he joined the U.S. Navy and saw action in the South Pacific, winning ten battle stars for his service.

Returning home after the war, Ford practiced law and entered politics, winning a House seat in 1948, the same year he married Betty Ann Bloomer, a vivacious young divorcée who worked in a Grand Rapids department store. Ford went on to represent Michigan's Fifth Congressional District for the next twenty-four years, rising to the top of Republican leadership ranks—all the while winning friends with his loyalty, warmth, and sincerity—attributes not always prized in Washington.

A moderately conservative Republican, he thought archconservative Goldwater had taken the party too far right. After the GOP's crushing defeat to LBJ in 1964, Ford became minority leader, and while he opposed much of Johnson's Great Society agenda, he attempted to find a more moderate path than obstructionism. He also did not want to align with the conservative Southern Democrats but sought instead a middle-of-the-road moderation. On Vietnam, he was very hawkish, advocating an escalating war effort and expanding the bombing campaign against North Vietnam.

In 1973, as the Watergate crisis was building, Vice President Spiro Agnew was forced to resign for evading taxes and accepting bribes. Ford's reputation for honesty made him Nixon's choice to replace Agnew under the Twenty-fifth Amendment—he needed someone who was literally "unimpeachable." Nixon and Ford had become friends as congressmen in the 1950s, and Nixon never forgot Ford's decency when he was at a low point after his 1962 loss in the California governor's race.

Ford had made rare headlines in 1970 when he moved for the impeachment of Supreme Court Justice William O. Douglas, one of the most vigorously liberal justices in history. Ostensibly criticizing Douglas for his ties to a private foundation while on the bench, Ford also targeted Douglas's opinions, including defense of a controversial Swedish film, *I Am Curious (Yellow)*, then deemed pornographic. At the time, Ford said, "An impeachable offense is whatever the House of Representatives considers it to be at a given moment in history." The line would be cited often during Richard Nixon's impeachment hearings and again when Bill Clinton faced impeachment in 1999. Ford also called Watergate the "most stupid political action I've known in my long career."[4]

How did WIN not help Ford win?

Ford came to office as the Watergate crisis swirled and the American economy was in a tailspin, created in part by the Arab use of an oil boycott as a political weapon in the Arab-Israeli conflict. The power of OPEC—the cartel of oil producers dominated by Saudi Arabia—helped create the highest rates of unemployment since the Depression and historically high inflation—a combination of low growth and rising prices termed "stagflation." This struck a severe blow to American prestige and confidence: Once built on the bedrock of cheap labor and cheap oil, the American economy no longer enjoyed either.

An inflationary cycle of double-digit dimensions had been set in motion, and it would take Americans through a decade that seemed beyond the control of the country's leadership. The crisis, begun in Nixon's final days, became Gerald Ford's problem. His response was a campaign called "WIN"—"Whip Inflation Now." But it was an inept, empty rallying slogan. Ford's failure to cope effectively with the economic crisis played a large part, along with post-Watergate disillusionment, in the 1976 election of Jimmy Carter, the little-known former governor of Georgia.

Final Judgment: Grade C

Ford presided as the country watched the fall of Saigon in 1975, with images of the last Americans fleeing the embassy roof by helicopter, and Communist forces took over the city that had been the center of America's Vietnam War era.

His image took another hit when he became the first American politician to become regular fodder for *Saturday Night Live* skits. Comedian Chevy Chase took Ford's pratfall while getting off Air Force One and turned it into a running gag in 1975, solidifying the image of Ford as an amiable "dunce." "From that moment on," Ford later said, "every time I stumbled or bumped my head or fell in the snow, reporters zeroed in on that to the exclusion of almost all else."[5]

Ford survived a primary challenge from the right wing of his party led by Ronald Reagan, the former governor of California, who considered Ford a "caretaker." He was also hurt by the revelations coming from a Congressional inquiry into a long history of CIA abuses. Then, in a debate with Jimmy Carter, he fumbled badly by asserting that the Soviet Union did not dominate Eastern Europe, something he wouldn't allow during his presidency, as if thirty years of Cold War in Europe hadn't happened. But it was the pardon of Richard Nixon that may well have cost him the election in 1976.

Ford may have not been a great president, but he may have been the president that America needed at the time. Many historians have pointed to the resounding policy failures of the Ford administration—some accidental, some by design. But his fundamental decency, humility, and commitment to healing a nation that had passed through an ordeal have softened the harshest critics. Watergate was a deep wound in America. Ford provided a brief restorative calm to a White House in crisis. It was not the Civil War. And the president was correct. He was a Ford, not a Lincoln.

Ford Administration Milestones[6]

1974

August 8	In a televised address to the nation, Richard M. Nixon resigns the presidency.
August 9	Gerald R. Ford is sworn in as the thirty-eighth president.
August 19	Ford selects Nelson A. Rockefeller, the former governor of New York, as his vice president.
September 8	Ford grants Richard Nixon a full pardon; his approval rating slips to 49 percent.
October 8	Speaking to a joint session of Congress, Ford calls for a temporary tax hike, cuts in federal spending, and the

creation of a voluntary inflation-fighting organization, named "Whip Inflation Now" (WIN).

November 5 In the wake of Watergate, Democrats gain forty-three House seats and three Senate seats, giving them a majority in both houses of Congress.

November 17 Ford makes the first visit to Japan by an American president.

November 21 The Freedom of Information Act is passed.

1975

January 4 Ford announces the creation of a presidential commission to review abuses by the Central Intelligence Agency.

March 27 Saigon falls to the North Vietnamese.

April 11 Cambodia falls to the Khmer Rouge.

November 20 Ronald Reagan challenges Ford for the Republican nomination.

1976

July 4 The Bicentennial is marked. President Ford speaks at Valley Forge and Independence Hall.

July 15 Former Georgia governor Jimmy Carter wins the Democratic nomination.

July 21 *Viking I* lands on Mars.

August 19 Following a primary battle between Ford and Ronald Reagan, the Republicans nominate Ford.

September 9 Mao Zedong dies.

October 6 In a second debate with Jimmy Carter, Ford blunders, declaring that there "is no Soviet domination of Eastern Europe and never will be under a Ford administration."

November 2 Jimmy Carter defeats Gerald Ford for the presidency, winning 49.9 percent of the popular vote to Ford's 47.9 percent.

MUST READS
Douglas Brinkley, *Gerald R. Ford*.

ONLINE RESOURCES
Library of Congress Resource Guide
   http://www.loc.gov/rr/program/bib/presidents/ford/index.html
National Archives
   http://www.archives.gov/research/arc/topics/presidents/ford.html
Miller Center of Public Affairs, University of Virginia
   http://millercenter.org/academic/americanpresident/ford
Ford Presidential Library and Museum
   http://www.fordlibrarymuseum.gov/
"Times Topics," *New York Times*: Gerald R. Ford
   http://topics.nytimes.com/top/reference/timestopics/people/f
   /gerald_rudolph_jr_ford/index.html
Obituary, *New York Times*
   http://www.nytimes.com/2006/12/27/washington/27webford.html

39

Man from Plains
James Earl Carter, Jr.

★ ★ ★

January 20, 1977–January 20, 1981

Milestones in James E. Carter's Life

October 1, 1924	Born in Plains, Georgia
1946–1953	Served as lieutenant in U.S. Navy
1963–1967	State senator in Georgia legislature
1971–1975	Governor of Georgia
1977–1981	Thirty-ninth president
2002	Awarded Nobel Peace Prize

PRESIDENTIAL VOICES

After four wars during 30 years, despite intensive human efforts, the Middle East, which is the cradle of civilization and the birthplace of three great religions, does not enjoy the blessings of peace. The people of the Middle East yearn for peace so that the vast human and natural resources of the region can be turned to the pursuits of peace and so that this area can become a model for coexistence and cooperation among nations.

The historic initiative of President Sadat in visiting Jerusalem and the reception accorded to him by the parliament, government and people of Israel, and the reciprocal visit of Prime Minister Begin to Ismailia, the peace proposals made by both leaders, as well as the warm reception of these missions by the peoples of both countries, have created an unprecedented opportunity for peace which must not be lost if this generation and future generations are to be spared the tragedies of war.

—JIMMY CARTER
Announcing Camp David Peace Accords
September 17, 1978[1]

W *hy Not the Best?* Jimmy Carter asked in a campaign autobiography intended to introduce him to the American people. "Jimmy Who?" was the reply.

A former peanut farmer—and nuclear submariner—the fairly obscure former governor of Georgia swept onto the American political scene as the ultimate "outsider" at a moment when Americans were thoroughly disgusted with Washington in the wake of Watergate.

A Deep South governor who was enlightened when it came to race. A Democrat with a seemingly commonsense approach to economics. A "born again" Christian who didn't threaten hellfire and damnation. In mid-seventies America, this was all remarkably refreshing and reassuring.

Fast Facts

RELIGION: Baptist
In 2000, Carter severed ties with the Southern Baptist Convention, saying parts of its doctrines violated "basic premises of my Christian faith."[2]

ASSOCIATIONS: Sons of the American Revolution

EDUCATION: Attended Georgia Southwestern College and Georgia Institute of Technology; graduated from U.S. Naval Academy

MILITARY SERVICE: Lieutenant, U.S. Navy (1946–1953)

CAREER BEFORE POLITICS: Farmer, naval officer

POLITICAL PARTY: Democratic

FIRST LADY: Eleanor Rosalynn Smith Carter (b. August 18, 1927)
CHILDREN: John, James III (Chip), Donnell (Jeff), and Amy.

* Carter was the first president born in a hospital.

* Emphasizing his "man of the people" qualities, Carter wore a business suit instead of formal attire to his inauguration; he also walked the entire route from the Capitol to the White House following his swearing-in ceremony.

* Carter is the only president to date ever interviewed by *Playboy* magazine. In a memorable 1976 issue, he told an interviewer, "I've committed adultery in my heart many times."[3]

* In 2002, Carter became the third president to win the Nobel Peace Prize, for his efforts at finding peaceful solutions to international conflicts; so far, he is the only presidential winner to receive the prize after leaving office. (The previous winners were Theodore Roosevelt and Woodrow Wilson, and in 2009, Barack Obama won.)

* Carter has written twenty-one books in his post-presidency and coauthored two others. Among these, the most controversial is *Palestine: Peace Not Apartheid* (2006), in which Carter contended that Israel's continued control and settlements on Palestinian land were the primary obstacles to a comprehensive peace agreement.

PRESIDENTIAL VOICES

If I'm elected at the end of four years or eight years I hope people will say, "You know, Jimmy Carter made a lot of mistakes, but he never told me a lie."
—JIMMY CARTER TO INTERVIEWER BILL MOYERS, 1976[4]

James—best known as "Jimmy"—Carter was born in Plains, a small southwest Georgia town. His father was a businessman and farmer and his mother a registered nurse. Descended from a Carter who arrived in America in 1635, he had at least one ancestor who fought in the American Revolution, while his great-grandfather served in the Confederate Army. A gifted student, he went to local public schools and, after attending Georgia Southwestern College and taking math courses at Georgia Tech, applied to the United States Naval Academy.

Hoping to make a career of the navy, Carter then served in the nuclear submarine program, once leading a team that dealt with a reactor core meltdown, an experience he said made him rethink nuclear weapons. After his father's death, he resigned his commission in 1953 and returned to Plains to run the family farm and peanut business.

Carter's political start came from serving on local school and hospital boards, until he was elected to the Georgia Senate and started to cast an eye on the statehouse. He lost in his first try in 1966 and spent four years building a base for a successful run in 1970. Carter promised to be the face of the "New South" that was trying to leave behind its staunchly segregationist past.

Sworn in as Georgia's governor in 1971, Carter served a single term, as required by Georgia law. But he had also prepared a campaign for the Democratic primaries in 1976. His surprise victory in the little-known (at that time) Iowa caucuses was followed by a win in the New Hampshire primary. In a short time, he went from "Jimmy Who?" to Democratic nominee, joined by his running mate, Minnesota senator Walter Mondale. In a close race with President Ford, Carter eked out a narrow popular and electoral victory, largely on a wave of post-Watergate rejection of incumbents in general and Republicans in particular.

PRESIDENTIAL VOICES

All the legislation in the world can't fix what's wrong with America. So I want to speak with you first tonight about a subject even more serious than energy or inflation. I want to talk to you right now about a fundamental threat to American democracy. . . .

The threat is nearly invisible in ordinary ways. It is a crisis of confidence. It is a crisis that strikes at the very heart and soul and spirit of our national will. We can see this crisis in the growing doubt about the meaning of our own lives and in the loss of a unity of purpose for our nation.

The erosion of our confidence in the future is threatening to destroy the social and the political fabric of America.

—JIMMY CARTER, JULY 15, 1979[5]

What was Carter's "malaise speech"?

Before the 1970s, Americans didn't think much about energy. Gas and oil were cheap and plentiful. Then OPEC turned off the spigots and the world came to a near standstill.

While America agonizingly transformed itself into a more efficient energy user and adjusted to new economic realities, it also began the search for alternative sources of energy. Under Carter, Congress funded development of wind and solar power and synthetic fuels. The American nuclear industry got a new boost as well. But there were still shocks to come. In 1978, Mohammad Reza Shah Pahlavi, established in power in 1954 through a CIA-backed coup, was overthrown by a fundamentalist Islamic revolution led by Ayatollah Ruholla Khomeini. Iran cut off its exports, setting off another mild oil shortage. A year later, America's energy future was further darkened when there was a major accident in the core of a nuclear reactor at Three Mile Island in Pennsylvania, which severely curtailed the planned development of nuclear power in this country. To make matters worse, that year OPEC announced another drastic price increase. And Nixon-era price controls were removed as oil prices were deregulated.

Although the nation did not have to resort to rationing again, as it had in 1973, there were frequent gasoline shortages. In 1979, there were once again long lines snaking out of gas stations, as drivers feared another round of government-designated days for buying gasoline. It didn't happen. But the mood of the country was bleak.

Responding to these oil shocks, combined with America's economic woes, Jimmy Carter offered a speech in July 1979 that suggested there was something more fundamentally wrong about the state of the country than high prices and unemployment—a "crisis of confidence." Carter's address would be called the "malaise speech" even though he never used the word. But it seemed to sum up his presidency.

Carter's call for a new American energy policy as the "moral equivalent of war" was reduced by commentators who derided his words as "MEOW." He was also mocked for installing a wood-burning stove in the White House living quarters and solar panels on the roof. This only enhanced Carter's image as an ineffectual "micro-manager" who personally scheduled the use of the White House tennis courts. James Fallows, who worked in the Carter White House, revealed that fact in a magazine article, in which he wrote more damningly that Carter lacked "the passion to convert himself from a good man into an effective one, to learn how to do the job."[6]

Carter's failure to translate his good intentions into effective action was highlighted by the situation in Iran, soon to move to the foreground of American consciousness, overshadowing Carter's historic achievement in negotiating the Camp David Peace Accords, a peace treaty between Egypt and Israel, in 1978. On November 4, 1979, some five hundred Iranians stormed the American embassy in Tehran, capturing ninety American diplomats and beginning a hostage crisis that ended Jimmy Carter's hopes for winning a second term. Carter's inability to free the hostages, including a disastrous, abortive rescue mission that ended with eight American soldiers dead in the Iranian desert, seemed to symbolize American powerlessness.

In 1980, the country turned to a man it thought represented old-style American ideals and strength. Ronald Reagan, former movie star and governor of California, soundly defeated Carter in 1980 by promising to restore American prestige, power, and economic health. At the moment of Reagan's inauguration, as a last insult to Jimmy Carter and an omen of the good fortune Reagan would enjoy, the hostages were freed by Iran.

Final Judgment: Grade D

Carter's inability to deal with the major forces arrayed against him and the American economy doomed him to a one-term presidency. He is best remembered for events that seemed to have overwhelmed him—inflation, the energy crisis, Russia's incursion into Afghanistan, and American hostages held in Iran.

Americans appreciated Jimmy Carter's honesty after Richard Nixon.

Americans didn't like his "malaise." They preferred Ronald Reagan's sunny optimism.

Far from the perfect manager or policy maker, Carter left office viewed as a weak and ineffectual president. He had frequently spoken of a new dedication to human rights while in office, as he did in his 1978 Annapolis commencement speech. There was an appreciation of the fact that he wanted American foreign policy to reflect a new concern for human rights, even though he seemed unable to formulate a realistic strategy to make that happen. His much-admired idealism ran up against the harsh reality of geopolitics in the 1970s.

But he made his greatest mark in that area after leaving office. In his post-presidency years, Carter became one of the most visible and vocal of former presidents, a passionate—if sometimes controversial—voice for human rights, winning the Nobel Peace Prize for his efforts to mediate conflicts around the world.

Carter Administration Milestones[7]

1977

January 20	Carter is inaugurated.
January 21	Carter pardons Vietnam War draft evaders.
February 2	Congress passes the Emergency Natural Gas Act, authorizing the president to deregulate natural gas prices due to a shortage in supply. He later proposes the establishment of a cabinet-level Department of Energy.
February 17	Soviet dissident Andrei Sakharov receives a written letter of support from President Carter.
April 18	In an address to the nation, Carter calls his program of energy conservation the "moral equivalent of war."
May 22	At Notre Dame University, Carter proposes a new direction in foreign policy, away from anti-Communism and focusing on support for human rights.
August 4	The Energy Department is created as a cabinet-level department.

1978

January 1	Carter visits the Shah of Iran in Tehran, calling Iran an "island of stability" in the Middle East.
January 17	In Utah, Gary Mark Gilmore becomes the first American prisoner to be executed in ten years.
March 9	Carter invokes the Taft-Hartley Act to end a strike by coal miners.
September 5–17	Carter mediates talks between Prime Minister Menachem Begin of Israel and President Anwar Sadat of Egypt, resulting in a peace treaty between the two nations—the "Camp David Accords."
December 15	The Carter administration grants full diplomatic status to the People's Republic of China.

1979

June 18	Carter signs the second Strategic Arms Limitation Treaty (SALT II) with the USSR. The U.S. Senate never ratifies the controversial treaty, although both nations comply with its terms.
July 15	Carter delivers what becomes known as his "malaise speech."
October 17	The Department of Education is created.
November 4	Iranian students take sixty-six Americans hostage at the American embassy in Tehran.

1980

January 3–4	Due to the USSR's invasion of Afghanistan, Carter asks the Senate to table its consideration of SALT II. He also places an embargo on grain sales to the Soviet Union and suggests boycotting the Summer Olympics in Moscow.
April 22	The U.S. Olympic Committee votes to boycott the Moscow summer Olympics.
April 25	Carter tells the nation that the Desert One mission failed to rescue the Iranian-held hostages, and that several American military personnel died in the operation.

May 18	Mount Saint Helens, a volcano in Washington, erupts, killing at least twenty-six people.
June	Carter's approval rating reaches the lowest mark of any president since 1945.
November 4	Ronald Reagan defeats Carter in a landslide; 489–49 in the electoral vote. Republicans also gain a majority in the Senate.

MUST READS

Julian E. Zelizer, *Jimmy Carter*.

ONLINE RESOURCES

Inaugural Address, Avalon Project, Yale University
  http://avalon.law.yale.edu/20th_century/carter.asp
National Archives
  http://www.archives.gov/research/arc/topics/presidents/carter.html
"Jimmy Carter," *The American Experience*, **PBS**
  http://www.pbs.org/wgbh/americanexperience/films/carter/
Miller Center of Public Affairs, University of Virginia
  http://millercenter.org/academic/americanpresident/carter
Jimmy Carter Presidential Library and Museum
  http://www.jimmycarterlibrary.gov/
The Carter Center
  http://www.cartercenter.org/index.html
Jimmy Carter Nobel Lecture
  http://nobelprize.org/nobel_prizes/peace/laureates/2002/carter
  -lecture.html
Jimmy Carter National Historic Site, National Park Service
  http://www.nps.gov/jica/index.htm
"Times Topics," *New York Times*: **Jimmy Carter**
  http://topics.nytimes.com/top/reference/timestopics/people/c
  /jimmy_carter/index.html

40

The Gipper
Ronald Wilson Reagan

★ ★ ★

January 20, 1981–January 20, 1989

Milestones in Ronald W. Reagan's Life

February 6, 1911	Born in Tampico, Illinois
1937	First appearance in a movie, *Love Is on the Air*
1942–1945	Served in U.S. Army during World War II
1967–1975	Governor of California
1981–1989	Fortieth president
March 30, 1981	Wounded in assassination attempt in Washington, D.C.
June 5, 2004	Died in Bel Air, California, aged ninety-three

PRESIDENTIAL VOICES

So, in your discussions of the nuclear freeze proposals, I urge you to beware the temptation of pride—the temptation of blithely declaring yourselves above it all and label both sides equally at fault, to ignore the facts of history and the aggressive impulses of an evil empire, to simply call the arms race a giant misunderstanding and thereby remove yourself from the struggle between right and wrong and good and evil.

I ask you to resist the attempts of those who would have you withhold your support for our efforts, this administration's efforts, to keep America strong and free, while we negotiate real and verifiable reductions in the world's nuclear arsenals and one day, with God's help, their total elimination.

While America's military strength is important, let me add here that I've always maintained that the struggle now going on for the world will never be decided by bombs or rockets, by armies or military might. The real crisis we face today is a spiritual one; at root, it is a test of moral will and faith.

—RONALD REAGAN, MARCH 8, 1983[1]

I t was, as one biographer who tracked former Hollywood star Ronald Wilson Reagan, put it, "The Role of a Lifetime."

After successful careers as a radio sports announcer, Hollywood movie actor, and television host, Ronald Reagan found his greatest stage in politics. When he defeated Jimmy Carter in 1980, Reagan took office with public confidence in government at its lowest ebb since the Great Depression. At the moment of Reagan's inauguration, as a last insult to Jimmy Carter and a seeming omen of the good fortune Reagan would enjoy, the hostages long held by Iran were set free. It was, as Reagan's campaign put it, "Morning in America."

Fast Facts

RELIGION: Disciples of Christ

EDUCATION: Eureka College (Eureka, Illinois)

MILITARY SERVICE: Captain, United States Army (1937–1945)

A member of the Reserve, he was classified for limited service because of poor eyesight. He later served in the First Motion Picture Unit, making training films and working on war bond drives.

CAREER BEFORE POLITICS: Actor

POLITICAL PARTY: Republican

FIRST LADY: Nancy Davis Reagan (b. July 6, 1921)

Ronald Reagan was the first divorced president. His first marriage to actress Jane Wyman ended in a divorce in 1948.

CHILDREN: Maureen and Michael, who was adopted.

Reagan met second wife actress Nancy Davis in 1949 when she

sought help from Reagan in his role as president of the Screen Actors Guild. They appeared in one film together, *Hell Cats of the Navy*. They were married in 1952.

CHILDREN: Patti Davis, Ron Reagan, Jr.

One of their two children together, Patti Davis, embraced more liberal viewpoints than her father and chose to use her mother's maiden name while attending the University of Southern California.

* Ronald Reagan was the oldest person ever to serve as president—he left office a few weeks before his seventy-eighth birthday.
* Reagan's 1981 inaugural was the warmest Inauguration Day recorded; his 1985 inauguration was the coldest ever.
* Reagan nominated Sandra Day O'Connor to be the first woman on the Supreme Court.

PRESIDENTIAL VOICES

Let us above all thank President Reagan for ending the West's retreat from world responsibility, for restoring pride and leadership of the United States, and for giving the West back its confidence. He has left America stronger, prouder, greater than ever before and we thank him for it.

—British Prime Minister Margaret Thatcher, 1988

Reaganites say that Reagan has lifted our "spirits"—correct if they mean he led the nation in a drunken world-record spending binge while leaving millions of American workers, consumers, and pollution victims defenseless.

—Consumer advocate Ralph Nader, 1989[2]

Ronald Reagan was born on February 6, 1911, in Tampico, Illinois. His family—father Jack, mother Nelle, and older brother Neil—moved to a succession of towns in the state, as his nomadic and alcoholic father searched for work. In 1920, the Reagans settled in Dixon, which Ronald considered his hometown.

Known by his boyhood nickname of "Dutch," Reagan graduated in 1928 from Dixon High School, where he showed interest in drama and journalism. He attended Eureka College, near Peoria, and paid his way through school with dishwashing and other jobs. Ronald Reagan was a solid C student but excelled in dramatics and football.

Following his graduation in June 1932, at a time when a quarter of Americans were unemployed, Reagan found work as a radio announcer, first in Davenport, Iowa, then later Des Moines. In time, Reagan became one of the best-known sports announcers in the Midwest, famous for his ability to improvise re-created play-by-play action from wire service summaries.

In 1937, Reagan went to California with the Chicago Cubs baseball team on spring training and was given a screen test at Warner Bros., which offered Reagan a contract for $200 a week, launching his film career. Although he would have to battle critics who derided movies like the 1951 *Bedtime for Bonzo*, in which Reagan's costar was a chimp, his iconic role came when he landed the part of George Gipp, legendary Notre Dame coach of Knute Rockne in *Knute Rockne—All American*. In a deathbed scene, Reagan got to say, "Win one for the Gipper," a line that would serve him in politics as well.

His most acclaimed dramatic role came in *Kings Row* (1942), in which his character's legs are amputated by a sadistic doctor and he wakes up to cry, "Where's the rest of me?" The line became the title of Reagan's later campaign autobiography. Throughout his political career, many friends and journalists called attention to the fact that Reagan had a knack for telling seemingly true stories that were actually from films he had made.

During the war, Reagan's poor eyesight kept him from active duty, so he made army training films and worked on war bond drives instead.

After the war, he was elected president of the Screen Actors Guild, at a time when the group was being investigated by the House Un-American Activities Committee for Communist infiltration. Though he didn't "name names" publicly, Reagan did so privately.

Once considering himself a New Deal Democrat, Reagan became

increasingly conservative through the 1950s, as he became a corporate spokesman or "roving ambassador" for General Electric, the company that also sponsored a television series hosted by Reagan. General Electric fired Reagan in 1962 for his criticism of the Tennessee Valley Authority, a major GE customer. Reagan supported archconservative Republican Barry Goldwater's 1964 presidential bid. Stridently anti-Communist and a low-tax, small government advocate, he entered politics himself, winning the governorship of California in 1966 by defeating Pat Brown, the man who had earlier beaten Richard Nixon. In 1970, Reagan was easily elected to a second term.

He then challenged Gerald Ford for the Republican nomination in 1976, but came up short. Four years later, he took the Republican nomination and easily defeated Jimmy Carter in a time of high inflation and general despair.

PRESIDENTIAL VOICES

Together, we not only cut the increase in government spending nearly in half, we brought about the largest tax reductions and the most sweeping changes in our tax structure since the beginning of this century. And because we indexed future taxes to the rate of inflation, we took away government's built-in profit on inflation and its hidden incentive to grow larger at the expense of American workers.

Together, after 50 years of taking power away from the hands of the people in their States and local communities, we have started returning power and resources to them.

—RONALD REAGAN
State of the Union Address
January 26, 1982[3]

What was "Reaganomics"?
When Ronald Reagan campaigned in 1980, he promised to cut taxes, reduce government deficits, reduce inflation, and rebuild America's

defenses. One of his Republican primary opponents called Reagan's ideas "voodoo economics." He was George H. W. Bush, later to become Reagan's loyal vice president and successor.

Resoundingly elected in 1980, Reagan brought a new conservative coalition to power in Washington—a group pledged to reverse what it saw as the damage done by decades of liberal Democratic control of American economic and social policy. The Reagan coalition featured the "neoconservatives," political theorists who put a new face on old-line anti-Communism; the so-called Moral Majority, evangelical Christians with a conservative social agenda; formerly Democratic Southerners, who responded to Reagan's call for a strengthened American defense and lower taxes as well as his call for "states' rights," once a code word for segregationists; and, perhaps most importantly but least visibly, a blue-collar majority who saw their paychecks disappearing in taxes and an endless inflationary spiral.

The theoretical underpinning of Reagan's plans was called "supply-side economics." The basic premise was that if taxes were cut, people would produce more goods and spend more money, creating more jobs and broader prosperity, which would lead to higher government revenues. Coupled with deep cuts in "wasteful" government spending, these revenues would provide a balanced budget.

There certainly was nothing new about this idea. President Carter had proposed tax cuts, smaller government, and tight credit to keep down inflation. Earlier in American history, another Republican administration had used a similar strategy. It had worked for Calvin Coolidge, a hero to Reagan, and Herbert Hoover had tried the same things during the Depression when the name for supply-side economics was "trickle-down economics."

And President Richard Nixon had championed what he called the "New Federalism," which directed money back toward the states and away from federally run programs. Reagan became the aggressive new champion of the "New Federalism," which he described in his 1982 State of the Union message, saying, "The time has come to control the uncontrollable."[4]

With strong popular support and the congressional backing of a bloc of conservative Southern Democrats known as "boll weevils," Reagan's economic package sailed through Congress in 1981. But there was no immediate relief, and the American economy was soon in the midst of a full-blown and devastating recession.

Unemployment was high, inflation continued, bankruptcies and business failures skyrocketed, and family farms went on the auction block. Committed to purging inflation from the world economic system, the Federal Reserve Board had adopted a policy of high interest rates to put the brakes on the economy. Without easy credit, houses don't get built, cars go unsold, and businesses and factories scale back or fold.

Oil had been at the root of the inflationary pressure, and it was only the eventual tumble in oil prices, caused in part by the falloff in demand as new sources of oil production developed in non-OPEC nations, that relieved that "oil pressure." With prices plunging, the heart of the inflationary dragon was cut out, and Ronald Reagan looked like St. George. Other pro-business Reagan policies, such as deregulating industry, fueled the recovery. Employment started to grow, and inflation, which had been running at 12 percent, dropped to around 5 percent. The tax cuts that passed in 1981, to be phased in over three years, also fueled resurgence in the financial markets and would reap a bonanza for the nation's wealthiest, but the poor and the middle class would feel few of their rewards.

The shift in tax policy was accompanied by a new reality in government spending. A succession of Reagan budgets slashed domestic spending in those areas that most affected the poor—the legacy of LBJ's Great Society. Welfare, housing, job training, drug treatment, and mass transportation all fell under the rubric of wasteful government spending.

Yet in spite of these cuts and the tax changes meant to stimulate government revenues, the federal deficits ballooned under Reagan. Apart from the reductions made by the tax cuts, the chief culprit in the deficits was the expansion of the defense budget. Although he pledged publicly to cut the budget, Reagan was overseeing a large transfer of funds from the domestic sector to the Pentagon.

And tax-cutting apostle that he was, Ronald Reagan was also pretty good at raising them, including one of the largest payroll tax increases in history. Overall, income taxes at the end of his administration stood at about the same rate they had been before—except for people in the highest tax brackets, who saw their taxes cut radically.

What was Iran-Contra?

The fact that the American embassy hostages held in Tehran were freed at the moment Reagan took office seemed to give the Reagan years the first blush of serendipity. This image got another boost when Reagan survived an assassination attempt by a young gunman, John Hinckley, on March 30, 1981, and the country reveled in press reports of how he joked with the emergency room staff. As *Washington Post* columnist David Broder wrote at the time, "A new legend has been born. The gunfire that shattered the stillness of a rainy Washington Monday afternoon . . . created a new hero in Reagan, the chipper 'Gipper' who took a .22 caliber slug in his chest but walked into the emergency room on his own power and joked with the anxious doctors on his way to surgery."[5]

Reagan emerged from the shooting with a surge in his approval polls that helped him ramrod through Congress the tax cuts and Pentagon spending plans he called for. After a generation of failed and disgraced presidents, Washington observers were marveling at Reagan's considerable power.

This gloss of invincibility and personal affability not only carried Reagan through a series of minor scandals in his administration, but even major policy disasters seemed to roll off his back. In 1983, the bombing of a U.S. Marine barracks in Beirut killed 239 marines who had been assigned to an indefensible position with no real justification for their presence other than to assert American interests in the area. Reagan assumed "responsibility" without any damage to his image and popularity. In 1986, an American air raid on the home of Libyan strongman Mu'ammar Khadafy failed in its goal to kill the Libyan leader and left two American pilots and an estimated fifteen Libyan civilians dead. (Rumors that the adopted daughter of the Libyan leader was killed later proved false.) Yet Reagan's popularity soared.

But his armor got its most severe dent with the series of events that came to be called Iran-Contra. Although President Reagan escaped this controversy unscathed, it crippled his administration's final days.

Essentially it boiled down to how to deal with American hostages once again being held in the Middle East. Among them was the CIA head of station in Beirut, a fact likely known to his kidnappers. Reagan was personally tormented by the plight of the hostages and their families, but publicly stuck to his guns that there would be no yielding to terrorist demands. Such a trade-off, it was stated, would only encourage further hostage taking.

Reagan's reputation was greatly tarnished when the public learned in late 1986 that members of the president's National Security Council staff had engineered an arms sale to Iran, then involved in a bloody war with Iraq, in an ill-conceived attempt to win the release of the Americans held hostage in Lebanon. Some of the proceeds from the arms sales were funneled to rebels ("Contras") opposing the Marxist government of Nicaragua. The two events became known as the Iran-Contra affair. On November 13, 1986, Reagan gave a national address in which he said that the United States had sent Iran "a small amount of defensive weapons" and "We did not trade weapons or anything else for hostages." Both assertions were completely false.

The immediate outcome of the episode was the formation of a presidential commission led by Senator John Tower, a conservative Republican from Texas. When the findings of the Tower Commission were released early in 1987, they constituted a scathing rebuke of Reagan and the publication was followed by a congressional investigation.

While never taken quite as seriously by the general public as Watergate had been, the abuses of Iran-Contra were dangerous: a president seemingly out of touch with events; junior officers in control of major foreign policy adventures without oversight; a plan to set up a secret CIA operation to circumvent the Congress; and an attempt to ignore a law by using a technicality, a maneuver that even the president's closest advisers said might be an impeachable offense. With images of Richard Nixon's resignation and departure in disgrace still vivid, the specter of another impeachment proceeding was more than speculation. But with Watergate memories still fresh, and Reagan's popularity still relatively strong, Congress had no appetite for impeachment.

In August 1993, eighty-one-year-old special prosecutor Lawrence E. Walsh issued the final report of the Iran-Contra affair.[6] Long-extended by the legal strategy of delays employed by some of the defendants in the case and the issuance of presidential pardons by President George H. W. Bush, Walsh's investigation had gone on for seven years. The report said the Iran-Contra operations "violated United States policy and law," and it criticized the Reagan and Bush administrations for involvement in a cover-up. However, Walsh acknowledged that there was no credible evidence that the president authorized or was aware of the diversion of the profits from the Iran arms sales to assist the Contras. Nonetheless, as Scott Spencer wrote at the time, "Walsh's won-lost record is surprisingly strong, considering the power of his opposition and the brick wall of 'national security' that was often hastily constructed when Walsh tried to obtain potentially incriminating documents. Of the 14 people against whom he brought criminal charges, 11 were convicted or pleaded guilty. (Two were pardoned before trial and one avoided trial because the Bush Administration refused to release pertinent documents.) While two of these convictions were overturned on appeal, the appeals turned mainly on the immunity the defendants had been granted for their testimony before Congress."[7]

PRESIDENTIAL VOICES

Come here to this gate! Mr. Gorbachev, open this gate! Mr. Gorbachev, tear down this wall!

—RONALD REAGAN
"Address from the Brandenburg Gate"
June 12, 1987[8]

Final Judgment: Grade A

In the years since his death Ronald Reagan has been widely praised for his leadership in the twilight of the Soviet Union and for restoring a sense of optimism to a nation at a low point. Early in 2012, a Harris

Poll confirmed that Americans hold the Gipper in high esteem, rank-ing Reagan as the best president of the post–World War II era.[9]

In a biography written after Reagan's death, veteran journalist and presidential chronicler Richard Reeves summed up the Gipper: "'Rea-ganism,' a word that defined his dominance. No other President be-came a noun in that way. Amazing things, good or bad, happened in the 1980s because President Reagan wanted them to happen. He knew how to be President. . . . His personal popularity remained remarkably high in the years after the recession of 1982, even though a majority of Americans disapproved of what he was doing in driving the country deep into debt, fighting little wars in Central America, secretly selling arms to Iran, or refusing to acknowledge the lethal spread of AIDS across the nation."[10]

Biographer Lou Cannon once called his approach to AIDS "halting and ineffective." Harsher critics blamed his administration's reluctance to attack AIDS more vigorously as the result of its connections to the evangelical right, which at the time painted AIDS as divine retribution on homosexuals. Cannon writes, "It is surprising that the president could remain silent as 6,000 Americans died, that he could fail to acknowledge the epidemic's existence. Perhaps his staff felt he had to, since many of his New Right supporters have raised money by campaigning against ho-mosexuals."[11]

The Iran-Contra scandal bedeviled Reagan during the last years of his presidency but did not overshadow his role in bringing the Cold War to a near conclusion. It was in foreign affairs that Reagan had his greatest successes—his assault on the "evil empire," the Soviet Union.

For years, Reagan had hectored the Soviets and built up American defenses in the belief that this would force them to spend as recklessly. But in the end, it was Reagan working diligently with the Soviet Union's new reform-minded leader, Mikhail Gorbachev, that changed the course of the Cold War. First they negotiated the 1987 Intermediate Nuclear Forces (INF) Treaty, the first treaty of the Cold War to reduce the number of nuclear missiles rather than stabilizing them at higher levels. With Reagan promising that he would "trust but verify," the INF Treaty paved the way for other agreements that reduced the nuclear arsenals of the superpowers.

Encouraged by the conservative British prime minister Margaret Thatcher—his ideological soul mate—Reagan believed that Gorbachev was a different sort of Soviet leader—a more modern realist, a reformer with whom he could do business. While the ultimate end of the Soviet Union did not come on Reagan's official presidential watch, the Communist nation that had been America's unflinching enemy for generations was in its death throes.

In a balanced assessment of Reagan's role in ending the Cold War, reporter James Mann wrote, "Unquestionably Gorbachev played the leading role in bringing the four-decade conflict to a close. Yet Reagan, overcoming considerable opposition of his own at home, played a crucial role by buttressing Gorbachev's position. . . . Reagan didn't win the Cold War; Gorbachev abandoned it."[12]

In the end, that supporting part may have really been Ronald Reagan's "Role of a Lifetime."

Milestones in the Reagan Years[13]

1981

January 20	Reagan is inaugurated.
	Fifty-two American hostages held in Iran since November 1979 are released.
February 18	In an Address to Congress, Reagan proposes increased defense spending, lower taxes, and domestic spending cuts.
March 10	Reagan budget proposal sent to Congress; it calls for spending $695.3 billion with a projected deficit of $45 billion. It includes funding cuts for two hundred programs in addition to those cuts already proposed by President Carter.
March 30	Reagan is shot in the chest by John Warnock Hinckley, Jr.
April 24	Reagan lifts a grain embargo imposed on the Soviet Union by President Carter.
July 7	Reagan nominates Sandra Day O'Connor, the first woman to sit on the Supreme Court.

August 5   Reagan orders the dismissal of thirteen thousand
                PATCO air traffic controllers out on strike, citing
                their violation of a federal law against industry strikes.

August 13   Reagan signs the tax cut into law.

October 2   Reagan declares that the United States will produce
                the B-1 bomber and MX missiles as part of a military
                buildup.

November 18   Reagan states that he will not deploy intermediate-
                range nuclear missiles in Europe if the Soviet Union
                agrees to dismantle similar weapons already in place.

December 28   Reagan imposes economic sanctions on Poland follow-
                ing that government's imposition of martial law.

1982

January 26   Reagan calls for a "New Federalism" in his State of the
                Union Address, advocating less federal spending and
                returning policy decisions to the states.

June 6   Reagan becomes the first U.S. president to address the
                combined Houses of Parliament, taking Britain's side
                in a conflict with Argentina over the Falkland Islands.

1983

January 5   Reagan signs into law a five-cents-per-gallon gasoline
                tax increase.

January 25   In his State of the Union Address, Reagan calls for a
                freeze on domestic spending and increases in military
                outlays.

March 23   Reagan urges development of the Strategic Defense
                Initiative (SDI), an attempt to create a high-
                technology antiballistic missile shield to protect the
                United States from nuclear attack.

April 20   The U.S. GNP shows dramatic growth for the first
                quarter of 1983, signaling the end of the recession.

June 18   Reagan nominates Paul Volcker to a second term as
                head of the Federal Reserve Board.

July 1   The final phase of the tax cut goes into effect.

1984

August 22	The Republican Party renominates Reagan and Bush.
November 6	Reagan is reelected president, defeating Democratic candidate Walter Mondale.

1985

January 20	Reagan is inaugurated for a second term.
May 1	The Reagan administration announces a trade embargo against Nicaragua.
November 19–21	Reagan and Soviet premier Mikhail Gorbachev hold a summit meeting in Geneva, Switzerland, the first such meeting since 1979.
December 12	Reagan signs the Gramm-Rudman deficit reduction bill.

1986

June 17	Supreme Court chief justice Warren Burger announces his retirement; Reagan elevates Justice William Rehnquist to the position of chief justice and nominates Anthony Scalia as an associate justice.
October 11–12	Reagan and Gorbachev meet again in Reykjavík, Iceland.
October 22	Reagan signs a revision of the tax code into law.
November 4	The Democrats win control of the Senate; both houses of Congress are in Democratic hands for the first time in Reagan's two terms.
November 13	The White House informs Congress that the United States secretly sold arms to Iran in violation of federal laws; the administration denies that the sales were part of an attempt to secure the release of American hostages held by Iranian-backed forces.
November 25	The administration admits that between $10 and $30 million was diverted from Iranian arms sales to the Nicaraguan rebels.

| November 26 | The Tower Commission is appointed to investigate the Iran-Contra affair as special prosecutor Lawrence Walsh investigates criminal wrongdoing. |

1987

| February 26 | The Tower Commission releases its report, finding no criminal wrongdoing at the White House but criticizing the administration. |
| December 7–10 | Gorbachev and Reagan meet in Washington, D.C., and sign the Intermediate Range Nuclear Forces Treaty. |

1988

January 29	The administration prohibits federally funded family-planning centers from providing assistance to women seeking abortions.
May 29–June 1	Reagan visits the Soviet Union for the first time.
August 15–18	The Republicans nominate Vice President George H. W. Bush for president.
November 8	Vice President George H. W. Bush defeats Democratic challenger Michael Dukakis.

1989

| January 20 | Reagan leaves office as the most popular president since Franklin D. Roosevelt. |

MUST READS

Lou Cannon, *President Reagan: The Role of a Lifetime*; James Mann, *The Rebellion of Ronald Reagan: A History of the End of the Cold War*; Richard Reeves, *President Reagan: The Triumph of Imagination*.

ONLINE RESOURCES

Inaugural Addresses, Avalon Project, Yale University
   1981: http://avalon.law.yale.edu/20th_century/reagan1.asp
   1985: http://avalon.law.yale.edu/20th_century/reagan2.asp

Miller Center of Public Affairs, University of Virginia
http://millercenter.org/president/reagan
National Archives
http://www.archives.gov/research/arc/topics/presidents/reagan
.html
Reagan Presidential Library and Foundation
http://www.reaganfoundation.org/
"Times Topics," *New York Times*: **Ronald Reagan**
http://topics.nytimes.com/top/reference/timestopics/people/r
/ronald_wilson_reagan/index.html?inline=nyt-per
Obituary, *New York Times*
http://www.nytimes.com/2004/06/06/us/ronald-reagan-dies-at-93
-fostered-cold-war-might-and-curbs-on-government.html
?ref=ronaldwilsonreagan

41

Bush 41
George Herbert Walker Bush

* * *

January 20, 1989–January 20, 1993

Milestones in George H. W. Bush's Life

June 12, 1924	Born in Milton, Massachusetts
1942–1945	Served in the U.S. Navy, World War II
1948–1964	Founded oil company in Texas
1966–1971	U.S. representative from Texas
1971–1972	U.S. ambassador to the United Nations under Nixon
1971–1972	Chairman of the Republican National Committee
1973–1974	Chief, U.S. Liaison Office, Beijing, China, under Ford
1976–1977	Director, Central Intelligence Agency, under Ford
1981–1989	Vice president under Reagan
1989–1993	Forty-first president

PRESIDENTIAL VOICES

I have spoken of a thousand points of light, of all the community organizations that are spread like stars throughout the Nation, doing good. We will work hand in hand, encouraging, sometimes leading, sometimes being led, rewarding. We will work on this in the White House, in the Cabinet agencies. I will go to the people and the programs that are the brighter points of light, and I will ask every member of my government to become involved. The old ideas are new again because they are not old, they are timeless: duty, sacrifice, commitment, and a patriotism that finds its expression in taking part and pitching in.

GEORGE BUSH
Inaugural Address, January 20, 1989[1]

G eorge H. W. "Poppy" Bush was the first vice president later elected to the Oval Office in his own right since Martin Van Buren in 1836. When someone gave Bush a portrait of Van Buren on Inauguration Day, he may have politely failed to mention that Van Buren served only a single term; he was turned out of office because of the terrible shape of the American economy back then.

The résumé of "41," as he is sometime called to distinguish him from his son George W. Bush, is a pedigree for presidential success: Proper family. The right schools. Distinguished military service. A series of elected and appointed posts. Two terms as vice president under a charismatic president. Few men have had the broad breadth of knowledge, credentials, and experience that George H. W. Bush brought to the Oval Office.

It was not enough.

Fast Facts

RELIGION: Episcopal
EDUCATION: Yale
ASSOCIATIONS: "Skull and Bones," undergraduate secret society at Yale
MILITARY SERVICE: U.S. Navy pilot, World War II
CAREER BEFORE POLITICS: Oil business
POLITICAL PARTY: Republican
FIRST LADY: Barbara Pierce Bush (b. June 8, 1925)

CHILDREN: George, Pauline (Robin), John Ellis ("Jeb"), Neil, Marvin, and Dorothy

President George H. W. Bush is the father of the forty-third president, George W. Bush; they are the second father-and-son presidents, after John and John Quincy Adams.

Son Jeb Bush is the former governor of Florida.

Since Abigail Adams, no woman had been both first lady and mother of a president. The matriarch of the Bush family, Barbara Bush, claims both distinctions, becoming one of the most admired first ladies in recent times. With a grandmotherly and compassionate public face, she embraced AIDS patients and victims of leukemia, which had claimed her own daughter Pauline's life. Almost every first lady stakes a claim to a cause, and for Barbara Bush it was literacy, convinced as she was that literacy held the key to solving some of America's other pressing social problems—AIDS and homelessness chief among them in the 1980s.

* Bush's father, Prescott, was a senator from Connecticut and a member of the moderate Eastern wing of the Republican Party (he was an early supporter of both Planned Parenthood and the United Negro College Fund). Although he was anti-Communist, Prescott Bush disagreed with Senator Joseph McCarthy's tactics and was one of the few men to say so publicly.

* After Pearl Harbor, when Bush turned eighteen, he enlisted in the navy. The youngest naval aviator commissioned (three days before his nineteenth birthday), he flew forty-four combat missions in the Pacific and was awarded the Distinguished Flying Cross.

* In all probability, Bush will be the last of the World War II generation of presidents.

PRESIDENTIAL VOICES

Communism died this year. Even as president, with the most fascinating possible vantage point, there were times when I was so busy helping to manage progress and lead change that I didn't always show the joy that was in my

heart. But the biggest thing that has happened in the world in my life, in our lives, is this: By the grace of God, America won the Cold War.
—George H. W. Bush
New York Times, January 29, 1992

Born and raised in New England in an old, established, and wealthy family, George H. W. Bush was educated at Phillips Academy in Andover, Massachusetts, before joining the U.S. Navy. Becoming the youngest naval pilot during World War II, he was shot down once, losing two crew members, and was afloat in a small rubber raft for hours before being rescued by submarine. Bush was later sent to a naval base in Michigan, where he trained pilots. While there, he married Barbara Pierce, whom he'd met at a prep school Christmas dance. They were engaged before he left for the navy.

When the war ended, Bush left the navy and attended Yale University, where he had been accepted before the war. Captain and first baseman of the Yale baseball team, he played in the first two College World Series and graduated in two and a half years, receiving a degree in economics. While he was at Yale, his son George W. Bush, the future president, was born in 1946. Bush 41 also joined Skull and Bones, as his father had (and later son George W. would). The secret society became a favorite of conspiracy theorists, who claimed it was part of a plan for control of the world or that it controlled the CIA, which Bush would later lead as director. In fact, in his history of the CIA, *Legacy of Ashes*, Tim Weiner calls the CIA "Skull and Bones with a billion-dollar budget."[2]

Setting out on his own after college, Bush moved his young family to Texas, where he made a success in the oil business, with the connections provided by his powerful businessman-turned-senator father, Prescott Bush. He eventually relocated to Houston, Texas, and became involved in Republican Party politics, winning two terms in the U.S. House of Representatives from Houston.

But most of his long years of experience came in appointed rather than elected posts. And moving the family became a Bush specialty, with some twenty-nine moves recorded in his professional and political career. After losing an election for a U.S. Senate seat in 1970, Bush was appointed the U.S. ambassador to the United Nations by President Richard Nixon. In 1974, he was asked to take over the thankless task of chairman of the Republican National Committee during the Watergate crisis. Under Gerald Ford, he served as U.S. envoy to China before full diplomatic relations with the Chinese were established.

Bush took on another daunting appointment when he returned to the United States to become director of Central Intelligence. It was a difficult post, as in the post-Watergate era, the agency was being investigated by Congress about revelations of assassination plots and other illicit covert activities during the 1970s. Bush thrived in the CIA and wanted incoming president Jimmy Carter to retain him as director. But Carter chose to replace him, and Bush returned to Houston, where he charted his first presidential run.

In the 1980 Republican primaries, Bush ran as a moderate candidate with years of experience, collecting a surprising win in the Iowa caucuses. When Ronald Reagan overwhelmed him in the other primary states, Bush agreed to run as his vice president to help attract moderates and bring foreign policy experience to the ticket, which won easily in both 1980 and 1984. As vice president in the 1984 election, one of Bush's memorable, though less than shining, moments came after he debated the first woman on a major national ticket, Geraldine Ferraro, the Democratic nominee for vice president. His post-debate remarks had the ring of frat-boy sexism but made no difference in Reagan's landslide victory.

In the 1988 presidential election, Bush's candidacy offered a continuation of the Reagan years. He ran against Massachusetts governor Michael Dukakis and his running mate, Texas senator Lloyd Bentsen, the man who had defeated Bush in the Texas Senate race in 1970. Bush wanted to soften some of Reagan's programs and promised "a kinder and gentler nation"—to which Mrs. Reagan archly inquired, "Kinder and gentler than who?" But he did not advocate radical change or propose sweeping new legislation. Bush was sworn in on January 20, 1989, as the United States navigated the end of the Cold War.

PRESIDENTIAL VOICES

Had we gone the invasion route, the United States could conceivably still be an occupying power in a bitterly hostile land.
— GEORGE H. W. BUSH AND BRENT SCOWCROFT
Commenting on the decision not to invade Iraq in the
Gulf War of 1991[3]

How did George Bush lead America into the first Persian Gulf War?

To many Americans, the Reagan years had completed a clean break with the long post-Vietnam, post-Watergate mood of the country. This was true despite the fact that budget deficits were ballooning, Wall Street was tottering through another periodic scandal—this time it was over manipulating "junk bonds"—and a banking crisis was costing taxpayers billions. Crack cocaine had become epidemic, bringing with it a deadly wave of urban crime. And the specter of AIDS and the epidemic's death toll had scarred the country.

Still, on the surface at least, the Reagan years seemed to have restored a semblance of confidence in the United States. And the chief beneficiary of that confidence was Reagan's vice president, George Bush.

In his first two years as president, Bush witnessed the stunning unraveling of Communism in Europe. The Berlin Wall crumbled, East and West Germany were united, once-captive nations embraced democracy, and, astonishingly, the Soviet Union, the longtime adversary that Ronald Reagan had called the "evil empire," simply and bloodlessly disintegrated.

Soviet leader Mikhail Gorbachev had attempted to restructure his nation's economy and loosen political restraints. But the Soviet Union ultimately buckled under its own weight. The Cold War was over. George Bush was the president on hand to usher in what he called a "New World Order."

As the "evil empire" unraveled, Bush's presidential high point came in a part of the world that has confounded every American president since Truman: the Middle East. In Bush's case, the crisis came from Iraqi dictator Saddam Hussein's August 1990 invasion of neighboring oil-rich Kuwait.

Mobilizing the United Nations against Hussein, Bush first ordered Operation Desert Shield, a defensive move to protect the vast oil fields of Saudi Arabia. A decisive thrust by Iraq's army into the Saudi kingdom would have given Iraq control of more than 40 percent of the world's oil reserves, a frightening prospect to the West.

Leading a coalition of thirty-nine other nations and with United Nations approval, the United States then spearheaded Operation Desert Storm, under the command of General Norman Schwarzkopf; it was a devastating air war, followed by a hundred-hour ground offensive.

The Gulf War lasted forty-two days: thirty-eight days of intense air strikes and four days of ground fighting. The U.S.-led coalition routed Saddam's army and "liberated" Kuwait. By halting the offensive against Iraq—without assaulting Baghdad and possibly overthrowing Saddam Hussein—President Bush and his advisers had fulfilled the UN's terms of the action against Iraq.

American losses for the operation were 148 killed in action and 7 missing in action. The Gulf War devastated Iraq. As many as 100,000 Iraqi soldiers were killed, and a great number of civilians also died. Iraqi roads, bridges, factories, and oil industry facilities were demolished. Water purification and sewage treatment facilities could not operate without electric power. A continuing trade embargo caused serious economic problems. In March 1991, Kurdish and Shiite Muslims rebelled against Saddam Hussein with encouragement from President Bush, who had promised American support that never came. But by April, Iraqi troops had put down most of the rebellions with brutal efficiency and the use of deadly chemical weapons.

In April, the UN Security Council officially declared an end to the war. Under the cease-fire agreement, Iraq agreed to destroy all of its biological and chemical weapons, its facilities for producing such weapons, and any facilities or materials it might have for producing nuclear weapons.

Final Judgment: Grade C

The euphoria of the quick victory over Iraq in the first Gulf War did not last long. The economy went into a deep recessionary tailspin, and a crisis over bailing out failed savings and loans—a scandal which involved one of Bush's other sons, Neil—had the country in a sour mood. After leading the war effort with such steady resolve, Bush seemed to have no good answers for getting the country out of its funk.

Presidential historian Robert Dallek points out, "Bush seemed less ready to address the more pressing domestic issues troubling the country at the end of the eighties—crime, drugs, massive government debts and deficits, bank failures, a faltering educational system, homelessness, increased poverty and racial divisions. With conventional bravado, Bush promised to grow the country out of its deficits with the memorable phrase, 'Read my lips: no new taxes,' a pledge he would come to regret."[4]

Slogans may be great for campaigning, but not necessarily for governing. President Bush broke the "no new taxes" pledge and paid a political price. His sterling leadership in the Gulf War and the end of the Cold War seemed like distant memories to American voters who were once again disillusioned by recession and unemployment.

Assessing Bush, biographer Timothy Naftali wrote: "Since 1940, with the exceptions of the election of Harry S. Truman in 1948 and Jimmy Carter in 1976, foreign policy had figured prominently in every presidential horse race. Presidents might not be elected on the basis of their foreign policy platforms, but if they did not seem credible in standing up to the Nazis or later the Soviets, they could not come close to winning. In 1992, with the Soviet Union gone, the American people judged leadership by a different standard, summarized by a poster in the war room of the Clinton campaign: 'It's the economy, stupid.' . . . George Bush learned he had failed that test."[5]

Like his long-ago predecessor Martin Van Buren, Bush would also be a one-term president—and one who was being measured up against a presidential giant: Jackson in Van Buren's case and Reagan in Bush's. But in eight years, President Bush would wake up under the White House roof once more. As the father of a president.

George H. W. Bush Administration Milestones[6]

1989

January 20	George H. W. Bush is inaugurated.
February 6	Bush introduces a bailout plan for troubled savings and loans banks. It provides for the sale of $50 billion in government bonds to finance the bailout.
March 24	The *Exxon Valdez* supertanker runs aground in southeastern Alaska, dumping 240,000 barrels of oil, the worst oil spill to date on American territory.
June 4	In Beijing's Tiananmen Square, the Chinese military use tanks and armored cars to suppress a burgeoning pro-democracy movement that encamped in the city's most prominent central square, site of Chairman Mao's mausoleum.
June 21	The Supreme Court rules that the government may not prevent people from burning the American flag as a form of protest.
August 9	The Financial Institutions Reform, Recovery, and Enforcement Act provides $166 billion to pay for the closure of insolvent savings and loan institutions.
August 10	Bush nominates Colin Powell to be chairman of the Joint Chiefs of Staff; he will become the first African-American in that post.
November 9	The Berlin Wall falls, marking the symbolic end of Communism in Eastern Europe.
December 2–3	Bush and Soviet president Mikhail Gorbachev hold their first meeting. Both leaders announce that the Cold War is effectively over.
December 20	In an effort to capture Manuel Antonio Noriega, Panama's military dictator, who was indicted in the United States on drug trafficking charges, twelve

thousand American soldiers invade the country. Noriega will surrender on January 3, 1990, and later be convicted and sent to prison.

1990

June 1   President Bush and Mikhail Gorbachev sign the broadest arms reduction agreement in two decades, reducing nuclear stockpiles.

August 2   Iraq invades Kuwait.

October 3   The two German states are formally reunited.

November 5   President Bush signs a budget law intended to reduce the federal budget; it includes $140 billion in new taxes.

1991

January 17   The Persian Gulf War, code-named Operation Desert Storm, begins with a massive, American-led air attack on Iraq.

February 24   Ground troops begin operations in Operation Desert Storm.

February 27   After liberating Kuwait, coalition troops advance rapidly into Iraqi territory, encountering no resistance. President Bush calls off the ground offensive.

July 3   President Bush and Mikhail Gorbachev meet in Moscow to sign a nuclear arms reduction treaty (START-I), which calls for both nations to make significant reductions in the number of nuclear warheads in their respective arsenals.

October 15   Clarence Thomas, nominated by President Bush to the Supreme Court, is confirmed by the Senate in a close 52–48 vote. His confirmation follows heated televised Judiciary Committee hearings during which Anita Hill, a former coworker in two government posts, testified that Thomas sexually harassed her.

December 31   The Union of Soviet Socialist Republics dissolves.

1992

April 1	President Bush announces a $24 billion aid plan to spur democratic and free market reforms in the former Soviet Union.
April 29–May 1	Los Angeles is torn by days of rioting following the jury acquittal of policemen who had been tried for beating an African-American man, Rodney King. On May 1, Bush orders marines and army troops to keep the peace in Los Angeles.
May 19	The Twenty-seventh Amendment goes into effect. It prevents Congress from changing its compensation until there has been an intervening election—in other words, Congress cannot give itself a raise. The amendment was first proposed in 1789.
May 23	The United States signs agreements with Russia, Belarus, Ukraine, and Kazakhstan, ensuring the continued participation of these nations in the nuclear arms reduction treaties signed by the USSR before its collapse in late 1991.
August 19–20	The Republicans nominate Bush for a second term.
October 1	After an earlier withdrawal, billionaire Ross Perot rejoins the presidential race as a third-party candidate. He joins a series of debates with President Bush and Bill Clinton.
November 3	Arkansas governor Bill Clinton, a Democrat, is elected president after defeating President Bush and Ross Perot, an independent from Texas. Clinton wins 43 percent of the vote and 370 electoral college votes, to Bush's 38 percent and 168 electors; Perot wins 19 percent but no electors.

MUST READS

George Bush and Brent Scowcroft, *A World Transformed*; Timothy Naftali, *George H. W. Bush*; Bob Woodward, *The Commanders*.

ONLINE RESOURCES

Inaugural Address, Avalon Project, Yale Law School
http://avalon.law.yale.edu/20th_century/bush.asp
Miller Center of Public Affairs, University of Virginia
http://millercenter.org/president/bush
George Bush Presidential Library and Museum, Texas A&M
http://bushlibrary.tamu.edu/
"Times Topics," *New York Times*: **George H. W. Bush**
http://topics.nytimes.com/top/reference/timestopics/people/b
/george_bush/index.html

42

Bubba
William Jefferson Clinton

★ ★ ★

January 20, 1993–January 20, 2001

Milestones in William J. Clinton's Life

August 19, 1946	Born in Hope, Arkansas
1973–1976	Taught law at the University of Arkansas
1976	Attorney general of Arkansas
1978	Governor of Arkansas
1980	Defeated in reelection bid
1983–1992	Governor of Arkansas
1993–2001	Forty-second president
1998	Impeached by the House of Representatives
February 12, 1999	Acquitted by the Senate

PRESIDENTIAL VOICES

Our democracy must be not only the envy of the world but the engine of our own renewal. There is nothing wrong with America that cannot be cured by what is right with America.

And so today, we pledge an end to the era of deadlock and drift; a new season of American renewal has begun. To renew America, we must be bold. We must do what no generation has had to do before. We must invest more in our own people, in their jobs, in their future, and at the same time cut our massive debt.

BILL CLINTON
First Inaugural Address, January 20, 1993[1]

F ew presidential stories are as compelling and yet as tawdry as the
rise and fall and rise again of Bill Clinton. He became the first
Democrat since FDR to win two terms in office in his own right. He
did it in the face of partisan fighting that had the intensity of a blow-
torch. And he did it despite personal lapses that often had him on the
brink of failure or worse. Yet he was always able to rebound—calling
himself the "Comeback Kid." Not even the second presidential impeachment in American history was enough to keep him down.

Fast Facts

RELIGION: Baptist

COLLEGE: Georgetown University, Oxford University, and Yale Law
School

PROFESSION BEFORE POLITICS: Attorney, professor of law

POLITICAL PARTY: Democratic

FIRST LADY: Hillary Diane Rodham Clinton (b. October 26, 1947)

CHILDREN: Chelsea

* Clinton is the only president who was a Rhodes Scholar.
* He and Al Gore were the first president and vice president from
  the baby boomer generation. Inaugurated at forty-six, Clinton was
  the third youngest president (after Theodore Roosevelt and John
  F. Kennedy).
* Clinton's 1997 inaugural ceremony was the first broadcast live on
  the Internet.
* The second president to be impeached, Clinton was charged with
  perjury related to testimony given under oath in a sexual harassment suit. The Senate, in a largely party-line vote, acquitted him.
* In spite of Clinton's impeachment and revelations of his sexual relationship with a White House intern, he left office with high public
  approval ratings.

* His wife, Hillary Clinton, was the first first lady to ever run for public office, becoming a U.S. senator from New York. After campaigning for the presidency in 2008, she lost the nomination to Barack Obama, who then selected Hillary Clinton as his secretary of state.

PRESIDENTIAL VOICES

As he officially began his campaign for reelection, there was no question that Bill Clinton was still the best politician of his generation. He had managed to confuse his enemies by giving into the wild-eyed Republicans of the 104th Congress as often as he opposed them. Perhaps more important, by acting more assertively on foreign policy and staying off television unless he had something to say, he was beginning to look presidential and act like the president.

RICHARD REEVES[2]

Born in 1946, a few months after his father died, Bill Clinton wanted to be president from a very early age. He attended public schools in Hot Springs, Arkansas, after moving there from Hope. As a boy he was obsessed with politics, winning student elections in high school and meeting JFK at the White House as part of the "Boy's Nation" program—film of this 1963 event now a Clinton-era icon.

After attending Georgetown University in Washington, D.C., Clinton worked on the staff of Senator William Fulbright of Arkansas and later went to Oxford University as a Rhodes Scholar. Following graduation from Yale Law School, Clinton briefly taught law at the University of Arkansas, but his eyes were always on a political career. He ran for the United States House of Representatives, losing in 1974, but was elected attorney general of Arkansas. In 1978, at age thirty-two, he became the youngest governor in the nation and in Arkansas history. After losing a bid for reelection, Clinton came back to win four terms, serving eight years as governor and positioning himself for a shot at the Democratic nomination for president in 1992.

He nearly undid that dream with a keynote address at the 1988 Democratic Convention that was widely derided as long and boring; some commentators thought his presidential dreams had been dashed. But the young man from Hope had a demonstrated knack for making big comebacks.

How did a third-party candidate help the young governor of a small state win the presidency?

Running as an "agent of change" who promised reforms, William Jefferson Clinton—Bill to most people, "Bubba" to some—and his running mate, Senator Al Gore of Tennessee, became the first baby boomers to win the White House. Their victory followed a raucous election that was noteworthy, among other reasons, for the third-party candidacy of H. Ross Perot.

Ross Perot had built Electronic Data Systems into a billion-dollar firm with large, profitable government contracts servicing Medicare records. But his Reform Party platform was built on assailing big government and excessive government spending. With his deep pockets, the amply financed Perot ran as an independent with a campaign aimed at overhauling government and opposing the North American Free Trade Act (NAFTA), favored by both major party candidates, which Perot memorably said would create a "great sucking sound" as American jobs migrated south to lower-wage Mexico.

Using infomercial-style television advertising, Perot actually had a lead in some polls in the early days of the campaign. His folksy style and can-do approach appealed to millions of American voters who were completely disenchanted with the two major political parties, whose differences seemed marginal. Announcing most of his major decisions and moves on Larry King's evening television talk show, Perot completely altered the landscape of American politics at the time.

While Clinton and Perot both adroitly used the media—Clinton appeared on MTV, where he was famously asked about wearing "boxers or briefs," and played saxophone on *The Arsenio Hall Show*, another popular nighttime talk program—President Bush seemed very behind the times. Attempts to have the World War II combat veteran seem in touch—shopping at a mall, for instance—just made him seem more awkward and remote.

But when Perot abruptly canceled his unorthodox campaign, with a claim that he was being threatened with revealing pictures of his daughter, he was dismissed as a wealthy kook. Going forward, the two main candidates focused on each other until only weeks before Election Day, when Perot stunned the political world by rejoining the fray.

Perot then participated in a series of three-man televised debates. But it was Clinton's campaign mantra—"It's the economy, stupid"— that ultimately mattered. An indelible debate moment came when a seemingly disinterested President Bush stared at his wristwatch as if he couldn't wait to get off the stage.

A week before the election, the Iran-Contra special prosecutor announced a grand jury indictment of Reagan administration official Caspar Weinberger, and questions about Bush's role in the Iran-Contra case (for full discussion, see Chapter 40, "Ronald Wilson Reagan") were once again in the headlines. (Years later, Bush's role in the Iran-Contra controversy was still unresolved. Late in 2011, however, documents released through the Freedom of Information Act revealed that the prosecutor at the time said Reagan and Bush were not criminally liable in the case, "reflecting an absence of evidence demonstrating that either man hid information from investigators."[3])

With the best third-party showing in the popular vote since Theodore Roosevelt finished second in 1912, helping elect Democrat Woodrow Wilson over the incumbent Republican William Taft, Perot took nearly twenty million votes (19 percent). Unlike Strom Thurmond and George Wallace, Southern segregationists who ran as third-party candidates, Perot won no electoral votes. But he clearly drew disaffected voters from Bush and probably skewed the race, allowing the Clinton-Gore ticket to win with 43 percent to Bush's 37 percent. In later years, Bush would claim that the indictment of Weinberger and the failure of Federal Reserve chairman Alan Greenspan to cut interest rates quickly enough doomed his presidency. But Ross Perot and the Reform Party, like several other successful third-party candidates in American history, probably made a difference, tipping the balance in a very closely divided and unhappy America.

If the government closes down, does anybody notice?

Bill Clinton's administration got off to a rocky start. Having pledged to overturn the ban on homosexuals serving in the military, Clinton found himself forced to accept a compromise "Don't Ask, Don't Tell" policy, under which homosexuals could serve in the military as long as they didn't reveal their sexual preference, and superiors were barred from inquiring into the sexual history or preferences of recruits or service members (the "Don't Ask" part).

But the biggest issue was "the economy, stupid" after all. A series of early setbacks to the administration, indicating fierce partisan opposition, were overshadowed by a recovering economy and, more surprisingly, the shrinking deficit. Risking that Americans wanted to be done with the excessive deficits, Clinton had gambled on a tax package that included tough deficit reduction restrictions in 1993. Passage of a free trade pact with Mexico and Canada (NAFTA) and a major anticrime package that included new handgun controls—known as the Brady Bill in honor of James Brady, the White House press secretary who had been severely wounded and permanently injured in the assassination attempt on Ronald Reagan—were also victories.

But Clinton could not escape his past. He was dogged by rumors of infidelity, past and present. A sexual harassment suit was filed in 1994 based on events that took place when he was governor of Arkansas. The case would ultimately be connected to an ongoing investigation of the Clintons' Arkansas investments and real estate deals, known as Whitewater. When White House aide Vincent Foster, a longtime Clinton friend, committed suicide, his death was tied to Whitewater as well, and Washington went into full-blown scandal-investigation mode. By August 1994, Special Prosecutor Kenneth Starr had begun an investigation of Whitewater that would expand to include other allegations against the Clintons[4] and eventually spill over into the impeachment proceedings against President Clinton. The investigation, denounced by Democrats as a "political witch hunt," would last several years and cost more than $60 million. (Starr's final report exonerated the Clin-

WILLIAM JEFFERSON CLINTON

tons over some aspects of the related cases; they were never charged with any crime, but a number of other Arkansas figures were convicted of a variety of crimes.)

The policy stumbles, personal embarrassments, and major missteps culminated in the 1993 defeat of Clinton's legislative keystone, the overhaul of the health care system. Establishing a commission to examine American health care policies, Clinton's first mistake may have been the choice of his wife, Hillary Rodham Clinton, to head the commission. A successful attorney twice named among America's most influential lawyers by the *National Law Journal*, she had been a member of the House Watergate impeachment legal staff. With some ill-considered campaign comments about not staying home and baking cookies, she had already become a controversial figure in her own right, once famously depicted in the conservative media as the "Lady Macbeth of Little Rock." As first lady, she stepped on congressional toes on the way to proposing a far-reaching plan that would cover all Americans. But the Clintons saw their prize project flame out, bucked by Congress and an intense lobbying effort by the health insurance industry.

In 1994, Republicans swept control of the House of Representatives for the first time in forty years. Georgia Representative Newt Gingrich, who became House speaker, trumpeted the "Contract with America," a conservative agenda containing a list of favorite Republican policy wishes and desires, including a balanced budget amendment, increased defense spending, term limits for congressional seats, an amendment to end legal abortion, and reform of the welfare system.

Recognizing the shifting political landscape in the new world of "talk show" politics, Clinton was able to co-opt some of the Contract with America ideas as he deftly moved to the political center. In November 1995, he regained the upper hand when he battled Gingrich and the Republican Congress over the budget, a stalemate that led to a partial shutdown of the United States government.

While nonessential federal workers were sent home because there was no funding to pay them, most Americans barely noticed that the government was on hiatus. A temporary spending bill resolved the problem, which then became an election issue in 1996 and greatly benefited Clinton, while the Gingrich-led Republicans in Congress were punished by voters. Clinton then beat the Republicans to the punch with one of the centerpieces of the Contract with America: He bucked his own party's history to champion an overhaul of the welfare system into what was widely called "workfare," or in some states "WorkFirst." Written by Republicans, the legislation eliminated the sixty-year-old federal entitlement of aid to poor women and dependent children, replacing it with block grants to the states, requiring most recipients to find work after two years, and limiting lifetime benefits to five years. It also allowed states to determine how their individual welfare and work programs would function. In 1996, Clinton signed another conservative-driven bill, the Defense of Marriage Act (DOMA), which recognized marriage as between a man and a woman and denied federal recognition of same sex marriages or "civil unions," which at that time had not been legalized in any state.

PRESIDENTIAL VOICES

As I write these words, a popular president presiding over an America prosperous and at peace has been impeached. Clinton's lawyers are skillfully defending him in a Senate trial against the charge that he committed perjury and obstructed justice to conceal his sexual affair with a twenty-two-year-old intern. The battle is all but over, and I'm still mystified by the Clinton paradox: How could a president so intelligent, so compassionate, so public-spirited, and so conscious of his place in history act in such a stupid, selfish, and self-destructive manner? I don't know how to answer that question, and I never thought I'd have to try.

—George Stephanopoulos[5]

Why was Bill Clinton the second president to be impeached?

Many presidents have iconic moments—images forever imprinted on the American psyche. FDR with Churchill. A jubilant Truman holding the newspaper that proclaimed DEWEY DEFEATS TRUMAN. JFK giving his ringing Inaugural Address. Ronald Reagan in Berlin, saying, "Tear down this wall."

Unfortunately for Bill Clinton, in one of his indelible images, he wags a finger as he indignantly tells America on January 26, 1998, "I did not have sexual relations with that woman, Miss Lewinsky."

Almost one year later, that image came back to make history. On December 19, 1998, Bill Clinton became the second president to be impeached by the House of Representatives. (The first was Lincoln's successor, Andrew Johnson; see Chapter 17.) The Republican-controlled Judiciary Committee sent four articles of impeachment to the House, but only two of them were adopted by the full House.

The seamy history of the Clinton impeachment case dated to Clinton's years as an elected official in Arkansas, and continued as he became president. Aided by his wife, Hillary, who sat by his side during a famous *60 Minutes* television interview in which the couple confessed that they had experienced past marital problems, Clinton had been able to maneuver past the rumors during the 1992 campaign. In 1994, the suit by Paula Jones accusing Clinton of sexual harassment while he was governor of Arkansas broke as the Clintons were being actively investigated by Special Prosecutor Kenneth Starr. Starr was examining the tangle of Arkansas real estate deals known as Whitewater, along with two separate cases involving misuse of FBI files by the Clinton White House and missing billing records from Hillary Clinton's Little Rock law firm.

Starr's investigations were essentially going nowhere, and Clinton's law team was successfully delaying the harassment suit until after the 1996 election—in which Clinton rather easily defeated veteran Republican senator Robert Dole, with Reform Party candidate Ross Perot playing a substantially diminished role.

In spite of these high-profile investigations, and in the midst of his reelection campaign, Clinton had become involved with Monica S. Lewinsky, then a twenty-one-year-old White House intern, in a sexual relationship that began in November 1995 and lasted until early in 1996. Questioned about this under oath, in a deposition in the harassment suit, Clinton denied the relationship. Prosecutor Starr received word of this denial and began an investigation into possible perjury and obstruction-of-justice charges.

In September 1998, just before the midterm congressional elections,

Starr released his report on the investigation to Congress. The expectation was that the report would damage the Democrats. But in a stunning reversal of American election tradition, the Democrats gained five seats in the House. (The party controlling the White House historically loses seats in the sixth year of a presidency.)

Voters seemed to be tired of the Republican obsession with the scandal. House speaker Newt Gingrich, who had gambled $10 million on last-minute advertising that attacked Clinton, was largely blamed for the party's dismal showing. Within a week of the election, Gingrich announced his resignation from the House. (His own infidelities would also be revealed soon after, as well as those of the next man in line for the speaker's position, Bob Livingston of Louisiana; he would also resign.)

The essence of the case for impeachment boiled down to an affair Clinton had clearly lied about while under oath. Was that the level of "high crimes and misdemeanors" that the framers had in mind when they drafted the Constitution?

During the framing of the Constitution in 1787, the rules regarding impeachment were vigorously debated by men who recognized the enormity of removing an official from office, especially an elected one. An initial draft called for removing the president only for bribery or treason. After heated discussion over the question of how easy such a removal should be, Virginia's George Mason offered a compromise phrase that dated from old English law: "high crimes and misdemeanors." And it is that phrase that has caused the most controversy.

Many historians hold that when the Constitution was composed, "high crimes and misdemeanors" referred specifically to offenses against the state or community, as opposed to a crime against people or property. Even so, many impeachment proceedings—and certainly the only other one brought against a president, Andrew Johnson—were politically motivated. As Gerald Ford said in 1970, as a member of the House, "An impeachable offense is whatever a majority of the House of Representatives considers it to be at a given moment in history."

On January 7, 1999, Chief Justice William H. Rehnquist formally opened the Senate impeachment trial. Five days later, the Senate voted to acquit President Clinton on both articles of impeachment.

In *A Vast Conspiracy*, a journalistic assessment of the impeachment, legal expert Jeffrey Toobin wrote of Clinton, "To be sure he will be remembered as the target of an unwise and unfair impeachment proceeding. But just as certainly, history will haunt Clinton for his own role in this political apocalypse, and for that, despite his best efforts, this president can blame only himself."[6]

Final Judgment: Grade B

Twenty-two million jobs created. A balanced budget and a budget surplus.[7] Crime reduced. Home ownership up. By most measures, it was a notable series of accomplishments for a president. Bill Clinton certainly went out on a high note, and he had the approval ratings to show for it.

Despite his very visible personal flaws, the American people seemed to be willing to accept Bill Clinton for what he had done in his private affairs and separate that from his public performance. They didn't necessarily like what Bill Clinton had *done*, but the majority of Americans still seemed to like *him*. There was, however, a very large segment of conservative Republican America who bitterly resented and despised him.

In a 2005 post-presidency assessment, journalist John Harris concluded, "However heedless he could be in his personal life, Clinton brought a dutiful sensibility to his public life. . . . Clinton had implemented a mild but innovative brand of liberalism that favored economic growth over redistribution, insisted that the government pay its way rather than rely on budget deficits, and embraced free trade rather than taking refuge in protectionism."[8]

The formula had worked but imperfectly, as other Clinton-era decisions would allow the financial dealings that ultimately led to the financial crisis and Great Recession of 2007. Chief among those Clinton decisions may have been the repeal of the Glass-Steagall Act, a piece of New Deal legislation that separated commercial and investment banks. That repeal, asserts writer Jeff Madrick, "led directly to the rise of huge financial institutions whose managers believed they could take on both highly risky investments and enormous debt as well. And his administration, along with many congressional Democrats, was consistently soft on Wall Street in other areas at a time when there were numerous accounting frauds, scams to sell high-technology new issues and hot money racing around the world to find easy profits, destabilizing foreign economies in the process."[9]

Clinton also left some unfinished business in the form of the growing threat of terrorism. After the World Trade Center in New York City was bombed in 1993, by a group of men with ties to Islamic terrorist groups, Clinton had been warned about the growing danger posed by Osama bin Laden's al-Qaeda group, which was believed to be responsible for an attack on embassies in Africa in 1998 and the USS *Cole* in October 2000, just weeks before the November election. While Clinton had signed a directive authorizing the CIA to capture bin Laden, or kill him if necessary, those efforts failed. In 1998, the navy had launched a cruise missile attack on bin Laden's training camps in Afghanistan, but that was also unsuccessful. The 9/11 Commission, in its report, found that while the Clinton administration had taken steps to address terrorism, "the United States did not, before 9/11, adopt as a clear strategic objective the elimination of al Qaeda."[10]

But the distinct possibility remained that Bill Clinton—although he said he would never run for office again—might well have made another of his famed "comebacks," if not for the constitutional prohibition against a third term.

Clinton Administration Milestones[11]

1993

January 20	William Jefferson Clinton is inaugurated.
January 25	President Clinton announces that Hillary Clinton will head the Task Force on National Health Care Reform.
February 26	Six people are killed and more than a thousand suffer injuries after a bomb planted under the World Trade Center in New York City explodes.
March 11	The Senate confirms Janet Reno as attorney general, the first woman to serve in the position.

April 19	In Waco, Texas, federal law enforcement officers end a fifty-one-day standoff against a religious cult. Fires destroy the cult's compound and kill at least seventy-five people.
June 26	The U.S. Navy, under President Clinton's orders, attacks Iraqi intelligence operations in downtown Baghdad after learning that Iraqis plotted to kill former President Bush during a 1993 visit to Kuwait.
July 20	Vince Foster, deputy counsel to the president, is found dead in a Northern Virginia park. Authorities rule his death a suicide.
August 3	The Senate confirms Ruth Bader Ginsburg's nomination to the Supreme Court; she is the second woman to sit on the high court.
September 22	President Clinton unveils a plan for universal health care.
October 3–4	American Special Forces searching for a Somali warlord in the capital, Mogadishu, are ambushed, leaving eighteen Americans dead. Three days later, Clinton announces the withdrawal of all American military personnel in Somalia.
November 30	The Brady Act requires background checks for handgun purchases.
December 8	The North American Free Trade Agreement (NAFTA), eliminating nearly every trade barrier between the United States, Canada, and Mexico, is approved.

1994

June 14	Clinton unveils a welfare reform initiative promising to "end welfare as we know it."
July 25	Clinton leads talks with Israel's Prime Minister Rabin and Jordan's King Hussein, resulting in peace between the Middle East neighbors.
November 8	In midterm congressional elections, the Republican Party wins control of both houses of Congress for the first time in more than forty years.

| December 5 | Clinton signs the Strategic Arms Reduction Treaty (START I). The treaty eliminates more than nine thousand warheads. |

1995

April 19	A truck bomb explodes in front of the Federal Building in Oklahoma City, Oklahoma, killing 168 people. It is the work of domestic terrorist Timothy McVeigh. He is captured, tried, and executed.
July 11	The United States extends full diplomatic recognition of Vietnam, twenty-two years after American forces withdrew from that country.
August 30	With a contingent of U.S. forces taking the lead, NATO begins two weeks of air attacks on Serbian positions.
November–December	Failure to reach a budget agreement leads to the shutdown of certain parts of the federal government.
November 21	Representatives of Bosnia, Croatia, and Serbia agree in principle to end three years of war in Bosnia.

1996

August 22	Clinton signs the "welfare to work" initiative.
September 3	Clinton orders a cruise missile strike against Iraq after Saddam Hussein leads a siege against the Kurdish city of Irbil.
November 5	Clinton defeats Senator Bob Dole for his second term. Clinton becomes the first Democratic president since Franklin Roosevelt to win reelection to a second term.
December 5	President Clinton selects Madeleine Albright to serve as his secretary of state; she becomes the first woman to hold the position.

1998

| August 7 | Terrorists bomb American embassies in Kenya and Tanzania, killing 224 people, including twenty Ameri- |

cans. United States intelligence believes that Osama bin Laden, a Saudi exile and alleged terrorist leader, is behind the attacks.

December 16   President Clinton orders a three-day bombing attack against Iraq after Saddam Hussein refuses to cooperate with United Nations weapons inspectors.

December 19   The House of Representatives votes to impeach President Clinton on charges of perjury and obstruction of justice.

1999

February 12   The Senate acquits President Clinton on both articles of impeachment, rejecting one article and splitting evenly on the second.

June 10   The NATO air campaign against Serbia ends after Serb forces agree on June 9 to withdraw from Kosovo.

2000

February 1   The Labor Department announces that the nation's business expansion has reached eight years and eleven months, marking the longest economic expansion in American history.

July 11–26   President Clinton hosts Israeli leader Ehud Barak and Palestinian leader Yasser Arafat at Camp David in the hope of reaching a peace agreement. After two weeks, the summit fails to reach an agreement when Arafat balks.

August 14   Vice President Al Gore wins the Democratic nomination. His Republican opponent is Texas governor George W. Bush.

October 12   In the Yemeni port of Aden, seventeen American sailors die when the USS *Cole* is attacked by suicide bombers.

November 7   On Election Day, Vice President Gore and Governor Bush run so closely that no winner can be declared.

December 13   The Supreme Court rules that there will be no recount of Florida's contested votes, forcing Gore to concede defeat.

MUST READS

David Maraniss, *First in His Class: The Biography of Bill Clinton*; Richard Reeves, *Running in Place: How Bill Clinton Disappointed America*; Jeffrey Toobin, *A Vast Conspiracy: The Real Story of the Sex Scandal That Nearly Brought Down a President*; Bob Woodward, *The Agenda: Inside the Clinton White House*.

ONLINE RESOURCES

Inaugural Addresses, Avalon Project, Yale University
1993: http://avalon.law.yale.edu/20th_century/clinton1.asp
1997: http://avalon.law.yale.edu/20th_century/clinton2.asp
National Archives
http://www.archives.gov/research/arc/topics/presidents/reagan.html
Miller Center of Public Affairs, University of Virginia
http://millercenter.org/academic/americanpresident/clinton
William J. Clinton Presidential Library and Museum
http://www.clintonlibrary.gov/
"Times Topics," *New York Times*: Bill Clinton
http://topics.nytimes.com/top/reference/timestopics/people/c/bill
_clinton/index.html
"Times Topics," *New York Times*: H. Ross Perot
http://topics.nytimes.com/topics/reference/timestopics/people/p
/ross_perot/index.html

43

Dubya
George Walker Bush

★ ★ ★

January 20, 2001–January 20, 2009

Milestones in George W. Bush's Life

July 6, 1946	Born in New Haven, Connecticut
1968–1973	Served in the Texas Air National Guard
1989–1993	Managing partner, Texas Rangers baseball team
1995–2000	Governor of Texas
2001–2009	Forty-third president

PRESIDENTIAL VOICES

North Korea is a regime arming with missiles and weapons of mass destruction, while starving its citizens.

Iran aggressively pursues these weapons and exports terror, while an unelected few repress the Iranian people's hope for freedom.

Iraq continues to flaunt its hostility toward America and to support terror . . .

States like these and their terrorist allies constitute an axis of evil, arming to threaten the peace of the world. By seeking weapons of mass destruction, these regimes pose a grave and growing danger. They could provide these arms to terrorists, giving them the means to match their hatred. They could attack our allies or attempt to blackmail the United States. In any of these cases, the price of indifference would be catastrophic.

—GEORGE W. BUSH
State of the Union Address, January 29, 2002[1]

Fast Facts

RELIGION Episcopal, United Methodist (after 1977)
EDUCATION: Yale, Harvard Business School
ASSOCIATIONS: "Skull and Bones"
MILITARY SERVICE: Texas Air National Guard
PROFESSION BEFORE POLITICS: Oil business, baseball team owner
PARTY: Republican
FIRST LADY: Laura Welch Bush (b. November 4, 1946)
CHILDREN: Barbara and Jenna
   Born on November 25, 1981, they are the only twins in a presidential family to date.

* George W. Bush and his father, George H. W. Bush, are the only father and son presidents to date other than John Adams and John Quincy Adams.
* "Dubya" is the only president to date with a master's in business administration; it is from Harvard Business School.
* After his father's election, Bush joined a group of investors who purchased the Texas Rangers baseball team.

PRESIDENTIAL VOICES

They still don't get it. Insteada goin' all out against al Qaeda and eliminating our vulnerabilities at home, they wanna fuckin' invade Iraq again. We have a token U.S. military force in Afghanistan, the Taliban are regrouping, we haven't caught bin Laden. . . . And they aren't going to send any more troops to Afghanistan to catch them or to help the government in Kabul secure the country. No, they're holding back waiting to invade Iraq. . . . There's no threat to us from Iraq, but 70 percent of the American people think Iraq attacked the Pentagon and the World Trade Center. You wanna know why? Because that's what the Administration wants them to think.
   —FOREIGN SERVICE OFFICER RANDY BEERS
   quoted by Richard A. Clarke in *Against All Enemies,* 2004[2]

Born in New Haven in 1946, while his father was completing his Yale education as a wartime veteran, George W. Bush is the oldest son in a very old, Eastern Establishment family. All of that changed when his father moved the family to West Texas when George was a toddler. Post–World War II Midland, Texas, was in the midst of an oil boom and was about as far as one could get from New England's staid traditions. An otherwise idyllic childhood was tempered by the death of his three-year-old sister, Robin, of leukemia in 1953. His other four siblings—three brothers and a sister—were born after Robin's death.

Following in the footsteps of his father and grandfather, Senator Prescott Bush, the younger George Bush attended prep school, first in Houston, then back East at Andover Academy, a prestigious boarding school. From there it was on to Yale, where he received a bachelor's degree in history in 1968, and then Harvard Business School, where he received a master's degree in 1975.

Between Yale and Harvard was a Vietnam War–era stint in the Texas Air National Guard, where Bush flew F-102 fighters. How he qualified for the spot and got the assignments he did would later cause some partisan controversy as it was suggested that his influential father had pulled strings to help him avoid the Vietnam War.

Bush moved back to Texas in the mid-1970s and went into the oil business. After a turning-point marriage to schoolteacher Laura Welch, he stabilized a life that he later admitted was too hard-drinking. His first stab at politics was an unsuccessful run for Congress in 1978, and then he put together the partnership that acquired the Texas Rangers baseball team, which threatened to leave the city of Arlington unless a new stadium was built. After the city used eminent domain to take property for the stadium, it was built with public financing based on an increased sales tax.[3] Of the maneuvering to make the stadium happen, which increased Bush's stake in the team enormously, he later wrote, "I had no objection to a temporary sales tax increase to pay for the park, so long as local citizens had a chance to vote on it."[4]

Bush was the public face of the Rangers front office until 1994, when he ran for governor of Texas. He defeated popular incumbent Ann Richards that year and won reelection in 1998 with 68 percent of the vote. Already, the Republican establishment was lining up behind Bush for a possible presidential run in 2000. Embracing Christianity and positioning himself as a "compassionate conservative," Bush then squared off against Vice President Al Gore.

Going into Election Day, it was the proverbial "too close to call" race.

Who won the 2000 election?

Vice President Al Gore won the most popular votes—not by much, but he won. But he did not become president. Late on election night on November 7, 2000, the networks called the election for Gore. But not so fast. The ballots in Florida were being called into question.

It was the beginning of a long, tortured process that ended up with the 2000 election being decided by the Supreme Court.

The issue was how to count certain paper ballots from the Florida polls that had been improperly marked. For nearly a month, the two sides fought in court and recounted ballots trying to decide which were and were not legitimate. The world learned that American elections depended on "chads"—the small pieces of paper that were pressed out of paper ballots. Were they "dimpled" or "pregnant"?— phrases that described paper ballots that had been insufficiently marked with a pointed stylus meant to cast a vote. It would have been absurdly funny except that the fate of the nation's future hung on these questions.

On December 1, the Supreme Court heard arguments in the case of *Bush v. Gore* and, on December 9, halted recounts of the Florida ballot. Finally, in a dramatic decision, the court ruled on December 12 that the Florida State Supreme Court's earlier ruling should be reviewed. But there was no time to do that before the legal deadline for the Florida ballots to be officially entered and recorded and counted by the electoral college. Because there was no time for a complete recount and certainly not for a rerun of the election in Florida, George W. Bush was declared winner of Florida's electoral votes by default. That provided his one vote margin of victory over Gore in the electoral contest. On December 13, Al Gore conceded.

The Florida recount had transfixed the nation and left many to wonder why the most powerful, technologically advanced country in the world depended on people poking a piece of paper with a stick to elect its leader and determine the nation's fate.

But more important, the commentary in this extraordinary and bizarre election also focused on the unprecedented role of the Supreme Court. Had the Rehnquist court, which was often divided between five conservative justices—William Rehnquist, Sandra Day O'Connor, Antonin Scalia, Clarence Thomas, and Anthony Kennedy—and four more liberal justices—Stephen Breyer, David Souter, Ruth Bader Ginsburg, and John Paul Stevens—acted properly in its decision? Or had the court gone beyond its legitimate bounds in reaching a decision that had the practical effect of electing the president?

The answer to that question, predictably, seemed to depend on political alliance. At one end of the spectrum were those who found the court's opinion perfectly acceptable, usually Republican Bush supporters. One constant in their view: the Supreme Court had to overturn a flawed and politically biased ruling made by the Democratic majority in the Florida State Supreme Court—even if that flew in the face of the Republican Party's professed devotion to "states' rights."

In the highly partisan post-decision atmosphere, it was difficult to find a conservative voice that disagreed with the Supreme Court. But, writing in the *Weekly Standard* (December 25, 2000), John J. DiIulio, Jr. (later to join the Bush administration) was one of the few who did: "To any conservative who truly respects federalism, the majority's opinion is hard to respect. . . . The arguments that ended the battle and 'gave' Bush the presidency are constitutionally disingenuous at best. They will come back to haunt conservatives and confuse, if they do not cripple, the principled conservative case for limited government, legislative supremacy, and universal civic deference to legitimate, duly constituted state and local public authority."

On the other end of the spectrum were those—generally Democratic

Gore supporters—who thought the decision a judicial outrage. Harvard's Alan Dershowitz called it the "single most corrupt decision in Supreme Court history."

The fact that the electoral college had once again overturned a close but nonetheless clear popular vote briefly rekindled the call to be rid of the electoral college once and for all. If the process of choosing electors who chose the president once had its usefulness as a means of guaranteeing that the president had to be elected by a diverse geographical population and not just those in a few large states, that rationale certainly no longer existed. The advent of mass media, televised debates, and more recently the Internet had completely eliminated the eighteenth- and nineteenth-century notion that the general electorate would be unable to get to know the candidates and make a fair judgment.

But any thoughts of reforming this process were short-lived. As the nation busied itself, a sense of resigned complacency about the election seemed to set in—except perhaps among a handful of Democratic true believers convinced that their man Gore was the "real" president. But in a broader historical sweep, the strange election of 2000 was more or less forgotten less than a year later, eclipsed by the events of September 11, 2001.

How did the events of 9/11 reshape the Bush years?

The coordinated attacks came on the morning of September 11, 2001, when a group of nineteen hijackers, all of them Arab men, seized four commercial airliners and crashed two of them into the World Trade Center in lower Manhattan—site of an earlier Islamic terrorist bombing in 1993—and a third into the Pentagon in Arlington, Virginia. The fourth plane was presumed to be heading toward another target in Washington, D.C., possibly the White House, when the passengers and crew attempted to retake the plane and it crashed into a field near Shanksville, in rural Pennsylvania, killing all on board.

The total number of victims in the attacks is officially listed as 2,973, with others claiming that a number of rescue workers at the World Trade Center site have died from ailments that came as a result of their work at the site—in essence, "collateral damage" from the hijackings.

Within minutes of the hijackings and crashes, the FBI opened what would become the largest criminal investigation in American history. Within seventy-two hours, the identities of the hijackers were known. All were from Arab nations: Saudi Arabia (eleven of the men), the United Arab Emirates, Lebanon, and Egypt.

The specific planning of the attacks was attributed to a man well known to American intelligence, Khalid Sheikh Mohammed, who grew up in Kuwait, attended college in the United States—where he had earned a degree in mechanical engineering in 1986—and eventually entered the anti-Soviet jihad ("holy war") in Afghanistan. Khalid Sheikh Mohammed was captured by Pakistani authorities in Pakistan in 2003 and transferred to the controversial American "detainee" prison built in Guantánamo, Cuba. According to official accounts, he had confessed to planning the 9/11 attacks along with a number of terrorist acts that were either foiled or carried out.

Just as the Civil War influenced politics for a generation in the nineteenth century, and the Cold War influenced nearly every decision for presidents after 1945, the terrorist attacks colored all of Bush's decisions going forward. And they would be momentous. Immediately afterward Bush's job approval ratings soared. He suddenly found himself leading a nation that was now fighting a shadowy "Global War on Terror" against an army of Islamic extremists operating out of some sixty countries under the direction of Osama bin Laden, who headed a worldwide terrorist organization called al-Qaeda. All of the rules governing America's military actions in the past were going to be challenged by the new realities of fighting an enemy that was not a nation but a movement.

Bush refocused his priorities, telling his aides that fighting al-Qaeda was now the primary mission of his administration. On October 7, 2001, the United States began air sorties against al-Qaeda terrorist camps in Afghanistan. But even as Afghanistan was the first target for sheltering Osama bin Laden and al-Qaeda's training camps, plans were being drawn to invade America's nemesis—Saddam Hussein's Iraq.

In a lopsided congressional vote on October 11, 2002, Bush received authorization to invade Iraq if the country did not turn over its presumed arsenal of biological and chemical weapons, as well as what was thought to be its reconstituted nuclear weapons research.

On March 19, 2003, Bush informed the American people—and the world—that the invasion of Iraq was on. The Bush administration made a concerted effort to connect the threads of the 9/11 plot to Saddam Hussein, even if—as evidence later proved—no such threads existed. By the time America went to war with Iraq, a large majority of the country had been convinced of that connection. Unlike the attack on Afghanistan, however, the invasion of Iraq had scant international support. Only the United Kingdom and a handful of other nations joined a so-called "coalition of the willing" in attacking Iraq. The United Nations, which had an inspection team on the ground searching for WMD and a set of sanctions against Iraq, would not condone the attack.

Bush went ahead. In what was described at the time as a "shock and awe" campaign, Baghdad and the rest of Iraq were devastated by American air power. Less than six weeks after the assault began, American troops were in nominal control of Baghdad. They had been accompanied by "embedded" journalists who were offering a close-up—if largely Pentagon-sanctioned—version of events on the ground. Iraqi armed forces had been killed, had surrendered, or had melted back into the general population. On May 1, 2003—at a time when only 137 American military personnel had been killed—Bush, dressed in a flight uniform, told the American people from the deck of the aircraft carrier USS *Abraham Lincoln* that major combat operations in Iraq had ended.

That announcement was beyond premature. Almost immediately after the invasion, Iraq was spiraling into complete chaos. Remnants of the old regime, joined by Islamic fighters surging into the country, kept up a steady insurgency. Sectarian violence, suicide bombings, and insurgent attacks were killing thousands of Iraqis. Iraqi politicians were unwilling or unable to form a meaningful, coherent government. Planning for the post-invasion period had been almost nonexistent. In spite of the serious concerns raised about America's misguided and misdirected war effort, Bush won a second term in 2004 over Senator John Kerry of Massachusetts, with slightly more than 50 percent of the popular vote; his electoral vote margin was larger than in 2000.

But in a short time after the election, world opinion had shifted strongly against the United States, and at home, a strong antiwar sentiment reenergized the Democratic Party as it looked toward 2008. As the situation in Iraq grew more deadly and chaotic, the Bush administration's handling of the invasion was increasingly seen as a fiasco. The consensus was that there was no sufficient plan for occupying Iraq and far too few troops to control the country. Assumptions about restoring Iraq's oil production were wildly optimistic, and a rising toll in American battlefield deaths and crippling injuries caused by the insurgents' favorite weapon, the roadside IED (Improvised Explosive Device), was raising concerns about the wisdom of the attack—as well as its extraordinary commitment of American financial resources.

In 2007, President Bush announced a new military policy featuring a "surge" of troops, accompanied by payment of large sums of money to Iraqi groups in an effort to pacify the country. By that time, it had also become clear that Saddam Hussein's feared "weapons of mass destruction"—the ostensible rationale for the war—simply did not exist.

"A president must be able to get a clear-eyed, unbiased assessment of the war," Bob Woodward, the veteran presidential observer, wrote in *The War Within*, one of a series of books about the Bush war against terror. "For years, time and again, President Bush has displayed impatience, bravado, and unsettling personal certainty about his decisions. The result has too often been impulsiveness and carelessness, and perhaps most troubling, a delayed reaction to realities and advice that ran counter to his gut."[5]

Final Judgment: Grade F

It is always difficult to assess a presidency so soon after its conclusion. But historians and the public seem to be of one mind. Three recent surveys of historians—by the *Wall Street Journal*, the *London Times*, and C-SPAN—all place George W. Bush near the bottom of presidential rankings. A Harris Poll of the public in 2012 showed a majority of Americans think the forty-third president was the worst in post–World War II America.

The response to 9/11, and in particular the two wars that the terrorist attacks spawned, were the centerpiece of the Bush years. As his second term went by, and the enormity and gravity of his administration's miscalculations and missteps became clear, the once popular president paid a price—just as his father had, for different reasons.

Set against the miscalculations that had made the Iraq War a costly fiasco were the other post-9/11 Bush policies that had become increasingly controversial and unpopular. The Patriot Act, legislation written in the immediate aftermath of the terrorist attacks and signed into law on October 24, 2001, greatly expanded government powers in conducting surveillance and investigations. But many critics saw the law as an overreaction that was an attack on basic civil liberties and constitutional protections.[6]

That controversy extended to the treatment of captured "enemy combatants," suspected terrorists who were denied the treatment dictated by the Geneva Convention and were placed in a prison camp on the U.S. military base at Guantánamo, Cuba. Critics' concerns over the prison there were only heightened when photographs of American troops abusing prisoners in Iraq's Abu Ghraib prison were published, further damaging American credibility and legitimacy in the Arab world and the rest of the international community.

Bush's presidential legacy is also affected by one of the most powerful and influential vice presidents: Richard Cheney.[7] A lightning rod for criticism, Dick Cheney was a veteran Republican official who had served under Donald Rumsfeld—George W. Bush's equally combative and controversial defense secretary—in the Nixon White House and later as Gerald Ford's chief of staff. After six terms in the House of Representatives from Wyoming, he became defense secretary under President George Bush (41), overseeing operations in the first Gulf War. He then served as CEO of the Halliburton oil services company from 1995 to 2000, when, after heading the Bush search team for a vice presidential running mate, Cheney himself joined the ticket. By all accounts, he wielded enormous power and influence in shaping Bush policies on the wars, national security, and the environment. Although he had "long been a skeptic of the CIA's skills," according to reporter Jane Mayer in *The Dark Side*, he was insistent on reviewing the CIA's raw data after 9/11. The cumulative effect, reported Mayer, "turned national security concerns into 'an obsession.'"[8]

Cheney was also a forceful proponent of the CIA's use of "extraordinary rendition." That term is a tidy euphemism for kidnapping people, transporting them to foreign prisons—in places that included Pakistan and Egypt, among other detention sites—where they are subjected to interrogations not permitted on American soil. Such practices included "water boarding," a controversial interrogation method later ruled to be torture and prohibited by the army.

As the hunt for Osama bin Laden and the search for the "WMD" both turned up empty, and Iraq slipped further into chaos, Bush's approval ratings went to a record low. They were only worsened by the failed response to Hurricane Katrina in 2005 and the financial crisis that began as a recession in 2007 and quickly grew into the worst economic catastrophe since the Great Depression. By most measures—lack of job creation, rising unemployment, the exploding deficit, and the first deep cracks in the great housing downturn—eight years of Bush's management of the economy were disastrous.

As Bush was preparing to leave office and the contest between Republican senator John McCain and Democratic senator Barack Obama took place, the American economy was approaching meltdown territory. Wall Street scandals, failing brokerages, international banking crises, and the bankruptcies of the major American automakers had the American economy on the brink of the worst scenario since the 1920s. McCain and Obama were put in the unusual position of sitting in as decisions about the economy were made, since one of them would inherit the economic catastrophe unraveling under Bush.

One result, writes Timothy Naftali, was that Bush's father was starting to look much better in hindsight. "Some critics of the Iraq war wondered why the son had not been persuaded by the logic that had kept his father from going into Baghdad a decade earlier. Others wondered whether the U.S. military had lost whatever chance it had to establish order because the son's administration had used half the number of troops for its invasion in 2003 as had the father in 1990–91. . . . When George W. Bush had spoken confidently in 1997 of how history would revise his father's reputation, he had no reason to assume that it would be because of his own shortcomings as president."[9]

George W. Bush Administration Milestones[10]

2000

December	In a 5–4 ruling, the U.S. Supreme Court stops the recount of votes in several contested Florida counties. The Democratic candidate, Vice President Albert Gore, Jr., concedes the election.

2001

January 20	George W. Bush is inaugurated.
January 22	Bush reinstates the Reagan-era ban on aid to international groups performing or counseling on abortion.
January 29	Bush creates the Office of Faith-Based and Community Initiatives. The new office will work to ease regulations on religious charities.
February 16	United States airplanes attack Iraqi radar sites to enforce a "no-fly zone."
March 29	The Bush administration abandons ratification of the Kyoto Protocol, an international treaty signed by 180 countries to reduce global warming.
June 7	President Bush signs a $1.35 trillion tax cut; it slashes income tax rates across the board and provides for the gradual elimination of the estate tax.
September 11	Terrorists hijack four commercial jets and crash them into the World Trade Center in New York City and the Pentagon in Washington, D.C.; one of them does not reach its target but crashes in the Pennsylvania countryside.

September 20	Before a joint session of Congress, Bush outlines the administration's plans to defeat world terrorism, singling out Osama bin Laden and his al-Qaeda organization as the primary targets.
October 7	President Bush announces the commencement of military action in Afghanistan.
December 2	The Enron Corporation files for Chapter 11 bankruptcy protection, the largest bankruptcy case in American history.

2002

January 8	An education reform bill known as "No Child Left Behind" is passed; providing for more local authority, the law requires standardized math and reading tests.
May 16	Congress presses the Bush administration for further information about warnings of the September 11 attacks. National security adviser Condoleezza Rice insists that there was no lapse in intelligence.
May 24	Bush and Russia's Vladimir Putin sign a nuclear arms treaty, vowing to reduce their arsenals by two-thirds over the next ten years.
June 6	Bush announces broad changes to security policy; the cabinet-level Office of Homeland Security will coordinate and oversee more than one hundred organizations.
September 4	Bush tells Congress that Iraqi strongman Saddam Hussein is a "serious threat," and mentions the concept of a regime change.
October 10	Congress broadly supports authorization to use force against Iraq.
November 5	In a sweeping midterm election victory, Republicans gain control of the Senate and maintain their edge in the House.

2003

| January 7 | Bush reveals a tax-cut plan of $674 billion over ten years. Democrats dismiss the plan as financially irresponsible and favorable to the rich. |

February 1	The seven-member crew of the shuttle *Columbia* dies in an explosion during reentry into the atmosphere.
March 16	Bush announces the U.S. intention to move against Iraq with its coalition of allies. Bush gives Iraqi leader Saddam Hussein and his sons forty-eight hours to leave Iraq.
March 19	At 10:15 p.m., Bush tells the American people that the United States is at war with Iraq.
May 1	Standing in front of a "Mission Accomplished" banner aboard the aircraft carrier USS *Abraham Lincoln*, Bush declares that major combat operations in Iraq are over.
May 28	Bush signs his $350 billion tax-cut package, the third largest in history.
July 11	CIA Director George Tenet accepts full responsibility for the incorrect statement in Bush's 2003 State of the Union Address regarding Iraq's alleged effort to obtain uranium from Africa.
July 24	The joint Congressional Committee on Intelligence report on 9/11 concludes that intelligence agencies failed to respond to alerts about potential targets and methods. The report faults the NSA, the CIA, and the FBI.
October 2	Chief U.S. weapons inspector David Kay reports that his fourteen-hundred-member team failed to find any biological, chemical, or nuclear weapons ("WMD") in Iraq.
November 5	A ban on late-term abortion is passed; it is the first law to ban an abortion procedure since the Supreme Court's 1973 decision in *Roe v. Wade*. The Supreme Court later upholds the ban.
December 8	Bush signs a bill overhauling Medicare; it includes the program's first prescription drug benefits, to begin in 2006.

2004

April 28	CBS broadcasts photographs of U.S. Army abuse of Iraqi prisoners in Abu Ghraib prison.

May 17 Massachusetts becomes the first state to offer marriage licenses to same-sex couples.

June 3 Bush announces the resignation of CIA director George Tenet, widely blamed for intelligence failures leading up to September 11.

June 8 The Senate Judiciary Committee presses Attorney General John Ashcroft regarding legal arguments for circumventing U.S. and international bans on torture, specifically for the questioning of terrorist suspects.

November 3 Bush wins a second term with 51 percent of the popular vote and 274 electoral votes to John Kerry's 252.

November 8 U.S. troops launch an assault to retake the rebel-controlled city of Fallujah in the largest military operation since the initial invasion of Iraq in March of 2003.

2005

January 20 Bush is sworn in for a second term.

August 28 Hurricane Katrina strikes the southern coast of the United States with devastating effects. The storm breaches the levee system in New Orleans, causing massive flooding and destruction of property. The Bush administration is harshly criticized for what is viewed as a grossly inadequate response.

September 29 John G. Roberts is confirmed as chief justice of the U.S. Supreme Court.

2006

March 21 Bush admits for the first time that the complete removal of U.S. troops from Iraq during the remainder of his term is improbable.

October 26 To stem illegal immigration, Bush signs a bill providing for the construction of a seven-hundred-mile fence along the border with Mexico.

November 7 Democrats recapture control of the U.S. House and Senate.

December 30	Former Iraqi President Saddam Hussein is hanged in Baghdad.

2007

January 4	Nancy Pelosi, a Democrat from California, takes office as the first female speaker of the House.
January 11	As an insurgency continues in Iraq, Bush announces what is called a "troop surge."
March 6	Scooter Libby, Vice President Cheney's chief of staff, is convicted of perjury and obstruction of justice in the case of CIA operative Valerie Plame Wilson, whose covert identity was exposed. Bush later commutes Libby's sentence.
October 9	The Dow Jones industrial average closes at 14,164, its all-time high.

2008

January 18	Faced with a slowing economy, Bush proposes a $145 billion stimulus package in response to a housing crisis and rapidly increasing oil prices.
June 3	After a bruising primary campaign against Hillary Clinton, one-term Illinois senator Barack Obama secures the Democratic nomination.
June 5	The Senate Select Committee on Intelligence finds, after a five-year study, that President Bush and other officials greatly exaggerated the evidence showing that Saddam Hussein held weapons of mass destruction.
June 30	In a new report issued on the situation in Iraq, the U.S. Army admits that while it was able to adequately topple Hussein's regime, it did not have the capability to rebuild Iraq into a fully functioning new country.
September 7	The U.S. government places the two mortgage agencies Fannie Mae and Freddie Mac under its control to prevent the institutions from going under and endangering more than half of the country's mortgages.

October 3	In full financial crisis, President Bush signs a $700 billion bailout plan for failing bank assets, the largest in U.S. history.
October 30	U.S. gross domestic product drops by 0.3 percent, the first time GDP has shrunk in seventeen years.
November 4	Barack Obama is elected.
November 25	The Treasury Department and the Federal Reserve agree to provide another $800 billion in lending programs to buy debt insured by Fannie Mae and Freddie Mac and to provide more small loans to consumers.
December 16	The Federal Reserve cuts interest rates to an all-time low of 0 percent as part of a plan to stimulate the economy.
December 19	Bush issues a $17.4-billion auto bailout to General Motors and Chrysler to keep the two auto giants from going bankrupt.

2009

January 20	Barack Obama, the first African-American president, is inaugurated.

MUST READS

George W. Bush, *Decision Points*; Michael R. Gordon and General Bernard E. Trainor, *Cobra !!: The Inside Story of the Invasion and Occupation of Iraq*; Jane Mayer, *The Dark Side: The Inside Story of How the War on Terror Turned Into a War on American Ideals*; George Packer, *The Assassins' Gate: America in Iraq*; Andrew Ross Sorkin, *Too Big to Fail: The Inside Story of How Wall Street and Washington Fought to Save the Financial System—and Themselves*; Bob Woodward, *Plan of Attack*; *State of Denial*; and *The War Within: A Secret White House History 2006–2008*.

ONLINE RESOURCES

Inaugural Addresses, Avalon Project, Yale University
  2001: http://avalon.law.yale.edu/21st_century/gbush1.asp
  2005: http://avalon.law.yale.edu/21st_century/gbush2.asp

Miller Center of Public Affairs, University of Virginia
http://millercenter.org/academic/americanpresident/clinton
New York Times **archive**
http://topics.nytimes.com/top/reference/timestopics/people/b
/george_w_bush/index.html?offset=25&s=newest
George W. Bush Presidential Library
http://www.georgewbushlibrary.gov/
George W. Bush Presidential Center
http://www.bushcenter.com/about-Us/about-the-bush-center

44

No Drama Obama
Barack Hussein Obama

★ ★ ★

January 20, 2009–

Milestones in Barack H. Obama's Life

August 4, 1961	Born in Honolulu, Hawaii
1985–1988	Worked as community organizer in Chicago, Illinois
1992–2004	Taught constitutional law at University of Chicago
1993–2003	Practiced law in Chicago
1995	Published autobiography, *Dreams from My Father*
1997–2005	Member of Illinois Senate
2004–2009	U.S. senator from Illinois
2006	Published second book, *The Audacity of Hope*
2009–	Forty-fourth president

PRESIDENTIAL VOICES

If there is anyone out there who still doubts that America is a place where all things are possible; who still wonders if the dream of our founders is alive in our time; who still questions the power of our democracy, tonight is your answer.

—Barack Obama
Election Night speech, November 4, 2008[1]

T here are probably few who imagined that the tall, angular, first-term senator from Illinois, who gave a ringing speech to the Democratic Convention in 2004, would challenge the party establishment for the nomination four years later. There were probably people who thought he couldn't possibly win the nomination when he announced his candidacy in Springfield, Illinois—the "Land of Lincoln."

Barack Obama had emerged from near obscurity to improbably defeat the heavily favored Hillary Clinton, the former first lady and senator from New York, who seemed to be assured of becoming the first woman to run for president from a major party.

With an enthusiastic campaign highlighted by Obama's "Hope and Change" mantra, and capitalizing on the new political power of social media, Obama stunned the party regulars and commentators with a breathtaking primary campaign. He went on to a fairly easy victory over Republican senator John McCain and his running mate, newcomer Alaska governor Sarah Palin. Although the GOP ticket was plagued by internal discord, the Republicans had bigger problems than the Alaska governor's inexperience and McCain's sluggish campaign. They were weighed down by two wars and an economy on the brink of a historic collapse that was George Bush's parting gift to his party.

Fast Facts

RELIGION: Christian (unaffiliated)

EDUCATION: Columbia University, Harvard Law School

CAREER BEFORE POLITICS: Community organizer, attorney, law professor

POLITICAL PARTY: Democratic

FIRST LADY: Michelle LaVaughn Robinson Obama (b. January 17, 1964)

CHILDREN: Malia and Natasha (Sasha)

* Barack Obama is the first African-American president. When Obama was born in 1961, his white mother and black father would not have been able to marry legally in sixteen American states, including Vir-

ginia. Only in 1967 did the Supreme Court's ruling in the *Loving v. Virginia* case end race-based restrictions on marriage in the United States.

* Obama's wife, First Lady Michelle Obama, is also an attorney, the third first lady with a postgraduate degree (Hillary Clinton and Laura Bush, her two predecessors, both have them). Once in the White House, she devoted her energy to bringing to light the epidemic of childhood obesity in America and campaigned for better food in schools and more exercise for America's children.

* Obama's first Supreme Court appointee, Sonia Sotomayor, became the first Hispanic on the court. With Obama's second appointment, Elena Kagan, the Supreme Court also had three sitting women justices for the first time in its history.

* In 2009, Obama was awarded the Nobel Peace Prize in recognition of his efforts to improve peaceful dialog in international affairs, becoming the fourth American president to win. (Theodore Roosevelt, Woodrow Wilson, and Jimmy Carter are the others.)

PRESIDENTIAL VOICES

The day will come—and it is not far off—when the legacy of Lincoln will finally be fulfilled at 1600 Pennsylvania Avenue when a black man or woman will sit in the Oval Office. When that day comes, the most remarkable thing about it will be how naturally it occurs.

—PRESIDENT GEORGE H. W. BUSH, 1990[2]

Although he was called the first African-American president, Barack Obama's life story was much more complex—and in a changing America, the complexity of that story seemed more familiar to people and a lot less scary. In 2008, America was no longer the *Ozzie and Harriet* landscape of 1958 black-and-white television.

The son of a white American mother and a black Kenyan father—also named Barack—the forty-fourth president was born in Honolulu in 1961.* His mother, from Kansas, was a student there and his father was a Kenyan exchange student. After his parents divorced, a young Obama was taken to Indonesia by his mother. He returned to Hawaii, where he grew up with his maternal grandparents, both Kansas natives. His grandfather had served in World War II and his grandmother had been a real "Rosie the Riveter," working in a wartime factory building bombers. They moved to Hawaii in 1960.

After attending a prestigious island prep school on a scholarship, Obama went to Occidental College in California, before a transfer to New York's Columbia University. He moved to Chicago after college, where he worked as a community organizer.

In 1988, he went to Harvard Law School, where he was later elected the president of the prestigious *Harvard Law Review*, the first African-American to hold that position. After his return to Chicago to work as an attorney and teach law at the University of Chicago, Obama met fellow lawyer Michelle LaVaughn Robinson in 1992. They married and had two daughters, Malia and Natasha (Sasha), born in 1998 and 2001, respectively.

Obama was elected to the Illinois State Senate in 1996 and served there for eight years. In 2004, he was elected by a record majority to the U.S. Senate from Illinois, and in February 2007, he announced his candidacy for president. One of his campaign promises was made to his wife, Michelle: He would stop smoking.

Does the president-elect always have to wait his turn?

After the Constitution was amended to fix the long "lame duck" period of the presidency by moving the inauguration up to January 20, it still left a two-month "transition period" for an incoming president to prepare to completely overhaul the presidency—a daunting task under ordinary circumstances.

---

* Despite evidence of his birth in Hawaii, Obama was dogged by an ongoing controversy, fueled by the Internet and Republican opponents, that he was born in Kenya and not Hawaii. In April 2011, the Obama White House released a so-called "long form" birth certificate, attesting to his birth in Honolulu in an attempt to end the controversy. http://www.whitehouse.gov/blog/2011/04/27/president-obamas-long-form-birth-certificate.

But by the time Barack Obama made history in November 2008, he was confronting challenges of an enormity that no president had faced besides FDR or Lincoln.

America was at war. The continuing conflicts in Iraq and Afghanistan, as well as the "Global War on Terror" that had American drones striking in Pakistan's territory, were grave enough. Obama learned the full extent of the dangers ahead when he got his first one-on-one national security briefing two days after his election. Besides the well-documented threats in Iraq and Afghanistan, Obama learned that the CIA had a three-thousand-man covert force in Afghanistan, that there were threats against his inauguration, and that the Chinese had hacked his and McCain's campaign computers in a "cyber attack." He reportedly said after the meeting, "I'm inheriting a world that could blow up any minute in half a dozen ways, and I will have some powerful but limited and perhaps even dubious tools to keep it from happening."[3]

While worrying about the world blowing up, President-elect Obama also had to worry about it melting down. America was in the midst of the so-called "Great Recession"; foreclosures of homes were multiplying and unemployment was rising fast. But more frighteningly, major banking institutions were in danger of failure, which would bring the entire complex and interrelated world financial network crashing down.

Obama did not need a secret presidential briefing to understand this crisis. It unfolded in the midst of the campaign against McCain. In late September, with the crisis at its peak, McCain called for a White House meeting with President Bush, his economic team, and Obama to discuss responding to the crisis. It was a gambit intended to make McCain look decisive, but it backfired. More than a polite "backgrounder" for the candidates, the meeting established that the two men running for president would potentially make decisions that affected the rescue of the world's financial system. Obama made what was described as a well-prepared, thoughtful presentation and promised that the Democrats in Congress would deliver the needed votes for the Bush team's rescue package. McCain fumbled.

When Barack Obama took office in 2009, he was confronted by a hydra of daunting problems. As journalist Bill Keller described it in 2011, "Obama inherited a country in such distress that his Inaugural

Address alluded to George Washington at Valley Forge, marking 'this winter of our hardship.' Unfunded wars, supply-side deficits, twin housing and banking crises enabled by an orgy of regulatory permissiveness— that was the legacy Obama assumed. In our political culture if you inherit a problem and don't fix it, you own it. So at some point it became the popular wisdom that Iraq and Afghanistan were 'Obama's wars,' and that the recession had become 'Obama's economy.' "[4]

PRESIDENTIAL VOICES

It has now been nearly a century since Theodore Roosevelt first called for health care reform, and ever since, nearly every President and Congress, whether Democrat or Republican, has attempted to meet this challenge in some way. A bill for comprehensive health reform was first introduced by John Dingell, Sr., in 1943. Sixty-five years later, his son continues to introduce that same bill at the beginning of each session.

Our collective failure to meet this challenge, year after year, decade after decade, has led us to the breaking point. Everyone understands the extraordinary hardships that are placed on the uninsured who live every day just one accident or illness away from bankruptcy. These are not primarily people on welfare; these are middle class Americans. . . .

We are the only democracy—the only advanced democracy on Earth—the only wealthy nation that allows such hardship for millions of its people.
—Barack Obama, September 9, 2009[5]

What is Obamacare?

Obama had come into office with one large goal—a major reform of the nation's health care system. Since the time of Harry Truman, every Democratic president had talked about national health care reform, and in 1965, Lyndon B. Johnson had secured the enactment of Medicare for older Americans and Medicaid for the poor.

But Obama's first order of business was dealing with the situation he had inherited. What would become known as the "Stimulus" or

"Recovery Act," a combination of tax cuts, aid to states, and so-called "shovel-ready" public works projects that weren't really ready, was prepared during the transition.

While Obama preached the hope of transforming Washington's culture with a new spirit of bipartisanship, he had entered a period of relentless and disciplined Republican obstructionism. Although he agreed to include ideas meant to appeal to Republicans in his stimulus plan, his hopes for achieving a new bipartisan moment in the Washington culture were doomed from the start. As Ron Suskind recorded, "Hastily constructed policy was matched by miscalculations of political strategy: all the accommodations to conservative principles and practice in the plan were never exchanged for hard commitments. On the way to his inauguration, Obama got word that Republicans in the House had committed, as a bloc, to oppose the stimulus plan."[6]

With solid Democratic support in the House and a few Republican votes in the Senate, Congress passed an emergency package in February 2009. Still committed to health care reform, Obama decided that his best chance of success to pass new legislation was during his first year in office, when his popularity was likely to be at its highest.

But passage of a health care reform bill, a policy and political disaster for Bill Clinton, faced major resistance from Republicans, who denounced the plan as "socialized medicine."

Although Democrats in Congress were united in support of reform, they were divided about what form it should take, with some insisting that the federal government offer a "public option" (that is, government-run) coverage plan and others urging that private coverage be extended to those who lacked it. More than three-fourths of Americans had private health insurance in some form, and despite the steeply rising costs of health care, many of them worried that changing the system might make their own situation worse and add to the federal budget deficit that the Recovery Act had already sent soaring to more than $1 trillion per year.

When members of Congress encountered angry opposition to the proposed health care legislation from the newly formed, grassroots conservative Tea Party, the president, frustrated that he was not getting through to the American people, spoke to Congress on September 9, 2009, in a prime-time address.

The speech helped build public and congressional support for reform. In an altered political environment, the president launched a successful campaign to persuade members of Congress in face-to-face meetings to pass the legislation. By year's end, both houses of Congress had passed different versions of health care reform legislation. In March 2010, after some elaborate legislative wrangling to get the House to pass the Senate bill, Obama signed the bill known as the Patient Protection and Affordable Care Act.

Everybody else now calls it "Obamacare."

The central features of the bill included an expansion of health insurance to cover the uninsured, a cap on premium increases, and permission for people to retain their coverage when they move or change jobs ("portability"). It also made it illegal for insurers to drop sick people or deny them coverage for preexisting conditions. But the central point of contention was a mandate that required every American to carry health coverage. In theory, bringing more healthy but uninsured people into the insurance pool will ultimately reduce premiums.

In addition to more protections for people with preexisting conditions, among its provisions the law provided tougher oversight of health insurers and expansion of coverage to millions of children and young adults who were uncovered by their parents' policies. According to a *New York Times* summary of the legislation, "The law was also forcing major institutions to wrestle with the relentless rise in health care costs."[7]

The passage of the act had given Republicans their cudgel against Obama as the 2010 midterm elections approached. Kentucky senator Mitch McConnell, the Republican minority leader at the time, underscored the party's attitude. He told *National Journal* magazine in October 2010, "The single most important thing we want to achieve is for President Obama to be a one-term president."

The passage of health care reform, discontent over the costly stimulus package that was designed to kick-start a recession-bound economy, the legacy of the Bush administration's assistance to banks under the Troubled Asset Relief Program (TARP), and a bailout for bankrupt carmakers all helped fuel an antigovernment mood that handed Obama a huge setback—in his words a "shellacking"—in the 2010 midterm elections, with the Republicans taking control of the House. (Democrats kept control of the Senate.)

The health care legislation was to be phased in over several years but was challenged by a number of states over one of its key provisions: a mandate that individuals must purchase health care insurance. The lawsuits were resolved by a 5–4 Supreme Court decision in June 2012, which upheld the Affordable Care Act and the individual mandate. The chief justice, John Roberts, wrote the opinion in which the law was found constitutional under the congressional power to tax.

Another test of Obamacare came in the 2012 presidential election. But its impact had been blunted by the Supreme Court decision as well as the fact that Obama's opponent, Republican Mitt Romney, had overseen the enactment of a similar law while he was governor of Massachusetts.

In 2013, congressional Republicans again attempted to use the law as an issue, threatening to "defund" Obamacare, an ultimately unsuccessful strategy that led to a temporary shutdown of parts of the federal government in October 2013. That shutdown, while damaging Obama's popularity, was even more problematic for congressional Republicans, whose public approval ratings fell to historic lows. The fallout to the GOP worsened a public image already battered by the loss to Obama in the 2012 election, which showed the party losing favor among younger voters, women, Hispanics, and other minorities—all key voting groups.

The shutdown came just as the federal website on which Americans were supposed to "shop" for individual insurance policies was opened. A wave of technical difficulties made the site nearly impossible to use, and Obamacare was once more a political albatross, bringing Obama's popularity to a new low as well.

The uncertain solution to these website problems, residual anger at the cancellation of some individual policies—which Obama himself had said consumers could keep if they were happy with them—and lingering questions over the long-range impact of the implementation of the Affordable Care Act combined to raise serious doubts about the law's future at the end of the first year of Obama's second term. Even allies and supporters of the president had to concede that his administration had seriously mishandled what was considered his signature piece of legislation.

Final Judgment: Grade I (Incomplete)

At the conclusion of the first year of his second term, Obama could not yet be fairly judged in the long stream of presidential history. Such judgments are tricky, especially given the fast pace of world events.

Three years into his first term, Lincoln was considered a disaster who wouldn't be nominated for a second term by his party, let alone reelected. And even after he won a second term in 1864, critics savaged Lincoln over the conduct of the Civil War. After his landslide victory in 1936, Franklin D. Roosevelt began his second term with the greatest legislative loss of his presidency over his court-packing plan.

As the 2012 election approached, Obama's popularity had fallen sharply due to the rising unemployment and moribund economy of his first term. But the public view of Congress was if anything worse. In fact, Obama's poll numbers were better than those of both Ronald Reagan and George W. Bush in the midst of the recessions during their respective terms in office.

But sharp partisan resistance had buffeted Obama as the election neared. The glow of his first few months and his promises of "Hope and Change" and a new conciliatory spirit in Washington had long been replaced by the gloom of a nation sharply divided and uncertain of its direction as the Great Recession continued to hold the economy back. The killing of al-Qaeda leader Osama bin Laden in Pakistan by navy SEALs in May 2011 provided a momentary surge in Obama's popularity. But it was soon dragged down by the stark political divide over America's finances.

As 2011 came to an end, Obama kept to a campaign pledge to withdraw the last American combat troops from Iraq, as the American war there ended on December 15. He was also sticking to a pledge to wind down the American combat commitment in Afghanistan, begun in the aftermath of September 11, 2001. But other promises, including one to close the prison at Guantánamo where "enemy combatants" had been held since early in the Bush years, had not been kept.

"The decline in Obama's political fortunes, the Great Disappointment, can be attributed to four main factors," Bill Keller of the *New York Times* wrote in 2011. "The intractable legacy bequeathed by George W. Bush; Republican resistance amounting to sabotage; the unrealistic expectations and inevitable disenchantment of some of the president's supporters; and, to be sure, the man himself."[8]

Heading into the presidential election, Barack Obama was also suffering the pains of every president with a sputtering economy. He did not get much credit as a "wartime" president, even though U.S. troops were still heavily engaged in Afghanistan.

Facing Mitt Romney, a Republican candidate who had been pulled far to the right by conservative GOP primary voters and the influence of the largely uncompromising Tea Party wing of the GOP, Obama did enjoy the luxury of a Democratic party that was largely united—although there was considerable unhappiness on his left wing that Obama had not fulfilled the loftiest aspirations of his "Hope and Change" campaign promise.

The victory over Romney in November 2012 was comfortably convincing, as such so-called swing states as Florida, Ohio, and Pennsylvania stayed in the Obama column, and he won 332 electoral votes in 26 states and the District of Columbia. (That was down from the 365 electoral votes he had won in 2008.) The culture wars of previous decades had also faded as a political weapon. Obama's endorsement of same-sex marriage and the end of the Pentagon's prohibition on homosexuals openly serving in the military no longer generated passionate opposition. It is also worth noting that Romney was the first Mormon nominee of a major party, but his religion was never an issue, which was remarkable given the historic enmity toward Mormons among many American Protestants.

The first year of Obama's second term would mostly be characterized by what was *not* being accomplished. The budgetary wars with Republicans continued unrelentingly as the "Sequester" took hold in March 2013. Under a 2011 bill, a wave of supposedly draconian, "across the board" budget cuts would automatically go into effect if there were no agreement on cuts to the federal budget. The Sequester took effect and the economy continued to limp along. In October 2013 another crisis point—the so-called "Fiscal Cliff"—was reached as the government was partially shut down and a deadline for authorizing an increase in the nation's borrowing ability (the "debt ceiling") also loomed. Failure to increase that limit might have led to an unprecedented default by the U.S. government on its obligations. A last-minute deal ended the shutdown and deferred the crisis.

Seen as cool and nonconfrontational, Barack Obama seemed to prize his "No Drama Obama" image. But he was increasingly criticized as aloof and detached from the legislative process by many, including some of his supporters. That may be one reason that a series of proposed gun control measures, drafted in the aftermath of a string of deadly mass shootings, was killed in the Senate.

As his fifth year in office came to a close, with most of his legislative agenda on hold, Obama publicly committed the rest of his presidency to the goal of addressing the nation's growing economic inequality. Five years after the Great Recession that had greeted Obama's inauguration, the Dow Jones Industrial Average and S & P 500 index had reached all-time highs, the housing market was well into recovery mode, American corporate profits were robust, and unemployment had fallen to 7 percent for the first time in five years.

But growing poverty rates and the spreading gap between the wealthiest Americans and the great majority of the country had never been larger. Committing the rest of his term to addressing that inequity in December 2013, Obama said, "The basic bargain at the heart of our economy has frayed." He added, "This increasing inequality is most pronounced in our country, and it challenges the very essence of who we are as a people. Understand, we've never begrudged success in America; we aspire to it, we admire folks who start new businesses, create jobs and invent the products that enrich our lives, and we expect them to be rewarded handsomely for it."[9]

Entering Obama's sixth year in office, controversy swirled over spying on Americans and foreign leaders by the National Security Agency following a massive leak of NSA secrets by Edward J. Snowden, a contractor who then fled the country and was given asylum in Russia. The use of drones to combat terrorism, a potential deal to halt Iran's nuclear program, and America's role in a civil war in Syria were all serious foreign policy questions. The growing economic and military power of China also marked a profound challenge to American policy.

But all of these issues seemed to pale beside the question that few presidents truly control: Would American prosperity continue and, with it, the American Dream?

Obama Administration Milestones[10]

2009

January 20	Barack Obama is inaugurated.
February 17	A stimulus bill is passed to provide new spending.
February 20	A series of "stress tests" are planned to measure the banking system's health.
April 3	Iowa's Supreme Court strikes down the law barring same-sex marriages in the state.
June 1	General Motors files for bankruptcy under a plan to reorganize with the government taking a large stake in the company.
June	According to the Business Cycle Dating Committee, the recession comes to an end; it was the longest in post–World War II American history.
August 6	Sonia Sotomayor is confirmed as an associate justice of the Supreme Court; she is the first Latina and third woman on the high court.
August 7	A popular "cash for clunkers" program provides funds for people to retire old gas-guzzling cars for more efficient new models.
December 1	Obama announces a "surge" of troops in Afghanistan.
December 6	Big banks begin to repay TARP funds.

2010

January 19	In a special election to fill the seat of the late Senator Ted Kennedy, Scott Brown, a Tea Party–backed Republican, is the surprise victor.
January 21	The Supreme Court overturns limits on corporate campaign spending, ruling that corporations have a

First Amendment right to spend to influence the outcome of elections.

January 27   Obama promises to end the "Don't Ask, Don't Tell" policy in the U.S. military.

March 3   Same-sex marriage is legalized in Washington, D.C.

March 23   Obama signs a landmark health care reform measure.

April 20   An oil-drilling platform explodes in the Gulf of Mexico, killing eleven people and beginning a massive oil spill into the Gulf waters. BP Oil is largely responsible for cleaning up the spill and reimbursing business and property owners for losses.

July 25   An archive of secret documents about the war in Afghanistan is released online by WikiLeaks; the documents chronicle a struggle against a revived Taliban insurgency in Afghanistan.

August 7   Elena Kagan is sworn in as a Supreme Court justice.

August 16   China surpasses Japan as the world's second largest economy.

August 31   Obama declares an end to the seven-year combat mission in Iraq. However, nearly 50,000 American forces remain in the country to provide security and training for Iraqi forces. More than 4,400 American soldiers and more than 70,000 Iraqis lost their lives in the conflict, according to figures cited by the *New York Times*.

September 9   A U.S. district judge rules that "Don't Ask, Don't Tell," which prohibits the military from seeking to learn someone's sexual orientation but allows discharge for homosexuality, is unconstitutional.

October 7   On the ninth anniversary of the invasion of Afghanistan, President Obama confirms that his troop withdrawal will still begin in July 2011.

November 2   The Republicans regain control of the House; many of the victors espouse the "Tea Party" movement.

November 17   General Motors returns to the stock market; the government's stake in the company is reduced by half.

| December 18 | Congress repeals "Don't Ask, Don't Tell." |
| December 22 | The new START Treaty reducing nuclear stockpiles is ratified by the Senate. |

2011

May 1	Obama announces that a U.S. military operation has killed Osama bin Laden in Pakistan.
June 24	New York State passes a law permitting same-sex marriage.
December 15	The war in Iraq is officially declared over as U.S. troops withdraw.
September 20	The Pentagon ends its "Don't Ask, Don't Tell" policy, enacted during the Clinton administration. Under new rules, gay men and lesbian women are permitted to serve openly in the armed forces.
October 20	Libyan rebel forces supported by NATO, including U.S. air power, kill Col. Muammar al-Qaddafi, who had seized power in Libya in 1969. National elections in Libya follow in July.

2012

May 9	Obama becomes the first sitting president to endorse same-sex marriage, days after Vice President Joe Biden and Education Secretary Arne Duncan voice their support for the measure.
June 28	In a 5–4 ruling, the Supreme Court upholds a key provision of the Affordable Care Act ("Obamacare") requiring individuals to buy health insurance or face a penalty.
September 11	Four Americans, including the ambassador to Libya, are killed when armed Islamic militants attack the U.S. consulate in Benghazi, Libya.
October 29	A major hurricane turned tropical storm named Sandy devastates the Northeast, killing an estimated 113 people in nine states and flooding many towns and

cities, including New York and the metropolitan area, just days before the presidential election.

November 6   Obama wins his second term, defeating Republican Mitt Romney, former governor of Massachusetts.

November 9   CIA director David Petraeus, the former army general who had overseen the "Surge" strategy in Iraq, resigns following revelations of an extramarital affair.

December 14   A mass shooting at the Sandy Hook Elementary School in Newton, Connecticut, leaves twenty children and six adult staff members dead. The shooter, who had earlier killed his mother, commits suicide. It is one in a string of deadly mass shootings in the United States and leads Obama to call for stricter gun control measures in January 2013.

2013

March 1   Under the terms of a bill passed in 2011, automatic spending cuts known as the "Sequester" begin to go into effect.

April 17   The Senate defeats several measures proposed by Obama to expand gun control.

June 6   An English newspaper, *The Guardian*, begins publishing a series of articles about electronic surveillance by the National Security Agency (NSA) and FBI. Edward J. Snowden, a young American contractor who flees the country, has leaked the material. The disclosures eventually reveal that the NSA has logs of virtually all telephone calls made in the United States; tracks the location and movement of hundreds of millions of cellphones outside the country; has collected e-mails of foreigners from the major American Internet companies; and spies on American allies and heads of state, such as German chancellor Angela Merkel.

June 25   In a pair of rulings on same-sex marriage, the Supreme Court strikes down the Defense of Marriage Act (DOMA), which restricted federal spousal benefits to marriages between a man and a woman; and, by declining to rule on a California case, effectively allows same-sex marriage in the nation's largest state. By the end of 2013, sixteen states and the District of Columbia allow same-sex marriage.

August 13 After widespread reports of the use of chemical weapons against civilians by Syria's government during a civil war, Obama prepares to ask Congress for authority to take military action against the Assad regime. In cooperation with Russia, the United States agrees instead to delay any attack in return for Syria's agreement to eliminate its chemical weapons under U.N. supervision.

October 1 The U.S. government is partially shut down amid congressional attempts to defund Obamacare.

October 1 Healthcare.gov, the website on which Americans are supposed to purchase mandated individual health insurance policies, fails to function properly, creating a firestorm of controversy over Obamacare.

October 17 The twin crises over the government shutdown and raising the federal debt ceiling end when Obama signs into law an appropriations act in a victory over the Republican-controlled House.

2014

January 6 The Senate confirms Janet L. Yellen as the chairwoman of the Federal Reserve, marking the first time that a woman leads the country's central bank in its hundred-year history.

MUST READS

Jonathan Alter, *The Promise: President Obama, Year One*; Barack Obama, *Dreams from My Father: A Story of Race and Inheritance*; David Remnick, *The Bridge: The Life and Rise of Barack Obama*.

ONLINE RESOURCES

Inaugural Address, Avalon Project, Yale Law School
   http://avalon.law.yale.edu/21st_century/obama.asp

Miller Center of Public Affairs, University of Virginia
http://millercenter.org/president/obama
"Times Topics," *New York Times*: **Barack Obama**
http://topics.nytimes.com/top/reference/timestopics/people/o
/barack_obama/index.html

What Should We Do with the President?

Oh that lovely title, ex-President.
—Dwight Eisenhower
New York Post, October 26, 1959

Though the President is Commander-in-Chief, Congress is his commander and, God willing, he shall obey. He and his minions shall learn that this is not a government of kings and satraps, but a Government of the people, and that Congress is the people.
—Representative Thaddeus Stevens
Speech in Congress, January 3, 1867

The answer to the runaway presidency is not the messenger-boy presidency. The American democracy must discover a middle ground between making the president a czar and making him a puppet.
—Arthur M. Schlesinger, Jr.[1]

As more than two hundred years of presidential history proves, the pendulum of power has swung widely. The decades of post-Lincoln presidents who largely deferred to Congress eventually gave way to the twentieth-century titans, especially the two Roosevelts and Lyndon Johnson, who made the White House and not Capitol Hill the seat of American power, stoking fears of an "imperial presidency." A succession of failed and disgraced presidents, beginning with Johnson's failure and Nixon's fall, and continuing through the ineffective Ford and Carter years, swung the pendulum back the other way. American presidential prestige stood at a fairly low point when Ronald Reagan was elected.

But these periodic shifts in the Washington, D.C., power game mask some larger questions that have mainly been confined to political science department debates, scholarly journals, and the world of the academy. Does the presidency still make sense? Is the job too big for one person? And more practically, is there a better way to pick the president?

What are the president's powers?

In their wisdom, the framers of the Constitution wrote Article II with a brief and fairly limited set of specific powers assigned to the president:

- Serves as commander in chief of the armed forces (but Congress has the power to declare war)
- Can grant pardons and reprieves to federal offenders

- Makes foreign treaties (subject to Senate approval)
- Appoints judges, ambassadors (and other "public ministers"), and other high officials (also requiring Senate confirmation)
- Approves or vetoes federal bills (When given a bill passed by Congress, the president has three choices: sign the legislation into law; return the bill to Congress without signing it—the veto; or do nothing. In the last case, the bill becomes law in ten days, unless Congress has adjourned. In that case, the bill dies after thirty days—the "pocket veto." The word "veto" is Latin for "I forbid.")
- Has authority to propose legislation
- Carries out federal laws ("Takes care that the Laws be faithfully executed," known as the "takes care" clause)
- Fills vacancies in federal offices while Congress is out of session ("recess appointments")
- Convenes both houses of Congress on "extraordinary occasions"

To preserve the "separation of powers," a central issue for the framers, and limit a "vigorous" executive from acquiring too much power, the Constitution also provides for a series of "checks" on presidential powers, just as the president can check the two other branches of government.

Key Checks on Executive Powers

- Congress can override presidential vetoes by a two-thirds vote
- The Senate can reject or refuse to confirm appointments or ratify treaties
- Congress can impeach and remove the president for "high crimes and misdemeanors"
- Congress can declare war
- The Supreme Court can declare executive acts unconstitutional (although this too was an implied, not stated, power)

But more than two hundred years of presidential actions have expanded the powers of the office well beyond the more narrowly circumscribed scope laid out in the Constitution. Many of these powers have caused controversy and even crisis over those two centuries, and these "implied powers" have been the subject of challenge by Congress and the courts.

Chief among these implied powers:

- **Budgeting:** As the saying goes, "The president proposes and Congress disposes." Congress controls the purse strings under the Constitution. But the budgeting process has evolved into one of the president's chief powers to determine policy. Especially in the second half of the twentieth century, the president has taken the central role in determining federal spending.

- **Executive Orders:** One of the least specific but most important powers given to the president is the "executive power" mentioned but never clearly defined in the Constitution. For the most part, these executive orders can establish executive branch agencies, modify rules, or give substance to existing laws.

- **Executive Privilege:** Although the specific term was coined during the Eisenhower administration, the idea that the president does not have to tell Congress everything goes back to George Washington's days. In essence, it means that the president has the right to withhold sensitive information from Congress or the courts. In theory, it gives presidents the freedom to receive a wide range of advice, whether or not they choose to act on that advice.[2]

  George Washington established this precedent when he refused to give Congress papers relating to a foreign treaty with England, the Jay Treaty. Jefferson refused to testify at the treason trial of his former vice president, Aaron Burr, under the concept.

  In 1974, Richard Nixon claimed executive privilege during the Watergate crisis when he refused to release tapes of conversations secretly recorded in the Oval Office. The Supreme Court forced Nixon to release the "Watergate Tapes," ultimately leading to his resignation.

  More recently, Vice President Richard Cheney refused to reveal information about an energy task force he consulted in 2001. Congress wanted information on the identities of the task force, as did the Sierra Club, which filed a suit in the case. But the courts ruled in Cheney's favor.

• **Emergency Powers:** In a crisis—and sometimes not—presidents may lay claim to extraordinary powers to preserve the nation. Again, this is not a power stated explicitly in the Constitution, and some presidents have used "emergency powers" under the general mandate to "preserve, protect and defend" the Constitution.

The most famous example is Lincoln's suspension of the constitutional writ of habeas corpus to jail opponents during the Civil War, leading to the charge that he was a "constitutional dictator." Harry Truman also invoked such an emergency after North Korea invaded South Korea in 1950 and also used these emergency powers to seize strike-threatened steel mills in 1952. The Supreme Court later ruled that seizure unconstitutional. Most recently, emergency powers were invoked by George W. Bush to authorize military tribunals to deal with accused foreign terrorists after the terrorist attacks of September 11, 2001.

• **War Powers:** Probably no idea scared the framers more than the notion of a single man in charge of the military. But they also recognized that a sudden attack on the nation demanded urgent action—"vigor" was their favorite word. The precise authority of the president as commander in chief, however, was left undefined.

Always looking to maintain a separation of powers and checks on each branch, the framers gave the president command of the military so that he could respond quickly to a direct threat. But Congress had the power to "declare" war (the word "declare" was substituted for "make"). Congress has formally done so only five times: the War of 1812, the Mexican-American War of 1846, the Spanish-American War in 1898, and the two World Wars (1917, 1941).

For most of American history, Congress has largely acquiesced to the expansion of presidential military and wartime powers, generally content with what the presidents were accomplishing. In the long, costly nineteenth-century wars with the Seminole of Florida, for instance, there was no formal war declaration by Congress.

More recently, when Truman took the country to war in Korea, there was some dispute, but he had the cover of the recently created United Nations, which authorized the military action with a Security Council resolution.

But the mostly compliant Congress finally changed its stance with the conflict in Vietnam, another undeclared war. In 1973, Congress enacted the War Powers Resolution over President Nixon's veto. It set a sixty-day limit on presidential commitment of troops overseas without specific congressional authorization.[3]

Obviously, the country has gone to war many other times in more than two hundred years. And the issue remains alive. Presidents continue to authorize military action without congressional approval. Bill Clinton did it in Kosovo in 1999. And when President Obama committed American forces to support the NATO attacks against Libya in 2011, congressional critics complained that he had exceeded his constitutional authority. As a candidate, Obama had said the president lacked the power to unilaterally authorize a military attack that did not involve a direct threat to America. Clearly, Obama learned, as others have, that being president is different than running for president.[4]

• **Signing Statements:** In recent years perhaps the most controversial of the created or "implied" powers, these statements are comments usually written when a president signs a bill into law. For the most part, these statements merely comment on the legislation. Although seldom used for most of the country's history, the "signing statement" has become controversial, as some presidents have claimed in their signing statements that they intend to ignore or not fully implement the legislation because they believe it is unconstitutional.

James Monroe issued what may have been the first such statement in 1822 over his authority to make appointments, according to the American Presidency Project at the University of California-Santa

Barbara.⁵ But the controversy has grown as several presidents since Ronald Reagan began to use the concept of the signing statement more aggressively.

In 2005, for example, President Bush signed a bill that included a ban on the use of torture. But he issued a statement that he could override Congress and the courts on a major part of the bill—implicitly the definition of "torture"—if he thought it conflicted with his role as chief executive.

President George W. Bush issued approximately 140 separate signing statements asserting he would enforce the law only as consistent with his understanding of the Constitution and the separation of powers.⁶ Sharply criticized by a panel of the American Bar Association and many constitutional scholars, Bush's use of signing statements was a "groundless assertion," according to a *New York Times* editorial. "In principle," said the *Times*, "a president should veto a bill if he believes that part of it is unconstitutional."⁷

PRESIDENTIAL VOICES

Each State shall appoint, in such Manner as the Legislature thereof may direct, a Number of Electors, equal to the whole Number of Senators and Representatives to which the State may be entitled in the Congress: but no Senator or Representative, or Person holding an Office of Trust or Profit under the United States, shall be appointed an Elector.
—UNITED STATES CONSTITUTION
Article II, Section 1.2

What kind of SAT scores do you need to get into the electoral college?
In creating the "electoral college"—a phrase not coined until the nineteenth century—the Constitution's authors gave each state presidential "electors" equal to the number of its senators and representatives in Congress. Under the original Constitution, these "electors," chosen by whatever means a state decided, would vote for two candidates. As this

section makes clear, the electors may not be elected officials. There is also no constitutional instruction or requirement specifying how electors may actually vote. The candidate with a majority of the electoral votes became president and the second-place finisher became vice president.

Article II of the Constitution and the Twelfth Amendment, which changed the means of electing the president and vice president, refer to "electors," but not to an "electoral college." In the Federalist Papers (number 68), Alexander Hamilton described the process of choosing the executive and simply described that "the people of each State shall choose a number of persons as electors," but he did not use the term "electoral college" either.

According to the National Archives, "The founders appropriated the concept of electors from the Holy Roman Empire (962–1806). An elector was one of a number of princes of the various German states within the Holy Roman Empire who had a right to participate in the election of the German king (who generally was crowned as emperor). The term 'college' (from the Latin *collegium*), refers to a body of persons that act as a unit, as in the college of cardinals who advise the Pope and vote in papal elections. In the early 1800s, the term 'electoral college' came into general usage as the unofficial designation for the group of citizens selected to cast votes for President and Vice President. It was first written into Federal law in 1845, and today the term appears in 3 U.S.C. section 4, in the section heading and in the text as 'college of electors.'"[8]

Was this democratic? Not really. But it would lead to more democracy, whether or not the framers envisioned that possibility.

One essential fail-safe built into this plan was the agreement that if the electoral vote failed to produce a clear winner, the election would be sent to the House of Representatives, where each state would get a single vote. Was this a sensible solution? Or, as many historians conclude, did the framers believe that after George Washington, no man could win the votes needed for election and the enlightened men in the Congress would make the decisions? It happened as soon as 1800, with Jefferson's ultimate victory over Aaron Burr and John Adams, and again in 1824, when John Quincy Adams was awarded the victory over Andrew Jackson.

And yet, the electoral college, this archaic relic of a hot Philadelphia summer—and clearly designed with slavery factored into its logic—remains alive. Today, the electoral college equals 538 votes; the 435 members of the House and 100 members of the Senate, plus three electoral votes for the District of Columbia (the result of another amendment to the Constitution, see Appendix II).

To many, the existence of the electoral college is difficult to justify. But it lives on chiefly because for years most people have believed in that old adage "If it ain't broke, don't fix it." Until the controversial Bush-Gore election of 2000, the electoral college system had basically affirmed the popular vote for more than one hundred years. Although there were other cases in which the popular winner lost the presidential election, these dated back to the nineteenth century.*

Promises of reform or a constitutional amendment to do away with the electoral college have always met serious resistance, especially from states and politicians who benefit from the system. An attempt to amend the Constitution and abolish the electoral college, replacing it with simple direct election of the president, was killed in the Senate in 1979. But the issue rears its head every four years, when people look around and wonder why America needs this antiquated contraption.

Another alternative to the electoral college does not require an amendment. Under an approach called the National Popular Vote, a state can pledge to give its electors to the winner of the national popular vote. In 2011, California became the eighth state to pass such legislation.[9]

PRESIDENTIAL VOICES

This is the beginning of a whole new concept. This is it. This is the way they'll be elected forevermore. The next guys up will have to be performers.

—ROGER AILES
During the 1968 Nixon campaign[10]

---

* The three earlier popular vote winners who did not become president were Andrew Jackson in 1828, Samuel Tilden in 1876, and Grover Cleveland in 1888.

(A media consultant to Richard Nixon, Ronald Reagan, and other Republican candidates and presidents, Roger Ailes was the creator of the Fox News Network, launched in October 1996.)

Is the White House "for sale"?

Apart from the constitutional debate over how to elect America's leader, the larger and, in many ways, more pressing debate is over how these campaigns are paid for. Running for president in America takes a lot of cash.

There is nothing new about that. From the days of providing rum punch for voters in colonial Virginia, to providing free beer and "walking around money" to precinct captains to ensure turnout on Election Day, to Joseph Kennedy's proverbial largess in 1960, money has always been the "mother's milk" of politics.

What has changed is the quantity of cash required and how it is spent. What changed, in a word, is television. Richard Nixon's 1968 victory, detailed in the campaign classic *The Selling of the President*, made it clear that candidates would have to be carefully packaged and marketed through the techniques of television advertising. And that required money, which to that time had been largely unregulated in federal election campaigns.

Nixon also changed that. His administration's illicit use of campaign funds and other abuses in the Watergate era underscored the need for campaign finance reform. Chief among the results was the Federal Election Commission, created in 1974 to regulate and enforce campaign laws. The idea of public financing of presidential campaigns for qualified candidates was also introduced at that time. Part of the eligibility for those funds was a candidate's agreement to limit spending. A politician who wanted the federal election money had to keep to strict spending limits. However, there were several ways around such limits. For instance, under the laws, "soft" money could flow to the parties, rather than the "hard" money contributed directly to individual candidates, often through Political Action Committees (PACs), which were not bound by the same spending limits. Finally, candidates could avoid spending limits by simply refusing public money, as several primary candidates, including Barack Obama, did in 2008.

Then in 2010, the Supreme Court reset all the rules, with a decision in the Citizens United case. A 5–4 opinion held that the First Amendment guarantee of free speech prohibits the government from limiting spending for political purposes by corporations and unions.[11]

The effects of this decision became vividly apparent during the Republican primary campaigns of 2012. The floodgates opened as wealthy donors funded "super PACs" that began heavy television advertising campaigns and altered the shape of the GOP primary. President Obama then announced that he was shifting from his earlier refusal to now cooperate with the super PAC supporting his reelection. In a rueful editorial in February 2012, the *New York Times* castigated Obama for his turnaround. "The announcement fully implicates the president, his campaign and his administration in the pollution of the political system unleashed by Citizens United and related court decisions. Corporations, unions and wealthy individuals are already writing huge checks —with no restrictions—to political action committees supporting individual candidates, which have become bag men for campaigns that still nominally operate under federal limits."[12]

By March 2012, the presidential candidates from both parties had raised more than $330 million.[13] That amount did not include independent spending by groups and individuals with no legal ties to a candidate but which have no limits. In early March 2012, these independent groups and individuals had spent at least $64.7 million, according to the *New York Times.*[14] Before the 2012 campaign began in earnest, there were predictions that President Obama, who raised more than $740 million from individuals and spent $427 million on media in the 2008 campaign, would raise $1 billion toward his reelection campaign.[15] By March 2012, after essentially securing the Republican nomination, Romney and his campaign looked to raise $800 million with the possibility of another $200 million spent by Super PACS on his behalf—bringing both candidates and their supporters near the billion-dollar mark.[16]

That would buy an awful lot of rum punch and free beer.

PRESIDENTIAL VOICES

Monarchy on the British model may be irrelevant or quaint in the late twentieth century. Could it be that Americans have something more dangerous: not an Imperial Presidency or an Imperiled but a plumb Impossible Presidency? A bundle . . . of contradictions ancient and modern, aggravated by all the institutional problems that political scientists analyze: the built-in clashes with Congress, the feuding and cross purposes within the Executive Department, the ever-growing public expectation that their republican monarch will be a politician and a statesman, an average citizen and a superman, a meditative dreamer and a tireless hustler?

MARCUS CUNLIFFE
The Presidency, 1987[17]

Setting aside the perennial partisan sniping between Congress and the White House and the larger historic seesaw swings between these two branches of American government, the American presidency has traveled an immense distance in more than two hundred years. We have come so far from those days when men like Benjamin Franklin and George Mason feared an "elected monarch." And certainly many of the founders would be shocked, if not appalled, by the power of the modern presidency, with all its ceremonial trappings.

On the other side of the ledger is concern voiced by presidential historian Marcus Cunliffe—the job of president is unwieldy, unmanageable, even impossible.

What this history of these men and their administrations has shown is that predicting presidential success is clearly a roll of the dice. As the long list of mediocre or worse presidents shows, many men who may have seemed well suited to the task fell short. And some of those least prepared—most notably Lincoln—or with exceedingly low expectations—Harry Truman comes to mind—stand above the rest.

It would be sublime if a presidential competency checklist could be compiled and the American people could use it to tick off boxes for each candidate—like ticking off the features we want when picking a hotel. But choosing a president is not as easy as choosing a vacation room, a new appliance, or an automobile. There is no Consumer Guide to one of the most important decisions Americans must make.

It is more like the old carnival barker's cry as you play the Wheel of Fortune: "You pays your money and you takes your chance."

Perhaps remarkably, the republic has survived more than two hundred years of that spinning wheel.

Appendices

The United States Constitution:
Article II

★

D rafted in the summer of 1787, the United States Constitution was submitted to the thirteen states for ratification in September 1787. When New Hampshire became the ninth state to ratify the Constitution on June 21, 1788, it went into effect.

The United States Constitution is the supreme law of the land. It is comprised of the "Preamble," which famously begins "We the People" and discusses the need for forming a "More perfect Union," and seven separate subdivisions, called Articles.

These "Articles," or main sections, of the Constitution establish the framework of America's national government, the relationships between the three branches of government, and rules that govern the country, including the mechanics for ratifying and changing, or amending, the Constitution.

The Articles, in brief:

Article I deals with the legislature—the Congress—and its two divisions: the House of Representatives, based on proportional representation, and the Senate, in which each state has two senators, regardless of population.

Article II deals with the powers, duties, and responsibilities of the executive branch—the president—as well as the mechanics of electing the president and removing him from office. (The complete text of Article II appears below.)

Article III deals with the judicial branch, including the Supreme Court and all of the lower federal courts. But the actual mechanics of the federal court system were left to Congress, which has passed numerous judiciary acts that established the number of Supreme Court justices and created the lower federal courts.

Article IV details the relationships between the states and provides rules for the admission of new states.

Article V lays out the procedure for amending the Constitution; in general, the Congress proposes amendments, which must pass both the House and Senate by a two-thirds majority and are then sent to the state legislatures; two-thirds of the states must also approve the amendment to ratify it.

Article VI contains one clause relating to national debts that is now obsolete; the other clauses state that the Constitution is the supreme law of the land and require that all office holders and members of government take an oath supporting the Constitution, but that "no religious test shall ever be required as a qualification."

Article VII provided the terms for the original ratification of the Constitution by the states.

Article II

Section 1.1 The executive Power shall be vested in a President of the United States of America. He shall hold his Office during the Term of four Years, and, together with the Vice President, chosen for the same Term, be elected, as follows:

1.2 Each State shall appoint, in such Manner as the Legislature thereof may direct, a Number of Electors, equal to the whole Number of Senators and Representatives to which the State may be entitled in the Congress: but no Senator or Representative, or Person holding an Office of Trust or Profit under the United States, shall be appointed an Elector.

NOTE: As this section makes clear, the electors may not be elected officials and the manner in which they are chosen is left to the states. There is also no constitutional instruction or requirement specifying how electors may actually vote. In *The Citizen's Constitution*, Seth Lipsky pointedly notes, "The word 'state' appears ten times in this and the following paragraph describing the procedure for choosing the President; the word 'people' does not appear at all."[1]

1.3 [*The Electors shall meet in their respective States, and vote by Ballot for two Persons, of whom one at least shall not be an Inhabitant of the same State with themselves. And they shall make a List of all the Persons voted for, and of the Number of Votes for each; which List they shall sign and certify, and transmit sealed to the Seat of the Government of the United States, directed to the President of the Senate. The President of the Senate shall, in the Presence of the Senate and House of Representatives, open all the Certificates, and the Votes shall then be counted. The Person having the greatest Number of Votes shall be the President, if such Number be a Majority of the whole Number of Electors appointed; and if there be more than one who have such Majority, and have an equal Number of Votes, then the House of Representatives shall immediately chuse by Ballot one of them for President; and if no Person have a Majority, then from the five highest on the List the said House shall in like Manner chuse the President. But in chusing the President, the Votes shall be taken by States, the Representation from each State having one Vote; A quorum for this Purpose shall consist of a Member or Members from two thirds of the States, and a Majority of all the States shall be necessary to a Choice. In every Case, after the Choice of the President, the Person having the greatest Number of Votes of the Electors shall be the Vice President. But if there should remain two or more who have equal Votes, the Senate shall chuse from them by Ballot the Vice President.*]

NOTE: The bracketed section in italics had been superseded by the Twelfth Amendment. (See Appendix II.)

1.4 The Congress may determine the Time of chusing the Electors, and the Day on which they shall give their Votes; which Day shall be the same throughout the United States.

NOTE: In the nation's early years, Election Day could be held on any day in a thirty-four-day period before the first Wednesday in December, determined by the state. That created problems, as some states waited to see what the others were doing before deciding on their Election Day. This led to the creation of a uniform national Election Day in 1845. The first Tuesday after the first Monday in November was chosen because it came after the fall harvest but before the worst winter weather.[2]

1.5 No Person except a natural born Citizen, or a Citizen of the United States, at the time of the Adoption of this Constitution, shall be eligible to the Office of President; neither shall any Person be eligible to that Office who shall not have attained to the Age of thirty five Years, and been fourteen Years a Resident within the United States.

1.6 In Case of the Removal of the President from Office, or of his Death, Resignation, or Inability to discharge the Powers and Duties of the said Office, the Same shall devolve on the Vice President, and the Congress may by Law provide for the Case of Removal, Death, Resignation or Inability, both of the President and Vice President, declaring what Officer shall then act as President, and such Officer shall act accordingly, until the Disability be removed, or a President shall be elected.

NOTE: This section was changed by ratification of the Twenty-fifth Amendment in 1967. (See Appendix II.) The Twenty-fifth Amendment clarified the rules of presidential disability and succession. It also allows for the appointment of a vice president if the vice president succeeds to the presidency. The Twenty-fifth Amendment was ratified on February 10, 1967. The Presidential Succession Act of 1947 is an act of Congress that established the current order of succession. (See Appendix III.)

1.7 The President shall, at stated Times, receive for his Services, a Compensation, which shall neither be encreased nor diminished during the Period for which he shall have been elected, and he shall not receive within that Period any other Emolument from the United States, or any of them.

1.8 Before he enter on the Execution of his Office, he shall take the following Oath or Affirmation: "I do solemnly swear (or affirm) that I will faithfully execute the Office of President of the United States, and will to the best of my Ability, preserve, protect and defend the Constitution of the United States."

Section 2.1 The President shall be Commander in Chief of the Army and Navy of the United States, and of the Militia of the several States, when called into the actual Service of the United States; he may require the Opinion, in writing, of the principal Officer in each of the executive Departments, upon any Subject relating to the Duties of their respective Offices, and he shall have Power to grant Reprieves and Pardons for Offences against the United States, except in Cases of Impeachment.

2.2 He shall have Power, by and with the Advice and Consent of the Senate, to make Treaties, provided two thirds of the Senators present concur; and he shall nominate, and by and with the Advice and Consent of the Senate, shall appoint Ambassadors, other public Ministers and Consuls, Judges of the supreme Court, and all other Officers of the United States, whose Appointments are not herein otherwise provided for, and which shall be established by Law: but the Congress may by Law vest the Appointment of such inferior Officers, as they think proper, in the President alone, in the Courts of Law, or in the Heads of Departments.

2.3 The President shall have Power to fill up all Vacancies that may happen during the Recess of the Senate, by granting Commissions which shall expire at the End of their next Session.

Section 3. He shall from time to time give to the Congress Information of the State of the Union, and recommend to their Consideration such Measures as he shall judge necessary and expedient; he may, on extraordinary Occasions, convene both Houses, or either of them, and in Case of Disagreement between them, with Respect to the Time of Adjournment, he may adjourn them to such Time as he shall think proper; he shall receive Ambassadors and other public Ministers; he shall take Care that the Laws be faithfully executed, and shall Commission all the Officers of the United States.

Section 4. The President, Vice President and all civil Officers of the United States, shall be removed from Office on Impeachment for, and Conviction of, Treason, Bribery, or other high Crimes and Misdemeanors.

Constitutional Amendments Affecting the Presidency, Presidential Elections, and Voting Rights

Amendment Twelve (proposed in 1803; ratified in 1804)
Passed after the controversial election of 1800, this amendment altered the manner of choosing the president and vice president.

The Electors shall meet in their respective states and vote by ballot for president and vice president, one of whom, at least, shall not be an inhabitant of the same state with themselves; they shall name in their ballots the person voted for as president, and in distinct ballots the person voted for as Vice President, and they shall make distinct lists of all persons voted for as president, and of all persons voted for as Vice President, and of the number of votes for each, which lists they shall sign and certify, and transmit sealed to the seat of the government of the United States, directed to the president of the Senate;—The president of the Senate shall, in presence of the Senate and House of Representatives, open all the certificates and the votes shall then be counted;—The person having the greatest number of votes for president, shall be the president, if such number be a majority of the whole number of Electors appointed; and if no person have such majority, then from the persons having the highest numbers not exceeding three on the list of those voted for as president, the House of Representatives shall choose immediately, by ballot, the president. But in choosing the president, the vote shall be taken by states, the representation from each state having one vote; a quorum for this purpose shall consist of a member or members from two thirds of the states, and a majority of all the states shall be necessary to a choice. [And if the House of representatives shall not choose a President whenever the right of choice shall devolve upon them, before the fourth day of March next following, then the Vice President, shall act as president, as in the case of the death or other constitutional disability of the president.] The person having the greatest number of votes as Vice President, shall be the Vice President, if such number be a majority of the whole number of Electors appointed, and if no person have a majority, then from the two highest numbers on the list, the Senate shall choose the Vice President; a quorum for the purpose shall consist of two thirds of the whole number of Senators, and a majority of the whole number shall be necessary to a choice. But no person constitutionally ineligible to the office of President shall be eligible to that of Vice President of the United States. [Bracketed portion was superseded by Section 3 of Amendment Twenty in 1933.]

NOTE: In America's presidential elections, a voter does not actually vote for the candidate but casts a ballot for a group of presidential electors, known as a "slate," selected by the various political parties within the state. The electors are then pledged to that party's candidate. In some states, the names of the electors actually appear on the ballot, but in many they do not.

The number of electors in each state is equal to the combined total of senators and representatives in the House from that state. Currently there are 538 electors: 435 House members, 100 Senate members, and an additional 3 electors granted to the District of Columbia, which has no representatives in either house of Congress.

To win the presidency, a candidate must win 270 electoral votes, one more than half of the 538 total electors.

In most states, there is a winner-take-all system, and the state's electors go to the winner of the popular vote in the state, no matter how close the vote. This is what makes it possible, as in the 2000 election of George Bush, for the president to be elected by a minority of the popular vote. As noted in this book, this has happened three other times in American history: In 1828, Andrew Jackson won the popular vote but lacked sufficient electoral votes; in 1876, Rutherford B. Hayes won the presidency over Samuel J. Tilden with a minority vote; and in

1888, Benjamin Harrison beat Grover Cleveland with a minority of the popular vote.

Amendment Fifteen (proposed by Congress in February 1869; ratified in February 1870)

Passed after the Civil War, this amendment gave black males the vote.

SECTION 1

The right of citizens of the United States to vote shall not be denied or abridged by the United States or by any States on account of race, color, or previous condition of servitude.

SECTION 2

The Congress shall have the power to enforce this article by appropriate legislation.

Amendment Seventeen (proposed by Congress in May 1912; ratified in April 1913)

Prior to passage of this amendment, U.S. senators were chosen by state legislatures; this amendment allowed direct election by popular vote and made the rules for filling a vacancy if a senator dies or leaves office.

The Senate of the United States shall be composed of two Senators from each State, elected by the people thereof, for six years; and each Senator shall have one vote. The electors in each State shall have the qualifications requisite for electors of the most numerous branch of the State legislatures.

When vacancies happen in the representation of any State in the Senate, the executive authority of such State shall issue writs of election to fill such vacancies: Provided, That the legislature of any State may empower the executive thereof to make temporary appointments until the people fill the vacancies by election as the legislature may direct. This amendment shall not be so construed as to affect the election or term of any Senator chosen before it becomes valid as part of the Constitution.

Amendment Nineteen (proposed by Congress in June 1919; ratified in August 1920)
This amendment established the nationwide vote for women.

The right of citizens of the United States to vote shall not be denied or abridged by the United States or by any State on account of sex.

Congress shall have the power to enforce this article by appropriate legislation.

NOTE: Although ratified by a sufficient number of states, this amendment was rejected by the following states: Alabama, Georgia, Louisiana, Maryland, Mississippi, South Carolina, and Virginia. While it guaranteed the vote to women, states could still enact their own voting requirements. The amendment also did not require states to allow women to serve on juries or make them eligible for public office. All states have since permitted women to serve on juries and serve in public office, but only after the Supreme Court ruled in 1975 that excluding women from juries was unconstitutional.

Amendment Twenty (proposed by Congress in March 1932; ratified in January 1933)
Before this amendment was ratified, Inauguration Day was on March 4. That created problems as the period following the election of the president created a large gap until the president-elect took office. This amendment changed that date. It also changed the date when the new Congress convened.

1. The terms of the President and Vice President shall end at noon on the 20th day of January, and the terms of Senators and Repre-

sentatives at noon on the 3d day of January, of the years in which such terms would have ended if this article had not been ratified; and the terms of their successors shall then begin.

2. The Congress shall assemble at least once in every year, and such meeting shall begin at noon on the 3d of January, unless they shall by law appoint a different day.

3. If, at the time fixed for the beginning of the term of the President, the President elect shall have died, the Vice President elect shall become President. If a President shall not have been chosen before the time fixed for the beginning of his term, or if the President elect shall have failed to qualify, then the Vice President elect shall act as President until a President shall have qualified; and the Congress may by law provide for the case wherein neither a President elect nor a Vice President elect shall have qualified, declaring who shall then act as President, or the manner in which one who is to act shall be selected, and such person shall act accordingly until a President or Vice President shall have qualified.

4. The Congress may by law provide for the case of the death of any of the persons from whom the House of Representatives may choose a President whenever the right of choice shall have devolved upon them, and for the case of the death of any of the persons from whom the Senate may choose a Vice President whenever the right of choice shall have devolved upon them.

5. Sections 1 and 2 shall take effect on the 15th day of October following the ratification of this article [October 1933].

6. This article shall be inoperative unless it shall have been ratified as an amendment to the Constitution by the legislatures of three fourths of the several States within seven years from the date of its submission.

NOTE: The old election schedule was a holdover from the time when travel and communications were much slower and the pace of the government very different. However, it meant that the Congress that convened in December possibly included defeated officials there to carry out the legislative and executive business of government in what was known as a "lame duck" session.

Under the revised rules, the old session of Congress adjourns before the elections and the new session begins in January with newly elected representatives taking their seats at once.

Of course, the sitting president remains in power until the president-elect is inaugurated in January. While Congress is not in session, the "lame duck" president still functions, and controversial decisions, executive orders, pardons, and appointments can be made during this period.

Amendment Twenty-two (proposed by Congress in March 1947; ratified in February 1951)

Passed after Franklin D. Roosevelt's four terms, this amendment sets presidential term limits.

> No persons shall be elected to the office of the President more than twice, and no person who has held the office of President, or acted as president, for more than two years of a term to which some other person was elected President shall be elected to the office of President more than once. But this article shall not apply to any person holding the office of president when this Article was proposed by the Congress.

> This article shall be inoperative unless it shall have been ratified as an Amendment to the Constitution by the legislatures of three fourths of the several states within seven years from the date of its submission to the States by the Congress.

NOTE: This amendment was proposed in 1947 and ratified in 1951, following the unprecedented and unequaled four terms of Franklin D.

Roosevelt, who died early in his fourth term, in April 1945. It limits a president to two terms, except in the case of a vice president who has succeeded to the presidency but serves two years or less of his predecessor's term.

Harry Truman, having served more than three years of FDR's fourth term and been elected to a term of his own, could have still run for a third term under the special provision of the amendment that made him an exception. Lyndon B. Johnson served only one year of President Kennedy's first term. He was then reelected in 1964 and was eligible to run again in 1968, but declined to do so. Had he run and won, he would have served a total of nine years. It is possible for a vice president who succeeds to office to serve as many as ten years, or two and one-half terms.[1]

Amendment Twenty-three (proposed by Congress in June 1960; ratified in March 1961)

This amendment gave voters in the District of Columbia the Presidential vote.

1. The District constituting the seat of Government of the United States shall appoint in such manner as the Congress may direct: A number of electors of president and vice president equal to the whole number of Senators and Representatives in Congress to which the District would be entitled if it were a State, but in no event more than the least populous state; they shall be in addition to those appointed by the States, but they shall be considered, for the purpose of the election of the President and Vice President, to be electors appointed by a State; and they shall meet in the District and perform such duties as provided by the twelfth article of amendment.

2. The Congress shall have power to enforce this article by appropriate legislation.

NOTE: Prior to this amendment, voters in the District of Columbia could not vote for president. The amendment guarantees that the District will always have at least three electoral votes, since even the states with the smallest populations have two senators and at least one representative. In 1970, Congress approved a single delegate from the District of Columbia to the House of Representatives. This member cannot vote on the floor but can vote in committee and participate in debates. The District has no representation in the Senate. If the District of Columbia were counted as the fifty-first state, it would rank fiftieth in population, behind Vermont but ahead of Wyoming, according to the 2010 census.

Amendment Twenty-four (proposed by Congress in August 1962; ratified in January 1964)

Passed during the civil rights era, this amendment outlaws poll taxes in federal elections.

1. The right of citizens of the United States to vote in any primary or other election for President or Vice President, of electors for President or Vice President, or for Senator or Representative in Congress, shall not be denied or abridged by the United States or any State by reason of failure to pay any poll tax or other tax.

2. The Congress shall have power to enforce this article by appropriate legislation.

NOTE: While some states had imposed some sort of poll tax—an income requirement in order to vote—following the Civil War Reconstruction era, many Southern states had imposed taxes as a specific means to limit black voter participation. Passed during the period of civil rights legislation that included the Voting Rights Act of 1964, this amendment was aimed at eliminating one more hurdle to voting rights for all Americans.

Amendment Twenty-five (proposed by Congress in July 1965; ratified in February 1967)

Passed after the assassination of John F. Kennedy, this amendment more clearly established the rules governing presidential disability and succession.

1. In case of the removal of the President from office or of his death or resignation, the Vice President shall become President.

2. Whenever there is a vacancy in the office of the Vice President, the President shall nominate a Vice President who shall take office upon confirmation by a majority vote of both Houses of Congress.

3. Whenever the President transmits to the President pro tempore of the Senate and the Speaker of the House of Representatives his written declaration that he is unable to discharge the powers and duties of his office, and until he transmits to them a written declaration to the contrary, such power and duties shall be discharged by the Vice President as Acting President.

4. Whenever the Vice President and a majority of either the principal officers of the executive departments or of such other body as Congress may by law provide, transmit to the President pro tempore of the Senate and the Speaker of the House of Representatives their written declaration that the President is unable to discharge the power and duties of his office, the Vice President shall immediately assume the powers and duties of the office as Acting President. Thereafter, when the President transmits to the President pro tempore of the Senate and the Speaker of the House of Representatives his written declaration that no inability exists, he shall resume the powers and duties of his office unless the Vice President and a majority of either the principal officers of the executive department or of such other body as Congress may by law provide, transmit within four days to the President pro tempore of the Senate and the Speaker of the House of Representatives their written declaration that the President is unable to discharge the powers and duties of his office. Thereupon Congress shall decide the issue, assembling within forty-eight hours for that purpose if not in session. If the Congress, within twenty-one days after receipt of the latter written

declaration, or if Congress is not in session, within twenty-one days after Congress is required to assemble, determines by two thirds vote of both Houses that the President is unable to discharge the powers and duties of his office, the Vice President shall continue to discharge the same as Acting President; otherwise, the President shall resume the powers and duties of his office.

NOTE: This amendment provided clearer rules for the succession in the presidency, in cases of death, removal, resignation, or disability. It covers temporary as well as permanent succession by the vice president. The first time this amendment was invoked came during President Reagan's 1985 cancer surgery, when Vice President Bush became the first "acting president." In 2002, Vice President Cheney became acting president while President George W. Bush underwent a colonoscopy and was sedated. Some observers, including physicians who treated Ronald Reagan, believe that the amendment should have been invoked while he was undergoing surgery after the 1981 assassination attempt.

Amendment Twenty-six (proposed by Congress in March 1971; ratified in June 1971)

This amendment extended voting rights to eighteen-year-olds.

1. The right of citizens of the United States, who are eighteen years of age or older, to vote shall not be denied or abridged by the United States or by any State on account of age.

2. The Congress shall have the power to enforce this article by appropriate legislation.

NOTE: The idea of lowering the voting age to eighteen began during World War II, and President Eisenhower recommended it in his State of the Union Address in 1954. Officially proposed[2] during the Vietnam War era, while many eighteen-year-olds were being drafted to fight but couldn't vote, and many others were vocally protesting the war, this amendment was ratified faster than any other in American history.

At the time, most states' drinking age was still eighteen, but since then almost every state has raised the minimum drinking age to twenty-one years. The only notable court case involving this amendment was the successful suit brought by college students who wanted to register to vote in the towns where they attended school. The court found that the students did have that right.

The Order of Presidential Succession

There is a curious little drama, or guessing game, that plays out every time the president comes to the Capitol to address a joint session of Congress, as in the State of the Union Address or at a presidential inauguration. Aside from all the pomp and circumstance, there are the senators and representatives in their best clothes, the Supreme Court justices all looking rather glum in black, and members of the military in their full dress regalia—then comes the cabinet. That is when the guessing game commences: Who isn't there?

Because the president must live in a worst-case-scenario world, there is always at least one cabinet member—one who must be eligible to serve as president—who doesn't come to the speech. Just in case.

In a true doomsday scenario, if something happened to the president, the Congress, and the rest of the cabinet, somebody has to be around to take charge.

Most people know that the vice president comes first. Some know that the speaker of the House comes after that. But where on the list of presidential succession does that "uninvited" cabinet secretary reside?

Here is the official order:

1. Vice President of the United States
2. Speaker of the House
3. President pro tempore of the Senate
   (This is the senator who has been serving the longest without interruption, and may be the most controversial post on the list, as it means that a usually elderly senator is number three

on the list; in 2011, Daniel K. Inouye, age eighty-seven,
was in this position.)

4. Secretary of State
5. Secretary of the Treasury
6. Secretary of Defense
7. Attorney General
8. Secretary of the Interior
9. Secretary of Agriculture
10. Secretary of Commerce
11. Secretary of Labor
12. Secretary of Health and Human Services
13, Secretary of Housing and Urban Development
14. Secretary of Transportation
15. Secretary of Energy
16. Secretary of Education
17. Secretary of Veterans Affairs
18. Director of Homeland Security

This order was established in 1947 when the Presidential Succession Act was passed. One change made then was to elevate the two members of Congress over the secretary of state, so an elected official rather than a presidential appointee took precedence. The order of the cabinet members is not a reflection of their relative importance. It is simply a list in the chronological order in which their offices were created.

When Barack Obama was inaugurated in 2009, Secretary of Defense William Gates was the odd man out.

"It's All About the Benjamins"
Presidents on Coins and Currency

Maybe you call them "Benjamins," in honor of Founding Father Benjamin Franklin, still featured on the $100 bill. But they are also known as "dead presidents." Yes, the money we all carry. And by law, the people whose portraits are on America's money must be dead— but not necessarily a president. A 1909 law stipulates that a person must be dead two years before his or her likeness can be used on American currency or coins. Before that time, there were no portraits on American coins, which instead featured a figure known as "Liberty." The Lincoln penny changed that, and since 1909, other coins featuring presidential portraits have been added.

American paper money is a different story. The long, winding history of America's paper money is closely tied to America's complicated history of national banks. But it actually begins in colonial times, when the Massachusetts Bay Colony issued the future America's first paper money in 1690. Other colonies did the same thing. The basic idea was that paper money could be redeemed for gold or silver coins. But the "guarantees" of redemption were sometimes sketchy and created a tremendous distrust of paper money that ran through early American history.

During the American Revolution, the Continental Congress issued paper money, known as "Continentals," and these notes proved to be so useless, because of insufficient backing, the high rate of inflation, and widespread counterfeiting, that a common expression entered the language: "Not worth a Continental."

In 1777, the first notes bearing the words "The United States" were issued and signed by revolutionary figures to give them credibility.

But the early American experience with paper money left a deep distrust of paper currency and many Americans wanted "hard money," meaning silver or gold coins.

After the Constitution was passed and the first National Bank was created in 1791, the bank issued paper notes. When Andrew Jackson vetoed the bank in 1832, it opened up a "Free Banking Era" in which state-chartered banks were created, but they lacked federal regulation or uniformity. The hodgepodge of banknotes issued by these state banks meant that many of these notes eventually proved worthless.

During the Civil War, the governments of both the United States and the Confederacy again had to turn to paper money to finance their war efforts. In 1861, Congress authorized "demand notes" in $5, $10, and $20 denominations, redeemable for coins. Black on one side and printed in green on the reverse, these were the first "greenbacks."

In 1862, these demand notes were switched to "legal tender notes," issued in denominations from $1 to $1,000 (later $5,000 and $10,000). The first $1 bill had on it a portrait of Salmon P. Chase, Lincoln's secretary of the Treasury, who also decided to include the words "In God We Trust" on the money. (The words were not legally part of American currency until an act of Congress in 1957.) In 1863, a National Banking Act created a uniform national currency. And in 1869, the $1 U.S. note was redesigned with a portrait of George Washington on it.

Another form of currency, gold and silver certificates, were printed in the later nineteenth century as periodic depressions and banking failures created a demand for gold. The silver certificates had many designs, including an "educational series" featuring Indians, military heroes, inventors like Robert Fulton, and the only piece of U.S. paper currency adorned with the portrait of a woman—Martha Washington appeared on the 1886 silver certificate. Over the years, many of these notes were produced featuring presidential portraits.

Currently, these are the presidential faces of U.S. currency:[1]

$1 note	George Washington
$2 note	Thomas Jefferson
$5 note	Abraham Lincoln
$20 note	Andrew Jackson
$50 note	Ulysses S. Grant

The two non-presidents on current American currency are:

| $10 note | Alexander Hamilton |
| $100 note | Benjamin Franklin |

The following notes are no longer in circulation:

$500 note	William McKinley
$1,000 note	Grover Cleveland
$5,000 note	James Madison
$10,000 note	Salmon P. Chase
$100,000 note	Woodrow Wilson

Presidents featured on current coins:

Penny	Lincoln
Nickel	Jefferson
Dime	Franklin D. Roosevelt
Quarter	George Washington
Half dollar	John F. Kennedy

Dollar coins: In 2005, Congress passed a bill to begin producing $1 coins with portraits of the presidents in order. The first twenty of these dollar coins included the presidents from Washington to James A. Garfield, released in November 2011.[2]

ACKNOWLEDGMENTS

The completion of this work is due to the efforts and assistance of a great many people. My gratitude begins with the wonderful librarians and researchers at all of the historical museums, presidential sites, research facilities and libraries around the country. They provide a great service to the country.

During my writing career, I have had the good fortune to be represented by the David Black Literary Agency, and I count among my allies and supporters there my good friend David Black, along with Allison Hemphill, Antonella Iannarino, Dave Larabell, Gary Morris, Susan Raihofer, and Luke Thomas. Thank you all.

During the more than twenty years that I have been writing the Don't Know Much About® series and other books, I have also been graced with the generous support, encouragement, and enthusiasm of many colleagues and friends, among them Gretchen Koss, Meg Walker, Laura Reynolds, Diane Burrowes, Virginia Stanley, Will Schwalbe, Michael Signorelli, and Carrie Kania.

This undertaking has brought me to a new publisher and I have been very pleased to work with the Hyperion team led by Ellen Archer. Thanks to Kristin Kiser, Diane Aronson, Karen Minster, Amy Vreeland, Navorn Johnson, Vincent Stanley, Christine Ragasa, Bryan Christian, Jon Bernstein, and Rick Willett, and to their ABC colleagues Edward O'Keefe and John Griffin.

It has been my great pleasure to work again with my editor, Elisabeth Dyssegaard, and her assistant, Sam O'Brien. I am extremely grateful for their encouragement, insights, and yeoman's work on this very large undertaking.

My greatest gratitude goes, as always, to my family: Jenny Davis, Colin Davis, and my wife, Joann, who has made it all possible.

NOTES

INTRODUCTION

1. Editor's Note in the *American Presidency* series (Times Books).
2. John Milton Cooper, Jr., *Woodrow Wilson: A Biography*, p. 11.

PART I:
THE MAKING OF A PRESIDENT

1. Cited in Edward J. Larson and Michael P. Winship, *The Constitutional Convention: A Narrative History from the Notes of James Madison*, p. 18.
2. Larson and Winship, p. 26.
3. Larson and Winship, p. 18.
4. Larson and Winship, p. 17.
5. Text of Northwest Ordinance (July 13, 1787), Avalon Project-Yale Law School, retrieved from http://avalon.law.yale.edu/18th_century/nworder.asp.
6. Ron Chernow, *Alexander Hamilton*, p. 224.
7. McCullough, *John Adams*, pp. 368–369.
8. Gordon S. Wood, *The Creation of the American Republic: 1776–1787*, p. 326.
9. Washington's diary cited by Catherine Drinker Bowen in *Miracle at Philadelphia*, p. 195.
10. Richard Beeman, *Plain, Honest Men: The Making of the American Constitution*, p. xi.
11. James McGregor Burns, *Vineyard of Liberty*, p. 112.
12. H. W. Brands, *The First American*, p. 673.
13. Washington, *Writings*, p. 652.
14. Brands, *The First American*, p. 673.
15. *Works of Benjamin Franklin*, cited in Beeman, p. 53.
16. Beeman, p. 53.
17. Richard Brookhiser, *Founding Father*, p. 61.
18. Larson and Winship, p. 20.
19. Akhil Reed Amar, *America's Constitution: A Biography*, p. 160.
20. http://www.nps.gov/history/history/online_books/constitution/bio31.htm.

21. Larson and Winship, p. 26.
22. Dahl, *How Democratic Is the American Constitution?*, pp. 64–65.
23. Larson and Winship, p. 26.
24. Cited in Richard Brookhiser, *Gentleman Revolutionary*, p. 87.
25. Brookhiser, p. 82.
26. Brookhiser, pp. 85–86.
27. Seth Lipsky, *The Citizen's Constitution*, p. 87.
28. Dahl, p. 67.
29. Yale's Akhil Reed Amar agrees. In *America's Constitution*, he notes, "a child born abroad of American parentage would be eligible, so long as the citizenship rules in place at the time of his birth so provided." Note 91, p. 554.
30. Amar, p. 151.
31. Reed, p. 158.
32. Clarence Lusane, *The Black History of the White House*, p. 15.
33. Woody Holton, *The Unruly Americans*, p. 189.
34. Larson and Winship, p. 156; Brands, p. 691.
35. Cited in David McCullough, *John Adams*, pp. 379–380.
36. John Ferling, *The Ascent of George Washington*, p. 272.
37. James Wilson, Pennsylvania Ratification Convention, 1787.
38. John Adams, *Works*, cited in McCullough, p. 380.
39. Henry May, *The Enlightenment in America*, p. 99.

PART II:
PRESIDENTIAL PROFILES

1. Cited in James M. McPherson, *"To the Best of My Ability": The American Presidents*, p. 26.
2. Cited in "TR: The Story of Theodore Roosevelt," *American Experience*, Public Broadcasting Service, retrieved from http://www.pbs.org/wgbh/american experience/features/general-article/tr-know.
3. David H. Donald, *Lincoln*, p. 13.

1. GEORGE WASHINGTON

1. http://avalon.law.yale.edu/18th_century/wash1.asp.
2. Richard Brookhiser, *Gentleman Revolutionary*, p. 26. A similar version of the story is cited by Walter Isaacson in *Benjamin Franklin* and a similar version appears in Richard Beeman's *Plain, Honest Men: The Making of the American Constitution*, p. 48.
3. Joseph J. Ellis, *His Excellency George Washington*, p. 273.
4. http://www.apva.org/MaryWashingtonHouse/MaryBallWashington.php.
5. William A. DeGregorio, *The Complete Book of U.S. Presidents*, p. 2.
6. Cited in Joseph Ellis, *His Excellency George Washington*, p. 9.

7. Ron Chernow, *Washington: A Life*, p. 61.
8. Ellis, p. 27.
9. Patricia Brady, *Martha Washington: An American Life*, p. 232.
10. Edwin G. Burrows and Mike Wallace, *Gotham*, p. 296.
11. Cathy Lynn Grossman, "No Proof Washington said 'so help me God'—will Obama?" *USA Today*, January 9, 2009, retrieved from http://www.usatoday.com/news/religion/2009-01-07-washington-oath_N.htm.
12. Chernow, p. 569.
13. Burrows and Wallace, *Gotham*, p. 298.
14. http://www.whitehousehistory.org/whha_timelines/timelines_decorative-arts-01.html.
15. Clarence Lusane, *The Black History of the White House*, p. 41.
16. Lusane, p. 46.
17. Ron Chernow, *Alexander Hamilton*, pp. 303–304.
18. Ron Chernow, *Washington*, p. 650.
19. Marshall cited in Jean Edward Smith, *John Marshall*, p. 170.
20. Eric Foner, Introduction to Thomas Paine, *The Rights of Man*, p. 21.
21. William Hogeland, "Why the Whiskey Rebellion Is Worth Recalling Now," http://hnn.us/articles/27341.html.
22. Richard Brookhiser, *Founding Father*, p. 90.
23. "George Washington's Distillery and Gristmill," retrieved from http://www.mountvernon.org/visit-his-estate/plan-your-visit/distillery-amp-gristmill.
24. John Ferling, *The Ascent of George Washington*, p. 285.
25. Dennis J. Pogue, "George Washington and the Politics of Slavery," *Historical Alexandria Quarterly*, Spring/Summer 2003.
26. Timeline sources: Miller Center, University of Virginia; Arthur M. Schlesinger, Jr., *The Almanac of American History*; Gorton Carruth, *What Happened When: A Chronology of Life and Events in America*.

2. JOHN ADAMS

1. Cited in McCullough, *John Adams*, p. 163.
2. McCullough, pp. 18–19.
3. McCullough, p. 67.
4. Cited in *Bartlett's Familiar Quotations*, edition 16, p. 338.
5. William A. DeGregorio, *The Complete Book of U.S. Presidents*, p. 27.
6. Robert Hendrickson, *QPB Encyclopedia of Word and Phrase Origins*, p. 135.
7. Cited in Joseph Ellis, *First Family: Abigail and John Adams*, p. 176.
8. Ellis, pp. 176–177.
9. Edith B. Gelles, *Abigail and John*, p. 249.
10. Ellis, p. 188.
11. Cited in McCullough, p. 553; Ellis, p. 208; Gelles, p. 262.
12. William Seale, *The President's House, Volume I*, p. 88.

13. Timeline sources: Miller Center, University of Virginia; Arthur M. Schlesinger, Jr., *The Almanac of American History;* Gorton Carruth, *What Happened When: A Chronology of Life and Events in America.*

3. THOMAS JEFFERSON

1. Jefferson Inaugural Address, retrieved from http://avalon.law.yale.edu/19th _century/jefinau1.asp.
2. Quote retrieved from John F. Kennedy Presidential Library and Museum, http://www.jfklibrary.org/Research/Ready-Reference/JFK-Quotations .aspx.
3. Garry Wills, *"Negro President": Jefferson and the Slave Power,* pp. xvi–xvii.
4. Quote about Martha's death and words on tombstone are cited in "Martha Wayles Skelton Jefferson," retrieved from Monticello.org, "The Thomas Jefferson Encyclopedia," http://www.monticello.org/site/jefferson/martha -wayles-skelton-jefferson.
5. "Thomas Jefferson and Sally Hemings: A Brief Account," retrieved from http://www.monticello.org/site/plantation-and-slavery/thomas-jefferson-and -sally-hemings-brief-account.
6. William A. DeGregorio, *The Complete Book of U.S. Presidents,* p. 41.
7. William Seale, *The President's House, Volume I,* pp. 106–107.
8. Text retrieved from Avalon Project, Yale Law School: Papers of Thomas Jefferson, http://avalon.law.yale.edu/18th_century/jeffsumm.asp.
9. Cited in DeGregorio, p. 40.
10. Cited in Wills, p. 1.
11. Wills, p. 2.
12. Bernard A. Weisberger, *America Afire,* p. 9.
13. Margaret Bayard Smith's recollection is cited in Robert V. Remini, *The House: The History of the House of Representatives,* p. 73.
14. Wills, p. 2.
15. Leonard L. Richards, *The Slave Power,* cited in Wills, p. 6.
16. Richard H. Brown, "The Missouri Crisis, Slavery, and the Crisis of Jacksonianism," *South Atlantic Quarterly* 65 (1966): 65. Cited in Wills, p. 7.
17. Text of Jefferson letter retrieved from Miller Center, University of Virginia, http://millercenter.org/scripps/archive/speeches/detail/3473.
18. Marshall letter to Charles Pinckney, cited in Wilentz, *The Rise of American Democracy,* p. 99.
19. Marshall's views of Jefferson cited in Jean Edward Smith, *John Marshall,* pp. 323 ff.
20. Jean Edward Smith, *John Marshall,* p. 324.
21. http://millercenter.org/scripps/archive/speeches/detail/3497.
22. Wilentz, p. 136.
23. "Jefferson's Cause of Death," retrieved from Monticello Research and Col-

lections, http://www.monticello.org/site/research-and-collections/jeffersons -cause-death.

24. Timeline sources: Miller Center, University of Virginia; Arthur M. Schlesinger, Jr., *The Almanac of American History*; Gorton Carruth, *What Happened When: A Chronology of Life and Events in America.*

4. JAMES MADISON

1. James Madison Inaugural Address, March 4, 1809, retrieved from "The American Presidency Project," University of California-Santa Barbara, http://www.presidency.ucsb.edu/ws/index.php?pid=25805#axzz1lKeAS1RH.
2. Richard Brookhiser, *James Madison*, p. 9.
3. Cited in David C. Whitney and Robin Vaughan Whitney, *The American Presidents*, p. 44.
4. Miller Center University of Virginia, "American President: A Reference Resource," http://millercenter.org/president/madison/essays/biography/3.
5. Retrieved from *The Founders' Constitution*, University of Chicago Press, http://press-pubs.uchicago.edu/founders/documents/amendI_religions43.html.
6. Retrieved from the Avalon Project, Yale Law School, http://avalon.law.yale.edu/18th_century/fed10.asp.
7. Clay cited in Robert Remini, *The House*, p. 88.
8. Catherine Allgor, *A Perfect Union*, p. 13.
9. All Dolley Madison quotes are cited in William Seale, *The President's House, Volume I*, p. 126.
10. Colin Calloway, *The Shawnee and the War for America*, p. 118.
11. Sean Wilentz, *The Rise of American Democracy*, pp. 155–156.
12. "U.S. historians pick top 10 presidential errors," Associated Press, February 18, 2006, retrieved from http://www.ctv.ca/CTVNews/World/20060218/presidential_errors_060218.
13. Seale, *Volume I*, pp.132–135.
14. *A Colored Man's Reminiscences of James Madison*, retrieved from Google Books, http://books.google.com/books?id=DoZDAAAAYAAJ&pg=PR1&lpg=PR1&dq=A+colored+man%27s+Reminiscences+of+James+Madison&source=bl&ots=pnKsPepUhY&sig=HlwTdkCO7vB5LeGoQrSrNpPpxbE&hl=en&ei=AdyhTufoMMn20gHW4ayvCg&sa=X&oi=book_result&ct=result&resnum=10&ved=0CHQQ6AEwCQ#v=onepage&q&f=false.
15. Rachel L. Swarns, "Madison and the White House, Through the Memoir of a Slave," *New York Times*, August 16, 2009.
16. Garry Wills, *James Madison*, p. 155.
17. Wills, p. 164.
18. Timeline sources: Miller Center, University of Virginia; Arthur M. Schlesinger, Jr., *The Almanac of American History*; Gorton Carruth, *What Happened When: A Chronology of Life and Events in America.*

5. JAMES MONROE

1. Retrieved from Avalon Project, Yale Law School, http://avalon.law.yale.edu /19th_century/monroe1.asp.
2. White House Historical Association, http://www.whitehousehistory.org/whha _timelines/timelines_first-ladies-05.html.
3. David C. Whitney and Robin Vaughan Whitney, *The American Presidents*, p. 56.
4. Retrieved from the White House Historical Association, http://www.white househistory.org/whha_timelines/timelines_architecture-01.html.
5. David I. Holmes, The Religion of James Monroe," *Virginia Quarterly Review*, Autumn 2003, retrieved from http://www.vqronline.org/articles/2003/autumn /holmes-religion-james-monroe.
6. Cited in *Quotations of James Monroe*, p. 57.
7. Jean Edward Smith, *John Marshall*, p. 98.
8. John Marshall cited by Smith, p. 63.
9. Andrew Burstein, *The Passions of Andrew Jackson*, pp. 131–133.
10. Frank Laumer, *Dade's Last Command*, p. 15.
11. Sean Michael O'Brien, *In Bitterness and in Tears*, p. 240.
12. Sean Wilentz, *The Rise of American Democracy*, pp. 236–237.
13. Jefferson's letter to John Holmes is cited in *Bartlett's Familiar Quotations*, p. 344.
14. Source: U.S Census Bureau: Selected Historical Decennial Census Population and Housing Counts, retrieved from http://www.census.gov/prod/www /abs/decennial/1820.html.
15. Timeline sources: Miller Center, University of Virginia; Arthur M. Schlesinger, Jr., *The Almanac of American History*; Gorton Carruth, *What Happened When: A Chronology of Life and Events in America*.

6. JOHN QUINCY ADAMS

1. John Quincy Adams Inaugural Address, retrieved from Avalon Project, Yale Law School, retrieved from http://avalon.law.yale.edu/19th_century/qadams .asp.
2. David C. Whitney and Robin Vaughan Whitney, *The American Presidents*, p. 60.
3. William A. DeGregorio, *The Complete Book of U.S. Presidents*, p. 93.
4. Cited in Lynn Hudson Parsons, *The Birth of Modern Politics*, p. 106.
5. Paul F. Boller, Jr., *Presidential Campaigns*, p. 34.
6. Cited in Paul F. Boller, Jr., *Presidential Campaigns*, p. 36.
7. Daniel Walker Howe, *What Hath God Wrought*, pp. 244–245.
8. Timeline sources: Miller Center, University of Virginia; Arthur M. Schlesinger, Jr., *The Almanac of American History*; Gorton Carruth, *What Happened When: A Chronology of Life and Events in America*.

7. ANDREW JACKSON

1. Andrew Jackson First Inaugural Address, retrieved from Avalon Project, Yale Law School, retrieved from http://avalon.law.yale.edu/19th_century/jackson1 .asp.

2. "Old Hickory, Rock Star President," *New York Times*, April 7, 2010, retrieved from http://theater.nytimes.com/2010/04/07/theater/reviews/07bloody.html.

3. "Should Andrew Jackson Be on the Twenty-dollar Bill?" retrieved from http://www.pbs.org/kcet/andrewjackson/edu/webquest2.html.

4. All citations about Jackson are in Robert Remini, *Andrew Jackson and the Course of American Empire 1767–1821*, p. 378.

5. The Jefferson and John Quincy Adams quotes are cited in William A. DeGregorio, *The Complete Book of U.S. Presidents*, p. 118.

6. Retrieved from the Hermitage, http://www.thehermitage.com/jackson-family /did-you-know.

7. William Seale, *The President's House, Volume I*, p. 197.

8. "Slavery," retrieved from the Hermitage, http://www.thehermitage.com/man sion-grounds/farm/slavery.

9. Arthur M. Schlesinger, Jr., *The Age of Jackson*, p. 6.

10. Cited in Jon Meacham, *American Lion*, p. 20.

11. Meacham, p. 21.

12. Meacham, p. 22.

13. Andrew Burstein, *The Passions of Andrew Jackson*, p. 106.

14. Cited in Paul F. Boller, Jr., *Presidential Wives*, p. 65.

15. Rachel and Andrew Jackson quotes cited in Meacham, p. 13ff.

16. Margaret Bayard Smith's account was published in *The First Forty Years of Washington Society* (1906), retrieved from http://www.eyewitnesstohistory.com /jacksoninauguration.htm.

17. Wilentz, *The Rise of American Democracy*, p. 308.

18. Wilentz, p. 317.

19. Wilentz, p. 319.

20. Jill Lepore, *New York Burning: Liberty, Slavery and Conspiracy in Eighteenth-Century Manhattan*, p. 23ff.

21. Steve Fraser, *Every Man a Speculator*, p. 50.

22. Meacham, p. 212.

23. Timeline sources: Miller Center, University of Virginia; Arthur M. Schlesinger, Jr., *The Almanac of American History*; Gorton Carruth, *What Happened When: A Chronology of Life and Events in America*.

8. MARTIN VAN BUREN

1. Retrieved from the American Presidency Project at the University of California-Santa Barbara, http://www.presidency.ucsb.edu/ws/index.php?pid=25812 #axzz1bSfThOFK.

2. David S. Reynolds, *The Waking Giant*, p. 316.
3. Sean Wilentz, *The Rise of American Democracy*, p. 324.
4. Martin Van Buren Inaugural Address, retrieved from http://www.presidency .ucsb.edu/ws/index.php?pid=25812#axzz1bSfThOFK.
5. "Struggles Over Slavery: The 'Gag Rule,'" retrieved from the National Archives, http://www.archives.gov/exhibits/treasures_of_congress/text/page10_text.html.
6. Dennis Tilden Lynch, *An Epoch and a Man: Martin Van Buren and His Times*, cited in William A. DeGregorio, *The Complete Book of U.S. Presidents*, p. 133.
7. Timeline sources: Miller Center, University of Virginia; Arthur M. Schlesinger, Jr. *The Almanac of American History*; Gorton Carruth, *What Happened When: A Chronology of Life and Events in America*.

9. WILLIAM HENRY HARRISON

1. Paul F. Boller, Jr., *Presidential Campaigns*, p. 77.
2. Retrieved from the National First Ladies Library, http://www.firstladies.org /TheWhiteHouse.aspx#pensions.

10. JOHN TYLER

1. "First Annual Message," retrieved from Miller Center, http://millercenter.org /president/speeches/detail/3549.
2. Adams and Tyler quotes from Robert J. Morgan, *A Whig Embattled*, cited in William A. DeGregorio, *The Complete Book of U.S. Presidents*, p. 257.
3. Ann Blackman, "Fatal Cruise of the *Princeton*," Naval Institute, 2005, retrieved from http://www.military.com/NewContent/0,13190,NH_0905_Cruise -P1,00.html.
4. Cited in James M. McPherson, ed., *"To the Best of My Ability*," p. 82.
5. Timeline sources: Miller Center, University of Virginia; Arthur M. Schlesinger, Jr., *The Almanac of American History*; Gorton Carruth, *What Happened When: A Chronology of Life and Events in America*; Kenneth C. Davis, *Don't Know Much About the Civil War*.

11. JAMES K. POLK

1. James K. Polk Inaugural Address, retrieved from http://avalon.law.yale.edu /19th_century/polk.asp.
2. Paul F. Boller, Jr., *Presidential Campaigns*, p. 80.
3. William Seale, *The President's House, Volume I*, p. 262.
4. Robert W. Merry, *A Country of Vast Designs*, p. 16.
5. Walter A. Borneman, *Polk: The Man Who Transformed the Presidency and America*, p. 12.
6. Hans Sperber, "'Fifty-Four Forty or Fight': Fact and Fictions," *American Speech* 32, no. 1 (February 1957), cited in Mark Stein, *The People Behind the Border Lines*, p. 151.

7. David S. Reynolds, *Waking Giant: America in the Age of Jackson*, p. 360.

8. Daniel Walker Howe, *What Hath God Wrought*, pp. 751–752.

9. Timeline sources: Miller Center, University of Virginia; Arthur M. Schlesinger, Jr., *The Almanac of American History*; Gorton Carruth, *What Happened When: A Chronology of Life and Events in America*; Kenneth C. Davis, *Don't Know Much About the Civil War.*

12. ZACHARY TAYLOR

1. Retrieved from the American Presidency Project, University of California-Santa Barbara, http://www.presidency.ucsb.edu/ws/index.php?pid=29490 #axzz1cSoI0LZV.

2. William Seale, *The President's House, Volume I*, p. 276.

3. Michael Marriott, "Verdict In: 12th President Was Not Assassinated," *New York Times*, June 27, 1991, http://www.nytimes.com/1991/06/27/us/verdict-in -12th-president-was-not-assassinated.html?ref=zacharytaylor17841850.

4. http://millercenter.org/president/taylor/essays/biography/2.

5. David Wilmot cited in Reynolds, *Waking Giant*, p. 370.

6. John S. D. Eisenhower, *Zachary Taylor*, p. 133.

7. Timeline sources: Miller Center, University of Virginia; Arthur M. Schlesinger, Jr., *The Almanac of American History*; Gorton Carruth, *What Happened When: A Chronology of Life and Events in America*; Kenneth C. Davis, *Don't Know Much About the Civil War.*

13. MILLARD FILLMORE

1. Millard Fillmore First Annual Message, December 2, 1850, retrieved from Miller Center, http://millercenter.org/president/speeches/detail/3552.

2. Thomas Vinciguerra, "Why He Gets the Laughs," *New York Times*, March 18, 2007, retrieved from http://www.nytimes.com/2007/03/18/weekinreview /18vince.html?ref=millardfillmore18001874.

3. "The Ordeal of Shadrach Minkins," retrieved from the Massachusetts Historical Society, http://www.masshist.org/longroad/01slavery/minkins.htm.

4. Frederick Douglass speech to National Free Soil Convention, August 11, 1852, retrieved from University of Rochester Frederick Douglass Project, http://www.lib.rochester.edu/index.cfm?PAGE=4385.

5. Debby Applegate, *The Most Famous Man in America*, p. 262.

6. Ted Widmer, "He Rested on the Seventh Day," *New York Times*, February 16, 2011.

7. Timeline sources: Miller Center, University of Virginia; Arthur M. Schlesinger, Jr., *The Almanac of American History*; Gorton Carruth, *What Happened When: A Chronology of Life and Events in America*; Kenneth C. Davis, *Don't Know Much About the Civil War.*

14. FRANKLIN PIERCE

1. Franklin Pierce Inaugural Address, retrieved from Avalon Project, Yale Law School, http://avalon.law.yale.edu/19th_century/pierce.asp.
2. William Seale, *The President's House, Volume I*, p. 302.
3. Seale, p. 309.
4. Richard Kluger, *Seizing Destiny*, p. 504.
5. James Rawley entry on Franklin Pierce in James M. McPherson, ed., *"To the Best of My Ability,"* p. 108.
6. Kluger, p. 490.
7. Hawthorne cited in David C. Whitney and Robin Vaughan Whitney, *The American Presidents*, p. 126.
8. Timeline sources: Miller Center, University of Virginia; Arthur M. Schlesinger, Jr., *The Almanac of American History*; Gordon Carruth, *What Happened When: A Chronology of Life and Events in America*; Kenneth C. Davis, *Don't Know Much About the Civil War.*

15. JAMES BUCHANAN

1. Jean Baker, *James Buchanan*, p. 25.
2. James Buchanan, "Inaugural Address," retrieved from http://www.presidency.ucsb.edu/ws/index.php?pid=25817#axzz1cwbgF5v3.
3. Paul F. Boller, Jr., *Presidential Campaigns*, p. 98.
4. Sean Wilentz, *The Rise of American Democracy*, p. 700.
5. Wilentz, p. 708.
6. John Brown at sentencing and note retrieved from University of Missouri-Kansas City School of Law, "Famous Trials," http://law2.umkc.edu/faculty/projects/ftrials/johnbrown/brownaddress.html; http://law2.umkc.edu/faculty/projects/ftrials/johnbrown/brownprisonletters.html.
7. Nicolay and Hay, eds., *Complete Works of Abraham Lincoln*, cited in William A. DeGregorio, *The Complete Book of U.S. Presidents*, p. 222.
8. William W. Freehling, "James Buchanan's Activist Blunder," *New York Times*, January 5, 2011.
9. Jean Baker, *James Buchanan*, p. 149.
10. Timeline sources: Miller Center, University of Virginia; Arthur M. Schlesinger, Jr., *The Almanac of American History*; Gorton Carruth, *What Happened When: A Chronology of Life and Events in America*; Kenneth C. Davis, *Don't Know Much About the Civil War.*

16. ABRAHAM LINCOLN

1. First Inaugural Address, retrieved from Avalon Project, Yale Law School, http://avalon.law.yale.edu/19th_century/lincoln1.asp.
2. William Seale, *The President's House, Volume I*, p. 372.

3. Doris Kearns Goodwin, *Team of Rivals*, p. 58.

4. Goodwin, p. 48.

5. Goodwin, p. 49.

6. Stephen B. Oates, *With Malice Toward None*, p. 11.

7. Abraham Lincoln, "House Divided" speech, retrieved from http://millercenter .org/scripps/archive/speeches/detail/3504.

8. Goodwin, p. xvi.

9. "Bayonets in Buffalo" by Ted Widmer, *New York Times*, February 15, 2011, retrieved from http://opinionator.blogs.nytimes.com/2011/02/15/bayonets-in -buffalo/?ref=abrahamlincoln.

10. Seth Lipsky, *The Citizen's Constitution*, p. 90.

11. Second Inaugural Address retrieved from Avalon Project, Yale Law School, http://avalon.law.yale.edu/19th_century/lincoln2.asp.

12. J. David Hacker, "Recounting the Dead," *New York Times*, September 20, 2011, retrieved from http://opinionator.blogs.nytimes.com/2011/09/20/recounting -the-dead/?scp=1&sq=civil%20war%20death%20toll&st=cse.

13. James L. Swanson, *Manhunt*, p. 376.

14. Timeline sources: Miller Center, University of Virginia; Kenneth C. Davis, *Don't Know Much About the Civil War*; Arthur M. Schlesinger, Jr., *The Almanac of American History*; Gorton Carruth, *What Happened When: A Chronology of Life and Events in America*.

17. ANDREW JOHNSON

1. Johnson quote is cited in Debby Applegate, *The Most Famous Man in America*, p. 357; also cited in Jean Edward Smith, *Grant*, p. 422.

2. William Seale, *The President's House, Volume I*, p. 412.

3. Jean Edward Smith, *Grant*, p. 418.

4. Trefousse, p. 20; Annette Gordon-Reed, *Andrew Johnson*, p. 20.

5. Trefousse, p. 21.

6. Frederick Douglass, *The Life and Times of Frederick Douglass*, cited in Annette Gordon-Reed, *Andrew Johnson*, p. 3.

7. Hans L. Trefousse, *Andrew Johnson: A Biography*, p. 242; cited in Jean Edward Smith, *Grant*, p. 426.

8. Lewis L. Gould, *Grand Old Party*, pp. 53–54.

9. Timeline sources: Miller Center, University of Virginia; Kenneth C. Davis, *Don't Know Much About the Civil War*; Arthur M. Schlesinger, Jr., *The Almanac of American History*; Gorton Carruth, *What Happened When: A Chronology of Life and Events in America*.

18. ULYSSES S. GRANT

1. Ulysses S. Grant First Inaugural Address, retrieved from http://avalon.law.yale .edu/19th_century/grant1.asp.

2. Roosevelt on Grant, cited in Theodore Roosevelt, *Theodore Roosevelt's History of the United States*, pp. 198–199.

3. The Garfield and Wilson quotes are cited in William A. DeGregorio, *The Complete Book of U.S. Presidents*, p. 275.

4. Kenneth T. Jackson, ed., *The Encyclopedia of New York*, pp. 500–501; "General Grant National Memorial," retrieved from http://www.nps.gov/gegr/historycul ture/index.htm.

5. Lloyd Paul Stryker, *Andrew Johnson: A Study in Courage*, cited in DeGregorio, p. 274.

6. Ulysses S. Grant, *Personal Memoirs*, p. 100.

7. Henry Adams cited in Brands, *American Colossus*, p. 39.

8. John Steele Gordon, *An Empire of Wealth*, p. 225.

9. Gordon, p. 226.

10. Candice Millard, *Destiny of the Republic*, p. 60.

11. Seale, The *President's House, Volume I*, p. 468.

12. Michael Korda, *Ulysses S. Grant: The Unlikely Hero*, p. 135.

13. Timeline sources: Miller Center, University of Virginia; Kenneth C. Davis, *Don't Know Much About the Civil War*; Arthur M. Schlesinger, Jr., *The Almanac of American History*; Gorton Carruth, *What Happened When: A Chronology of Life and Events in America*.

19. RUTHERFORD B. HAYES

1. Rutherford B. Hayes Inaugural Address, retrieved from http://avalon.law.yale .edu/19th_century/hayes.asp.

2. Lewis L. Gould, *Grand Old Party*, p. 76.

3. Hayes, *The Diary and Letters of Rutherford B. Hayes, 19th President of the United States*, Volume IV, p. 354, retrieved from http://www.ohiohistory.org/onlinedoc /hayes/Volume04/Chapter45/December4.txt.

4. Hayes, retrieved from http://www.ohiohistory.org/onlinedoc/hayes/quotes .html.

5. Timeline sources: Miller Center, University of Virginia; Arthur M. Schlesinger, Jr., *The Almanac of American History*; Gorton Carruth, *What Happened When: A Chronology of Life and Events in America*.

20. JAMES A. GARFIELD

1. James A. Garfield Inaugural Address, March 4, 1881, retrieved from http:// millercenter.org/president/speeches/detail/3559.

2. Cited in Candice Millard, *Destiny of the Republic*, p. 26.

3. Millard, pp. 156 ff and 212 ff.

4. Timeline sources: Miller Center, University of Virginia; Arthur M. Schlesinger, Jr., *The Almanac of American History*; Gorton Carruth, *What Happened When: A Chronology of Life and Events in America*.

21. CHESTER A. ARTHUR

1. Chester A. Arthur, First Annual Message, December 6, 1881, retrieved from "The American Presidency Project," University of California-Santa Barbara, http://www.presidency.ucsb.edu/ws/index.php?pid=29522#axzz1saSnNot8.
2. Paul Grondahi, "The President with 80 Pairs of Pants," *Albany Times Union*, September 21, 2006, retrieved from http://www.union.edu/N/DS/s.php?s=6633.
3. Thomas Reeves, *Gentleman Boss: The Life of Chester A. Arthur*, p. 275, cited in William A. DeGregorio, *The Complete Book of U.S. Presidents*, p. 315.
4. DeGregorio, p. 308.
5. Zachary Karabell, *Chester Alan Arthur*, p. 3.
6. Iris Chang, *The Chinese in America*, p. 134.
7. H. W. Brands, *American Colossus*, pp. 256–257.
8. Cited in David C. Whitney and Robin Vaughan Whitney, *The American Presidents*, p. 186.
9. Timeline sources: Miller Center, University of Virginia; Arthur M. Schlesinger, Jr., *The Almanac of American History*; Gorton Carruth, *What Happened When: A Chronology of Life and Events in America*.

22. GROVER CLEVELAND

1. First Inaugural Address of Grover Cleveland, March 4, 1885, retrieved from http://avalon.law.yale.edu/19th_century/cleve1.asp.
2. Paul F. Boller, Jr., *Presidential Campaigns*, p. 149.
3. Whitney, *The American Presidents*, p. 191.
4. "Baby Ruth," retrieved from http://www.snopes.com/business/names/babyruth.asp.
5. Cited in William A. DeGregorio, *The Complete Book of U.S. Presidents*, p. 351.
6. Daniel Ruddy, *Theodore Roosevelt's History of the United States*, p. 213.
7. Ruddy, p. 214.
8. Henry F. Graff, *Grover Cleveland*.
9. Timeline sources: Miller Center, University of Virginia; Arthur M. Schlesinger, Jr., *The Almanac of American History*; Gorton Carruth, *What Happened When: A Chronology of Life and Events in America*.

23. BENJAMIN HARRISON

1. "Inaugural Address of Benjamin Harrison," March 4, 1889, retrieved from http://avalon.law.yale.edu/19th_century/harris.asp.
2. William Seale, *The President's House, Volume I*, p. 571.
3. Paul Boller, Jr., *Presidential Campaigns*, p. 161.
4. Boller, p. 158.
5. Charles W. Calhoun, *Benjamin Harrison*, p. 60.
6. Benjamin Harrison, *Views of an Ex-President*, cited in DeGregorio, p. 342.

7. Timeline sources: Miller Center, University of Virginia; Arthur M. Schlesinger, Jr., *The Almanac of American History*; Gorton Carruth, *What Happened When: A Chronology of Life and Events in America.*

24. GROVER CLEVELAND

1. Grover Cleveland, Second Inaugural Address, March 4, 1893, retrieved from http://avalon.law.yale.edu/19th_century/cleve2.asp.
2. Steve Fraser, *Every Man a Speculator*, p. 111.
3. Ron Chernow, *The House of Morgan*, p. 75.
4. H. W. Brands, *American Colossus*, p. 535.
5. Henry F. Graff, *Grover Cleveland*, epilogue.
6. Timeline sources: Miller Center, University of Virginia; Arthur M. Schlesinger, Jr., *The Almanac of American History*; Gorton Carruth, *What Happened When: A Chronology of Life and Events in America.*

25. WILLIAM MCKINLEY

1. William McKinley, First Annual Message, December 6, 1897, retrieved from http://www.presidency.ucsb.edu/ws/index.php?pid=29538#axzz1eJz0RIyc.
2. Scott Miller, *The President and the Assassin*, p. 20.
3. Theodore Roosevelt letter to his sister dated July 20, 1896, cited in Theodore Roosevelt, *Theodore Roosevelt's History of the United States*, p. 226.
4. Roosevelt, pp. 230–231.
5. McKinley cited in Seale, *The President's House, Volume I*, p. 596.
6. McKinley quoted in *Bartlett's Familiar Quotations*, p. 549.
7. Paul F. Boller, *Presidential Campaigns*, p. 180.
8. Morton Keller in McKinley entry in James M. McPherson, ed., *"To the Best of My Ability,"* p. 178.
9. Kevin Phillips, *William McKinley*, p. 1.
10. Timeline sources: Miller Center, University of Virginia; Arthur M. Schlesinger, Jr., *The Almanac of American History*; Gorton Carruth, *What Happened When: A Chronology of Life and Events in America.*

26. THEODORE ROOSEVELT

1. Theodore Roosevelt, "The American Boy," in *The Strenuous Life: Essays and Addresses* (1900), retrieved from http://www.bartleby.com/58/10.html.
2. Edmund Morris, *The Rise of Theodore Roosevelt*, p. 10.
3. Cited in Morris, *The Rise of Theodore Roosevelt*, p. 230.
4. Morris, *The Rise of Theodore Roosevelt*, p. 396.
5. Cited in Morris, *The Rise of Theodore Roosevelt*, p. 532.
6. Cited in Edmund Morris, *Theodore Rex*, pp. 54-55.
7. Edmund Morris, *Theodore Rex*, p. 53.
8. Morris, *Theodore Rex*, p. 169.

9. Theodore Roosevelt, "Man in the Arena," retrieved from the "Almanac of Theodore Roosevelt," http://www.theodore-roosevelt.com/trsorbonnespeech.html.

10. Henry Beach Needham, "The College Athlete," *McClure's Magazine*, retrieved from http://babel.hathitrust.org/cgi/pt?id=mdp.39015011718304;page =root;view=image;size=100;seq=127;num=115.

11. Roosevelt's Harvard speech retrieved from the "Almanac of Theodore Roosevelt: The Complete Speeches of Theodore Roosevelt," http://www.theodore -roosevelt.com/trspeechescomplete.html.

12. Timeline sources: Miller Center, University of Virginia; Arthur M. Schlesinger, Jr., *The Almanac of American History*; Gorton Carruth, *What Happened When: A Chronology of Life and Events in America*.

27. WILLIAM HOWARD TAFT

1. Inaugural Address of William Howard Taft, March 4, 1909, retrieved from http://avalon.law.yale.edu/20th_century/taft.asp.

2. Cited in William A. DeGregorio, *The Complete Book of U.S. Presidents*, p. 396.

3. Retrieved from *First Lady Biography: Helen Taft*, National First Ladies' Library, http://www.firstladies.org/biographies/firstladies.aspx?biography=27.

4. William Seale, *The President's House, Volume II*, p. 19.

5. Theodore Roosevelt, *Theodore Roosevelt's History of the United States*, p. 304.

6. Roosevelt, p. 304.

7. Timeline sources: Miller Center, University of Virginia; Arthur M. Schlesinger, Jr., *The Almanac of American History*; Gorton Carruth, *What Happened When: A Chronology of Life and Events in America*.

28. WOODROW WILSON

1. Woodrow Wilson First Inaugural Address, March 4, 1913, retrieved from http://avalon.law.yale.edu/20th_century/wilson1.asp.

2. "The President's State of the Union Message: Frequently Asked Questions," retrieved from http://www.senate.gov/artandhistory/history/resources/pdf /stateoftheunion.pdf.

3. John Milton Cooper, Jr., *Woodrow Wilson*, p. 548.

4. "Woodrow Wilson," *American Experience*, Public Broadcasting Service, transcript retrieved from http://www.pbs.org/wgbh/amex/wilson/filmmore/fm _trans2.html.

5. Woodrow Wilson, "Address to Congress Requesting a Declaration of War," retrieved from University of Virginia-Miller Center, http://millercenter.org /president/speeches/detail/4722.

6. Cooper, *Woodrow Wilson*, p. 540.

7. Cooper, *Woodrow Wilson*, p. 11.

8. Timeline sources: Miller Center, University of Virginia; Arthur M. Schlesinger, Jr., *The Almanac of American History*; Gorton Carruth, *What Happened When: A*

Chronology of Life and Events in America; Kenneth C. Davis, *Don't Know Much About History*.

9.   John Steele Gordon, *An Empire of Wealth*, p. 298.

29. WARREN GAMALIEL HARDING

1.   Paul F. Boller, Jr., *Presidential Campaigns*, p. 213.
2.   William Seale, *The President's House, Volume II*, p. 95.
3.   Warren G. Harding, Second Annual Message to Congress, December 8, 1922, retrieved from Miller Center, University of Virginia, http://millercenter .org/president/speeches/detail/3805.
4.   Daniel Okrent, *Last Call*, p. 129.
5.   Alice Longworth cited in Okrent, p. 130.
6.   John Milton Cooper, Jr., *Woodrow Wilson*, p. 589.
7.   Hoover quote from *Memoirs of Herbert Hoover*, cited in William A. DeGregorio, *The Complete Book of U.S. Presidents*, p. 443.
8.   Timeline sources: Miller Center, University of Virginia; Arthur M. Schlesinger, Jr., *The Almanac of American History*; Gorton Carruth, *What Happened When: A Chronology of Life and Events in America*.

30. CALVIN COOLIDGE

1.   Calvin Coolidge Inaugural Address, March 4, 1925, retrieved from Miller Center, University of Virginia, http://millercenter.org/scripps/archive/speeches /detail/3569.
2.   "Silent Cal's Home Speaks Volumes," *New York Times*, June 4, 2000.
3.   Reagan quoted in *Cleveland Plain Dealer*, May 29, 1981, cited in William A. DeGregorio, *The Complete Book of U.S. Presidents*, p. 460.
4.   Alfred E. Smith quoted in *Meet Calvin Coolidge*, cited in William A. DeGregorio, *The Complete Book of U.S. Presidents*, p. 461.
5.   Alice Longworth cited in Daniel Okrent, *Last Call*, p. 227.
6.   Okrent, p. 228.
7.   Steve Fraser, *Every Man a Speculator: A History of Wall Street in American Life*, p. 375.
8.   Benjamin Strong cited in Liaquat Ahamed, *Lords of Finance*, p. 277.
9.   Mencken cited in DeGregorio, p. 460.
10. Timeline sources: Miller Center, University of Virginia; Arthur M. Schlesinger, Jr., *The Almanac of American History*; Gorton Carruth, *What Happened When: A Chronology of Life and Events in America*.

31. HERBERT HOOVER

1.   Herbert Hoover, "Rugged Individualism" campaign speech, October 22, 1928, retrieved from http://www.teachingamericanhistory.org/library/index .asp?document=953.

2. Bob Jones quoted in Daniel Okrent, *Last Call*, p. 305.
3. Amity Shlaes, *The Forgotten Man*, p. 6.
4. Liaquat Ahamed, *Lords of Finance*, p. 6.
5. Cited in David Shipley, "Editorial Notebook; Remembering Herbert Hoover," *New York Times*, August 10, 1992, retrieved from http://www.nytimes.com /1992/08/10/opinion/editorial-notebook-remembering-herbert-hoover.html ?ref=herbertclarkhoover.
6. Timeline sources: Miller Center, University of Virginia; Arthur M. Schlesinger, Jr., *The Almanac of American History*; Gorton Carruth, *What Happened When: A Chronology of Life and Events in America*.

32. FRANKLIN DELANO ROOSEVELT

1. Franklin D. Roosevelt First Inaugural Address, March 4, 1933, retrieved from the Avalon Project, Yale Law School, http://avalon.law.yale.edu/20th _century/froos1.asp.
2. Inauguration of the President: Franklin D. Roosevelt: U.S. Senate, retrieved from http://inaugural.senate.gov/history/chronology/fdroosevelt1933.cfm.
3. James Roosevelt cited in Doris K. Goodwin, *No Ordinary Time*, p. 16.
4. Anthony Badger, *FDR: The First Hundred Days*, pp. 14–15.
5. H. W. Brands, *Traitor to His Class*, p. 12.
6. Eleanor Roosevelt cited in Goodwin, p. 17.
7. Franklin D. Roosevelt First Inaugural Address, March 4, 1933, retrieved from Avalon Project, Yale Law School, http://avalon.law.yale.edu/20th _century/froos1.asp.
8. PBS "Online Newshour" biography of Ronald Reagan, retrieved from http:// www.pbs.org/newshour/biography_pages/reagan/biography.html.
9. Alf Landon cited in William A. DeGregorio, *The Complete Book of U.S. Presidents*, p. 504.
10. ranklin D. Roosevelt State of the Union ("Four Freedoms" speech), January 6, 1941, retrieved from Miller Center, University of Virginia, http://millercenter .org/president/speeches/detail/3320.
11. Goodwin, p. 10.
12. "Mother Teresa Voted by American People as Most Admired Person of the Century," retrieved from http://www.gallup.com/poll/3367/Mother-Teresa -Voted-American-People-Most-Admired-Person-Century.aspx.
13. Badger, pp. 172–173.
14. Goodwin, p. 10.
15. Brands, *Traitor to His Class*, p. 818.
16. Timeline sources: Miller Center, University of Virginia; Arthur M. Schlesinger, Jr.. *The Almanac of American History*; Gorton Carruth, *What Happened When: A Chronology of Life and Events in America*; Kenneth C. Davis, *Don't Know Much About History*.

17. Franklin D. Roosevelt, Second Inaugural Address, retrieved from http://
    millercenter.org/president/speeches/detail/3308.

33. HARRY S. TRUMAN

1. William Seale, *The President's House, Volume II*, p. 250.
2. Cited in David C. Whitney and Robert Vaughan Whitney, *The American
   Presidents*, p. 311.
3. "Assassination Attempt on President Truman's Life," retrieved from Truman
   Library, http://www.trumanlibrary.org/trivia/assassin.htm.
4. Truman quotes are from James David Barber, *The Presidential Character*, and
   Hope Ridings Miller, *Scandals in the Highest Office*, both cited in William
   A. DeGregorio, *The Complete Book of U.S. Presidents*, p. 523.
5. Richard Rhodes, *The Making of the Atomic Bomb*, p. 690.
6. Rhodes, p. 630.
7. David McCullough, *Truman*, p. 457.
8. "Special Message to the Congress on Greece and Turkey: The Truman Doctrine," retrieved from Harry S. Truman Library and Museum, http://www
   .trumanlibrary.org/publicpapers/index.php?pid=2189&st=&st1=.
9. Sam Tanenhaus, *Whittaker Chambers: A Biography*; "The Alger Hiss Trials,"
   University of Missouri-Kansas City Law School Famous Trials Homepage,
   retrieved from http://law2.umkc.edu/faculty/projects/ftrials/hiss/hiss.html.
10. David Halberstam, *The Fifties*, p. 55.
11. Truman quote on McCarthy cited in McCullough, *Truman*, p. 768.
12. Halberstam, pp. 49–55.
13. McCullough, p. 463.
14. Halberstam, p. 22.
15. Robert Dallek, *Harry S. Truman*, "Epilogue."
16. Timeline sources: Miller Center, University of Virginia; Arthur M. Schlesinger,
    Jr., *The Almanac of American History*; Gorton Carruth, *What Happened When: A
    Chronology of Life and Events in America*; "Truman Chronologies," Harry S. Tru-
    man Library and Museum, http://www.trumanlibrary.org/chron/index.html.

34. DWIGHT D. EISENHOWER

1. Dwight D. Eisenhower, "A Chance for Peace" speech, April 16, 1953, retrieved
   from http://millercenter.org/scripps/archive/speeches/detail/3357.
2. Tom Wicker, *Dwight D. Eisenhower*, p. 2.
3. Wicker, p. 8.
4. Michael Beschloss, *Presidential Courage*, p. 228.
5. David Halberstam, *The Fifties*, p. 685.
6. Dwight D. Eisenhower Farewell Address, January 17, 1961, retrieved from
   http://millercenter.org/scripps/archive/speeches/detail/3361.
7. Michael Korda, *Ike*, p. 714.

8. Wicker, p. 139.

9. Timeline sources: Miller Center, University of Virginia; Arthur M. Schlesinger, Jr., *The Almanac of American History*; Gorton Carruth, *What Happened When: A Chronology of Life and Events in America*.

35. JOHN F. KENNEDY

1. Inaugural Address of John F. Kennedy, January 20, 1961, retrieved from Miller Center, University of Virginia, http://avalon.law.yale.edu/20th _century/kennedy.asp.

2. William Seale, *The President's House, Volume II*, pp. 350–351.

3. Robert Dallek, *An Unfinished Life*, p. 130.

4. Dallek, p. 129.

5. Randall Balmer, *God in the White House: A History*, pp. 12ff.

6. Garry Wills, *Bare Ruined Choirs: Doubt, Prophecy, and Radical Religion*, cited in Balmer, *God in the White House*, p. 12.

7. "The Bay of Pigs," retrieved from John F. Kennedy Presidential Library and Museum, http://www.jfklibrary.org/JFK/JFK-in-History/The-Bay-of-Pigs.aspx.

8. Tim Weiner, *Legacy of Ashes*, pp. 214–215.

9. "Cuban Missile Crisis," retrieved from John F. Kennedy Presidential Library and Museum, http://www.jfklibrary.org/JFK/JFK-in-History/Cuban-Missile -Crisis.aspx.

10. "La Presidente," *Time*, June 9, 1961, retrieved from http://www.time.com /time/magazine/article/0,9171,938093,00.html.

11. Chris Matthews, *Jack Kennedy*, p. 9.

12. Gerald Posner, *Case Closed*, p. 403.

13. Dallek, pp 710–711.

14. Cited in William A. DeGregorio, *The Complete Book of U.S. Presidents*, p. 561.

15. Timeline sources: Miller Center, University of Virginia; Arthur M. Schlesinger, Jr., *The Almanac of American History*; Gorton Carruth, *What Happened When: A Chronology of Life and Events in America*.

36. LYNDON B. JOHNSON

1. Lyndon B. Johnson Address to Joint Session of Congress, November 27, 1963, retrieved from Miller Center, University of Virginia, http://millercenter.org/ president/speeches/detail/3381.

2. Fulbright quote in Alfred Steinberg's *Sam Johnson's Boy*, cited in William A. DeGregorio, *The Complete Book of U.S. Presidents*, p. 578.

3. Robert Dallek, *Flawed Giant*, Preface.

4. Lyndon B. Johnson "Remarks at University of Michigan," May 22, 1964, retrieved from Miller Center, University of Virginia, http://millercenter.org /president/speeches/detail/3383.

5. Stanley Karnow, *Vietnam: A History*, p. 390.

6. Karnow, p. 392.

7. Lyndon B. Johnson, "Remarks on Decision Not to Seek Re-election," March 31, 1968, retrieved from Miller Center, University of Virginia, http://miller center.org/president/speeches/detail/3388.

8. Robert Dallek, *Hail to the Chief*, p. 158.

9. Dallek, p. 161.

10. Timeline sources: Miller Center, University of Virginia; Arthur M. Schlesinger, Jr., *The Almanac of American History*; Gorton Carruth, *What Happened When: A Chronology of Life and Events in America*; Kenneth C. Davis, *Don't Know Much About History*.

37. RICHARD M. NIXON

1. Richard M. Nixon, "Address to the Nation Announcing Decision to Resign the Office of President," August 8, 1974, retrieved from Miller Center, University of Virginia, http://millercenter.org/scripps/archive/speeches/detail/3871.

2. Elizabeth Drew, *Richard M. Nixon*, p. 1.

3. David Halberstam, *The Fifties*, p. 313.

4. Eisenhower and Truman quotes cited in William A. DeGregorio, *The Complete Book of U.S. Presidents*, p. 600.

5. Halberstam, p. 318.

6. "GOP Ignored Black Vote," *Boston Globe*, July 15, 2005, retrieved from http://www.boston.com/news/nation/articles/2005/07/15/gop_ignored_black_vote _chairman_says.

7. Miller Center, University of Virginia "Presidential Recording Program: Watergate Collection," retrieved from http://whitehousetapes.net/transcript/nixon /cancer-presidency.

8. Carter quoted in Kandy Stroud, *How Jimmy Won*, p. 146, cited in William A. DeGregorio, p. 600.

9. Halberstam, p. 315.

10. David A. DeVoss, "Ping-Pong Diplomacy" *Smithsonian*, April 2002, retrieved from http://www.smithsonianmag.com/history-archaeology/pingpong.html.

11. Bob Woodward, *Shadow*, Introduction.

12. Timeline sources: Miller Center, University of Virginia; Arthur M. Schlesinger, Jr., *The Almanac of American History*; Gorton Carruth, *What Happened When: A Chronology of Life and Events in America*.

38. GERALD R. FORD

1. Gerald R. Ford, "Remarks on Taking the Oath of Office," August 9, 1974, retrieved from Miller Center, University of Virginia, http://millercenter.org /president/speeches/detail/3390.

2. Johnson quoted in Jerald F. terHost, *Gerald Ford and the Future of the Presidency*,

p. 83, cited in William A. DeGregorio, *The Complete Book of U.S. Presidents*, p. 615.

3. Ford quote cited in Douglas Brinkley, *Gerald R. Ford*, p. 6.

4. Brinkley, p. 43.

5. Ford quotation cited by Laura Kalman in Ford entry in James M. McPherson, ed., *"To the Best of My Ability,"* p. 280.

6. Timeline sources: Miller Center, University of Virginia; Arthur M. Schlesinger, Jr., *The Almanac of American History*; Gorton Carruth, *What Happened When: A Chronology of Life and Events in America.*

39. JAMES CARTER

1. Jimmy Carter, "Camp David Accords," September 17, 1978, retrieved from Avalon Project, Yale Law School, http://avalon.law.yale.edu/20th_century/campdav.asp.

2. "Carter Sadly Turns Back on National Baptist Body," Somini Sengupta, *New York Times*, October 21, 2000, retrieved from http://www.nytimes.com/2000/10/21/us/carter-sadly-turns-back-on-national-baptist-body.html.

3. Robert Scheer, "The Playboy Interview: Jimmy Carter," *Playboy*, November 1976.

4. Carter quoted in Carter entry by Douglas Brinkley in James M. McPherson, ed., *"To the Best of My Ability,"* p. 282.

5. Jimmy Carter, "Crisis of Confidence," July 15 1979, retrieved from http://www.pbs.org/wgbh/americanexperience/features/primary-resources/carter-crisis.

6. James Fallows, "The Passionless Presidency," *Atlantic*, May 1979, retrieved from http://www.theatlantic.com/magazine/archive/1979/05/the-passionless-presidency/8516.

7. Timeline sources: Miller Center, University of Virginia; Arthur M. Schlesinger, Jr., *The Almanac of American History*; Gorton Carruth, *What Happened When: A Chronology of Life and Events in America.*

40. RONALD REAGAN

1. Ronald Reagan, "Evil Empire" speech, March 8, 1983, retrieved from http://millercenter.org/scripps/archive/speeches/detail/3409.

2. Thatcher quote cited in *USA Today*, November 16, 1988; Nader quote from *Washington Post*, January 18, 1989. Both cited in William A. DeGregorio, *The Complete Book of U.S. Presidents*, p. 659.

3. Ronald Reagan State of the Union Address, January 26, 1982, retrieved from University of California-Santa Barbara, http://www.presidency.ucsb.edu/ws/index.php?pid=42687#axzz1gLkZlkPl.

4. Ronald Reagan State of the Union Address, January 26, 1982, retrieved from University of California-Santa Barbara, http://www.presidency.ucsb.edu/ws/index.php?pid=42687#axzz1gLkZlkPl.

5. David Broder cited in Richard Reeves, *President Reagan*, p. 44.
6. "Final Report of the Independent Counsel for Iran/Contra Matters," retrieved from http://www.fas.org/irp/offdocs/walsh.
7. Scott Spencer, "Lawrence Walsh's Last Legal Battle," New *York Times*, July 4, 1993, retrieved from http://www.nytimes.com/books/97/06/29/reviews/iran-profile.html.
8. Ronald Reagan, "Address from the Brandenburg Gate [Berlin Wall]," June 12, 1987, retrieved from Miller Center, University of Virginia, http://millercenter.org/president/speeches/detail/3415.
9. "Among Presidents Since WWII, Ronald Reagan is the Best and George W. Bush is the Worst," February 15, 2012, Harris Interactive, retrieved from http://www.harrisinteractive.com/NewsRoom/HarrisPolls/tabid/447/ctl/ReadCustom%20Default/mid/1508/ArticleId/962/Default.aspx.
10. Reeves, "Introduction."
11. Cited in "Reagan's AIDS Legacy," *San Francisco Chronicle*, June 8, 2004, retrieved from http://www.sfgate.com/cgi-bin/article.cgi?f=/c/a/2004/06/08/EDG777163F1.DTL#ixzz1mKRgB6Ig.
12. James Mann, *The Rebellion of Ronald Reagan*, pp. 345–346.
13. Timeline sources: Miller Center, University of Virginia; Arthur M. Schlesinger, Jr., *The Almanac of American History*; Gorton Carruth, *What Happened When: A Chronology of Life and Events in America*.

41. GEORGE H. W. BUSH

1. George Bush Inaugural Address, January 20, 1989, retrieved from Avalon Project, Yale Law School, http://avalon.law.yale.edu/20th_century/bush.asp.
2. Tim Weiner, *Legacy of Ashes*, p. 402.
3. George Bush and Brent Scowcroft, *A World Transformed*, p. 489.
4. Robert Dallek, *Hail to the Chief*, pp. 37–38.
5. Timothy Naftali, *George H.W. Bush*, p. 149.
6. Timeline sources: Miller Center, University of Virginia; Arthur M. Schlesinger, Jr., *The Almanac of American History*; Gorton Carruth, *What Happened When: A Chronology of Life and Events in America*; Kenneth C. Davis, *Don't Know Much About History*.

42. WILLIAM JEFFERSON CLINTON

1. William J. Clinton Inaugural Address, January 20, 1993, retrieved from Avalon Project, Yale Law School, http://avalon.law.yale.edu/20th_century/clinton1.asp.
2. Richard Reeves, *Running in Place*, p. xiv.
3. "Prosecutor: Reagan, Bush Not Criminally Liable," AP, November 25, 2011, retrieved from http://news.yahoo.com/prosecutor-reagan-bush-not-criminally-liable-205745501.html.

4. "Whitewater Time Line," *Washington Post*, retrieved from http://www.wash ingtonpost.com/wp-srv/politics/special/whitewater/timeline.htm.

5. George Stephanopoulos, *All Too Human*, prologue.

6. Jeffrey Toobin, *A Vast Conspiracy*, p. 368.

7. "The Budget and Deficit Under Clinton," retrieved from FactCheck.org, a project of the Annenberg Public Policy Center, http://www.factcheck.org/2008 /02/the-budget-and-deficit-under-clinton/.

8. John F. Harris, *The Survivor*, p. 432.

9. Jeff Madrick, "What Bill Clinton Would Do," *New York Times*, December 9, 2011.

10. National Commission on Terrorist Attacks Upon the United States, "Responses to Al Qaeda's Initial Assaults," retrieved from http://www.9-11commission.gov /report/911Report_Ch4.htm.

11. Timeline sources: Miller Center, University of Virginia; Arthur M. Schlesinger, Jr., *The Almanac of American History*; Gorton Carruth, *What Happened When: A Chronology of Life and Events in America*.

43. GEORGE W. BUSH

1. George W. Bush State of the Union Address, January 29, 2002, retrieved from Miller Center, University of Virginia, http://millercenter.org/president /speeches/detail/4540.

2. Richard A. Clarke, *Against All Enemies*, p. 241.

3. Molly Ivins, *Shrub: The Short But Happy Political Life of George W. Bush*, p, 37.

4. George W. Bush, *Decision Points*, p. 47.

5. Bob Woodward, *The War Within*, p. 433.

6. "Times Topics," *New York Times*, USA Patriot Act, retrieved from http://topics .nytimes.com/top/reference/timestopics/subjects/u/usa_patriot_act/index .html?scp=1-spot&sq=patriot%20act&st=cse.

7. "Times Topics," *New York Times*: Dick Cheney, retrieved from http://topics .nytimes.com/top/reference/timestopics/people/c/dick_cheney/index.html; "Angler: The Cheney Vice Presidency," *Washington Post*, retrieved from http:// voices.washingtonpost.com/cheney.

8. Jane Mayer, *The Dark Side*, p. 5.

9. Timothy Naftali, *George H.W. Bush*, p . 176.

10. Timeline sources: Miller Center, University of Virginia; Arthur M. Schlesinger, Jr., *The Almanac of American History*; Gorton Carruth, *What Happened When: A Chronology of Life and Events in America*.

44. BARACK HUSSEIN OBAMA

1. Barack Obama, text of remarks on Election Night, November 4, 2008, retrieved from http://millercenter.org/scripps/archive/speeches/detail/4424.

2. George Bush, quoted in *New York Times*, April 4, 1990.

3. Bob Woodward, *Obama's Wars*, p. 11.
4. Bill Keller, "Fill in the Blanks," *New York Times*, September 19, 2011.
5. Barack Obama, "Address to Congress on Health Care," September 9, 2009, retrieved from Miller Center, University of Virginia, http://millercenter.org /president/speeches/detail/5548.
6. Ron Suskind, *Confidence Men*, p. 163.
7. "Times Topics," *New York Times*: Health Care Reform," retrieved from http:// topics.nytimes.com/top/news/health/diseasesconditionsandhealthtopics/health _insurance_and_managed_care/health_care_reform/index.html?scp=1-spot &sq=obamacare&st=cse.
8. Bill Keller, "Fill in the Blanks," *New York Times*, September 19, 2011.
9. "Full Transcript: President Obama's December 4 Remarks on the Economy," *Washington Post*, (December 4, 2013) http://www.washingtonpost.com/politics/ running-transcript-president-obamas-december-4-remarks-on-the-economy /213/12/04/7cec31ba-5cff-11e3-be07-006c776266ed_story.html   Retrieved December 9, 2013.
10. Timeline sources: *The World Almanac and Book of Facts: 2011; Time Almanac: 2012; The World Almanac and Book of Facts: 2013; New York Times.*

PART III:
WHAT SHOULD WE DO WITH THE PRESIDENT?

1. Arthur M. Schlesinger, Jr., *The Imperial Presidency*, Preface.
2. Eric Weiner, "What Is Executive Privilege, Anyway?" National Public Radio, June 28, 2007, retrieved from http://www.npr.org/templates/story/story.php ?storyId=11527747.
3. Times Topics," *New York Times*: War Powers Act of 1973, retrieved from http://topics.nytimes.com/top/reference/timestopics/subjects/w/war_powers _act_of_1973/index.html?inline=nyt-classifier.
4. "Attack Renews Debate Over Congressional Consent," *New York Times*, March 21, 2011, retrieved from http://www.nytimes.com/2011/03/22/world /africa/22powers.html?_r=1&partner=rss&emc=rss.
5. "Presidential Signing Statements," American Presidency Project, retrieved from http://www.presidency.ucsb.edu/signingstatements.php#axzz1gRn8xF6f.
6. Library of Congress Law Library, http://www.loc.gov/law/help/statements.php.
7. "On Signing Statements," *New York Times*, March 16, 2009, retrieved from http://www.nytimes.com/2009/03/17/opinion/17tue3.html?scp=8&sq=signing %20statements&st=cse.
8. National Records and Archives Administration, http://www.archives.gov/federal -register/electoral-college/faq.html#history.
9. "California: Brown Signs Electoral College Revision," Associated Press, August 8, 2011, retrieved from http://www.nytimes.com/2011/08/09/us /09brfs-BROWNSIGNSEL_BRF.html?ref=electoralcollege.

10. Cited in Joe McGinniss, *The Selling of the President*, p. xxii.

11. "Justices, 5–4, Reject Corporate Spending Limit," *New York Times*, January 21, 2010, retrieved from http://www.nytimes.com/2010/01/22/us/politics/22scotus.html.

12. "Another Campaign for Sale," *New York Times*, February 7, 2012, retrieved from http://www.nytimes.com/2012/02/08/opinion/another-2012-campaign-for-sale.html?ref=campaignfinance.

13. "The 2012 Money Race: Compare the Candidates," *New York Times*, retrieved from http://elections.nytimes.com/2012/campaign-finance.

14. "Independent Spending, Week by Week," *New York Times*, retrieved from http://elections.nytimes.com/2012/campaign-finance/independent-expenditures/week/2012-02-27.

15. Jim Meyers, "2012 Election Price tag: $8 Billion," *Newsmax*, April 14 2011, retrieved from http://www.newsmax.com/InsideCover/election-cost-price-tag/2011/04/14/id/392926.

16. "$800 Million Target for Romney Campaign and Republican Committee," *New York Times*, retrieved from http://thecaucus.blogs.nytimes.com/2012/04/16/800-million-target-for-romney-campaign-and-republican-committee/?ref=todayspaper.

17. Marcus Cunliffe, *The Presidency*, p. 386.

APPENDIX I

1. Seth Lipsky, *The Citizen's Constitution*, p. 121.
2. Lipsky, p. 124.

APPENDIX II

1. Angela Roddey Holder and John Thomas Roddey Holder, *The Meaning of the Constitution*, p. 108.
2. Seth Lipsky, *The Citizen's Constitution*, p. 285.

APPENDIX IV

1. Source: http://moneyfactory.gov/home.html.
2. http://www.frbservices.org/operations/currency/new_coin_presidential.html.

BIBLIOGRAPHY

General Readings, References, Collective Biographies, and Individual Non-Presidential Biographies

Ahamed, Liaquat. *Lords of Finance: The Bankers Who Broke the World.* New York: Penguin Books, 2009.

Alterman, Eric. *When Presidents Lie: A History of Official Deception and Its Consequences.* New York: Viking, 2004.

Anderson, Fred and Andrew Cayton. *The Dominion of War: Empire and Liberty in North America, 1500–2000.* New York: Viking Penguin, 2005.

Applegate, Debby. *The Most Famous Man in America: The Biography of Henry Ward Beecher.* New York: Doubleday, 2006.

Balmer, Randall. *God in the White House: How Faith Shaped the Presidency from John F. Kennedy to George W. Bush.* New York: HarperOne, 2008.

Barber, James D. *The Presidential Character: Predicting Performance in the White House,* revised 4th edition. Upper Saddle River, New Jersey: Longman/Prentice Hall, 2008.

Bartlett, John and Justin Kaplan, editors. *Familiar Quotations (Sixteenth Edition).* Boston: Little, Brown, 1992.

Beschloss, Michael. *Presidential Courage: Brave Leaders and How They Changed America, 1789–1989.* New York: Simon & Schuster, 2007.

Boller, Paul F., Jr. *Presidential Inaugurations.* New York: Harcourt, 2001.

_____. *Presidential Wives: An Anecdotal History.* New York: Oxford University Press, 1998.

Brands, H. W. *The Age of Gold: The California Gold Rush and the New American Dream.* New York: Doubleday, 2002.

_____. *American Colossus: The Triumph of Capitalism.* New York: Doubleday, 2010.

Burns, James MacGregor. *The Vineyard of Liberty.* New York: Knopf, 1982.

Burrows, Edwin G. and Mike Wallace. *Gotham: A History of New York City to 1898.* New York: Oxford University Press, 1998.

Calloway, Colin G. *The Shawnees and the War for America.* New York: Viking Penguin, 2007.

Carruth, Gorton. *What Happened When: A Chronology of Life and Events in America.* New York: Signet, 1991.

Carter, Graydon, ed. *Vanity Fair's Presidential Profiles.* New York: Abrams, 2010.

Chang, Iris. *The Chinese in America: A Narrative History.* New York: Viking Penguin, 2003.

Chernow, Ron. *Alexander Hamilton.* New York: Penguin Press, 2004.

_____. *The House of Morgan: An American Banking Dynasty and the Rise of Modern Finance.* New York: Grove Press, 1990.

Cohen, I. Bernard. *Science and the Founding Fathers: Science in the Political Thought of Thomas Jefferson, Benjamin Franklin, John Adams and James Madison.* New York: Norton, 1995.

Colbert, David, ed. *Eyewitness to America: 500 Years of American History in the Words of Those Who Saw It Happen.* New York: Pantheon, 1997.

Cunliffe, Marcus. *The Presidency*, 3rd edition, Boston: Houghton Mifflin, 1987.

Dallek, Robert. *Hail to the Chief: The Making and Unmaking of American Presidents.* New York: Hyperion, 1996.

DeGregorio, William A. *The Complete Book of U.S. Presidents*, 4th edition. New York: Barricade Books, 1993.

Ellis, Joseph J. *Founding Brothers: The Revolutionary Generation.* New York: Knopf, 2001.

Ellis, Richard J., ed. *Founding the American Presidency.* Lanham, Maryland: Rowman & Littlefield, 1999.

Fleming, Thomas. *Liberty!: The American Revolution.* New York: Viking, 1977.

Fraser, Steve. *Every Man a Speculator: A History of Wall Street in American Life.* New York: HarperCollins, 2005

Gaustad, Edwin, and Leigh Schmidt. *The Religious History of America.* New York: Harper, 2002.

Goldberg, Vicki. *The White House: The President's Home in Photographs and History.* New York: Little, Brown, 2011.

Goldwag, Arthur. *Cults, Conspiracies, and Secret Societies: The Straight Scoop on Freemasons, the Illuminati, Skull and Bones, Black Helicopters, and many, many more.* New York: Random House, 2009.

Gordon, John Steele. *An Empire of Wealth: The Epic History of American Economic Power.* New York: HarperCollins, 2004.

Gould, Lewis L. *Grand Old Party: A History of the Republicans.* New York: Random House, 2003.

Graff, Henry F., ed. *The Presidents: A Reference History*, 2nd edition. New York: Scribner's, 1997.

Hendrickson, Robert. *QPB Encyclopedia of Word and Phrase Origins*. New York: Facts on File, 1997.

Hochschild, Adam. *To End All Wars: A Story of Loyalty and Rebellion, 1914–1918*. New York: Houghton Mifflin Harcourt, 2011.

Irons, Peter. *A People's History of the Supreme Court*. New York: Viking Penguin, 1999.

Jackson, Kenneth T., ed. *The Encyclopedia of New York*. New Haven: Yale University Press, 1995.

Janssen, Sarah, ed. *The World Almanac and Book of Facts 2012*. New York: World Almanac, 2011.

Kessler, Ronald. *Inside the White House: The Hidden Lives of the Modern President and the Secrets of the World's Most Powerful Institution*. New York: Pocket Books, 1995.

Kiernan, Denise, and Joseph D'Agnese. *Signing Their Lives Away: The Fame and Misfortune of the Men Who Signed the Declaration of Independence*. Philadelphia: Quirk Books, 2009.

Kluger, Richard. *Seizing Destiny: How America Grew from Sea to Shining Sea*. New York: Knopf, 2007.

Knauer, Kelly and the Editors of *Time* magazine. *Time Almanac 2012*. New York: Time Almanac, 2012.

Kolchin, Peter. *American Slavery: 1619–1877*. New York: Hill and Wang, 1993.

Lepore, Jill. *New York Burning: Liberty, Slavery and Conspiracy in Eighteenth-Century Manhattan*. New York: Knopf, 2005.

Lusane, Clarence. *The Black History of the White House*. San Francisco: City Lights Books, 2011.

Mayer, Henry. *All on Fire: William Lloyd Garrison and the Abolition of Slavery*. New York: Norton, 1998.

McCullough, David. *1776*. New York: Simon & Schuster, 2005.

McPherson, James M. *Battle Cry of Freedom: The Civil War Era*. New York: Oxford University Press, 1988.

McPherson, James M., ed. *"To the Best of My Ability": The American Presidents*. New York: Dorling Kindersley, 2000.

Mihm, Stephen. *A Nation of Counterfeiters: Capitalists, Con Men, and the Making of the United States*. Cambridge, Massachusetts: Harvard University Press, 2007.

Miller, Nathan. *Star-Spangled Men: America's Ten Worst Presidents*. New York: Scribner, 1998.

Okrent, Daniel. *Last Call: The Rise and Fall of Prohibition*. New York: Scribner, 2010.

Peters, Gerhard, ed. *The Presidency A to Z (Fourth Edition).* Washington, D.C.: CQ Press, 2008.

Raphael, Ray. *Founders: The People Who Brought You a Nation.* New York: The New Press, 2009.

Rediker, Marcus. *The Slave Ship: A Human History.* New York: Viking, 2007.

Remini, Robert V. *The House: The History of the House of Representatives.* New York: Smithsonian/Collins, 2006.

Roberts, Cokie. *Founding Mothers: The Women Who Raised Our Nation.* New York: Morrow, 2004.

Ruddy, Daniel, ed. *Theodore Roosevelt's History of the United States.* New York: Smithsonian/HarperCollins, 2010.

Schlesinger, Arthur M., Jr., ed. *The Almanac of American History.* New York: Barnes & Noble, 2004.

_____. *The Imperial Presidency.* New York: Mariner Books, 2004.

Seale, William. *The President's House: A History,* 2nd edition. Baltimore: The Johns Hopkins University Press, 2008.

Sides, Hampton. *Blood and Thunder: The Epic Story of Kit Carson and the Conquest of the American West.* New York: Doubleday, 2006.

Smith, Gary Scott. *Faith and the Presidency: From George Washington to George W. Bush.* New York: Oxford University Press, 2006.

Smith, Jean Edward. *John Marshall: Definer of a Nation.* New York: Henry Holt, 1996.

Stein, Mark. *The People Behind the Border Lines.* Washington, D.C.: Smithsonian Books, 2011.

Viola, Herman J. *Diplomats in Buckskins: A History of the Indian Delegations in Washington City.* Bluffton, South Carolina: Rivolo Books, 1995.

Waldman, Steven. *Founding Faith: Providence, Politics, and the Birth of Religious Freedom in America.* New York: Random House, 2008.

Weiner, Tim. *Legacy of Ashes: The History of the CIA.* New York: Anchor Books, 2008.

White, Richard. *Railroaded: The Transcontinentals and the Making of Modern America.* New York: Norton, 2011.

Whitney, David C., and Robin Vaughan Whitney. *The American Presidents: Biographies of Our Chief Executives,* 11th edition. New York: Madison Park Press, 2009.

Wilentz, Sean. *The Rise of American Democracy: Jefferson to Lincoln.* New York: Norton, 2005.

Wood, Gordon S. *The Creation of the American Republic: 1776–1787.* Chapel Hill, North Carolina: University of North Carolina Press, 1998.

_____. *Empire of Liberty: A History of the Early Republic.* New York: Oxford University Press, 2009.

Woodward, Bob. *Shadow: Five Presidents and the Legacy of Watergate.* New York: Simon & Schuster, 1999.

Yafa, Stephen. *Big Cotton: How a Humble Fiber Created Fortunes, Wrecked Civilizations, and Put America on the Map.* New York: Viking Penguin, 2005.

Constitutional History and Reference

Amar, Akhil Reed. *America's Constitution: A Biography.* New York: Random House, 2005.

Beard, Charles A. *An Economic Interpretation of the Constitution of the United States.* Mineola, New York: Dover, 2004. (Unabridged republication of 1913 work published by Macmillan.)

Beeman, Richard. *Plain, Honest Men: The Making of the American Constitution.* New York: Random House, 2009.

Bowen, Catherine Drinker. *Miracle at Philadelphia: The Story of the Constitutional Convention, May to September 1787.* New York: Little Brown, 1966.

Brands, H. W. *The First American: The Life and Times of Benjamin Franklin.* New York: Doubleday, 2000.

Brookhiser, Richard. *Gentleman Revolutionary: Gouverneur Morris —The Rake Who Wrote the Constitution.* New York: Free Press, 2003.

Collier, Christopher, and James Lincoln Collier. *Decision in Philadelphia: The Constitutional Convention of 1787.* New York: Random House, 1986.

Dahl, Robert A. *How Democratic Is the American Constitution?*, 2nd edition. New Haven, Connecticut: Yale University Press, 2003.

Holder, Angela Roddey, and John Thomas Roddey Holder. *The Meaning of the Constitution*, 3rd edition. Hauppauge, New York: Barron's Educational Series, 1997.

Holton, Woody. *Unruly Americans and the Origin of the Constitution.* New York: Hill & Wang, 2007.

Isaacson, Walter. *Benjamin Franklin: An American Life.* New York: Simon & Schuster, 2003.

Ketcham, Ralph, ed. *The Anti-Federalist Papers and the Constitutional Convention Debates.* New York: New American Library/Penguin, 1986.

Larson, Edward J., and Michael P. Winship. *The Constitutional Convention: A Narrative History from the Notes of James Madison.* New York: Modern Library, 2005.

Levy, Leonard W. *Origins of the Bill of Rights.* New Haven: Yale University Press, 2001.

Lipsky, Seth. *The Citizen's Constitution: An Annotated Guide.* New York: Basic Books, 2009.

Madison, James. *Notes of Debates in the Federal Convention of 1787.* New York: Norton, 1987.

May, Henry F. *The Enlightenment in America.* New York: Oxford University Press, 1976.

Paine, Thomas. *Collected Writings.* New York: Library of America, 1995.

Rakove, Jack N. *Original Meanings: Politics and Ideas in the Making of the Constitution.* New York: Vintage Books, 1997.

Rossiter, Clinton, ed. *The Federalist Papers.* New York: New American Library/Penguin, 1961, 1999. (Many other editions available.)

Presidential Campaigns

Boller, Paul F., Jr. *Presidential Campaigns.* New York: Oxford University Press, 1984.

Cummins, Joseph. *Anything for a Vote: Dirty Tricks, Cheap Shots, and October Surprises in U.S. Presidential Campaigns.* Philadelphia: Quirk Books, 2007.

McGinnis, Joe. *The Selling of the President.* New York: Penguin Books, 1988. (Originally published in 1969 as *The Selling of the President, 1968.* New York: Simon & Schuster.)

Parsons, Lynn Hudson. *The Birth of Modern Politics: Andrew Jackson, John Quincy Adams and the Election of 1828.* New York: Oxford University Press, 2009.

Weisberger, Bernard A. *America Afire: Jefferson, Adams and the First Contested Election.* New York: Morrow, 2000.

Wright, Jordan M. *Campaigning for President: Memorabilia from the Nation's Private Collection.* Smithsonian/HarperCollins, 2008.

Presidents
1. GEORGE WASHINGTON

Brady, Patricia. *Martha Washington: An American Life.* New York: Viking, 2005.

Brookhiser, Richard. *Founding Father: Rediscovering George Washington.* New York: Free Press, 1996.

Chernow, Ron. *Washington: A Life.* New York: Penguin Press, 2010.

Ellis, Joseph J. *His Excellency George Washington.* New York: Knopf, 2004.

Ferling, John. *The Ascent of George Washington: The Hidden Political Genius of an American Icon.* New York: Bloomsbury Press, 2009.

Fischer, David Hackett. *Washington's Crossing.* New York: Oxford University Press, 2004.

Fleming, Thomas. *Washington's Secret War: The Hidden History of Valley Forge.* New York: Smithsonian/HarperCollins, 2005.

Flexner, James Thomas. *Washington: The Indispensable Man*. New York: Little, Brown, 1966, 1974.

Paine, Thomas. *Rights of Man*. New York: Viking Penguin, 1984.

Schama, Simon. *Rough Crossings: The Slaves, the British, and the American Revolution*. New York: Harper, 2006.

Washington, George. *George Washington: Writings*. New York: Library of America, 1997.

Wiencek, Henry. *An Imperfect God: George Washington and His Slaves*. New York: Farrar, Straus and Giroux, 2003.

Williams, Glenn F. *Year of the Hangman: George Washington's Campaign Against the Iroquois*. Yardley, Pennsylvania: Westholme Publishing, 2005.

2. JOHN ADAMS

Ellis, Joseph. *First Family: Abigail and John Adams*. New York: Knopf, 2010.

_____. *Passionate Sage: The Character and Legacy of John Adams*. New York: Norton, 1993.

Ferling, John. *John Adams: A Life*. New York: Oxford University Press, 2010.

Gelles, Edith B. *Abigail and John: Portrait of a Marriage*. New York: Morrow, 2009.

Holton, Woody. *Abigail Adams*. New York: Free Press, 2009.

McCullough, David. *John Adams*. New York: Simon & Schuster, 2001.

3. THOMAS JEFFERSON

Adams, William Howard. *Jefferson's Monticello*. New York: Abbeville Press, 1983.

Ellis, Joseph J. *American Sphinx: The Character of Thomas Jefferson*. New York: Random House, 1996.

Fleming, Thomas. *Duel: Alexander Hamilton, Aaron Burr and the Future of America*. New York: Basic Books, 1999.

Gordon-Reed, Annette. *The Hemingses of Monticello: An American Family*. New York: Norton, 2008.

_____. *Thomas Jefferson and Sally Hemings: An American Controversy*. Charlottesville, Virginia: University of Virginia Press, 1997.

Isenberg, Nancy. *Fallen Founder: The Life of Aaron Burr*. New York: Viking, 2007.

Jefferson, Thomas. *Jefferson: Public and Private Papers*. New York: Library of America, 1990.

Kranish, Michael. *Flight from Monticello: Thomas Jefferson at War*. New York: Oxford University Press, 2010.

Wills, Garry. *"Negro President:" Jefferson and the Slave Power*. Boston: Houghton Mifflin, 2003.

4. JAMES MADISON

Allgor, Catherine. *A Perfect Union: Dolley Madison and the Creation of the American Nation.* New York: Holt, 2006.

Borneman, Walter R. *1812: The War That Forged a Nation.* New York: Harper, 2004.

Brookhiser, Richard. *James Madison.* New York: Basic Books, 2011.

Langguth, A. J. *Union 1812: The Americans Who Fought the Second War of Independence.* New York: Simon & Schuster, 2006.

Madison, James. *Madison: Writings.* New York: Library of America, 1999.

Wills, Garry. *James Madison (The American Presidents Series).* New York: Times Books/Henry Holt, 2002.

5. JAMES MONROE

Hart, Gary. *James Monroe (The American Presidents Series).* New York: Times Books, 2005.

Monroe, James. *Quotations of James Monroe,* Charlottesville, Virginia: Ash-Lawn Highland, 2010.

Unger, Harlow Giles. *The Last Founding Father: James Monroe and a Nation's Call to Greatness.* New York: Da Capo Press, 2009.

6. JOHN QUINCY ADAMS

Howe, Daniel Walker. *What Hath God Wrought: The Transformation of America, 1815–1848.* New York: Oxford University Pres, 2004.

Nagel, Paul C. *John Quincy Adams: A Public Life, a Private Life.* Boston: Cambridge University Press, 1999.

Remini, Robert V. *John Quincy Adams (The American Presidents Series).* New York: Times Books, 2002.

7. ANDREW JACKSON

Brands, H. W. *Andrew Jackson: His Life and Times.* New York: Doubleday, 2005.

Burstein, Andrew. *The Passions of Andrew Jackson.* New York: Random House, 2003.

Davis, Kenneth C. *A Nation Rising.* New York: Smithsonian/HarperCollins, 2010.

Heidler, David S., and Jeanne T. Heidler. *Old Hickory's War: Andrew Jackson and the Quest for Empire.* Baton Rouge, Louisiana: Louisiana State University Press, 1996, 2003.

Meacham, Jon. *American Lion: Andrew Jackson in the White House.* New York: Random House, 2008.

O'Brien, Sean Michael. *In Bitterness and in Tears: Andrew Jackson's Destruction of the Creeks and Seminoles.* Guilford, Connecticut: Lyons/Globe Pequot, 2003.

Remini, Robert V. *Andrew Jackson.* New York: Twayne Publishers, 1966.

_____. *Andrew Jackson: The Course of American Empire*, vol 1. Baltimore: Johns Hopkins University Press, 1998.

Reynolds, David S. *Waking Giant: America in the Age of Jackson.* New York: HarperCollins, 2008.

Schlesinger, Arthur M., Jr. *The Age of Jackson.* Boston: Back Bay Books, 1945.

8. MARTIN VAN BUREN

Laumer, Frank. *Dade's Last Command.* Gainesville, Florida: University Press of Florida, 2008.

Widmer, Ted. *Martin Van Buren (The American Presidents Series).* New York: Times Books, 2004.

9. WILLIAM HENRY HARRISON

Owens, Robert M. *Mr. Jefferson's Hammer: William Henry Harrison and the Origins of American Indian Policy.* Norman, Oklahoma: University of Oklahoma Press, 2011.

Sugden, John. *Tecumseh: A Life.* New York: Henry Holt, 1998.

10. JOHN TYLER

Crapol, Edward P. *John Tyler: The Accidental President.* Chapel Hill: University of North Carolina Press, 2006.

Fehrenbach, T. R. *Lone Star: A History of Texas and the Texans.* Cambridge, Massachusetts: Da Capo Press, 2000.

May, Gary. *John Tyler (The American Presidents Series).* New York: Times Books, 2008.

11. JAMES KNOX POLK

Borneman, Walter R. *Polk: The Man Who Transformed the Presidency and America.* New York: Random House, 2008.

Eisenhower, John S. D. *So Far from God: The U.S. War with Mexico, 1846–1848.* New York: Random House, 1989.

Merry, Robert W. *A Country of Vast Designs: James K. Polk, the Mexican War, and the Conquest of the American Continent.* New York: Simon & Schuster, 2009.

12. ZACHARY TAYLOR

Eisenhower, John S. D. *Zachary Taylor (The American Presidents Series).* New York: Times Books, 2008.

Heidler, David S., and Jeanne T. Heidler. *Henry Clay: The Essential American.* New York: Random House, 2010.

13. MILLARD FILLMORE

Finkelman, Paul. *Millard Fillmore (The American Presidents Series).* New York: Times Books, 2011.

14. FRANKLIN PIERCE

Holt, Michael. *Franklin Pierce (The American Presidents Series).* New York: Times Books, 2010.

Reynolds, David S. *John Brown, Abolitionist: The Man Who Killed Slavery, Sparked the Civil War, and Seeded Civil Rights.* New York: Knopf, 2005.

15. JAMES BUCHANAN

Baker, Jean. *James Buchanan (The American Presidents Series).* New York: Times Books, 2004.

16. ABRAHAM LINCOLN

Davis, Kenneth C. *Don't Know Much About the Civil War.* New York: Morrow, 1996.

Donald, David Herbert. *Lincoln.* New York: Simon & Schuster, 1995.

Epstein, Daniel Mark. *Lincoln's Men: The President and His Private Secretaries.* New York: Smithsonian/Collins, 2009.

Foner, Eric. *The Fiery Trial: Abraham Lincoln and American Slavery.* New York: Norton, 2010.

Goodwin, Doris Kearns. *Team of Rivals: The Political Genius of Abraham Lincoln.* New York: Simon & Schuster, 2005.

Kunhardt, Philip B., Jr., Philip B. Kunhardt III, and Peter W. Kunhardt. *Lincoln: An Illustrated Biography.* New York: Knopf, 1993.

Lincoln, Abraham. *Abraham Lincoln: Speeches and Writings*, 2 volumes. New York: The Library of America, 1989.

Neely, Mark E., Jr. *The Abraham Lincoln Encyclopedia.* New York: Da Capo Press, 1982.

Oates, Stephen B. *With Malice Toward None: The Life of Abraham Lincoln.* New York: Harper and Row, 1977.

Swanson, James L. *Manhunt: The Twelve-Day Chase for Lincoln's Killer.* New York: William Morrow, 2006.

White, Ronald C., Jr. *A. Lincoln: A Biography.* New York: Random House, 2009.

Wills, Garry. *Lincoln at Gettysburg: The Words That Remade America.* New York: Simon & Schuster, 1992.

Winik, Jay. *April 1865: The Month That Saved America.* New York: HarperCollins, 2001.

17. ANDREW JOHNSON

Foner, Eric. *A Short History of Reconstruction.* New York: HarperCollins, 1990. (An abridged version of the author's *Reconstruction: America's Unfinished Revolution.*)

Gordon-Reed, Annette. *Andrew Johnson (The American Presidents Series).* New York: Times Books, 2011.

Trefousse, Hans L. *Andrew Johnson: A Biography.* New York: Norton, 1989.

18. ULYSSES S. GRANT

Grant, Ulysses S. *Personal Memoirs.* New York: Modern Library, 1999.

Korda, Michael. *Ulysses S. Grant: The Unlikely Hero.* New York: HarperCollins, 2004.

McFeely, William S. *Grant: A Biography.* New York: Norton, 1981.

Smith, Jean Edward. *Grant.* New York: Simon & Schuster, 2001.

19. RUTHERFORD B. HAYES

Trefousse, Hans. *Rutherford B. Hayes.* New York: Henry Holt, 2002.

20. JAMES A. GARFIELD

Millard, Candice. *Destiny of the Republic: A Tale of Madness, Medicine and the Murder of a President.* New York: Doubleday: 2011.

21. CHESTER A. ARTHUR

Karabell, Zachary. *Chester Alan Arthur (The American Presidents Series).* New York: Times Books, 2004.

22. and 24. GROVER CLEVELAND

Graff, Henry F. *Grover Cleveland (The American Presidents Series).* New York: Times Books, 2002.

23. BENJAMIN HARRISON

Brown, Dee. *Bury My Heart at Wounded Knee: An Indian History of the American West.* New York: Holt, 1971.

Calhoun, Charles W. *Benjamin Harrison.* New York: Times Books, 2005.

25. WILLIAM MCKINLEY

Miller, Scott. *The President and the Assassin: McKinley, Terror and Empire at the Dawn of the American Century.* New York: Random House, 2011.

Phillips, Kevin. *William McKinley (The American Presidents Series).* New York: Times Books, 2003.

26. THEODORE ROOSEVELT

Brinkley, Douglas. *The Wilderness Warrior: Theodore Roosevelt and the Crusade for America.* New York: HarperCollins, 2009.

McCullough, David. *Mornings on Horseback: The Story of an Extraordinary Family, a Vanished Way of Life and the Unique Child Who Became Theodore Roosevelt.* New York: Simon & Schuster, 1982.

_____. *The Path Between the Seas: The Creation of the Panama Canal, 1870–1914.* New York: Simon & Schuster, 1977.

Millard, Candice. *The River of Doubt: Theodore Roosevelt's Darkest Journey.* New York: Doubleday, 2005.

Morris, Edmund. *The Rise of Theodore Roosevelt.* New York: Random House, 1979. (The first volume of a trilogy tracing the life and times of Theodore Roosevelt.)

_____. *Theodore Rex.* New York: Random House, 2001.

_____. *Colonel Roosevelt.* New York: Random House, 2010.

Roosevelt, Theodore. *Theodore Roosevelt's History of the United States: His Own Words,* selected and arranged by Daniel Ruddy. New York: Smithsonian/HarperCollins, 2010.

27. WILLIAM HOWARD TAFT

Chace, James. *1912: Wilson, Roosevelt, Taft & Debs—The Election That Changed the Country.* New York: Simon & Schuster, 2004.

Gould, Lewis L. *The William Howard Taft Presidency.* Lawrence, Kansas: University Press of Kansas, 2009.

28. WOODROW WILSON

Cooper, John Milton. *Woodrow Wilson: A Biography.* New York: Knopf, 2009.

29. WARREN G. HARDING

Pietrusza, David. *1920: The Year of Six Presidents.* New York: Basic Books, 2009.

30. CALVIN COOLIDGE

Greenberg, David. *Calvin Coolidge.* New York: Times Books, 2006.

Shlaes, Amity. *The Forgotten Man: A New History of the Great Depression.* New York: HarperCollins, 2007.

31. HERBERT CLARK HOOVER

Leuchtenberg, William E. *Herbert Hoover (The American Presidents Series).* New York: Times Books, 2009.

32. FRANKLIN D. ROOSEVELT

Badger, Anthony J. *FDR: The First Hundred Days.* New York: Hill & Wang, 2008.

Brands, H. W. *Traitor to His Class: The Privileged Life and Radical Presidency of Franklin Delano Roosevelt.* New York: Doubleday, 2008.

Cook, Blanche Wiesen. *Eleanor Roosevelt, Volume I: 1884–1933.* New York: Penguin, 1993.

_____. *Eleanor Roosevelt, Volume II: The Defining Years, 1933–1938.* New York: Penguin, 1999.

Egan, Timothy. *The Worst Hard Time: The Untold Story of Those Who Survived the Great American Dust Bowl.* New York: Houghton Mifflin, 2006.

Fraser, Steve. *Every Man a Speculator: A History of Wall Street in American Life.* New York: HarperCollins, 2005.

Goodwin, Doris Kearns. *No Ordinary Time: Franklin and Eleanor Roosevelt: The Home Front in World War II.* New York: Simon & Schuster, 1994.

Gordon, John Steele. *An Empire of Wealth: The Epic History of American Economic Power.* New York: HarperCollins, 2004.

Roberts, Andrew. *The Storm of War: A New History of the Second World War.* New York: Penguin, 2011.

Shlaes, Amity. *The Forgotten Man: A New History of the Great Depression.* New York: HarperCollins, 2007.

33. HARRY S. TRUMAN

Dallek, Robert. *Harry S. Truman.* New York: Times Books, 2008.

Halberstam, David. *The Coldest Winter: America and the Korean War.* New York: Hyperion, 2007.

_____. *The Fifties.* New York: Random House, 1993.

McCullough, David. *Truman.* New York: Simon & Schuster, 1992.

Rhodes, Richard. *The Making of the Atomic Bomb*. New York: Simon & Schuster, 1986.

Tanenhaus, Sam. *Whittaker Chambers: A Biography*. New York: Random House, 1997.

34. DWIGHT D. EISENHOWER

Korda, Michael. *Ike: An American Hero*. New York: HarperCollins, 2007.

Wicker, Tom. *Dwight D. Eisenhower*. New York: Times Books/Henry Holt, 2002.

35. JOHN F. KENNEDY

Dallek, Robert. *An Unfinished Life: John Kennedy 1917–1963*. New York: Little, Brown, 2003.

Matthews, Chris. *Jack Kennedy: Elusive Hero*. New York: Simon & Schuster, 2011.

Posner, Gerald M. *Case Closed: Lee Harvey Oswald and the Assassination of JFK*. New York: Anchor Books, 1994.

Schlesinger, Arthur M., Jr. *A Thousand Days: John F. Kennedy in the White House*. New York: Mariner Books, 2002.

36. LYNDON B. JOHNSON

Caro, Robert A. *The Years of Lyndon Johnson: The Path to Power*. New York: Knopf, 1982.

_____. *The Years of Lyndon Johnson: Means of Ascent*. New York: Knopf, 1990.

_____. *The Years of Lyndon Johnson: Master of the Senate*. New York: Knopf, 2002.

Dallek, Robert. *Flawed Giant: Lyndon Johnson and His Times, 1961–1973*. New York: Oxford University Press, 1999.

Goodwin, Doris Kearns. *Lyndon Johnson and the American Dream*. New York: St. Martin's Press, 1976.

Reeves, Richard. *President Kennedy: Profile of Power*. New York: Simon & Schuster, 1993.

Schlesinger, Arthur M., Jr. *A Thousand Days: John F. Kennedy in the White House*. New York: Mariner Books, 2002.

Wyden, Peter. *Bay of Pigs*. New York: Simon & Schuster, 1979.

37. RICHARD M. NIXON

Drew, Elizabeth. *Richard M. Nixon (The American Presidents Series)*. New York: Times Books, 2007.

Karnow, Stanley. *Vietnam: A History*. New York: Viking, 1983.

McGinniss, Joe. *The Selling of the President*. New York: Penguin Books, 1988.

Nixon, Richard. *Six Crises*. New York: Doubleday, 1962.

Reeves, Richard. *President Nixon*. New York: Simon & Schuster, 2001.

Woodward, Bob and Carl Bernstein. *All the President's Men*. New York: Simon & Schuster, 1973

_____. *The Final Days*. New York: Simon & Schuster, 1976.

38. GERALD R. FORD

Brinkley, Douglas. *Gerald R. Ford (The American Presidents Series)*. New York: Times Books, 2007.

39. JAMES EARL "JIMMY" CARTER

Witcover, Jules. *Marathon: The Pursuit of the Presidency 1972–1976*. New York: Viking, 1977.

Zelizer, Julian E. *Jimmy Carter (The American Presidents Series)*. New York: Times Books, 2010.

40. RONALD WILSON REAGAN

Cannon, Lou. *President Reagan: The Role of a Lifetime*. New York: Public Affairs, 2000.

Kleinknecht, William. *The Man Who Sold the World: Ronald Reagan and the Betrayal of America*. New York: Nation Books, 2009.

Mann, James. *The Rebellion of Ronald Reagan: A History of the End of the Cold War*. New York: Viking Penguin, 2009.

Reeves, Richard. *President Reagan: The Triumph of Imagination*. New York: Simon & Schuster, 2006.

41. GEORGE HERBERT WALKER BUSH

Bush, George and Brent Scowcroft, *A World Transformed*. New York: Knopf, 1998.

Naftali, Timothy. *George H. W. Bush (The American Presidents Series)*. New York: Times Books, 2007.

Woodward, Bob. *The Commanders*. New York: Simon & Schuster, 1991.

42. WILLIAM JEFFERSON "BILL" CLINTON

Branch, Taylor. *The Clinton Tapes: Wrestling with History with the President*. New York: Simon & Schuster, 2009.

Clinton, Bill. *My Life*. New York: Knopf, 2004.

Harris, John. *The Survivor: Bill Clinton in the White House*. New York: Random House, 2005.

Maraniss, David. *First in His Class: The Biography of Bill Clinton*. New York: Simon & Schuster, 1995.

Reeves, Richard. *Running in Place: How Bill Clinton Disappointed America*. Kansas City, Missouri: Andrews McMeel, 1996.

Stephanopoulos, George. *All Too Human*. New York: Little, Brown, 1999.

Toobin, Jeffrey. *A Vast Conspiracy: The Real Story of the Sex Scandal That Nearly Brought Down a President*. New York: Simon & Schuster, 1999.

Woodward, Bob. *The Agenda: Inside the Clinton White House*. New York: Simon & Schuster, 2005.

_____. *Shadow: Five Presidents and the Legacy of Watergate*. New York: Simon & Schuster, 1999.

43. GEORGE W. BUSH

Bush, George W. *Decision Points*. New York: Crown, 2010.

Clarke, Richard A. *Against All Enemies: Inside America's War on Terror*. New York: Free Press, 2004.

Gordon, Michael R., and General Bernard E. Trainor. *Cobra !!: The Inside Story of the Invasion and Occupation of Iraq*. New York: Pantheon Books, 2006.

Hersh, Seymour M. *Chain of Command: The Road from 9/11 to Abu Ghraib*. New York: HarperCollins, 2004.

Ivins, Molly and Lou Dubose. *Shrub: The Short but Happy Political Life of George W. Bush*. New York: Random House, 2000.

Lewis, Charles, and the Center for Public Integrity. *The Buying of the President 2004: Who's Really Bankrolling Bush and His Democratic Challengers—and What They Expect in Return*. New York: HarperCollins, 2004.

Mann, James. *The Rise of the Vulcans: The History of the Bush War Cabinet*. New York: Penguin, 2004.

Mayer, Jane. *The Dark Side: The Inside Story of How the War on Terror Turned Into a War on American Ideals*. New York: Doubleday, 2008.

Packer, George. *The Assassins' Gate: America in Iraq*. New York: Farrar, Straus and Giroux, 2005.

Sorkin, Andrew Ross. *Too Big to Fail: The Inside Story of How Wall Street and Washington Fought to Save the Financial System—and Themselves*. New York: Viking, 2009.

Woodward, Bob. *Plan of Attack*. New York: Simon & Schuster, 2004.

_____. *State of Denial*. New York: Simon & Schuster, 2007.

_____. *The War Within: A Secret White House History 2006–2008*. New York: Simon & Schuster, 2008.

44. BARACK HUSSEIN OBAMA

Alter, Jonathan. *The Promise: President Obama, Year One*. New York: Simon & Schuster, 2010.

Heilemann, John, and Mark Halperin. *Game Change: Obama and the Clintons, Mc-Cain and Palin and the Race of a Lifetime*. New York: Harper, 2010.

Mitchell, Greg. *Why Obama Won: The Making of a President 2008*. New York: Sinclair Books, 2008.

Obama, Barack. *Dreams from My Father: A Story of Race and Inheritance*. New York: Three Rivers Press, 1995, 2004.

Remnick, David. *The Bridge: The Life and Rise of Barack Obama*. New York: Knopf, 2010.

Staff of the *Washington Post. Landmark: The Inside Story of America's New Health-Care Law and What It Means for Us All*. New York: Public Affairs, 2010.

Suskind, Ron. *Confidence Men: Wall Street, Washington, and the Education of a President*. New York: Harper, 2011.

Tesler, Michael, and David O. Sears. *Obama's Race: The 2008 Election and the Dream of a Post-Racial America*. Chicago: University of Chicago Press, 2010.

Woodward, Bob. *Obama's Wars*. New York: Simon & Schuster, 2010.

Online Resources

Historical Election Results, National Archives
http://www.archives.gov/federal-register/electoral-college/votes/index.html

"The Presidents," *The American Experience,* **Public Broadcasting System**
http://www.pbs.org/wgbh/amex/presidents/about.html#programs

National Park Service
http://www.nps.gov/nr/travel/presidents/list_of_sites.html

Smithsonian Museum of American History: "The American Presidency"
http://americanhistory.si.edu/presidency/home.html

Miller Center of Public Affairs, University of Virginia, the American President Online Reference
http://millercenter.org/academic/americanpresident

University of California–Santa Barbara, the American Presidency Project
http://www.presidency.ucsb.edu/

Avalon Project, Yale Law School: Inaugural Addresses
http://avalon.law.yale.edu/subject_menus/inaug.asp

Avalon Project, Yale Law School: Presidential Papers
http://avalon.law.yale.edu/subject_menus/presiden.asp

The Founders' Constitution, University of Chicago Press
http://press-pubs.uchicago.edu/founders/help/about.html

"Charters of Freedom," National Archives
http://archives.gov/exhibits/charters/constitution.html

Legal Information Institute, Cornell Law School
http://www.law.cornell.edu/constitution/overview

Library of Congress, Primary Documents of American History
http://www.loc.gov/rr/program/bib/ourdocs/Constitution.html

National Constitution Center, Philadelphia
http://constitutioncenter.org/ncc_progs_Constitution_Day.aspx

Avalon Project, Yale Law School: "The American Constitution: A Documentary Record"
http://avalon.law.yale.edu/subject_menus/constpap.asp

HarpWeek: Cartoons from Harper's Weekly: Elections from 1860 to 1912
http://elections.harpweek.com/introduction.htm

INDEX